Thermodynamics for Chemical Engineers

Thermodynamics for Chemical Engineers

by

K. E. BETT, J. S. ROWLINSON *and* G. SAVILLE

Department of Chemical Engineering and Chemical Technology,
Imperial College of Science and Technology,
University of London

THE ATHLONE PRESS *of the University of London* 1975

Published by
THE ATHLONE PRESS
UNIVERSITY OF LONDON
4 *Gower Street London* WC 1

Distributed by Tiptree Book Services Ltd
Tiptree, Essex

© *University of London* 1975

ISBN 0 485 12023 2

Set in 10/12 *pt Linotron Times*
at The Universities Press, Belfast
and printed by photolithography
in Great Britain by J. W. Arrowsmith Ltd, Bristol

Preface

All scientists and engineers must learn something of thermodynamics, but they do not all approach the subject in the same way, nor are they all interested in the same applications. There are, therefore, innumerable books on thermodynamics for physicists, chemists and mechanical engineers. This book is intended for chemical engineers, who have been less lavishly provided for, and is based on the undergraduate course taught at Imperial College.

We aim to approach the subject along a route which will lead the chemical engineer most naturally to those fields in which he is interested, and to cover all the principles of classical thermodynamics he needs in order to study both the engineering and the chemistry which comprise chemical engineering. We have not, however, written a textbook of those parts of chemical engineering in which thermodynamics is widely used, such as fluid mechanics, heat exchangers, gas liquefaction, or distillation. This distinction between the thermodynamics and the field in which it is used is not an easy one, and we have been influenced by the attention paid to these other fields in most courses of chemical engineering. Thus fluid mechanics is usually taught as a separate course, whilst gas liquefaction often forms part of a thermodynamics course; hence we discuss the former topic rather more briefly than the latter. We have, similarly, not attempted to describe apparatus in any detail since we envisage that all students will be taking practical courses in both chemistry and engineering laboratories. We aim only to make clear the principles of each piece of apparatus or machine. We hope our choice in this matter reflects tolerably well the consensus of views in other universities.

Most of the material here is covered in our undergraduate course of three years. During this time the students' abilities improve, and so the standard of the book rises continuously through the nine chapters. We expect a student starting the course to know the elements of physics, chemistry and classical mechanics, and so do not, for example, define such terms as pressure or work. We assume also that he understands the concept of mechanical energy, and the conditions for its conservation. In mathematics we expect him to know the elements of differential and integral calculus and of numerical analysis, but include an appendix on partial differentiation.

Illustrative material has been divided into examples and exercises in the text, and problems at the ends of the chapters. The first, which we use sparingly, are an essential part of the text, since our explanation of later material requires that they be understood. The second are not part of the main development, but may contain statements of minor results which form an integral part of the subject. The third serve, as usual, to illustrate the use of the principles set out in the text. Many are based on examination questions.

Some of the examples and problems require thermodynamic tables. Except where otherwise stated, the necessary information is to be found in 'Thermodynamics and Transport Properties of Fluids' by Y. R. Mayhew and G. F. C. Rogers (2nd edn.), published by Blackwell, Oxford (1968).

The last chapter poses difficult problems. A proper understanding of modern methods of predicting thermodynamic properties requires an understanding of statistical thermodynamics, a subject on which there are already many excellent elementary textbooks. However, the engineer who wishes to use intelligently these methods of prediction can do so if he is willing to take on trust a few easily expounded results of statistical and quantum mechanics. It is, in fact, often more important that he understands the practical limitations of these subjects than their foundations. The last chapter is, therefore, an attempt to describe methods of prediction which bear in mind these needs of the engineer.

Units and Symbols

The basic units of this book are those of the Système Internationale (SI), of which the following are used in thermodynamics:

Mass	kilogramme	symbol kg
Length	metre	symbol m
Time	second	symbol s
Temperature	kelvin	symbol K
Amount of substance	mole	symbol mol

Decimal multiples and sub-multiples are used freely, as convenience dictates. The derived units used most frequently are:

Energy	$kg\,m^2\,s^{-2}$	or	joule (J)
Force	$kg\,m\,s^{-2}$	or	newton (N)
Pressure	$kg\,m^{-1}\,s^{-2}$	or	$N\,m^{-2}$ or pascal (Pa).
Power	$kg\,m^2\,s^{-3}$	or	watt (W)

The practical unit of pressure is the bar ($10^5\,N\,m^{-2}$), which is conveniently close to atmospheric pressure. 1 atmosphere (atm) is defined to be $101\,325\,N\,m^{-2}$. The quantity of material is specified here either by its *mass*, or by its *amount of substance*. The latter phrase describes the quantity by specifying the number of atomic or molecular units it contains. Its unit is the mole, which is formally defined as follows:

'The mole is the amount of substance which contains as many elementary units as there are atoms in 0.012 kilogramme of carbon-12. The elementary unit must be specified and may be an atom, a molecule, an ion, a radical, an electron, a photon, etc., or a specified group of such entities.'

A capital letter, such as V for volume, is used for the property of a system of arbitrary size. We use lower case letters, v, etc., for the ratio of volume, etc.

to quantity of substance, where the latter can be specified either by its mass or by its amount of substance. The former is more convenient in those parts of thermodynamics which deal with the flow of material and its compression, expansion, etc. The latter is more convenient in chemical thermodynamics. Thus the symbol v can denote either

$$v = V/m \quad \text{specific volume,} \quad \text{measured, eg. in m}^3 \text{ kg}^{-1}$$
$$v = V/n \quad \text{molar volume,} \quad \text{measured, eg. in m}^3 \text{ mol}^{-1}$$

The risk of confusion between these two uses is, we think, more tolerable than the inconvenience of different symbols, for many of the equations can be interpreted correctly in either sense.

If conversion is required, however, it can be conveniently made by using n_m, the amount of substance per unit mass, defined as

$$n_m = n/m$$

Equations are generally written so that they can be used with any consistent set of units. If the units have to be shown, then we use what is commonly called the *quantity calculus*. Thus, if a molar heat capacity is a linear function of temperature, we write,

$$c_P/\text{J K}^{-1}\text{mol}^{-1} = 21.1 + 0.037 \, (T/\text{K})$$

rather than

$$c_P = 21.1 + 0.037 \, T$$

where c_P is in $\text{J K}^{-1}\text{mol}^{-1}$ and T is in K.

This way of reducing equations to pure numbers is convenient for writing logarithms and exponentials. Thus,

$$\ln(P/\text{bar}) \quad \text{or} \quad \exp(-\Delta h/\text{J mol}^{-1})$$

Many of the equations are valid only for a perfect gas. Such restriction is made clear in the text but, to guard against misuse, we add the symbol (pg) at the end of the line. Thus,

$$PV = nRT \hspace{3cm} \text{(pg)} \quad (3.53)$$

We are grateful to the following colleagues and visitors to the department for their comments on the manuscript; D. A. Armitage, M. D. Carabine, P. T. Eubank, D. Kivelson, H. J. Michels, G. A. Morrison and D. H. Napier. We wish to thank most warmly Kay Bond for typing and re-typing the palimpsest that was our manuscript.

Contents

Principal Symbols

A	Helmholtz free energy	P	pressure
a	van der Waals' constant	P	number of phases
$\mathscr{A}$	area	p	probability; molecular momentum
B	stream availability; second virial coefficient	$\mathscr{P}$	power
b	van der Waals' constant	Q	heat; configurational integral
C	heat capacity; third virial coefficient; clearance ratio	R	specific or, more usually, molar gas constant
C	number of components	r	molecular position, or separation
D	availability in a closed system		
E	electromotive force; energy of a system (Chapter 9)	S	entropy
		T	thermodynamic temperature
F	force; Faraday's constant	t	time
F	degrees of freedom	U	internal energy
f	fugacity; function defined by (9.89); ratio of intermolecular energies	u	intermolecular energy
		$\mathscr{U}$	configurational energy
		V	volume
G	Gibbs free energy	$\mathscr{V}$	speed
g	gravitational constant	W	work
H	enthalpy	$\mathscr{W}$	speed of sound
h	Planck's constant; ratio of intermolecular volumes	x	mole fraction, specifically in a liquid; quality
I	moment of inertia	y	mole fraction, specifically in a gas
j	rotational quantum number		
K	equilibrium constant for liquid-vapour equilibrium or for chemical reaction	Z	compression factor; partition function
		z	ionic charge; molecular partition function
k	Boltzmann's constant		
L	latent heat of evaporation $(=\Delta_e H)$	KE	kinetic energy
		PE	potential energy
m	mass; molality	α	coefficient of thermal expansion; volatility ratio
$\mathscr{M}$	relative molar mass (or 'molecular weight')	β	coefficient of performance; coefficient of compressibility; reciprocal vibrational temperature
N	number of molecules		
N_A	Avogadro's constant		
$\mathscr{N}_M$	Mach number	Γ	adsorption
n	amount of substance	γ	the ratio C_P/C_V; activity coefficient; surface tension
n_m	amount of substance per unit mass		

Δ	difference between two states	ν	stoichiometric coefficient; frequency
ε	energy of a system (Chapter 9); intermolecular energy; volumetric efficiency ε_{vol}	ξ	extent of a chemical reaction; parameter defined by (9.139)
η	efficiency; parameter defined by (9.140)	ρ	density
Θ	characteristic rotational temperature	σ	symmetry number; intermolecular distance
Λ	degree of reaction (of a turbine)	ϕ	volume fraction
		ω	intermolecular angle; acentric factor
μ	chemical potential	Ω	frequency

In general we use subscript letters for *processes* and superscript letters and, in the earlier part of the book, subscript and superscript numbers for *states*; thus

Subscripts   *Superscripts*

e	evaporation	c	critical
f	fusion	E	excess
m	melting	f	freezing point
r	reduced	g	gas
s	sublimation	l	liquid
x	substance equivalent to a mixture	m	melting point
		s	solid
σ	along the saturation line	t	triple point
i,j	running suffixes for components	α,β	running suffixes for different phases
$1,2$	particular components	σ	surface

$g_{2x} = (\partial^2 g/\partial x^2)_{P,T}$ in Chapter 7

A time derivative is denoted by a dot, thus $\dot{m}$ is (dm/dt)
For $\int X\, dY_Z$, see Section 3.14

Standard States

The conventions used here are demonstrated for the chemical potential. Thus:

μ_i potential of component i, a function of P, T, x

μ_i° potential of pure i, a function of P, T

$\mu_i^{\dagger}$ potential of i in a particular fixed or standard state chosen for its convenience in treating the problem in hand. (see eg. Section 6.9)

$\mu_i^{\ominus}$ potential of pure i in what is usually called *the standard state*, a function of T. This state is defined formally in Sections 6.4, 6.7 and 8.3, but the definitions may be summarised:

for a perfect gas   —the pressure is $P^{\ominus}$ (Section 6.4)

for a real gas   —the equivalent perfect gas is at a pressure $P^{\ominus}$ (Sections 6.7 and 8.3)

for a solid or liquid—the pressure is $P^{\ominus}$ (Section 8.3)

The standard pressure $P^{\ominus}$ is almost always taken to be

$$1 \text{ atm} = 101\ 325 \text{ N m}^{-2}$$

$\mu_i^{\square}$ potential of ideal solution at unit molality, a function of T

(Section 6.13).

Useful Constants

Faraday's constant	$F = 96\ 487 \text{ C mol}^{-1}$
Planck's constant	$h = 6.626 \times 10^{-34} \text{ J s}$
Boltzmann's constant	$k = 1.3805 \times 10^{-23} \text{ J K}^{-1}$
Avogadro's constant	$N_A = 6.023 \times 10^{23} \text{ mol}^{-1}$
Molar gas constant	$R = 8.314 \text{ J K}^{-1} \text{ mol}^{-1}$
Temperature conversion	$0\,°C = 273.15 \text{ K}$
$\mathcal{M}$ for air	$= 28.96$

1 Heat and Work

1.1 Introduction

Thermodynamics is the study of the interconversion of heat, work and other forms of energy. It is called a phenomenological subject in that it treats of the phenomena that occur in real macroscopic systems and not of their microscopic or molecular causes. Thus, if we heat a liquid at atmospheric pressure we find that it expands, if we heat it at a fixed volume we find that the pressure rises. Thermodynamics is that part of science which gives us relations between such quantities as the amount of heat supplied in each case, the increase of volume and the rise of pressure. Some of these quantities may be difficult to measure, and one of the principal uses of thermodynamics is their calculation from the more accessible quantities. Such calculations tell us nothing, however, of the molecular mechanisms in the liquid that cause the increase in volume or the rise of pressure.

If we wish to calculate, not one macroscopic property in terms of another, but to estimate both from our knowledge of the behaviour of molecules, then we must go beyond the relations of classical thermodynamics. This extension is called statistical thermodynamics, and we touch on some of its engineering uses in the last chapter. The bulk of the book is, however, confined to the principles and chemical engineering applications of classical thermodynamics.

Heat and work are particularly important forms of energy as far as thermodynamics is concerned. Historically, all of the early work on the subject involved these two forms of energy and their interconversion. Thus, in the early years of the nineteenth century, the steam engine was in regular use and attempts to improve its efficiency, for the conversion of thermal energy into mechanical energy, were of great economic importance. Conversion in the opposite direction had been observed many years earlier and perhaps the most famous reported observation is that of Rumford who, in 1798, noticed that during the boring of cannon, tremendous amounts of heat were generated. Interpretation of observations such as these were clouded at the time by the credence given to the old caloric theory of heat, and it was not until the 1840s and the work of Joule that thermodynamics, as we know it, began to see the light of day.[1]

In spite of apparent preoccupation with heat and work, particularly in the early parts of this book, much of what we say will ultimately have a much wider interpretation. We shall be applying our results to situations which, at first sight, do not appear to involve them in any important way. We shall examine not only physical processes, which may involve both heat and work, but also chemical processes, where their role is less obvious. We could, although we shall not do so, examine processes which take place in strong magnetic or electric fields (work being done against the field), but the study of such situations is more appropriate to physics textbooks. We could also examine biological processes, such as the exchange of chemical and mechanical energy in muscle, but we leave them to books on biochemistry. Thermodynamics has applications in all branches of science and engineering, but in this textbook we select material which is important to the chemical engineer.

1.2 Equilibrium

Before going further, we must introduce the concept of equilibrium. This is something which is difficult to define formally, and we do not attempt a rigorous definition. A system is said to be in equilibrium if (a) it does not change over the time scale of interest to us, and (b) a small change made to it may be reversed, so returning the system to its starting point. The time scale of interest varies with the situation and each case must be examined individually. For example, if a hot aqueous solution of a soluble salt is cooled, a point will be reached at which we would expect crystallisation to occur. However, if the cooling process is slow, it is possible to 'supercool' the solution, no crystallisation taking place. Let us maintain it at the temperature then reached and ask whether the situation is in equilibrium. If our time scale is measured in minutes, then we would usually find no further change in the supercooled solution and we can say the solution is in a state of equilibrium. If, however, our time scale is measured in days, in all probability crystallisation will occur due to nucleation and our supercooled state cannot be considered to be the equilibrium one; this description belongs to the crystallised state.

What we have just described is very similar to equilibrium in the mechanical situations represented in Figure 1.1. Ball A sitting at the bottom of the valley is in a position of *stable equilibrium* and this corresponds to the crystallised solution. Ball B in a local depression at the top of the hill is said to be in *metastable equilibrium*, and corresponds to the supercooled solution; formally we say that ball B is stable with respect to small displacements, but not to large ones. Ball C is in a *non-equilibrium* position, as it is spontaneously rolling downhill.

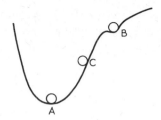

Figure 1.1. Equilibrium in a mechanical situation

We give two more examples to clarify our ideas on equilibrium.

(a) A mixture of hydrogen and oxygen at room temperature is at equilibrium. If we introduce a catalyst, chemical reaction occurs, and not until reaction stops is equilibrium restored. By analogy with Figure 1.1, we would say that the unreacted mixture was in metastable equilibrium and the final state in stable equilibrium. But we can make quite large changes in the pressure and temperature of the hydrogen-oxygen mixture, and we can then reverse these, thus restoring the system to its original state. In the absence of a catalyst these large changes do not cause reaction, and so the region of metastability is far from small, that is in this case, it is more like a deep hole in the side of the hill, rather than the shallow depression of Figure 1.1. The metastable system is therefore coming close to what can quite properly be called stable equilibrium and, conversely, what we usually think of as stable equilibrium is really nothing more than the limiting case of metastable equilibrium, for even the fully reacted system, water, might under appropriate circumstances, undergo nuclear reaction to a state of even lower energy.

(b) A vessel containing gas at a uniform temperature and pressure is at equilibrium. If there is a temperature gradient present we would not normally consider it to be at equilibrium. But, when the vessel is a very long capillary tube, our time of interest is small compared to the time thermal conduction takes to even out the temperature gradient, and when we consider only changes which, when reversed, allow the original temperature gradient to be restored, then the system may be taken as being at equilibrium. Thus, for example, a long capillary tube made of rubber and containing gas can be squeezed uniformly by application of an external pressure. This changes the state of the gas within the tube, but there will not necessarily be a significant flow of gas molecules along the tube. Thus, if the external pressure is relaxed, we can return the gas to its original state and with the original temperature gradient intact. It therefore conforms to our requirements for an equilibrium state. The situation is analogous to example (a) where the unreacted hydrogen-oxygen mixture is at equilibrium with respect to changes in pressure and temperature only if the chemical reaction is 'frozen' in the unreacted state.

Thermodynamics deals only with equilibrium situations and, in particular, changes from one equilibrium situation to another, such as from A to B in Figure 1.1, or vice versa. The change may pass through non-equilibrium positions en route, as clearly happens if the ball rolls down the hill, but this does not affect the applicability of thermodynamics. It is required only that the initial and final positions are in equilibrium with respect to the change we are considering.

The inability of thermodynamics to deal with other than equilibrium situations has one very important consequence. We are unable to say anything about the rate at which a process happens, for any natural or spontaneous process goes through a series of non-equilibrium positions. If a process is undergoing change, we can describe the position (thermodynamically) when it comes to a stop, but we can say nothing about the rate at which it gets there. In the hydrogen-oxygen reaction we can investigate the products of reaction and even, as we shall see, predict what they are, but thermodynamics gives us no clue as to whether the reaction takes one second or one year to come to completion. There have, in recent years, been developments in a subject called 'non-equilibrium thermodynamics', which attempts to deal with rate processes, but apart from the title its connection with 'equilibrium thermodynamics', which is what we are concerned with here, is small and will not be discussed in this book.

1.3 Temperature

An understanding of the concepts of work and pressure is essential to the study of mechanical systems, and we presume the reader to be familiar with them. They are also important in thermodynamics, but here we have, in addition, the concepts of heat and temperature to contend with. We examine now some of the properties of the latter.

Consider two bodies well separated from one another. Each will be separately at equilibrium in the sense given in Section 1.2. If we bring the bodies into contact so that energy, in the form of heat, can flow from one to the other, we notice that the heat flow takes place in one direction only, and we say that the body which gives up heat is hotter than the other. After the bodies have been in contact for some time, we notice that heat flow falls off and then stops. We now have equilibrium between them, and we say that they are at the same 'temperature', this being the quantity we use to measure 'hotness'. If we bring the two bodies together and find no heat flow, we conclude that both are at the same temperature. The same is true of any third body which we may bring up and which, when in contact with the other two, does not transfer any heat in either direction.

It is pertinent to ask, at this point, how in fact we know that there has been a flow of heat. It is our experience that we can only infer that heat has flowed if the two bodies we have brought into contact have changed in some observable way. Thus, if they are two pieces of metal, measurements of their volume (or length) tells us whether any change is taking place; if we have gas contained in a vessel of fixed volume, measurement of pressure does the same. We use these observations, not only to determine equality of temperature, but to provide a monotonic scale of temperature. We do this by associating a numerical value of temperature with each measurement of volume in the case of our pieces of metal, or with each measurement of pressure for the gas at constant volume. The way we do this is quite arbitrary. We could, for example, choose a scale in which the temperature was proportional to the pressure in the case of the gas at constant volume; or we could choose to make it inversely proportional. The most frequently used thermometer is one which uses the expansion of a liquid, typically alcohol or mercury, in a glass vessel, but there is no reason to suppose that, even if we define our temperature scale as being linear in changes of the liquid volume, both alcohol and mercury will give the same value for the measurement of any arbitrary temperature. It is clear, therefore, that we have available an almost infinite number of thermometric devices and a similarly large number of temperature scales.

The observations which we have made in this section are often embodied in the so-called *zeroth law of thermodynamics* ('zeroth' since it is more primitive than the first, second and third laws which, nevertheless, preceded it historically). In science, a law is a statement of an important generalisation from experience and, in general, the title is reserved for basic ideas which are fundamental to the subject. Clearly, the existence of the quantity 'temperature' and its measurable properties fit this requirement. The zeroth law is:

if, of three bodies, A, B and C, A and B are separately in thermal equilibrium with C, then A and B are in thermal equilibrium with one another.

It is, in many respects, a trivial statement, almost, one might say, a statement of the obvious. Nevertheless, it is a statement which has to be made before it is possible to quantify the concept of temperature.

We leave temperature, for the moment, in this somewhat unsatisfactory state, with its multiplicity of scales, to return to it later in Chapter 3 after we have introduced the second law of thermodynamics. We shall see there that it is possible to choose one particular scale having thermodynamically desirable properties. However, it will help, in the meantime, if the reader thinks of temperature as expressed on the scale of the constant volume gas thermometer, that is, the temperature as indicated by measurements of the pressure of a gas contained in a vessel of constant volume. This leads to temperatures which are never negative and in which large numbers are associated with hot bodies, small numbers with cold.

1.4 Definitions

In thermodynamics, the part of the physical world which we are investigating is called the *system*. It may be a very simple part, such as a beaker in which a chemical reaction is carried out on the laboratory bench, or it may be very much more complex, such as a complete air liquefaction plant.

That part of the remainder of the physical world which can in any significant way affect or be affected by the system we call the *surroundings*. Thus, the burner which supplies heat to the beaker is part of the surroundings. The Earth's atmosphere, which supplies air to the liquefaction plant, forms part of the surroundings in the second example. It is true that the atmosphere is in contact with the beaker in the first example also, but we do not need to consider it as part of the surroundings unless it has a significant effect on the reaction taking place.

In general, we expect the interaction between the system and its surroundings to result in the transfer of (a) thermal energy, i.e. heat, (b) mechanical energy, i.e. work and (c) material from one to the other. If the nature of the system is such that only heat and/or work is transferred to or from the surroundings, we call the system *closed*. If, in addition, there is transfer of material, that is molecules, then the system is said to be *open*. Thus, the chemical reaction taking place in the beaker is a closed system, provided that there is no loss or gain of gaseous material to or from the atmosphere. The air liquefaction plant is an open system since it takes in material from the atmosphere, that is from the surroundings.

A system which is thermally isolated from the surroundings is said to be *adiabatic*. It is as though the system were surrounded by walls which are impenetrable by heat. This is not a completely hypothetical concept, for a double-walled vacuum flask with silvered walls (Dewar vessel) is an excellent approximation to an adiabatic enclosure. In fact, without such a vessel, the experimental aspects of thermodynamics, particularly calorimetry, would be impracticable. In an adiabatic closed system, the only way that any changes can be made to the system is by transferring energy in the form of work.

In the design of large chemical plant, the chemical engineer might therefore ask how is he to decide what constitutes his system. Consider the case of a methane liquefier, Figure 1.2. Methane is stored under pressure in a series of cylinders. The methane gas is fed, via the compressor, to the liquefaction unit. Since the latter requires an input stream at a constant pressure of e.g. 100 bar, the compressor must be operated in such a way as to boost the dwindling gas

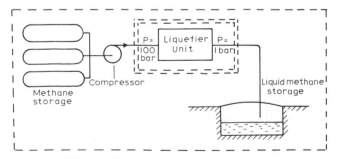

Figure 1.2. Methane liquefaction plant

pressure in the storage cylinders to this figure. The liquid methane leaves the liquefier at 1 bar pressure and is led to a storage tank. If the engineer takes as his system the whole plant, that is the whole area within the singly broken lines on the diagram, then he clearly has a closed system since, although heat and work (the latter is needed to drive the compressor) pass through this boundary, no methane does so. However, the engineer could, quite justifiably, focus his attention on the liquefier unit since this is the most difficult part of the plant to design, so that he defines his system as that which is enclosed by the double broken lines. Now the system is open since we have a gaseous methane input stream and a liquid methane output stream; the remainder of the plant forms part of the surroundings. During start up, we have gaseous methane going in and no liquid methane coming out. However, once the plant has been operating for some time, we reach a steady state in which the amount of gaseous methane entering, equals the amount of liquid methane flowing out. There is now no net change in the amount of material within the system. Such a state of affairs is of sufficient importance to warrant its being classified as a *steady state flow system*. In general, the chemical engineer attempts to design the various components of a plant to operate under steady state flow conditions. The reasons for this are largely economic, and they become more and more compelling, the larger the plant under consideration. In this book we are only rarely concerned with open systems in which the amount of material is changing with time. Most of the discussion is on closed systems and on steady state flow systems.

In order to be quantitative about what happens inside a system, we shall find it necessary to talk about its *properties*. If the system is a simple one, such as a piece of metal, then mass, volume and temperature are obvious candidates for the name property. Pressure might be added as another property, and is obviously appropriate if the system is a gas. However, what constitutes a property in the case of the methane liquefier discussed above? Mass and volume are both reasonable for we can evaluate the mass and volume of the whole plant by summing over its various components. But pressure and temperature are more difficult since these vary throughout the plant. There is not just one value of pressure, for example, which can be ascribed to the plant. We must, therefore, define a property more formally, and consider which properties are relevant to thermodynamics.

We define a property by describing methods of measuring it. The value of that property, at any one time, is the result of the measuring operation performed at that time. The value must be unique, so that different methods of measurement of the same property give the same result, and it must be independent of the past history of the object or system, that is, a property is a characterisation of the system as we find it now. Clearly, mass, volume, pressure and temperature conform to this definition, even in the case of the methane liquefier. We may take a measurement of pressure by inserting a probe into the plant *at some point*, and measuring the pressure at that point. The result will be a meaningful value and, therefore, may be classed as a property. Clearly, we can make many pressure measurements at points throughout the plant. The values obtained will, in general, be different, and so we find that many properties of the plant or system are measurements of pressure. This is obviously inconvenient in any thermodynamic computation and so we nearly always break down our plant into simpler components, choosing these so that, as far as possible, the pressure and temperature, for example, are uniform throughout that component. Thus, in the methane liquefier, one component would be the gaseous methane storage. A second one would be the liquid methane storage. This leaves a residual number of components, in this case the compressor and the liquefier unit, in which there are pressure and temperature gradients. We shall see later how it is possible to avoid the need for a detailed knowledge of these, and how to base our calculations on the characteristics of the input and output streams only.

We can divide the properties considered so far, mass, volume, pressure and temperature, into two classes. The first, mass and volume, can be evaluated for a whole system by summation over the component parts. Such properties are called *extensive*. The second, temperature and pressure, may be looked upon more as point values, or, more precisely, as properties whose values approach a finite and non-zero limit as the size of a system which includes the selected point approaches zero. These properties are called *intensive*. The two classes do not embrace all possible properties. Thus, V^2 is a property. If a volume V is considered as made up of two parts V_1 and V_2 then, since

$$V^2 \neq V_1^2 + V_2^2 \tag{1.1}$$

V^2 cannot be classed as extensive. It is clearly not intensive either. Properties of this type are hardly ever useful in thermodynamics, and in this book we are concerned only with intensive and extensive properties.

When we know the values of a sufficient number of properties of a system so as to specify it completely, we say that we know the *state* of the system. Thus, if two systems are to be in the same state, then they must both have the same value for every property. Since a system has, in general, a large number of properties, our aim is to find a set of the *minimum number* of properties which specify its state. We should like also to find the rules which enable us to calculate as many other properties as is possible from this minimum set.

The minimum number of properties necessary to specify the state of a system can be determined only from our experience of the physical world; it cannot be found in any theoretical way. Consider the case of a sample of gas, which we assume to be homogeneous. Our experience tells us that if we know the values of pressure, temperature and amount of material, we have specified completely the state of the gas. It has just one value for the volume, given by an expression of the type

$$V = f(P, T, n) \tag{1.2}$$

We see that P, T and n do not form a unique set of properties which may be used to specify the state of the system; P, T and V, or V, T and n, etc. also form adequate sets.

The minimum number of properties needed to specify the state of a system varies with the latter's complexity. Thus, to take a simple extension to the example above, if the gas is a two-component mixture, in addition to P, T and n, we need to determine the composition.

Although any type of property may be used to specify the state of a system, we find that when we come to determine the rules relating one property to another, we can do this only if we restrict our considerations to the intensive and extensive properties which describe systems at equilibrium. The properties in this subject are termed *functions of state* or *state functions*.

Functions of state have a number of important mathematical properties. Consider the case of the volume, V, of a system. Any infinitesimal change in the volume can be denoted by dV, that is as a differential of the function of state. Thus, if in any process the volume of the system changes, and if the process can be represented by a series of infinitesimal steps, the total volume change is given by

$$\text{Volume change} = \int_1^2 dV = V_2 - V_1 \qquad (1.3)$$

where the limits on the integral sign imply that the system starts in state 1 with volume V_1, and the process continues until the system reaches state 2 with volume V_2. The value of the integral $(V_2 - V_1)$ is independent of the particular path or route by which the volume was changed. The process may have been such that the volume increased uniformly from V_1 to V_2, or there may have been an initial contraction followed by an expansion, or any other more complex process. The value for the change in volume, however, is independent of all of this, and depends only on the properties of the system in state 1 and on the properties in state 2. Mathematically, a differential quantity such as dV, which may be integrated in this way, is called a *perfect differential*, or a *total differential*, or an *exact differential*.

Differences in the values of state functions, of which $V_2 - V_1$ is just one example, are frequently encountered in thermodynamics, and for convenience we use the shorthand notation

$$V_2 - V_1 \equiv \Delta V \qquad (1.4)$$

This 'capital delta' notation is used only for changes in state functions and not for any other purpose.

Finally, it is clear from the argument above that if the material in a closed system starts in state 1, and the process is such that the system is ultimately returned to state 1, there will have been no net change in any of the functions of state. Thus, in the case of the volume we can write

$$\Delta V = \oint dV = 0 \qquad (1.5)$$

where the symbol $\oint$ is used to show that the integral is over a closed path. The same is true for steady flow of unit amount of material through a series of processes if they ultimately return the material to state 1. A process which brings the material back to its original state in this way is called a *cycle*.

1.5 Heat and work

Heat and work are quantities quite different in character from the properties—functions of state—which we have considered so far. Thus, if our system consists of a gas contained within a vessel, although it is perfectly proper to talk of the pressure of the gas or of its volume, it is meaningless to talk of its heat or work. If, however, our gas, which we assume to be at sufficiently high pressure, is allowed to push a piston along a cylinder, and if we connect the piston to a crank by means of a connecting rod, as in an internal combustion engine, we can perform useful mechanical work. That is, we can transfer energy, in the form of work, from the system to some other object or system in the surroundings. Similarly, if we have a vessel which contains substances which react together exothermically,* we can transfer energy, this time in the form of heat, to another body in the surroundings merely by bringing them into thermal contact. We can thus look upon both work and heat as 'energy in transit' to the surroundings from the system, or vice versa.

That heat and work are not functions of state can be seen clearly by considering a simple example. Let us assume that we wish to increase the temperature of a piece of metal from, say 20 °C to 30 °C. One way to do this would be to supply the necessary heat from a suitable burner. Clearly no work is involved in this process. A second way would be to rub the piece of metal on a rough surface and thereby increase the temperature by friction. This time, work will have been performed in overcoming friction, but no heat will have been supplied. Thus, although the state of the metal is the same at the end of each process—same temperature, pressure and mass—and the changes in these properties are the same in each process—as is required for a function of state—the work done in the first case differs from that done in the second, as also does the heat supplied. Therefore, neither heat nor work can be functions of state.

This example shows that work can be converted into heat by friction. A paddle wheel rotating in a vessel of liquid has the same effect. Strictly speaking, both processes result in an increase in the temperature of the system rather than in the direct conversion of work into heat. But material at a temperature above ambient can act as a source of thermal energy, and we may therefore talk loosely of the conversion of work into heat. Such conversion, by means of a paddle wheel, was the one carried out by Joule in the mid-nineteenth century. He took great pains to measure accurately the amount of energy in the form of work which he had to supply to raise the temperature of a certain mass of water.

---

* An exothermic reaction is one which, when carried out at constant temperature, gives out heat.

Knowing the amount of heat which he would have had to supply to obtain the same temperature rise, he calculated the constant of proportionality, known as the 'mechanical equivalent of heat', relating the work supplied to the heat to which it was equivalent. Subsequent investigations on other situations in which work is converted into heat have shown that, provided the effect of the work is purely one of raising the temperature of the system, the constant of proportionality has always the same value. We might say that conversion of work into heat can be carried out with 100% efficiency. In the SI system of units advantage has been taken of this fact, and the mechanical equivalent of heat set equal to unity, so that both heat and work can be measured in the same units, namely joules. Its constancy, in all circumstances, is also the essential content of the first law of thermodynamics which we consider in Chapter 2.

In contrast, our experience with the conversion of heat into work always leads to a conversion efficiency of less than 100%. For example, the mechanical energy provided by a steam turbine is often only 40–50% of the thermal energy supplied to raise the steam. Some of the inefficiency arises from mechanical difficulties such as friction, but this represents only a small part of the loss. There is, therefore, something more fundamental involved, and we shall see what this is when we come to consider the second law of thermodynamics.

It is often said that work represents a higher form of energy than heat. That is, we can always convert a given quantity of work into heat whenever we wish, but once we have got the energy as heat, we cannot go back to work without some losses in the process. The maximum efficiency of the latter process we consider in Chapter 3 under the heading 'availability'.

Thermodynamics is a quantitative subject and in the earlier part of this book we are concerned with calculating the heat or work which is transferred to or from a system. To take a concrete example, let us assume that we wish to know how much work we need to supply a compressor in order to compress a given amount of air. We have the choice of either measuring this at the motor, using a dynamometer, or of calculating it from the known dimensions, etc., of the compressor. The first method involves an investigation of what is happening in the surroundings, the second of what is happening in the system. Since both measure the same quantity we can choose whichever is the more convenient. However, only in a few cases can we do the necessary calculations on the system, and we are often forced to examine what is happening in the surroundings.

When a particular system is undergoing a certain process, we can transfer heat and/or work to or from it. Since it is more convenient to treat heat and work as algebraic quantities in calculations, we require a convention as to their sign. Whenever heat, symbol Q, or work, symbol W, is transferred to the system from the surroundings, we shall treat it as positive. Thus, for example, a system which is losing heat to its surroundings will be characterised by Q having a negative value. This convention is the one recommended by the

International Union of Pure and Applied Chemistry (IUPAC) and is used by many authors. Unfortunately, however, many other authors, particularly of the older textbooks, adhere to this convention for Q but use the opposite one for W.

There is a second convention for Q and W. In solving a problem it is frequently convenient to set up a differential equation to represent an infinitesimal change in the process, and then to evaluate the total process by integration. This equation may involve the differentials of state functions such as dV and dP, together with differentials of the non-state functions heat and work. The latter we represent by dQ and dW as a reminder that they are not state functions. dQ and dW may be integrated just as dV and dP but, whereas the value obtained by integration of a state function (such as dV or dP) depends only on the initial and final states of the system, the one obtained by integration of dQ or dW depends also on the route taken during the process.

1.6 Work

The transfer of mechanical energy, as work, can take place in many ways. For example, in the generation of electricity, mechanical energy is first produced by a steam turbine. This is transferred, as work, to an electrical generator. This, in turn, produces electricity which can perform electrical work. If we use this electrical work to drive a motor, then once more we have mechanical energy. This interconversion of one form of work into another can, in principle, be carried out with 100% efficiency provided we can eliminate losses from friction, etc. This interconvertibility is characteristic of all forms of work.

Perhaps the simplest situation in which we can calculate the work required to bring about a process, is the lifting of a mass against the force of gravity. If the mass m is raised a distance h, then the increase in the potential energy of the mass, and therefore the work required to raise it is

$$W = mgh \qquad (1.6)$$

where g is the acceleration due to gravity. If, however, the mass were not constant, as would be the case if we used for the mass a leaky bucket which, though initially full of water, steadily lost its contents, we should have to break down the process into a large number of small steps, each of height dh and for which the small amount of work required would be

$$dW = mg\, dh \qquad (1.7)$$

where m would now be a variable quantity. The total work required is obtained by integration

$$W = \int dW = g \int m\, dh \qquad (1.8)$$

The expression for dW is of the form

$$dW = \text{force} \times \text{distance through which the force moves}$$

$$= mg \times dh \qquad (1.9)$$

and this is what we generally find for all of the various types of work which we consider.

Since, in principle, one form of work can be converted into another with 100% efficiency, we frequently have recourse to the work done in raising a mass against gravity as a device for calculating the work involved in other, more complex, situations. All we require is that we can postulate some machinery which will convert the actual work into 'raising against gravity' work.

1.7 Work in a closed system

The commonest situation involving work in a closed system is the one in which a three-dimensional system expands or contracts against an external pressure. For simplicity, let the system be a rectangular object of sides $a \times b \times c$, and let the external pressure which is supplied by the surroundings be P_{ext}. Since pressure is, by definition, the force per unit area acting on the surface and normal to it, the total force acting on one side of the box $a \times b$ is $P_{ext}ab$, Figure 1.3. If now dimension c increases to $c + dc$ the surroundings are 'pushed back' a

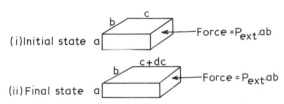

Figure 1.3. The expansion of a rectangular object

distance dc and the system (the box) does work on the surroundings numerically equal to $P_{ext}ab \, dc$.

On our convention of the work done on the system being counted as positive, the work done on the system by the surroundings during the infinitesimal expansion process is

$$dW = -P_{ext}ab \, dc \tag{1.10}$$

Since the increase in the volume of the box

$$dV = ab \, dc \tag{1.11}$$

we can simplify (1.10) to

$$dW = -P_{ext} \, dV \tag{1.12}$$

where dV is the change in volume of the system, and not of the surroundings.

It is readily seen that if the other two dimensions of the box increase in a similar manner, the work done on the system is given by similar equations, and provided that P_{ext} is the same on all faces of the box, summing the various work terms gives (1.12) again, where dV now refers to the total change in the volume of the box, no matter on which face or faces it takes place. A simple extension to the argument shows that (1.12) holds for systems of arbitrary shape.

Exercise

Show that (1.12) applies for the work done when a sphere expands uniformly against an external pressure.

If the system expanding against an external pressure is a rigid cylinder containing gas sealed by a frictionless piston, Figure 1.4, then the only external pressure we need concern ourselves with is the one acting on the piston.

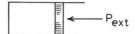

Figure 1.4. The expansion of gas against an external pressure

Comparison with the three-dimensional object expanding in one dimension which we considered above leads again to

$$dW = -P_{ext}\,dV \qquad (1.12)$$

The pressure of the gas in the cylinder is irrelevant in evaluating the work done by the surroundings on the system (the gas). Any displacement of the piston means that work is done as given by (1.12). In practice, if the gas pressure inside differs from that outside, then some mechanical restraints or catches are required to hold the piston in any chosen position, but the operation of such a catch need not involve the performance of a significant amount of work.

An alternative calculation of the work performed by a gas expanding against an external pressure can be made by placing the cylinder so that its axis is vertical and, instead of supplying a restraining force on the piston from an external pressure, supplying an equal force by placing a mass m on the piston, Figure 1.5. If we assume that the pressure of the surrounding atmosphere is

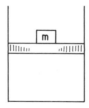

Figure 1.5. The expansion of gas against a gravitational force

zero, and that the piston is weightless and of area $\mathscr{A}$, then, with the value of m given by

$$mg = P_{ext}\mathscr{A} \qquad (1.13)$$

the force on the piston will be the same as before. A displacement of the piston upwards by a distance dh raises the mass m by this same amount and thereby does work on the mass, of $mg\,dh$. Since we consider the mass as part of the surroundings, we have once more the work done by the surroundings on the system

$$dW = -mg\,dh$$
$$= -P_{ext}\mathscr{A}\,dh$$
$$= -P_{ext}\,dV \tag{1.14}$$

If there are no pressure gradients within the cylinder and the (uniform) pressure P of the gas within it is equal to the external pressure P_{ext} we can write

$$dW = -P\,dV \tag{1.15}$$

and now *both* properties on the right hand side of this equation are properties of the system.

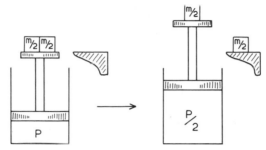

Figure 1.6. Raising a mass by means of expansion of a gas

Consider gas at pressure P in a cylinder, Figure 1.6, and sealed by a weightless piston which can slide freely without friction. Again we take the surrounding pressure as zero. If the gas pressure is to be equal to the external pressure, here supplied by a mass m on the piston of area $\mathscr{A}$, then

$$P = mg/\mathscr{A} \tag{1.16}$$

Let us slide off sideways on to a suitably placed platform one half of the mass m. This operation clearly does not involve the performance of work. The forces on the piston are now unbalanced and it rises until the pressure of the gas is $\frac{1}{2}P$, when the internal pressure is once more balanced by the external force supplied by the mass $\frac{1}{2}m$, which is equivalent to an external pressure

$$P_{ext} = \tfrac{1}{2}mg/\mathscr{A} = \tfrac{1}{2}P \tag{1.17}$$

The calculation of the work done by the surroundings on the system we have already done in differential form (1.14), and integration of this gives

$$W = -\int_{V_1}^{V_2} P_{ext}\,dV$$
$$= -P_{ext}(V_2 - V_1)$$
$$= -\tfrac{1}{2}P(V_2 - V_1) \tag{1.18}$$

where V_1 is the initial volume of the gas and V_2 the final volume.

Although the external pressure is equal to the internal (gas) pressure (i) at the beginning when $P_{ext} = P$, and (ii) at the end when $P_{ext} = \frac{1}{2}P$, it is clearly not so during the expansion, and we cannot replace P_{ext} in (1.18) by the internal pressure as an alternative method of integration. However, we can imagine that the mass m is divided into a large number of parts, as it would be if it were formed from a pile of fine sand, Figure 1.7. Consider first the case in which the process takes place adiabatically, that is the system neither gains nor loses

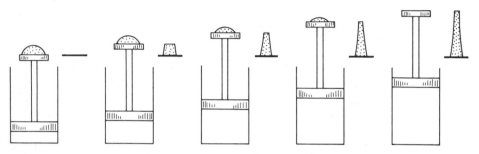

Figure 1.7. Raising a pile of sand by expansion of a gas

thermal energy from the surroundings. If we remove the grains of sand from the piston one by one, piling them so that they remain at the level at which they are removed from the piston, we have the sequence depicted. Since the removal of any one grain unbalances the forces exerted on the piston only by a very small amount, and only a small displacement of the piston is needed to restore equilibrium, we can consider the device as being essentially in equilibrium all of the time. Let the mass of sand on the piston be m when the height of the piston is h, and the mass of each grain of sand removed from the piston be the differential quantity dm, and let dh be the corresponding distance which the piston rises. Then the work done by the surroundings (sand) on the system (gas) by the removal of one grain is

$$dW = -mg\, dh$$
$$= -P_{ext}\, dV$$
$$= -P_{gas}\, dV \tag{1.19}$$

where we have used the fact that P_{ext} and P_{gas} differ only infinitesimally during the removal of one grain. Thus, for the whole process in which a substantial amount of sand is removed from the piston, the work done on the system is

$$W = \int dW$$
$$= -\int P_{gas}\, dV \tag{1.20}$$

This process is essentially equivalent to a *single* expansion stroke of the engine shown in Figure 1.8, in which the piston drives a flywheel via a crank

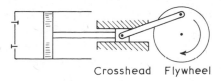

Crosshead   Flywheel

Figure 1.8. Reciprocating expansion engine

and crosshead. If a source of high pressure gas is momentarily connected to the cylinder when the piston is near the cylinder head (in an internal combustion engine this is done by igniting a hydrocarbon/air mixture), the forces on the piston will be approximately balanced during the expansion stroke, the compressive forces within the connecting rod varying in such a manner as to keep them so. In view of the interconvertibility of mechanical work, the work done during one stroke of this rather complicated machine can be calculated from the changing properties of the gas by solving the much simpler problem of a mass of sand being raised against gravity.

A process of this type, in which the system goes through a series of infinitesimally small steps, keeping essentially at equilibrium all the time, we call a *reversible* process. It is reversible in the sense that if we replace the grains of sand, one by one, on top of the piston, taking them from the pile by the side in the reverse order to that in which they were placed there, the process can be made to reverse itself. It retraces exactly the path which it took during expansion. No additional work is needed to lift on the grains of sand as all their movements are sideways. At the end of the reverse process the device is indistinguishable from its state at the beginning. Contrast this situation with that needed to reverse Figure 1.6. Any reversal requires that we first lift the mass $\frac{1}{2}m$ from the platform on to the piston, and this requires us to supply work. At the end of the process, therefore, the surroundings have lost energy and so the conditions for reversibility are not fulfilled. We say that such a process is *irreversible*.

For the reversible process described above, we can plot the instantaneous values of pressure and volume of the gas on a *P-V* diagram represented in Figure 1.9a by the line 1–2. We call this the path of the process, and it follows from (1.20) that the work done on the gas is the negative of the area under line $1 \rightarrow 2$.

If the reversible process is not adiabatic, and heat is supplied to the gas as it is expanding, the instantaneous values of pressure will be greater than in the adiabatic case, and we must expect the value of the integral in (1.20) to be numerically larger. Again we analyse the situation by using the pile of sand device, taking off the grains adiabatically one by one, but in between the removal of each grain we supply a small amount of heat, keeping the volume constant as we do it. The path of this process is shown in Figure 1.9b and by making the steps smaller and smaller, we have in the limit the situation shown

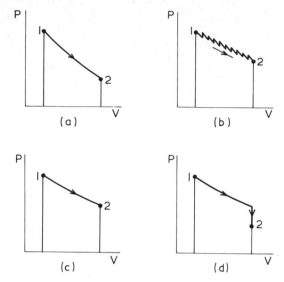

Figure 1.9. Reversible expansion processes

in Figure 1.9c, which represents a process in which heat is supplied continuously to the gas as it expands. In Figure 1.9b the number of steps is arbitrary, but the shape of each step, and in particular the length of each vertical constant volume element of it, is determined by the amount of heat supplied to the system as it expands. If heat is removed they will, of course, occur in the opposite direction.

The process depicted in Figure 1.9b is reversible in the same way that the corresponding adiabatic process was. The only difference between the two return paths is that in this latter example we must remove exactly the same amount of heat from the gas as we supplied in the forward path at each particular step in the process. We defer consideration of how heat can be transferred reversibly until Chapter 3. It is sufficient, at this point, to know that, as far as the system is concerned, there is no problem in the reversible absorption of heat provided that we do not allow temperature gradients to develop within the gas.

Since no work is done during the heating stages in Figure 1.9b (there is no change in volume and so $P\,dV$ is zero) all the work comes from the adiabatic stages, and once more we find that the total work done on the gas is equal to the negative of the area under the line $1 \rightarrow 2$. This applies also to the limiting case in Figure 1.9c. Now if we extend the process shown in c to d, that is if we cool the gas at constant volume until the final values of P and V are the same as in a, no additional work is done, and the total work done remains equal to the negative of the area under the curve. This area, in Figure 1.9d, is not equal to that in Figure 1.9a, in spite of the fact that the initial and final conditions, 1 and 2, are the same in each case.

Thus we see that the work accompanying a change in volume in a closed system is $-\int P\,dV$ whatever the path and whatever the process. It is a result which is applicable without exception to all closed system reversible processes and, for example, applies even to the expansion part of the work (usually termed P-V work) in a process which involves, in addition, electrical work. A battery would form one such system.

The argument given shows also, see Figure 1.9b, that it is always possible to devise a reversible route between any two states provided that both can be represented uniquely on a P-V diagram. This latter requires that, for a fixed amount of material, only two additional independent variables, such as P and V, are necessary to determine the state of the system. If the system is, say, a binary mixture, the composition, if it changes, must be considered as an additional independent variable, and the points 1 and 2 in Figure 1.9 no longer represent unique states. The figure therefore tells us nothing about the existence, or otherwise, of a reversible route between them, but, if we have other evidence which shows that one or more reversible processes in a binary system do indeed follow the route as represented on the P-V diagram of Figure 1.9, then the work done is $-\int P\,dV$, as indicated.

Although the work of the type we have been considering (P-V work) is by far the most important encountered in chemical engineering, it is not the only one. We examine here one other example: electrical work. If the surroundings supply electrical energy to a system then we can write that the work done by them on the system in taking an infinitesimal charge dq through a potential difference φ is

$$\mathrm{d}W = \varphi \cdot \mathrm{d}q = \varphi i \cdot \mathrm{d}t \qquad (1.21)$$

where we have used that $dq = i \cdot dt$ (i = current and t = time). That the energy supplied is work rather than heat is apparent from the fact that a motor can be used to convert the electrical energy into mechanical energy with 100% efficiency, assuming that there are no losses from friction, etc.

1.8   Work in a steady state flow system

A machine operating under steady flow conditions must produce, or be supplied with, work at a constant rate. Such machines are usually rotary, e.g. a compressor, a fan, a blower or a turbine. These are used to compress a fluid by the input of work, or, in the case of expanders, to produce work from a source of high pressure fluid. A thermodynamic analysis shows that these machines are all essentially equivalent, a fact which we illustrate by considering just two machines: (a) a turbine and (b) a reciprocating compressor.

Turbine

A turbine is a steady state flow device for obtaining work from a source of high pressure fluid. It consists of a series of banks of blades fixed alternately to the

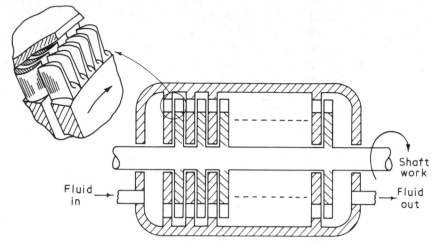

Figure 1.10. Turbine (schematic)

casing and the rotor, see Figure 1.10. The blades are shaped so that, when fluid flows through the turbine, the rotor turns and does work outside the turbine. This useful work is called *shaft work* or, more briefly just *work*. Shaft work is not the only form of mechanical energy which is involved in the operation of a turbine. The moving fluid has kinetic energy and as its speed may change as it passes through the turbine, so also will its kinetic energy.

In general, if we wish to determine the amount of shaft work performed by a given turbine, we can do this only by attaching a suitable machine to the turbine shaft and measuring how much work is done on this external machine per unit mass of fluid flowing through the turbine. A suitable external machine would be a dynamometer, and since this is equivalent to raising a weight against gravity, we can in effect convert the turbine output into 'raising against gravity' work. Clearly, this approach to the analysis of the operation of a turbine does not involve a knowledge of what happens inside the turbine casing, we are examining only the interaction between the 'system' and its 'surroundings'. However, just as in certain closed systems it is possible to calculate the work from a knowledge of the behaviour within the system itself, so also is it possible to determine shaft work in certain steady state flow systems by considering only the system. A full study of this belongs more properly to the field of fluid mechanics, but we consider here sufficient of it for our purposes.

We take as our example an idealised version of an impulse turbine, since this is the simplest from a mathematical point of view. Consider one flow channel through the first stage of the turbine, as shown in Figure 1.11 (a fixed plus moving pair of banks of blades forms a stage). The fixed blades form a converging channel, usually termed a nozzle, so that the fluid flowing through is accelerated, driven by the pressure drop across it. The emerging fluid has, therefore, a higher kinetic energy, but a lower pressure than the ingoing fluid.

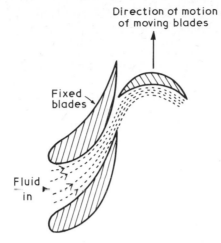

Figure 1.11. Turbine (detail) showing flow of fluid through the blades

This accelerated fluid impinges on the particular blade in its path—the blade being attached to the rotor—and drives it round, thus contributing to the shaft work from the turbine. The fluid loses kinetic energy in the process. In an impulse turbine, it is usually arranged that (i) all of the kinetic energy gained in the flow through the fixed blades is given up to the moving blades immediately following, and (ii) there is no pressure drop in the fluid flowing through the moving blades, that is, all pressure drops take place in the fixed bank of blades.

If there are no frictional losses, the flow is considered 'one-dimensional', even if the channel is curved, and we can calculate the kinetic energy which the fluid stream gains on passing through the fixed blades and, if all of it is transferred to the moving blades, this is equal to the shaft work which the turbine performs. Consider an element of fluid within a nozzle, Figure 1.12. The input velocity of the fluid entering the element is $\mathcal{V}$, and the exit velocity $\mathcal{V} + d\mathcal{V}$. If $\mathscr{A}$ is the cross sectional area at that point then,

$$\text{the net force on this element of fluid} = -\mathscr{A}\ dP \qquad (1.22)$$

and

$$\text{the mass flow rate, } \dot{m}, = \mathscr{A}\mathcal{V}/v \qquad (1.23)$$

where v is the volume of the fluid per unit mass under the conditions of pressure and temperature prevailing within this element of the nozzle. From the laws of

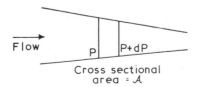

Figure 1.12. Fluid flow through an element of a nozzle

mechanics the net force on the element of fluid must be equal to the rate of change of momentum. Thus

$$-\mathscr{A}\,dP = \dot{m}\,d\mathscr{V}$$

$$= \mathscr{A}\mathscr{V}/v\,d\mathscr{V} \qquad (1.24)$$

or

$$v\,dP + \mathscr{V}\,d\mathscr{V} = 0 \qquad (1.25)$$

We multiply this equation by $\dot{m}$ and integrate over the whole length of the turbine ($\dot{m}$ is constant during this integration), obtaining

$$-\int_{\text{input}}^{\text{output}} \dot{m}v\,dP = [\tfrac{1}{2}\dot{m}\mathscr{V}^2]_{\text{input}}^{\text{output}} \qquad (1.26)$$

and we observe that the right hand side of this equation is the rate of increase in kinetic energy of the fluid as it passes through the nozzle. We can write the left hand side of (1.26) in terms of the volumetric flow rate $\dot{V}$ by noting that $\dot{V} = \dot{m}v$, but an even more general formulation leaves unspecified the time taken for a given mass of fluid to flow through the nozzle, viz:

$$-\int_1^2 V\,dP = \text{KE}_{\text{out}} - \text{KE}_{\text{in}} \qquad (1.27)$$

where P_1 and V_1 refer to the pressure and volume of the given mass of gas at the input to the nozzle and P_2 and V_2 refer similarly to the output.

For a frictionless impulse turbine the gain in kinetic energy by the fluid as it passes through the nozzle is equal to shaft work produced by the complete stage of the turbine of which it is part. Thus, following the convention given in Section 1.5, that we consider work supplied to a system as positive,

$$\text{the work supplied to the turbine} = +\int_1^2 V\,dP \qquad (1.28)$$

In a multistage turbine, the output of one stage immediately forms the input to the next stage. Adding the various integrals gives

$$\text{Total work} = \int_1^a V\,dP + \int_a^b V\,dP + \cdots + \int_z^2 V\,dP = \int_1^2 V\,dP \qquad (1.29)$$

where the limits 1 and 2 now refer to the overall P and V for the whole turbine and the limits a, b, c, etc. refer to the values at the intermediate stages.

We see that in a multistage turbine it is not necessary for all the kinetic energy gained by the fluid in moving through one nozzle to be entirely converted into shaft work by the blades immediately following, for any excess kinetic energy is not lost, but merely carried over to the next stage. The situation regarding the kinetic energy of the fluid entering the first stage and leaving the last stage is more complicated. If the kinetic energy of the input stream equals that of the output stream then there is no net effect on the magnitude of the shaft work which remains $\int_1^2 V\,dP$. If, however, there is an imbalance, the deficiency must be made up from the shaft work, that is

$$\text{shaft work} = \int_1^2 V \, dP + KE_{out} - KE_{in} \tag{1.30}$$

Similarly, if the input and output streams of the turbine are at different levels, work must be done against gravity in raising the fluid; this too must be done at the expense of the shaft work, giving

$$\text{shaft work} = \int_1^2 V \, dP + KE_{out} - KE_{in} + PE_{out} - PE_{in} \tag{1.31}$$

Fortunately, in the majority of steady state flow systems of interest to chemical engineers, the changes in kinetic energy and potential energy are small compared with the other energy changes. In such cases we may neglect these smaller terms and this is implied throughout this book unless a statement is made to the contrary.

The machine we have been considering as a turbine, that is a device for producing work from a source of high pressure fluid, can be operated in reverse, when it becomes a turbo-compressor. This requires a source of low pressure fluid to be connected to what was the output side of the turbine and an external source of work to be connected to the rotor shaft. Provided that the same assumption of frictionless flow through the machine remains true, the analysis of the turbo-compressor is the same as that of the turbine; the magnitude of the various forces remains the same, but they act in the opposite direction. The shaft work to be supplied to the compressor is, therefore, also

$$\int_1^2 V \, dP + KE_{out} - KE_{in} + PE_{out} - PE_{in} \tag{1.32}$$

It is not the negative of (1.31), since what was considered the input stream for a turbine is the output stream for a turbo-compressor, whereas subscript 1, by convention, always refers to the input stream of whatever device is under investigation. If kinetic and potential energy can be neglected

$$\text{Shaft work} = \int_1^2 V \, dP \tag{1.33}$$

These machines are called reversible since when operated in the reverse direction all aspects of the process are retraced in the opposite direction. Thus, for example, the magnitude of the heat and work, pressure and temperature changes, will remain the same, but are of opposite sign. In a practical turbo-compressor or turbine there will be frictional losses and if these assume significant proportions the machines are not reversible. A given turbo-compressor (say) may in principle be operated in reverse as a turbine; if there is friction, in neither case is the shaft work given by $\int_1^2 V \, dP$. We may compare this situation with that prevailing in the closed system where the work to be supplied is equal to $\int_1^2 - P \, dV$ only if the process is reversible.

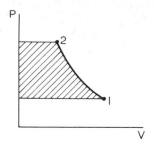

Figure 1.13. Work done in a steady state flow process

Evaluation of the shaft work $\int_1^2 V \, dP$ requires a knowledge of how the volume per unit mass v ($V = mv$) varies with pressure P along the length of the turbine or turbo-compressor. Once this path is known, work may be evaluated as the area shown shaded in Figure 1.13.

Reciprocating compressor

Figure 1.14 shows in diagrammatic form a reciprocating compressor which has spring loaded inlet and outlet valves. The vessels on the inlet and outlet pipes are for damping out the pressure fluctuations which would otherwise occur.

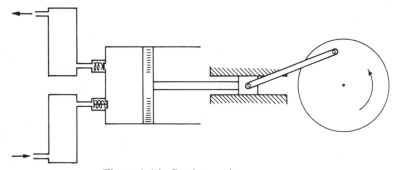

Figure 1.14. Reciprocating compressor

Thus, although compression of the fluid in the cylinder is carried out in 'batches', provided the frequency of compression strokes is high enough, the overall performance of the cylinder plus pulsation dampeners results in steady state flow compression. In a modern reciprocating compressor the approximation is a good one, even if the pulsation dampeners are only lengths of tubing.

As for the turbine, we can always determine the work required for compression by examining the work supplied by the motor driving the compressor. However, we can again in certain cases determine it from what happens within the compressor itself.

In an idealised reciprocating compressor, we assume that the piston displaces completely all material within the cylinder and thus, at the beginning of the intake stroke, the volume and pressure can be represented as point 4, Figure

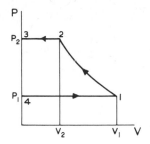

Figure 1.15. *P-V* diagram for a reciprocating compressor (V = instantaneous volume of cylinder)

1.15. During the intake stroke the pressure is maintained essentially constant, represented by the horizontal line 4–1. Once the compression stroke begins, point 1, the input valve closes and the pressure rises until the output pressure P_2 is reached, point 2. The output valve then opens and the compressed gas displaced at an essentially constant pressure P_2.

The work done per cycle may be evaluated as the sum of the various steps, but this is complicated by the fact that, although step 1–2 is closed and no work is done in step 3–4, steps 4–1 and 2–3 are open and the gas flows non-steady state. However, since the piston is solely responsible for the transfer of work to the gas, we can, where necessary, examine the forces on the piston as a means of determining these particular work terms.

We consider the case of a compressor in which all movements of the piston are carried out reversibly (see Section 1.7 on reversible processes in a closed system)—an adequate approximation if a flywheel is interposed between the piston and driving motor—and where the external pressure is zero. The only forces of the piston arise, therefore, on one side from the gas being compressed, and on the other from the compressive forces in the connecting rod. In a reversible process they are equal. Thus, during the intake stroke 4–1, if $\mathscr{A}$ is the cross sectional area of the piston, the work done on the piston is equal to the product of the stroke ($V_1/\mathscr{A}$), and the force on the piston ($P_1\mathscr{A}$), that is

$$\text{Work done on the piston by the gas} = V_1/\mathscr{A} \cdot P_1\mathscr{A} = P_1 V_1 \qquad (1.34)$$

and similarly, during the displacement stroke 2–3,

$$\text{Work done by the piston on the gas} = P_2 V_2 \qquad (1.35)$$

Using the result already obtained for the work done during step 1–2 (a closed system), the total work done by the piston during one complete cycle, which is equal to the work input to the gas, is

$$W_{\text{cycle}} = -P_1 V_1 + \int_1^2 -P\, dV + P_2 V_2$$

$$= \int_1^2 V\, dP \qquad (1.36)$$

The final step, identifying W_{cycle} with $\int_1^2 V\,dP$, is made by examining the areas in Figure 1.15 which represent $P_1 V_1$, $\int_1^2 -P\,dV$ and $P_2 V_2$. The work done on the gas per cycle is, therefore, represented as the area enclosed by 1–2–3–4.

Exercise

Show that (1.36) still holds when the pressure external to the compressor is P_{atm}, and constant.

1.9 Conclusions

We can generalise the results of Sections 1.7 and 1.8 as 'in all reversible processes, the work done in closed and steady state flow systems is $-\int_1^2 P\,dV$ and $\int_1^2 V\,dP$ respectively, provided that changes of kinetic energy can be neglected'. Although formally we have proved this only for the systems discussed there, it is a result which has been found to hold for all reversible processes. Thus, for example, in a real reciprocating compressor, the piston cannot displace all of the gas as some is trapped in the ports leading to the inlet and outlet valves. Figure 1.15 no longer represents accurately the compression process, for the volumes of gas within the compressor at points 3 and 4 are not zero. Nevertheless, as we shall show in Chapter 5, if the compressor acts in a reversible manner, the work done is still expressible as $\int_1^2 V\,dP$. If the process is not reversible, we cannot calculate the work by these methods. In the case of a closed system we can use $\int_1^2 -P_{ext}\,dV$ but this has no steady state flow counterpart. For these irreversible steady state flow systems we can determine the work only by examining what is happening in the surroundings, by the use of a dynamometer or similar device, or by conversion of the work into heat and the measurement of this.

Finally, we note that (1.36) explains why the work involved in a closed system process is not normally equal to the shaft work involved in the corresponding steady state flow process. The difference between these two work terms is the net work, $(P_2 V_2 - P_1 V_1)$, often called flow work, required to get the material into and out of the steady state flow device and whether this is positive or negative depends entirely on the relative magnitude of $P_2 V_2$ and $P_1 V_1$.

Problems

1. An ordinary electrically powered domestic refrigerator is operated in a closed, thermally insulated room. What happens to the 'average temperature' in the room (a) if the refrigerator door is kept shut, and (b) if it is left open?

2. One of the largest Newcomen 'atmospheric' steam engines built in the eighteenth century used a cylinder of 1.8 m diameter, fitted with a piston with a

stroke of 3 metres. In operation, the cylinder was first filled with steam at atmospheric pressure to extend the piston fully, and then a spray of cold water was injected to condense the steam very rapidly, leaving the cylinder essentially evacuated. Atmospheric pressure would then push the piston into the cylinder and, by means of suitable attachments to the piston rod, do work. Taking atmospheric pressure as 1 bar, how much work could an ideal Newcomen engine do per stroke? If the engine operates at 10 strokes per minute, what is the power?

3. The pressure on 1 kg of silver is increased at a constant temperature, from 1 to 1000 bar. The density at 1 bar is $10\,500\;\mathrm{kg\,m^{-3}}$ and the compressibility constant at $10^{-11}\;\mathrm{m^2\,N^{-1}}$. Calculate the work of compression.

4. A pump is used to deliver $0.001\;\mathrm{m^3\,s^{-1}}$ of hydraulic oil, assumed incompressible, at a pressure of 1 kbar ($= 1000$ bar) from a reservoir at 1 bar. What power is required to operate it?

5. A turbo-compressor is used to compress carbon dioxide from 1 to 20 bar. Assuming that the process can be carried out reversibly and isothermally at 300 K, calculate the work required per mole, given that at 300 K the P-V-T properties of carbon dioxide follow the equation $P(v-b)=RT$ with $b=-0.000\,11\;\mathrm{m^3\,mol^{-1}}$.

Answers

1. If the compressor motor runs continuously, the average temperature rises by the same amount in both (a) and (b) since the rate of supply of electrical energy (the only energy input) is unchanged. If the motor runs intermittently under thermostatic control, the temperature rise will be greater in (b) than in (a) since the 'on' period is greater.

2. Work $= -P_{ext}\,\Delta V = -760$ kJ.
   Power $= 127$ kW.

3. Work $= -\int P\,dV = 4.75$ J.

4. Work $= \int V\,dP$, hence power $= 99.9$ kW.

5. Work $= \int V\,dP = RT\,\ln(P_2/P_1) + b(P_2 - P_1) = 7.26\;\mathrm{kJ\,mol^{-1}}$.

Note

1. D. S. L. Cardwell, *From Watt to Clausius, the rise of thermodynamics in the early industrial age*, Heinemann, London, 1971.

2 First Law of Thermodynamics

2.1 Introduction

In classical mechanics, we frequently use the observation that energy is conserved. Thus, if two elastic bodies collide, the total kinetic energy before collision is equal to the kinetic energy after collision; or, if a body is projected upwards, it rises until all of the initial kinetic energy has been converted into potential energy. Thus, for a perfectly elastic system the sum of the kinetic and potential energies is a constant. If the bodies are not perfectly elastic, these energies are not conserved, but are eventually 'degraded' to heat or thermal energy. We find now that the total energy, that is kinetic plus potential plus thermal, is conserved. It is a matter of experimental observation, to which we give the name of the First Law of Thermodynamics, that *in all processes the total energy is conserved.* The forms of energy with which we are concerned here are mechanical, thermal and, later in the book, chemical, but the first law applies also to processes in which these are exchanged with other forms, such as electrical or magnetic.

In Chapter 1 we considered two means of energy transfer, heat and work, and in the paddle-wheel experiment of Joule we saw how energy transfer as either heat or work can have the same effect, since they both raise the temperature of water. Let us examine how the law of conservation of energy applies to this process. In the first part of the experiment where only work was supplied, the energy transferred was stored by the system. Similarly, in the second part of the experiment, where energy was transferred as heat, storage again took place. However, since the final state of the system was the same in each case, the storage mechanism did not distinguish between energy supplied as heat, and energy supplied as work. In the particular case of Joule's experiment, the observations led us to suggest that this energy storage was in some way linked with an increase in temperature.

In general, we must expect a system to have several ways of storing energy. Apart from the storage mechanism which was operating in Joule's experiment, we can immediately think of the kinetic energy of motion of the system and of its potential energy relative to the ground or some arbitrary reference point; but there are others. We begin this chapter by considering energy storage in relatively simple systems and, in particular, in ones in which kinetic and potential energies are sufficiently small to be neglected. Later we include them and examine how they change the conclusions we have reached.

2.2 The first law applied to a closed system

Let us first consider a closed system, that is one in which no material flows through the boundaries enclosing it. Thus, the only quantities passing through the boundaries will be work and heat. We assume that the system is at rest, both at the beginning and at the end of any process, but do not preclude movement during the process, and we assume that there is no difference in the potential energy of the system at the beginning and at the end. For illustrative purposes we shall speak of the system as though it were homogeneous, such as a gas or a liquid (we do not include the container in the system), and one in which no chemical reactions take place, so that only two properties, e.g. pressure and volume, are needed to specify the state of the system. However, we shall see in retrospect that the results have a more general validity and can be used with any system which is at equilibrium.

Let the pressure and volume of the material in the system, before we perform any work on it, or allow it to absorb any heat, be P_1 and V_1 (Figure 2.1), and after we have performed some operation involving heat and work, let them be P_2 and V_2. In Chapter 1 we saw that, if the process was carried out reversibly, we could expect to find any number of routes between 1 and 2, each differing in the amount of work required, since the work required in a

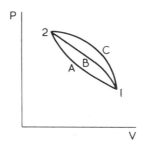

Figure 2.1. Representation of processes on a P-V diagram

reversible process is the area under the P-V curve. If we allow the process to be irreversible, then we have even more ways of getting from 1 to 2. However, in these cases, the details of the path cannot be found from thermodynamics alone, nor can we represent it as a line on a P-V diagram (see further in Chapter 3). To find the work involved in an irreversible process we must determine how much work is being supplied by machinery in the surroundings.

The lines in Figure 2.1 represent three routes between 1 and 2. These are quite arbitrary and are not to be assumed to be either reversible or irreversible. On any chosen route, both heat and work may be supplied to the system, and these are specified by the arbitrary algebraic quantities Q and W. For convenience, we shall use the following shorthand:

$${}_1^2W_A = \text{the work transferred to the system in going}$$
$$\text{from 1 to 2 along path A}$$

$${}_2^1Q_B = \text{the heat transferred to the system in going}$$
$$\text{from 2 to 1 along path B}$$

etc.

Consider the cycle formed by using process A to go from 1 to 2, and process B to return to 1 again. The total energy gained by the system in this cycle is

$$\text{Total energy gain} = {}_1^2Q_A + {}_1^2W_A + {}_2^1Q_B + {}_2^1W_B \qquad (2.1)$$

(Note, we cannot assume ${}_2^1W_B = -{}_1^2W_B$ etc. since this implies reversibility.) The system is now back at its starting point, and so is indistinguishable from its original condition. However, during the process described, we have supplied energy in the form of both heat and work, and this has been stored by the system. If the law of conservation of energy is to hold, the net amount of energy stored must be zero once we return to the starting point. Thus, we have

$$ {}_1^2Q_A + {}_1^2W_A + {}_2^1Q_B + {}_2^1W_B = 0 \qquad (2.2)$$

We can form an alternative cycle by using process C to go from 1 to 2, but retaining B for the return path. This gives

$$ {}_1^2Q_C + {}_1^2W_C + {}_2^1Q_B + {}_2^1W_B = 0 \qquad (2.3)$$

and hence

$$ {}_1^2Q_A + {}_1^2W_A = {}_1^2Q_C + {}_1^2W_C \qquad (2.4)$$

Since paths A and C were chosen quite arbitrarily, it follows that $(Q + W)$ must have the same value for all paths between 1 and 2. The quantity $(Q + W)$, has therefore the properties of a function of state, or, more precisely, of a change in a function of state. Just as the change in pressure ΔP, $(P_2 - P_1)$, in going from 1 to 2 has a definite value, so also has $(Q + W)$. We therefore define a new state function U, such that

$$\Delta U = Q + W \tag{2.5}$$

Since $(Q + W)$ is the total amount of energy supplied to the system during the process, ΔU is the amount of energy stored in the system, and for this reason the state function U is called the *internal energy*.

We can generalize the argument to include inhomogeneous systems and chemical reactions. Thus, for example, the derivation of (2.5) is essentially unchanged when we consider a chemical reaction which proceeds in the forward direction along A and C, and in the reverse direction along B.

2.3   The first law applied to a steady state flow system

Once more we consider a number of routes for going from state 1 to state 2 (Figure 2.1), only this time we take each route as operating under steady state flow conditions. To set up a cycle equivalent to the one for a closed system requires an arrangement of the kind shown in Figure 2.2. The assumptions regarding the nature of the processes are essentially the same as those for the closed system, that is homogeneous fluid flowing into and out of each process, which can be either reversible or irreversible. However, the requirement of negligible kinetic energy needs some comment. If material is flowing, then it has kinetic energy, but in this Section we assume that it is small compared with the heat and shaft work which are supplied to each process. If the process uses a turbo-device, then we have seen in Section 1.8 that conversion of work to kinetic energy and vice versa is inherent in the operation of the machine, but this does not prevent us requiring that the input and output kinetic energies be small.

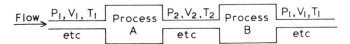

Figure 2.2.   Cyclic process using steady state flow systems

Thus, in Figure 2.2, P_1, V_1 and T_1 are properties of the input material—for a specified mass or time in the case of the extensive property V—and similarly for P_2, V_2 and T_2. Since the properties of the material leaving B are the same as those entering A, the law of conservation of energy requires that no net energy is stored in the flowing material. Thus, after the given amount of material has passed through both processes

$$_1^2Q_A + {}_1^2W_A + {}_2^1Q_B + {}_2^1W_B = 0 \tag{2.6}$$

which is formally a similar equation to the one we obtained for a closed system, but where W is now shaft work. Replacing process A by process C, gives the corresponding equation in terms of B and C, and hence, by an argument analogous to the one which we applied to a closed system, we find that $(Q + W)$ has the same value for all processes between two states 1 and 2. Again there is no assumption as to reversibility and irreversibility. This quantity, therefore, has the properties of a state function which we define as *enthalpy*, and to which we give the symbol H. In a steady state flow system

$$\Delta H = Q + W \qquad (2.7)$$

If Q and W are expressed per given mass of material flowing through process A, say, then ΔH is the amount of energy stored by this mass of material, and is the same no matter what process is used to get from state 1 to state 2. Enthalpy is thus seen to be a property of the substance which is passing through the system, a steady state reactor (in which any physical or chemical process takes place), rather than of the system itself. In this it behaves in the same way as the other state functions P, V and T.

2.4 Relation between enthalpy and internal energy

In the above discussion of the first law, we postulated that, whereas energy is stored by a closed system in one way, U, it is stored differently, H, by the flowing material in a steady state flow system. The two equations which express this energy storage (2.5) and (2.7) are often called the 'First Law Equations'. To see how U and H differ, consider the hypothetical process depicted in Figure 2.3. The steady state reactor is supplied with heat and work by any suitable means, and the input material is supplied by a piston moving steadily inside a cylinder. The output stream is taken off by a similar piston also moving steadily, the two pistons being coupled in such a way that the amount of material within the reactor remains constant. We examine the situation when the pistons reach the positions shown dotted. The amount of material displaced by the left-hand piston is equal to that taken up by the cylinder on the right.

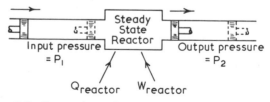

Figure 2.3. Comparison of closed and steady state flow systems

We can consider the process to be either a closed or a steady state flow system, depending on where we draw the boundaries. If we consider everything which happens between the two pistons we have a closed system, since no material is lost or gained. If we consider only the reactor, we have a steady state flow system. We examine the closed case first. To maintain a steady movement of the input piston, we have to supply a steady pressure (or its equivalent) which is infinitesimally greater than P_1. Similarly, the pressure on the output piston must be infinitesimally smaller than P_2. Let V_1 be the volume displaced by the first piston and V_2 by the second, where V_1 and V_2 are the volumes of the same mass of material measured at the input and output conditions. The total input of work to the closed system is

$$P_1 V_1 + W_{reactor} - P_2 V_2 \qquad (2.8)$$

since the work done by the input piston on the system = stroke × force on piston

$$= (V_1/\mathscr{A}) P_1 \mathscr{A} = P_1 V_1$$

where $\mathscr{A}$ is the area of piston, and similarly for the output piston. The only heat supplied to the system is $Q_{reactor}$, supplied to the reactor, and we have, using the appropriate form of the first law $(\Delta U = Q + W)$,

$$\Delta U = Q_{reactor} + P_1 V_1 + W_{reactor} - P_2 V_2 \qquad (2.9)$$

where ΔU is the gain in internal energy of the material which has passed through the reactor, the internal energy of the reactor plus contents being unchanged in any steady state flow process.

If now we examine only the steady state flow reactor, the first law gives us, neglecting kinetic and potential energy,

$$\Delta H = Q + W$$
$$= Q_{reactor} + W_{reactor} \qquad (2.10)$$

where ΔH is also a property only of the material which has passed through the reactor. Hence

$$\Delta H = \Delta U + P_2 V_2 - P_1 V_1$$
$$= \Delta U + \Delta(PV) \qquad (2.11)$$

Since all of the quantities in this equation are functions of state, that is ΔH, ΔU, $\Delta(PV)$ are independent of the way in which the process is carried out and depend only on the initial and final states, it follows that

$$H = U + PV \qquad (2.12)$$

Although this equation is a 'derived' equation, its utility extends far beyond merely relating the behaviour of a closed to a steady state flow system. Since it involves only state functions, it may be used in any situation, and for this reason it has the standing of a definition in thermodynamics.

2.5 Internal energy and enthalpy

We have seen how both of these quantities are introduced naturally as a consequence of the first law of thermodynamics. Both are state functions and have the dimensions of energy, and both are expressing quantitatively a means of energy storage. In Chapter 9 we describe the molecular mechanisms by which energy storage takes place, but by considering a few simple examples at this point, we can see in outline how it comes about.

In a perfect gas it is assumed that the molecules move about independently of one another, although there are collisions. If the molecules are monatomic (helium, argon, krypton, etc.) then the only means of energy storage available to them is an increase in the kinetic energy of the individual atoms (molecules), or what amounts to the same thing, an increase in the average kinetic energy of all of the molecules, since we cannot say what happens to one particular molecule. We must be careful to distinguish here between the kinetic energy of the randomly moving molecules in a stationary gas and the additional ordered kinetic energy of that gas when it is moving bodily in one particular direction. This ordered kinetic energy can be converted into the random variety by allowing the moving gas stream to collide with a stationary object, the increase in the random kinetic energy of the gas molecules being detectable as an increase in temperature.

If the molecules contain two or more atoms, then there are additional modes of energy storage within each molecule—vibrational energy and rotational energy. In the case of a diatomic molecule, for example, the bond is not of constant length but is repeatedly stretching and contracting in a periodic manner, that is, the molecule is vibrating. Such a vibrating system can store more energy by increasing the amplitude of vibration. A molecule which is rotating also stores energy by virtue of its moment of inertia; an increase in the angular speed of rotation takes place when the energy is increased.

In a real gas, the molecules exert forces on one another, and since energy = force × distance, energy can be stored by rearranging the average positions of the molecules in space, which, in practice, means changing the volume of the container. At low pressure the thermodynamic effect of the forces between molecules is small, and the main modes of energy storage are kinetic (often called translational), vibration and rotation. At higher pressures intermolecular forces provide an increasingly important additional mode of energy storage. In the limit of liquid and solid phases the intermolecular forces assume the dominant role.

However, although it may help us conceptually to consider the various modes of energy storage in this detail, it is not necessary to the thermodynamic method that we should do so. Thermodynamics describes a macroscopic world, and the relation between the various macroscopic quantities, and the existence of an underlying molecular description is not important. However, when we come to consider the prediction of thermodynamic properties in Chapter 9, we shall find that we can do this only by making use of molecular properties.

Equations (2.5) and (2.7) which express the first law, were developed assuming that a finite but non-zero change was taking place in the system. If we are considering only microscopic changes, the analogous equations are

$$\begin{array}{cc} \text{closed} & \text{steady state flow} \\ dU = dQ + dW & dH = dQ + dW \end{array} \qquad (2.13)$$

and are the ones to use if the solution to a problem is being sought by the use of calculus.

2.6 Systems involving potential and kinetic energy

If, in any of the above processes, the speed of flow, and therefore also the kinetic energy, of the substances change materially during the process, then conservation of energy requires that this additional energy be supplied or removed, as necessary. Kinetic energy, therefore, is a mode of energy storage additional to that involved in the changes of U and H. A similar argument holds for changes in potential energy consequent upon changes in vertical height and the need to do work against gravity. Thus (2.5) and (2.7) become:

$$\Delta U = Q + W - (KE_{out} - KE_{in}) - (PE_{out} - PE_{in}) \tag{2.14}$$

$$\Delta H = Q + W - (KE_{out} - KE_{in}) - (PE_{out} - PE_{in}) \tag{2.15}$$

Only rarely is the first of these equations used in thermodynamics, but the second is more important, particularly in the field of fluid mechanics. There, we are frequently concerned with calculations of the flow of fluids through passages (called ducts, pipes or nozzles according to application) and the kinetic energy may be far from negligible. In Section 1.8 we showed that for frictionless (i.e. reversible) flow of a fluid through an infinitesimal part of a nozzle

$$-V \, dP = d(KE) \tag{2.16}$$

If the nozzle is inclined to the horizontal so that we have to consider changes in the potential energy, then we extend this equation to

$$-V \, dP = d(KE) + d(PE) \tag{2.17}$$

a result established by Bernoulli in the eighteenth century and which therefore predates thermodynamics. Comparing this equation with (1.31) and (1.32) we see that it is nothing more than the differentiated form of the equation for a hypothetical reversible turbo-device which requires no work input or output, viz.

$$\int_1^2 V \, dP + KE_{out} - KE_{in} + PE_{out} - PE_{in} = 0 \tag{2.18}$$

and may be used to calculate changes in kinetic energy of a fluid flowing through a passage. An alternative approach to the calculation of the change in kinetic energy in such cases is to set $W = 0$ in (2.15) giving

$$\Delta H - Q + KE_{out} - KE_{in} + PE_{out} - PE_{in} = 0 \tag{2.19}$$

This is particularly valuable when the flow is adiabatic, $(Q = 0)$, for we have replaced the evaluation of an integral, $\int V \, dP$ by the determination of the enthalpy at the beginning, H_1, and at the end, H_2, of the flow process, since by definition, $\Delta H = H_2 - H_1$.

In this book, we are rarely concerned with systems in which changes of kinetic and potential energies are significant. We can therefore use

$$\Delta H = Q + W \tag{2.20}$$

and this restricted equation is implied unless a statement is made to the contrary.

2.7 Heat capacities

The heat capacity of a substance is conventionally defined as the amount of heat required to raise the temperature by one unit under the conditions specified, but this definition leads to difficulties when the heat capacity is varying rapidly with temperature. It is more useful to define a heat capacity as the limiting value of dQ/dT as dT, and therefore also dQ, go to zero. This leads to an unambiguous value no matter how rapidly the heat capacity varies. Let us apply the first law to this measurement. Consider first the heat capacity at constant volume, C_V. Experimentally, we place the substance, assumed to be a fluid, in a rigid container, supply a small amount of heat and measure the resulting temperature increase. The system is a closed one and the appropriate form of the first law is

$$dU = dQ + dW \tag{2.21}$$

The definition of C_V gives us that

$$dQ = C_V \, dT \tag{2.22}$$

and the work is given by

$$dW = -P_{ext} \, dV = 0 \tag{2.23}$$

since dV is clearly zero in a constant volume process. Thus, $dU = C_V \, dT$ for the experiment described, which is more succinctly expressed by the partial differential calculus as

$$\left(\frac{\partial U}{\partial T}\right)_V = C_V \tag{2.24}$$

where the subscript V on the differential indicates that the differentiation is performed subject to V remaining constant.

The measurement of the heat capacity at constant pressure C_P of a liquid or solid can be performed merely by supplying heat to the sample under a constant (and usually atmospheric) pressure. Once more the appropriate first law equation is (2.21), but this time

$$dQ = C_P \, dT \tag{2.25}$$

and $dW = -P_{ext} \, dV$ is not zero. From the nature of the experiment, we see that

$P_{ext} = P$, where P is the pressure of the sample itself, and hence

$$dU = dQ + dW$$
$$= C_P \, dT - P \, dV \tag{2.26}$$

Since $H = U + PV$, (2.12) differentiation gives

$$dH = dU + P \, dV + V \, dP \tag{2.27}$$

In the measurement of C_P, P is constant and so $dP = 0$. Hence substituting (2.27) in (2.26) gives

$$dH = C_P \, dT \tag{2.28}$$

or

$$\left(\frac{\partial H}{\partial T}\right)_P = C_P \tag{2.29}$$

The heat capacity at constant pressure of a liquid or gas is frequently measured in a flow calorimeter. This is a device through which the fluid flows steadily, being heated electrically as it does so. Determination of the temperature before and after the device completes the measurement. This time, it is appropriate to apply the steady state flow version of the first law,

$$dH = dQ + dW \tag{2.30}$$

If the temperature rise produced is dT, then the heat supplied

$$dQ = C_P \, dT \tag{2.31}$$

The shaft work done, dW is zero, since a flow calorimeter has no connection with any device for supplying or removing work, thus

$$dH = C_P \, dT \tag{2.32}$$

$$\left(\frac{\partial H}{\partial T}\right)_P = C_P \tag{2.33}$$

Thus we see that however the heat capacity C_P is measured, its relation to H is the same.

If, instead of supplying infinitesimal amounts of heat, we supply substantial amounts of heat, the total effect may be found by integration of (2.24) and (2.33). Thus, for heat supplied at constant volume

$$\Delta U = \int_{T_1}^{T_2} C_V \, dT = \text{total heat supplied} \tag{2.34}$$

and at constant pressure

$$\Delta H = \int_{T_1}^{T_2} C_P \, dT = \text{total heat supplied} \tag{2.35}$$

Both of these expressions can be evaluated, even if C_V and C_P vary with temperature.

It must not be presumed that C_P and C_V depend only on temperature. Take C_P for example. Measurement of this quantity can be made at any pressure provided it is constant, and although the majority of such experiments are performed at a pressure of about 1 bar there have been many measurements at other pressures. These show that C_P is indeed a function of pressure as well as temperature, and to indicate this fact we can write

$$C_P = f(P, T)$$

which is often condensed to $C_P(P, T)$, a formalism which we shall use frequently in this book. In the case of C_V, the analogous expression is $C_V(P, T)$ but, in practice, it is more useful to take V and T as the independent variables and we shall therefore use $C_V(V, T)$.

2.8 Measurement of heat capacities

In view of the importance of heat capacities to quantitative thermodynamics—we have already seen how they relate to enthalpy and internal energy—we consider in this section the more important aspects of their measurement, with particular stress on the accuracy of each method. There is no point in carrying out calculations involving H to four or five significant figures if the enthalpy is based on heat capacities which are only accurate to 1%. We set the scene with a few general observations on the accuracy of modern experimental methods. Calorimetric measurements near to room temperature can usually be made with 1% accuracy by using an ordinary Dewar flask and very simple instrumentation (a calorimetric measurement can be defined as any measurement involving heat which is carried out quantitatively). Measurements to 0.1% are very much more difficult, measurements to 0.01% are virtually impossible, with one or two isolated exceptions. As we move away from room temperature the difficulty of a given measurement increases substantially and, for example, at the extremes of temperature it can be as difficult to achieve 1% accuracy as it is to achieve 0.01% accuracy at room temperature.

Below about 700 K, virtually all reliable measurements of heat capacity are electrical; a known amount of substance is heated electrically and the temperature rise measured. By making the temperature rise small, about 1 kelvin in most cases, the value of $Q/\Delta T$ approaches the true heat capacity, dQ/dT. Of course, if the heat capacity is varying rapidly with temperature, much smaller increments may need to be used. The system in which this is done can be either closed (for solid, liquid or gas) or steady state flow (liquid or gas). We consider here the measurement of the heat capacity of a solid by the closed system technique and of a gas by the flow technique, and indicate how each may be extended to the other phases. McCullough and Scott[1] give a detailed description of these, and other experimental methods.

Figure 2.4 shows schematically the apparatus used to measure the heat capacity of a solid over a wide range of temperature. It is shown in the form

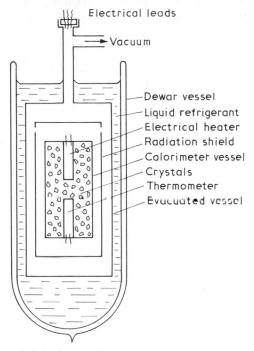

Figure 2.4. Adiabatic calorimeter for heat capacity measurements

used for temperatures below 300 K. The solid is in a sealed metal calorimeter (made of copper or a similarly good-conducting material) and provided with a thermometer (usually a platinum-resistance thermometer) and a heater. To make useful measurements we must eliminate, or at least determine, the heat leaks from the calorimeter to its surroundings, and it is the difficulty of doing this which has led to the complexity of the modern calorimeter. Heat transfer is by conduction, convection and radiation. The first two can be eliminated, in practice, by providing a high vacuum environment, although in the most precise work it is necessary to consider heat leaks down electrical leads to the calorimeter, and also down the calorimeter supports. Radiation can be eliminated by arranging for the calorimeter to 'see' only surfaces at the same temperature as itself. Thus we interpose a 'radiation shield', see Figure 2.4, between the calorimeter and its surroundings, and by providing it with its own thermometer and heater, we maintain its temperature equal to that of the calorimeter which is then said to be operating under adiabatic conditions; hence the name *adiabatic calorimeter* which is usually applied to apparatus of this type. The surroundings of the radiation shield are lower in temperature than the calorimeter and it is usual to immerse the whole evacuated apparatus into a Dewar vessel containing a refrigerant. Thus, in Figure 2.4 a bath of liquid nitrogen would be used when making measurements in the range 80 to 300 K.

The success of the method described depends critically on the accuracy with which the temperature of the radiation shield can be made equal to that of the calorimeter. The amount of radiation from a surface is proportional to T^4 so that if two surfaces differ in temperature by δT, the amount of heat exchanged by radiation is proportional to $T^3 \delta T$. Since one can never make δT exactly zero, the errors are worse at high temperatures than at low. At temperatures below 20 K we can dispense with the radiation shield. At high temperatures, radiation heat exchange is the limiting factor on accuracy, and the upper limit of about 700 K for the adiabatic calorimeter is determined by this. As might be expected, the accuracy at these temperatures is considerably less than those made at lower temperatures. At 700 K accuracies of 1% can be achieved with difficulty, whereas below room temperature 0.1% is achieved as a matter of routine.

Once we understand the principle behind the adiabatic calorimeter used for measuring the heat capacity of a solid, we can suggest ways in which it can be used with liquids and gases. If the liquid can be poured or distilled in, we can fill the calorimeter on the bench before incorporation into the apparatus, just as we did for a solid. Alternatively, we can connect a long, thin capillary tube from the calorimeter, when installed in the vacuum part of the apparatus, to the outside, so that we can fill the calorimeter without taking it out. This increases the heat leak and introduces a few additional uncertainties, but there is a substantial gain in convenience. In this form, the calorimeter can be used for gases, but in view of the smallness of the heat capacity of the gas contained within a copper calorimeter compared with the heat capacity of the latter, it is not a good method unless the pressure is high. But it is difficult to make the calorimeter sufficiently strong, and the method is not often used.

The essential part of the apparatus used to measure the heat capacity C_P of a gas by the flow method is shown in Figure 2.5. Since it uses a stirred liquid thermostat, its range is generally 150 K to 600 K. In practice, the lower limit of 150 K is no great handicap since, as we shall see, C_P for substances which have a significant vapour pressure, or are still above the critical point (for the meaning of this see Chapter 4), at 150 K, may be calculated more accurately than they can be measured by the methods of Chapter 9. The upper limit of 600 K is more of a handicap and the methods of Chapter 9 only provide a partial solution to it.

The experimental procedure involves supplying a steady stream of gas to the heat exchanger (Figure 2.5), thus bringing its temperature up to that of the thermostat, passing it over thermometer 1, then the heater and finally thermometers 2 and 3. Hence, knowing the flow rate and the electrical power supplied, the heat capacity can be calculated, if we can allow for any heat leak. Here we notice a fundamental difference between the adiabatic calorimeter for solids and the flow calorimeter for gases. In the adiabatic calorimeter, the temperature variation is with time as the independent variable and at any one instant the calorimeter has an essentially uniform temperature. In the flow

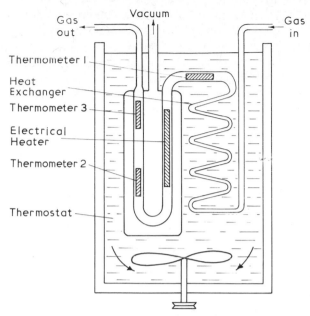

Figure 2.5. Flow calorimeter for gases

calorimeter the temperature variation is spatial and there is always a temperature gradient. Thus, although we can use vacuum to eliminate conduction and convection heat transfer, as is indicated in Figure 2.5, a radiation shield with a temperature gradient along it is rather impractical, although some attempts have been made to use one. The more usual way of allowing for radiation heat leaks is to use the ability of the flow calorimeter to operate at different flow rates for, in theory, if the flow rate is infinite the radiation heat leak can be ignored. In practice, this means making measurements at several flow rates and extrapolating to infinite flow rate. Analysis shows that for the apparatus in question the apparent C_P (C_P ignoring heat leaks) varies as the reciprocal of the flow rate, see Figure 2.6, and that the slope of the line is proportional to T^3.

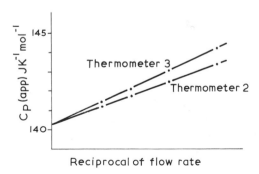

Figure 2.6. Apparent heat capacity versus reciprocal of flow rate

With two exit thermometers, we have a check that the extrapolation procedure is valid, as both lines should provide the same intercept. Again we notice that at high temperatures the uncertainty in the derived value of the heat capacity becomes large since a line of large slope has an uncertain intercept.

The method we have described can clearly be used for liquids as well as gases, although the large heat capacity of the former, per unit volume, means lower volumetric flow rates and quite different dimensions for the apparatus.

Above 700 K, and then only for solids and liquids, the only method available to us is the drop calorimeter, shown in Figure 2.7. The sample, in a container if necessary, is heated in a furnace to the experimental temperature. It is then dropped into a calorimeter at or near to room temperature. Figure 2.7 shows a metal block calorimeter in which a block of copper, with a hole in the middle to

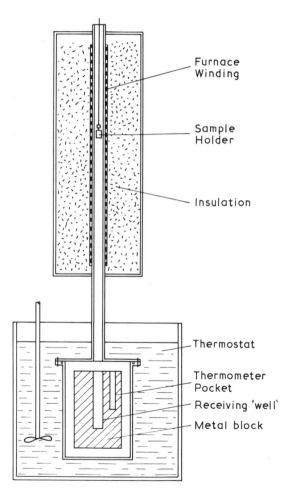

Figure 2.7. High temperature drop calorimeter

receive the sample and a thermometer to measure its temperature, is in a thermally isolated enclosure. Usually, it is sufficient that the outer container be maintained at a constant temperature close to that of the copper block, but arrangements similar to the adiabatic calorimeter, described above, have been used. Thus a measurement of the rise in temperature of the copper block, combined with its known heat capacity (this is usually arranged to be about 100 times larger than that of the sample so that the temperature rise is only a few kelvin) gives a value for the increase in enthalpy of the copper block. This is equal to the heat given up by the hot sample and this, in turn, is equal to its enthalpy decrease. Thus we get the enthalpy difference for the sample between furnace temperature and final temperature. We cannot, in general, divide ΔH by ΔT to get the heat capacity unless we require only a 'mean' heat capacity, for the temperature range is so large that the heat capacity will almost certainly not be constant. If true heat capacities are needed, they can be obtained from experiments at sets of closely spaced furnace temperatures and calculating differences, but the method is not very accurate, particularly if C_P is varying rapidly with T.

The overall accuracy of enthalpy differences determined by the drop method is, with a well designed apparatus, between 0.1 and 1.0%.

2.9   Latent heat

The latent heat of a phase change, L, is the amount of heat absorbed when the phase change takes place under the prevailing (constant) pressure. Closed system thermodynamics is appropriate here, and the first law gives

$$\Delta U = Q + W$$
$$= L - P_{ext} \Delta V \tag{2.36}$$

where ΔV is the volume change accompanying the phase change. Since the external pressure equals the pressure of the substance, P, we can write $P_{ext} = P$. Also $H = U + PV$ which on differentiating and setting dP to zero, since P is constant, gives

$$dH = dU + P\,dV \tag{2.37}$$

and for a macroscopic change, by integration

$$\Delta H = \Delta U + P\,\Delta V \tag{2.38}$$

We see then that (2.36) gives

$$\Delta H = L \tag{2.39}$$

Exercise

Show that (2.39) is also obtained when the phase change takes place in a steady state flow device.

It is observed experimentally that the latent heat of a phase change varies with the temperature, and hence, in practice, also with the pressure, at which it takes place. As an example, let us consider the evaporation of a liquid. We assume, Figure 2.8, that we have made a measurement of the latent heat L_1 at temperature T_1. To determine how L varies with temperature we investigate separately how the enthalpy of the gas phase, and of the liquid phase, increase with temperature (full lines in Figure 2.8), and hence calculate the enthalpy change, that is the latent heat L_2, at temperature T_2, by making use of the state function properties of enthalpy. However, if we increase the temperature, we also increase the vapour pressure. In a homogeneous system, fixing two properties determines the state of the system. Thus for the gas phase alone,

$$H^g = f^g(P, T) \tag{2.40}$$

which may be differentiated to give

$$dH^g = \left(\frac{\partial H^g}{\partial P}\right)_T dP + \left(\frac{\partial H^g}{\partial T}\right)_P dT \tag{2.41}$$

and a similar equation applies to the liquid. Thus for a temperature only infinitesimally greater than T_1, the latent heat is

$$L_1 + dH^g - dH^l$$
$$= L_1 + \left[\left(\frac{\partial H^g}{\partial P}\right)_T - \left(\frac{\partial H^l}{\partial P}\right)_T\right] dP + \left[\left(\frac{\partial H^g}{\partial T}\right)_P - \left(\frac{\partial H^l}{\partial T}\right)_P\right] dT \tag{2.42}$$

In Section 3.24, we show that we can neglect the term in dP for liquid-gas phase transitions provided that the temperature is sufficiently low for the vapour pressure to be small (say, less than 1 bar). Thus substituting C_P for $(\partial H/\partial T)_P$ and integrating (2.42), we obtain

$$L_2 = L_1 + \int_{T_1}^{T_2} (C_P^g - C_P^l)\, dT \tag{2.43}$$

which is often written as

$$L_2 = L_1 + \int_{T_1}^{T_2} \Delta C_P\, dT \tag{2.44}$$

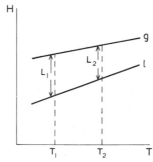

Figure 2.8. Variation of latent heat with temperature

This is an example of *Kirchoff's equation* whose general form is

$$\Delta_2 H = \Delta_1 H + \int_{T_1}^{T_2} \Delta C_P \, dT \qquad (2.45)$$

where Δ_2 and Δ_1 refer to a process carried out at T_2 and T_1 but at the same pressure. It is only when P is sufficiently low for its change from T_1 to T_2 to be neglected that (2.44) is valid.

2.10 Measurement of latent heat

Latent heat is measured in an apparatus similar to the adiabatic calorimeter used for measuring heat capacity. Although not ideally suitable, a heat capacity calorimeter fitted with an inlet capillary tube for work on liquids will often double as a latent heat calorimeter. The principle of a latent heat calorimeter is the evaporation of a liquid by heat supplied electrically and the collection of the vapour by condensation or freezing so as to determine the amount evaporated. If heat leaks can be reduced to insignificance, the molar latent heat is the electrical work supplied divided by the amount of substance evaporated. Clearly, the adiabatic shield of the heat capacity calorimeter provides an ideal way of achieving this and is used in all modern latent heat calorimeters. Since the temperature does not vary during a determination, it is possible to simplify the ways used to maintain constancy of temperature of the shield. The main disadvantage in using a heat capacity calorimeter for latent heat determinations is the absence of stirring, for this usually means that the rate of evaporation must be kept low enough for temperature gradients and 'bumping' to be avoided. A calorimeter designed specifically for the job usually has a stirrer, or uses the same natural convection which takes place in a coffee percolator, and much higher heating rates are possible. Since latent heat is a function of pressure (or temperature, as the two are related via the saturated vapour pressure) it is usual to control the pressure of the evaporating liquid by a control valve, external to the calorimeter, and placed in the connecting tube to the condenser.

Latent heats determined in this way have an accuracy close to that of a heat capacity determined in a similar apparatus. Generally, this accuracy is of the order of 0.1%; only rarely do we require the latent heat of evaporation of a substance which is still liquid at high temperatures, and so most determinations are, therefore, in the experimentally easy range of temperatures below 700 K. Further details are given in the book by McCullough and Scott referred to in Section 2.8.

2.11 Use of H and U in constant pressure and constant volume processes

The examples in the sections on heat capacity and latent heat show that the utility of U and H is not restricted to closed and steady state flow systems respectively. Equations (2.29) and (2.39) show that for constant pressure (or *isobaric*) processes, H is a more appropriate state function than U, even if the processes are carried out in a closed system, as in the measurement of C_P or L. We can extend this observation to all closed constant pressure processes which do no work other than that involved in expansion of the system against the constant pressure.

Formally, the work done,

$$dW = -P_{ext}\, dV = -P\, dV \qquad (2.46)$$

where the last step can be made since the pressure in the system equals the external pressure. Thus, the first law for a closed system gives

$$dU = dQ - P\, dV \qquad (2.47)$$

By using $dH = dU + P\, dV + V\, dP$, and observing that $dP = 0$, this becomes

$$dH = dQ \quad \text{(constant } P) \qquad (2.48)$$

which is clearly simpler than (2.47). This equation applies to both reversible and irreversible processes, the only restrictions are that, at all times, the pressure within the system equals the external pressure, and that no other work is done.

We can examine a constant volume (or *isochoric*) process in a similar manner. In a closed system, the expansion work ($P\, dV$) is clearly zero and, if no other work is done, $dW = 0$ and

$$dU = dQ \quad \text{(constant } V) \qquad (2.49)$$

If the process is carried out under steady state flow conditions work will have to be supplied to maintain the constancy of volume. Provided no other work is done, $dW = V\, dP$, and

$$dH = dQ + V\, dP \qquad (2.50)$$

Hence, using $dH = dU + P\, dV + V\, dP$, remembering that $dV = 0$, we have

$$dU = dQ \qquad (2.51)$$

and this equation, therefore, applies to constant volume processes in both closed and steady state flow processes.

2.12 Energy zeros for internal energy and enthalpy

We have seen how changes in internal energy and enthalpy may be evaluated by measuring the amount of heat and work involved in the appropriate process used to measure it. However, an absolute scale of (e.g.) enthalpy does not exist. There is no pressure and temperature combination at which we can unambiguously state that the enthalpy of the particular substance is zero. In this it is unlike pressure and volume, both of which quantities have perfectly well defined zero values. Recourse must, therefore, be made to defined scales with defined zeros. This inevitably means proliferation of a number of different scales, all having different zeros. These we shall consider in detail in Chapters 4 and 8, but as most of the time we are concerned with changes in enthalpy, or changes in internal energy, the choice of scale is relatively unimportant. However, care is clearly needed when extracting values from several tables at the same time.

Problems

1. (a) 2.0 m³ of a gas are compressed adiabatically to 1.0 m³, during which the temperature rises from 20 °C to 150 °C. If the work input is 100 kJ, what is the internal energy change?
(b) 2.0 m³ of the same gas at the same initial pressure and temperature as (a) are heated at constant volume to 150 °C, requiring 95 kJ of heat. What is the internal energy change for this process?
(c) if the 2.0 m³ of gas at 150 °C of (b) are now compressed at this constant temperature to a volume of 1.0 m³, during which 185 kJ of heat are removed, what is the internal energy change and how much work is required?

2. Calculate W, Q, ΔU and ΔH when 1 kg of liquid carbon tetrachloride is heated from 0 °C to 50 °C at a pressure of 1 bar. The coefficient of thermal expansion is 0.0012 K⁻¹, the density at 0 °C is 1590 kg m⁻³ and the heat capacity C_P is 0.84 kJ K⁻¹ kg⁻¹.

3. The densities of ice and water at 0 °C and 1 atm ($= 1.013\,25$ bar) pressure are 917 and 1000 kg m⁻³ respectively. Calculate the difference between ΔU and ΔH of fusion of 1 kg of ice at this temperature. If the corresponding densities for liquid water and steam at 100 °C and 1 atm are 958.4 and 0.596 kg m⁻³, calculate also this difference for the evaporation of water at atmospheric pressure.

4. Steam enters a nozzle at 10 bar with a speed of 200 m s⁻¹ and leaves at 1 bar having been accelerated to 800 m s⁻¹. If heat losses can be neglected, what is the change in enthalpy per kilogram of steam?

5. A turbine is supplied with steam at the rate of 3 kg s⁻¹. If the initial and final values of the enthalpy of the steam are 630 kJ kg⁻¹ and 500 kJ kg⁻¹ respectively and the heat loss from the turbine is 40 kJ s⁻¹, calculate the power output.

6. It has been suggested that the bottom of a waterfall should be hotter than the top. What temperature difference would you expect in the case of Niagara Falls (height approximately 50 m)? For water, $C_P = 4.2$ kJ K⁻¹ kg⁻¹.

Answers

1. (a) $\Delta U = 100$ kJ; (b) $\Delta U = 95$ kJ; (c) $\Delta U = 5$ kJ, $W = 190$ kJ.

2. $W = -3.8$ J kg^{-1}, $Q = 42$ kJ kg^{-1}, $\Delta U = Q + W \approx 42$ kJ kg^{-1},
$\Delta H = C_P \, \Delta T = 42$ kJ kg^{-1}.

3. For fusion $\Delta H - \Delta U = -9.2$ J kg^{-1},
for evaporation $\Delta H - \Delta U = 171$ kJ kg^{-1}.

4. $\Delta H = -600$ kJ kg^{-1} [use equation (2.15)].

5. Power output $= 350$ kW [use equation (2.7)].

6. $\Delta T = 0.12$ K [use equations (2.15) and (2.35)].

Note

1. J. P. McCullough and D. W. Scott, *Experimental Thermodynamics*, Vol. 1, 'Calorimetry of Non-reacting systems', Butterworth, London (I.U.P.A.C.), 1968.

3 Second Law of Thermodynamics

3.1 Introduction

The first law of thermodynamics is essentially concerned with the conservation of energy during a process. Thus, when we wind up the spring of a clock, energy is conserved in that we supply manual work, derived from chemical energy, to the spring, and this is stored as potential energy. As the clock winds down of its own accord, energy is again conserved, the potential energy being converted to kinetic energy of the clock mechanism and thence to heat. However, although the process is not precluded by the first law, we cannot rewind the clock merely by supplying heat, that is, the reverse of the winding-down process, but we must supply more manual work. It is the object of the second law of thermodynamics to deal quantitatively with this one-way nature of processes. Before we can do this, we must introduce a device called a 'heat engine' and also extend our ideas on reversible and irreversible processes.

3.2 Heat engine

This is a device which operates in a cyclical manner and exchanges only heat and work with its surroundings. The cycle is, therefore, closed in the thermodynamic sense, no material being lost or gained. Perhaps the simplest heat engine is a pair of thermocouples in which heat flows in from the surroundings at the higher temperature (say T_1) into the region of the junction J_1, and flows out to the surroundings at junction J_2 where the temperature is lower. The thermocouples generate electricity which, in turn, drives an electric motor, and so produces mechanical work, Figure 3.1.

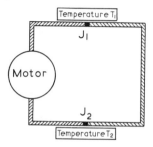

Figure 3.1. The thermocouple heat engine

A more complicated heat engine is the steam power plant, Figure 3.2. Liquid water from the feed pump is evaporated in the steam generator by an input of heat at high temperature. The high pressure, high temperature steam drives a turbine, thereby producing work. The stream leaving the turbine at a much lower temperature and pressure is condensed to liquid water, by low temperature coolant, before being returned to the pump. Although each of the sections of the plant are operating under conditions of steady state flow, the plant as a whole is closed since no water is lost from the cycle at any point.

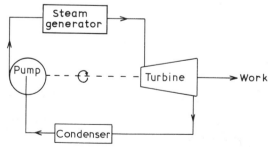

Figure 3.2. Steam power plant heat engine

A simple heat engine can be made from a piston and cylinder, Figure 3.3. A freely moving piston, which is not of negligible mass, supports a platform which comes to level A when the piston rests on the lower stops, and level B when it is pressed against the upper stops. We assume that the device initially contains gas at a sufficiently low temperature and pressure for the piston, with an empty platform, to lie on the lower stops, Figure (a). The weight resting on the shelf at level A may be raised to level B by sliding the weight on to the platform and bringing the heat source Y into contact with the bottom of the cylinder, Figure (b). The flow of heat into the confined gas causes its pressure to rise, thus, first lifting the piston off the stops and then raising it until the platform becomes level with shelf B, Figure (c). Finally the weight is slid on to the higher shelf. The device can be made ready to lift the next weight by replacing the heat source Y by the cooling apparatus Z (commonly called a heat sink in thermodynamics), Figure (d), when the pressure of the confined gas falls, thus restoring the piston to its original position against the lower stops, Figure (a). Clearly, this device fulfills the requirements of a heat engine in that the complete cycle can be repeated any number of times without renewing any part of the engine or its working fluid.

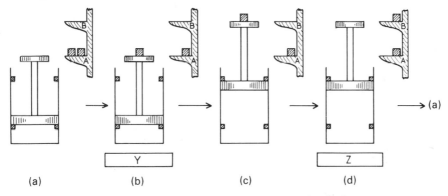

Figure 3.3. Heat engine using a piston and cylinder

Figure 3.4 shows the path taken by the working fluid in P-V and T-V coordinates. The two steps 1–2–3 take place when the heat source Y is in contact with the cylinder and the steps 3–4–1 when heat sink Z is in contact. We have assumed that only sufficient heat is supplied by the source to raise the piston to its upper stops. Extra heat would raise the pressure beyond that shown, since the stops prevent further expansion. A similar argument applies to the amount of heat removed by the heat sink.

The two characteristics these above examples have in common are, firstly, the use of a source of heat at some high temperature and, secondly, the use of a heat sink at a lower temperature. If Q_1 is the heat absorbed by the engine at the higher temperature, and Q_2 the heat absorbed at the lower temperature (in the examples Q_2 is negative) then, by the first law of thermodynamics, which

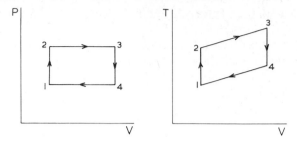

Figure 3.4. Thermodynamic path of heat engine in Figure 3.3

for a closed system is $\Delta U = Q + W$, we have

$$Q_1 + Q_2 + W = 0 \qquad (3.1)$$

since if the working fluid is taken round a cycle, the original thermodynamic state is restored and $\Delta U = 0$. Thus, if the heat engine is to produce useful work (which means that W must be negative) we require Q_1 to be numerically larger than Q_2. Further, since in practice the heat sink would be the atmosphere or a large body of cooling water (sea, river or lake), the thermal, and hence here the economic cost of running a heat engine is mainly that of providing the heat at the higher temperature. We may thus define a positive efficiency, η, as

$$\frac{\text{Work output from the machine}}{\text{Heat input at the higher temperature}}$$

which, in our case, is

$$\eta = -\frac{W}{Q_1} = \frac{Q_1 + Q_2}{Q_1} \qquad (3.2)$$

and it is less than unity since Q_2 is negative.

This equation prompts consideration of what happens if Q_2 is zero, for this gives a heat engine with an efficiency of unity, that is all heat input is converted into mechanical work. Such a machine would be highly desirable for it would permit us to obtain work without a source of high temperature heat. Clearly, when only one source is involved, the concept of high and low temperature sources is irrelevant, any single temperature will do. Thus, we could run an engine with a single heat source such as the atmosphere and use no fuel at all. It is our experience that such an engine does not exist, and hence that all real heat engines must have both a source and a sink, one to supply heat and the second to remove it. Expressed in more formal terms, this experimental observation was proposed by Kelvin and by Planck as a formulation of the second law of thermodynamics, but we defer consideration of this until Section 3.7.

3.3 Reversible and irreversible processes

In Chapter 1 we introduced the concept of reversibility as applied to compression and expansion machinery. However, the classification of an operation as either reversible or irreversible is quite general and can be extended to cover all processes. Formally, we define a process as reversible if, after it has been carried out, it is possible by any means whatsoever to restore both the system and its surroundings to their original states, or at most have them differ from these by infinitesimal amounts. This definition does not require that we use, as the reverse path, an exact reversal of the forward path, but in examining a process for reversibility it is often convenient to do so, for certainly such a path must exist. Thus, when we were considering adiabatic expansions in Chapter 1, we used exact reversal as our test for reversibility.

Reversible processes are important in thermodynamics in that they are the most efficient (proof of this will follow later in the chapter), and are free from 'lossy' effects such as friction. Take, for example, the piston raising sand under adiabatic conditions as in Chapter 1, Section 1.7. If there is friction between the piston and the walls of the cylinder, rather more sand will have to be removed from the piston before it begins to move; one grain is no longer enough. The force exerted by the sand on the piston is thus less than the force exerted on it by the gas by a substantial, non-zero amount. Since this applies throughout the whole of the adiabatic expansion, the result is the raising of a smaller amount of sand. Now, if we reverse the process and add sand to force the piston back down, we find that no movement takes place until a substantial amount of sand has been *added* to the piston, again because of friction. Thus, when the piston has been restored to its starting position, and the volume of the gas is the same as it was initially, we find that more sand was required to depress the piston than was originally raised by it. Moreover, we find that the temperature and pressure are also higher. As we now show, this follows from the first law, which for an adiabatic process ($Q = 0$) is,

$$\Delta U = W \tag{3.3}$$

For the initial expansion, represented as a process going from state 1 to state 2,

$$U_2 - U_1 = {}^2_1W \tag{3.4}$$

and for the compression from state 2 to state 3 (state 3 has the same volume as state 1, but not the same temperature or pressure)

$$U_3 - U_2 = {}^3_2W \tag{3.5}$$

since we have found that ${}^3_2W > -{}^2_1W$, it follows that

$$U_3 > U_1 \tag{3.6}$$

In Chapter 2, we showed that for any constant volume process between two states, in this case 1 and 3,

$$U_3 - U_1 = \int_1^3 C_V \, dT \qquad (3.7)$$

which, since C_V is always positive, means that if U_3 is greater than U_1, T_3 is greater than T_1. This same result applies even if the piston is frictionless for the return stroke. Thus, to restore the system to its original state we must cool the gas, the heat removed being taken up by the surroundings. Clearly, the conditions for reversibility have not been met, for the heat and work will have changed the thermodynamic state of the surroundings even though the system itself has returned to its starting point. We note also that the amount of sand raised by the piston is less than the amount raised by the reversible, frictionless piston in Chapter 1. Thus, in this example, irreversibility and low efficiency go together.

Friction between the piston and cylinder is not the only type of friction which results in irreversibility; the viscous flow of a gas or liquid is another example. Thus, if the grains of sand were removed so quickly that, due to viscous flow, the gas in the cylinder was unable to adjust its pressure to uniformity before the next grain was removed, the gas immediately below the piston would, on the average, be at a lower pressure than if the pressure were uniform. This again results in a diminution of the amount of sand raised. This position is now as it was in the example above where the friction was between the piston and the cylinder, and so we may conclude that fluid friction also results in irreversibility and lowered efficiency.

We now have the basic requirements for reversibility in an expansion: (i) the balancing of internal and external pressures across the moving boundary, (e.g. the piston); (ii) no friction; and (iii) a process which is slow compared with the time to re-establish equilibrium. This last condition means that a reversible process takes place through a series of equilibrium states so that if the process is stopped at any stage, the system is indistinguishable from one which has been at that position of equilibrium for an indefinite period of time. Reversible processes are therefore possible only between equilibrium states. In the example above, where there was a non-uniform pressure in the cylinder due to rapid removal of sand, the gas was not allowed to reach an equilibrium state, in this case characterised by uniform pressure, before the next grain was removed. If the removal of sand is slow, so as to have reversibility, then we can stop the process at any stage and the system remains in equilibrium.

In testing for reversibility, it is necessary that all three conditions in the paragraph above are satisfied. If even one condition is not satisfied, the process is irreversible. Two examples help to make this clear.

(i) A paddle wheel, or stirrer, rotating in a bath of fluid will dissipate heat due to the viscous forces (i.e. friction) acting on it. The process is therefore irreversible.

(ii) A stream of gas flows through a capillary orifice into a region of lower pressure, Figure 3.5. The process is irreversible since there is a pressure imbalance across the capillary.

$(P_1 > P_2)$

Figure 3.5. Apparatus for demonstrating free expansion

These examples show irreversibility in an essentially mechanical system. However, irreversibility is also found in heat transfer. We usually heat an object by bringing it into contact with a body which is at a substantially higher temperature. Thus, the latter could be hot combustion gases at a temperature of about 2000 °C, whereas the object being heated is much closer to room temperature. If we apply the fundamental definition of reversibility to this situation, we see that since the heated object is still much colder than the combustion gases, and since there is no way in which it alone can transfer the heat it has gained back to the flame, the process is clearly irreversible. However, consider a highly efficient heat exchanger in which stream A, Figure 3.6, is only infinitesimally warmer than stream B. Heat is now transfer-

Figure 3.6. Heat exchanger

red to stream B reversibly since, if we consider stream B to be part of the surroundings and stream A the system, we need only make an infinitesimal reduction in the temperature of A for the direction of heat flow to be back from B to A, and for both system and surroundings to be unchanged at the end, apart from this infinitesimal change in temperature. This observation is quite general; if heat transfer to the system from the surroundings is across an infinitesimal temperature difference, it is carried out reversibly. If the temperature difference is non-zero, the transfer is irreversible.

In the reversible processes described above, there is some degree of spontaneity. In free expansion the gas at high pressure rushes spontaneously through the orifice into the region of lower pressure; placing a system in a high temperature environment results in the immediate transfer of heat to it. In general, all spontaneous processes are irreversible. If this were not so we would have the possibility of a process which could proceed spontaneously in the forward direction and also spontaneously in the backward direction, a state of affairs which is obviously absurd. We can, therefore, use spontaneity as a simple test for irreversibility. Thus, if vessel A in Figure 3.7 contains one

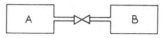

Figure 3.7. A mixing process

gas, and vessel B contains a second gas at the same pressure, then on opening the valve the gases will mix spontaneously by diffusion and this is, therefore, an irreversible process. Similarly, a mixture of hydrogen and oxygen at room temperature will not react, but introduction of a suitable catalyst brings about immediate reaction. Since this is a spontaneous process, the reaction is carried out irreversibly. In general, we shall find that mixing processes and chemical reactions are almost always carried out irreversibly.

It must not be thought that if a process is not spontaneous then it must be reversible. Consider the reversible lifting of the sand in Section 1.7. If the grains of sand, after removal from the piston, are simply dropped by the side of the cylinder instead of being carefully placed on the level at which each one was removed, then from the point of view of the system and the surroundings together, the process is irreversible, but it certainly cannot be considered to be a spontaneous process. However, we are often interested only in what happens in the system; the behaviour of the surroundings is secondary. Since what happens here in the system is the same as what happens in the corresponding reversible process, we call the process *internally reversible*. As an example of an internally reversible process involving the transfer of heat to a system, consider the evaporation of water at a constant temperature of 100 °C. If the source of heat is a flame, the process is irreversible when considered from the point of view of the system and surroundings, but if the temperature of the source is only infinitesimally greater than 100 °C, then the process is reversible. But from the point of view of the system (water) there is no difference between these two sources of heat, *provided that the flame does not produce any temperature gradients within the liquid water*, and thus, subject to this proviso, the process is internally reversible.

3.4 Carnot engine

This is a heat engine of particularly simple design conceived by Carnot in 1824. It is, as we shall see, an efficient engine and, although difficult to implement mechanically, it does indicate the thermodynamic characteristics which one would ideally incorporate into designs of practical heat engines. Ultimately, it is the standard against which these designs are judged. In a more fundamental vein, we shall use the Carnot engine to define a thermodynamically useful temperature scale, something the zeroth law (see Chap-

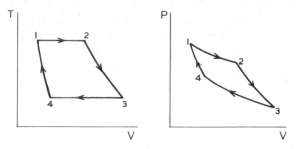

Figure 3.8. The Carnot Cycle

ter 1) does not do. Carnot engines may be designed using mechanical devices operating under either flow or non-flow conditions, and for any arbitrary working fluid.

The basis of the engine is a sequence of four steps known as the Carnot cycle. They may be represented on P-V and T-V diagrams, see Figure 3.8. Steps 1–2 and 3–4 are carried out reversibly and isothermally, whereas steps 2–3 and 4–1 are reversible and adiabatic.

The simplest way of implementing this engine in a non-flow system is to contain the working fluid, assumed for convenience to be a gas, in a cylinder with a piston which can slide without friction. The piston is connected to a device for supplying or extracting work reversibly, for example, the pile of sand used in Chapter 1, and the necessary sources and sinks of heat are available to supply or remove heat during the two isothermal steps.

A steady state flow Carnot engine needs four separate machines, see Figure 3.9. A and B are expansion turbines for obtaining work from the fluid as it expands, and C and D are compressors. The numbers 1, 2, 3 and 4 on the diagram correspond to those in Figure 3.8, and thus represent the thermodynamic state of the fluid at each point in the engine. Whereas B and D are adiabatic (thermal insulation is indicated in Figure 3.9), A and C require heat

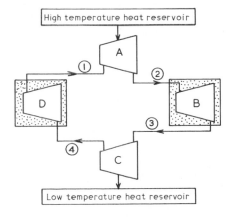

Figure 3.9. A steady state flow Carnot engine

input and output as shown. Of course, in any practical implementation all machines would be linked mechanically, probably by sharing a common shaft which would also supply any work input or output to the engine as a whole.

We examine the overall performance of the engine by examining each step in detail.

Reversible isothermal expansion of the gas from 1 to 2

During this step, the gas does work, for example, on a pile of sand, and since this would lower its temperature, heat is supplied continuously during the expansion to prevent this. The extraction of work and supply of heat must both take place reversibly. We have seen above how this can be done and, for the heat supply, we need a source at a temperature which is only infinitesimally greater than T_{high}, the temperature at points 1 and 2. We treat both heat and work inputs algebraically in accordance with our earlier convention, and represent the heat and work supplied by the surroundings as $_1^2Q$ and $_1^2W$. For a non-flow Carnot engine

$$_1^2W_C = -\int_1^2 P\,dV \qquad (3.8)$$

and for a steady state flow engine

$$_1^2W_S = \int_1^2 V\,dP \qquad (3.9)$$

(Subscripts C and S indicate closed and steady state flow respectively.) We do not expect the two work terms to be equal. Although we might expect the same to be true for $_1^2Q_C$ and $_1^2Q_S$, this is not the case. The thermodynamic state of the working fluid is the same when it reaches 2, whether this was by a closed or a steady state flow process is irrelevant. Thus ΔU is the same in each process, as is also ΔH (since both are state functions). Applying the first law to an infinitesimal step in each process gives

$$dU = dQ_C - P\,dV \qquad (3.10)$$
$$dH = dQ_S + V\,dP \qquad (3.11)$$

(we have replaced $d\,W_C$ and $d\,W_S$ by the corresponding reversible quantity) and combining the two equations, making use of the fact that $dH = dU + P\,dV + V\,dP$ (the differentiated form of $H = U + PV$),

$$dQ_C = dQ_S \qquad (3.12)$$

Integration immediately gives

$$_1^2Q_C = _1^2Q_S \qquad (3.13)$$

Reversible adiabatic expansion of the gas from 2 to 3

Again, the gas does work on the surroundings, and

$$_2^3W_C = -\int_2^3 P\,dV; \qquad _2^3W_S = \int_2^3 V\,dP \tag{3.14}$$

but, since the process is adiabatic

$$_2^3Q_C = 0; \qquad _2^3Q_S = 0 \tag{3.15}$$

and this time the temperature of the gas falls.

Reversible isothermal compression of the gas from 3 to 4

Qualitatively, this is a reversal of the first stage; the surroundings now do work on the gas and the heat flow is out of and not into the gas. The condition of reversibility requires a heat sink at temperature T_{low}, which is infinitesimally lower than that at points 3 and 4. The work transferred is

$$_3^4W_C = -\int_3^4 P\,dV; \qquad _3^4W_S = \int_3^4 V\,dP \tag{3.16}$$

and the heat transferred is

$$_3^4Q_C = {_3^4}Q_S \tag{3.17}$$

Reversible adiabatic compression of the gas from 4 to 1

For this

$$_4^1W_C = -\int_4^1 P\,dV; \qquad _4^1W_S = \int_4^1 V\,dP \tag{3.18}$$

$$_4^1Q_C = 0 \qquad _4^1Q_S = 0 \tag{3.19}$$

Thus, the net result of operating a non-flow Carnot engine for one complete cycle is the absorption of heat equal to $_1^2Q_C + {_3^4}Q_C$ and of work equal to $_1^2W_C + {_2^3}W_C + {_3^4}W_C + {_4^1}W_C$. Since $\Delta U = 0$, the first law of thermodynamics, $\Delta U = Q + W$, gives us

$$_1^2Q_C + {_3^4}Q_C = -({_1^2}W_C + {_2^3}W_C + {_3^4}W_C + {_4^1}W_C) \tag{3.20}$$

As all parts of the cycle were carried out reversibly, the magnitude of $_1^2W_C$ (say) is equal to the area under the line joining points 1 and 2, which represents the path of the process on the P-V diagram (see Figure 3.8). Thus, for a non-flow Carnot engine, the net work done by the engine in one cycle [the right-hand side of (3.20)] is equal in magnitude to the area enclosed by that cycle when represented on a P-V diagram. It follows from (3.20) that this area is also equal to the net amount of heat taken in by the engine, $_1^2Q_C + {_3^4}Q_C$, which will be a positive quantity, since we expect the net work, $_1^2W_C + _2^3W_C + _3^4W_C + _4^1W_C$, to be negative (an engine does work on the surroundings).

A similar analysis applied to the steady state flow case supplies the parallel result:

$$_1^2Q_s + _3^4Q_s = -(_1^2W_s + _2^3W_s + _3^4W_s + _4^1W_s) \tag{3.21}$$

and also the fact that the net work done is equal in magnitude to the area enclosed by the cycle when represented on a P-V diagram.

Since, henceforth, we shall be interested only in the net work rather than the individual terms which constitute it, we drop the subscripts C and S and allow the equations to apply to both flow and non-flow Carnot engines.

We can now write the efficiency, η, of a Carnot engine as (3.2)

$$\eta = -(_1^2W + _2^3W + _3^4W + _4^1W)/_1^2Q \tag{3.22}$$

or, using (3.20) or (3.21),

$$\eta = (_1^2Q + _3^4Q)/_1^2Q \tag{3.23}$$

3.5 Carnot refrigerator and heat pump

Devices which use the same four operations as the Carnot engine performed in the reverse order are a Carnot refrigerator and a Carnot heat pump. The procedure is, see Figure 3.10:

  (i) Reversible adiabatic expansion from 1 to 4,
  (ii) Reversible isothermal expansion from 4 to 3 (this requires a heat source infinitesimally higher in temperature than T_{low}, the temperature of points 3 and 4),
  (iii) Reversible adiabatic compression from 3 to 2,
  (iv) Reversible isothermal compression from 2 to 1 (requiring a heat sink infinitesimally below T_{high}).

An analysis of this cycle similar to that given above for the Carnot engine gives the net heat input as $_2^1Q + _4^3Q$ and the net work input as $_2^1W + _3^2W + _4^3W + _1^4W$, and the first law gives

$$_2^1Q + _4^3Q = -(_2^1W + _3^2W + _4^3W + _1^4W) \tag{3.24}$$

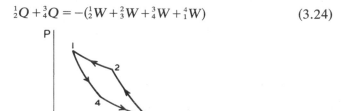

Figure 3.10. Carnot refrigerator and heat pump

As in the Carnot engine, the magnitude of the net work input is equal to the area enclosed within the cycle on the P-V diagram.

In a refrigerator we extract heat from an object at a low temperature, generally below ambient, and reject it to some convenient sink, such as the atmosphere. The Carnot device we have just described can do this; the isothermal expansion from 4 to 3 takes place at T_{low} and absorbs heat. This is rejected, together with the net work input, to the heat sink at the higher temperature T_{high}. As a measure of the effectiveness of such a refrigerator, we define its coefficient of performance, β, as

$$\frac{\text{Heat extracted at the lower temperature}}{\text{Work input to the machine}}$$

which in our case is

$$\beta = \frac{{}^3_4Q}{{}^1_2W + {}^2_3W + {}^3_4W + {}^4_1W} = -\frac{{}^3_4Q}{{}^1_2Q + {}^3_4Q} \tag{3.25}$$

If we take the same piece of machinery described above as a refrigerator and, instead of rejecting the heat at temperature T_{high} into the atmosphere we use it, say, to heat a room, we have a plant which is perhaps somewhat misleadingly called a heat pump. The object being cooled at T_{low} is now unimportant; any convenient source of 'low temperature heat' can be used such as the atmosphere or a river, it being presumed that these are below the temperature of the room being heated. The appropriate measure of the effectiveness of a heat pump is its coefficient of performance, β', defined as:

$$\frac{\text{Heat supplied to object at higher temperature}}{\text{Work input to the machine}}$$

which in our case is

$$\beta' = -\frac{{}^1_2Q}{{}^1_2W + {}^2_3W + {}^3_4W + {}^4_1W} = \frac{{}^1_2Q}{{}^1_2Q + {}^3_4Q} \tag{3.26}$$

3.6 The second law of thermodynamics

In the section on the Carnot engine there was a presumption that the net work input was negative, and for the Carnot refrigerator that it was positive. These may seem obvious, for we cannot expect, for example, to be able to transfer heat from a body at a low temperature to one at a higher temperature without doing something to bring it about. Nor can we expect to find a situation in which we can extract heat from a body at a lower temperature and convert part of it into work and reject the remainder at some higher temperature. Our experience of everyday life leads us to believe that these processes are impossible. We cannot prove that they are impossible, but it is our invariable experience that they are so. This observation is very important and when stated formally it is termed the second law of thermodynamics.

It is impossible to construct a machine operating in a cyclical manner which is able to convey heat from one reservoir at a lower temperature to one at a higher temperature and produce no other effect on any other part of the surroundings. This formulation of the second law is essentially that proposed by Clausius.

The term 'cyclical manner' ensures that at least the thermodynamic state of the machine is unchanged at the end, that is after completion of an integral number of cycles. Moreover, it is essential to the law, for we can devise a non-cyclic machine which can transfer heat from a low to a high temperature and have no other effect on the surroundings. Consider the reversible process represented by path 1–2–3–4 in Figure 3.11. Stage 1–2 is a reversible isothermal expansion, heat being taken in from the cold reservoir at T_1. Stage 2–3 is

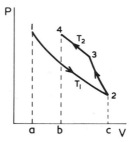

Figure 3.11. An incomplete cycle and the second law of thermodynamics

adiabatic compression to temperature T_2 and is followed by isothermal compression, 3–4, in which heat is rejected to the hot reservoir at T_2. If we arrange that the area 1–2–c–a equals the area 4–3–2–c–b on the P-V diagram, we have, for reversible processes, arranged that no net work is done by the system on the surroundings. The latter are, therefore unchanged apart from the heat which has been transferred from a low to a high temperature. But of course, the cycle has not been closed so there is no violation of the second law. If we do close it, we can see from the diagram that there must be an input of work and this changes the state of the surroundings, again in accord with the second law.

3.7   Carnot principle

This may be expressed by making two statements:

(i)   No heat engine can be more efficient than a reversible engine operating between the same two heat reservoirs.

(ii)   All reversible heat engines operating between the same two heat reservoirs have the same efficiency.

We may prove both of these propositions by means of the second law of thermodynamics.

Consider two engines, the first, the one we wish to test, which may or may

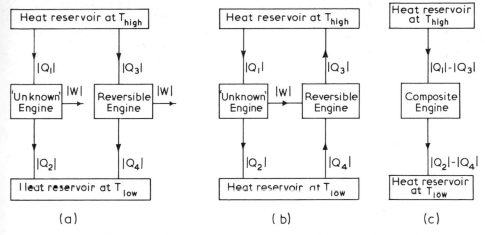

Figure 3.12. Comparison of an 'unknown' engine with a reversible engine

not be reversible, and the second a reversible engine, such as a Carnot engine. Both of these engines are presumed to operate between the same two heat reservoirs and to produce the same net amount of work per cycle (see Figure 3.12a). Heat flows into and out of the engines as indicated.*

If we reverse the direction of the operation of the reversible engine, that is use it as a refrigerator, the magnitudes of $|Q_3|$, $|Q_4|$ and $|W|$ remain the same—the definition of a reversible process—but the flows are opposite in direction. Thus, we can use the work output of the 'unknown' engine to drive the refrigerator, giving us the situation in Figure 3.12b. Since there is no reason why the two engines should be regarded as separate any longer, we can join them together to form the composite machine, Figure 3.12c, which has only heat inputs and outputs, but no work. By the first law it follows that

$$|Q_1| - |Q_3| = |Q_2| - |Q_4| \qquad (3.27)$$

and from the second law that

$$|Q_1| - |Q_3| \geqslant 0 \qquad (3.28)$$

since if $|Q_3| > |Q_1|$ there is net heat flow from a cold reservoir to a hot reservoir without there being any other change to the surroundings, in contravention of Clausius's statement of the second law.

Thus from (3.28) we have

$$\frac{|W|}{|Q_1|} \leqslant \frac{|W|}{|Q_3|} \qquad (3.29)$$

that is, the efficiency of the reversible engine is greater than or equal to that of the 'unknown' engine, and the first proposition of Carnot's principle is proved.

---

* In this section, and also in two of those following, all Q's and W's will be treated as numerical quantities, symbol $|W|$ etc., and the direction of heat or work flow indicated either on a diagram or in words.

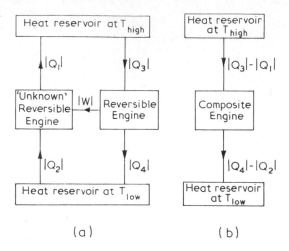

Figure 3.13. Comparison of two reversible engines

Now if the 'unknown' engine were also reversible we could change its direction of motion and drive it with the first reversible engine, as in Figure 3.13a, which is equivalent to Figure 3.13b. From the first law

$$|Q_3| - |Q_1| = |Q_4| - |Q_2| \tag{3.30}$$

and from the second law

$$|Q_3| - |Q_1| \geqslant 0 \tag{3.31}$$

Hence

$$\frac{|W|}{|Q_1|} \geqslant \frac{|W|}{|Q_3|} \tag{3.32}$$

There is only one way that (3.29) and (3.32) can both be satisfied at the same time, and that is if

$$\frac{|W|}{|Q_1|} = \frac{|W|}{|Q_3|} \tag{3.33}$$

Thus, both the reversible engines have the same efficiency, and this proves Carnot's second proposition.

We have proved Carnot's principle without making any assumptions about the working fluid in the engines; our conclusions are perfectly general. However, we have not said anything about how the efficiency of a reversible engine varies with the temperatures of its two reservoirs. We might express this variation as

$$\eta = f(T_{low}, T_{high}) \tag{3.34}$$

it is important that there are only two independent variables in this equation, the temperatures of the two reservoirs, for if there were others, such as the pressure at some point in the cycle, then it would be possible to devise machinery which would violate the second law. It is also important that the function f is a universal function and has the same form whatever the working fluid. This is a consequence of Carnot's Principle.

Exercise

Kelvin and Planck proposed the second law in the form 'it is impossible to construct a machine operating in a cyclic manner which produces no effect other than the extraction of heat from a reservoir and the performance of an equal amount of mechanical work'. By linking such a machine to a heat engine which has both a heat source and sink, show that if the former existed, Clausius's statement of the second law could be violated.

3.8 Thermodynamic scales of temperature

We shall define as 'thermodynamic' any temperature scale which is compatible with the Carnot Principle and, in particular, one which allows (3.34) to be satisfied. Henceforth we use the symbol T only to represent a temperature measured on one of these scales.

Consider the experimental arrangement shown in Figure 3.14 (Q and W are again treated as numerical quantities in this section.) The machine at the left-hand side is a Carnot engine operating between T_1 and T_2, whereas the right-hand machine consists of two Carnot engines in series. The sizes of the engines are such that there is no net heat gain by the reservoir at T_3, and that the heat flows into engines 1 and 2 are both equal to $|Q_1|$. For engine 1 the efficiency

$$\eta = \frac{|W_1|}{|Q_1|} = f(T_1, T_2) \tag{3.35}$$

or since $|W_1| = |Q_1| - |Q_2|$

$$\frac{|Q_1| - |Q_2|}{|Q_1|} = f(T_1, T_2) \tag{3.36}$$

Hence

$$\frac{|Q_2|}{|Q_1|} = 1 - f(T_1, T_2) = F(T_1, T_2) \tag{3.37}$$

similarly

$$\frac{|Q_3|}{|Q_1|} = F(T_1, T_3) \tag{3.38}$$

and

$$\frac{|Q_4|}{|Q_3|} = F(T_3, T_2) \tag{3.39}$$

for engines 2 and 3, where the mathematical form of $F(T_a, T_b)$ is the same in all three cases.

We may look upon engines 2 and 3, taken together, as one engine with a heat input of $|Q_1|$ at temperature T_1, a heat rejection of $|Q_4|$ at T_2, and a work output of $|W_2| + |W_3|$. By the Carnot Principle this must have the same efficiency as engine 1. Therefore,

$$\eta = \frac{|W_1|}{|Q_1|} = \frac{|W_2| + |W_3|}{|Q_1|} \qquad (3.40)$$

and hence

$$|W_1| = |W_2| + |W_3|; \qquad |Q_2| = |Q_4| \qquad (3.41)$$

and (3.39) becomes

$$\frac{|Q_2|}{|Q_3|} = F(T_3, T_2) \qquad (3.42)$$

which, combined with (3.38) and equated to (3.37) gives

$$\frac{|Q_2|}{|Q_1|} = F(T_3, T_2) \cdot F(T_1, T_3) = F(T_1, T_2) \qquad (3.43)$$

This implies that the effect of T_3 in the product of $F(T_3, T_2)$ and $F(T_1, T_3)$ cancels if the result is to be equal to $F(T_1, T_2)$. This can only be so if $F(T_a, T_b)$ can be separated into $F_1(T_a)/F_1(T_b)$ as any other mathematical form does not permit cancellation. Thus

$$\frac{|Q_2|}{|Q_1|} = \frac{F_1(T_1)}{F_1(T_2)} \qquad (3.44)$$

and this is the equation which all thermodynamically useful temperature scales must satisfy. Clearly, there are any number of scales which satisfy this equation.

The scale of temperature which is used almost exclusively in science and engineering is one defined by

$$F_1(T) = A/T \qquad (3.45)$$

where A is a constant of proportionality. This definition gives

$$\frac{|Q_2|}{|Q_1|} = \frac{T_2}{T_1} \qquad (3.46)$$

and the efficiency of a Carnot engine is

$$\eta = \frac{|W_1|}{|Q_1|} = \frac{|Q_1| - |Q_2|}{|Q_1|} = \frac{T_1 - T_2}{T_1} \qquad (3.47)$$

We shall see later that this scale corresponds to the perfect gas scale of temperature.

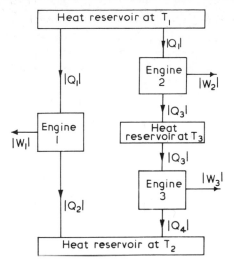

Figure 3.14. Carnot engines and thermodynamic temperature

Clearly, if engine 1, Figure 3.14, is driven in reverse as a refrigerator or heat pump, we have

(i) the coefficient of performance of a refrigerator

$$\beta = \frac{|Q_2|}{|W_1|} = \frac{|Q_2|}{|Q_1| - |Q_2|} = \frac{T_2}{T_1 - T_2} \tag{3.48}$$

(ii) the coefficient of performance of a heat pump

$$\beta' = \frac{|Q_1|}{|W_1|} = \frac{|Q_1|}{|Q_1| - |Q_2|} = \frac{T_1}{T_1 - T_2} \tag{3.49}$$

Whereas the efficiency of a Carnot engine η is always less than 1, we see that the coefficient of performance of a refrigerator β can be greater than 1, and that the coefficient of performance of a heat pump β' is always greater than 1.

Other proposals for the form of $F_1(T)$ have been made but have never gained wide acceptance. Thus, if the function is defined as $F_1(T) = CT$, where C is a constant,

$$\frac{|Q_2|}{|Q_1|} = \frac{T_1}{T_2} \tag{3.50}$$

and one has a 'reciprocal' temperature scale. If $F_1(T) = Ce^{-T}$,

$$\frac{|Q_2|}{|Q_1|} = e^{(T_1 - T_2)} \tag{3.51}$$

and one has an 'exponential' temperature scale.

Perfect gas and thermodynamic scales of temperature

The results above indicate that the Carnot engine can be used as a thermometric device with the valuable property that it always gives the same result whatever the working fluid. Compare this with the performance of two liquid-in-glass thermometers filled with different liquids. If both are calibrated at the same two points, say melting ice and boiling water, and a linear variation of temperature with volume is assumed between them, then we find that the two thermometers do not agree at an intermediate temperature. On the other hand, the Carnot engine is not a convenient device to use to measure a temperature. We therefore search for a more practical device which can be proved to give the same temperature as that given by the thermodynamic scale of (3.47). We find the solution in the properties of real gases at low pressure.

Experimental measurements on the pressure-volume-temperature $(P\text{-}V\text{-}T)$ relationship for real gases at low pressure may be summarised in the laws of Boyle and Charles, both of which can be included in the single equation

$$PV = nR\theta \tag{3.52}$$

where n is the amount of material, R is a constant and θ is a temperature on a scale whose zero is at the temperature at which the extrapolated pressure of the gas at constant volume becomes zero (Charles's Law). This equation is, of course, only an approximation to the behaviour of real gases, but becomes better the lower the pressure. However, it has one other important property; experiment shows that the constant R is the same whatever the gas.

We state now, and prove later in Section 3.12, that we may replace θ in (3.52) by the thermodynamic temperature T as defined by (3.47). This gives

$$PV = nRT \qquad \text{(pg)}* \tag{3.53}$$

and we call 'perfect gases' those hypothetical substances whose $P\text{-}V\text{-}T$ properties conform *exactly* to this equation for all values of pressure and temperature. We may thus use a perfect gas thermometer as a means of reproducing what is usually termed 'the thermodynamic scale of temperature'. In older literature it is often called the 'absolute' scale of temperature. In as far as a real gas at low pressure approximates a perfect gas, then the gas thermometer, as used in practice, approximates the thermodynamic temperature scale and it does not matter what gas is used in the thermometer provided the pressure is sufficiently low. We emphasise that, although we have introduced the perfect gas thermometer at this early stage, this is purely to help us conceptually. The discussion in Sections 3.9 to 3.11 is based solely on the thermodynamic temperature as defined by (3.47).

It remains only for us to fix the size of the 'degree'. We can do this by

---

*Equations which apply only to the perfect gas are indicated throughout by (pg).

defining only one temperature on the thermodynamic scale since all other temperatures can be related to this via the efficiency of the Carnot engine which operates between these two temperatures

$$\eta = \frac{T_1 - T_2}{T_1} \qquad (3.54)$$

or via, say, the constant volume, perfect gas thermometer which gives

$$\frac{P_1}{P_2} = \frac{T_1}{T_2} \quad (\text{pg}) \qquad (3.55)$$

By international agreement, the triple point of water (see Chapter 4 for the meaning of triple point) has been defined as being at a temperature of 273.16 K *exactly* where the kelvin, symbol K, is the unit of temperature. This figure has been chosen since the melting point of water at 1 atm pressure (the so-called 'ice-point' which is ~ 0.01 K lower than the triple point) is then at 273.15 K approximately and the boiling point at 1 atm pressure (the so-called 'normal boiling point') is at 373.15 approximately, thus making the size of the thermodynamic unit of temperature very close to that of the older Celsius (or Centigrade) degree.

3.9 Entropy

(In this section we continue to treat Q and W as numerical quantities and indicate the direction of the heat or work flow by arrows on a diagram.)

Figure 3.15a shows a Carnot engine represented on a T-V diagram. It may be operating either under non-flow or steady state flow conditions, for, as we saw in Section 3.4, we need not distinguish between them; the results we derive are applicable to both. If, instead of considering the four steps of the Carnot cycle as all operating in the same direction, we treat the steps as two alternative ways of getting from point 1 to point 3, the first route being via 2 and the second via 4, see Figure 3.15b, then we must reverse the direction of heat flow in the isothermal step at the lower temperature. Since this step is reversible, the magnitude of the heat flow is unchanged. In Section 3.8 we

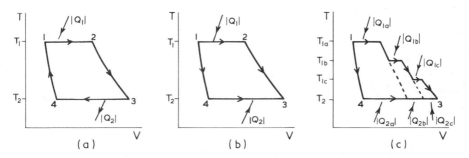

Figure 3.15. Carnot cycle and the representation of reversible processes

showed that for a Carnot cycle

$$\frac{|Q_1|}{|Q_2|} = \frac{T_1}{T_2} \tag{3.56}$$

and, therefore,

$$\frac{|Q_1|}{T_1} = \frac{|Q_2|}{T_2} \tag{3.57}$$

Figure 3.15c shows another way of getting from point 1 to point 3, via three isothermal/adiabatic steps. These additional adiabatic lines have been projected (shown dotted) until they cross the isothermal line joining points 3 and 4, thus forming three smaller Carnot cycles within the main diagram. (Note, the adiabatic lines cannot cross at any point, otherwise we can set up an engine using two adiabats and one isotherm which therefore generates work by taking in heat only at one temperature, thus violating the second law.) Each of the smaller cycles can then be treated in the same way as Figure 3.15a and b, giving

$$\frac{|Q_{1a}|}{T_{1a}} = \frac{|Q_{2a}|}{T_2} \; ; \qquad \frac{|Q_{1b}|}{T_{1b}} = \frac{|Q_{2b}|}{T_2} \; ; \qquad \frac{|Q_{1c}|}{T_{1c}} = \frac{|Q_{2c}|}{T_2} \tag{3.58}$$

Since

$$|Q_2| = |Q_{2a}| + |Q_{2b}| + |Q_{2c}|$$

we have

$$\frac{|Q_{1a}|}{T_{1a}} + \frac{|Q_{1b}|}{T_{1b}} + \frac{|Q_{1c}|}{T_{1c}} = \frac{|Q_2|}{T_2} \tag{3.59}$$

Clearly, this can be generalised to any path between points 1 and 3 which consists alternately of reversible isotherms and adiabats. If we make the individual steps infinitesimally small we can so represent any reversible path between points 1 and 3. Thus the quantity

$$\int_1^3 \frac{dQ_{rev}}{T} \tag{3.60}$$

is independent of the path between those points. In the integral, dQ_{rev} is the small amount of heat taken in at temperature T, which generally varies throughout the integration. The subscript rev on dQ serves as a reminder that the process is reversible.

A quantity which is independent of the path between two points was shown in Chapter 1 to be a state function, or, more accurately, a change in a state function. We may therefore define a function 'entropy' with symbol S by

$$\Delta S = \int \frac{dQ_{rev}}{T} \tag{3.61}$$

where the integral is to be performed over any reversible path between the initial and final states.

In this derivation, we assumed that Q was a numerical quantity (i.e. positive) and that as far as $\int dQ_{rev}/T$ was concerned that the heat flows were into the system. If the heat flows are out of the system, as they would be if we were to go backwards from point 3 to point 1 in Figure 3.15, ΔS would be negative, but equal in magnitude to its forward value since it is a state function. This is clearly covered by (3.61) if we allow dQ_{rev} to revert to its conventional algebraic definition, with heat flows into the system represented by positive values and heat flows out by negative.

Temperature—entropy diagram

The definition of entropy

$$\Delta S = \int \frac{dQ_{rev}}{T} \quad \text{or} \quad dS = \frac{dQ_{rev}}{T} \tag{3.62}$$

can be arranged as

$$dQ_{rev} = T \, dS \quad \text{and} \quad Q_{rev} = \int T \, dS \tag{3.63}$$

and this suggests the use of temperature and entropy as suitable coordinates to show the heat transfer during a reversible process. Figure 3.16 shows an arbitrary reversible process between points 1 and 2. Equation (3.63) tells us that the heat input during this process is equal to the shaded area, provided that the temperature is expressed on the thermodynamic (or kelvin) scale

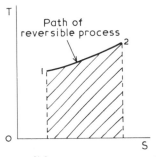

Figure 3.16. Path of a reversible process as represented on a T-S diagram

from an axis at zero. The temperature-entropy diagram is thus complementary to the pressure-volume diagram, the latter showing the work input to the system during a reversible process as the area under the path representing the process (see Section 1.7).

The Carnot cycle may be represented on a T-S diagram, Figure 3.17, in which the arrows are drawn in the direction applicable to a heat engine. The isothermal parts of the cycle are, of course, horizontal, and as a consequence of the definition of entropy (3.61) the adiabatic reversible parts of the cycle

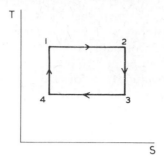

Figure 3.17. A Carnot cycle represented on a T-S diagram

are vertical lines. Adiabatic reversible processes are often, therefore, termed *isentropic*.

3.10 Entropy changes in irreversible processes

We have seen how to represent the path of a reversible process on a T-S diagram. However, it is not clear how we can represent an irreversible process on such a diagram, for it is a characteristic of such a process that, although we may know the initial and final states of the system, we know little, if anything of the path taken. Irreversible processes are therefore frequently shown on T-S and other diagrams as a cross-hatched line between the initial and final states, Figure 3.18. The actual route taken by the cross-hatched line has no physical meaning and so it might just as well be drawn straight. Cross-hatching also serves as a reminder that we cannot evaluate the heat input as the area under it.

In an irreversible adiabatic process, i.e. a spontaneous process under thermally isolated conditions, there is no reason to suppose that the entropy change will be zero as for a reversible process. Consider two possible irreversible adiabatic processes, one in which the entropy increases, and one in which it decreases. Figure 3.19a and b represent these on a T-S diagram. To

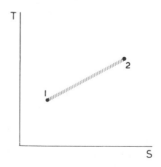

Figure 3.18. An irreversible process (represented on a T-S diagram)

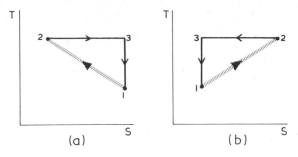

Figure 3.19. Examination of two possible irreversible adiabatic processes (represented on a T-S diagram)

determine whether either or both are thermodynamically feasible, we examine a return path which is reversible. For convenience, we choose a two-step process, a reversible isothermal change followed by a reversible adiabatic one, shown by full lines in the figure. Both diagrams (a) and (b) now represent cycles for which the first law (in either non-flow or steady state flow form) gives

$$ {}_1^2W + {}_2^3W + {}_3^1W + {}_2^3Q = 0 \qquad (3.64) $$

where ${}_1^2W$ = work input to the system during step 1–2, etc. and where we have made use of the fact that steps 1–2 and 3–1 are both adiabatic. If ${}_2^3Q$ is positive, the result of the operation of the cycle is the conversion of heat into work, that is we have a heat engine. However, we saw that an engine taking in heat at one temperature and converting it into work without rejecting heat at a lower temperature was an impossible device; it violates the second law. Thus the situation shown in Figure 3.19a cannot exist. On the other hand, that in Figure 3.19b requires ${}_2^3Q$ to be negative and the cycle is merely a device for converting work into heat, an unexceptionable process.

Although both diagrams in Figure 3.19 show an irreversible process taking place during an increase in temperature, the argument is unchanged when the temperature falls, and only marginally changed when it is constant (${}_3^1W$ is now zero). In all cases we find, therefore, that entropy cannot fall during an irreversible adiabatic process. We summarise our results as

$$ \Delta S_{\text{adiabatic process}} \geqslant 0 \qquad (3.65) $$

where the equality sign applies in the limit of a reversible process, and (3.65) applies equally to closed and steady state flow irreversible processes.

If there is exchange of heat between the system and its surroundings, that is, a non-adiabatic process, then we cannot, in general, say anything about the entropy of the system without considering what is happening in the surroundings. So that we may use the result we have already obtained for an adiabatic system, it is convenient to define an 'enlarged system', Figure 3.20, which

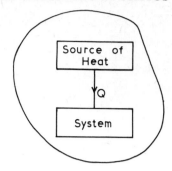

Figure 3.20. 'Enlarged system' containing both system and source of heat in the surroundings

contains not only the system of interest, but also the source of heat within the surroundings. This enlarged system has now an adiabatic boundary and we may therefore write

$$\Delta S_{\text{system}} + \Delta S_{\text{surroundings}} \geqslant 0 \qquad (3.66)$$

where the subscript 'surroundings' implies that we consider only those parts of the surroundings which exchange heat with the system.

This is a perfectly general result and applies to any process, but it suffers from the defect of being rather difficult to use since we rarely know sufficient about the state of the surroundings. Moreover, it can be simplified only if we make assumptions about the nature of the system or surroundings. We consider just one or two such simplifications here.

Consider the case of but a single source of heat in the surroundings, which is at a temperature T_{sur}. If Q_{sys} is the amount of heat absorbed by the system from the surroundings then

$$Q_{\text{sur}} = -Q_{\text{sys}} \qquad (3.67)$$

If the heat source in the surroundings is large, as is necessary if its temperature is to remain constant, its loss of heat is an internally reversible process. Thus

$$\Delta S_{\text{sur}} = \frac{Q_{\text{sur}}}{T_{\text{sur}}} = \frac{-Q_{\text{sys}}}{T_{\text{sur}}} \qquad (3.68)$$

and substitution in (3.66) gives

$$\Delta S_{\text{sys}} \geqslant \frac{Q_{\text{sys}}}{T_{\text{sur}}} \qquad (3.69)$$

If, in addition, the temperature of the system is constant during the process and equal to that of the surroundings, $T_{\text{sys}} = T_{\text{sur}}$, we have

$$\Delta S_{\text{sys}} \geqslant \frac{Q_{\text{sys}}}{T_{\text{sys}}} \qquad (3.70)$$

and we have an inequality expressed only in terms of quantities relating to the system.

3.11 Relationship between entropy and other thermodynamic functions for systems of constant composition

In this section, we derive a number of thermodynamic equations which are applicable to all systems which do not change composition during the process in question, i.e. we restrict consideration to systems which, for a given amount of material, may be completely specified by fixing only two independent variables such as P and V. They apply, therefore, to systems containing a single molecular species and also to systems containing a mixture provided that the composition remains constant both in time and in space throughout the system. We do not consider here mixtures in which there are chemical reactions or phase equilibria. For example, we can apply the results of this section to air provided that there is no chemical reaction between the nitrogen and oxygen, and provided also that we do not study the liquefaction process for, in the case of liquid-vapour equilibrium in a mixture, the liquid and vapour phases differ in composition. But, if the system is all liquid or all vapour and no phase change occurs during the process, we have constant composition and this section is applicable. Such systems are effectively 'single component systems', although we defer until Chapter 7 a formal definition of the word 'component'. Many of the equations we derive are especially valuable and may be called the 'working equations' of thermodynamics. We indicate these by a box drawn around them.

We consider the effect of making small changes in the state of a system of fixed composition. If we do this reversibly, and we saw in Section 1.7 that there must exist at least one reversible route between any two states provided that only two independent variables (P and V) are necessary to specify them, then for a closed system

$$dQ = T\,dS \quad \text{and} \quad dW = -P\,dV \tag{3.71}$$

if only P-V work is involved, and hence by the first law ($dU = dQ + dW$), we have

$$\boxed{dU = T\,dS - P\,dV} \tag{3.72}$$

which may be applied to any infinitesimal process, reversible or irreversible, since it involves only state functions—we have used the reversible path purely as a means of deriving it. Similarly, if the displacement is carried out in a steady state flow system

$$dQ = T\,dS \quad \text{and} \quad dW = V\,dP \tag{3.73}$$

and so

$$\boxed{dH = T\,dS + V\,dP} \tag{3.74}$$

(3.72) and (3.74) are particularly useful, and we shall use them frequently. Although the method of derivation given here may imply that (3.72) can only be used in a closed system and (3.74) only in a steady state flow system, this is not so. Both equations can be used in either situation since they involve only state functions. We can see this if we take (3.72) and substitute in it the differentiated form of $H = U + PV$, i.e. $dH = dU + P\,dV + V\,dP$, for then we obtain (3.74).

Since U, S and V are functions of state, there exists, for a system which can be specified by only two independent variables, an equation of the form $U = f(S, V)$ whose total differential is (see Appendix A)

$$dU = \left(\frac{\partial U}{\partial S}\right)_V dS + \left(\frac{\partial U}{\partial V}\right)_S dV \qquad (3.75)$$

Comparing this equation with (3.72) we note that the total differentials involved are the same in each case, namely dU, dS and dV. Bearing in mind the physical meaning of (3.75) and therefore also of (3.72), that if we make small arbitrary and independent changes in S and V of magnitude dS and dV, the resulting change in U is dU in both equations. Hence the two equations can both be true only if

$$\boxed{T = \left(\frac{\partial U}{\partial S}\right)_V} \qquad (3.76)$$

and

$$\boxed{-P = \left(\frac{\partial U}{\partial V}\right)_S} \qquad (3.77)$$

Similarly, if we take $H = f(S, P)$ and differentiate to give

$$dH = \left(\frac{\partial H}{\partial S}\right)_P dS + \left(\frac{\partial H}{\partial P}\right)_S dP \qquad (3.78)$$

comparison with (3.74) shows that

$$\boxed{T = \left(\frac{\partial H}{\partial S}\right)_P} \qquad (3.79)$$

and

$$\boxed{V = \left(\frac{\partial H}{\partial P}\right)_S} \qquad (3.80)$$

From (3.76)–(3.80) we derive four more useful equations. If we differentiate (3.76) partially with respect to V, keeping S constant and (3.77) with respect to S, keeping V constant, we have

$$\left(\frac{\partial T}{\partial V}\right)_S = \left[\frac{\partial}{\partial V}\left(\frac{\partial U}{\partial S}\right)_V\right]_S \quad \text{or} \quad \left(\frac{\partial^2 U}{\partial V\,\partial S}\right) \qquad (3.81)$$

and

$$-\left(\frac{\partial P}{\partial S}\right)_V = \left[\frac{\partial}{\partial S}\left(\frac{\partial U}{\partial V}\right)_S\right]_V \quad \text{or} \quad \left(\frac{\partial^2 U}{\partial S\, \partial V}\right) \tag{3.82}$$

The 'mixed' second derivative is independent of the order in which the two differentiations are carried out (see Appendix A) and so the right-hand sides of (3.81) and (3.82) are equal. Consequently,

$$\boxed{\left(\frac{\partial T}{\partial V}\right)_S = -\left(\frac{\partial P}{\partial S}\right)_V} \tag{3.83}$$

Similarly, a second differentiation of (3.79) and (3.80) gives

$$\boxed{\left(\frac{\partial T}{\partial P}\right)_S = \left(\frac{\partial V}{\partial S}\right)_P} \tag{3.84}$$

Substituting

$$\left(\frac{\partial T}{\partial V}\right)_S \left(\frac{\partial V}{\partial S}\right)_T \left(\frac{\partial S}{\partial T}\right)_V = -1 \quad \text{(see Appendix A)}$$

into (3.83) followed by rearrangement gives

$$\boxed{\left(\frac{\partial S}{\partial V}\right)_T = \left(\frac{\partial P}{\partial T}\right)_V} \tag{3.85}$$

and similarly from (3.84)

$$\boxed{\left(\frac{\partial S}{\partial P}\right)_T = -\left(\frac{\partial V}{\partial T}\right)_P} \tag{3.86}$$

(3.83)–(3.86) are the four *Maxwell Equations*, named after James Clerk Maxwell who first derived them.

We use these equations to relate entropy to the heat capacities C_P and C_V. If we take $dU = T\, dS - P\, dV$ and consider the case when the volume is constant ($dV = 0$), dividing throughout by dT gives

$$\left(\frac{\partial U}{\partial T}\right)_V = T\left(\frac{\partial S}{\partial T}\right)_V \tag{3.87}$$

Since the left-hand side of this equation is the heat capacity at constant volume C_V, we have

$$\boxed{C_V = T\left(\frac{\partial S}{\partial T}\right)_V} \tag{3.88}$$

Similarly, if we take $dH = T\, dS + V\, dP$ and divide by dT when P is constant we have

$$\left(\frac{\partial H}{\partial T}\right)_P = T\left(\frac{\partial S}{\partial T}\right)_P \tag{3.89}$$

and hence

$$\boxed{C_P = T\left(\frac{\partial S}{\partial T}\right)_P}$$

(3.90)

Equations (3.88) and (3.90) suggest a universal way of defining a heat capacity, viz.,

$$C_X = T\left(\frac{\partial S}{\partial T}\right)_X$$

(3.91)

where X is any constraint, and this is the definition used in Chapter 4. C_P and C_V are the most frequently encountered heat capacities but as an illustration of the way (3.91) may be used in other situations, consider what happens when we heat a vessel which is almost completely full of a pure liquid with only a very small vapour phase above it. If the vapour phase contains only the same molecular species as the liquid, that is there is no inert atmosphere present, the liquid and vapour phases are in equilibrium and we say that the liquid and vapour are 'saturated'. The pressure of the system is the 'saturated vapour pressure' or, more briefly, just 'vapour pressure'. If we now heat this system, the temperature rises. There is also some evaporation of liquid into vapour phase, but by adjusting P and V to keep this of negligible volume compared with the liquid, the uptake of latent heat can be neglected. We can, therefore, talk of 'the heat capacity' of the saturated liquid for this process, but it is neither C_P—the vapour pressure changes with temperature—nor C_V—the volume of the liquid changes owing to thermal expansion. Nevertheless, there is the constraint that the system should remain saturated. Hence we define a 'saturation heat capacity' C_σ (σ meaning 'saturation'),

$$C_\sigma = T\left(\frac{\partial S}{\partial T}\right)_\sigma$$

(3.92)

where the derivative is evaluated along the path which the liquid takes during the heating process.

The difference between the two principal heat capacities C_P and C_V is frequently needed and is obtained from (3.88) and (3.90):

$$C_P - C_V = T\left[\left(\frac{\partial S}{\partial T}\right)_P - \left(\frac{\partial S}{\partial T}\right)_V\right]$$

(3.93)

For systems of fixed composition, two variables are necessary to specify the state, hence $S = f_1(T, P)$, the total differential of which is

$$dS = \left(\frac{\partial S}{\partial T}\right)_P dT + \left(\frac{\partial S}{\partial P}\right)_T dP$$

(3.94)

But we can also write $S = f_2(T, V)$. It is shown in Appendix A that this means that in (3.94) we can 'divide by dT and apply the constraint $V = $ constant', giving

$$\left(\frac{\partial S}{\partial T}\right)_V = \left(\frac{\partial S}{\partial T}\right)_P + \left(\frac{\partial S}{\partial P}\right)_T \left(\frac{\partial P}{\partial T}\right)_V \tag{3.95}$$

Combining this with (3.93) and the Maxwell equation (3.86) we find

$$\boxed{C_P - C_V = T \left(\frac{\partial V}{\partial T}\right)_P \left(\frac{\partial P}{\partial T}\right)_V} \tag{3.96}$$

which shows that the difference between the heat capacities C_P and C_V is determined solely by the P-V-T properties.

Often, a coefficient of thermal expansion, α, is defined as

$$\alpha = \frac{1}{V} \left(\frac{\partial V}{\partial T}\right)_P \tag{3.97}$$

and a coefficient of isothermal compressibility, β_T, as

$$\beta_T = -\frac{1}{V} \left(\frac{\partial V}{\partial P}\right)_T \tag{3.98}$$

In terms of these quantities (3.96) becomes (see A.10)

$$\boxed{C_P - C_V = \frac{T\alpha^2 V}{\beta_T}} \tag{3.99}$$

We conclude this section by examining the way internal energy and enthalpy vary with volume and pressure respectively.

For any substance,

$$dU = T\,dS - P\,dV \tag{3.100}$$

and hence, dividing by dV and keeping T constant

$$\left(\frac{\partial U}{\partial V}\right)_T = T \left(\frac{\partial S}{\partial V}\right)_T - P \tag{3.101}$$

using the appropriate Maxwell equation, (3.85) gives

$$\boxed{\left(\frac{\partial U}{\partial V}\right)_T = T \left(\frac{\partial P}{\partial T}\right)_V - P} \tag{3.102}$$

Similarly,

$$dH = T\,dS + V\,dP \tag{3.103}$$

and dividing by dP, keeping T constant followed by use of the appropriate Maxwell equation gives

$$\boxed{\left(\frac{\partial H}{\partial P}\right)_T = -T \left(\frac{\partial V}{\partial T}\right)_P + V} \tag{3.104}$$

Equations (3.102) and (3.104) are sometimes called the *thermodynamic equations of state*, since they express the change of the thermal properties U and H, with volume and pressure, in terms of the $(P\text{-}V\text{-}T)$ properties of the system.

3.12   Identity of the gas thermometer and thermodynamic scales of temperature

In Section 3.8 we asserted that the perfect gas thermometer and thermodynamic scales of temperature were identical. We now prove this proposition and, at the same time, show how real gases can be used in their implementation.

Experiment leads us to believe that all real gases conform to Boyle's and Charles's Laws when the density (and therefore the pressure) tends to zero. We shall, therefore, take it as established experimental fact that for any real gas

$$PV = nR\theta \tag{3.105}$$

in the limit of n/V going to zero and this equation defines a 'limiting density' gas thermometer temperature scale, symbol θ. Experiment also shows that, at a given temperature, as the pressure (and therefore n/V) is increased from zero, the $P\text{-}V$ behaviour can be expressed as

$$PV = n(R\theta + BP + C'P^2) \tag{3.106}$$

and that this equation is valid up to moderately high pressures. The coefficients B and C' vary from substance to substance but are otherwise functions only of temperature.

Equation (3.104) is a convenient starting point for comparing θ with the thermodynamic temperature T defined by (3.47), since experimental measurements of $(\partial H/\partial P)_T$ can be made without requiring a knowledge of the value of the thermodynamic temperature. For the experimental procedure see Section 3.17.

Figure 3.21 shows the results of some experimental measurements made on nitrogen; those for other gases are similar. If we consider one mole of material and differentiate (3.106) with respect to T when P is constant

$$P\left(\frac{\partial V}{\partial T}\right)_P = R\frac{d\theta}{dT} + P\frac{dB}{dT} + P^2\frac{dC'}{dT} \tag{3.107}$$

and substitution in (3.104) gives

$$\left(\frac{\partial H}{\partial P}\right)_T = \frac{R}{P}\left(\theta - T\frac{d\theta}{dT}\right) + B - T\frac{dB}{dT} + P\left(C' - T\frac{dC'}{dT}\right) \tag{3.108}$$

We observe, Figure 3.21, that in the limit of P being zero, $(\partial H/\partial P)_T$ remains finite. We see also that the right hand side of (3.108) is finite under these

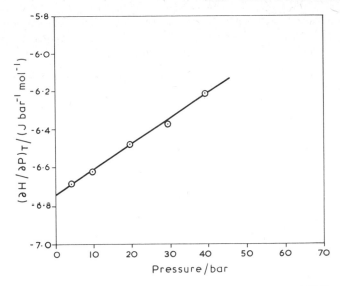

Figure 3.21. The derivative $(\partial H/\partial P)_T$ for nitrogen at 15 °C

conditions only if

$$\theta - T\frac{d\theta}{dT} = 0 \qquad (3.109)$$

that is, if

$$\theta/T = \text{const} \qquad (3.110)$$

Choosing the constant as unity ensures the equality of the gas thermometer and thermodynamic temperature scales.

3.13 The perfect gas

The perfect gas is a particularly valuable concept in thermodynamics for, although no real gas behaves exactly like it, it is often an adequate approximation to the behaviour of real gases at low or moderate pressures. Also, as we have seen, it enables us to implement the thermodynamic scale of temperature. In this section we investigate in detail its thermodynamic properties, and remind the reader that (pg) attached to an equation means that it applies *only* to a perfect gas.

We define a perfect gas as a substance whose P-V-T properties obey the equation

$$PV = nRT \qquad \text{(pg)} \qquad (3.111)$$

for all values of pressure P and thermodynamic temperature T. We place no other restrictions on the properties of this gas that do not conflict with this definition. Thus we find, for example, that the heat capacities C_P and C_V may vary with temperature, but, as we show below, they may not vary with pressure.

We begin by investigating the internal energy and enthalpy of a perfect gas. Equation (3.102) expresses the way the internal energy of any substance varies with volume:

$$\left(\frac{\partial U}{\partial V}\right)_T = T\left(\frac{\partial P}{\partial T}\right)_V - P \tag{3.112}$$

Differentiation of $PV = nRT$, gives

$$T\left(\frac{\partial P}{\partial T}\right)_V = P \qquad \text{(pg)} \tag{3.113}$$

and hence

$$\left(\frac{\partial U}{\partial V}\right)_T = 0 \qquad \text{(pg)} \tag{3.114}$$

Since for a perfect gas, P and V are necessarily linked, such that at a constant temperature, as V increases, P must decrease, it follows immediately that

$$\left(\frac{\partial U}{\partial P}\right)_T = 0 \qquad \text{(pg)} \tag{3.115}$$

The corresponding derivatives of enthalpy, with respect to pressure and volume, may be shown to be zero in a similar way. Taking (3.104)

$$\left(\frac{\partial H}{\partial P}\right)_T = -T\left(\frac{\partial V}{\partial T}\right)_P + V \tag{3.116}$$

which is true for all substances, differentiating $PV = nRT$ to obtain $(\partial V/\partial T)_P$, and substitution gives

$$\left(\frac{\partial H}{\partial P}\right)_T = 0 \qquad \text{(pg)} \tag{3.117}$$

and hence also

$$\left(\frac{\partial H}{\partial V}\right)_T = 0 \qquad \text{(pg)} \tag{3.118}$$

These results are often summarised in the statement 'the internal energy and enthalpy of a perfect gas are a function of temperature only, and do not depend on the pressure or volume'.

We note that in Figure 3.21 the intercept on the $(\partial H/\partial P)_T$ axis, which is equal to $B - T(dB/dT)$, is not zero for a real gas in the limit of zero pressure. This example shows that, although for some properties such as PV/nRT the value for a real gas in the limit of zero pressure is equal to that of a perfect gas, for other properties, in this case $(\partial H/\partial P)_T$, this is not so. Care must therefore always be exercised when replacing the zero pressure value of a property for a real gas with its corresponding perfect gas value.

Since the heat capacities C_V and C_P are the derivatives $(\partial U/\partial T)_V$ and $(\partial H/\partial T)_P$

respectively, we might surmise, correctly, that C_V and C_P for a perfect gas are also functions of temperature only. We give here a formal proof for C_V.

The heat capacity C_V for any substance can be expressed in terms of entropy as see (3.88)

$$C_V = T\left(\frac{\partial S}{\partial T}\right)_V \qquad (3.119)$$

Differentiating with respect to V, keeping T constant, gives

$$\left(\frac{\partial C_V}{\partial V}\right)_T = T\left[\frac{\partial}{\partial V}\left(\frac{\partial S}{\partial T}\right)_V\right]_T = T\left[\cdot\frac{\partial}{\partial T}\left(\frac{\partial S}{\partial V}\right)_T\right]_V \qquad (3.120)$$

since as before the order in which the differentiations are carried out is immaterial.

Replacing $(\partial S/\partial V)_T$ by $(\partial P/\partial T)_V$—one of Maxwell's equation (3.85)—gives

$$\left(\frac{\partial C_V}{\partial V}\right)_T = T\left(\frac{\partial^2 P}{\partial T^2}\right)_V \qquad (3.121)$$

an equation which is true for all substances. For a substance obeying the equation of state $PV = nRT$, $(\partial^2 P/\partial T^2)_V = 0$, hence

$$\left(\frac{\partial C_V}{\partial V}\right)_T = 0 \qquad \text{(pg)} \qquad (3.122)$$

Thus for a perfect gas, C_V is a function of temperature only.

Exercise

Show similarly that

$$\left(\frac{\partial C_P}{\partial P}\right)_T = -T\left(\frac{\partial^2 V}{\partial T^2}\right)_P \qquad (3.123)$$

and hence that for a perfect gas,

$$\left(\frac{\partial C_P}{\partial P}\right)_T = 0 \qquad \text{(pg)} \qquad (3.124)$$

i.e. that for a perfect gas C_P is a function of temperature only.

These properties of perfect gases make the evaluation of internal energy and enthalpy changes in any process particularly simple. Consider a process in which both pressure and temperature are changing and, say, we wish to evaluate the enthalpy change. Since in general, $H = H(P, T)$, we have

$$dH = \left(\frac{\partial H}{\partial P}\right)_T dP + \left(\frac{\partial H}{\partial T}\right)_P dT \qquad (3.125)$$

We have already seen that $(\partial H/\partial P)_T = 0$ for a perfect gas, and so substituting C_P

for $(\partial H/\partial T)_P$

$$dH = C_P \, dT$$

or

$$\Delta H = \int dH = \int C_P \, dT \quad \text{(pg)} \qquad (3.126)$$

Similarly, we may show that for a perfect gas in any arbitrary process

$$\Delta U = \int dU = \int C_V \, dT \quad \text{(pg)} \qquad (3.127)$$

Thus, unlike the situation for most real substances, ΔH and ΔU are independent of the way the pressure (or volume) changes during a process in a perfect gas.

   This observation allows us to derive a very simple relationship between the heat capacities C_P and C_V for a perfect gas. We may replace PV by nRT in $H = U + PV$, giving

$$H = U + nRT \quad \text{(pg)} \qquad (3.128)$$

This may be differentiated for any arbitrary process:

$$dH = dU + nR \, dT \quad \text{(pg)} \qquad (3.129)$$

Replacing dH by $C_P \, dT$ and dU by $C_V \, dT$, (3.126) and (3.127) and equating coefficients of dT thus gives

$$C_P = C_V + nR \quad \text{(pg)} \qquad (3.130)$$

which, when expressed per mole of material, gives

$$c_P = c_V + R \quad \text{(pg)} \qquad (3.131)$$

(We use lower case letters to indicate extensive quantities expressed per unit amount of material.) This equation could also have been derived from the general expression for $C_P - C_V$ (3.96).

   In thermodynamics we frequently encounter reversible isothermal and reversible adiabatic processes. We use the results above to investigate these processes for a perfect gas. For the reversible isothermal process 1–2, Figure 3.22, carried out in a closed system designated by the subscript C, the work done on the system, $_1^2W_C$, is

$$_1^2W_C = \int_1^2 -P \, dV \qquad (3.132)$$

which, on substitution by $PV = nRT$ gives

$$_1^2W_C = -\int_1^2 \frac{nRT}{V} \, dV \quad \text{(pg)}$$

$$= nRT \ln(V_1/V_2) \quad \text{(pg)} \qquad (3.133)$$

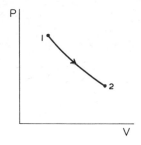

Figure 3.22. Reversible process in a perfect gas

Similarly, if the same reversible isothermal process is carried out in a steady state flow system designated by the subscript S, we have

$$_1^2W_S = \int_1^2 V \, dP$$

$$= nRT \ln(P_2/P_1) \qquad \text{(pg)} \qquad (3.134)$$

For a perfect gas at constant temperature, $P_1 V_1 = P_2 V_2$, and hence

$$_1^2W_C = {}_1^2W_S = nRT \ln(P_2/P_1) \qquad \text{(pg)} \qquad (3.135)$$

We have shown that the internal energy and enthalpy do not change during any isothermal process in a perfect gas. Thus the first law gives

$$_1^2W = -{}_1^2Q \qquad (3.136)$$

and therefore

$$_1^2Q_C = {}_1^2Q_S = -nRT \ln(P_2/P_1) \qquad \text{(pg)} \qquad (3.137)$$

for an isothermal process.

To analyse an adiabatic process we start with (3.72) $dU = T \, dS - P \, dV$, since it applies to both closed and steady state flow systems and we do not, therefore, need to consider them separately. We saw in Section 3.9 that reversible adiabatic processes are isentropic, that is

$$dS = 0 \qquad (3.138)$$

Thus,

$$dU = -P \, dV \qquad (3.139)$$

Using (3.127) for a perfect gas, we have

$$C_V \, dT = -P \, dV \qquad \text{(pg)} \qquad (3.140)$$

If we differentiate $PV = nRT$ to give $P \, dV + V \, dP = nR \, dT$ and substitute this, together with $C_V = nc_V$, into (3.140), we obtain

$$(c_V + R)P \, dV + c_V V \, dP = 0 \qquad \text{(pg)}$$

or

$$c_P P \, dV + c_V V \, dP = 0 \qquad \text{(pg)} \qquad (3.141)$$

where we have used that $c_P = c_V + R$ for a perfect gas. This equation is more frequently written in the form

$$\gamma \frac{dV}{V} + \frac{dP}{P} = 0 \qquad \text{(pg)} \qquad (3.142)$$

with $\gamma = c_P/c_V$. This equation is, in differential form, that of the adiabats of a perfect gas.

In general, this is as far as we can take the derivation, for experiment shows that for most substances c_P, and therefore also γ, vary with temperature. However, there are a number of substances for which c_P is independent of temperature, notably the rare gases, and a number of others, particularly the diatomic molecules, for which the variation is small if the temperature change is not too large. Thus, for these substances we can integrate (3.142) to give

$$PV^\gamma = \text{const} \qquad \text{(pg)} \qquad (3.143)$$

We can use this equation to determine the final temperature when a perfect gas of constant γ is compressed from an initial state of P_1, T_1 to pressure P_2. Equation (3.143) gives

$$P_1 V_1^\gamma = P_2 V_2^\gamma \qquad \text{(pg)}$$

and for a perfect gas,

$$P_1 V_1 = nRT_1 \quad \text{and} \quad P_2 V_2 = nRT_2 \qquad \text{(pg)}$$

Hence by elimination of V_1 and V_2 from these equations we obtain

$$\frac{T_2}{T_1} = \left(\frac{P_2}{P_1}\right)^{(\gamma-1)/\gamma} \qquad \text{(pg)} \qquad (3.144)$$

3.14   Calculation of entropy changes

For any system of fixed composition,

$$dS = \left(\frac{\partial S}{\partial T}\right)_V dT + \left(\frac{\partial S}{\partial V}\right)_T dV \qquad (3.145)$$

If we substitute in this (3.88) and (3.85), viz:

$$C_V = T\left(\frac{\partial S}{\partial T}\right)_V \quad \text{and} \quad \left(\frac{\partial S}{\partial V}\right)_T = \left(\frac{\partial P}{\partial T}\right)_V$$

we obtain

$$dS = \frac{C_V}{T} dT + \left(\frac{\partial P}{\partial T}\right)_V dV \qquad (3.146)$$

This equation applies to any infinitesimal step, reversible or irreversible.

Similarly, combining

$$dS = \left(\frac{\partial S}{\partial T}\right)_P dT + \left(\frac{\partial S}{\partial P}\right)_T dP \qquad (3.147)$$

with

$$C_P = T\left(\frac{\partial S}{\partial T}\right)_P \quad \text{and} \quad \left(\frac{\partial S}{\partial P}\right)_T = -\left(\frac{\partial V}{\partial T}\right)_P$$

gives

$$dS = \frac{C_P}{T} dT - \left(\frac{\partial V}{\partial T}\right)_P dP \qquad (3.148)$$

Both of these equations may be used to determine the change in entropy of the system as it goes from state 1 (characterised by values P_1, V_1 and T_1) to state 2 (P_2, V_2 and T_2). We need only choose a convenient path of integration. One such path might be from T_1 to T_2 while the pressure remains constant at P_1, followed by P_1 to P_2 while the temperature remains constant at T_2, giving

$$S_2 - S_1 = \int_1^2 dS = \int_{T_1}^{T_2} \frac{C_P}{T} dT_{P_1} - \int_{P_1}^{P_2} \left(\frac{\partial V}{\partial T}\right)_P dP_{T_2} \qquad (3.149)$$

(We use an integral written in the form $\int_{X_i}^{X_2} Z \, dX_{Y_n}$ to represent the integration of argument Z, which is a function of two independent variables X and Y, with respect to X when Y is held constant at the value Y_n.) This particular path is used frequently since all quantities involved are experimentally accessible.

If the material is a perfect gas then $(\partial V/\partial T)_P = nR/P$ and so, per unit amount of material

$$S_2 - S_1 = \int_{T_1}^{T_2} \frac{C_P}{T} dT_{P_1} - \int_{P_1}^{P_2} \frac{R}{P} dP_{T_2} \qquad \text{(pg)} \qquad (3.150)$$

which integrates to

$$S_2 - S_1 = C_P \ln(T_2/T_1) - R \ln(P_2/P_1) \qquad \text{(pg)} \qquad (3.151)$$

if C_P is independent of temperature.

For real substances, we do not have these simplifications and it is frequently necessary to resort to numerical integration. Most measurements of C_P have been made at a pressure of 1 atm (1.013 25 bar). If we are to use these measurements to evaluate ΔS, then P_1 in (3.149) must be 1 atm. If, therefore, we wish to determine ΔS for changes in temperature at a constant pressure of 1 atm, (3.149) simplifies to

$$\Delta S \ (P = \text{const}) = \int_{T_1}^{T_2} \frac{C_P}{T} dT \qquad (3.152)$$

and numerical integration of C_P/T where C_P is the experimentally determined heat capacity, gives ΔS directly. We shall see in Chapter 8 that values of ΔS determined in this way are particularly useful in studying chemical equilibria.

The presence of a phase change within the temperature range complicates things when evaluating $\int (C_P/T)\, dT$. Associated with a phase change there is absorption of latent heat and since this is taken in over an infinitesimal temperature range one might consider it as an infinite heat capacity over that range. However, this does not make $\int (C_P/T)\, dT$ indeterminate, for the constancy of T during the phase change, (see later, Section 3.23) allows us to write it as $(1/T)\int C_P\, dT$, and $\int C_P\, dT$ over a phase change is merely the latent heat, or more accurately, the enthalpy of transformation, since the process takes place at constant pressure. Including terms of this type in (3.152) we obtain

$$\Delta S\,(P = \text{const}) = \int_{T_1}^{T_2} \frac{C_P}{T}\, dT + \sum_{\substack{\text{all phase}\\ \text{transformations}}} \frac{\Delta_{tr}H}{T^{tr}} \qquad (3.153)$$

where the summation is taken over all phase transformations which take place within the temperature range T_1 to T_2, $\Delta_{tr}H$ the enthalpy of transformation and T^{tr} the temperature at which it takes place. $\Delta_{tr}H/T^{tr}$ is often called the entropy of the transformation $\Delta_{tr}S$. Thus we can speak of the entropies of evaporation, melting and sublimation for the three principal phase changes.

Example

Figure 3.23 shows C_P/T for water between $0\,°C$ and $200\,°C$ at 1 atm pressure. To evaluate the entropy change between these two temperatures we

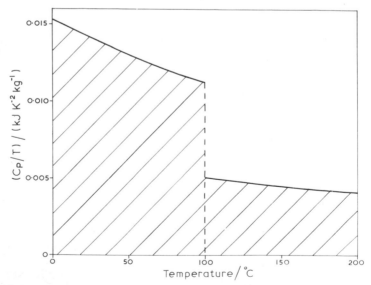

Figure 3.23. Use of a graph of C_P/T against temperature (for water) in the evaluation of entropy changes

consider the process to take place in three stages

   (i)   liquid water from 0 °C to 100 °C
  (ii) evaporation at 100 °C
 (iii) water vapour from 100 °C to 200 °C

The entropy changes in stages (i) and (iii) are evaluated from the area under the relevant regions of the graph giving 1.31 kJ K^{-1} kg^{-1} and 0.47 kJ K^{-1} kg^{-1} respectively. (These units are more properly J K^{-1} g^{-1} since it is not necessary to use the prefix in both numerator and denominator. We follow, however, the more usual engineering practice of retaining the kg as the unit of mass.) The entropy change for the evaporation step is

$$\Delta_e s = \frac{\text{latent heat}}{\text{temperature}} = \frac{\Delta_e h}{T^b} = \frac{2257 \text{ kJ kg}^{-1}}{373.15 \text{ K}} = 6.05 \text{ kJ K}^{-1} \text{ kg}^{-1}$$

Thus the total change of entropy is 7.83 kJ K^{-1} kg^{-1}.

3.15 Zero of entropy

Since all the methods described above are concerned with changes in entropy, rather than 'absolute' values of entropy, we can use a defined origin as we did for enthalpy and internal energy. Indeed, there are a number of tables and charts which use such defined zeros of entropy; thus most steam tables[1] take $S = 0$ for liquid water at 0 °C and 1 atm. However, a third law of thermodynamics, see Chapter 8, suggests a far more useful zero to be that of the solid at 0 K, and unless a statement is made to the contrary we assume that entropies have been expressed in this way.

If we are to express the entropy of a substance relative to its value at 0 K, we clearly need measurements of the heat capacity down to this temperature in order to evaluate $\int (C_P/T) \, dT$. Figure 3.24a and b show the heat capacity C_P

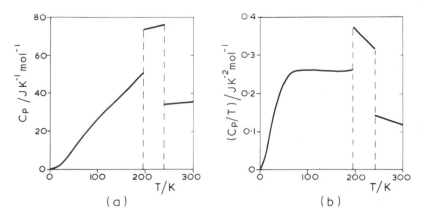

Figure 3.24. C_P and C_P/T for ammonia at 1 atmosphere pressure

and C_P/T for ammonia, for a pressure of 1 atm. Figure 3.24a, as well as showing the discontinuities in the heat capacity curve which occur at the phase changes (195.42 K and 239.74 K) shows that the heat capacity falls to zero at 0 K. This is not entirely the result of experimental measurements down to 0 K since one corollary of the third law is that 0 K is unattainable in a finite number of operations. Measurements have in fact been made down to 15.0 K, where the value of C_P has fallen to 0.7 J K^{-1} mol^{-1}. The extrapolation over the remaining few kelvin has been made according to the requirements of statistical thermodynamics which are that near to 0 K, $C_V \simeq C_P = \text{const} \times T^3$, a result due to Debye, but whose derivation is outside the scope of this book. This T^3 behaviour of C_P means that when we come to evaluate C_P/T near to 0 K, see Figure 3.24b, the value of the quotient does not become indeterminate since near to 0 K C_P/T varies as T^2.

3.16 Joule-Thomson expansion

In a Joule-Thomson expansion, fluid flows steadily through a constriction or throttle, suffering a fall in pressure as it does so, Figure 3.25. The constriction used by Joule and Thomson was a plug of porous material, but an orifice plate

Figure 3.25. Joule-Thomson expansion

or a partially opened valve performs equally well. In general, a change in the temperature of the fluid is observed as it flows through the throttle. We saw earlier that the Joule-Thomson expansion is an irreversible process, but the flow from the orifice has also another non-uniform characteristic. For the flow rates and pressure drops which we normally encounter in chemical engineering, the orifice is usually small in area compared with the inlet and outlet pipes. Hence we have a high velocity jet emerging from the orifice into a larger amount of relatively slow-moving fluid. A little way downstream, the kinetic energy of this jet will have been dissipated by molecular collisions so that there is essentially uniform flow in the outlet pipe and, most importantly, a return to a low value for the kinetic energy of the stream.

Thus, if we measure the properties of the fluid sufficiently far away from the orifice, we can apply the steady state flow version of the first law, neglecting potential and kinetic energy:

$$\Delta H = Q + W \tag{3.154}$$

In the absence of any means of extracting work from the system, W is zero. In an actual Joule-Thomson expansion, the orifice is usually well insulated to reduce heat transfer. If we assume the insulation is perfect, $Q = 0$. Hence

$$\Delta H = 0 \tag{3.155}$$

Usually we are interested in determining the temperature change accompanying the pressure drop as the fluid flows through the throttle. Since the expansion is irreversible we cannot follow the temperature change through the actual throttle. However, we can use the property of state functions that the change in one is determined solely by the initial and final states of the system, and not by the process used to link them. We can, therefore, for the purposes of calculation, replace the irreversible process by a convenient reversible process, and perform the calculations on this. Since the overall change in enthalpy during a Joule-Thomson expansion is zero, an obvious choice is a reversible process taking place at constant enthalpy. We are interested in determining the temperature change accompanying a pressure change in this constant enthalpy process. Thus, for an infinitesimal step, we require the value of

$$\left(\frac{\partial T}{\partial P}\right)_H$$

known as the *Joule-Thomson coefficient.*

If the throttling process takes place without a phase change, the Joule-Thomson coefficient can be expressed in terms of more useful quantities. (If a phase change takes place, the equations below become indeterminate, see Section 7.6.) We write

$$\left(\frac{\partial T}{\partial P}\right)_H = -\left(\frac{\partial T}{\partial H}\right)_P \left(\frac{\partial H}{\partial P}\right)_T \tag{3.156}$$

and after using (3.104), namely

$$\left(\frac{\partial H}{\partial P}\right)_T = -T\left(\frac{\partial V}{\partial T}\right)_P + V \tag{3.157}$$

we obtain

$$\left(\frac{\partial T}{\partial P}\right)_H = \frac{1}{C_P}\left[T\left(\frac{\partial V}{\partial T}\right)_P - V\right] \tag{3.158}$$

Since $(\partial V/\partial T)_P$ can be evaluated from experimental P-V-T measurements, this permits the Joule-Thomson coefficient to be calculated as a function of P and T.

For a perfect gas, differentiation of $PV = nRT$ gives

$$P\left(\frac{\partial V}{\partial T}\right)_P = nR \qquad \text{(pg)} \tag{3.159}$$

and hence $\left(\frac{\partial T}{\partial P}\right)_H = 0$. It is instructive to compare this with the value of the Joule-Thomson coefficient for a real gas in the limit of zero pressure. At low pressures, a real gas obeys the equation of state $PV = n(RT + BP + C'P^2)$ where the parameters B and C' are functions of temperature but not of pressure. Differentiation of this gives

$$\left(\frac{\partial V}{\partial T}\right)_P = n\left(\frac{R}{P} + \frac{dB}{dT} + P\frac{dC'}{dT}\right) \tag{3.160}$$

and the Joule-Thomson coefficient is

$$\left(\frac{\partial T}{\partial P}\right)_H = \frac{1}{C_P}\left[T\frac{dB}{dT} - B + PT\frac{dC'}{dT} - PC'\right] \tag{3.161}$$

where C_P is to be evaluated at the temperature and pressure of interest. Clearly, even when $P = 0$, the Joule-Thomson coefficient is not zero thus providing another example of the fact that the properties of a real gas in the limit of zero pressure are not necessarily those of a perfect gas.

For non-zero pressure drops across the throttle, (3.158) must be integrated. This is not simple for we must also allow for the fact that C_P varies with T and P, and so we usually resort to numerical integration procedures of the initial value type. Alternatively, a thermodynamic chart can be used (see Chapter 4 for a description of charts). Figure 3.26 shows lines of constant enthalpy on a pressure-temperature chart for nitrogen. Included also is the liquid-gas saturation line terminating at the critical point C, shown inset to a larger scale. The region above the saturation line represents liquid, whereas the region below and to the right represents gas. Upon expansion through a throttle, the state of the gas undergoing a Joule-Thomson expansion follows one of the lines of constant enthalpy down to lower pressures. Consider gas at 1000 bar and 607 K (corresponding to the top of the 26 kJ/mol isenthalp). As the pressure falls during expansion, the temperature steadily rises reaching 654 K when the outlet pressure is close to zero. But at a lower initial temperature, such as 370 K, corresponding to the 18 kJ/mol isenthalp for an initial pressure of 1000 bar, although there is a rise in temperature to begin with, to 397 K when the pressure is 330 bar, further expansion results in a decrease in

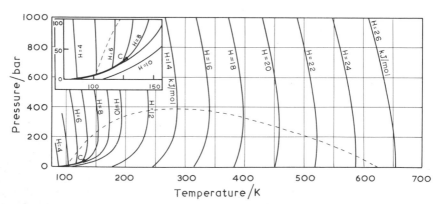

Figure 3.26. P-T chart for nitrogen showing isenthalps and the Joule-Thomson inversion curve.

temperature, eventually to 380 K. The line drawn through the points where the isenthalps have maximum slope, that is when the Joule-Thomson coefficient $(\partial T/\partial P)_H$ is zero, is called the *Joule-Thomson inversion curve*, and is shown dashed in Figure 3.26. The locus of this curve can be found from (3.158) which indicates that the Joule-Thomson coefficient passes through zero when $T(\partial V/\partial T)_P = V$. The Joule-Thomson expansion is frequently used in refrigeration and liquefaction and is discussed in detail in Chapter 5. We consider here just a few more fundamental aspects. As a fall in temperature is the aim in both of these processes, Figure 3.26 indicates that it is desirable to work at temperatures and pressures which lie within the inversion curve. Thus, if our aim is to liquefy nitrogen, and we start with gas at 285 K, then the diagram indicates that to get the maximum cooling effect we require an initial pressure of about 380 bar (corresponding to the 14 kJ/mol isenthalp), but even after a Joule-Thomson expansion down to a pressure of approximately 1 bar, the temperature is 245 K, still well above the normal boiling point, 78 K. However, if we use this cold gas to cool another stream of nitrogen at 380 bar, then this gas at 380 bar and 250 K (the temperature is 5 K higher to allow for incomplete cooling) can be expanded in a similar manner (along the 12.5 kJ/mol isenthalp) down to 200 K and further similar steps will ultimately allow 78 K to be reached. The way in which this is achieved is discussed in Chapter 5.

For refrigeration and liquefaction, the temperature at which the inversion curve cuts the temperature axis has a particular significance. Above this temperature, no matter what the initial pressure, a Joule-Thomson expansion always results in an increase in temperature. It is called the *Joule-Thomson inversion temperature*. For nitrogen, this temperature is 620 K, which is well above room temperature, but for hydrogen and helium it is 200 K and 35 K respectively and thus to liquefy these gases by Joule-Thomson expansion they must be precooled below these temperatures.

3.17 Isothermal Joule-Thomson experiment

This is a modern variant on the classical (or adiabatic) Joule-Thomson experiment which is especially valuable for the determination of thermodynamic properties. Moreover, it is the experiment which allowed us, in Section 3.12, to prove the identity of the thermodynamic and gas thermometer scales of temperature. It may be used with any gas which cools as it passes through a throttle, as for example will be the case if the initial pressure and temperature lie within the inversion curve of Figure 3.26. Figure 3.27 shows the essential components of the isothermal Joule-Thomson experiment. The gas at high pressure P_1 flows steadily through a throttle as in the adiabatic Joule-Thomson experiment but, on leaving the throttle, the gas passes over an electric heating element, the power to which is adjusted so that the temperature of the low pressure gas, at P_2, is the same as that of the high pressure gas

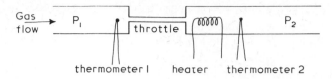

Figure 3.27. Isothermal Joule-Thomson experiment (schematic)

entering the throttle. The experiment is well insulated to eliminate heat transfer to the surroundings, a task which can be made simpler by using an apparatus of the design shown in Figure 3.28. The external surface is at an almost constant temperature thus permitting the use of the techniques of calorimetry, as described in Section 2.8.

Applying the first law for a steady state flow process to the experiment,

$$\Delta H = Q \tag{3.162}$$

since no work is involved, i.e. W is zero. ΔH is the enthalpy change for the process: gas at P_1, $T \rightarrow$ gas at P_2, T, hence

$$\Delta H = \int_{P_1}^{P_2} \left(\frac{\partial H}{\partial P}\right)_T dP_T \tag{3.163}$$

Thus, from a series of measurements of Q for a range of values of P_1 and P_2 at one temperature T we obtain, by taking slopes of the appropriate graphs, $(\partial H/\partial P)_T$ as a function of pressure. An example of a graph obtained in this way is shown in Figure 3.21.

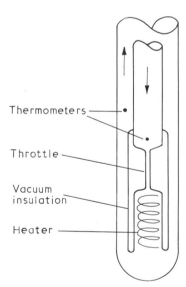

Figure 3.28. Isothermal Joule-Thomson experimental Cell (Counterflow design)

$(\partial H/\partial P)_T$ is related to the Joule-Thomson coefficient $(\partial T/\partial P)_H$. We can write (see Appendix A)

$$\left(\frac{\partial H}{\partial P}\right)_T \left(\frac{\partial P}{\partial T}\right)_H \left(\frac{\partial T}{\partial H}\right)_P = -1 \tag{3.164}$$

and rearrangement gives

$$\left(\frac{\partial H}{\partial P}\right)_T = -\left(\frac{\partial H}{\partial T}\right)_P \left(\frac{\partial T}{\partial P}\right)_H$$

$$= -C_P \left(\frac{\partial T}{\partial P}\right)_H \tag{3.165}$$

Thus, when the Joule-Thomson coefficient is zero, as in the case of a perfect gas, so also is the isothermal Joule-Thomson coefficient.

3.18 Joule expansion

This is the closed system counterpart of the Joule-Thomson expansion, but does not have the same technological importance. In a Joule expansion, gas initially contained in vessel A, Figure 3.29, is allowed to expand into vessel B.

Figure 3.29. Joule experiment

Although at the end of the process the pressure in A is equal to that in B, we have no reason to suppose that the temperatures will be equal, nor that either is the same as that of the gas originally in A. However, the first law still applies; in the absence of any means of extracting work, $W = 0$, and if we presume that the system is well insulated with no heat losses, then $Q = 0$ as well. Thus, for the Joule expansion

$$\Delta U = 0 \tag{3.166}$$

Without further information about the details of the system we are unable to say anything about the temperatures of the gas in the two vessels. Although it would be a rather idealised situation, we can obtain a solution along the lines of the one given above for the Joule-Thomson expansion, if we assume that the two vessels have a negligible heat capacity, and that they and their contents are allowed to come to thermal equilibrium with one another after the expansion has taken place. This gives

$$\left(\frac{\partial T}{\partial V}\right)_U = -\frac{1}{C_V}\left[T\left(\frac{\partial P}{\partial T}\right)_V - P\right] \tag{3.167}$$

Exercise
   Derive (3.167) and show that $(\partial T/\partial V)_U$ is zero for a perfect gas.

3.19 Speed of sound

Sound is propagated through a gas or liquid as a plane wave in which the elements of fluid oscillate perpendicularly to the wave front. The local density at a fixed point oscillates about that of the undisturbed fluid and results in the 'compressions and rarefactions', as they are usually called. To a first approximation we can consider these to take place adiabatically and reversibly; adiabatically because they take place too rapidly for heat to be conducted from one part of the sound wave to another, and reversibly since each element of the sound wave is in an essentially equilibrium state over the time scale of interest (see Section 1.2) and differs only infinitesimally from its neighbour. Transmission of sound is therefore an isentropic process and thermodynamics can be applied to it. We find[2] that the speed of sound $\mathcal{W}$ is given by

$$\mathcal{W}^2 = -v^2 \left(\frac{\partial P}{\partial v}\right)_s \qquad (3.168)$$

where v is the specific volume ($m^3 \, kg^{-1}$ if SI units used) at the pressure and temperature of the gas.

Since $\mathcal{W}$ is relatively easy to measure, it provides a convenient source of thermodynamic information. We therefore examine the approximations involved in deriving (3.168). They are primarily concerned with the reversibility of the process. Firstly, the compressed regions of gas are hotter than the expanded regions. This results in conduction of heat from the hot to the cold regions, an irreversible process. The time available for conduction is less at high frequencies than at low frequencies but this factor is more than compensated for by the shorter wavelength over which the heat is conducted. Secondly, movement of gas from a compression region to a rarefaction region, and vice versa, implies viscous forces and dissipation of energy—again an irreversible process. Once more it is at its worst at high frequencies. Thirdly, we presumed each element of the sound wave to be at equilibrium. But at high frequencies, the rate of compression is high and although re-establishment of equilibrium in the translational mode of energy storage is rapid, re-establishment of equilibrium in the rotational and, more particularly, the vibrational modes of polyatomic molecules is relatively slow and our assumption may be invalid (see Section 9.3 for a discussion of these different modes of storing energy). In an extreme case, we can have a situation in which the vibrating molecules are totally unaware that a sound wave is passing through them and, paradoxically, this is again tantamount to equilibrium although not the one we usually encounter.

These considerations suggest the use of a low frequency to measure the speed of sound, but now we encounter practical difficulties, for the sound wave is plane only if the dimensions of the apparatus are large compared with the wavelength. Compromise is necessary and most work is done at frequencies in the range 0.1 to 1.0 MHz, frequencies which are more accurately termed 'ultrasonic' rather than 'sonic'. The independence of the experimental result to change in frequency over the range used is a convenient check on its suitability, but strictly, it is based only on a condition which is necessary and not one which is also sufficient.

Exercise

Show that for a perfect gas

$$\mathcal{W}^2 = n_m \gamma RT \qquad (\text{pg}) \tag{3.169}$$

where $\gamma = C_P/C_V$ and $n_m =$ amount of substance per unit mass. Calculate the wavelength in air ($\mathcal{M} = 29$, $\gamma = 1.40$) at 300 K for a frequency of 1 MHz.

3.20 Free energy functions

Although in principle any thermodynamic calculation can be performed in terms of the functions of state already introduced, it is in practice found to be convenient to define two new functions: the Helmholtz free energy, A, and the Gibbs free energy, G. Their definitions are

$$A = U - TS \tag{3.170}$$

$$G = H - TS \tag{3.171}$$

from which it follows (since $H = U + PV$)

$$G = A + PV \tag{3.172}$$

Both equations can be differentiated, thus (3.170) gives

$$dA = dU - T\,dS - S\,dT \tag{3.173}$$

and if we consider systems in which there is no change in composition,

$$dU = T\,dS - P\,dV \tag{3.174}$$

and hence

$$dA = -S\,dT - P\,dV \tag{3.175}$$

Similarly, differentiation of (3.171) followed by substitution of

$$dH = T\,dS + V\,dP \tag{3.176}$$

gives

$$dG = -S\,dT + V\,dP \tag{3.177}$$

Equations (3.174) to (3.177) are often called the 'fundamental equations' and they apply to any change in a system of one component (see Section 3.11). They are fundamental in the sense that if we take one of them, say (3.177), we can express all other thermodynamic functions in terms of the one on the left hand side of the equation, in this case G. Thus, at constant temperature (3.177) becomes

$$V = \left(\frac{\partial G}{\partial P}\right)_T \tag{3.178}$$

and at constant pressure

$$-S = \left(\frac{\partial G}{\partial T}\right)_P \tag{3.179}$$

Putting these results into (3.171) and (3.172) gives

$$H = G - T\left(\frac{\partial G}{\partial T}\right)_P \tag{3.180}$$

$$A = G - P\left(\frac{\partial G}{\partial P}\right)_T \tag{3.181}$$

$$U = G - T\left(\frac{\partial G}{\partial T}\right)_P - P\left(\frac{\partial G}{\partial P}\right)_T \tag{3.182}$$

and we have V, S, H, A and U in terms of G. We note that in (3.178)–(3.182) P and T have a special role as common independent variables, P and T are also just the two variables which occur as differentials in (3.177). We shall call P and T the *proper* or *natural* variables for the Gibbs free energy G. In a similar way, V and T are the proper variables for A, S and V for U, and S and P for H.

Exercise

Show that

$$S = -\left(\frac{\partial A}{\partial T}\right)_V \tag{3.183}$$

$$P = -\left(\frac{\partial A}{\partial V}\right)_T \tag{3.184}$$

$$U = A - T\left(\frac{\partial A}{\partial T}\right)_V \tag{3.185}$$

$$G = A - V\left(\frac{\partial A}{\partial V}\right)_T \tag{3.186}$$

$$H = A - T\left(\frac{\partial A}{\partial T}\right)_V - V\left(\frac{\partial A}{\partial V}\right)_T \tag{3.187}$$

3.21 Zeros for G and A

In considering internal energy and enthalpy, (Section 2.12), we had to use arbitrarily defined zeros or origins in order to tabulate these properties as functions of, say, temperature and pressure. Similarly, defined zeros are often used for entropy, (Section 3.15), although as was pointed out, a third law of thermodynamics does indicate the way in which a less arbitrary zero for entropy can be chosen. Fortunately, this arbitrariness in the choice of zero is of no practical disadvantage since we are usually interested only in changes in the property concerned.

In the case of the Gibbs and the Helmholtz free energy the situation is more complicated. Thus the change in G resulting from a change in P and T can be calculated by integration of

$$dG = -S\, dT + V\, dP \qquad (3.188)$$

choosing as the path of integration a process of constant temperature followed by one of constant pressure, that is,

$$\Delta G = G_2 - G_1 = \int_1^2 dG = -\int_{T_1}^{T_2} S\, dT_{P_2} + \int_{P_1}^{P_2} V\, dP_{T_1} \qquad (3.189)$$

Although integration with respect to P presents no problems, the value of the integral with respect to T will depend on the choice of origin for S. Taking $S = 0$ for the solid at 0 K will give a different result for this integral from that obtained by taking $S = 0$ for the substance at 0 °C. We see, therefore, that not only do we need a defined zero for G, but that the actual 'scale' of G depends on our choice of zero for S. We resolve this difficulty by choosing as *the* scale of free energy one based on the entropy of the solid being zero at 0 K. This still leaves us free to define the position of the zero on this scale as we wish. We return to the conventions in this matter in Chapter 8.

Very often we are interested in evaluating changes in the free energy, ΔG or ΔA at constant temperature. We see that in (3.189) the integral involving S does not then contribute, nor does the corresponding integral in the expression for ΔA. We may, therefore, use G and A quite freely under these conditions without fear of introducing inconsistencies.

Exercise

Show that for pressure and volume changes in a perfect gas at constant temperature

$$\Delta G = \Delta A = RT \ln(P_2/P_1) = RT \ln(V_1/V_2) \qquad \text{(pg)} \qquad (3.190)$$

where

$$\Delta G = G_2 - G_1 \quad \text{and} \quad \Delta A = A_2 - A_1$$

3.22 Free energy changes in an irreversible process

We saw in Section 3.10 that when a system is in thermal contact with its surroundings, for any change in its state

$$\Delta S_{\text{system}} + \Delta S_{\text{surroundings}} \geq 0 \qquad (3.191)$$

where the equality sign applies to reversible changes, and the inequality to irreversible. For an adiabatic process this reduces to $\Delta S_{sys} \geq 0$, and for a non-adiabatic process in which the temperature of the system remains equal to that of the surroundings we found that

$$T_{sys} \, \Delta S_{sys} \geq Q_{sys} \tag{3.192}$$

(3.70), where Q_{sys} is the heat taken in by the system from the surroundings. All of these equations hold however much work W is supplied to the system during the process.

If, in addition to this equality of temperature, the pressure of the system remains unchanged throughout the process and equal to that of the surroundings, then we can make a further simplification if no work is done other than that involved in expansion of the system against the surrounding pressure. We saw in Section 2.11 that for such a process

$$\Delta H_{sys} = Q_{sys} \tag{3.193}$$

irrespective of whether the conditions were closed or steady state flow.

Substitution of (3.193) into (3.192) gives

$$T \, \Delta S \geq \Delta H \tag{3.194}$$

(where we have dropped the subscript $_{sys}$ since we shall now only be concerned with the system). From the definition of the Gibbs free energy, (3.171), we have, for a process taking place at constant temperature,

$$\Delta G = \Delta H - T \, \Delta S \tag{3.195}$$

Hence,

$$\Delta G \leq 0 \tag{3.196}$$

for a process taking place at constant pressure and temperature.

We can investigate what happens in a process of constant temperature and volume in a similar manner. Section 2.11 also gave us that for a constant volume process involving no work other than that needed to keep the volume constant,

$$\Delta U_{sys} = Q_{sys} \tag{3.197}$$

Substitution into (3.192) gives

$$T \, \Delta S \geq \Delta U \tag{3.198}$$

and from the definition of the Helmholtz free energy for a process taking place at constant temperature

$$\Delta A = \Delta U - T \, \Delta S \tag{3.199}$$

giving

$$\Delta A \leq 0 \tag{3.200}$$

for a process of constant temperature and volume.

We summarise these results as:

for any process $\qquad\qquad \Delta S_{sys} + \Delta S_{sur} \geqslant 0$ $\qquad\qquad\qquad$ (3.201)

for an adiabatic process $\qquad\qquad \Delta S \geqslant 0$ $\qquad\qquad\qquad\qquad$ (3.202)

for a constant P, T, process $\qquad \Delta G \leqslant 0$ $\Big\}$ Provided no work done $\quad$ (3.203)

$\qquad\qquad\qquad\qquad\qquad\qquad\qquad\qquad\quad$ other than as indicated

for a constant V, T, process $\qquad \Delta A \leqslant 0$ $\Big\}$ in the text $\qquad\qquad$ (3.204)

The last three criteria apply to functions of the system alone and are clearly more convenient than the first *if they can be used*. It is fortunate that very many processes are carried out under conditions of nearly constant pressure so that the expression in terms of the Gibbs free energy is applicable.

Exercise

In a similar manner, show that in a constant P and T process if additional work W is done,

$$\Delta G \leqslant W \qquad\qquad (3.205)$$

and in a constant V and T process

$$\Delta A \leqslant W \qquad\qquad (3.206)$$

3.23 Systems at equilibrium

We use the inequalities (3.201)–(3.204) to examine systems which are either at, or are approaching, equilibrium. If a system is undergoing changes which bring it closer to equilibrium then they are spontaneous changes; they take place in one direction only. Thus in the Joule expansion, Section 3.18, the spontaneous process is the flow of gas from A to B and the equilibrium state which is finally reached is characterised by equality of pressures in the two vessels. The use of the word spontaneous suggests irreversibility and indeed the approach to equilibrium is irreversible whatever the process. It is the inequality signs in (3.201)–(3.204) which are appropriate to systems approaching equilibrium. Hence, if the Joule expansion is carried out adiabatically we require $\Delta S > 0$ for the system, that is, the entropy rises until equilibrium is reached. Now, it is possible to imagine an 'overshoot' in which gas continues to flow from A to B even after the system has reached equilibrium, thus generating a greater pressure in B than in A. Our experience leads us to believe that if this were to happen, it would correct itself quickly and the system would return to the *same* equilibrium position that it had just passed through. Since the correcting procedure is spontaneous, it too takes place with $\Delta S > 0$. Thus, we can plot the entropy of the system as in Figure 3.30, and the maximum in the curve corresponds to the equilibrium situation. To the

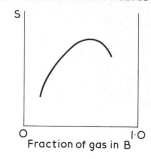

Figure 3.30. Variation of entropy during Joule expansion

left of the maximum we have the forward Joule expansion, and to the right we have the 'overshoot' region. Mathematically, therefore, the problem becomes one of determining the maximum in the curve of the entropy of the system as it goes through the process.

If a process is carried out under constant P and T or constant V and T, the appropriate criteria are G or A, but since the inequalities are $\Delta G < 0$ and $\Delta A < 0$, the diagrams corresponding to Figure 3.30 have a minimum rather than a maximum. We shall see, in Chapters 6 to 8, that these two criteria are particularly suitable for the study of both phase equilibria and chemical equilibria in multicomponent systems.

In a single component system, we frequently encounter the equilibrium between two phases, such as between liquid and vapour, liquid and solid, solid and vapour, or between one allotropic solid and another. As an example, let us consider the equilibrium between a liquid and its vapour. We can set up this equilibrium situation by putting the liquid into a previously evacuated vessel, Figure 3.31a, and allowing as much of the liquid to evaporate as is necessary to fill the remaining space with vapour. We observe that, at a fixed temperature, provided the amount of material added is such that both liquid and vapour coexist when equilibrium is reached, the pressure in the system does not depend on the amount of material introduced in the first place. That this must be so we can see from Figure 3.31b and c. We imagine the vessel shown in (a) to have two sliding partitions. In (b), one of these is used to partition off a certain volume of the vapour. In (c) the second partitions off an equal

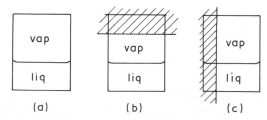

Figure 3.31. Equilibrium between a liquid and its vapour

volume, but this time of both liquid and vapour. Since the density of the liquid phase is greater than that of the vapour, (b) and (c) have the same volume but contain different total amounts of material. Clearly, sliding in the partitions does not disturb the pressure, and thus our observation is confirmed. The pressure exerted by the two coexisting phases in this example we call the saturation or saturated vapour pressure, or more concisely, simply the *vapour pressure*.

We study this equilibrium thermodynamically by disturbing the system in some way and examining what happens. If we carry out the disturbance at constant pressure and temperature, an appropriate variable would be the volume of the system. Increasing this will result in the evaporation of liquid to keep the pressure constant and we have to supply heat to maintain the temperature constant. This new state is perfectly stable and at equilibrium. It has no tendency to revert spontaneously to the previous state via an irreversible process. Thus the inequality in (3.203) does not apply and we have

$$\Delta G = 0 \qquad (3.207)$$

for the evaporation process, i.e. the gain in G in the vapour phase equals the loss in G in the liquid phase. Since the gain of the material in the vapour phase equals the loss of material in the liquid phase, this requires that the Gibbs free energy per unit amount of material (mole, kg, g, etc.) in the vapour phase equals that for the liquid phase, that is

$$g^g = g^l \qquad (3.208)$$

where a lower case g is used to indicate the Gibbs free energy per unit amount of material and superscript ^{g} and ^{l} indicate gaseous and liquid phases respectively.*

This argument is clearly applicable to all phase changes involving a single substance and not just to liquid-vapour equilibrium. Thus at 96 °C and 1 bar pressure, monoclinic and rhombic sulphur are in equilibrium and the molar Gibbs free energies of the two forms are equal.

3.24 Clapeyron's equation

Clapeyron first showed how the equilibrium between two phases (such as liquid-vapour) varies with temperature in a single component system. Consider the situation above in which a closed volume contains both liquid and vapour in equilibrium at temperature T, the pressure being the vapour pressure P, and for which

$$g^g(T) = g^l(T) \qquad (3.209)$$

---

* We use gas and vapour interchangably in the text of this book, the word chosen for a given situation being governed by conventional usage, but for consistency we use only superscript g in equations.

If the temperature of the system is raised by an infinitesimal amount dT the vapour pressure rises by dP and at this new temperature

$$g^s(T+dT) = g^l(T+dT) \tag{3.210}$$

or

$$dg^s = dg^l \tag{3.211}$$

($dg^s = g^s(T+dT) - g^s(T)$, and similarly for dg^l). The fundamental equation (3.177) for the Gibbs free energy is $dG = V\,dP - S\,dT$. Thus for a unit amount (mole, kg, g, etc.) of gas and liquid we obtain, respectively

$$dg^s = v^s\,dP - s^s\,dT \tag{3.212}$$
$$dg^l = v^l\,dP - s^l\,dT \tag{3.213}$$

where v and s are the corresponding volume and entropy for a unit amount of the substance. Substituting (3.212) and (3.213), in (3.211) gives

$$v^s\,dP - s^s\,dT = v^l\,dP - s^l\,dT \tag{3.214}$$

and hence

$$\left(\frac{\partial P}{\partial T}\right)_\sigma = \frac{s^s - s^l}{v^s - v^l} \tag{3.215}$$

where the derivative (dP/dT) has been written as a partial derivative with the constraint σ (meaning constant saturation) as a reminder that the derivative only applies along the vapour pressure curve. This equation describes how the vapour pressure of a liquid varies with temperature.

In view of the cautions in Section 3.21 about the use of free energy when the temperature is varying, the argument we have just given raises the question as to why the origin used for entropy and its influence on free energy scales does not affect the result. The reason is that we are taking differences which, provided we use the same origin throughout, become independent of that origin. This is seen clearly in (3.215) where $(s^s - s^l)$ obviously does not depend on the choice of origin for entropy s.

The quantity $(s^s - s^l)$ is the entropy of evaporation of the liquid per unit amount of material, and we saw in Section 3.14 that this is related to the latent heat of evaporation by

$$\Delta_e s = s^s - s^l = \frac{l}{T} \tag{3.216}$$

where l is the latent heat (or enthalpy) of evaporation per unit amount of material. Thus we obtain

$$\left(\frac{\partial P}{\partial T}\right)_\sigma = \frac{l}{T(v^s - v^l)} \tag{3.217}$$

which is *Clapeyron's Equation*.

Although this equation was derived for liquid-vapour equilibrium, it applies also to all other phase changes. For solid-vapour equilibrium, it gives the variation of sublimation pressure with temperature. In solid-liquid equilibrium the function we are investigating is usually termed the 'melting line' rather than a saturation pressure. We have

$$\left(\frac{\partial P}{\partial T}\right)_{\text{melting}} = \frac{l}{T(v^l - v^s)} \tag{3.218}$$

where l is the latent heat of fusion per unit amount of solid, and the derivative expresses how the melting point varies with pressure.

Example 1

For ice and water at 0 °C,

$$v_{\text{ice}} = 19.6 \times 10^{-6} \, \text{m}^3 \, \text{mol}^{-1}$$

$$v_{\text{water}} = 18.0 \times 10^{-6} \, \text{m}^3 \, \text{mol}^{-1}$$

and the latent heat is 6000 J mol^{-1}. Hence

$$\left(\frac{\partial P}{\partial T}\right)_{\text{melting}} = -1.4 \times 10^7 \, \text{N m}^{-2} \, \text{K}^{-1}$$

or

$$\left(\frac{\partial T}{\partial P}\right)_{\text{melting}} = -7.2 \times 10^{-8} \, \text{K N}^{-1} \, \text{m}^2$$

$$= -0.0072 \, \text{K bar}^{-1}$$

we see that the change of melting point with pressure is quite small.

Example 2

For water and vapour at 0 °C

$$v_{\text{water}} = 18.0 \times 10^{-6} \, \text{m}^3 \, \text{mol}^{-1}$$

$$v_{\text{water vapour}} = 3.71 \, \text{m}^3 \, \text{mol}^{-1}$$

$$\text{latent heat} = 45\,000 \, \text{J mol}^{-1}$$

Thus

$$\left(\frac{\partial P}{\partial T}\right)_\sigma = 44.5 \, \text{N m}^{-2} \, \text{K}^{-1}$$

The above examples show the crucial role of Δv, the difference in volume of the two phases. If both phases are condensed, Δv is small and $(\partial P/\partial T)$ is large, whereas if one phase is gaseous, Δv is large and $(\partial P/\partial T)$ is small. Furthermore, if the volume of the 'high temperature' phase is greater than the 'low temperature' phase $(\partial P/\partial T)$ is positive, whereas it is negative if the reverse is true since latent heats are always positive. Thus in equilibrium between gas and a condensed phase, $(\partial P/\partial T)$ is always positive, but if the two phases are both condensed (solid and liquid or allotropic solid I and allotropic solid II) we have no such rule. Sometimes the liquid is more dense than the solid, as with water, but more often the solid is more dense than the liquid.

The uses we make of the Clapeyron equation depend on our information. If we measure the vapour pressure of a liquid as a function of temperature and know the molar volumes of the coexisting liquid and gas phases, we can calculate l. Similarly, if we know the vapour pressure (as a function of T), the latent heat and the molar volume of the liquid, we can calculate the molar volume of the gas. These calculations are particularly valuable when carried out in conjunction with an equation of state of the gas and are dealt with at greater length in Chapter 4.

Let us examine the situation when the gas phase can be represented by the equation of state

$$PV = n(RT + BP) \tag{3.219}$$

where B is a function of temperature but not of pressure. For most substances, this is an adequate approximation up to about 3 bar. The volume of the gas phase is now given by

$$v^g = RT/P + B \tag{3.220}$$

and substitution into (3.217) gives

$$B - v^l = -\frac{T}{P}\left[R - \frac{lP}{T^2}\left(\frac{\partial T}{\partial P}\right)_\sigma\right] \tag{3.221}$$

thus, for example, measurements of l, v^l, $(\partial T/\partial P)_\sigma$ and P enable B to be calculated.

Example

Measurements of the vapour pressure and latent heat of evaporation of oxygen give the following values at the normal boiling point ($P = 1.013\,25$ bar).

$$T = 90.18 \text{ K}$$

$$l = 6820 \pm 10 \text{ J mol}^{-1}$$

$$(P/T^2)(\partial T/\partial P)_\sigma = 0.001\,174 \pm 0.000\,001 \text{ K}^{-1}$$

Thus

$$B - v^l = -\frac{90.18}{1.013\,25 \times 10^5}[8.314 - 6820 \times 0.001\,174]$$

$$= -0.890 \times 10^{-3}[8.314 - 8.007]$$

$$= -0.273 \times 10^{-3} \text{ m}^3 \text{ mol}^{-1}$$

$$= -273 \text{ cm}^3 \text{ mol}^{-1}$$

Taking
$$v^l = 28 \text{ cm}^3 \text{ mol}^{-1}$$
we obtain
$$B = -245 \text{ cm}^3 \text{ mol}^{-1}$$

In assessing this value of B, we note that the expression in square brackets consists of two terms each of approximately equal magnitude but of opposite sign. Taking the uncertainties of l and $(P/T^2)(\partial T/\partial P)_\sigma$ as given, the number 8.007 is uncertain to about 1 part in 600, say 0.013. If we examine how this uncertainty propagates through the calculation we find that we should write

$$B = -250 \pm 12 \text{ cm}^3 \text{ mol}^{-1}$$

Thus the calculation of B is 'ill-conditioned' and quite small errors in the original experimental data propagate to become substantial fractional errors in B. In this case we see physically why this comes about, for B measures the degree of imperfection in a gas which is not very far from perfect. However, ill-conditioned calculations occur all too frequently in thermodynamics and since, as a rule, we do not draw attention to them in the text, we must always be alert to the possibility that a calculation is of this type.

Clapeyron-Clausius equation

This is an approximate equation which may be applied to liquid-vapour or solid-vapour phase equilibria of a single component.

If we approximate the behaviour of the vapour phase to that of a perfect gas

$$v^g = RT/P \qquad \text{(pg)} \tag{3.222}$$

where P is the saturated vapour pressure. In situations in which we can use the perfect gas approximation, we find that v^g is so very much greater than v^l or v^s that these quantities can be ignored. Thus Clapeyron's equation simplifies to

$$\left(\frac{\partial P}{\partial T}\right)_\sigma = \frac{lP}{RT^2} \tag{3.223}$$

which is often rearranged as

$$\left(\frac{\partial \ln(P/P^\dagger)}{\partial T}\right) = \frac{l}{RT^2} \tag{3.224}$$

where $P^\dagger$ is the unit of pressure we are using.* Equation (3.224) is known as the *Clapeyron-Clausius equation.*

---

* Equation (3.224) is mathematically less valid when written, as it frequently is, with the logarithm of a dimensioned quantity as
$$\left(\frac{\partial \ln P}{\partial T}\right)_\sigma = \frac{l}{RT^2}$$
and this is a practice which we do not advocate.

Exercise 1

Show that the vapour pressure of a liquid varies with temperature as

$$\ln(P/P^\dagger) = A + B/T \tag{3.225}$$

if we assume that the latent heat of evaporation is independent of temperature and that the pressure is sufficiently low for the vapour to be perfect.

This same equation is frequently used, as in Section 6.11, to represent approximately the variation of vapour pressure over wide ranges of temperature, even up to the critical point. Since l is far from constant—it becomes zero at the critical point—and the gas is far from perfect at pressures well above 3 bar, give qualitative reasons for its success. (Refer to Section 4.3 for the variation of saturation volume with temperature.)

Exercise 2

Show that for a liquid and gas under saturation conditions

$$\left(\frac{\partial(\Delta h)}{\partial T}\right)_\sigma = \left(\frac{\partial(\Delta h)}{\partial T}\right)_P + \left(\frac{\partial(\Delta h)}{\partial P}\right)_T \left(\frac{\partial P}{\partial T}\right)_\sigma \tag{3.226}$$

where

$$\Delta h = h^g - h^l = l \tag{3.227}$$

and hence

$$\left(\frac{\partial(\Delta h)}{\partial T}\right)_\sigma = \Delta c_P + \frac{\Delta h}{T} - \frac{\Delta h}{\Delta v}\left(\frac{\partial(\Delta v)}{\partial T}\right)_P \tag{3.228}$$

where

$$\Delta c_P = c_P^g - c_P^l \tag{3.229}$$

$$\Delta v = v^g - v^l \tag{3.230}$$

Show that this reduces to Kirchhoff's equation, (2.44) Section 2.9, if $v^g \gg v^l$ and the gas is perfect.

Equation (3.228) is valid for all phase changes, not only for liquid-gas. We see, therefore, that Kirchhoff's equation applies also to the sublimation of a solid at low pressure, but not to its fusion.

3.25   Availability and maximum work

The chemical engineering industry uses a large amount of mechanically driven machinery, particularly compressors. Also used are machines for obtaining mechanical work from material at high temperature and pressure, such as steam turbine power plants. In the electricity generating industry, the supply of steam comes from the heat produced by a nuclear reactor or from the combustion of coal or hydrocarbons. In the chemical industry many reactions are carried out which are exothermic, and there is here a potential source of heat for generating power. For example, the oxidation of ammonia to nitric acid evolves a large amount of heat, and it makes economic sense to consider whether this might be used to generate power rather than be wasted.

The designer of this machinery aims at the highest efficiency, by which we mean, in the case of a compressor, that the work which we supply should be as small as possible, and in the case of the power plant that we require the largest possible output of work. Since we treat work, W, as an algebraic quantity which is positive when added to a system, we require that W is a minimum with respect to changes made to the process in question. It would be useful to be able to calculate this minimum value of W without having to consider the details of the process. We show in this section that this can be done by means of a quantity called the availability.

Closed system

We consider the case of a material in state 1, characterised by P_1, V_1, T_1, U_1, etc., a closed system, in an environment of temperature T_0 and pressure P_0, and examine how much work is involved in bringing the system to the temperature and pressure of the environment. In most practical cases, T_0 and P_0 are the atmospheric temperature and pressure. It probably aids understanding if we take T_1 and P_1 to be a high temperature and pressure as in a cylinder containing super-heated steam under pressure, Figure 3.32. However, the argument we give applies whatever the relative magnitudes of P_1, P_0, T_1 and T_0, for we are treating all quantities as algebraic. We see from the

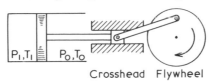

Crosshead Flywheel

Figure 3.32. Single stroke expansion engine (closed system)

diagram that the steam in the cylinder drives the piston outwards as long as P_1 is greater than P_0 and, at the same time, does work on the flywheel via the crosshead and crank. During this process we expect P_1 and T_1 to fall, exchanging heat with the surroundings as necessary, until they reach P_0 and T_0 when no further work can be done. We showed in (3.69) that for any process taking place in surroundings at temperature T_{sur} and exchanging heat only with those surroundings.

$$\Delta S_{sys} \geqslant \frac{Q_{sys}}{T_{sur}} \qquad (3.231)$$

where Q_{sys} is the heat absorbed from the surroundings by the system and the inequality applies to an irreversible process, the equality to a reversible one. Thus, for the process we are considering, if S_0, U_0, H_0, etc. are the thermodynamic properties of the steam when it reaches atmospheric temperature and pressure T_0 and P_0 (3.231) becomes

$$S_0 - S_1 \geqslant \frac{Q}{T_0} \qquad (3.232)$$

Since the first law gives

$$U_0 - U_1 = Q + W \qquad (3.233)$$

substitution gives

$$T_0(S_0 - S_1) \geqslant U_0 - U_1 - W \qquad (3.234)$$

or

$$W \geqslant (U_0 - T_0 S_0) - (U_1 - T_0 S_1) \qquad (3.235)$$

We require W to be a minimum (algebraically) which is the case if the 'equals' sign applies, that is if the process is carried out reversibly, giving

$$W = (U_0 - T_0 S_0) - (U_1 - T_0 S_1) \qquad (3.236)$$

W includes both the work done on the flywheel, that is useful work, and work done in driving the piston against atmospheric pressure P_0 which is not normally useful. This latter work, W_{atm}, is given by

$$W_{atm} = -P_0(V_0 - V_1) \qquad (3.327)$$

Thus the useful work is given by

$$W_{useful} = W - W_{atm} = (U_0 + P_0 V_0 - T_0 S_0) - (U_1 + P_0 V_1 - T_0 S_1) \qquad (3.238)$$

This expression depends only on the initial thermodynamic properties of the system and on the properties at ambient conditions. The actual path taken is irrelevant *provided that it is reversible*.

This expression for the useful work has been called by Keenan[3] the 'availability' of the system, which we give the symbol D, defined as

$$D = (U_1 + P_0 V_1 - T_0 S_1) - (U_0 + P_0 V_0 - T_0 S_0) \qquad (3.239)$$

This definition ($D = -W_{useful}$) treats the availability of material in a power generating machine as being positive at the beginning of the expansion stroke. It thus represents the maximum work which the engine can produce if the end state of the material is at ambient pressure and temperature. This definition makes physical sense when only heat engines are being considered, but it conflicts with our usual convention that additions to a system are treated as positive changes. Furthermore, the chemical engineer is more frequently concerned with machines requiring a power input than with those giving a power output. Nevertheless, since we do not wish to coin a new thermodynamic property, we retain Keenan's definition until such time as usage dictates otherwise.

The general expression for availability can be simplified under certain conditions.

(i) If the initial pressure is 'atmospheric', that is $P_1 = P_0$, we can use the equation $H = U + PV$ for both initial and ambient conditions, giving

$$D = (H_1 - T_0 S_1) - (H_0 - T_0 S_0) \qquad (3.240)$$

(ii) If, in addition to $P_1 = P_0$, we have $T_1 = T_0$, the equation is simplified further by using $G = H - TS$, which gives

$$D = G_1 - G_0 \qquad (3.241)$$

Steady state flow system

The machine corresponding to Figure 3.32 but operating under steady state flow conditions is represented in Figure 3.33 in which material flowing into the machine at P_1, T_1, H_1, etc. produces shaft work, absorbs heat Q from the surroundings as necessary and exhausts at ambient conditions P_0, T_0, etc. Equation (3.232) still applies to this system, but the first law, neglecting kinetic and potential energy changes, is now

$$H_0 - H_1 = Q + W \qquad (3.242)$$

where W is shaft work, so that there is now no need to be concerned with the work of 'driving back the atmosphere'. Thus, in place of (3.234) we have

$$T_0(S_0 - S_1) \geqslant H_0 - H_1 - W \qquad (3.243)$$

which for W to be a minimum requires

$$W = (H_0 - T_0 S_0) - (H_1 - T_0 S_1) \qquad (3.244)$$

To distinguish this quantity from the availability in a closed system Keenan termed it the 'stream availability' B defined as

$$B = (H_1 - T_0 S_1) - (H_0 - T_0 S_0) \qquad (3.245)$$

(an alternative name is 'exergy' used particularly by German authors). Keenan also considered the effect of kinetic and potential energy changes on the stream availability, full details of which are given in his book.[3] This definition, like that for closed system availability, also takes the function as positive for the material entering a heat engine.

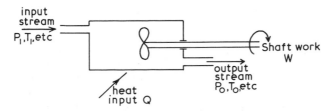

Figure 3.33. Expansion engine (steady state flow system)

Stream availability is much more appropriate to the analysis of engineering processes than is closed system availability and we therefore concentrate our attention on it. If we are to use the concept of availability, we need suitable tables and charts (see Chapter 4). Unfortunately, few of these exist and recourse must be made to tables of enthalpy and entropy, from which the stream availability is calculated by means of (3.245) rearranged in the form

$$B = (H_1 - H_0) - T_0(S_1 - S_0) \qquad (3.246)$$

One of the problems in tabulating B as a function of P and T is that it depends on the value of T_0. However, when we come to use B we find that this is not a serious objection for either the quantity we are calculating is not sensitive to small changes in value of ambient temperature T_0, or small corrections for the variation of T_0 can easily be applied.

In his pioneering paper on availability Keenan,[4] produced a B-S chart for water and Figure 3.34 gives an outline version of this but based on more

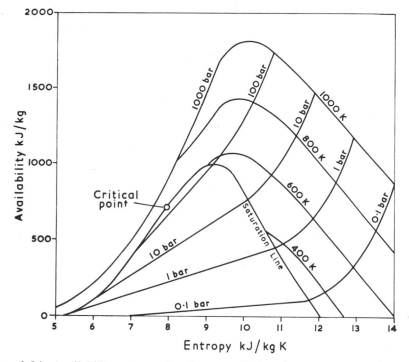

Figure 3.34. Availability-entropy chart for water. Reference temperature and pressure are 290 K and 1 bar. Zero of availability is liquid water at 290 K and 1 bar. Zero of entropy is ice at zero kelvin.

modern experimental measurements. In the absence of similar charts for other substances, a relatively simple construction on an H-S chart can be used, and full details are given in Section 4.18.

3.26 Use of availability in the analysis of processes

One use of the availability function is to answer such questions as 'if I have a supply of carbon dioxide at 350 °C and 8 bar pressure—such as the coolant stream from a nuclear reactor—what is the maximum work I can generate from it?', or, 'what is the minimum work needed to liquefy methane gas, initially at 20 °C, if both liquid and gas are to be at 1 bar pressure?' This use might be termed 'performing initial design calculations' for it gives a first estimate of the work involved in a projected process, as well as a target to aim for, a target which cannot, of course, be exceeded.

These calculations can be readily carried out using the tables and charts referred to above, if the process is carried out under steady state flow conditions. However, for illustrative purposes we calculate, without using tables, the maximum work which a steady stream of nitrogen at 700 K can produce. Ambient temperature is 300 K and the pressure of the hot nitrogen and of the surroundings are both 1 bar. By assuming that the heat capacity of nitrogen C_P, at 1 bar does not depend on temperature, we can so simplify the calculation as not to need tables.

The maximum work is the availability of the hot nitrogen stream. We calculate $(H_1 - H_0)$ and $(S_1 - S_0)$ from (2.35) and (3.152). Thus

$$H_1 - H_0 = \int_0^1 C_P \, dT \qquad (3.247)$$

and

$$S_1 - S_0 = \int_0^1 \frac{C_P}{T} \, dT \qquad (3.248)$$

Since C_P is independent of temperature, we have

$$H_1 - H_0 = C_P(T_1 - T_0) \qquad (3.249)$$
$$S_1 - S_0 = C_P \ln(T_1/T_0) \qquad (3.250)$$

Taking

$$C_P = 58.0 \text{ J K}^{-1} \text{ mol}^{-1}$$

we obtain

$$H_1 - H_0 = 58.0(700 - 300) = 23\,200 \text{ J mol}^{-1}$$
$$S_1 - S_0 = 58.0 \ln(700/300) = 49.0 \text{ J K}^{-1} \text{ mol}^{-1}$$

and

$$B = 23\,200 - 300 \times 49.0$$
$$= 8500 \text{ J mol}^{-1}$$

which is the maximum work obtainable.

It frequently happens that the process we consider does not end up at the same temperature and pressure as the surroundings. Thus, in the production of liquid methane starting with gaseous methane stored in cylinders under pressure, but at ambient temperature, the process neither starts nor finishes at ambient conditions of temperature and pressure. We can determine the work required for this process from the change of availability. Thus, if state 1 is the initial one, gaseous methane under pressure, and state 2 is the final one, liquid methane, then

$$\text{maximum work output} = D_1 - D_2 \text{ for a closed system} \qquad (3.251)$$

and

$$= B_1 - B_2 \text{ for a steady state flow system}$$
$$(3.252)$$

If the quantity calculated is negative, as, for example, if B_1 and B_2 are both positive but $B_2 > B_1$, then the physical meaning becomes one of minimum work input.

When there are no tables of availability and we use tables of enthalpy and entropy (as in the case of a steady state flow system) then some simplification is possible. Subtracting

$$B_1 = (H_1 - H_0) - T_0(S_1 - S_0) \qquad (3.253)$$

and

$$B_2 = (H_2 - H_0) - T_0(S_2 - S_0) \qquad (3.254)$$

gives the maximum work output as

$$(H_1 - H_2) - T_0(S_1 - S_2) \qquad (3.255)$$

which requires only a knowledge of the enthalpy and entropy in the initial and final states.

For illustration, we consider the production of liquid methane at its normal boiling point (111.67 K) from a supply of gaseous methane at 100 bar, 300 K. Tables give the following values

	$H/\text{J mol}^{-1}$	$S/\text{J K}^{-1}\text{mol}^{-1}$
Saturated liquid methane at 111.67 K	4600	79.3
Gaseous methane at 300 K, 100 bar	17600	143.9

Substitution in (3.255), taking $T_0 = 300$ K, gives

$$\text{maximum work output} = (17600 - 4600) - 300(143.9 - 79.3)$$
$$= -6400 \text{ J mol}^{-1}$$

Thus the minimum work which must be supplied to produce the liquid methane is 6400 J mol^{-1}.

The other main use of the availability function is to determine how closely an actual process or part of a process comes to the ideal (ideal being, as we shall see, synonymous with reversible). In this way, analysis of each part of a plant serves to pinpoint the more thermodynamically weak aspects of the design and indicates where further effort might be worthwhile in that it would produce the largest gains. We illustrate such analysis by considering the performance of a heat exchanger.

Heat exchangers are used in the chemical industry both for removal of waste heat from a process stream, the heat removed being rejected to the air, or to cooling water from a river or lake, and for transfer of heat from one process fluid to another. The first case does concern us here since we do not wish to extract work from either the fluid used as a coolant or from the cooled process stream. We can, by means of availability calculations, determine how much work we are 'throwing away' by cooling the process stream in this way, but this is the type of calculation we have already described.

Heat exchangers of the second type are most frequently encountered in power generation, refrigeration and gas liquefaction plant. They are often very large, with huge throughputs, and their high efficiency is vital. Efficiency in a heat exchanger means two things: (1) the largest possible amount of heat transfer per unit surface area of contact, and (2) thermodynamic efficiency. The first of these belongs more appropriately to the study of heat transfer and is not considered in this book. As for thermodynamic efficiency, consider the situation in which a stream of methane gas passes through a heat exchanger to be cooled, ultimately to the liquid phase. The stream passing down the other side of the heat exchanger must be a material which has undergone a refrigeration process. Continuous refrigeration requires a machine and an input of work. Clearly, we do not wish to waste this work and we must ask ourselves whether there is any way that the operation of the heat exchanger can lead to such a loss. Similarly, to take an example from the power generation industry, hot carbon dioxide from the core of a nuclear reactor (of the 'Magnox' type) is passed through a heat exchanger to raise steam, which then drives a turbine generator. Again, we ask ourselves how the performance of the heat exchanger affects the efficiency of the conversion of heat into work.

In this latter example, the generation of power, the hot carbon dioxide has a certain capacity for doing work—as measured by its availability—as it enters the heat exchanger. When it leaves the heat exchanger at some lower temperature, the availability is less. In an ideal heat exchanger, the whole of this decrease in availability is transferred to the second process stream, in this case water/steam. However, when a real heat exchanger is examined we find that the increase in availability in this second stream is always less than the decrease in the first, that is, there is a 'loss' of availability in the operation of the heat exchanger. Since the aim is the generation of power, this is undesirable and may be termed 'thermodynamic inefficiency'.

Figure 3.35 shows a heat exchanger of the countercurrent type. We use A and B to represent the material of the two streams and numbers 1 to 4 to represent the thermodynamic states of the streams entering and leaving the exchanger. If the unit loses no heat to the surroundings, that is the process is adiabatic as far as the surroundings are concerned, and since no work is done

Figure 3.35. Countercurrent heat exchanger

within the unit, the first law for a steady state flow system gives

$$\Delta H = 0 \qquad (3.256)$$

If the amount of material flowing through A per unit time is $\dot{n}_A$, and similarly for B we have

$$\dot{n}_A\,{}_1h_A + \dot{n}_B\,{}_3h_B = \dot{n}_A\,{}_2h_A + \dot{n}_B\,{}_4h_B \qquad (3.257)$$

where the enthalpies ${}_1h_A$ to ${}_4h_B$ are per mole. The rate of loss of availability for the whole heat exchanger is

$$\dot{n}_A\,{}_1b_A + \dot{n}_B\,{}_3b_B - \dot{n}_A\,{}_2b_A - \dot{n}_B\,{}_4b_B \qquad (3.258)$$

where ${}_1b_A$ to ${}_4b_B$ are the availabilities per mole. Substituting $b = h - T_0 s$ into this and incorporating (3.256) gives

$$\text{Rate of loss of availability} = T_0[\dot{n}_A({}_2s_A - {}_1s_A) + \dot{n}_B({}_4s_B - {}_3s_B)] \qquad (3.259)$$

This equation applies even if there is a pressure drop in either stream of the heat exchanger. The only assumption, introduced via the first law, is that changes in potential and kinetic energy are negligible. We note also that although the equations were derived in terms of amount of material, they are equally true when mass is used instead.

To understand how this loss in availability occurs, we examine what happens within the heat exchanger. Figure 3.36 shows a small element of a countercurrent heat exchanger. We assume that the properties of stream A, when it enters the element, are T_A, P_A, s_A, etc. and that each increases by an amount dT_A, dP_A, ds_A, etc. within it. A similar symbolism will be used for stream B. We can apply the loss in availability, equation (3.259) to this infinitesimal element giving

$$\text{Rate of loss of availability} = T_0(d\dot{S}_A + d\dot{S}_B) \qquad (3.260)$$

where we have used the fact that $d\dot{S}_A = \dot{n}\,ds_A = \dot{n}_A({}_2s_A - {}_1s_A)$ and a similar

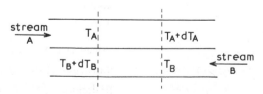

Figure 3.36. Element of heat exchanger in Figure 3.35

equation for B. Since there is no heat loss to the surroundings over the infinitesimal element, we can use (3.65) giving

$$d\dot{S}_A + d\dot{S}_B \geqslant 0 \tag{3.261}$$

or,

$$\dot{n}_A(_2s_A - _1s_A) + \dot{n}_B(_4s_B - _3s_B) \geqslant 0 \tag{3.262}$$

thus proving that the availability loss is never negative. For stream A,

$$T_A \, d\dot{S}_A = d\dot{H}_A - \dot{V}_A \, dP_A \tag{3.263}$$

and similarly for B, hence

$$\text{Rate of loss of availability} = T_0 \left(\frac{d\dot{H}_A - \dot{V}_A \, dP_A}{T_A} + \frac{d\dot{H}_B - \dot{V}_B \, dP_B}{T_B} \right) \tag{3.264}$$

We have seen above that $d\dot{H}_A + d\dot{H}_B = 0$, and if stream A is at a higher temperature than stream B, exchanging heat of magnitude $|d\dot{Q}|$,

$$|d\dot{Q}| = -d\dot{H}_A = d\dot{H}_B \tag{3.265}$$

Thus,

$$\begin{aligned}
\text{Rate of loss of availability} &= T_0 \left\{ \frac{|d\dot{Q}|}{T_B} - \frac{|d\dot{Q}|}{T_A} - \left[\frac{\dot{V}_A \, dP_A}{T_A} + \frac{\dot{V}_B \, dP_B}{T_B} \right] \right\} \\
&= T_0 \left\{ |d\dot{Q}| \left(\frac{T_A - T_B}{T_A T_B} \right) - \left[\frac{\dot{V}_A \, dP_A}{T_A} + \frac{\dot{V}_B \, dP_B}{T_B} \right] \right\} \quad (3.266)
\end{aligned}$$

This equation gives us all the information we need to improve the design of our heat exchanger. Firstly, since dP_A and dP_B are both negative, the contribution of a pressure drop is always to increase the availability loss. The other term can be reduced only by making T_A equal T_B as closely as possible. In the limit of T_A being only infinitesimally greater than T_B, the availability loss is at a minimum and the transfer of heat from stream A to stream B is close to reversible. Since the loss in availability for the whole heat exchanger is just the sum of the losses in each infinitesimal element, the most efficient heat exchanger is the one that maintains the streams close to equality in temperature all along its length. A countercurrent heat exchanger is therefore necessarily more efficient than a co-current one as Figure 3.37a and b show.

The ideal of a small temperature difference between the two streams is one which may be impossible, or at least very difficult, to achieve in practice. First, a heat exchanger operating on a small temperature difference must have a large heat transfer area for a given amount of heat exchange, and so is expensive. However, there are also thermodynamic factors which we illustrate by considering the design of a simple heat exchanger which would have been suitable for use on the Calder Hall nuclear reactor.[5] Of course, the actual heat exchanger used was considerably more complicated than that described here.

This reactor has a carbon dioxide cooled core with heat exchange to

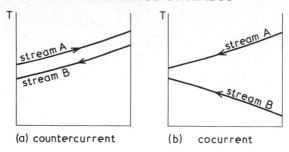

Figure 3.37. Temperature profiles in countercurrent and cocurrent heat exchangers

water/steam for power generation. To obtain the required reactor cooling, the carbon dioxide is circulated at a pressure of about 8 bar with inlet and outlet temperatures of about 140 °C and 340 °C. We examine the design of a simple countercurrent heat exchanger in which liquid water enters at low temperature, is raised to its boiling point at the prevailing pressure, evaporated, and then superheated until it reaches a temperature of 320 °C, the 20 K difference, often called the 'approach', between the hot carbon dioxide and the superheated steam being determined by the need to keep the size of the heat exchanger within economic bounds. We can represent the thermodynamic paths for both fluids in the heat exchanger on a T-H diagram, Figure 3.38, which superimposes the diagram for carbon dioxide on top of the one for water. This superimposition is possible only if the enthalpies are expressed in terms of the amounts of material flowing through the heat exchanger per unit time and not per unit mass, as is more usual. Since the amount of heat exchanged is equal to the enthalpy change, dropping a vertical from any point on the carbon dioxide line to the water line links the thermodynamic properties of the materials exchanging heat at that point in the exchanger. Consideration of the overall enthalpy change determines the relative flow rates which, in our case, comes out as 13.96 kg of carbon dioxide for each kilogram of water.

Certain qualitative observations can be made from the T-H diagram. Firstly, since carbon dioxide remains gaseous throughout the whole heat exchanger, its path on the diagram is smooth, although not a straight line since C_P varies with temperature. Secondly, the liquid water stream is evaporated when the boiling point is reached, taking in latent heat, and this produces the horizontal portion to the path on the T-H diagram. It also produces a large temperature difference between the two streams, particularly in the superheat region.

In plotting the path of the steam side of the heat exchanger, a constant pressure was assumed. In practice, there would be substantial pressure drops because the steam would be generated in the tubes of a 'shell and tube' heat exchanger. However, at the low pressures we are considering, the enthalpy of

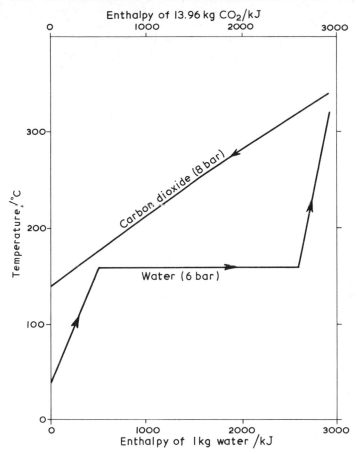

Figure 3.38. *T-H* diagram for a carbon dioxide/water heat exchanger

the liquid and of the vapour do not vary much with pressure and we therefore take the pressure of the whole steam side of the plant to be equal to that in the boiler. The water/steam pressure of 6 bar is not arbitrary. If the pressure is lower than this, the horizontal portion of the path is at a lower temperature, and this leads to even greater thermodynamic inefficiency owing to larger temperature differences between the two streams. Conversely, if the pressure is increased, the horizontal line might, in theory, be raised until the steam line crosses the carbon dioxide one. However, this is physically impossible for it requires that heat be transferred from a low temperature stream to a high temperature one. Thus, taking 20 K as the minimum temperature difference between the two streams (for the economic reasons given), 6 bar is the maximum pressure for the water/steam side.

This consequence of the non-crossing rule is known to designers as the 'pinch effect' when it occurs at a point within the heat exchanger, and it can occur even in the absence of phase changes if the two substances have markedly different variations in their heat capacities with temperature. The inefficiency which this causes can be substantial, and it is particularly difficult to reduce.

We conclude this discussion by examining the actual losses of availability in the heat exchanger described in Figure 3.38. Table 3.1 gives the necessary

Table 3.1. Thermodynamic properties of carbon dioxide and water

	$t/°C$	$h/kJ \, kg^{-1}$	$s/kJ \, K^{-1} \, kg^{-1}$
Carbon dioxide	140	908.7	4.749
	340	1118.1	5.156
Water	40	167	0.572
	320	3090	7.442

thermodynamic information, taken from published tabulations of thermodynamic properties. Using (3.255) we see that the loss in availability by the carbon dioxide stream (for 13.96 kg) is

$$[(1118.1 - 908.7) - 290 \times (5.156 - 4.749)] \times 13.96 = 1276 \, kJ$$

and the gain by the water stream (for 1 kg)

$$[(3090 - 167) - 290 \times (7.442 - 0.572)] = 931 \, kJ$$

taking ambient temperature as 290 K.

Thus we see that approximately 25% of the maximum possible work is lost owing to irreversibilities in the heat exchanger. This also means that the maximum possible gain to be obtained by use of a more sophisticated system of heat exchangers, such as by use of two or more water/steam streams at different pressures, as is sometimes used in gas liquefaction processes, see Section 5.19f, is just this 25%.

It is instructive to compare the availability gain of the water stream (931 kJ) with the total heat exchanged as given by the enthalpy change of the water (2923 kJ). Thus, assuming a perfect turbine stage, the efficiency of the plant is

$$\frac{931}{2923} = 0.32$$

That is, at the most, one-third of the thermal energy delivered by the reactor can be converted into mechanical, and hence electrical, energy.

Problems

1. 10 kW of power is required to maintain a house at 20 °C when the outside is 0 °C. If instead of using direct electrical heating, a reversible heat pump is used to perform the same duty, what would be the minimum power required?

2. Prove that

$$\left(\frac{\partial P}{\partial V}\right)_S = \gamma \left(\frac{\partial P}{\partial V}\right)_T$$

where $\gamma = C_P/C_V$. In Section 4.2 we see that $(\partial P/\partial V)_T$ is always negative. Show that this means that in a typical Carnot cycle as represented in Figure 3.10, we can with confidence draw the isentropes steeper than the isotherms.

3. Show that

$$\left(\frac{\partial T}{\partial V}\right)_S = -\frac{T}{C_V}\left(\frac{\partial P}{\partial T}\right)_V \quad \text{and} \quad \left(\frac{\partial T}{\partial P}\right)_S = -\frac{T}{C_P}\left(\frac{\partial V}{\partial T}\right)_P$$

4. Show that for a gas which obeys the van der Waals equation of state, $(P + a/v^2)(v - b) = RT$, C_V is a function of temperature only whereas C_P is a function of both pressure and temperature.

5. Prove that

$$\left(\frac{\partial U}{\partial V}\right)_P = C_P\left(\frac{\partial T}{\partial V}\right)_P - P \quad \text{and} \quad \left(\frac{\partial U}{\partial P}\right)_V = C_V\left(\frac{\partial T}{\partial P}\right)_V$$

show that for a perfect gas

$$\left(\frac{\partial U}{\partial V}\right)_P = \frac{C_V P}{R} \quad \text{and} \quad \left(\frac{\partial U}{\partial P}\right)_V = \frac{C_V V}{R} \qquad \text{(pg)}$$

6. Show that for a perfect gas undergoing reversible adiabatic expansion

$$PV^{\gamma_0} \exp(\{\gamma_0 - 1\}C_{V_0}AT/R) = \text{constant}$$

if C_V varies with temperature as

$$C_V = C_{V_0}(1 + AT)$$

(A is constant) and $\gamma_0 = (C_{V_0} + R)/C_{V_0}$.

7. The heat capacity, C_P, of beryllium in the range 0 to 20 K can be represented as

$$C_P/(\text{J K}^{-1}\,\text{kg}^{-1}) = 0.025(T/K) + 0.000\,138(T/K)^3$$

Calculate the difference in entropy of beryllium between 0 K and 20 K.

8. Show that for a van der Waals gas, the Joule-Thomson inversion temperature is given by $T = 2a/bR$.

9. Show that for a van der Waals gas, the speed of sound $\mathcal{W}$ is given by

$$\mathcal{W}^2 = n_m\gamma[RTv^2/(v - b)^2 - 2a/v]$$

where $\gamma = C_P/C_V$ and n_m = amount of substance per unit mass.

10. The Helmholtz free energy of a gas is often represented as

$$A = -RT \ln(V - b) + (a/T^{1/2}b) \ln(V/\{v + b\}) + f(T)$$

where a and b are constants and $f(T)$ is a function which depends only on temperature. Derive an expression for the pressure of the gas.

11. Determine the boiling point of water at a pressure of 2 bar given that the boiling point at 1.013 25 bar (1 atm) is 100 °C and that the enthalpy of evaporation is essentially constant at 2257 kJ kg^{-1}.

12. Liquid mercury has a density of 13 690 kg m^{-3} and solid mercury a density of 14 190 kg m^{-3}, both measured at the melting point of −38.87 °C under a pressure of 1 bar. The latent heat of fusion under the same conditions is 11.62 kJ kg^{-1}. How high would the pressure have to be if the melting point is to be raised to 0 °C?

13. The melting points and the Δv of fusion of carbon tetrachloride at various pressures are given below. Calculate Δh and Δs of fusion at 1 bar and 6000 bar.

P/bar	T/°C	Δv/cm^3 mol^{-1}
1	−22.6	3.97
1000	14.8	3.07
2000	48.0	2.53
5000	128.8	1.55
7000	173.6	1.12

14. Calculate the maximum amount of work which can be produced by a turbine (per mole of material) when supplied with nitrogen at (a) 1000 K, 50 bar, and (b) 200 K, 100 bar. You may assume that nitrogen behaves as a perfect gas and that C_P is given by

$$C_P/(\text{J K}^{-1} \text{ mol}^{-1}) = 58.0 + 0.005 \, T/\text{K}$$

Atmospheric surroundings are 300 K, 1 bar.

15. Hot process gases at 800 K, 1 bar flow through a heat exchanger and are cooled to 700 K without significant pressure drop. Heat exchange is to air which enters the exchanger at 470 K and 1 bar. If the mass flow rate of air is twice that of the process gas determine (a) the temperature of the emerging air, (b) the availability decrease of the process gas, (c) the availability increase of the coolant (air), and (d) the overall loss in availability due to operation of the heat exchanger. Assume that all gases are perfect; $C_P = 1.08$ kJ K^{-1} kg^{-1} for the process gas and $C_P = 1.05$ kJ K^{-1} kg^{-1} for air, both independent of temperature; and ambient conditions are 20 °C, 1 bar.

Answers

1. Power $= 680$ watts.

4. Hint, use equations 3.121 and 3.123.

7. $\Delta S = 0.868 \, \text{J K}^{-1} \, \text{kg}^{-1}$.

8. Hint, use $T(\partial V/\partial T)_P = V$ to find the locus and take the limit of the resulting equation as $V \to \infty$.

10. The equation is $P = RT/(V-b) - a/(T^{1/2}V\{V+b\})$, which is the Redlich-Kwong equation of state—see Section 4.13.

11. Boiling point $= 120.8 \, ^\circ\text{C}$.

12. $P = 7500$ bar.

13. At 1 bar, $\Delta h = 2.58 \, \text{kJ mol}^{-1}$, $\Delta s = 10.3 \, \text{J K}^{-1} \, \text{mol}^{-1}$
    at 6000 bar, $\Delta h = 2.47 \, \text{kJ mol}^{-1}$, $\Delta s = 5.9 \, \text{J K}^{-1} \, \text{mol}^{-1}$.

14. (a) work $= 31\,000 \, \text{J mol}^{-1}$
    (b) work $= 12\,800 \, \text{J mol}^{-1}$.

15. (a) $521.4 \, \text{K}$
    (b) $66 \, \text{kJ kg}^{-1}$
    (c) $22 \, \text{kJ kg}^{-1}$
    (d) $22 \, \text{kJ}$ per kg of process gas.

Notes

1. See e.g. J. H. Keenan, F. H. Keyes, P. G. Hill and J. G. Moore, *Steam Tables, thermodynamic properties of water* (*International edition—metric units*), Wiley, New York, 1969.

2. See e.g. J. S. Rowlinson, *The Perfect Gas*, Pergamon Press, Oxford, 1963.

3. J. H. Keenan, *Thermodynamics*, M.I.T. Press, Cambridge, Mass., 1970, Chapter 17.

4. *Mech. Engng, N.Y.*, **54** (1932), 195–204.

5. 'The World's Reactors, No. 6 Calder Hall', *Nucl. Engng, Lond.*, **1** (1956), No. 9.

4   Gases, Liquids and Solids

4.1   Introduction

Experience tells us that substances can exist as solids, liquids or gases. Under ambient conditions iodine is a solid, bromine a liquid and chlorine a gas, but each of these substances can appear in a different phase if the pressure or temperature is changed sufficiently. We consider how the phase behaviour and thermodynamic properties of a substance may be presented. Initially, we confine our attention to the directly measurable properties, pressure, volume and temperature, because the relations between these, the so-called *P-V-T* properties, are important in many problems such as the compression and metering of fluids. We then show how derived thermodynamic properties, such as changes in internal energy, enthalpy and entropy, may be calculated from *P-V-T* and other directly measurable properties. In this chapter we are concerned only with pure substances; the properties of mixtures are discussed in Chapters 6 and 7.

4.2   *P-V-T* surface of a typical pure substance

A thorough understanding of the phase behaviour of pure substances is facilitated by studying, or preferably by constructing, a three-dimensional

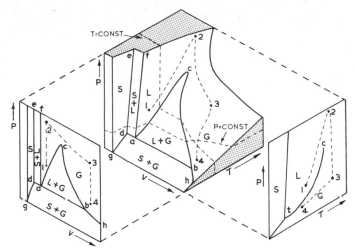

Figure 4.1. P-v-T surface for a typical pure substance which contracts on freezing.
S = solid, L = liquid, G = gas or vapour

model such as that illustrated in Figure 4.1, in which the pressure, specific
volume and temperature for the stable states of the substance are plotted in
perpendicular coordinates. Before discussing it in detail, we must remember,
from the discussion in Chapter 1, that a pure substance may assume various
states, but that only those states which are in equilibrium persist indefinitely,
and only states of stable equilibrium persist if the state is disturbed.

A system at equilibrium satisfies certain thermodynamic conditions of
stability, which we summarise here since they are needed later in the chapter.
The condition for thermal stability is that

$$\left(\frac{\partial T}{\partial S}\right)_V > 0 \quad \text{or} \quad \frac{T}{C_V} > 0 \tag{4.1}$$

Thus temperature increases when heat is added at constant volume. Hence it
is a condition of thermal stability that the heat capacity at constant volume, or
strictly its reciprocal, be positive.

The condition for mechanical equilibrium is that

$$\left(\frac{\partial P}{\partial V}\right)_T < 0 \quad \text{or} \quad \frac{1}{V\beta_T} > 0 \tag{4.2}$$

where β_T is the coefficient of isothermal bulk compressibility, see Sections
3.11 and 4.15. Thus, when the pressure is increased reversibly and isothermally, the volume decreases. Hence the condition of mechanical stability is
that the reciprocal of the isothermal coefficient of compressibility be positive.
Although these conditions for thermal and mechanical stability may be derived formally from the second law, a few moments reflection will reveal that
both are necessary and sufficient for the stability of systems whose interaction
with their surroundings is confined to the exchange of heat and work.

The phase rule, which is discussed fully in Chapter 7, requires that a system of one phase, solid (S), liquid (L), or gas (G), is completely defined if the pressure and temperature are specified; hence all points representing the state of single phase lie on curved parts of the P-V-T surface which have been labelled with the appropriate phase. A system of two co-existent phases (S+L), (S+G) or (L+G) is defined *either* by the pressure *or* by the temperature; hence all points representing such a system lie on ruled surfaces which are made up of straight lines parallel to the specific volume axis. For a pure material the point of highest temperature and pressure at which liquid and gas can co-exist is the *gas-liquid critical point c*, which is usually abbreviated to *critical point*. If three phases (S+L+G) are present, then points which represent their mixture lie on a line known as the *triple-phase line* formed at the intersection of two ruled surfaces. Thus in Figure 4.1, section da of the triple-phase line db is formed by the intersection of the ruled surface representing mixtures (S+G) with that representing mixtures (S+L), whereas section ab is formed at its junction with surface (L+G). All stable states are represented by points on the P-V-T surface of the model; hence the paths of all reversible, i.e. equilibrium, processes must lie on the surface, as do the isothermal and isobaric paths shown in Figure 4.1.

Under certain conditions mentioned on page 143 it is possible for a substance to be in a state of metastable equilibrium represented by a point above or below the surface, but such a state is not stable and a disturbance will cause a spontaneous irreversible change which restores the substance to a state of stable equilibrium lying on the surface.

Although the curved area of the P-V-T surface in Figure 4.1 representing the fluid phase is divided into liquid and gaseous regions, this division is not clear cut. Fluid at point 1 on that part of the surface labelled (L) can be changed to fluid at point 4 in the gaseous (G) region by heating at constant volume to 2, expanding at constant temperature to 3, and then cooling at constant volume to 4. At no point in this three-stage process is there a change of phase, and no dividing meniscus is observed, such as that which separates liquid from gas in the two-phase (L+G) region. The two fluids differ only in degree; that on the high pressure (low specific volume) side of the two-phase (L+G) region is termed a liquid, whereas that on the low pressure (high specific volume) side is a gas or vapour. Any attempt to divide the fluid state at temperatures and pressures higher than the critical is even more artificial. One arbitrary distinction that is sometimes made is to call a fluid of high specific volume a vapour if it can be liquefied at room temperature by isothermal compression, and gas if it cannot. Thus, for example, methane ($T^c = 191$ K) would be described as a gas and carbon tetrachloride ($T^c = 566$ K) a vapour. As was stated in the previous chapter, we make no distinction between these two terms and use them almost interchangeably throughout the book.

The P-V-T surfaces of most substances are similar to that shown in Figure

4.1, but the ranges of pressure, specific volume and temperature vary widely, as may be seen from the triple-phase and critical point data given in Table 4.1.

Table 4.1. Critical and triple points

	Triple point		Critical point		
Substance	$\dfrac{P^t}{\text{bar}}$	$\dfrac{T^t}{\text{K}}$	$\dfrac{P^c}{\text{bar}}$	$\dfrac{T^c}{\text{K}}$	$\dfrac{v^c}{\text{cm}^3\,\text{g}^{-1}}$
⁴Helium	—	—	2.291	5.2	14.43
Hydrogen	0.07	14	12.8	33	33.2
Carbon Dioxide	5.18	220.6	73.82	304.21	2.146
Water	0.006	273.16	221.2	647.3	3.17
Mercury	1.3×10^{-9}	234.3	1150	1765	~0.2

Triple phase temperatures extend from 14 K for hydrogen to temperatures too high for accurate measurement, as for carbon; the corresponding pressures are never high, that of carbon dioxide being one of the highest at 5.2 bar. Critical temperatures also span an enormous range starting with that at 5 K for helium and extending to temperatures beyond measurement. The corresponding pressures are more uniform, those of water and mercury being unusually high at 221.2 bar and 1150 bar and those of helium and hydrogen being unusually low at 2 bar and 13 bar respectively.

Unfortunately, few models of the P-V-T surfaces are available outside museums, and most students have to make do with a two-dimensional representation, such as that shown in Figure 4.1, or with a projection of the P-V-T surface on the PV, TV or PT planes. It is, therefore, important to bear in mind that the volume scale of this and similar representations found in textbooks has been distorted to make the projections intelligible. The change in specific volume between points a and b is many times that between d and a, and the specific volume at the critical point is about three times that at point a. Since little use is made of the T-V projection, it is not shown in Figure 4.1, although its form is obvious from the model. We will now examine the more important P-V and P-T projections in greater detail.

4.3 *P-V* diagram

If gas or vapour, represented by the point 5 in Figure 4.2 is compressed slowly and isothermally, the pressure rises until the vapour becomes *saturated* and the first drop of liquid appears at conditions corresponding to point 6. If the compression is continued, condensation takes place at a constant pressure known as the *saturation pressure* for the given temperature; conversely this temperature is called the *saturation temperature* (or boiling point) at the corresponding pressure. For a pure substance the relationship between the saturation pressures and temperatures is given by measurements of this

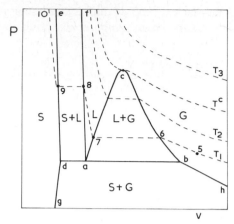

Figure 4.2. P-v projection of the surface shown in Figure 4.1

vapour pressure. At any point on the line between 6 and 7, saturated liquid and saturated vapour are in equilibrium; at point 7 the vapour phase disappears and only saturated liquid remains. The co-existence of two phases is not necessary in order to have a saturated phase; a phase is saturated even if it exists alone, as long as it is at a pressure and temperature under which two (or more) phases could exist in equilibrium.

A large increase in pressure is needed to compress the liquid; hence the path of the isothermal compression 7–8, is steep. At 8 the first trace of saturated solid is formed; as the specific volume of the system moves from 8 to 9, an increasing amount of liquid solidifies until the system is entirely solid at 9. Further compression results in a rapid increase in pressure along the path, 9–10. At points on the lines 5–6, 7–8 and 9–10, the substance is in the vapour, liquid and solid state respectively. Along 6–7 there is equilibrium between (L+G) and along 8–9 between (L+S). Although the specific volume of a two-phase system changes continuously as the relative amounts of the two phases change, the specific volumes of the saturated phases are fixed at a particular temperature. Thus the specific volumes of the saturated liquid and solid in equilibrium along line 8–9 are those of points 8 and 9, while the specific volumes of the saturated vapour and liquid in equilibrium along line 6–7 are those of points 6 and 7.

At temperatures above T_1 the differences between the specific volumes of the co-existing liquid and gas phases get progressively smaller until, at the critical temperature T^c, they become zero and the two phases are no longer distinguishable. The isotherm at T^c is called the critical isotherm, and the point of inflection at which

$$(\partial P/\partial v)_{T^c} = 0 \quad \text{and} \quad (\partial^2 P/\partial v^2)_{T^c} = 0 \tag{4.3}$$

is the critical point.

The lowest temperature at which liquid and vapour can coexist is the triple phase temperature T'; all mixtures of liquid and vapour are represented by points within the two-phase region bounded by the triple phase line ab, the *saturated liquid curve* ac and the *saturated vapour curve* bc. Saturated vapour, liquid and solid at the triple phase temperature and pressure are represented by points b, a and d respectively. Points on the triple phase line between d and a represent mixtures of solid and liquid, solid and vapour, or of all three phases, whereas points on the line between b and a represent mixtures of solid and vapour, liquid and vapour, or of all three phases. At temperatures and pressures below the triple phase line, solid-vapour mixtures are represented by the area bounded by the triple phase line, the saturated solid line gd, and the saturated vapour line bh. At temperatures and pressures above the triple phase line, mixtures of solid and liquid are represented by points in the region bounded by lines ed, da and af. Whereas the saturated liquid and saturated vapour boundaries meet at the critical point, there is no evidence that the corresponding boundaries de and af for the solid-liquid ever meet in a solid-liquid critical point. For helium, the solid-liquid boundary has been followed to 7400 bar and 50 K, a pressure which is over 3000 times and a temperature which is 25 times that for the gas-liquid critical point. With many substances the solid undergoes polymorphic transformations as the pressure is raised; at very much higher pressures it is thought that first the molecular and then the atomic structure undergo rearrangement, but these speculations are beyond the scope of this book.

4.4 P-T diagram

When the P-V-T surface is projected on to the P-T plane, as in Figure 4.1, the $(S+G)$ surface projects to form the *sublimation curve*, the $(S+L)$ surface the *melting curve*, and the $(G+L)$ surface the *evaporation* or *vapour pressure*

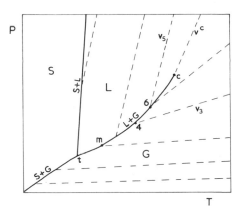

Figure 4.3. *P-T* projection of the surface shown in Figure 4.1

curve. The latter extends from the triple point, *t*, a projection of the triple phase line to the critical point, *c*.

An enlarged *P-T* projection is shown in Figure 4.3 on which *isochores* or lines of constant specific volume have been plotted, from which it may be seen that the isochore corresponding to the critical volume, v^c, is co-linear with the vapour pressure curve. For all substances the slopes of the sublimation and evaporation curves are positive, but the slope of the melting curve may be positive or negative. Most substances expand on melting, that is, $(v^l - v^s)$ is positive, and for these Clapeyron's equation (3.218) shows that the slope of the melting curve $(\partial P/\partial T)_m$ is also positive as illustrated in Figure 4.1. Water is an exception in that it expands on solidification; hence $(\partial P/\partial T)_m$ is negative, as illustrated in Figure 4.4. Examination of its *P-V* projection shows that point a can represent (S) a_1; (S+L) a_2 or (L or G) a_3, whereas point b can represent (S) b_1; (S+L) b_2 or (L+G) b_3. Because the *P-T* projection, unlike the *P-V* projection, shows the phase boundaries unambiguously, it is often called the *phase diagram*.

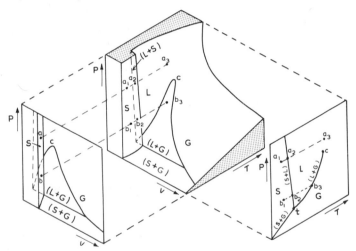

Figure 4.4. *P-v-T* surface of a pure substance which expands on freezing

4.5   Gas-liquid region

If saturated gas or vapour at temperature T_σ represented by point g in Figure 4.5 is heated at constant pressure, the vapour is said to be *superheated* (superheated vapour is *unsaturated vapour*). At point 1 when the temperature is T_1 the temperature difference $(T_1 - T_\sigma)$ is the *degree of superheat*. Similarly, if saturated liquid at T_σ represented by point *l* is cooled at constant pressure, the liquid is said to be *sub-cooled* indicating that the temperature is lower than the saturation temperature. At point 2 where the temperature is T_2 the liquid is said to be sub-cooled by $(T_\sigma - T_2)$. Alternatively the state of the

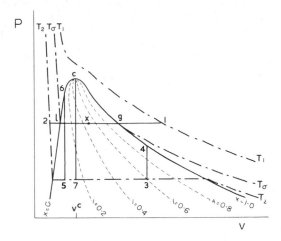

Figure 4.5. P-v projection of the fluid regions of a pure substance showing lines of constant quality

liquid at the point 2 may be described as that of a *compressed liquid,* implying that the pressure at 2 is greater than the saturation pressure corresponding to temperature T_2. In a like manner, a solid at a temperature below its saturation temperature is called a *compressed solid.* The adjectives, compressed, sub-cooled and superheated, are generally used only when their omission might imply the existence of saturation conditions.

The *quality* of a mixture of vapour and liquid is denoted by the symbol x, and is defined as the mass or mole fraction of vapour in the mixture; it has no meaning for states of compressed liquid or superheated vapour. The limiting values of quality are 0 for the saturated liquid and 1 for saturated vapour. Saturated vapour with no liquid present ($x = 1$) is sometimes called *dry satu-rated vapour,* and vapour mixed with liquid ($0 < x < 1$) *wet vapour.* These terms are misleading and should not be used because the properties of the saturated vapour are the same whether or not liquid is present.

If the specific volume of a liquid-vapour mixture represented by the point x in Figure 4.5 is v^x, while that of the saturated liquid l is v^l and that of the saturated vapour g is v^g, then

$$v^x = (m^l v^l + m^g v^g)/(m^l + m^g) \qquad (4.4)$$

where m^l and m^g denote the mass of liquid and vapour respectively. Since the quality x is given by

$$x = m^g/(m^l + m^g) \qquad (4.5)$$

Then

$$v^x = (1-x)v^l + xv^g \qquad (4.6)$$

or

$$v^x = v^l + x(v^g - v^l) \tag{4.7}$$

Equation (4.6) or (4.7) is usually known as the *lever rule*. The same equations are obtained if the v^x etc. are molar and not specific volumes.

A line that joins the thermodynamic states of two co-existent phases in such a way that the position of a point on the line is a measure of the relative amounts of the phases is called a *tie line*. Thus, from (4.6) or (4.7) lines such as *lg* in Figure 4.5 are tie lines; however, the triple phase line in Figure 4.2 is not a tie line since the composition of three co-existent phases represented by a point on the line cannot be determined solely by the position of the point. Equation (4.7) enables lines of constant quality, such as those in Figure 4.5 to be drawn in the two phase region.

In order to understand the significance of the critical point, it may be helpful to consider the phase changes which occur when a pure substance is heated at constant volume in a sealed vertical glass tube. If the tube is filled completely with either saturated liquid or saturated vapour, the heating is represented on Figure 4.5 by vertical lines which start on, but lie entirely above, the two phase boundary; hence no phase change is observed. If the tube is only partially filled with liquid (the remainder being vapour in equilibrium with the liquid) heating leads to a change of phase, but what is observed depends on the quality of the mixture. For example, at point 3, $x = 0.6$, and the meniscus separating the phases is near the base of the tube. As the tube is heated the meniscus falls and disappears as the last drop of liquid evaporates at 4. If the meniscus is initially near the top of the tube, as at point 5, ($x = 0.1$), then the volume of liquid increases on heating until at 6 it completely fills the tube. When the initial position of the meniscus is such that the specific volume of the mixture of saturated liquid and vapour, 7, corresponds to the specific volume at the critical point v^c, then the meniscus rises slowly on heating, but only to the middle of the tube (for further discussion, see Section 4.17, p. 161). At a temperature just below the critical, the meniscus becomes hazy, then vanishes at the critical point after being momentarily obscured by a phenomenon known as *critical opalescence*. At the critical point the compressibility is infinite, and so spontaneous fluctuations in density are no longer restrained by the pressure in the fluid. The fluctuations extend over distances comparable with the wave-length of light and are responsible for the strong scattering of light which we see as opalescence.

Before heating, all three mixtures are represented by the point *m* on the *P-T* diagram, Figure 4.3. On heating, all follow the vapour pressure curve, but that of the mixture having the highest quality follows isochore v_3 into the superheated vapour region when the last drop of liquid evaporates at 4, and that having the lowest quality follows isochore v_5 into the liquid region when all the vapour condenses at 6. The mixture of specific volume v^c follows the vapour pressure curve to the critical point and thence along the critical isochore v^c into the super-critical fluid region.

4.6 P-V-T measurements

Much experimental work is needed to obtain the P-V-T data required to construct models such as those illustrated in Figure 4.1 and Figure 4.4. In the case of water, measurements extend to 1000 K and pressures up to 22 kbar, but their accuracy varies widely over these ranges. For most substances the vapour pressure from the triple to the critical temperature and the saturated molar volumes of the liquid and vapour have been measured extensively by methods described elsewhere.[1,2]

Critical constants

The unusual mechanical, thermal and optical properties of fluids near the critical point makes difficult the precise measurement of the critical constants. At the critical point $(\partial V/\partial P)_T$ is infinite and the earth's gravitational field produces large density gradients even in small samples of fluid. Furthermore, it is shown in Section 4.18 that C_P and probably C_V are infinite, hence it is hard to achieve thermal equilibrium. The critical temperature is the easiest of the three constants to measure and is usually found by observing the temperature at which critical opalescence occurs in a system of overall density approximately equal to the critical, as discussed in Section 4.5. For measurements of moderate precision, say, 0.05 K to 0.1 K, no great care is needed to load the tube exactly to the critical density for a slight error only causes opalescence to occur a little above or below the centre of the tube at a height at which the local density is equal to the critical. However, this lack of sensitivity to the loading density means that this method cannot be used for any but the roughest measurements of the critical volume.

If the tube is not sealed but open at its lower end to a reservoir of mercury, then the density of the fluid may be altered and the critical pressure measured at the same time as the critical temperature. The critical volume is the most difficult of the constants to measure accurately, and the method which is most commonly used is to extrapolate the mean of the saturated liquid and saturated vapour densities up to the critical temperature using the empirical law of *rectilinear diameters*. It has been found experimentally (see Figure 4.6) that the mid points M_1, M_2 etc. of the isotherms lie on a straight line known as the rectilinear diameter which, when extrapolated, cuts the horizontal line $T = T^c$ at the critical density ρ^c $(= 1/v^c)$. Thus, the rectilinear diameter can be represented by the equation

$$(\rho^l + \rho^g)/2 = a - bT \tag{4.8}$$

where a and b are constants for each substance. Since this line cuts the saturation boundary at the critical point

$$(\rho^l + \rho^g)/2 = \rho^c + b(T^c - T) \tag{4.9}$$

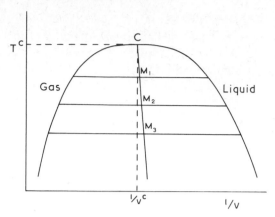

Figure 4.6. The law of rectilinear diameters

and as the temperature approaches the critical (4.9) reduces to

$$v^g - v^c = v^c - v^l \qquad (4.10)$$

The critical constants for a large number of substances may be found in reviews.[3,4,5]

Homogeneous fluid

Apart from the saturation boundary and critical point the most important part of the P-V-T surface is the single-phase fluid region. In this region the P-V-T relations are usually found either by measuring the pressure of a known mass of fluid as a function of volume at a series of fixed temperatures, or by measuring pressure as a function of temperature at a series of fixed volumes. The former enables $(\partial P/\partial V)_T$ to be calculated, and so determines an isotherm, whereas the latter leads to $(\partial P/\partial T)_V$ and so determines an isochore. Although measurements at constant pressure could provide the same information as those at constant volume or temperature, they are difficult to carry out and so are seldom made. As will be seen later in this chapter, the mathematical procedures used for calculating derived thermodynamic properties require that mass, pressure, volume and temperature be measured to about 1 part in 10^5 if the uncertainty in the derived properties is to be less than 1 part in 10^3. This need for P-V-T measurements of the highest precision over wide ranges of pressure and temperature has led to the development of many different experimental techniques. Some of the more important of these are described elsewhere[6,7] and here we give only a brief account of general principles.

The isothermal procedure may be carried out by determining the displacement of, and the load on, a piston of known area when it is forced into a cylinder containing the fluid, and the isochoric procedure by measuring the pressure change which accompanies a temperature change when the fluid is contained in a vessel of fixed volume. However, the former method is not very accurate and for precise work, the procedure must be modified (see below).

In any case, whether the method is isothermal or isochoric, allowance must be made for unwanted volume changes. All vessels change in volume when the temperature is varied, and this is often the largest cource of error in a volume calibration. Increasing the pressure of the fluid inside a vessel whilst the outside is at atmospheric pressure increases the internal volume because of the elasticity of the material of construction; even for vessels of simple shape, it is impossible to calculate this volume change accurately. This difficulty can be reduced by pressure compensation that is, the inner

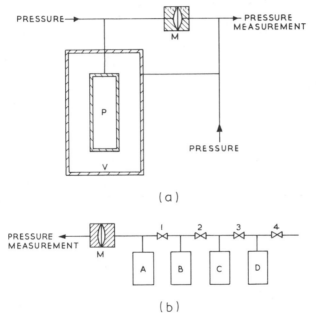

Figure 4.7. Diagram of equipment used to measure the *P-v-T* properties of fluids: (a) Pressure balanced piezometer, (b) Series of expansion vessels

experimental vessel, known as the piezometer, is surrounded by another vessel in which the pressure is kept equal to that in the piezometer, as in Figure 4.7a. With this arrangement the fractional change of volume of the piezometer is independent of its shape and is equal to $P\beta_T$, where β_T is the isothermal coefficient of bulk compressibility of the material of construction.

Precise isothermal measurements on gases can be made by having a series of separate vessels of known volume maintained at a uniform temperature, as in Figure 4.7b. Initially, the fluid at a known temperature is confined to vessel A, then, after opening valve 1 to allow the fluid to distribute itself between vessels A and B, the pressure is remeasured. Successive opening of valves 2,

3, 4 etc., followed by the measurement of the pressure, enables a series of values of pressure and volume to be obtained for a fixed mass of gas at constant temperature. Clearly the way the pressure is measured has a bearing on the constancy of the volumes. For example, it is not sufficient to attach a mercury manometer to vessel A, in Figure 4.7b, for the volume of gas in the pipe leading to the mercury meniscus would be an unknown and variable quantity. It is usual to reduce this uncertainty by using a null-manometer, M, which is often a thin metal diaphragm clamped between two hollowed plates whose position is located electrically. A second fluid has to be used to maintain a pressure exactly equal to that in the experimental vessels, as detected by the null-manometer. This reference pressure can then be measured accurately by any suitable primary pressure gauge; it can serve also to pressure compensate the piezometer as shown in Figure 4.7a.

The solid phase is not as experimentally accessible nor as important to the chemical engineer as the fluid phases, and so less effort has been devoted to the accurate measurements of its P-V-T properties. As will be seen in Chapter 7, many substances, e.g. water, can exist in more than one solid phase, with the result that a 'true to scale' P-V-T surface for water, showing all the solid phases, is very complex.[8] A full description of the techniques used to study the phase equilibria and P-V-T properties of solids is given by Bridgeman.[9]

4.7 Deviations of real gas behaviour from that of a perfect gas

In view of the great use which has been made in earlier chapters of the perfect gas equation

$$PV = nRT \qquad \text{(pg)} \qquad (4.11)$$

we begin our quantitative discussion of P-V-T properties of a pure substance by comparing them with those of a perfect gas. Since the condensation of a gas at sub-critical temperatures to form a liquid is not implicit in (4.11) this discussion must of necessity be confined to the gaseous phase.

4.8 Compression factor

It is apparent from Figure 4.5 that, in the gaseous region, the shapes of the isotherms deviate increasingly from the rectangular hyperbola of a perfect gas as the temperature approaches the critical. The most common way of expressing this deviation is to evaluate the ratio of the molar volume of the gas, v, under given temperature and pressure conditions to the molar volume of a perfect gas, v_{pg}, under the same conditions. This ratio Z is usually called the compressibility factor, but to avoid confusion with the term compressibility defined in Chapter 3, we follow recommended terminology and refer to it as the *compression factor*.

Thus

$$Z = v/v_{pg} = Pv/RT \qquad (4.12)$$

For the perfect gas $Z = 1$ and so is independent of pressure and temperature, but for a real gas it is a function of these variables.

In Figure 4.8a the compression factor Z, for several gases at 273 K, has

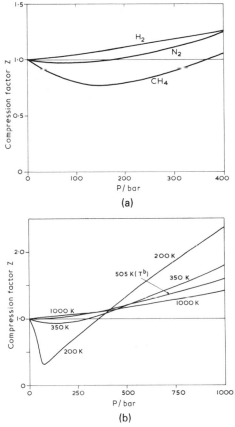

(a)

(b)

Figure 4.8. Compression factor as a function of pressure: (a) Hydrogen ($T^c = 33.2$ K), Nitrogen ($T^c = 126.2$ K), and Methane ($T^c = 191.1$ K), all at 273 K, (b) Methane at various temperatures

been plotted against pressure. As the critical temperature of the gas approaches 273 K the compression factor decreases below the perfect gas value of unity. For hydrogen the critical temperature is sufficiently below 273 K for the compression factor to be greater than unity at all pressures. In Figure 4.8b the compression factors for methane are presented as a function of pressure at a number of temperatures. At high temperatures the compression factor is always greater than unity but as the temperature approaches the critical it becomes less than unity in the low pressure region. At some intermediate temperature known as the *Boyle temperature*, T^b, $(\partial Z/\partial P)_T$ is zero at zero pressure; for methane $T^b = 505$ K.

4.9 Fugacity

In later chapters a property known as *fugacity* is used to describe phase and reaction equilibria. However, this is a convenient point to introduce the concept because the fugacity of a pure gas is related to the deviation of the P-V-T properties from those of a perfect gas. For the moment it may be helpful to regard fugacity as a pseudo-pressure which, when substituted for pressure in the simple equations derived for a perfect gas, enable them to be used for real gases without error.

The application of (3.188) to the isothermal change of a perfect gas gives

$$dg = v\, dP = RT\frac{dP}{P} \qquad \text{(pg)} \tag{4.13}$$

In order to use this equation to calculate the isothermal change in the molar Gibbs free energy of a real gas we substitute the fugacity of the gas for its pressure.

Thus

$$dg = v\, dP = RT\frac{df}{f} \tag{4.14}$$

where f is the fugacity of the gas at P and T. Clearly, for an isothermal process, the change in fugacity is related to the change in the Gibbs free energy of a real gas, in the same way as the pressure change is related to the Gibbs free energy change of a perfect gas. Such a function is of little use unless it can be related easily to measurable properties, and this we do as follows.

By subtracting $RT(dP/P)$ from both sides of (4.14)

$$v\, dP - RT\frac{dP}{P} = RT\frac{df}{f} - RT\frac{dP}{P} \tag{4.15}$$

Hence

$$RT\, d\ln\left(\frac{f}{P}\right) = \left(v - \frac{RT}{P}\right)dP \tag{4.16}$$

Integrating at constant temperature from zero pressure to the particular pressure P' at which the fugacity is required gives

$$RT\ln\left(\frac{f}{P}\right)_{P=P'} - RT\ln\left(\frac{f}{P}\right)_{P=0} = \int_0^{P'}\left(v - \frac{RT}{P}\right)dP \tag{4.17}$$

When the pressure is low enough for the gas to obey the perfect gas law the fugacity is equal to the pressure. Thus, as P approaches zero, f/P approaches unity.

Hence

$$RT \ln\left(\frac{f}{P'}\right) = \int_0^{P'} \left(v - \frac{RT}{P}\right) dP \qquad (4.18)$$

Equation (4.18) serves not only to define fugacity but enables it to be calculated from P-V-T data. This equation can be expressed in a more convenient form in terms of the compression factor defined by (4.12);

$$\ln\left(\frac{f}{P'}\right) = \int_0^{P'} \left(\frac{Z-1}{P}\right) dP \qquad (4.19)$$

We will call the dimensionless ratio f/P the *fugacity-pressure ratio*; it is also known as the *activity coefficient* but we restrict the use of this term to mixtures (see Chapter 6). Graphical representation, as in Figure 4.9, or tabulation of the fugacity-pressure ratio as a function of pressure is a useful way of summarising departures from the perfect gas laws. The data also enable the work for reversible isothermal compression to be evaluated easily.

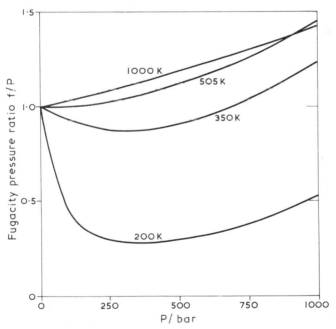

Figure 4.9. Fugacity—pressure ratio for methane

4.10 Equations of state

The choice of a perfect gas as a standard of normal behaviour is acceptable at moderate pressures but, as may be seen from Figure 4.8b, the deviations from perfect behaviour are very large at high pressures and it is more convenient, in general, to use an empirical algebraic function of the form $f(P, v, T) = 0$ to represent the P-V-T properties. Such a function is called an *equation of state*. Of the many which have been proposed, none is capable of representing the solid, liquid and vapour phase properties and only few can be used to represent the properties of both fluid phases. First we confine our attention to the equations of state which are used to represent the properties of the vapour phase and then consider those which can be used for both liquid and vapour.

4.11 Virial equation

This is an open equation of state in which the compression factor is expressed as a power series in molar density, that is in inverse powers of molar volume. Thus

$$Z = \frac{Pv}{RT} = 1 + \frac{B}{v} + \frac{C}{v^2} + \frac{D}{v^3} + \cdots \tag{4.20}$$

The coefficients $B, C, D, \ldots$, known as the second, third, fourth virial coefficients, are functions only of temperature, and their size and temperature-dependence vary from gas to gas. The term virial is derived from the latin word for force and by the methods of statistical thermodynamics (Chapter 9) it can be shown that the second virial coefficient B is related to the forces between pairs of molecules, the third C to triplets, and so on. As will be seen in Chapter 6 this property is valuable in the discussion of gas mixtures.

An analogous power series in which pressure is substituted for molar density may be written

$$Z = \frac{Pv}{RT} = 1 + B'P + C'P^2 + D'P^3 + \cdots \tag{4.21}$$

in which the coefficients B', C', $D' \cdots$ are also functions of temperature only. Although these coefficients do not have the simple theoretical significance of the virial coefficients, they may be related to them. Thus

$$B' = B/RT \tag{4.22}$$

$$C' = (C - B^2)/(RT)^2 \tag{4.23}$$

and there are similar but more complicated equations for the higher coefficients. We follow modern practice and restrict the name *virial* to the coefficients of (4.20). Equation (4.21) is often used to correlate the P-V-T properties of gases because the independent variables P and T are the quantities generally measured. This apparent advantage is offset by the fact that, for a given number of terms, the density series is usually capable of representing a set of experimental results more accurately than the pressure series. The relations between the virial coefficients and the coefficients in the pressure series, (4.22), (4.23) etc., are exact only for the infinite series; hence it is dangerous to use a truncated pressure series to make a convenient but poor fit of experimental results and then to use the coefficients B' and C' to determine B and C using (4.22) and (4.23). The virial expansion (4.20) is not a truly convergent series at high densities (probably above about the critical density), but an empirical polynomial representation of Z as a function of $(1/v)$ is often useful to densities two or three times the critical. Only the second and third coefficients of the infinite series (4.20) can be measured accurately. The expression of the compression factor as a sixth or seventh order polynomial in density is useful for interpolation, but its coefficients should not be identified with those of (4.20) and they usually show such an irregular variation with temperature that they are of little use for calculating other thermodynamic functions. The most reliable way to evaluate the lower virial coefficients from experimental measurements is to plot $(Z-1)v$ against $(1/v)$; when, as may be seen from (4.20), B is the intercept of the resulting curve and C the limiting slope as $(1/v)$ approaches zero.

Typical graphs showing the second virial coefficient, B, as a function of temperature, are plotted in Figure 4.10. At low temperatures the coefficient is

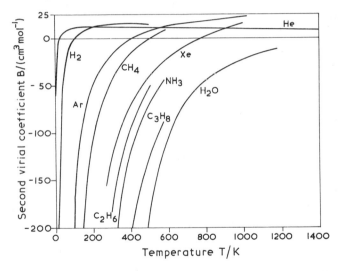

Figure 4.10. The second virial coefficient of various gases as a function of temperature

negative; with increasing temperature it becomes positive, passes through a very flat maximum, and finally decreases very slowly. The maximum has been observed only for helium, hydrogen and neon (not shown), but there is little doubt that all other chemically stable substances would show one if the measurements extended to high enough temperatures. The third virial coefficient, C, behaves similarly, but the maximum is at much lower temperatures. The sign of the fourth coefficient, D, is uncertain at low temperatures but is usually positive at high. Further information on the virial coefficients of different gases is to to be found in several monographs.[10,11]

4.12   van der Waals' equation

The best known equation of state, that of van der Waals, was published in 1873 as a semi-theoretical improvement to the perfect gas equation, and has the form

$$P = \frac{RT}{v-b} - \frac{a}{v^2} \tag{4.24}$$

where v is the molar volume and a and b are parameters which vary from one substance to another. The parameter b is intended to correct for the molecular size, while the term (a/v^2) takes account of the intermolecular forces of attraction. Although van der Waals' equation is crude, it is of considerable interest since it is the simplest form of equation that gives a qualitatively adequate account of the process of condensation and the properties of the

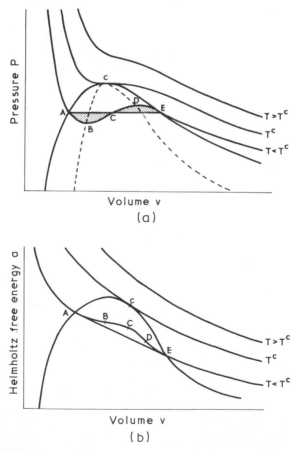

Figure 4.11. Schematic representation of the isotherms calculated from the van der Waals' equation of state: (a) P-v co-ordinates, (b) a-v co-ordinates

fluid phases. Its merits are that it is easy to manipulate algebraically, and it never predicts physically absurd results; so it is convenient to use for a quick, qualitative examination of a new problem. The van der Waals equation is cubic in v and if, for a number of temperatures, P is plotted against v a family of isotherms such as those shown schematically in Figure 4.11a is obtained. At low temperatures each isotherm passes through a maximum and a minimum; the locus of these turning points, shown as a broken line in Figure 4.11a is represented by

$$P = \frac{a}{v^2}\left(1 - \frac{2b}{v}\right) \tag{4.25}$$

which has been obtained by evaluating $(\partial P/\partial v)_T = 0$ from (4.24).

The general thermodynamic description of a critical point is

$$P > 0; \qquad \left(\frac{\partial P}{\partial V}\right)_T = 0; \qquad \left(\frac{\partial^2 P}{\partial V^2}\right)_T = 0; \qquad \left(\frac{\partial^3 P}{\partial V^3}\right)_T < 0 \tag{4.26}$$

and this corresponds to point c on Figure 4.11a. It is the maximum in the broken line referred to above, and lies on the isotherm in which the maximum and minimum turning points coalesce to form a point of inflexion. The critical isotherm labelled T^c in Figure 4.11a is tangent to the maximum in the locus of turning points given by (4.25). We see immediately that $(\partial^3 P/\partial V^3)_T$ is negative along the critical isotherm at the critical point in conformity with (4.26). This inequality must be included in the description of a critical point to ensure that the fluid is stable at volumes immediately above and below that of the critical point. By differentiating (4.24) to obtain both $(\partial P/\partial v)_T$ and $(\partial^2 P/\partial v^2)_T$, and setting them to zero, the coordinates of the critical point are obtained as

$$v^c = 3b; \qquad P^c = a/27b^2 \quad \text{and} \quad T^c = 8a/27Rb \tag{4.27}$$

At any temperature below T^c that portion of the isotherm to the left of the minimum point, B, represents the liquid state, and that to the right of the maximum point, D, the vapour state. The portion of the curve between B and D represents a mechanically unstable state, since $(\partial P/\partial V)_T > 0$, and so it has no real existence.

However, we must also qualify our observations regarding the state of the material represented by AB and DE in Figure 4.11. Experimentally, we find that we can compress a vapour beyond saturation, corresponding to E in Figure 4.11, without producing immediate condensation. This state is described as supersaturated or, alternatively, super-cooled, since it may also be produced by cooling saturated vapour. The portion of the isotherm beyond E, leading towards D, may be taken to represent this state. Similarly, it is possible, although less easy, to expand a saturated liquid to a pressure below that corresponding to point A in the diagram. This state is described as superheated, since it may also be produced by heating a saturated liquid. Both conditions are metastable in that they are stable for small disturbances but unstable for large ones.

We saw in Section 3.23 that, for liquid and vapour to coexist at equilibrium, the two phases must be at the same pressure and temperature and have the same value for the molar Gibbs free energy. Thus if we represent the equilibrium by the tie-line ACE, point A representing the saturated liquid and point E the saturated vapour, then

$$g_A^l = g_E^g \tag{4.28}$$

and so we require

$$\int_A^E \left(\frac{\partial g}{\partial P}\right)_T dP = 0 \tag{4.29}$$

where the integral is to be evaluated along the hypothetical isotherm $ABCDE$ in Figure 4.11a. From (3.178)

$$\left(\frac{\partial g}{\partial P}\right)_T = v \tag{4.30}$$

and for equilibrium,

$$\int_A^E v\, dP = 0 \tag{4.31}$$

This condition can be interpreted graphically by breaking the integral into several parts so that

$$\int_A^B v\, dP + \int_B^C v\, dP + \int_C^D v\, dP + \int_D^E v\, dP = 0 \tag{4.32}$$

which rearranges to

$$\int_B^C v\, dP - \int_B^A v\, dP = \int_E^D v\, dP - \int_C^D v\, dP \tag{4.33}$$

The left hand side of this equation represents the area ABC and the right hand side CDE. Thus, for equilibrium, we must draw the tie-line ACE so that it divides the hypothetical isotherm into two loops of equal area; a process known as the *Maxwell equal-area construction*, after its discoverer.

Exercise

Show that the Maxwell construction is equivalent to equating the fugacity-pressure ratio for the coexisting liquid and vapour phases.

Exercise

Show that the molar Helmholtz free energy a, as a function of v, is as shown in Figure 4.11b, for temperatures below at and above T^c [Hint, $P = -(\partial a/\partial v)_T$]. Hence, show that Maxwell's construction on the P-V diagram is equivalent in the A-V diagram to drawing a common tangent to the two portions of the isotherm for $T < T^c$.

For van der Waals' equation we can solve (4.29) analytically to obtain the pressure and volumes of the coexisting phases. We begin by modifying (4.31) to make it more suitable for use with an equation of state in which v is the independent variable:

$$\int_{A}^{E} v \left(\frac{\partial P}{\partial v}\right)_T dv = 0 \tag{4.34}$$

From (4.24)

$$\left(\frac{\partial P}{\partial v}\right)_T = \frac{-RT}{(v-b)^2} + \frac{2a}{v^3} \tag{4.35}$$

Eliminating a and b in (4.35) by (4.27) and substituting in (4.34) gives

$$\ln\left[\frac{3v^l - v^c}{3v^s - v^c}\right] + \frac{v^c}{3v^s - v^c} - \frac{v^c}{3v^l - v^c} + \frac{9v^cT^c(v^s - v^l)}{4Tv^lv^s} = 0 \tag{4.36}$$

The temperature may be eliminated from (4.36) by substituting from (4.24) into

$$P^l = P^s \tag{4.37}$$

and the equation rearranged to give

$$\chi^l = \frac{(r+1)\ln r - 2(r-1)}{r^2 - 2r \ln r - 1} \tag{4.38}$$

$$\chi^s = r\chi^l \tag{4.39}$$

where

$$\chi^l = \frac{v^c}{3v^l - v^c} \quad \text{and} \quad \chi^s = \frac{v^c}{3v^s - v^c} \tag{4.40}$$

The saturated liquid and vapour volumes may be found by choosing an arbitrary value of the ratio $r \leqslant 1$, calculating v^l and v^s from (4.38)–(4.40), and the temperature and vapour pressure by substituting these values in (4.24) to give a pair of linear simultaneous equations.

In Figure 4.12 we compare the experimentally measured molar densities of argon along the saturation boundary with those obtained from the van der Waals equation. Both density and temperature are expressed in dimensionless or reduced form. Figure 4.13 shows the corresponding calculated and experimentally measured vapour pressure curves. The most noticeable discrepancy, apart from the experimentally observed intervention of the solid state below $T/T^c = 0.56$, is the difference in curvature of the density curves in the region of the critical point; the significance of this is discussed in Section 4.14.

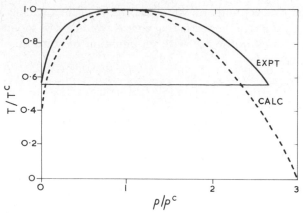

Figure 4.12. The density of argon along the saturated vapour-liquid boundary, measured experimentally and calculated from van der Waals' equation

Although we see that the van der Waals equation is not a good equation for the representation of the $P\text{-}V\text{-}T$ behaviour of a real substance, it does serve to illustrate the general procedure used with every equation of state which can represent both liquid and vapour regions. For the more complex equations described in the next section algebraic methods of solution, such as (4.34)–(4.40), cannot be found and we must resort to numerical procedures.

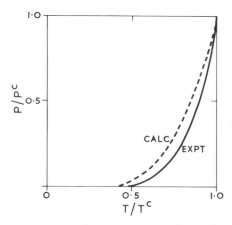

Figure 4.13. The vapour pressure of argon, measured experimentally and calculated from van der Waals' equation

4.13 Equations of practical importance

The two empirical equations which are most widely used are those of Redlich and Kwong and of Benedict, Webb and Rubin, usually known as the BWR equation. There are many other equations which have been proposed and critically reviewed[12] but which will not be discussed here.

The Redlich and Kwong equation

$$P = \frac{RT}{v - b} - \frac{a}{T^{1/2}v(v + b)}$$

(4.41)

is clearly based on that of van der Waals, but has greater numerical accuracy. However, since it contains only two arbitrary constants, it cannot reproduce the P-V-T behaviour of widely different types of fluids over extensive ranges of density with an accuracy approaching that of experimental measurements. Its utility stems from its simplicity, and the fact that, like the van der Waals equation, it is a well-behaved function which can be used to represent vapour phase properties over a wide range of pressure with moderate accuracy. At the critical point, where $(\partial P/\partial v)_T = 0$ and $(\partial^2 P/\partial v^2)_T = 0$, it may be shown that

$$a = \frac{0.4278 \; R^2 (T^c)^{2.5}}{P^c}$$

(4.42)

and

$$b = 0.0867 \frac{RT^c}{P^c}$$

(4.43)

However, the constants a and b should be determined by fitting (4.41) to experimental results in the region of interest. Table 4.2 gives them in dimensionless form for a few typical substances calculated first using saturated

Table 4.2. Dimensionless constants $\Omega_a = aP^c/R^2(T^c)^{2.5}$ and $\Omega_b = bP^c/RT^c$ in the Redlich-Kwong equation of state computed from (a) the P-V-T data for the saturated vapour (b) P-V-T data for saturated liquid

	Saturated Vapour		Saturated Liquid	
	Ω_a	Ω_b	Ω_a	Ω_b
Methane	0.4278	0.0867	0.4546	0.0872
Nitrogen	0.4290	0.0870	0.4540	0.0875
Benzene	0.4450	0.0904	0.4100	0.0787
Carbon Dioxide	0.4470	0.0911	0.4184	0.0794

vapour and secondly saturated liquid data. Had the constants been evaluated from (4.42) and (4.43) the values would have been $\Omega_a = 0.4278$ and $\Omega_b = 0.0867$ for all fluids. The Redlich and Kwong equation is no better than the van der Waals equation in correlating the P-V-T properties in the region of the critical point.

The BWR equation may be expressed in the form

$$P = \frac{RT}{v} + \left(B_0 RT - A_0 - \frac{C_0}{T^2}\right)\frac{1}{v^2} + \frac{(bRT - a)}{v^3} + \frac{a\alpha}{v^6}$$

$$+ \frac{c(1 + \gamma/v^2)}{v^3 T^2} e^{-\gamma/v^2}$$

(4.44)

This equation contains eight arbitrary constants A_0, B_0, C_0, a, b, c, α and γ, which may be evaluated from experimentally measured P-V-T data by using published procedures[13] to give a satisfactory representation of the fluid properties except in the immediate vicinity of the critical point. It was originally formulated for twelve hydrocarbons and the constants for these substances[14] enable the pressure in the vapour phase to be estimated to within an average deviation of 0.5% at densities up to 1.8 times the critical. It has now been applied to many other substances; a recent compilation[15] lists the constants for 38 compounds including polar (SO_2) and quantum (He) molecules. As its use increased, its shortcomings in correlating the P-V-T properties at a density greater than 1.8 times the critical density became apparent, and its accuracy has been improved by adding more temperature-dependent parameters. The increasing complexity of the modified equations can be handled without penalty by computers, and a recent equation of state of this type which is being used for scientific applications contains as many as twenty constants.[16]

4.14   Scaling equations

All equations of state used to represent the P-V-T properties of a pure substance in the liquid and gaseous regions assume that pressure is an analytic function of volume and temperature at and near the critical point. Although the assumption cannot be reconciled with the requirements for mechanical stability, that the isothermal compressibility is everywhere positive, this difficulty can be overcome by the device of Maxwell's construction. Moreover, we saw in Figure 4.12 that the densities of argon on the saturation curve calculated from van der Waals's equation differed from the observed values as the temperature approached the critical. This difference close to the critical point may be expressed quantitatively by writing

$$(\rho^l - \rho^g)_T = \text{const} \times (T^c - T)^\beta \tag{4.45}$$

The experimental results for argon show that $\beta = 0.34$, whereas the van der Waals equation requires that $\beta = \frac{1}{2}$. This difference in β does not arise because of experimental uncertainty in the results for argon or because of the particular form of the van der Waals equation, since values around 0.34 are found for other substances, whilst equations of state such as Redlich and Kwong, BWR, etc. all lead to $\beta = \frac{1}{2}$. Indices analogous to β in (4.45) can be defined which denote the rate at which other properties become zero as the critical point is approached. Thus,

$$1/C_V = \text{const} \times |T^c - T|^\alpha \tag{4.46}$$

describes the rate at which $1/C_V$ becomes zero along the critical isochore for a real gas (it is never zero for a gas which conforms to van der Waals' equation),

$$(\partial P/\partial v)_T = \text{const} \times (T - T^c)^\gamma \tag{4.47}$$

the rate at which the derivative $(\partial P/\partial v)_T$ becomes zero as the critical point is approached from $T > T^c$ along the critical isochore, and

$$P - P^c = \text{const} \times |V^c - V|^\delta \qquad (4.48)$$

describes the way in which the pressure approaches the critical along the critical isotherm. The indices in (4.45)–(4.48) are those commonly used to describe critical phenomena and must not be confused with α, the coefficient of thermal expansion, β_T, the coefficient of isothermal compressibility etc. discussed in Section 4.15.

Arguments based on the requirements for thermodynamic stability, which are outside the scope of this book, can be used to show that the indices must satisfy the following inequalities

$$\alpha + \beta(\delta + 1) \geqslant 2 \qquad (4.49)$$

$$\alpha + 2\beta + \gamma \geqslant 2 \qquad (4.50)$$

$$\gamma - \beta(\delta - 1) \geqslant 0 \qquad (4.51)$$

From the van der Waals equation $\alpha = 0$, $\beta = \frac{1}{2}$, $\gamma = 1$ and $\delta = 3$; hence the inequalities are satisfied as equations. The experimentally determined indices are independent of the nature of the fluid to within experimental uncertainty, as may be seen from Table 4.3. The mean values $\alpha = 0.1 \pm 0.1$, $\beta = 0.35 \pm 0.01$, $\gamma = 1.2 \pm 0.1$ and $\delta = 4.4 \pm 0.4$ are irreconcilable with the van der Waals result

Table 4.3. Critical constants and indices for carbon dioxide and methane

	Carbon dioxide	Methane
$v^c/\text{cm}^3\,\text{g}^{-1}$	2.146	6.143
T^c/K	304.21	190.53
P^c/bar	73.825	45.945
α	0.065	0.057
β	0.347	0.3566
γ	1.241	1.230
δ	4.576	4.450

and lead to the conclusion that pressure is not an analytic function of volume and temperature at the critical point. In practice this means that no analytic equation of state, however complicated, represents accurately the thermodynamic properties near the critical point. Should such a representation be needed, we must use a special non-analytic function known as a *scaling equation*,[17] of which there are several versions. One of these must be incorporated into the equation of state to force a fit in the critical region. Although the resulting set of equations enables the observed P-V-T behaviour to be reproduced accurately over the whole range of density and temperature, it is complex since its form must be such that the scaling, non-analytic part dominates at the critical point then fades away to enable the conventional, analytic part to take over in the regions away from the critical point.[18] For most applications the limitations of a conventional equation of state are not serious since it provides a convenient analytical representation of P-V-T data which can be used everywhere except around the critical point for interpolation or subsequent computation of other thermodynamic properties.

4.15 *P-V-T* relationships for condensed phases

The P-V-T behaviour of solids and liquids is complex and it has not been possible to devise an equation of state of simple form from which the three derivatives $(\partial V/\partial T)_P$, $(\partial V/\partial P)_T$ and $(\partial P/\partial T)_V$ can be calculated. The results of their experimental measurement are usually presented in terms of the following coefficients

$(1/V)(\partial V/\partial T)_P$; the coefficient of bulk (or cubic) thermal expansion, α_P

$-(1/V)(\partial V/\partial P)_T$; the coefficient of isothermal bulk compressibility, β_T (note the inclusion of the negative sign to make β_T positive)

$(1/P)(\partial P/\partial T)_V$; known in German as the Spannungskoeffizient, there is no recognised name in English although $(\partial P/\partial T)_V$ is frequently called the thermal pressure coefficient γ_V.

For a pure substance the coefficient that is most readily measured is the thermal expansion of the saturated liquid. However, when a saturated liquid is heated its vapour pressure increases, and so the volume change of a liquid in contact with its own vapour is not that at constant pressure but that at constant saturation. It is denoted by

$$\alpha_\sigma = (1/V)(\partial V/\partial T)_\sigma \tag{4.52}$$

There are reliable tables[19] (see Section 4.19) of saturated liquid density ($\rho_\sigma = 1/v_\sigma$), for many substances which extend over the whole liquid range, and from which α_σ may be evaluated. At the critical point it is infinite. Measurement of the volume or density of a liquid in contact with air at atmospheric pressure gives α_P, but such measurements are possible only at low temperatures where the vapour pressure is small. It follows from the rules for partial differentiation (see Appendix A) that

$$\left(\frac{\partial V}{\partial T}\right)_P = \left(\frac{\partial V}{\partial T}\right)_\sigma - \left(\frac{\partial V}{\partial P}\right)_T \left(\frac{\partial P}{\partial T}\right)_\sigma \tag{4.53}$$

or

$$\alpha_P = \alpha_\sigma + \beta_T \gamma_\sigma \tag{4.54}$$

where $\gamma_\sigma = (\partial P/\partial T)_\sigma$ is the slope of the vapour pressure curve.

As will be seen later in this section, β_T is small; hence the difference between the coefficient of expansion at constant pressure α_P and that along the saturation curve α_σ is negligible, provided the rate of increase of vapour pressure with temperature is small. This is the case at temperatures below the normal boiling point.

For most solids and all liquids α_P is positive, but there are a few substances for which it is negative over a small range of temperature, for example, water between $0\,°C$ and $4\,°C$.

Exercise

Show that

$$\alpha_P = \beta_T \gamma_V \tag{4.55}$$

and

$$\gamma_V - \gamma_\sigma = \alpha_\sigma / \beta_T \tag{4.56}$$

Most compressibility measurements have been made by observing the change in volume of the liquid as the pressure is increased isothermally in steps of about 100 bar to pressures of 1000 bar or more. The coefficient of isothermal compressibility β_T may be derived from the slope of the curve representing the change of volume as a function of pressure. The coefficient decreases as the pressure increases. At low pressure the minute volume change is difficult to measure accurately because the effect of small variations in temperature is comparable to that produced by the change in pressure. Hence, to obtain accurate values of β_T at the vapour pressure of the liquid, great care is needed in the extrapolation of the results.

Exercise

Show that

$$\beta_T = \beta_S + \frac{TV\alpha_P^2}{C_P} \tag{4.57}$$

where $\beta_S = -(1/V)(\partial V/\partial P)_S$ is the adiabatic coefficient of bulk compressibility which can be determined from the speed of sound (3.168).

Thus, a knowledge of the speed of sound and the other thermodynamic properties in the second term of the right-hand side of (4.57) as a function of temperature at atmospheric pressure provides an accurate method for calculating the coefficient of isothermal compressibility at atmospheric pressure.

The coefficient of isothermal compressibility and its dependence on pressure are different for each substance and for each of the condensed phases but, as was mentioned in Section 4.2, it is a condition for mechanical stability that the coefficient be positive. Values of β_T are small, usually of the order of 10^{-6} to 10^{-5} bar^{-1}. For accurate values it is still often necessary to turn to the early work of the French physicist Amagat and the pioneering work of Bridgman, whose book[9] is still an important source of knowledge of the volumetric behaviour of liquids and solids at high pressures. If, as is usually the case, the compressions have been measured along a number of isotherms, then α_P and γ_V may be calculated from the results by cross-plotting; the three coefficients are related by (4.55).

Although direct measurement of the thermal pressure coefficient γ_V is somewhat easier than that of β_T, results are not plentiful. This coefficient changes smoothly with temperature along the saturation curve, as may be seen from Figure 4.14. The full lines to the right of the saturation curve show

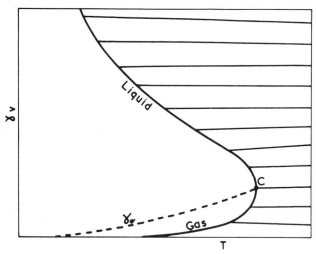

Figure 4.14. The variation of the thermal pressure coefficient $\gamma_V = (\partial P/\partial T)_V$ with temperature for the saturated gas and liquid, and for the homogeneous fluid at temperatures above saturation

γ_V along a set of isochores, for each of which the volume is the saturated volume at the temperature at which the isochore cuts the saturation curve. The slope of the vapour pressure curve γ_σ is shown by the dashed line which cuts the saturation curve at the critical point c, where $\gamma_\sigma = \gamma_V^c$, as may be seen from Figure 4.3.

The thermal pressure coefficient γ_V is a much more convenient function for interpolation and extrapolation than α_P or β_T because the rate of change of the coefficient with temperature in the compressed liquid region is always small. Furthermore, unlike α_P or β_T, it remains finite up to the critical point where its value is determined easily from vapour pressure measurements. A systematic procedure for obtaining the best values of α_P, β_T and γ_V along the saturation boundary has been described elsewhere.[20]

4.16 Calculation of thermodynamic properties

In principle all the thermodynamic functions of a pure substance can be evaluated from P-V-T properties, together with a heat capacity, either C_P or C_V, as a function of temperature along any one isobar or isochore respectively. In this section discussion is confined to the saturation boundary and vapour phase. However, if accurate P-V-T data for the condensed phases are available, the calculations may be extended to give the properties of the compressed liquid and solid regions.

The earliest attempts to calculate thermodynamic properties from P-V-T data were based on crude graphical differentiations and integrations, which were subsequently refined by plotting, not the actual measurements, but their deviations from some analytic expression using a technique known as graphical residuals. During the past decade the widespread use of computers has led to the development of a large number of multi-regression analytical procedures which vary with the type and extent of the available data. We are concerned here, solely, with the principles of these calculations, and to illustrate them we assume that the following measurements are available for a pure substance as a function of temperature:

(a) Saturated vapour pressure;
(b) Gas phase P-V measurements over a wide range of P and T;
(c) Density of saturated liquid;
(d) Isobaric heat capacity at low pressure.

The first step in the calculation of a complete set of thermodynamic properties for the saturated liquid, saturated vapour and super-heated vapour is to determine the coefficients of an equation for the vapour pressure curve which accurately represents the experimental measurements. An equation of the form

$$\ln(P/\text{bar}) = a + b/T + cT + dT^2 \qquad (4.58)$$

has often been used, but this is only one of a number of suitable empirical equations.[21]

The second step is to determine an equation of state for the gaseous region. As was mentioned in Section 4.10, there are many forms of equation which can be used; and, apart from the essential requirement of accuracy, it is an advantage if the equation is in a form suitable for differentiation.

Although the virial equation (4.20) can represent experimental P-V-T results with fewer terms than (4.21), the latter is frequently more convenient to use. From (4.21)

$$v = \frac{RT}{P}[1 + B'P + C'P^2 + D'P^3 \cdots] \qquad (4.59)$$

By using sufficient coefficients B', C', D', etc. this equation can represent gas densities very accurately, but it should not be extrapolated beyond the range of pressure for which experimental results are available as this can lead to large errors. Since the coefficients are functions of temperature only,

$$\left(\frac{\partial v}{\partial T}\right)_P = \frac{R}{P}\left[1 + \left(B' + T\frac{dB'}{dT}\right)P + \left(C' + T\frac{dC'}{dT}\right)P^2 + \left(D' + T\frac{dD'}{dT}\right)P^3 \cdots\right]$$

$$(4.60)$$

Hence, to obtain $(\partial v/\partial T)_P$ we must derive empirical relations between B' and C' and the temperature, from which the derivatives dB'/dT and dC'/dT can be calculated. The equation of state can now be used to evaluate the specific volume of the superheated vapour at given temperatures and pressures. In addition, the specific volume of the saturated vapour at a given temperature may be found by substituting the saturation pressure from the vapour pressure curve into the equation of state. The procedure for calculating the properties may be followed from Figure 4.15 in which the enthalpy and entropy of the saturated liquid, at state 1, have been arbitrarily set to zero.

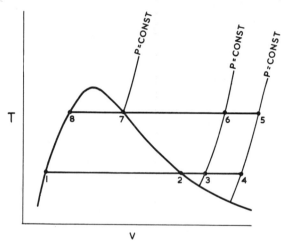

Figure 4.15. T-v projection to illustrate the procedure used to calculate the thermodynamic properties in the fluid region

The enthalpy of evaporation $\Delta_e h$ may be calculated from Clapeyron's equation (3.217), which may be written

$$\Delta_e h = h_2 - h_1 = T(v_2 - v_1)(\partial P/\partial T)_\sigma \qquad (4.61)$$

Hence, if $h_1 = 0$, the enthalpy of saturated vapour, h_2, can be calculated from a knowledge of the slope of the vapour pressure curve and the specific volumes of the saturated liquid and vapour (the latter being obtained from the equation of state).

The entropy at state 2 is found readily since

$$\Delta_e s = \Delta_e h/T \qquad (4.62)$$

Hence, when $h_1 = 0$, $s_1 = 0$

$$s_2 = h_2/T \qquad (4.63)$$

From state 2 we can now proceed along an isotherm into the superheated region. For an isothermal process integration of (3.104) and (3.86) gives

$$(h_3 - h_2)_T = \int_{P_2}^{P_3} [v - T(\partial v/\partial T)_P]\, dP_T \qquad (4.64)$$

and

$$(s_3 - s_2)_T = -\int_{P_2}^{P_3} (\partial v/\partial T)_P \, dP_T \tag{4.65}$$

As in Section 3.14 we write

$$\int_{X_1}^{X_2} Z \, dX_{Y_n}$$

to represent the integration of Z, a function of two independent variables X and Y, with respect to X, when Y is held constant at the value Y_n. Thus the enthalpy and entropy changes from 2 to 3 can be calculated from v and $(\partial v/\partial T)_P$ along the isotherm, both of which may be found from the equation of state.

The properties at point 4, where the pressure corresponds to that at which measurements of c_P have been made, are found similarly. The change in enthalpy and entropy between states 4 and 5 can be calculated by integrating (2.28) and (3.90) along the isobaric path.

$$(h_5 - h_4)_P = \int_{T_4}^{T_5} c_P \, dT_P \tag{4.66}$$

$$(s_5 - s_4)_P = \int_{T_4}^{T_5} (c_P/T) \, dT_P \tag{4.67}$$

In order to evaluate these integrals we express the heat capacity as a function of temperature by an empirical equation of the form

$$c_P = a + bT + cT^2 + dT^3 \tag{4.68}$$

The heat capacity can be measured directly (Section 2.8) or calculated at $P = 0$ from spectroscopic data (Section 9.4).

The properties at states 6 and 7 are calculated from those at 5 in the same way as the properties at states 3 and 4 were calculated from those at 2. Similarly the enthalpy and entropy for the saturated liquid, state 8, are found from those at state 7 by using the Clapeyron equation. The internal energy can be calculated from $u = h - pv$. Thus, the pressure, temperature, volume, enthalpy, entropy and internal energy of the saturated liquid, saturated vapour and superheated vapour can be tabulated for the region for which there are experimental data. Although the actual values of the enthalpy, entropy and internal energy depend on the chosen reference point, this in no way limits the usefulness of the tables since it is only the differences in these properties which are needed in thermodynamic calculations. If low temperature calorimetric data are available extending down to temperatures around 10 K, we can set both entropy and enthalpy at zero for the perfect solid at 0 K, as was suggested in Section 3.15. Compilations of tables in common use employ several different arbitrary reference states.[6] *

* References in square brackets are listed in Section 4.19.

When dealing with heat transfer at high pressures, the chemical engineer generally uses values of enthalpy and does not have to consider heat capacity. However, it is sometimes convenient to use the heat capacity to calculate thermal effects, but very few direct measurements of it have been made for gases at high pressures. We must, therefore, calculate the effect of pressure on heat capacity using the integral form of (3.123). For the difference between states 3 and 4 in Figure 4.15

$$(c_{P_4} - c_{P_3})_T = -T \int_{P_3}^{P_4} (\partial^2 v/\partial T^2)_P \, dP_T \tag{4.69}$$

Alternatively, if we know the heat capacity at constant volume as a function of temperature, then from (3.121)

$$(c_{V_4} - c_{V_3})_T = T \int_{v_3}^{v_4} (\partial^2 P/\partial T^2)_V \, dv_T \tag{4.70}$$

The derivative $(\partial^2 v/\partial T^2)_P$ may be cumbersome to handle if v is the independent variable in the equation of state. It may then be simpler to calculate c_P from (4.70) and (4.71). We have from (3.96) and (A.8)

$$(c_P - c_V)_T = T(\partial P/\partial T)_V(\partial v/\partial T)_P = -T(\partial P/\partial T)_V^2/(\partial P/\partial v)_T \tag{4.71}$$

If we are to obtain reliable values of the heat capacities, we need not only precise P-V-T data, but the equation of state from which the second derivatives are calculated must be well-behaved and reproduce the data accurately. In practice, there may be several independent sets of P-V-T results in those regions of the vapour phase readily accessible to experiment, and the weight to be placed on each set of data is a matter for careful judgement. On the other hand, in other regions there may be a shortage, or even a complete absence, of data, and alternative measurements such as the temperature change of gas when it is subjected to a Joule-Thomson expansion, or measurements of the speed of sound at various pressures and temperatures, may have to be used.

Exercise

From the expression for the Joule-Thomson expansion given in (3.158) show that the difference between (V/T) at two points on an isobar is

$$\Delta \left(\frac{V}{T} \right)_P = \int_{T_1}^{T_2} \frac{\mu C_P}{T^2} \, dT_P \tag{4.72}$$

where

$$\mu = (\partial T/\partial P)_H \tag{4.73}$$

Thus, if the Joule-Thomson coefficient μ and the heat capacity C_P are known as functions of temperature at constant pressure, (4.72) can be used to give the change in (V/T) and hence in V, between the temperature limits of integration.

In the simple example described in this section, we assumed that the vapour pressure and saturated liquid densities were available. Had this not been so, we should have used an equation of state such as the BWR, or preferably one of its later developments, which represents the properties of both fluid phases, to calculate the properties along the saturation boundary with the aid of Maxwell's construction. The error in the derived thermodynamic properties would then have been larger, both because of the limitation of the equation of state and as a result of the lack of experimental data. If the thermodynamic properties are to be calculated with a high accuracy by using multi-regression techniques, we must have a wide variety of experimental data covering extended ranges of pressure and temperature for both fluid phases. The computation of thermodynamic functions is a skilled task and all compilations should be accompanied by a report which contains the sources of the original data, the methods of computation and correlation, and an estimate of the accuracy of the properties in different regions. If, as is often the case with earlier computations, a report is not available, the user is strongly advised to check the data for thermodynamic consistency. For example, the Gibbs free energy of the saturated liquid should be the same as that of the vapour with which it is in equilibrium. Alternatively, integral forms of (3.74) provide the basis for other tests. At constant temperature

$$(h_b - h_a)_T = \int_{P_a}^{P_b} v \, dP_T + T(s_b - s_a)_T \tag{4.74}$$

or at constant entropy

$$(h_b - h_a)_s = \int_{P_a}^{P_b} v \, dP_s \tag{4.75}$$

4.17 Tables of thermodynamic properties

In general, tables of thermodynamic properties may be separated into two groups, those to be used for the calculation of heat and work and those for the calculation of chemical equilibria. We are concerned here with the former; the latter are discussed in Section 8.5.

Tables for the fluid phases of a pure substance are set out in two sections, one of which gives the properties on the saturated vapour-liquid boundary and the other those of the single-phase homogeneous fluid. Since pressure and temperature are related in the two-phase region, the properties on the saturated boundary may be compiled at regularly spaced intervals of pressure or of temperature or of both. Comprehensive compilations such as steam tables[26] give both so as to reduce the interpolation required. The minimum of properties required as a function of pressure and/or temperature are the specific (or molar) volume, enthalpy and entropy for the saturated liquid and saturated vapour. For convenience many tables give also the enthalpy of evaporation $\Delta_e h$, entropy of evaporation $\Delta_e s$, the density ρ, and the internal energy u, of the saturated liquid and vapour, all of which can be calculated from the first set of properties listed. A property which is sometimes tabulated and cannot be calculated easily from the first set is the heat capacity at saturation. Section (a) of skeleton Table 4.4 gives the minimum number of properties for benzene along the saturation boundary, as a function of round values of pressure. The only difference between this table and the one from which the values have been abstracted is that the original table[33] gives more properties at smaller and more regularly spaced intervals of pressure.

In the single phase, fluid pressure and temperature are independent variables, and several different methods of presentation are used. One is to tabulate separately the values for each property as a function of pressure and temperature as in references[2] and [6]. A second method is to draw up a table of all properties of interest as a function of temperature at a particular pressure as in references [26] and [30]. Other methods of presentation are also used, the choice depending on the number of properties to be tabulated. Whereas the specific or molar volume, enthalpy and entropy suffice for many calculations, and are the only properties given for this region in the main body of steam tables,[26] other tables may include one or more of the following: compression factor, fugacity-pressure ratio, heat capacity at constant volume, heat capacity at constant pressure, heat capacity ratio and Joule-Thomson coefficient. In section (b) of Table 4.4 v, h and s are given as a function of temperature on three widely spaced isobars.

Table 4.4. Thermodynamic properties of benzene

(a) Saturation

P bar	T K	ρ^l kg/m³	v^g m³/kg	h^l kJ/kg	h^g kJ/kg	s^l kJ/kg K	s^g kJ/kg K
0.1	293.09	878.99	3.0993	376.30	813.50	2.1888	3.6805
0.2	308.41	862.60	1.6237	403.41	829.21	2.2790	3.6596
0.3	318.31	851.93	1.1131	421.04	839.73	2.3352	3.6505
0.4	325.81	843.78	0.85157	434.56	847.88	2.3771	3.6457
0.5	331.93	837.10	0.69187	445.69	854.63	2.4109	3.6430
1	352.81	813.96	0.36289	484.44	878.38	2.5240	3.6405
2	377.08	786.20	0.18978	531.51	907.19	2.6526	3.6489
5	415.85	738.98	0.07949	611.33	955.21	2.8530	3.6799
10	451.66	690.27	0.04009	691.07	1000.4	3.0352	3.7201
15	475.80	652.96	0.02624	749.07	1030.0	3.1587	3.7491
16	479.89	646.15	0.02446	759.35	1034.8	3.1798	3.7539
17	483.79	639.47	0.02288	769.21	1039.4	3.2000	3.7584
18	487.53	632.91	0.02147	778.72	1043.7	3.2193	3.7627
20	494.57	620.08	0.01905	796.99	1051.6	3.2558	3.7705
30	523.53	557.84	0.01150	876.59	1079.6	3.4088	3.7967
40	545.83	488.59	0.007334	945.91	1090.9	3.5348	3.8005
48.98	562.16	303.95	0.003290	1043.1	1043.1	3.7057	3.7057

(b) isobaric

T K	1 bar v m³/kg	h kJ/kg	s kJ/kg K	5 bar v m³/kg	h kJ/kg	s kJ/kg K	20 bar v m³/kg	h kJ/kg	s kJ/kg K
360	0.3713	887.97	3.6674						
370	0.3829	901.59	3.7048						
380	0.3943	915.55	3.7420						
390	0.4057	929.83	3.7791						
400	0.4169	944.45	3.8161	0.08066	962.15	3.6965			
410	0.4281	959.41	3.8530	0.08342	978.93	3.7360			
420	0.4392	974.69	3.8898	0.08607	995.84	3.7749			
430	0.4503	990.29	3.9265	0.08863	1012.9	3.8133			
440	0.4614	1006.2	3.9632	0.09117	1030.2	3.8512			
450	0.4724	1022.5	3.9997	0.09367	1047.7	3.8888			
460	0.4834	1039.0	4.0361	0.09611	1065.4	3.9261			
470	0.4943	1055.9	4.0724	0.09853	1083.3	3.9630			
480	0.5052	1073.1	4.1086	0.1009	1101.5	3.9997			
490	0.5160	1090.6	4.1446	0.1033	1119.9	4.0362			
500	0.5269	1108.4	4.1805	0.1057	1138.5	4.0724	0.01968	1063.9	3.7954
510	0.5378	1126.4	4.2163	0.1080	1157.4	4.1083	0.02076	1086.0	3.8392
520	0.5486	1144.8	4.2519	0.1057	1176.5	4.1440	0.02172	1107.5	3.8810
530	0.5594	1163.4	4.2874	0.1080	1195.8	4.1796	0.02263	1128.7	3.9213
540	0.5703	1182.3	4.3228	0.1103	1215.4	4.2149	0.02348	1149.7	3.9605
550	0.5812	1201.5	4.3580	0.1127	1235.3	4.2149	0.02431	1170.6	3.9989
560	0.5919	1220.9	4.3930	0.1150	1255.3	4.2499	0.02509	1191.5	4.0365
570	0.6027	1240.6	4.4279	0.1173	1275.6	4.2849	0.02585	1212.4	4.0735
580	0.6135	1260.6	4.4626	0.1196	1296.2	4.3195	0.02661	1233.4	4.1100
590	0.6244	1280.8	4.4971	0.1218	1316.9	4.3541	0.02733	1254.4	4.1460
600	0.6351	1301.3	4.5315	0.1241	1337.9	4.3884	0.02805	1275.6	4.1816
610	0.6459	1321.9	4.5657	0.1264	1359.1	4.4225	0.02876	1296.9	4.2168
620	0.6568	1342.9	4.5997	0.1287	1380.5	4.4564	0.02946	1318.4	4.2517
630	0.6675	1364.0	4.6336	0.1310	1402.2	4.4902	0.03015	1340.0	4.2863
640	0.6783	1385.4	4.6672	0.1333		4.5237	0.03083	1361.8	4.3206
650	0.6889	1407.0	4.7007	0.1355			0.03152	1383.7	4.3546

Since pressure has little effect on the properties of a liquid, a separate table is sometimes provided for the compressed liquid in which the differences between the properties and those along the saturated liquid boundary, rather than the actual properties, are given as a function of pressure and temperature.

Before illustrating the use of the tables we must show how the properties of a two-phase liquid-vapour mixture are calculated from a knowledge of the properties on the saturation boundary. At constant pressure and temperature they can be obtained by using the lever rule of Section 4.5. Although (4.4), (4.6) and (4.7) were expressed in terms of specific volume, similar equations can also be written for the specific properties u, h and s. Thus from (4.6)

$$k^x = (1-x)k^l + xk^g \tag{4.76}$$

or

$$x = (k^x - k^l)/(k^g - k^l) \tag{4.77}$$

where k is any specific property and superscript x denotes the properties of the mixture of quality x.

The quality of a two-phase mixture changes as a result of evaporation or condensation when the temperature and pressure are changed, whilst some property k is held constant. The change of quality can be calculated as follows.

Suppose the mixture consists of mass x_1 of saturated vapour of specific property k_1^g and mass $(1-x_1)$ of saturated liquid of specific property k_1^l. Let Δx of liquid evaporate when the temperature is raised from T_1 to T_2 whilst the property of the mixture k^x is kept constant.

At T_1

$$k_1^x = (1-x_1)k_1^l + x_1 k_1^g \tag{4.78}$$

At T_2

$$k_2^x = (1-x_2)k_2^l + x_2 k_1^g \tag{4.79}$$

Since

$$k_2^x = k_1^x$$

Then

$$\Delta x = x_2 - x_1 = \frac{k_1^x - k_2^l}{\Delta_e k_2} - \frac{k_1^x - k_1^l}{\Delta_e k_1} \tag{4.80}$$

An example of the use of these equations is the calculation given later in this section of the work needed for the reversible adiabatic compression of a mixture of benzene liquid and vapour.

Exercise

Show by means of the lever rule that

$$\left(\frac{\partial x}{\partial T}\right)_k = -\left[(1-x)\left(\frac{\partial k^l}{\partial T}\right)_\sigma + x\left(\frac{\partial k^g}{\partial T}\right)_\sigma\right] \bigg/ \Delta_e k \tag{4.81}$$

and hence that for an isentropic process

$$\left(\frac{\partial x}{\partial T}\right)_s = -[(1-x)c_\sigma^l + xc_\sigma^g]/T \, \Delta_e s \tag{4.82}$$

If the variation of the specific heat capacities along the saturated liquid and vapour boundaries and the change in the entropy of evaporation are known as functions of temperature, (4.82) can be integrated from initial conditions T_1, x_1 to final conditions T_2, x_2. It is seldom that the values of the derivatives along the saturation boundary are tabulated as a function of temperature; hence (4.81) is useful only for the analytical solution of certain problems. For example, from (4.81) the condition for the position of the meniscus to remain unchanged in the constant volume experiment described in Section 4.5 is that $(1-x)v^l\alpha_\sigma^l + xv^g\alpha_\sigma^g = 0$.

Examples of the use of thermodynamic tables

1. From Table 4.4(a) calculate the latent heat of benzene at 5 bar from the entropy of evaporation, and compare the value with that in the table.
   From (3.153)

$$\Delta_e h = T_\sigma \, \Delta_e s = T_\sigma(s^g - s^l)$$

Hence

$$\Delta_e h = 415.85(3.6799 - 2.8530)$$
$$= 343.89 \text{ kJ kg}^{-1}$$

While using the enthalpy tabulations directly,

$$\Delta_e h = h^g - h^l$$
$$= 955.21 - 611.33 = 343.88 \text{ kJ kg}^{-1}$$

This simple example shows that tables must be thermodynamically consistent.

2. Calculate the work done on 1 kg of saturated liquid benzene as it evaporates reversibly at 5 bar in a closed system.
   From (1.20)

$$w = -\int P \, dv$$
$$= -P(v^g - v^l) = -P(v^g - 1/\rho^l)$$
$$= \frac{-5 \times 10^5}{10^3}\left(0.07949 - \frac{1}{738.98}\right) \text{ kJ}$$
$$= -39.07 \text{ kJ}$$

3. If benzene vapour at 1 bar and 360 K is compressed reversibly and adiabatically to 20 bar in a steady state flow device, what is the state of the vapour when it leaves the compressor, and how much work has to be done per

kg of vapour compressed? Table 4.4(a) shows that at 1 bar $T_\sigma = 352.81$ K; hence the gas entering the compressor (state 1) is superheated, and we must therefore turn to Table 4.4(b) for the properties in this state.

At 1 bar 360 K

$$s_1 = 3.6674 \text{ kJ K}^{-1} \text{ kg}^{-1}$$
$$h_1 = 887.97 \text{ kJ kg}^{-1}$$

Reversible adiabatic compression is an isentropic process; hence, at discharge conditions (state 2),

$$s_2 = s_1 = 3.6674 \text{ kJ K}^{-1} \text{ kg}^{-1}$$

At 20 bar

$$s_2^g = 3.7705 \text{ kJ K}^{-1} \text{ kg}^{-1}$$

Hence the benzene leaving the compressor is a mixture of saturated liquid and vapour.

The quality of the vapour at state 2 follows from (4.77)

$$x_2 = \frac{s_2 - s_2^l}{s_2^g - s_2^l} = \frac{3.6774 - 3.2558}{3.7705 - 3.2558} = 0.800$$

From (4.76) the enthalpy of the vapour at state 2 is

$$h_2 = h_2^l + x_2(h_2^g - h_2^l) = 796.99 + 0.800(1051.6 - 796.99)$$
$$= 1000.6 \text{ kJ kg}^{-1}$$

Hence from (2.7) the work required $= h_2 - h_1$

$$= 1000.6 - 887.97$$
$$= 112.6 \text{ kJ kg}^{-1}$$

For most substances (see Section 4.18) reversible adiabatic compression of a vapour increases the superheat but the shape of the saturated vapour boundary for benzene is such that condensation can occur, as in this example. In practice we should have to pre-heat the vapour before it entered the compressor so that no liquid is formed which might damage the close-clearance compression equipment.

At 20 bar $s^g = 3.7705 \text{ kJ K}^{-1} \text{ kg}^{-1}$; therefore to prevent condensation the temperature of the suction gas at 1 bar would have to be such that $s \geqslant 3.7705 \text{ kJ K}^{-1}\text{kg}^{-1}$. By linear interpolation in Table 4.4(b), the required suction gas temperature T_1 must be equal to or greater than $380 + 10(3.7705 - 3.7420)/(3.7420 - 3.7048) = 387.7$ K.

4. A mixture of saturated liquid and saturated vapour, of specific volume of $0.30 \text{ m}^3 \text{ kg}^{-1}$ at 1 bar, is compressed reversibly and adiabatically until the specific volume is reduced to $0.01 \text{ m}^3 \text{ kg}^{-1}$. Calculate the pressure and temperature of the compressed mixture.

At 1 bar from (4.77) and the data in Table 4.4(a)

$$x_1 = \frac{v_1^x - v_1^l}{v_1^g - v_1^l} = \frac{0.30 - 1/813.96}{0.36289 - 1/813.96} = 0.826$$

From (4.76)

$$s_1^x = (1 - x_1)s_1^l + x_1 s_1^g = 0.174 \times 2.5240 + 0.826 \times 3.6405$$
$$= 3.4463 \text{ kJ K}^{-1} \text{ kg}^{-1}$$

The final pressure P_2 has to be calculated by trial and error. Assume $P_2 = 15$ bar

$$x_2 = \frac{s_1^x - s_2^l}{s_2^g - s_2^l} = \frac{3.4463 - 3.1587}{3.7491 - 3.1587} - 0.487$$

Hence

$$v_2^x = (1 - x_2)v_2^l + xv_2^g = \frac{0.513}{652.96} + 0.487 \times 0.02624$$
$$= 0.01357 \text{ m}^3 \text{ kg}^{-1}$$

The following values of x_2 and v_2^x can be calculated similarly at other final pressures.

P_2	x_2	v_2^x
17	0.441	0.01097
18	0.418	0.00989
20	0.370	0.00806

Thus the pressure of the mixture when compressed to $0.01 \text{ m}^3 \text{ kg}^{-1}$ is about 18 bar and the temperature 487.5 K. From the quality of the mixture before and after compression we can calculate the change of specific internal energy $\Delta u = \Delta h - \Delta(Pv)$, which is equal to the work of compression per unit mass of mixture.

4.18 Thermodynamic charts

A pure substance has, at most, two independent variables; hence, by using only two thermodynamic properties as co-ordinates, we can draw a chart to scale which shows all other properties as parameters. The advantage of this method of presentation will have become apparent from the number of diagrams used in earlier chapters in which reversible processes were plotted in P-V, T-S, or H-S co-ordinates. These diagrams were used there to illustrate certain thermodynamic principles, but actual calculations can also be made with such charts, which are therefore widely used in the chemical industry. All charts are equivalent, and provided the necessary parameters are included, engineers should be able to carry out calculations on any one of them, interpolating as necessary. The choice of co-ordinates is arbitrary, but this does not mean that all charts are equally convenient for carrying out a particular calculation. As is shown in Chapter 5, power plant calculations are performed most conveniently with an *H-S* chart, heat exchanger calculations with an *H-T* chart, and refrigeration calculations with an *H-P* chart. When there is more than one component, the situation is much more complex and is discussed in Chapter 7.

T-S chart

The frequent assumption of reversible and adiabatic, i.e. isentropic, processes in the analysis of plant prompts the adoption of entropy as one of the co-ordinates, and the *T-S* chart is one of the most popular. The *T-S* diagram for a substance which contracts on freezing is illustrated in Figure 4.16. Path

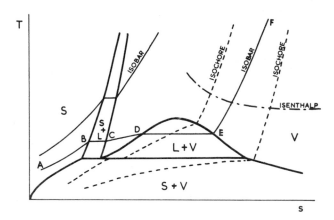

Figure 4.16. *T-s* diagram for a pure substance which contracts on freezing

AF is a typical isobar which represents a series of reversible isobaric processes in which solid is transformed finally into superheated vapour. Thus *AB* represents isobaric heating of solid to its melting point, *BC* isobaric-isothermal melting, *CD* isobaric heating of liquid to its boiling point, *DE* isobaric-isothermal evaporation and *EF* isobaric superheating of the vapour.

Since $q_{rev} = \int T \, ds$, the area below any line on a *T-S* diagram, down to the $T = 0$ axis, is the heat transferred during the process, provided that it is reversible. If the process is also at constant pressure, then $\Delta h = q_{rev}$. Thus the area under the line *BC* is the enthalpy of melting, $\Delta_m h$, at the particular temperature, and the area under the line *DE*, the enthalpy of evaporation, $\Delta_e h$. On the triple phase line the enthalpy of sublimation is equal to the sum of the enthalpy of melting and the enthalpy of evaporation. The corresponding entropy changes associated with sublimation, melting and evaporation may be read off the entropy axis directly; they are related to the enthalpy changes since, for an isobaric-isothermal process $\Delta g = 0$, or $\Delta s = \Delta h / T$.

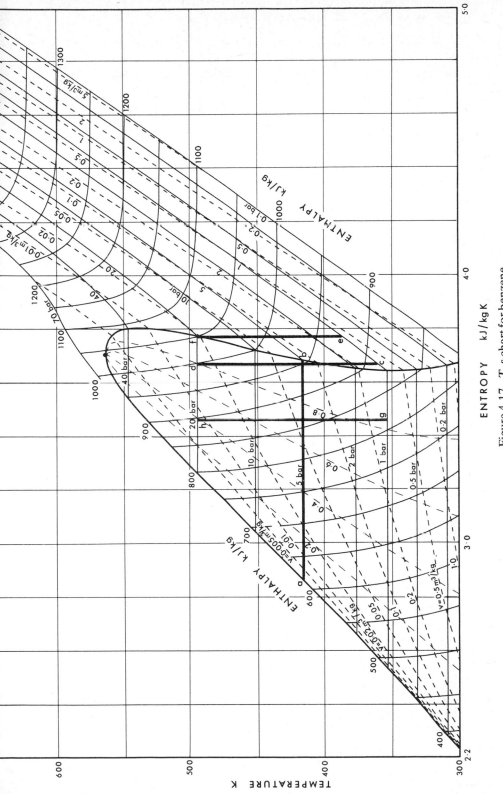

ENTROPY kJ / kg K

Figure 4.17. *T*-*s* chart for benzene

The area within any closed path is the net heat received or rejected by the system as it passes reversibly round the cycle, and according to the first law this area is the net work done on, or delivered by, the system. Hence

$$\oint T \, ds = \oint_{rev} dq = -\oint_{rev} dw \qquad (4.83)$$

When the flow of material or the order of the processes is such that the cycle is executed in a clockwise direction, the area is the net heat absorbed and the net work done by the system; if anti-clockwise, the net heat rejected and the net work done on the system.

The exact path of an irreversible process is seldom known and so cannot be represented on a chart because the system is not in equilibrium at all times. Even if the path is known, the area beneath it has no significance and, as a reminder of this, the path is shown as a broken or cross-hatched line.

Figure 4.17 shows a T-S chart for benzene. By using the lever rule, lines of constant enthalpy, volume and quality have been plotted in the two-phase region. One of the reasons for using charts is that these lines avoid the trial-and-error calculations which we had to make when using tabulated data in the two-phase region.

Examples of the use of thermodynamic charts

We illustrate the use of the chart shown in Figure 4.17 by solving again the problems at the end of the previous section.

1. Evaporation at 5 bar is represented by the line ab; hence

$$\Delta_e h = h^g - h^l = 955 - 615 = 340 \text{ kJ kg}^{-1}$$

Instead of interpolating between isenthalps it is easier to read the temperature of evaporation from the vertical axis, and the entropy change from the horizontal axis.
   Hence

$$\Delta_e h = 415(3.67 - 2.85) = 340 \text{ kJ kg}^{-1}$$

2. It is difficult to estimate the specific volume of saturated liquid at point a. However, since it is small compared with that of the saturated vapour it can be neglected.
   Hence

$$w = -\int P \, dv \simeq -Pv^g = \frac{-5 \times 10^5}{10^3} \times 0.08 = -40 \text{ kJ}$$

3. Since the compression is reversible and adiabatic, a vertical line cd can be drawn from the initial state c (360 K and 1 bar) to d, the point of intersection

with the isobar at 20 bar. From the position of d, we see that the fluid leaving the compressor is a mixture of saturated liquid and vapour of quality 0.8.

$$w = h_d - h_c = 995 - 887 = 108 \text{ kJ kg}^{-1}$$

Point e at 387 K on the isentrope ef represents the lowest temperature which can be used if condensation is to be avoided during the compression.

4. Point g on the isentropic line gh can be located (not without difficulty) at 1 bar and 0.30 m³ kg⁻¹ and h is fixed at the intersection of the line with the 0.01 m³ kg⁻¹ isochore. Thus the pressure, 18 bar, temperature, 490 K, and other properties of the compressed fluid can be interpolated from the lines on the chart without a trial-and-error calculation.

For low-boiling gases such as hydrogen and helium, for which we need the properties in both the two-phase region and homogeneous fluid phase, it is better to plot $\ln(T/K)$ versus S so that a large range of temperature can be covered with the same relative accuracy. Such a diagram illustrates the differences between the heat capacities.
From (3.91)

$$C_x = T(\partial S/\partial T)_x$$

Hence

$$C_x = [\partial S/\partial \ln(T/K)]_x \qquad (4.84)$$

where x is the property held constant.
Thus, in Figure 4.18 the slopes of an isochore are $(C_V)^{-1}$, those of an isobar $(C_P)^{-1}$ and those of the saturation curve $(C_\sigma)^{-1}$. Point l represents saturated liquid and g saturated vapour at the same pressure and temperature. $(C_P)^{-1}$ for the saturated liquid is the slope of the isobar al at l, $(C_V)^{-1}$ the slope of the isochore bl at l, and $(C_\sigma)^{-1}$ the slope of the saturated liquid boundary itself at

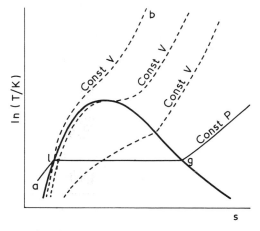

Figure 4.18. $\ln(T/K) - s$ diagram for the fluid regions of a pure substance

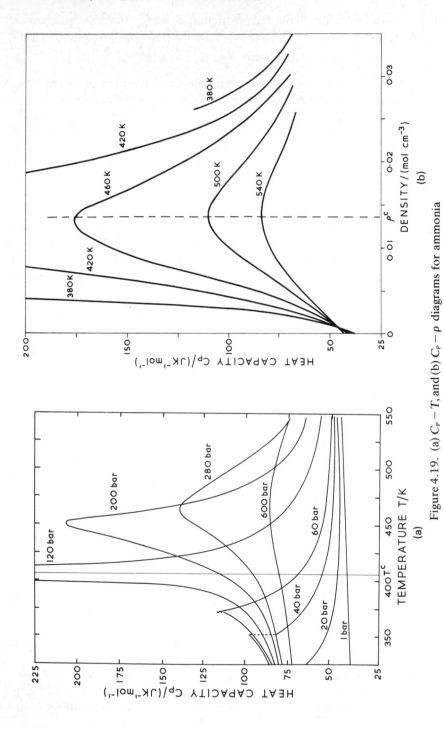

Figure 4.19. (a) $C_P - T$, and (b) $C_P - \rho$ diagrams for ammonia

l. Hence for the saturated liquid $C_V^l < C_\sigma^l < C_P^l$, and for the two-phase region, C_P is infinite. At the critical point both C_V and C_P are infinite, as is the ratio (C_P/C_V). In this figure C_σ is negative on the saturated vapour boundary and so reversible adiabatic compression of the saturated vapour cannot cause condensation. However, in the worked example in the previous section, we saw how isentropic compression of benzene vapour resulted in condensation because the heat capacity on the saturated vapour boundary is positive for this substance.

From (A.13)

$$\left(\frac{\partial S}{\partial T}\right)_\sigma = \left(\frac{\partial S}{\partial T}\right)_V + \left(\frac{\partial S}{\partial v}\right)_T \left(\frac{\partial V}{\partial T}\right)_\sigma \qquad (4.85)$$

Therefore

$$C_\sigma = C_V + T \left(\frac{\partial P}{\partial T}\right)_V \left(\frac{\partial V}{\partial T}\right)_\sigma \qquad (4.86)$$

or

$$C_\sigma^g = C_V^g + TV\gamma_V^g \alpha_\sigma^g \qquad (4.87)$$

It is a condition of thermal stability that C_V is positive and for most substances the last term in (4.87), which is negative, is large enough to make C_σ^g negative. However, for large molecules such as benzene, toluene, diphenyloxide and certain fluorinated and chlorinated hydrocarbons, C_σ^g is positive because their large heat capacity at constant volume is greater than $TV\gamma_V^g \alpha_V^g$. The difference in the shape of the saturation boundary may be seen by comparing the *T-S* chart for water in Appendix C, which has small C_v^g and a large entropy of evaporation, with that of benzene in Figure 4.17.

It is inconvenient to obtain the specific heat capacity at constant pressure, which is important for process design, from the slope of a *T-S* chart and so we often use tables or graphs in which C_P is given as a function of temperature at various pressures. Figure 4.19a shows the specific heat capacity at constant pressure for ammonia as a function of temperature, but a more simple graph is obtained if it is plotted against density as in Figure 4.19b.

H-S chart

In Figure 4.20 line *ABCDEF* on the *H-S* chart represents a reversible isobaric transition from solid at *A* to vapour at *F*. Since from (3.79), $(\partial H/\partial S)_P = T$, all lines of sublimation, melting and evaporation are straight, and the higher the temperature the steeper is the slope. Isotherms and isobars coincide in the two-phase regions, and although these lines are no longer parallel to either axis, they are tie-lines, and so the proportion of the two phases represented by a point on the lines is given by the lever rule.

The *H-S* chart, often known as a Mollier chart after its proponent, is frequently used for power-plant calculations because, as is shown in Chapter 5, the heat and work can be obtained directly. Work that appears as kinetic

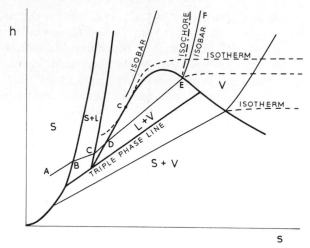

Figure 4.20. h-s diagram for a pure substance which contracts on freezing

energy in the reversible adiabatic flow of gases through nozzles ($\Delta s = 0$), or the change of state in an adiabatic throttling process ($\Delta h = 0$), are also obtained easily. The availability may be calculated by the simple construction shown in Figure 4.21. If a line of slope T_0 is drawn through the point P_0, T_0, then the stream availability B at any point on the chart is equal to the vertical distance of that point above this line. Points above the line have a positive

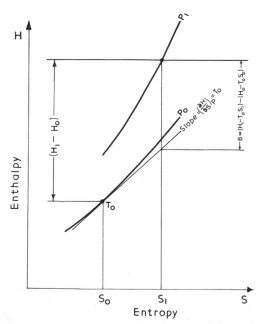

Figure 4.21. Construction used to calculate stream availability B on an H-S diagram

value for the availability, whereas points below it have a negative value. Hence the loss of availability arising from irreversible effects such as heat exchange through a non-zero difference of temperature (see Section 3.26) and by mixing two streams of the same material in different states, may be obtained.

P-H chart

The chief use of this chart is in the analysis of refrigeration processes; this is discussed in Chapter 5. The general features of the chart are shown in Figure 4.22; from (3.80), $(\partial h/\partial P)_s = v$, and so the slope of a line of constant entropy is the specific volume. If we need to show properties over a wide range of pressure, then it is more convenient to plot $\log (P/\text{bar})$ versus h, as in the chart for dichlorodifluoromethane in Appendix C.

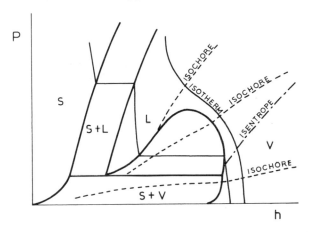

Figure 4.22. *P-h* diagram for a pure substance which contracts on freezing

It might appear from the *T-S*, *H-S* and *P-H* diagrams in Figures 4.16, 4.20 and 4.22, that there is little order in the directions which the lines of constant property take in relation to the coordinates of the diagram or in the direction across the lines of constant property along which that property increases. However, as Gibbs first pointed out, the direction and order of the lines follow certain rules which stem from the requirements for thermal and mechanical stability.[22]

We have discussed only charts of general application which are widely used to analyse thermodynamic processes. Many others have been produced for special purposes, e.g., stream availability $b = h - T_0s$ can be plotted against entropy for a fixed sink temperature T_0 and this chart used to calculate the loss of availability at each stage of a complex process. An auxiliary scale may be provided to correct for changes in the sink temperature and so increase the usefulness of the chart, but at the cost of making it less simple. Charts are generally used to carry out a rapid exploration of the thermodynamic consequences of a proposed process.

Table 4.5. Pure substances for which the thermodynamic properties are available in tabular or chart form

Substance	Reference No.
Acetylene	(6) (11k) (19)
Ammonia	(6) (17) (18a) (19)
Argon	(2) (6) (17) (21) (23) (30)
Benzene	(11l) (33)
i-Butane	(1) (11f) (19)
n-Butane	(1) (11d) (17) (19)
1-Butene	(5) (11j) (19)
Carbon Dioxide	(2) (4) (5) (6) (17) (18b) (19) (20)
Carbon Monoxide	(2) (6) (13) (18c) (19)
Carbon Tetrafluoride	(17)
Cyclopropane	(27)
n-Decane	(1)
Dichlorodifluoromethane	(17)
Dichloromonofluoromethane	(17)
Dichlorotetrafluoroethane	(17)
Ethane	(1) (6) (11b) (17) (19) (29)
Ethylene	(3) (6) (11h) (17) (19) (35)
Helium	(7) (10) (17) (32)
n-Hexane	(11g) (19)
n-Hydrogen	(2) (15) (17) (18d) (19)
p-Hydrogen	(12) (17)
Hydrogen sulphide	(5)
Methane	(1) (6) (8) (11a) (17) (19) (24) (28)
Methyl Chloride	(17)
Monochlorodifluoromethane	(17)
Monochlorotrifluoromethane	(17)
Neon	(16) (17)
Neopentane	(33)
Nitrogen	(1) (6) (9) (17) (18e) (19) (23)
Nitrous Oxide	(17)
n-Nonane	(5)
Oxygen	(2) (17) (18f) (19) (23) (25) (31)
n-Pentane	(1) (11e) (19)
Perfluorocyclobutane	(14)
Propane	(1) (6) (11c) (17) (19)
Propylene	(5) (11i) (17) (19)
Sulphur Dioxide	(17) (18g) (19)
Trichloromonofluoromethane	(17)
Trichlorotrifluoroethane	(17)
Water	(2) (18h) (19) (22) (26)

Their use avoids the trial-and-error calculations and interpolations often involved in using tables, but their accuracy is limited by their size. Although large charts have been published,[6] it is better to use tables in the final analysis. We see, therefore, that charts and tables are complementary. However, thermodynamic tables, unlike logarithm tables, are not always accurate to the number of significant figures given and their extrapolation is dangerous.

In spite of much experimentation over the past century, the properties of many substances have not been measured, or are not known as accurately as might be wished, over the wide ranges of pressure and temperature used in chemical processes. A bibliography of the main sources of information on the properties needed for the calculation of heat and work is given in the following section. We see from Table 4.5 that there are relatively few substances for which we have thermodynamic charts and tables; hence, we often need to predict the properties of substances from what we know of their constituent molecules. We cannot do this by the methods of classical thermodynamics alone, and so defer the subject to Chapter 9.

4.19 Bibliography of thermodynamic tables and charts

This bibliography includes only references to publications after 1950 in which values of P, T, v, h and s for the pure substances listed in Table 4.5 are presented in tabular or chart form; it does not include abridged thermodynamic tables compiled for the solution of problems by students. In many references other thermodynamic properties such as compression factors, fugacity-pressure ratios and heat capacities are given. An extensive review[23] of the literature published since 1950 up to the end of 1971 should be consulted for sources of information on individual thermodynamic properties for pure substances not included in Table 4.5.

References in chronological order

1. B. H. Sage and W. N. Lacey, Monograph on API Research Project 37, American Petroleum Institute, New York, 1950.
2. J. Hilsenrath et al., Nat. Bur. Stand. Circular 564, Washington, 1955.
3. H. Benzler and A. V. Koch, Chem. Ing. Tech. 27 (1955), 71.
4. F. Cramer, Chem. Ing. Tech. 27 (1955), 484.
5. B. H. Sage and W. N. Lacey, Monograph on API Research Project 37, American Petroleum Institute, New York, 1955.
6. F. Din, Thermodynamic Functions of Gases, Vol. 1-3, Butterworth, London, 1956-61.
7. D. B. Mann and R. B. Stewart, Nat. Bur. Stand. Tech. Note 8, Washington, 1959.
8. W. C. Edmister, Applied Hydrocarbon Thermodynamics, Gulf Publishing Co., Houston, 1961.
9. T. R. Strobridge, Nat. Bur. Stand. Tech. Note 129, Washington, 1962.
10. D. B. Mann, Nat. Bur. Stand. Tech. Note 154, Washington, 1962.
11. L. N. Canjar et al., Hydrocarbon processing and petroleum refiner, (a) 41 (1962), (9) 291; (b) (10) 149; (c) (11) 203; (d) (12) 115; (e) 42 (1963), (1) 129; (f) (8) 127; (g) 43 (1964), (6) 177; (h) 44 (1965), (9) 219; (i) (10) 137; (j) (10) 141; (k) (11) 293; (l) (11) 297.
12. H. M. Roder, L. A. Weber and R. D. Goodwin, Nat. Bur. Stand. Monograph 94, Washington, 1963.
13. J. G. Hurst and R. B. Stewart, Nat. Bur. Stand. Tech. Note 202, Washington, 1963.
14. R. H. Harrison and D. R. Douslin, Perfluorocyclobutane: the thermodynamic properties of the real gas, U.S. Dept. of Interior, Bureau of Mines, Washington (1964).

15. R. F. Kubin and L. L. Presley, *Nat. Aero. Space Admin.* S.P.3002, Washington, 1964.

16. R. D. McCarty and R. B. Stewart, *Advances in Thermophysical Properties at Extreme Temperatures and Pressures*, ASME, New York, 1965, p. 84.

17. *ASHRAE Thermodynamic Properties of Refrigerants*, Am. Soc. of Heating Refrig., Air. Cond. Engrs., New York, 1969.

18. L. N. Canjar *et al.*, *Hydrocarbon Processing* **45** (1966), (a) (1) 135;   (b) (1) 139;   (c) (2) 158;   (d) (2) 161;   (e) (3) 137;   (f) (3) 143;   (g) (4) 161;   (h) (4) 165.

19. L. N. Canjar and F. S. Manning, *Thermodynamic Properties and Reduced Correlations for Gases*, Gulf Publishing Co., Houston, 1967.

20. M. P. Vukalovich and V. V. Altunin, *Thermophysical Properties of Carbon Dioxide*, Colletts, London, 1968.

21. A. L. Gosman, R. D. McCarty and J. G. Hurst, *National Standards Reference Data Series NSRDS-NBS* 27, Washington, 1969.

22. J. H. Keenan, F. G. Keyes, P. G. Hill and J. G. Moore, *Steam Tables—International Edition in S.I. Units*, Wiley, New York, 1969.

23. A. A. Vasserman and V. A. Rabinovich, *Thermophysical Properties of Liquid Air and its Properties*. Israel Program for scientific translations, Jerusalem, 1970.

24. V. A. Zagoruchenko and A. M. Zhuravlev, *Thermophysical Properties of Gaseous and Liquid Methane*, U.S. Dept. Commerce, Washington, 1970.

25. L. A. Weber, *J. Res. Nat. Bur. Stand.* **74A** (1970), 93.

26. *U.K. Steam Tables in SI Units*, Arnold, London, 1970.

27. D. C. K. Lin, J. J. McKetta and I. H. Silberberg, *J. chem. Eng. Data* **16** (1971), 416.

28. K. E. Starling, *Hydrocarbon processing*, **50** (1971), (4) 139.

29. K. E. Starling and Y. C. Kwok, *Hydrocarbon processing*, **50** (1971), (4) 140.

30. S. Angus and B. Armstrong, *International Thermodynamic Tables of the Fluid State, Argon 1971*, Butterworth, London, 1972.

31. H. M. Roder and L. A. Weber, *Oxygen Technology Survey*, vol. 1, 'Thermophysical properties', N.A.S.A., Washington, 1972.

32. R. D. McCarty, 'Thermophysical properties of helium-4', *Nat. Bur. Stands. Tech. Note* 622, U.S. Dept. Commerce, Washington, (1972).

33. 'Thermodynamic properties of benzene', Engineering Sciences Data Unit, Item No. 73009, London, 1973.

34. P. P. Dawson and J. J. McKetta, *J. chem. Eng. Data* **18** (1973), 76.

35. S. Angus, B. Armstrong and K. M. de Reuck, *International Thermodynamic Tables of the Fluid State, Ethylene, 1972*, Butterworth, London, 1974.

Problems

1. Some textbooks give the conditions of thermal and mechanical stability as $(\partial S/\partial T)_P > 0$ and $(\partial P/\partial V)_S < 0$ respectively. Show that these conditions are consistent with those given in equations (4.1) and (4.2).

2. A three-phase system consisting of ice, liquid water and water vapour has an overall specific volume of $50 \text{ m}^3 \text{ kg}^{-1}$ and an enthalpy of 500 kJ kg^{-1} calculated on the basis that the enthalpy of liquid water at the triple point is zero. From tables of the thermodynamic properties of steam determine the relative masses of the three phases present.

3. Use the tabulated properties of water to show that at the triple point the sublimation curve in P-T co-ordinates has a greater slope than the vapour pressure curve.

4. From the data given in Table 4.4 calculate what percentage of the volume of a tube must be occupied by liquid benzene at 1 bar pressure (the remainder being benzene vapour) so that when the tube is sealed and heated the contents will pass through the critical state. How much heat must be added to the contents of the tube between 1 bar and the critical state if the enclosed volume is 5 cm^3?

5. From Figure 4.8b estimate the pressure which would be developed by storing 120 kg of methane in a vessel of 0.5 m^3 at 350 K.

6. From the values of the fugacity–pressure ratio for methane given in Figure 4.9 estimate the work needed to compress 1 mole of methane from 250 bar to 1000 bar at 350 K.

7. From the following table of experimentally measured compression factors for methane at 181.9 K evaluate the second and third virial coefficients and compare the former with that given in Figure 4.10.

P/bar	Z
30.58	0.652
24.74	0.745
18.82	0.819
13.67	0.875
9.62	0.915
6.62	0.943

8. The equation of state of a gas may be written

$$Pv = RT + B''P + C''P^2$$

in which the coefficients B'' and C'' are functions of temperature only. Derive an equation for the Joule-Thomson inversion curve in the form $P = f(T, B'', C'')$.

9. Express the van der Waals equation in the form of the virial equation and obtain an expression for the second virial coefficient in terms of the van der Waals constants.

10. The relationships between the van der Waals constants and the critical properties are given in equation (4.27). For a van der Waals gas show (a) that the Boyle temperature $T^b = 27T^c/8$, and compare the experimentally measured value for methane given in Figure 4.8b with that calculated from the

critical temperature given in Table 4.3; and (b) that the compression factor at the critical point $Z^c = \frac{3}{8}$, and compare this value with those calculated for the substances given in Table 4.1.

11. Calculate the van der Waals constants for carbon dioxide from the critical pressure and temperature given in Table 4.1 thence the volume occupied by 5 kg of the gas at 50 bar and 100 °C. Compare the calculated value with that obtained from tables of the thermodynamic properties of carbon dioxide see ref. 6, page 173.

12. Show that the slope of a line at constant temperature on an H-S chart is equal to $[T-(1/\alpha)]$ and that of a line at constant volume is equal to $[T+(\gamma-1)/\alpha]$ where $\gamma = C_P/C_V$ and $\alpha = (1/V)(\partial V/\partial T)_P$.

13. Sketch the T-s diagram for a perfect gas showing lines of constant P, v, u and h. Show that at a given temperature the slope of a line at constant volume is greater than that of the line at constant pressure and that the ratio of the two slopes is $\gamma = C_P/C_V$. For a real gas show that

$$(\partial T/\partial S)_U = (T/C_V)[1-(T/P)(\partial P/\partial T)_V]$$
$$(\partial T/\partial S)_H = (T/C_P)[1-(T/V)(\partial V/\partial T)_P]$$

14. With the aid of tables of the thermodynamic properties of steam, calculate (a) the quality of steam at a pressure of 9 bar, if, after adiabatic throttling to 1.013 bar, the temperature is 115 °C; (b) the minimum temperature to which steam at 30 bar must be superheated if no saturated water is to form as a result of reversible adiabatic expansion to 1 bar.

15. With the aid of the P-h chart for dichlorodifluoromethane given in Appendix C, estimate for this substance

(a) the boiling point at 1 bar;
(b) the vapour pressure at 340 K;
(c) the latent heat of evaporation at 1 bar;
(d) the entropy of evaporation at 1 bar;
(e) the final temperature if gas at 1 bar 300 K is compressed reversibly and adiabatically in a steady state flow device to 100 bar;
(f) the work required for process (e);
(g) the heat transfer, if gas at 1 bar 400 K is compressed reversibly and isothermally in a steady state flow device to 100 bar;
(h) the work required for process (g);
(i) the quality of the resulting mixture if gas at 100 bar 400 K is throttled adiabatically to 5 bar;
(j) the drop in temperature during process (i);

(k) the maximum pressure on the downstream side of the throttle in process (i) to ensure that all the liquid is evaporated;

(l) at any convenient point on the chart, confirm that $(\partial h/\partial P)_s = v$.

16. With the aid of the T-s chart for water given in Appendix C, estimate:

(a) the temperature at which saturated steam at 0.1 bar completely condenses;

(b) the heat transfer needed in process (a);

(c) the volume change in process (a);

(d) the temperature at which the last drop of water will evaporate if steam of quality 0.1 at 1 bar is heated at constant volume;

(e) the heat required to evaporate the water in process (d);

(f) the drop in temperature if steam at 200 bar 1000 K is throttled adiabatically to 1 bar;

(g) the drop in temperature if steam at 200 bar 1000 K is expanded reversibly and adiabatically in a steady state flow device to 1 bar;

(h) the work obtained from process (g);

(i) the quality of the steam leaving the steady state flow device in process (g);

(j) the work needed to compress 1 kg of steam at 0.05 bar 720 K reversibly and isothermally to 200 bar in a closed system.

(k) the heat which has to be removed in process (j);

(l) c_P for steam at 1 bar 700 K;

(m) c_V for steam at 1 bar 700 K.

Answers

2. $m^s : m^l : m^g = 0.316 : 0.442 : 0.242$.

4. Percentage occupied $= 37.1$, heat required $= 822$ J.

5. $P = 550$ bar.

6. Work $= 5.03$ kJ mol^{-1}.

7. $B = -125$ cm^3 mol^{-1}, $C = 4200$ cm^6 mol^{-2}.

8. $P = -[T(dB''/dT) - B'']/[T(dC''/dT) - C'']$.

9. $B = b - a/(RT)$.

10. (a) Calculated Boyle temperature $= 645$ K, experimental $= 505$ K. (b) Z^c for helium $= 0.306$, for hydrogen $= 0.312$, for carbon dioxide $= 0.276$, for water $= 0.235$, for mercury $= 0.41$.

11. $a = 0.3656 \, \text{N m}^4 \, \text{mol}^{-2}$, $b = 4.283 \times 10^{-5} \, \text{m}^3 \, \text{mol}^{-1}$, calculated volume = $0.06115 \, \text{m}^3$, experimental volume = $0.06025 \, \text{m}^3$.

14. Quality = 0.97. Temperature = 546 °C.

15. (a) 243 K   (b) 18 bar   (c) 169 kJ kg^{-1} (d) 0.69 kJ kg^{-1} K^{-1}
    (e) 515 K   (f) 110 kJ kg^{-1} (g) -214 kJ kg^{-1} (h) 109 kJ kg^{-1}
    (i) 0.8   (j) 110 K   (k) 0.35 bar.

16. (a) 320 K   (b) 2420 kJ kg^{-1} (c) 14 m^3 kg^{-1} (d) 480 K
    (e) 1800 kJ kg^{-1} (f) 50 K   (g) 625 K   (h) 1400 kJ kg^{-1}
    (i) 0.93   (j) 2620 kJ   (k) 3020 kJ   (l) ~ 2.1 kJ kg^{-1} K^{-1}
    (m) ~ 1.7 kJ kg^{-1} K^{-1}.

Notes

1. A. Weissberger and B. W. Rossiter, *Physical Methods of Chemistry*, Part V, 'Determination of thermodynamic and surface properties'. Wiley, Chichester, 1971, p. 47.

2. D. Ambrose, *Chemical Thermodynamics*, Vol. 1, Chapter 7, 'Vapour Pressures'. The Chemical Society, 1973, p. 218.

3. K. A. Kobe and R. E. Lynn, *Chem. Rev.* **52** (1953), 117.

4. A. P. Kudchadker, G. H. Alani and B. J. Zwolinski, *Chem. Rev.* **68** (1968), 659.

5. J. F. Matthews, *Chem. Rev.* **72** (1972), 71.

6. J. S. Rowlinson, 'The Properties of Real Gases' in *Handbuch der Physik*, Vol. 12, Chapter 1 (ed. S. Flügge), Springer, Berlin, 1958.

7. G. Saville, *Experimental Thermodynamics*, Vol. 2, 'Measurement of P-V-T-Properties of Gases and Gas Mixtures at Low Pressure', Butterworth, London, 1971, p. 321.

8. M. W. Zemansky, *Heat and Thermodynamics*, 4th edn, McGraw-Hill, New York, 1957, p. 205.

9. P. W. Bridgman, *The Physics of High Pressure*, Bell, London, 1952.

10. J. H. Dymond and E. B. Smith, *The Virial Coefficients of Gases—A critical compilation*, Clarendon Press, Oxford, 1969.

11. E. A. Mason and T. H. Spurling, *The Virial Equation of State*, Pergamon Press, Oxford, 1969.

12. J. J. Martin, *Ind. Eng. Chem.* **59** (1967), (12) 34.

13. M. Benedict, G. B. Webb and L. C. Rubin, *Eng. Chem. Progress*, **47** (1951), 419.

14. M. Benedict, F. Solomon and L. C. Rubin, *Ind. Eng. Chem.* **37** (1945), 55.

15. H. W. Cooper and J. C. Goldfrank, *Hydrocarbon Processing*, **46** (12) (1967), 141.

16. E. Bender, *The calculation of phase equilibria for a thermal equation of state applied to the pure fluids argon, nitrogen, oxygen and their mixtures*, Müller, Karlsruhe, 1973.

17. H. E. Stanley, *Introduction to Phase Transitions and Critical Phenomena*, Clarendon Press, Oxford, 1971; M. Vincenti-Missoni, in *Phase Transitions and Critical Phenomena*, Chapter 2 (ed. C. Domb and M. S. Green), Academic Press, London, 1972.

18. G. A. Chapela and J. S. Rowlinson, *J.C.S. Faraday Trans.* I, **70** (1974), 584, 2368.

19. J. Timmermans, *Physico-chemical Constants of Pure Organic Compounds,* Elsevier, New York, Vol. 1, 1950, Vol. 2, 1965.

20. J. S. Rowlinson, *Liquids and Liquid Mixtures,* 2nd edn, Butterworth, London, 1969, p. 32.

21. *Chemical Thermodynamics,* Vol. 1, The Chemical Society, London, 1973, p. 254.

22. J. H. Keenan, *Thermodynamics,* Chapter 14, M.I.T. Press, Cambridge, Mass., 1970.

23. *Chemical Thermodynamics,* Vol. 1., The Chemical Society, London, 1973.

5 Devices for the transfer of heat and work

In this chapter we apply the first and second laws of thermodynamics to plant for the compression, expansion, cooling and liquefaction of gases, and to the simultaneous production of heat and work for chemical processes. Gas turbines and reciprocating internal combustion engines are not discussed since they are not considered to be of prime importance to chemical engineers, and reference should be made to other texts[1] for an analysis of these machines.

Only those mechanical details needed to understand the thermodynamic processes are included, and it must be remembered that the design of any plant involves other sciences, such as the mechanics of machines and the strength of materials. Throughout this chapter emphasis is placed on establishing the limiting thermodynamic efficiency of various processes against which actual plant performance, governed in part by economic considerations, may be assessed.

In many applications involving the flow of fluids, the principles of both fluid mechanics and thermodynamics must be applied, and there is no clear distinction between the areas covered by these subjects. We begin this chapter with a short account of the flow of fluids through ducts, so that we may discuss the performance of turbo-compressors and expanders which play an important part in refrigeration and gas liquefaction without having to use concepts which are more appropriate to a study of fluid mechanics.

5.1 Flow of fluids in ducts

The application of thermodynamics to the flow of fluids in ducts is limited to interrelating the various energy terms and to establishing ideal flow conditions. Thermodynamics cannot answer questions related to the mechanism of flow, such as the pressure drop arising from friction between the fluid and the walls of the duct, or within the fluid itself. These topics form the subject of *fluid dynamics*, and in particular that branch dealing with compressible flow known as *gas dynamics*.

We confine our discussion to the steady-state flow of a fluid in a horizontal duct for which there is no change in potential energy. If no work is done by the fluid then from (2.15) the first law for the system may be written

$$\Delta H = Q - (\text{KE}_{\text{out}} - \text{KE}_{\text{in}}) \tag{5.1}$$

Or, in differential form,

$$dH = dQ - d(\text{KE}) \tag{5.2}$$

It was shown from mechanical considerations, see (2.18), that for reversible (that is, frictionless) flow

$$\int V\,dP + (\text{KE}_{\text{out}} - \text{KE}_{\text{in}}) = 0 \tag{5.3}$$

or, in differential form

$$V\,dP + d(\text{KE}) = 0 \tag{5.4}$$

(We note also that this equation can be derived from the fundamental equation $dH = T\,dS + V\,dP$ (3.74), since for a reversible process $dQ = T\,dS$, and substitution into (5.2) gives (5.4).)

The requirement of reversibility is a severe restriction when applied to flow through ducts. Viscous forces, turbulence and other frictional resistances all causes irreversibility and if equations based on reversibility are to hold, the thermal energy generated by them must be small compared with the $\int V\,dP$ of (5.3). This will be so only if the duct is short and the pressure drop sufficiently large; but in addition, since the latter necessitates changes in cross-sectional area along the length of the duct, negligible turbulence requires the transition from one region to the next to be smooth, as in Figure 5.1. In practice, the equations we derive are applicable to flow through valves or similar constrictions, to flow through the nozzles of a turbine and to flow through ejectors and injectors used for pumping fluids. They are not applicable to flow through pipelines.

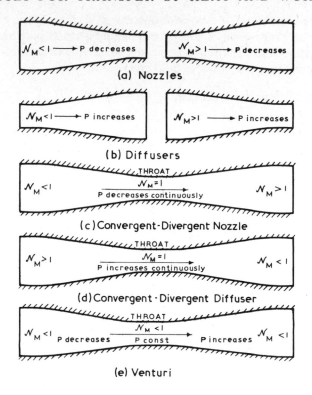

Figure 5.1. Flow in ducts of varying area

We further restrict our discussion to situations in which the flow velocity is sufficiently high for the process to be adiabatic. In such cases, the entropy of the fluid is the same at all positions along the duct whatever its shape, and changes in cross-sectional area produce changes only in other thermodynamic properties.

Equations (5.1) and (5.3) applied to two sections, 1 and 2, perpendicular to the stream give, for flow of unit mass of fluid,

$$(h_2 - h_1) + \tfrac{1}{2}(\mathcal{V}_2^2 - \mathcal{V}_1^2) = 0 \tag{5.5}$$

and

$$\int_1^2 v \, dP + \tfrac{1}{2}(\mathcal{V}_2^2 - \mathcal{V}_1^2) = 0 \tag{5.6}$$

The mass flow rate $\dot{m}$ through the duct is constant; hence, the flow velocity $\mathcal{V}$ at any position along the duct is given by

$$\mathcal{A}\mathcal{V}/v = \dot{m} = \text{const} \tag{5.7}$$

where $\mathcal{A}$ is the area of the duct at the section under consideration.

A duct of varying area, so designed that a drop in pressure from inlet to outlet accelerates the flow, is called a *nozzle*, whereas a *diffuser* is so shaped that the fluid flowing through it decelerates thus producing an increase in pressure. For frictionless flow through a nozzle or diffuser, from (5.4),

$$v \, dP + \mathcal{V} \, d\mathcal{V} = 0 \tag{5.8}$$

and from (5.7)

$$d\mathcal{A}/\mathcal{A} + d\mathcal{V}/\mathcal{V} - dv/v = 0 \tag{5.9}$$

hence,

$$\frac{d\mathcal{A}}{\mathcal{A}} = v \, dP \left(\frac{1}{\mathcal{V}^2} + \frac{1}{v^2} \frac{dv}{dP} \right) \tag{5.10}$$

Since the flow is isentropic, from (3.168)

$$\left(\frac{dP}{dv} \right)_s = - \frac{\mathcal{W}^2}{v^2} \tag{5.11}$$

and thus

$$\frac{d\mathcal{A}}{\mathcal{A}} = v \, dP \left(\frac{1}{\mathcal{V}^2} - \frac{1}{\mathcal{W}^2} \right) \tag{5.12}$$

where $\mathcal{W}$ is the local speed of sound in the fluid at the section where the pressure is P and the specific volume v.

Equation (5.12) enables us to draw the following conclusions about the correct shapes of nozzles and diffusers. For a nozzle, $dP < 0$; if flow is subsonic ($\mathcal{V} < \mathcal{W}$), (5.12) gives $d\mathcal{A} < 0$, that is, the nozzle converges; if flow is supersonic ($\mathcal{V} > \mathcal{W}$), $d\mathcal{A} > 0$ and the nozzle diverges. For a diffuser, $dP > 0$; if flow is subsonic ($\mathcal{V} < \mathcal{W}$), $d\mathcal{A} > 0$ and the diffuser diverges; if flow is supersonic ($\mathcal{V} > \mathcal{W}$), $d\mathcal{A} < 0$ and the diffuser converges. These conclusions are summarised in Figure 5.1a and b in which the Mach number $\mathcal{N}_M$ is defined as

$$\mathcal{N}_M = \mathcal{V}/\mathcal{W}$$

When $\mathcal{N}_M = 1$, that is, the fluid velocity is equal to the speed of sound, $d\mathcal{A} = 0$. Thus sonic velocity can be achieved only in that region of the nozzle or diffuser known as the *throat* where the area is constant. Conversely, if a duct has a throat and the pressure gradient does not change sign at any point along it, then $\mathcal{V} = \mathcal{W}$ in the throat. Thus if flow is to be accelerated continuously from subsonic to supersonic velocity in a nozzle or decelerated from supersonic to subsonic in a diffuser, both nozzle and diffuser must have a throat, see Figure 5.1c and d.

The presence of a throat does not necessarily mean that the velocity there is sonic. Figure 5.1e shows a *venturi*, that is, a duct in which subsonic flow is first accelerated and then decelerated without sonic velocity ever being reached. In this case, the condition in the throat is characterised by $d\mathcal{V} = 0$, and hence $dP = 0$.

Although these conclusions apply to all fluids, the high speed of sound in liquids, $\sim 1500 \text{ m s}^{-1}$, makes it impracticable to achieve sonic liquid velocities. Hence nozzles for high velocity liquid jets, such as those used for rock-cutting or fire-fighting, are always convergent.

Problems involving the isentropic flow of a fluid from state 1 to state 2 can be solved by using either (5.5) or (5.6). Equation (5.5) requires a table or chart of thermodynamic properties of the fluid, whereas (5.6) requires an equation of state for the fluid from which v may be evaluated as a function of P along a path of constant entropy.

5.2   Isentropic expansion of fluids in nozzles

We now examine the flow of fluid through a nozzle of arbitrary shape. For simplicity we assume that the cross-sectional area $\mathscr{A}_1$ at the inlet to the nozzle, see Figure 5.2a, is so large that $\mathscr{V}_1$ is negligible.

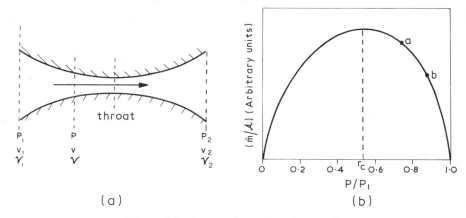

Figure 5.2. Converging—diverging nozzle

(a) Incompressible fluid

If the fluid is incompressible, that is the volume, v, is independent of P, then from (5.3)

$$v(P - P_1) + \tfrac{1}{2}(\mathscr{V}^2 - \mathscr{V}_1^2) = 0 \tag{5.13}$$

Since $\mathscr{V}_1 = 0$

$$\mathscr{V}^2 = 2v(P_1 - P) \tag{5.14}$$

From (5.7)

$$\left(\frac{\dot{m}}{\mathscr{A}}\right)^2 = \left(\frac{\mathscr{V}}{v}\right)^2 = \frac{2(P_1 - P)}{v} \tag{5.15}$$

and, since P falls steadily from inlet to outlet, where the pressure is P_2, the nozzle must be everywhere convergent.

Under most conditions, liquids have small coefficients of compressibility and equations (5.13) and (5.15) may be used without appreciable error. The equations, however, are not restricted to liquids and, in texts on fluid mechanics, a gas is often treated as *incompressible* (the term *uncompressed* would be more appropriate), if conditions are such that the density changes little during the process. Under these approximations, the first law equation becomes

$$\Delta h = v\,\Delta P$$

and the temperature change can be calculated from

$$\Delta h = c_P\,\Delta T$$

if the heat capacity does not vary with pressure and temperature. Note that, although incompressible flow implies constant volume, it is Δh which is the appropriate energy change and not Δu (cf. Section 2.11).

Example

Calculate the mass flow rate and the velocity of a jet of water emerging from a converging nozzle of outlet diameter 1 cm, if the water supply is at a pressure 10 bar above atmospheric.

$$\{2(P_1 - P_2)/v\}^{1/2} = \{2\times 10^6/10^{-3}\}^{1/2} = 4.47\times 10^4 \text{ kg m}^{-2}\text{ s}^{-1}$$

$$\text{Mass flow rate } \dot{m} = 4.47\times 10^4\times(\pi\times 0.005^2) = 3.51 \text{ kg s}^{-1}$$

$$\text{Velocity of jet } \mathcal{V}_2 = 4.47\times 10^4\times 10^{-3} = 44.7 \text{ m s}^{-1}$$

(b) Perfect gas

From (3.143) the isentropic expansion of unit mass of a perfect gas can be represented by

$$Pv^\gamma = \text{const} \qquad \text{(pg)} \qquad\qquad (5.16)$$

if $\gamma = c_P/c_V$ is independent of temperature, as we assume here. Hence,

$$\int v\,dP = \gamma(Pv - P_1 v_1)/(\gamma - 1) \qquad \text{(pg)} \qquad\qquad (5.17)$$

From (5.6), putting $\mathcal{V}_1 = 0$

$$\int v\,dP + \tfrac{1}{2}\mathcal{V}^2 = 0 \qquad\qquad (5.18)$$

From (5.16), (5.17) and (5.18)

$$\mathcal{V}^2 = \frac{2\gamma}{\gamma - 1}P_1 v_1\left\{1 - \left(\frac{P}{P_1}\right)^{(\gamma-1)/\gamma}\right\} \qquad \text{(pg)} \qquad\qquad (5.19)$$

From (5.7) and (5.16)

$$\frac{\dot{m}}{\mathscr{A}} = \frac{\mathscr{V}}{v} = \frac{\mathscr{V}}{v_1}\left(\frac{P}{P_1}\right)^{1/\gamma} \quad \text{(pg)} \tag{5.20}$$

and from (5.19) and (5.20)

$$\left(\frac{\dot{m}}{\mathscr{A}}\right)^2 = \frac{2\gamma}{\gamma-1}\frac{P_1}{v_1}\left\{\left(\frac{P}{P_1}\right)^{2/\gamma} - \left(\frac{P}{P_1}\right)^{(\gamma+1)/\gamma}\right\} \quad \text{(pg)} \tag{5.21}$$

Figure 5.2b shows $\dot{m}/\mathscr{A}$ plotted as a function of P/P_1 for $\gamma = 1.4$. We observe that $\dot{m}/\mathscr{A}$ goes through a maximum, which means the duct has a throat in which the velocity of flow, $\mathscr{V}$, is sonic. The pressure ratio at which it occurs is called the *critical pressure ratio* r_c (not to be confused with the gas-liquid critical point defined in Section 4.2, with which it has no connection). For a perfect gas with constant γ, we find that r_c is independent of P and T, and its value can be found by differentiating (5.21) with respect to P and setting the resulting equation to zero. We obtain:

$$r_c = \frac{P_t}{P_1} = \left(\frac{2}{\gamma+1}\right)^{\gamma/(\gamma-1)} \quad \text{(pg)} \tag{5.22}$$

where P_t is the pressure in the throat. For a monatomic gas (which has $\gamma = \tfrac{5}{3}$), $r_c = 0.49$; for simple diatomic gases such as oxygen and nitrogen ($\gamma = \tfrac{7}{5}$), $r_c = 0.53$; and for more complicated molecules, r_c is slightly higher still.

Exercise

Show that for the isentropic expansion of a perfect gas with constant γ, the velocity in the throat is

$$\mathscr{V}_t^2 = \frac{2\gamma}{\gamma+1}P_1v_1 \quad \text{(pg)} \tag{5.23}$$

and that this is equal to the local speed of sound.

We conclude that if a nozzle is to be used for reducing the pressure of a flowing fluid to the extent that P_2/P_1, see Figure 5.2a, is less than r_c, then it must be of the converging-diverging type. Furthermore, the divergent part of the nozzle following the throat must expand to exactly the right area if the pressure reduction is to be brought about reversibly. If it does not, the flow will be irreversible (see next section). Thus, we can calculate from Figure 5.2b that if the pressure is to be reduced until $P_2/P_1 = 0.2$, the area of the nozzle at the outlet should be 1.34 times that at the throat.

Substituting (5.22) into (5.21) gives the mass flow rate per unit throat area as

$$\left(\frac{\dot{m}}{\mathscr{A}_t}\right)^2 = \frac{P_1}{v_1}\gamma\left(\frac{2}{\gamma+1}\right)^{(\gamma+1)/(\gamma-1)} \quad \text{(pg)} \tag{5.24}$$

or

$$\left(\frac{\dot{m}}{\mathscr{A}_t}\right)^2 = \frac{P_1^2}{n_mRT_1}\gamma\left(\frac{2}{\gamma+1}\right)^{(\gamma+1)/(\gamma-1)} \quad \text{(pg)} \tag{5.25}$$

where v_1 is replaced by $n_m RT_1/P_1$ where n_m is the number of moles per unit mass. Thus provided that P_2 is sufficiently small for P_2/P_1 to be less than r_c, the mass flow rate per unit throat area is a function only of the nature of the gas and the inlet conditions.

If the pressure drop through the nozzle is such that P_2/P_1 is greater than r_c, (5.24) and (5.25) do not apply and we must return to (5.21). We see from this, and from Figure 5.2b, that for these small pressure drops a simple converging nozzle will suffice, the value of $\dot{m}/\mathscr{A}$ being obtained by replacing P by P_2. However, an alternative solution is the venturi. This is a converging-diverging duct in which the sonic flow characteristics described above are suppressed by the high discharge pressure P_2. As the fluid flows through the duct, the state follows the path starting at $\dot{m}/\mathscr{A} = 0$, $P/P_1 = 1$ as before, see Figure 5.2b, but the throat is reached, e.g. at a, before the curve has reached its maximum. Since the duct now opens out, the state can only retrace its path back towards the origin, the pressure increasing again as it does so. That is, the diverging section of the venturi is a diffuser. If the exit of the duct is reached at b, no further compression results and the pressure at this point is therefore P_2. Clearly, at no point in the duct does the value of P/P_1 fall to r_c. We note also that for a given duct, the mass flow rate $\dot{m}$ is always less in the case of a venturi than when the same duct is used as a nozzle in which the velocity in the throat is sonic. Thus (5.25) gives the maximum possible flow rate for reversible flow of fluid through a converging-diverging nozzle, and, as we see in the next section, it is not exceeded even when flow is irreversible. For this reason (5.25) is frequently used to calculate the relieving capacity of safety valves.

Example

A safety valve with a discharge area of 1 cm^2 at its narrowest section is used to vent a receiver for nitrogen when the pressure exceeds 10 bar. What is the flow rate through the valve?
For nitrogen
$$\gamma = 1.4$$
$$n_m = 1000/28 = 35.7 \text{ mol kg}^{-1}$$

If ambient pressure is ~1 bar, P_2/P_1 is less than the critical ratio r_c $(= 0.53)$ and we can use (5.25). Assuming ambient temperature is 290 K

$$\frac{\dot{m}}{\mathscr{A}_t} = 10^6 \left\{ \frac{1.4}{35.7 \times 8.314 \times 290} \left(\frac{2}{2.4} \right)^{2.4/0.4} \right\}^{1/2}$$
$$= 2330 \text{ kg m}^{-2} \text{ s}^{-1}$$
$$\dot{m} = 2330 \times 10^{-4} = 0.223 \text{ kg s}^{-1}$$

(c) Real fluid

In the case of a real fluid for which approximations (a) and (b) are inadequate, the flow characteristics within the nozzle, $\mathscr{V}$ and $\dot{m}/\mathscr{A}$, can be obtained from

(5.5) and (5.7) and tables or charts of the thermodynamic properties of the substance. Figure 5.3a illustrates the four types of reversible adiabatic path. Path ab is entirely in the liquid, cd begins in the liquid and ends in the two-phase region, ef begins in the gas and ends in the two-phase region and gh is entirely in the gas. The quantities $\mathcal{V}$ and $\dot{m}/\mathcal{A}$ can both be represented most conveniently as functions of P/P_1, where P_1 is the inlet pressure and P is the pressure at some

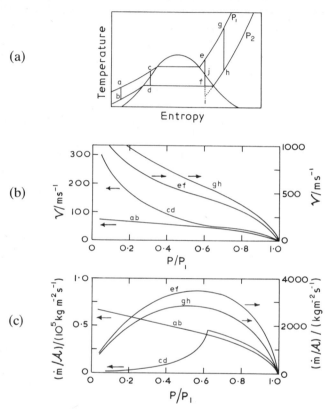

Figure 5.3. Flow characteristics for the isentropic expansion of water and steam

section within the nozzle. Figures 5.3b and 5.3c give the results of calculations on water. The inlet pressure, P_1, is 25 bar in each case and the initial temperatures, corresponding to points a, c, e and g, are 360 K, 470 K, 530 K and 790 K respectively. In both cd and ef, it is assumed that, once the two-phase region has been entered, the liquid and vapour are in equilibrium at all positions along the nozzle. This is probably true in practice for cd, but condensation, as in ef, is not usually instantaneous and may not have time to occur in a nozzle where the flow velocity is high. An alternative procedure, therefore, involves extrapolation of the gas-phase isobars into the two-phase region so that, for example, the state along the isobar P_2 is represented by i rather than f. Between j and i, the gas is said to be *supersaturated* or *supercooled* and the path metastable (see Section 1.2).

The curves ab are similar to those for an incompressible fluid derived from (5.14) and (5.15). There is no maximum in $\dot{m}/\mathcal{A}$, since the nozzle must converge everywhere. The curves gh resemble those for a perfect gas as discussed above. Again, the maximum in $\dot{m}/\mathcal{A}$ means that, if a pressure ratio P_2/P_1 of less than about 0.5 is required, the nozzle must have a throat (in which the velocity will equal the local speed of sound). Similar considerations apply to curves cd and ef but, since they enter the two phase region (at $P/P_1 = 0.58$), the curves will show discontinuties in slope. These can be clearly seen on cd but hardly at all on ef.

For a reversible nozzle, the relative lengths of the convergent and divergent passages and the rate at which they converge and diverge are unimportant. The exact shape required to ensure that irreversibilities are small, however, is a question of fluid mechanics and so outside the scope of this book.

5.3   Effect of back pressure on flow in nozzles

The application of back pressure to a nozzle illustrates how the flow characteristics can be changed from reversible to irreversible. We start with a back pressure equal to the inlet pressure and to study what happens as the back pressure is reduced.

(a) Convergent nozzle

In the arrangement shown in Figure 5.4, we assume that the inlet pressure P_1 is maintained constant. When the back pressure P_B is equal to P_1, there is no pressure drop along or flow through the nozzle, curve (a), but, as it is reduced from P_1 by opening the valve, the pressure distribution follows curve (b) and the mass flow rate $\dot{m}$ increases. This behaviour continues until P_B/P_1 is equal to the critical pressure ratio r_c, as in (c), when the mass flow rate reaches a maximum. At this stage, $P_2 = P_B = P_1 r_c$, where P_2 is the pressure at the exit of the nozzle. For a perfect gas the critical pressure ratio is given by (5.22) and the maximum gas flow rate by (5.24). Further reduction in P_B does not reduce P_2, which remains equal to $P_1 r_c$; nor does it alter the flow rate. Under these conditions the nozzle is said to be *choked*. On leaving the nozzle, the fluid undergoes an unrestrained and irreversible expansion to P_B as illustrated by (d) and the flow may no longer be analysed simply.

(b) Convergent-divergent nozzle

Initially, as the back pressure of a convergent-divergent duct, see Figure 5.5, is reduced from P_1, the duct acts as a venturi, and the pressure and velocity

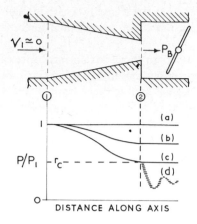

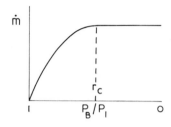

Figure 5.4. Flow characteristics of a convergent nozzle
Curve (a) $P_B = P_2 = P_1$
Curve (b) $P_B = P_2 > P_1 r_c$
Curve (c) $P_B = P_2 = P_1 r_c$
Curve (d) $P_B < P_1 r_c = P_2$

distributions are as shown by curves (a). When, as in (b), the back pressure P_B is such that $P_t = P_1 r_c$, the throat is choked and further reductions in P_B do not increase the mass flow rate. For the duct to function as a reversible nozzle, P_B must be lowered further until the pressure decreases and the velocity increases continuously as in curves (c); these correspond to the situations discussed in Section 5.2(b). Further reductions in P_B do not affect the pressure at the exit of the nozzle P_2; they result only in irreversible expansion outside the nozzle (d). An alternative description is that the ratio of the outlet area of the nozzle to the throat area is too small to maintain reversibility with such a large pressure drop. For values of P_B intermediate between those corresponding to (b) and (c), the nozzle is either the wrong shape (if $P_B/P_1 > r_c$) or of too large an outlet area (if $P_B/P_1 < r_c$) for reversible flow and an isentropic solution is not possible. This results in a discontinuity known as a *shock wave* being formed in the flow. A description of this phenomenon is outside the scope of this book and reference should be made to standard texts.[2]

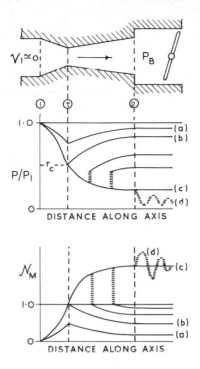

Figure 5.5. Flow characteristics of a convergent-divergent nozzle

5.4 Nozzle efficiency

Although flow through a nozzle is approximately adiabatic, frictional effects lead to an increase in entropy. In nozzle design, it is usual to base all calculations on isentropic flow and then to make an allowance for friction by using a coefficient of efficiency. A typical nozzle expansion between P_1 and P_2 is shown in Figure 5.6; path ab represents the ideal isentropic expansion and ac the actual irreversible adiabatic expansion. Three coefficients are used depending on the application. The *nozzle efficiency* is defined by the ratio of the actual enthalpy drop to the isentropic enthalpy drop between the same pressures, i.e.

$$\text{Nozzle efficiency} = \frac{h_a - h_c}{h_a - h_b} \qquad (5.26)$$

A *velocity coefficient* defined as the ratio of the actual exit velocity to that which would have been obtained had the flow been isentropic between the same pressures i.e.

$$\text{Velocity coefficient} = \mathcal{V}_c / \mathcal{V}_b \qquad (5.27)$$

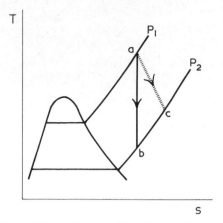

Figure 5.6. Reversible and irreversible adiabatic flow through a nozzle

Exercise

Show that when the inlet velocity is negligible, the velocity coefficient is the square root of the nozzle efficiency.

When as with venturi flow meters and safety valves, we are interested in the mass flow passed by the nozzle, we use a *coefficient of discharge,* defined as the ratio of the actual mass flow rate through the nozzle to that which would be passed if the flow were isentropic i.e.

$$\text{Coefficient of discharge} = \frac{\dot{m}_{\text{actual}}}{\dot{m}_{\text{isentropic}}} \tag{5.28}$$

Nozzles of circular section with straight axes usually have efficiencies as defined by (5.26) ranging from 0.94 to 0.99, whereas those with curved axes, as used in turbines, range from 0.90 to 0.95.

In this section we have used the methods of thermodynamics to analyse the flow of fluids through ducts of simple shape. A more complete analysis which avoids the need to assume a negligible inlet velocity as was done in (5.14) to (5.25), is possible once the concept of total (or stagnation) temperature is introduced. However, we consider this concept to be more appropriate to a study of gas dynamics than thermodynamics.

5.5 Heat and work effects in the compression and expansion of fiuids

We begin by collecting the equations developed in earlier chapters for the heat and work in steady state compression and expansion processes but put them in molar form. As indicated in the preface, a lower case letter, which we now use, can represent a specific quantity (i.e. per unit mass) as well as a molar one. The equations we give here are valid on this basis also provided only that we replace the molar gas constant R by $n_m R$ where n_m is the amount of substance per unit mass.

From (2.15), the first law for a system which exchanges only heat and work with the surroundings may be written per unit mass as (5.29) and, in the absence of changes in kinetic and potential energy as (5.30)

$$\Delta h = q + w - \Delta(\text{KE}) - \Delta(\text{PE}) \tag{5.29}$$

$$\Delta h = q + w \tag{5.30}$$

If the compression and expansion process is reversible, then from (1.32) and (3.63)

$$w = \int v \, dP + \Delta(\text{KE}) + \Delta(\text{PE}) \tag{5.31}$$

$$q = \int T \, ds \tag{5.32}$$

evaluation of which presupposes a knowledge of the P-V-T properties of the fluid and the path taken during the process.

For simplicity, we assume in the following sections that changes in kinetic and potential energy may be neglected. In a steady state flow device, the potential energy term is seldom important, but the size of the kinetic energy term must always be examined and included in the calculation if necessary.

(a) Reversible incompressible flow

It was mentioned in Section 5.2(a) that incompressible flow is not restricted to liquids whose compressibility is small. A gas may be treated as incompressible if the process is such that its density changes little. In which case from (5.31)

$$w = (P_2 - P_1)v \tag{5.33}$$

(b) Reversible isothermal change of a perfect gas

From (3.134) and (3.136),

$$q = -w = -RT \ln(P_2/P_1) \qquad \text{(pg)} \tag{5.34}$$

From (3.135)

$$= RT \ln(v_2/v_1) \qquad \text{(pg)} \tag{5.35}$$

From (3.63)

$$= T(s_2 - s_1) \tag{5.36}$$

(c) Reversible adiabatic change of a perfect gas

For a perfect gas for which γ is independent of temperature, from (3.143)

$$Pv^\gamma = \text{const} \qquad \text{(pg)} \tag{5.37}$$

$$w = \int_{P_1}^{P_2} v \, dP \tag{5.38}$$

$$= \gamma(P_2 v_2 - P_1 v_1)/(\gamma - 1) \qquad \text{(pg)} \tag{5.39}$$

$$= R\gamma(T_2 - T_1)/(\gamma - 1) \qquad \text{(pg)} \tag{5.40}$$

$$= RT_1 \frac{\gamma}{\gamma - 1} \left[\left(\frac{P_2}{P_1}\right)^{(\gamma - 1)/\gamma} - 1 \right] \qquad \text{(pg)} \tag{5.41}$$

$$= P_1 v_1 \frac{\gamma}{\gamma - 1} \left[\left(\frac{P_2}{P_1}\right)^{(\gamma - 1)/\gamma} - 1 \right] \qquad \text{(pg)} \tag{5.42}$$

Since the process is adiabatic and reversible,

$$\Delta s = 0 \tag{5.43}$$

(Equation (5.41) is obtained from (5.40) by substituting for T_2, using (3.144).)

(d) Reversible adiabatic and isothermal changes of a real gas

Heat and work in reversible adiabatic and isothermal processes between known pressure limits can be obtained easily from thermodynamic tables or charts. Thus, if, as in Figure 5.7, a gas is compressed adiabatically from 1 to 2,

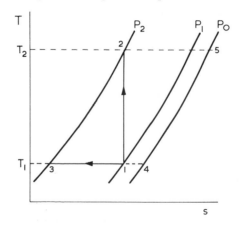

Figure 5.7. Reversible adiabatic and isothermal compressions

the final temperature T_2 is given by the point of intersection of the P_2 isobar and the isentrope through 1, whilst $w = (h_2 - h_1)$. Similarly, for the reversible isothermal process between the same pressure limits, $q = T(s_3 - s_1)$ and $w = (h_3 - h_1) - T(s_3 - s_1)$, which can be read from a T-S chart or table. If neither is available, then the heat and work can be calculated from an equation of state for the gas and the isobaric heat capacity at low pressure (needed for the non-isothermal process), using the following procedure which is the inverse of that given in Section 4.16.

To calculate the enthalpy change, and hence work, for a reversible adiabatic change such as that shown in Figure 5.7, it is necessary first to determine the final temperature T_2. We assume that the isobaric heat capacity is known as a function of temperature at pressure P_0.

Since the compression process is isentropic, then

$$(s_4 - s_1) + (s_5 - s_4) + (s_2 - s_5) = 0 \tag{5.44}$$

From (4.65) and (4.67)

$$-\int_{P_1}^{P_0} (\partial v/\partial T)_P \, dP_{T_1} + \int_{T_1}^{T_2} (c_P/T) \, dT_{P_0} - \int_{P_0}^{P_2} (\partial v/\partial T)_P \, dP_{T_2} = 0 \tag{5.45}$$

Using an iterative procedure, sometimes referred to as an 'entropy balance', a temperature T_2 may be evaluated, such that equation (5.45) is satisfied. For the adiabatic compression process

$$w = (h_2 - h_1) = (h_4 - h_1) + (h_5 - h_4) + (h_2 - h_5)$$

Hence, from (4.64) and (4.67)

$$w = \int_{P_1}^{P_0} [v - T(\partial v/\partial T)_P] \, dP_{T_1} + \int_{T_1}^{T_2} c_P \, dT_{P_0} + \int_{P_0}^{P_2} [v - T(\partial v/\partial T)_P] \, dP_{T_2} \tag{5.46}$$

which can be evaluated once T_2 has been determined.

In the case of the reversible isothermal compression

$$q = T_1(s_3 - s_1)$$

and

$$w = (h_3 - h_1) - T_1(s_3 - s_1)$$

Hence, from (4.64) and (4.65)

$$q = -T_1 \int_{P_1}^{P_2} (\partial v/\partial T)_P \, dP_{T_1} \tag{5.47}$$

$$w = \int_{P_1}^{P_2} [v - T(\partial v/\partial T)_P] \, dP_{T_1} + T_1 \int_{P_1}^{P_2} (\partial v/\partial T)_P \, dP_{T_1} \tag{5.48}$$

It follows from (4.57) that $-(\partial P/\partial V)_s > -(\partial P/\partial V)_T$. Hence, in any reversible steady state flow device, the work required to compress adiabatically a given mass of fluid is greater than that required to compress it isothermally through the same pressure range. Thus, the minimum work needed to compress a fluid continuously through a given pressure range is the reversible isothermal work, whereas the maximum work which may be obtained from a steady state expansion process through the same pressure range is the reversible adiabatic work.

It is impossible to design a steady-state flow compressor which operates isothermally and, as will be seen in Section 5.7(c) the best that can be done is to cool with air or water the container in which the gas is compressed, so that the path of the process lies between that of an isotherm and that of an adiabat. In the case of an expander, conditions are seldom adiabatic because of heat transfer between the fluid which may be at a higher or lower temperature than the surroundings. Thus, we have the problem of calculating the work and heat exchange in a process which is neither adiabatic nor isothermal.

(e) Polytropic analysis of reversible processes

This analysis provides a general method for calculating heat and work in processes involving real fluids, which, although approximate, is found in practice to be remarkably accurate. The initial and final states of a compression or expansion process can be determined from measurements of the inlet and discharge pressures and temperatures. Occasionally measurements are made of the overall heat and work but it is seldom that the exact path of the process is known. In a real process this path is irreversible to some extent, but we ignore this for the moment and consider only those paths which are reversible.

A path along which both heat and work are transferred is known as a *polytropic path*. However, since there are an infinite number of reversible polytropic paths between any two states, in order to proceed with the analysis we must choose one which is both physically plausible and mathematically convenient. One such path of great utility is defined by

$$T(ds/dT) = c \qquad (5.49)$$

where the constant $c = 0$ for an adiabatic process.

The applicability of this polytropic path is based on the assumption that equal temperature increments along the path result in the same amount of heat being transferred. On integration, (5.49) gives

$$q = \int_1^2 T \, ds = c(T_2 - T_1) \qquad (5.50)$$

and

$$s_2 - s_1 = c \ln(T_2/T_1) \qquad (5.51)$$

Hence,

$$q = \frac{(s_2 - s_1)(T_2 - T_1)}{\ln(T_2/T_1)} \qquad (5.52)$$

and the work is

$$w = (h_2 - h_1) - q \qquad (5.53)$$

Thus, from a knowledge of the initial and final states, say, the pressures and temperatures and the thermodynamic properties of the fluid, both q and w can be calculated.

Exercise

Show that for a reversible polytropic path defined by $T(ds/dT) = c$

$$\frac{dP}{P} - \frac{v}{P}\left[\left(\frac{c_P - c}{c_V - c}\right)\left(\frac{\partial P}{\partial v}\right)_T\right]\frac{dv}{v} = 0 \qquad (5.54)$$

and

$$\frac{dT}{T} = \left[\frac{P}{c_P - c} \left(\frac{\partial v}{\partial T} \right)_P \right] \frac{dP}{P} \qquad (5.55)$$

Alternative polytropic paths which have been widely used are defined by

$$Pv^n = \text{const} \qquad (5.56)$$

or

$$P^m/T = \text{const} \qquad (5.57)$$

The polytropic exponents n and m, both of which are constant for the path are obtained by fitting (5.56) or (5.57) to the known initial and final conditions. Thus,

$$n = \ln(P_2/P_1)/\ln(v_1/v_2) \qquad (5.58)$$

and

$$m = \ln(T_2/T_1)/\ln(P_2/P_1) \qquad (5.59)$$

Equations (5.56) and (5.57) are intuitive extensions of (3.143) and (3.144) for the reversible adiabatic change of a perfect gas, without the assumption that $n = \gamma$ and $m = (\gamma - 1)/\gamma$. Indeed it is our experience that with real gases, even in the case of an adiabatic process, $\gamma = c_P/c_V$ often gives a very poor estimate of n and m. Polytropic paths defined by $Pv^n = \text{const}$ are more frequently used than those defined by $P^m/T = \text{const}$, since the work and heat are obtained more easily.

For a steady state process which follows the path $Pv^n = \text{const}$, the work, calculated as in Section 5.5(c), but without assuming that the gas is perfect, is given by

$$w = \frac{n}{n-1} (P_2v_2 - P_1v_1) \qquad (5.60)$$

$$= P_1v_1 \frac{n}{n-1} \left[\left(\frac{P_2}{P_1} \right)^{(n-1)/n} - 1 \right] \qquad (5.61)$$

From a knowledge of the enthalpy change of the fluid, the heat transfer is given by the first law equation, $q = (h_2 - h_1) - w$.

Although this procedure may appear convenient, polytropic paths defined by $Pv^n = \text{const}$ suffer from limitations not found for those defined by $T(ds/dT) = c$. Figure 5.8a shows a skeleton T-S chart for dichloro-difluoromethane on which lines of constant n for reversible compression processes from 1 bar and 300 K have been superimposed. At low pressures and high values of n, the paths behave sensibly, in that the gas temperature increases during the compression in accordance with observations made on compressors in which the water cooling is efficient. But, although the reduction in temperature at pressures sufficiently great for the gas density to exceed $0.7 \rho^c$ and at low values of n is not prohibited thermodynamically, it is contrary to experience and leads us to doubt the validity of this polytropic path. On the

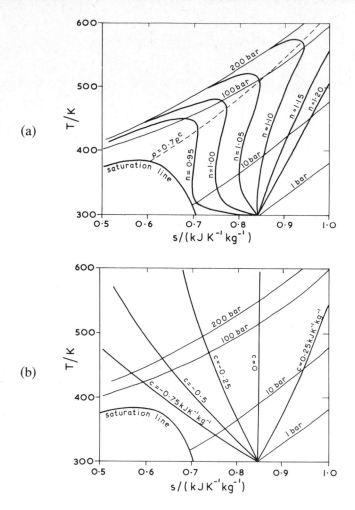

Figure 5.8. Skeleton T-s charts for dichlorodifluoromethane, showing (a) lines of constant n, and (b) lines of constant $T(ds/dT)$

other hand, paths defined by $T(ds/dT) = c$, shown in Figure 5.8b, show no such abnormalities; negative values of c indicate the removal and positive values the absorption of heat. Polytropic paths defined by $P^m/T = \text{const}$ are well behaved also but this equation has not been widely used since the heat and work can be obtained only by numerical integration. Thus use of $Pv^n = \text{const}$ to define a polytropic process must be restricted to low pressure ranges if meaningful results are to be achieved. Within these ranges the difference between paths defined by $Pv^n = \text{const}$ and $T(ds/dT) = c$ are often small. Indeed for a perfect gas, with constant heat capacities, c_P and c_V, the two paths are identical and are the same as that defined by $P^m/T = \text{const}$.

Exercise

Show that for a perfect gas for which c_P and c_V are constant

$$n = (c_P - c)/(c_V - c) \quad \text{(pg)} \tag{5.62}$$

and

$$m = (c_P - c_V)/(c_P - c) \quad \text{(pg)} \tag{5.63}$$

The near equality of the two polytropic paths defined by (5.49) and (5.56) can be illustrated by calculating for both paths, using the procedures outlined above, the work needed to compress dichlorodifluoromethane between arbitrarily chosen pairs of states. If the pressure ratio does not exceed 10, the two paths generally give the same value to within 1% and at pressure ratios of 100 the difference seldom exceeds 10%. On the other hand, if one of the two states is in the high density region where path (5.56) ceases to behave sensibly, the difference increases to as much as 20% even for quite small pressure ratios.

It is clear that there are a number of ways of evaluating the heat and work transfer in a reversible polytropic process between known thermodynamic states. Equations (5.50) to (5.53), based on a path defined by $T(ds/dT) = c$, give the most reliable results but, for most practical applications, particularly those for which the perfect gas approximation is justified, those based on $Pv^n = $ const are equivalent.

In many applications, the final temperature for a polytropic process may not be known and it may be necessary to calculate this and so obtain the work from a knowledge of the initial conditions, the final pressure and an estimate of the heat transfer. In the case of a real gas of known thermodynamic properties, an iterative calculation using (5.52) enables the final temperature to be determined and hence the work from (5.53). If the thermodynamic properties of the gas are not known, then the entropy and enthalpy must be obtained as a function of pressure and temperature, using the method of corresponding states described in Chapter 9.

(f) Irreversible effects

In the previous sections we have considered only reversible processes, but in practice all compressors and expanders involve irreversible effects, such as friction and leakage, which lead to an increase in entropy above that which would otherwise be expected. Hence, the actual enthalpy change differs from that of the reversible process. Furthermore, work delivered by or to the shaft will not be the same as that calculated from the change of enthalpy, because of bearing friction and other external mechanical losses, which, unlike the internal ones, do not affect the state of the fluid. These internal and external losses are allowed for by experimentally measured efficiencies, a knowledge of which is essential to estimate the actual work required or obtained.

The efficiency of a machine involves a comparison between the actual measured performance under given conditions and that which would have been achieved in an ideal process. Unfortunately, it is not always clear from published data which ideal process has been used as a basis for comparison, how the ideal performance has been calculated or whether the measured performance includes external losses. This difficulty stems from the fact that it is quite impossible, even in the simplest of cases, to define a uniquely appropriate 'ideal' path.

For example, in the case of a gas compressor, there are a number of ideal processes with which the actual performance can be compared. If no provision is made for cooling the gas during compression other than the unavoidable heat transfer between the compressor and the surroundings, the ideal process could be taken as the reversible adiabatic process between the known inlet state and the discharge pressure. If the work per unit mass flow through the compressor for this isentropic process is w_S and the actual work w_a, then the *adiabatic* or *isentropic efficiency*, η_S, is equal to w_S/w_a. On the other hand, if an attempt is made to cool the gas during compression, it might be considered that the more appropriate ideal process is reversible and isothermal even though the amount of heat transferred may be small in practice. If w_T is the work for the reversible isothermal process between the given inlet state and discharge pressure, and w_a the actual work, the *isothermal efficiency* η_T is equal to w_T/w_a. Alternatively, we could base the ideal process on the reversible polytropic path between the actual initial and final states (that is, the same final pressure and temperature as in the actual process, and not just the same final pressure as in η_S). If the work calculated for this process is w_P, the *polytropic efficiency*, η_P, is equal to w_P/w_a. Most authors restrict the use of η_P to adiabatic processes and this is a practice which we adhere to, but there is no reason in principle why polytropic paths cannot be applied to processes involving heat transfer and, indeed, we make this application below.

Let us consider first an adiabatic process and the calculation of its adiabatic efficiency η_S (polytropic efficiency is more appropriate to turbomachinery and is dealt with in Section 5.13(b)). We presume that external energy losses, such as those due to bearing friction, have been subtracted from the shaft work to give the actual work w_a. With reference to the compression process shown in Figure 5.9a, the adiabatic efficiency is defined as

$$\eta_S = \frac{\text{work of reversible adiabatic compression from state 1 to 3}}{\text{work of actual adiabatic compression from state 1 to 2}}$$

(5.64)

Hence, from the First Law, if there is no change in kinetic energy

$$\eta_S = \frac{w_S}{w_a} = \frac{(h_3 - h_1)}{(h_2 - h_1)}$$

(5.65)

In the case of the expansion process shown also in Figure 5.9a, the definition of the adiabatic efficiency is modified to conform to the convention that an efficiency is never greater than unity.

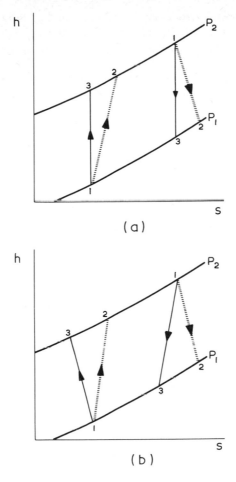

Figure 5.9. Effect of irreversibility on (a) adiabatic and (b) polytropic compression and expansion

Hence,

$$\eta_S = \frac{\text{work of actual adiabatic expansion from state 1 to 2}}{\text{work of reversible adiabatic expansion from state 1 to 3}} \qquad (5.66)$$

If there is no change in kinetic energy, then

$$\eta_S = \frac{w_a}{w_S} = \frac{(h_2 - h_1)}{(h_3 - h_1)} \qquad (5.67)$$

Since irreversibilities lead to an increase in entropy, there should be no difficulty in deciding which work term is the numerator and which the denominator, to ensure that the adiabatic efficiency is less than 1.

In the case of adiabatic compressors and expanders, (5.64) and (5.66) enable

w_a, the actual work done on or by the gas, to be calculated from a knowledge of the reversible work and the experimentally measured adiabatic efficiency of the machine. The adiabatic efficiency of a reciprocating machine, see Section 5.7, may vary from 0.50 to 0.95, depending on the cylinder design and the pressure ratio; highest values are achieved with the largest pressure ratios.

For processes in which the heat transfer is insufficiently small to be negligible, there is no generally accepted procedure for calculating the effects of irreversibility. The following method, however, allows us to calculate an efficiency which is related logically to the adiabatic efficiency, in that it reduces to η_s when the heat transfer is zero. The initial and final states of an actual compression process in a cooled compressor are represented in Figure 5.9b by points 1 and 2, fixed by the measured suction and discharge pressures and temperatures.

Now

$$h_2 - h_1 = q + w_a \tag{5.68}$$

and it is assumed that the heat transfer, q, has been measured or calculated using (5.68) from measurements of actual work, w_a, done on the gas. We assume that, from heat transfer considerations, an equation of the form

$$q = K'K''(T_m - T_0) \tag{5.69}$$

can be used to represent the heat transfer, where $T_m = (T_2 + T_1)/2$ and T_0 are the mean temperatures of the gas during compression and of the cooling medium, K' is a constant for the compressor and K'' is a constant related to the heat transfer coefficient and which varies from gas to gas.

From (5.69),

$$K' = q/[K''(T_m - T_0)] \tag{5.70}$$

We define a process efficiency η for compression in an analogous way to that which we used for adiabatic efficiency:

$$\eta = w/w_a \tag{5.71}$$

where w is the reversible polytropic work for a path starting at 1 and ending at the same pressure as the real process, whilst exchanging the same amount of heat, q. If the final state of this path is 3, then

$$h_3 - h_1 = q + w \tag{5.72}$$

We assume that the reversible polytropic path is defined by $T \, ds/dT = c$ and, hence, from (5.52)

$$q = (s_3 - s_1)(T_3 - T_1)/\ln(T_3/T_1) \tag{5.73}$$

From (5.68), (5.71) and (5.72)

$$h_2 - h_3 = w(1 - \eta)/\eta \tag{5.74}$$

Thus, if we know the thermodynamic properties of the gas, T_3 can be calculated from the heat transfer in the actual process, using (5.73), K' from (5.70), w from (5.72), and hence η from (5.74). Having obtained K' and η, we can calculate T_2 and w_a for the same machine operating between the same pressures but on a different gas by an iterative procedure starting with a guessed value of T_2 and solving successively for q, w_a and T_3 before obtaining the next estimate of T_2 from (5.70) and (5.73).

If a knowledge of the actual shaft work is required, the external machine losses must be allowed for by dividing w_a by a mechanical efficiency factor. For most compressors and expanders, this ranges from 0.95 to 1.0, but does not include losses in the driver itself.

5.6 Classification of compressors and expanders

Pressures which range from high vacuum to about 3500 bars are used industrially. Hence, machines which compress fluids by the application of work or which produce work from the expansion of fluids are a common feature of many processes.

Machines for compressing liquids are almost always called pumps and there is a wide variety of types of which the centrifugal is the most common. The energy which can be recovered from compressed liquid by an expander is very small, nevertheless, in recent years, situations have arisen where it was worthwhile.[3]

Machines used for compressing gases may be classified (see Figure 5.10) as *positive displacement* or as *dynamic*. In a positive displacement machine, gas is

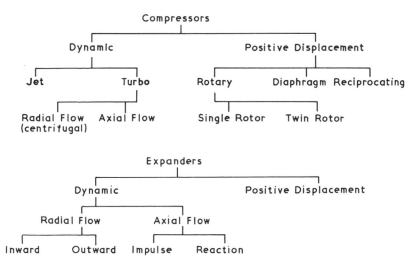

Figure 5.10. Classification of compressors and expanders, based on operating principles

prevented from flowing back down the pressure gradient by a solid boundary. Such machines include *piston* or *reciprocating compressors,* in which the volume changes are brought about by a piston in a cylinder, *diaphragm compressors* in which the change in volume is effected by the elastic deflection of a membrane, and *rotary compressors* of various types which employ either a single rotor, as in the sliding vane compressor or twin rotors, as in the screw compressor. In the dynamic devices, pressure is increased by imparting a high velocity to the gas, which is then converted to pressure in a diffuser. *Radial (centrifugal)* or *axial flow* machines, sometimes collectively known as *turbo-machines,* employ a multi-bladed rotor or impeller to increase the velocity of the gas, whereas in the *jet compressor,* which has no moving parts, a high velocity jet of water, steam or air is used to compress the gas.

Machines with intake pressures which are well below atmospheric and which discharge gases at about atmospheric pressure are generally known as *vacuum pumps* or *exhausters.* They do not differ in principle from those which take in gas at atmospheric pressure and discharge it at higher pressure. A machine which is used solely to overcome the resistance to flow at about atmospheric pressure is known as a *fan,* but when it operates at elevated pressures it is called a *recirculating compressor.*

Positive displacement machines for the expansion of gases are usually known as *expansion engines,* whereas the dynamic types are always referred to as *turbines.* In a turbine, the fluid enters at a high pressure and acquires increased kinetic energy as it expands to low pressure in a ring of nozzles, as in the *impulse turbine,* or through passages in a stator, as in the *reaction turbine.* The stream of fluid then undergoes a change of momentum as it flows through passages between the rotor blades so as to produce a torque at the shaft.

On the basis of this classification, we discuss positive displacement machines first for compressing, and then for expanding fluids. Turbo-machines are dealt with in Sections 5.11 and 5.12.

Positive Displacement Compressors

5.7 Reciprocating piston compressors

It was shown in Section 1.8 that a reciprocating compressor (see Figure 1.14) may be regarded as a steady-state flow machine to which work is supplied at a uniform rate. Figure 5.11a and b show how the pressure and quantity of gas in the cylinder vary with the position of the piston during one revolution of the crank shaft, i.e. during one cycle. In the following analysis, we assume the machine is ideal, in that all processes are reversible, the state of the fluid at suction and discharge conditions is constant, and kinetic energy negligible.

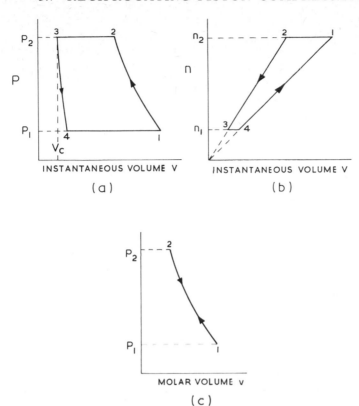

Figure 5.11. Reciprocating compressor: (a) ideal indicator diagram; (b) quantity of gas enclosed within cylinder at various stages during process; (c) path of compression and expansion

Step 1 → 2 n_2 moles of gas, not necessarily perfect, are compressed reversibly from state 1 to state 2, both discharge and suction valves being closed.

Step 2 → 3 $(n_2 - n_1)$ moles of gas, state 2, are displaced through the discharge valve without further change of state.

Step 3 → 4 n_1 moles of gas trapped in the clearance volume V_c at the end of the cylinder expand reversibly from state 2 to state 1, both valves being closed.

Step 4 → 1 $(n_2 - n_1)$ moles of gas, state 1, are drawn through the suction valve into the cylinder where they mix with n_1 moles already present in the same state, to give n_2 moles.

Figure 5.11a does not represent the thermodynamic state of the gas during the various stages of the cycle; V is the instantaneous volume of gas enclosed by the piston. The actual thermodynamic process, see Figure 5.11c, consists of compressing n_2 moles from state 1 to state 2, and expanding n_1 moles from 2 to 1, the net effect being to compress $(n_2 - n_1)$ moles.

(a) Power requirements

The work of compression may be calculated by considering the forces acting on the piston during the machine cycle, as was done in Section 1.8. Thus,

$$W_{cycle} = {}_1^2W + {}_2^3W + {}_3^4W + {}_4^1W \tag{5.75}$$

During steps $1 \to 2$ and $3 \to 4$, the quantity of gas is constant and the work is given by (5.5), whereas from (1.34) the work done during the constant pressure steps $2 \to 3$ and $4 \to 1$ is given by $P \Delta V$. Hence,

$$W_{cycle} = -\int_1^2 P \, dV - P_2(V_3 - V_2) - \int_3^4 P \, dV - P_1(V_1 - V_4) \tag{5.76}$$

$$= -\oint P \, dV \tag{5.77}$$

Thus, the enclosed area on the pressure-instantaneous volume diagram represents the work done.

Now, $V_1 = n_2 v_1$; $V_2 = n_2 v_2$; $V_3 = n_1 v_2$ and $V_4 = n_1 v_1$ where v_1 and v_2 are the molar volumes at states 1 and 2. From (5.76)

$$W_{cycle} = -n_2 \int_1^2 P \, dv - P_2(n_1 v_2 - n_2 v_2) - n_1 \int_3^4 P \, dv - P_1(n_2 v_1 - n_1 v_1) \tag{5.78}$$

If we assume that the path of the expansion process is the same as that for the compression, then

$$-\int_3^4 P \, dv = \int_1^2 P \, dv$$

Hence,

$$W_{cycle} = (n_2 - n_1)\left(P_2 v_2 - P_1 v_1 - \int_1^2 P \, dv\right)$$

$$= (n_2 - n_1)\int_1^2 v \, dP \tag{5.79}$$

Thus, we can treat a reciprocating compressor with finite clearance as a steady-state flow device and calculate the work needed to compress $(n_2 - n_1)$ moles of gas from state 1 to 2 as in Section 5.5.

For the reversible adiabatic compression of a perfect gas, from (5.42)

$$W_{cycle} = (n_2 - n_1)P_1 v_1 \frac{\gamma}{\gamma - 1}\left[\left(\frac{P_2}{P_1}\right)^{(\gamma-1)/\gamma} - 1\right] \quad \text{(pg)} \tag{5.80}$$

Now

$$n_2 - n_1 = \frac{V_1}{v_1} - \frac{V_4}{v_1}$$

Thus,

$$W_{cycle} = V_I P_1 \frac{\gamma}{\gamma - 1}\left[\left(\frac{P_2}{P_1}\right)^{(\gamma-1)/\gamma} - 1\right] \quad \text{(pg)} \tag{5.81}$$

where $V_I = V_1 - V_4$ is the intake volume of gas at suction conditions drawn into

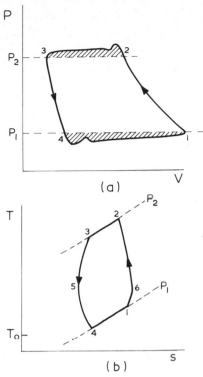

Figure 5.12. Typical performance of a reciprocating compressor in (a) P-V and (b) T-s co-ordinates

the cylinder each cycle. The power required, $\mathscr{P} = W_{\text{cycle}}\Omega$, where Ω is the frequency of the cycle.

An actual pressure-instantaneous volume diagram, usually known as an *indicator diagram*, may be obtained using an *engine indicator*[4] to record cylinder pressure as a function of piston movement. From the cross-sectional area of the piston, an indicator diagram can be derived, the area of which gives the *indicated work* per cycle. The *indicated power* can be obtained from the indicated work per cycle and the rotational speed of the machine.

Figure 5.12a shows a typical indicator diagram for a reciprocating compressor. The corners of the diagram are rounded because the spring-loaded suction and delivery valves do not open instantaneously, whilst the pressure oscillations during suction and delivery result from 'valve bounce' caused by the high initial pressure difference across the valve needed to overcome the inertia of the moving parts. Even when the valves are fully open, some pressure drop across them, shown in Figure 5.12 by cross-hatching, is inevitable because of fluid friction.

The ratio of the area of the entire indicator diagram to its area between the lines representing the suction and delivery pressures is a measure of the overall losses due to throttling and pressure differences across the valves. For ammonia compressors, this ratio usually ranges from 1.04 to 1.10, but may be as low as 1.015 if the machine speed is low; on the other hand, the ratio for fluorocarbon compressors ranges from 1.12 to 1.29 because of the higher density and viscosity of these fluids. If the indicator diagram is plotted on logarithmic scales, it is found that, provided the pressures are low and the pressure ratio not too large, the compression and expansion paths are approximately straight and that the exponent, n, in (5.56) is somewhat smaller for the expansion process. The lack of equality and constancy of the two exponents is caused by differences in heat transfer to and from the compressed gas and is best discussed on the basis of a T-S diagram, such as that shown in Figure 5.12b. This may be constructed from an indicator diagram and the mass flow-rate of compressed gas, if it is assumed that no gas leaks past the valves and piston and that the temperature of the gas at the beginning of the expansion stroke is equal to that being delivered. During expansion stroke 3 to 4, the hot gas is at first cooled by the cylinder wall; at 5, the gas temperature has fallen to that of the cylinder containing it and throughout the rest of the expansion, heat flow is from the cylinder to the fluid. The temperature, T_4, of the gas remaining in the cylinder at 4 is higher than that of the suction gas, T_0, and together with heat taken from the cylinder walls during the suction stroke (4 to 1), results in temperature T_1 being greater than T_0. In the diagram we also show T_1 as greater than T_4 although this is not necessarily always the case. During the compression stroke 1 to 2, the temperature of the gas increases; from 1 to 6, heat is transferred to and, from 6 to 2, from the gas at a rate which increases as the temperature difference increases. During delivery heat continues to flow from the fluid and the temperature falls to T_3. The heat transfers per unit mass of gas during $1 \rightarrow 2$ and $3 \rightarrow 4$, where the amount of gas within the system remains constant, are given by the areas under the curves concerned.

(b) Effect of clearance ratio

It may be seen from (5.79) that the clearance volume has no effect on the work per mole of gas compressed. However, n_1 increases as the clearance increases and thus the quantity of gas $(n_2 - n_1)$ compressed each cycle decreases.

The ratio of the volume of gas actually compressed each cycle, referred to suction conditions, V_I, to the volume swept by the piston, V_S, is known as the volumetric efficiency of the compressor. Thus,

$$\varepsilon_{vol} = V_I/V_S \qquad (5.82)$$

In terms of the quantities usually measured

$$\varepsilon_{vol} = \frac{\dot{n}v_1}{\Omega V_S}$$

where $\dot{n}v_1$ is the free gas delivery, i.e. the volumetric flow rate at suction pressure and temperature.

Exercise

Show that, for the isentropic expansion and compression of a perfect gas, the volumetric efficiency of a reciprocating compressor operating in accordance with the ideal cycle, Figure 5.11a, is given by

$$\varepsilon_{vol} = \frac{V_I}{V_S} = 1 - C\left[\left(\frac{P_2}{P_1}\right)^{1/\gamma} - 1\right] \qquad \text{(pg)} \qquad (5.83)$$

where the intake volume, $V_I = (V_1 - V_4)$ the swept volume, $V_S = (V_1 - V_3)$ and the clearance ratio, $C = V_3/V_S$.

The measured volumetric efficiency of a real gas differs from that calculated from (5.83) for a number of reasons. First, the gas may be imperfect; secondly the compression and expansion may not be isentropic; thirdly, the state of the gas changes during the suction stroke because of the heat transferred; lastly, there is always some leakage past the valves and piston. Thus, although an apparent volumetric efficiency can be calculated or deduced from an indicator diagram, its value in assessing compressor performance is limited. Nevertheless, (5.83) shows that, in a machine of fixed clearance ratio, the volumetric efficiency decreases as the pressure ratio increases. In the limit, $V_I/V_S = 0$, when

$$\frac{P_2}{P_1} = \left(\frac{C+1}{C}\right)^\gamma \qquad \text{(pg)} \qquad (5.84)$$

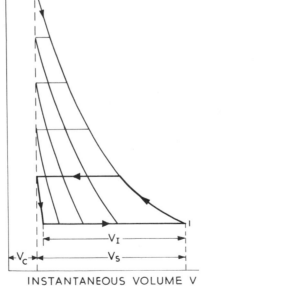

Figure 5.13. Effect of increasing the pressure ratio of a reciprocating compressor on the ideal indicator diagram

It may be seen from Figure 5.13 that, as the pressure ratio increases, the intake volume V_I, decreases, until ultimately there is no flow of gas through the machine and the gas within the cylinder is repeatedly compressed and re-expanded along isentrope 1–2. This situation corresponds to (5.84).

From (5.81) and (5.83)

$$W_{\text{cycle}} = \frac{\gamma}{\gamma-1} P_1 V_S \left\{1 - C\left[\left(\frac{P_2}{P_1}\right)^{1/\gamma} - 1\right]\right\}\left\{\left(\frac{P_2}{P_1}\right)^{(\gamma-1)/\gamma} - 1\right\} \quad \text{(pg)}$$

(5.85)

Hence,

$$\mathscr{P} = \Omega W_{\text{cycle}} \tag{5.86}$$

where $\mathscr{P}$ is the power and Ω the frequency of the cycle.

(c) Multistage compression and interstage cooling

Increasing the pressure ratio also increases the discharge temperature, which, for isentropic compression of a perfect gas, is given by

$$T_2 = T_1(P_2/P_1)^{(\gamma-1)/\gamma} \quad \text{(pg)} \tag{5.87}$$

Hence, the temperature of a gas such as oxygen or nitrogen, for which $\gamma = 1.40$, increases from 20 °C to 290 °C if adiabatically compressed through a pressure ratio of 10. Even if the cylinder were water cooled, the discharge temperature of the gas is unlikely to be reduced by more than 10 K. If a pressure ratio greater than about 10 is required, the process should be carried out in a *multistage compressor* in which the gas is cooled between stages. This proce-dure improves the overall volumetric efficiency of the process, reduces the maximum temperature, so easing the problem of lubricating the piston rings,

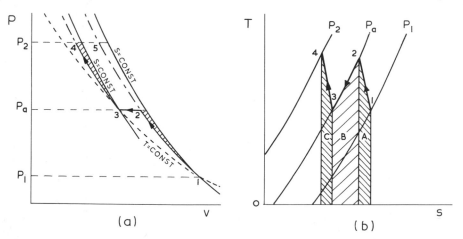

Figure 5.14. Stage compression with interstage cooling: (a) saving in work resulting from cooling during compression and between stages; (b) heat transfer during compres-sion and between stages

and reduces the work of compression. In Figure 5.14a, path $1 \rightarrow 2$ represents reversible compression of a gas from P_1 to an intermediate pressure, P_a in a water cooled cylinder, followed by isobaric cooling, such that at 3 the temperature of the compressed gas is the same as that at 1. Further reversible compression results in a change of state from $3 \rightarrow 4$. Had the compression been carried out in one stage, the process would have followed path 125. Hence the work saved per mole of gas compressed is the area 2345. The cross-hatched areas are the work saved by water-cooling the compressor cylinders. In Figure 5.14b, areas A, B and C are the heat transferred from the first stage cylinder, the inter-stage cooler and the second stage cylinder respectively.

(d) Optimum interstage pressures

We now consider the relationship between the interstage pressures, P_a, etc., to the suction pressure, P_1, and the discharge pressure, P_2, for minimum work. We assume the gas is perfect, the heat capacity ratio, γ, is independent of temperature, each stage of compression is reversible and adiabatic, and that, after each stage, the gas is cooled to the suction temperature of the first stage. The total work per mole of compressed gas, w, is the sum of the work done in m stages. Thus, from (5.42)

$$w = \frac{\gamma}{\gamma - 1} \sum_{i=1}^{m} P_i v_i \left[\left(\frac{P_{i+1}}{P_i} \right)^{(\gamma - 1)/\gamma} - 1 \right] \qquad \text{(pg)} \qquad (5.88)$$

Since the quantity and temperature of gas entering each stage is the same,

$$P_i v_i = P_1 v_1$$

and

$$w = \frac{P_1 v_1}{x} \sum_{i=1}^{m} \left[\left(\frac{P_{i+1}}{P_i} \right)^{x} - 1 \right] \qquad \text{(pg)} \qquad (5.89)$$

where

$$x = (\gamma - 1)/\gamma$$

Since

$$\sum_{i=1}^{m} (P_{i+1} - P_i) = P_2 - P_1 \qquad (5.90)$$

the interstage pressures cannot be varied independently and the method of Lagrange multipliers[5] is used to obtain the condition for minimum work. In this particular example, the method is equivalent to assuming that the interstage pressures can be varied independently. Hence, the criterion for minimum work is that

$$\frac{\partial w}{\partial P_i} = 0$$

From (5.89)

$$\frac{\partial w}{\partial P_i} = \frac{P_1 v_1}{x} \left(x \frac{P_i^{x-1}}{P_{i-1}} - x P_{i+1} P_i^{-x-1} \right) = 0$$

and

$$\frac{P_i}{P_{i-1}} = \frac{P_{i+1}}{P_i}$$

Thus, the condition for minimum work is that the pressure ratio, r, is the same for all stages.

Hence,

$$r = (P_2/P_1)^{1/m} \tag{5.91}$$

In this case, the work in each stage is the same and the total work is

$$w = mP_1v_1\frac{\gamma}{\gamma-1}\left\{\left(\frac{P_2}{P_1}\right)^{(\gamma-1)/m\gamma} - 1\right\} \quad \text{(pg)} \tag{5.92}$$

As

$$m \to \infty \qquad w \to P_1v_1 \ln(P_2/P_1) \quad \text{(pg)} \tag{5.93}$$

which is the work required for isothermal compression of a perfect gas, and is the minimum possible.

In calculations on an actual compressor it is necessary to allow for the pressure drops through the interstage coolers, by increasing the discharge pressure from each stage to include half of the pressure drop, and to subtract the other half from the suction pressure of the following stage. These pressure drops do not affect the theoretical optimum pressure ratio per stage, but they do affect the cumulative power required to do the work of total compression.

Although substantial savings in power can result from multistage compression with intercooling, the increased cost of the equipment means that even for pressures as high as 3000 bar, it is seldom economic to use more than four or five stages. But in addition to thermodynamic gains, there are also two mechanical ones. Firstly, only the small high pressure cylinder need be designed to withstand the full delivery pressure, and secondly, it is easier to balance the machine loads, provided all stages use a common drive-shaft.

(e) Operating characteristics

Many compressors work at constant suction and discharge pressures and their selection presents no difficulty. However, if, as is often the case, they have to accommodate fluctuations in both suction and discharge pressure caused by variations in process conditions, it is important that the machine is not overloaded. In Figure 5.15, a number of constant-power curves calculated from (5.85) and (5.86) have been drawn for a compressor of fixed clearance, running at constant speed, as a function of discharge and suction pressure. The points A and B give the minimum suction and discharge pressures respectively for which the power input corresponds to that of the curve on which they lie. If the normal operating conditions are at A, variations in discharge pressure at constant suction pressure will result in a reduction in the power required. On

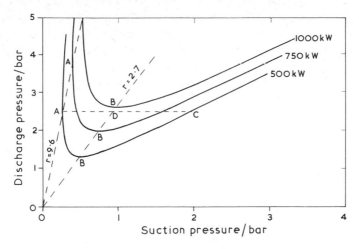

Figure 5.15. Power characteristics of a reciprocating compressor ($C = 0.1, \gamma = 1.4$) as a function of suction and discharge pressure

the other hand, if the suction pressure is increased whilst maintaining the discharge pressure constant, the locus of conditions will move along the line AC and the power requirement will pass through a maximum at point D, in spite of the fact that the pressure ratio at this point is less than that at A.

Exercise

From equations (5.85) and (5.86), show that, if P_2 is varied, the pressure ratio, $r = P_2/P_1$, for maximum power input is given by

$$r^{(1-\gamma)/\gamma} + \frac{(\gamma - 1)(1+C)}{C} r^{-1/\gamma} = \gamma \qquad (5.94)$$

and that, if P_1 is varied, the pressure ratio for maximum power input is given by

$$r^{(\gamma-1)/\gamma} + \frac{C(\gamma-1)}{1+C} r^{1/\gamma} = \gamma \qquad (5.95)$$

In Figure 5.15, the pressure ratio along line OA may be calculated from (5.94) and that along line OB from (5.95).

The main field of application of the reciprocating piston compressor is for relatively small mass flows at high pressure. Although the efficiency of the machine is high, the saving in power is offset by the high maintenance costs which stem from its intermittent operation. The difficulty of lubricating the piston rings and preventing valve and piping failures resulting from mechanical vibration induced by pressure pulsations, are just a few of the problems which beset the piston compressor. Not surprisingly therefore, the centrifugal compressor, which does not operate in this intermittent way, see Section 5.12(b), has taken over many of the duties formerly performed by the reciprocating machine. However, the centrifugal has a lower efficiency than the reciprocating compressor at the design throughput and whereas the throughput can be reduced by about 65% for a reciprocating compressor without any marked loss in efficiency, this is far from true for the centrifugal machine. For pressures above about 500 bar, there is no alternative to the reciprocating compressor and multi-stage machines are currently in use powered by 7.5 MW motors, which will compress 100 m³ s⁻¹ of ethylene to a pressure of 3500 bar.

The ranges of pressure and capacity over which the more important types of compressor discussed in this chapter are used are given in Figure 5.16. The capacity of a compressor is usually expressed in terms of the volume of gas measured at 1 atm = 1.0133 bar and in the U.K. at 20 °C, but elsewhere in Europe at 0 °C.

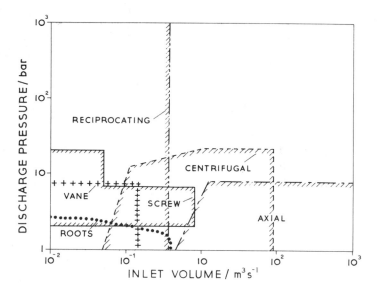

Figure 5.16. Duties of various compressors

5.8 Rotary compressors

Rotary compressors are smaller than reciprocating machines for comparable flow rates, because their continuous rotary action enables higher speeds to be used and, since they are generally uncooled, the rapid action results in conditions which are approximately adiabatic. They have small clearance volumes and are not equipped with suction or discharge valves; hence, the throughput is determined by the pressures in the systems to which the suction and discharge lines are connected.

Rotary compressors are of the single or twin rotor types. The sliding vane compressor, see Figure 5.17a, consists of a single rotor which is mounted eccentrically in a casing and slotted to house vanes. The volume trapped between the rotor and casing decreases from suction to discharge port; hence, compression begins as each vane moves past the suction port. If, as is usually the case, the pressure in the receiver connected to the discharge line is higher than that of the gas prior to discharge, there will be irreversible back flow of gas into the compressor as each vane reaches the discharge port. Finally, gas is displaced with only the very small amount of compression needed to restore the receiver pressure. The cycle may be represented by the ideal indicator diagram, see Figure 5.17b, in which path $1 \rightarrow 3$ represents the initial (internal) compression assumed isentropic and $3 \rightarrow 2$ the irreversible back flow. As a result of the irreversible step in the compression process, this machine requires more work than a reciprocating compressor operating between the same pressure limits.

There are a number of different types of twin rotor compressors which, from a thermodynamic point of view, may be distinguished by the amount of initial compression. For example, that illustrated in Figure 5.17c and d is a Roots blower in which there is no initial compression whatsoever (the term *blower* is often used for a rotary machine which discharges at a pressure below about 2 bar). In this machine pockets of gas (volume V_1 and pressure P_1) are trapped between the rotors (both of which are driven) and the casing and transported from suction to discharge port without change of pressure. The compression is brought about by irreversible back flow of gas from the receiver at P_2 after which the compressed gas is displaced, suffering a slight increase in pressure during the process. On the other hand, the Lysholm or screw compressor, as it is commonly called, has virtually no irreversible back flow, see Figure 5.17e, and is capable of developing a pressure ratio of 10 as a result of the almost complete intermeshing of the male and female rotors. The degree of initial compression is represented by the cross-hatched areas which show the volume occupied by the gas at the inlet and discharge ends of the rotors.

For maximum efficiency, the initial compression should be matched to the required duty. If the initial compression is to a pressure below that required, as in Figure 5.17b, or to a pressure greater, then the work required per cycle will be increased by the final irreversible compression or expansion step.

The necessary clearances between the moving parts of rotary compressors have an increasingly adverse effect on volumetric efficiency as the pressure ratio increases. This problem can be reduced by carrying out the compression in a number of stages or, in the case of the sliding vane and screw compressors, by injecting large quantities of oil into the compressor. This serves not only to seal the moving parts but also to absorb some of the heat generated during compression. Single stage oil-flooded screw compressors can operate with compression ratios as high as 20.

The approximate capacities and pressure ranges within which the three types of compressor described in this section operate are shown in Figure

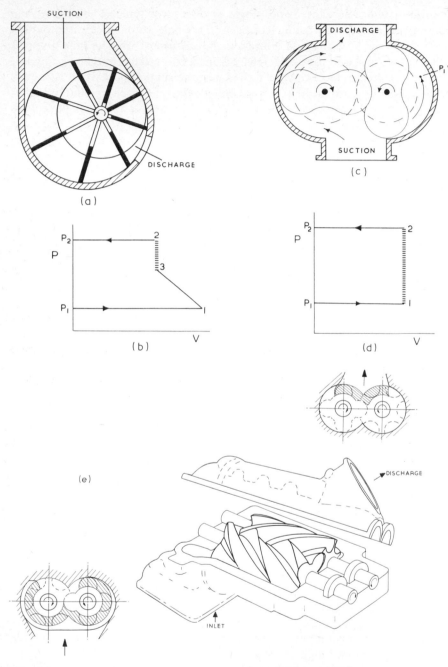

Figure 5.17. Positive displacement rotary compressors: (a) sliding vane compressor; (b) ideal indicator diagram for sliding vane compressor; (c) Roots blower; (d) ideal indicator diagram for Roots blower; (e) screw compressor

5.16. A detailed description of these and other rotary compressors has been given by Chlumsky[6] and others.[7]

Positive Displacement Expanders

5.9 Reciprocating expansion engines

Reversible expansion of a gas is used either for the production of power or low temperatures. For both applications, the continuous rotary action of a turbine (see Section 5.11) is preferred, but these machines are difficult to design when the inlet pressure and the pressure ratio are high, and are very inefficient when the flow rate is small; for these special applications a reciprocating expansion engine is generally employed.

The ideal indicator diagram for a reciprocating expansion engine cycle, operating on a perfect gas, is shown bold in Figure 5.18a. This is a compressor cycle in reverse but, unlike the compressor, the inlet and exhaust valve of an expansion engine must be operated mechanically and this makes it possible to open and close them at any point in the cycle. Four steps make up the basic cycle:

Step 2 to 1 n_2 moles of gas expand reversibly from state 2 to state 1, both inlet and exhaust valves being closed during the process.

Step 1 to 4 $(n_2 - n_1)$ moles of gas state 1 are displaced through the exhaust without further change of state.

Step 4 to 3 n_1 moles of gas left in the cylinder after the exhaust valve closes are compressed reversibly, point 4 being chosen so that the final pressure is equal to P_2.

Step 3 to 2 $(n_2 - n_1)$ moles of gas are admitted through the inlet valve and mix reversibly with n_1 moles trapped in the clearance volume at the end of the compression stroke.

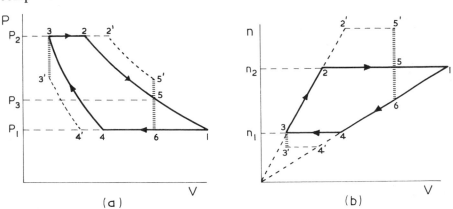

Figure 5.18. Reciprocating engine: (a) ideal indicator diagram (b) quantity of gas enclosed within cylinder at various stages during process

The indicator diagram for an actual engine differs from the ideal because of pressure differences or leakage across valves, and heat transfer between the fluid and cylinder wall. However, the overall expansion process is made as near adiabatic as possible by preventing heat losses in the case of a steam engine, or heat gains in the case of an expansion engine used for refrigeration.

At low pressures, $-(\partial v/\partial P)_s$ is large and the rapid increase in molar volume during expansion necessitates a long stroke machine, which is mechanically undesirable. The stroke length may be reduced from $(V_1 - V_3)$ to $(V_5 - V_3)$, if the exhaust valve is opened at point 5 to allow the gas at P_3 to expand to P_1 irreversibly through the valve. The reduction in work output per machine cycle is given by area 156 in Figure 5.18a. Since some of the gas passing through the engine is expanded irreversibly from P_3 to P_1, the thermodynamic process is no longer isentropic and the adiabatic efficiency of the ideal machine is less than 1.

The work done per cycle may be increased by closing the inlet valve later, say point 2' but the adiabatic efficiency is reduced since a larger proportion of the increased gas flow expands irreversibly. A similar effect may be achieved by delaying the closing of the exhaust valve to, say point 4', and again although this increases gas throughput it decreases efficiency, see Figure 5.18b. Inefficiency arises because the pressure at point 3' is below supply pressure so that when the inlet valve is opened, the gas supply raises the cylinder pressure irreversibly.

Thus, the optimum positions for opening and closing the valves depend on the relative importance of work output (as in a steam engine) and discharge temperature (as in an expander used for refrigeration).

The expansion process may be made more efficient by *compounding*, i.e. by carrying out the process in two or more stages. In the case of a steam engine, this has mechanical advantages, in that the large volume of low pressure steam can be handled in a cylinder of large diameter and, in addition, the range of temperature variation in each stage is reduced. Alternatively, a turbine may be used to complete the expansion of the low pressure steam because, as will be seen in Section 5.11, it is very efficient at high rates of flow.

Details of the design of reciprocating engines for low temperature applications are given by Blackford, Halford and Tantam.[8]

5.10 Dynamic compressors and expanders

(a) Jet ejector

Large volumes of vapour at low pressure may be compressed to atmospheric pressure, or slightly above, in an *ejector*. This consists of a converging-diverging nozzle, see Figure 5.19a, through which is passed the driving fluid, usually steam. This fluid leaves the nozzle at supersonic velocity and the vapour to be compressed is drawn into the mixing cone by the turbulence

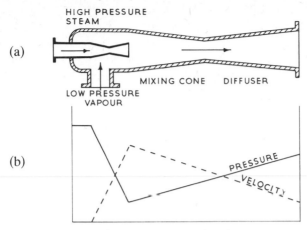

Figure 5.19. Steam jet ejector

formed at the nozzle outlet. The mixture then passes into a converging-diverging diffuser from which the stream emerges at subsonic velocity having been compressed to the discharge pressure as shown in Figure 5.19b. In the case of a *steam ejector* used to compress water vapour as in the refrigeration process described in Section 5.16d, the steam discharged from the ejector is condensed, but it could be passed into a second ejector prior to condensation. The processes occurring in the ejector are highly irreversible and the efficiency low; nevertheless, these devices are widely used in the chemical industry because they contain no moving parts and maintenance costs are low. The design is largely empirical and for fuller details see reference.[9]

(b) Turbo-machines

In Section 1.8, we described how in a turbo-expander, known as a *turbine*, high pressure fluid acquires increased kinetic energy as it expands to a lower pressure in a ring of nozzles. The fluid then undergoes a change of momentum as it flows through passages between blades attached to a rotor and in so doing generates shaft work. A *turbo-compressor* operates in the reverse manner in that an externally applied torque imparts a change of momentum to the fluid passing between rotor blades. Having acquired an increased velocity, the fluid then decelerates with an accompanying rise of pressure, whilst flowing through a ring of diffusers.

There are two main types of turbo-machines, *axial flow* and *radial flow*, see Figure 5.20. In a radial flow machine, the flow during that part of the process in which work is transferred, may be either inwards, *centripetal*, or outwards, *centrifugal*. By considering the change in fluid momentum between the inlet, 1, and outlet, 2, in an arbitrary passage within a rotor, see Figure 5.20b, it may be shown that

$$\mathscr{P} = \dot{m}(u_2 \mathscr{V}_{t_2} - u_1 \mathscr{V}_{t_1}) \tag{5.96}$$

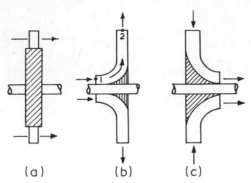

Figure 5.20. Flow through turbo-machinery: (a) axial flow; (b) radial outflow (centrifugal); (c) radial inflow (centripetal)

where $\mathscr{P}$ is the power or rate of work transfer
$\dot{m}$ is the mass flow rate of fluid;
u is the linear velocity of any point on the rotor
and $\mathscr{V}_t$ is the component of the fluid velocity tangential to the plane of rotation of the rotor at the same point.

Thus no work is transferred unless there is a change in the product $u\mathscr{V}_t$, known as the *whirl* or *whirl velocity*.

Equation (5.96) is applicable to steady one-dimensional flow, irrespective of the path through the rotor. The tangential component of the fluid velocity is a function of flow rate, rotor speed and geometry, and reference should be made to texts on fluid mechanics for details of the vector diagrams used in its calculation and subsequent application to design.

Thermodynamic analysis of turbomachinery is primarily concerned with calculating the energy losses. Since the speed of flow of fluid through a turbomachine is usually high, small machines can handle large mass flow rates and transfer large amounts of power under conditions which are approximately adiabatic. Thus the energy losses arise mainly from the irreversible nature of the flow and in the following sections where we discuss the nature of these losses, it will be necessary to understand enough of the mechanical details to identify the sources of irreversibility.

5.11 Turbines

The turbine is used either for the production of power or for the generation of low temperatures. For power generation, the axial flow turbine is preferred to the radial type, except for small flow rates when it is inefficient. On the other hand, the inward flowing radial turbine is of particular importance to chemical engineers, as nearly all the expanders for air separation and liquefaction plants are of this type.

(a) Axial flow turbine

These turbines are of the *impulse* or *reaction* type. The characteristic feature of the impulse turbine is that all pressure changes occur within a fixed ring of nozzles. These nozzles may be in the form of a number of convergent-divergent ducts of circular cross-section as in Figure 5.21a, or convergent channels between fixed blades, see Figure 1.11, so shaped that the emerging fluid has higher kinetic energy but lower pressure than the ingoing fluid. The blades attached to the discs of an impulse turbine form flow passages of approximately constant cross-sectional area, so that the reduction in kinetic energy of the fluid as it does work on the blades takes place at constant pressure. The variation in pressure and fluid velocity through three simple impulse stages is shown in Figure 5.21a. A number of different arrangements are used to reduce the high speed of rotation which results when fluid of high kinetic energy impinges on a single row of blades. The reduction in energy across the stage shown in Figure 5.21b is split between two rows of moving blades, so that the speed of rotation is lower than that for a simple impulse stage of similar power output. The fixed blades serve to redirect the flow to the correct angle to enter the second row of moving blades and the passages between them are of constant cross-sectional area to ensure that the velocity and pressure remain unchanged.

The reaction turbine shown in Figure 5.21c consists of rows of blades mounted alternately on the rotor and casing. The passages between the fixed blades accelerate the fluid and direct it onto the moving blades, the passages between which are shaped so as to permit fluid pressure to decrease. Thus, the fluid expands continuously through both fixed and moving blades and it is the additional reaction generated on the moving blades above that which would be obtained if the pressure within the blades remained constant, that gives its name to the turbine. The degree of reaction of an individual stage Λ is defined as the fraction of the total enthalpy change which occurs across the moving blades. Hence, for the isentropic expansion process in Figure 5.22

$$\Lambda = (h_3 - h_2)/(h_3 - h_1) \tag{5.97}$$

Exercise

Show that, for a perfect gas expanding isentropically, the pressure ratios across the fixed and moving blades are equal when the degree of reaction is 0.5.

The degree of reaction normally used in modern steam turbine plant is about 0.5. This enables both the fixed and moving blades of a given stage to have the same shape; furthermore, an identical blade profile can be used for all stages if the length of the blades and/or drum diameter is increased in proportion to the increase in volume of the expanding fluid, see Figure 5.21c.

The aim in the design of a turbine is to make the expansion process as reversible as possible and to carry it out in the smallest number of stages. There are two main sources of irreversibility: first, losses caused by fluid friction in the nozzle and rotor blade passages and secondly losses caused by

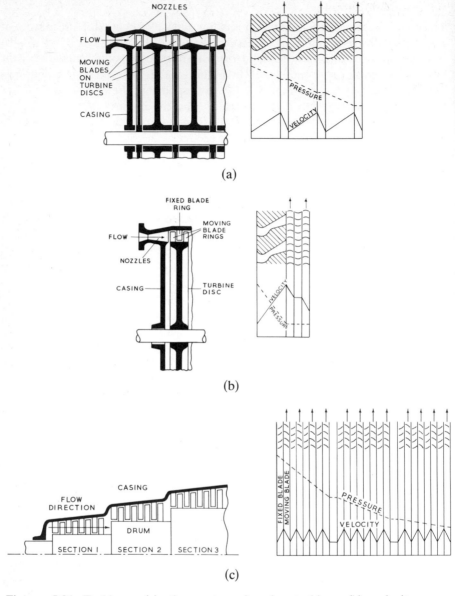

Figure 5.21. Turbines: (a) three stage impulse turbine; (b) velocity compounded impulse stage; (c) twelve stage reaction turbine

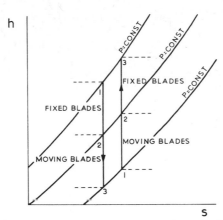

Figure 5.22. Isentropic expansion and compression in a single stage reaction turbo-
machine

irreversible expansion of the fluid through the gaps between the moving and
stationary parts of a turbine. A reaction stage has lower friction losses than an
impulse stage, but the opposite is true for leakage losses. Hence, in general,
leakage losses exceed friction losses at the high pressure end of a turbine of
high pressure ratio, whereas at the low pressure end or throughout a turbine
of low pressure-ratio friction losses predominate. This is why in high
pressure-ratio steam turbines it is usual to use at least two machines in series:
a high-pressure turbine with impulse stages, followed by a low pressure
reaction turbine.

(b) Radial flow turbine

When the pressure ratio through which the fluid is expanding is large, the flow
must be outward so that the volume increase on expansion can be partly
accommodated by the increase in flow area with diameter. The outward flow
turbine, see Figure 5.23a, consists of concentric rows of blades attached to the
opposing faces of two rotor discs which rotate in opposite directions. The blade
length is decreased initially since the increase in flow area with rotor diameter
is greater than required, but as the diameter increases still further it has to be
increased.

If the expansion of the fluid is relatively small, it is possible to obtain the
required increase in flow area with an inward flow arrangement, such as that
shown in Figure 5.23b. Fluid enters the turbine via a volute, and flows
through a row of fixed nozzles situated round the periphery of the rotor. The
high velocity stream then flows inward between vanes attached to the side of
the rotor, the passages being so shaped that the flow exhausts in the axial
direction.

The turbines used on gas-liquefaction plant (see Section 5.19) are usually of
the single stage, radial inflow type and are used for inlet pressures up to

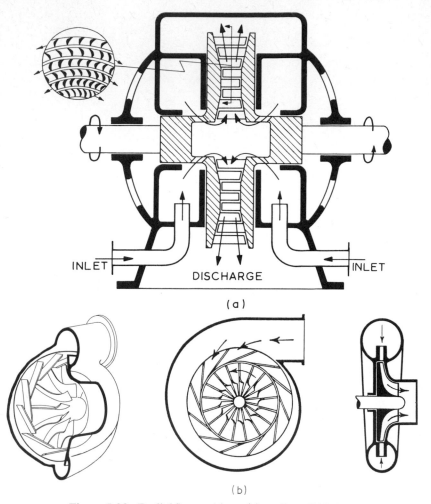

Figure 5.23. Radial flow turbines: (a) outflow; (b) inflow

200 bar, at throughputs of 30 m^3 s^{-1}. Since many operate at temperatures below 140 K, good insulation is necessary to reduce heat transfer by conduction and radiation. The ducting necessary for compounding a radial turbine is tortuous and is rarely used, because the density of the low temperature fluid is sufficiently high to enable a pressure ratio of about 8 to be achieved in a single stage.

In cryogenic applications, such as the liquefaction of hydrogen and helium, very high speed miniature turbines are used which operate at temperatures below 90 K.

It is not the primary purpose of a low temperature turbine to produce usable power; nevertheless, this must be absorbed if the temperature of the expanding fluid is to decrease. Although an electric generator is one of the most satisfactory ways of loading a turbine, the cost of equipment makes it uneconomic to recover less than about 30 kW, in which case a direct coupled air blower or oil pump can be used to absorb smaller power outputs and at the same time to perform a limited amount of useful work.

5.12 Turbo-compressors

As with turbines, flow through a turbo-compressor may be in the axial direction, in which case the machine is known as an *axial flow compressor*, or in the radial direction, when it is known as a *centrifugal* or *radial flow compressor*.

(a) Axial flow compressor

From the point of view of the exchange of energy between the fluid and the rotor, this compressor may be regarded as a reaction turbine operating in reverse. Thus, if fluid were to flow through the turbine shown in Figure 5.21c in the reverse direction, the passages between the fixed and moving blades would act as diffusers and the pressure would increase. As for a turbine, losses arising from irreversibility are a function of the degree of reaction which, for a compressor, is defined as the fraction of the total enthalpy increase which occurs in the moving blades. Hence, from Figure 5.22,

$$\Lambda = (h_2 - h_1)/(h_3 - h_1)$$

It is found that losses caused by fluid friction and leakage past the tips of the blades are a minimum when the pressure, and hence enthalpy, rise is approximately equally divided between the rotating and fixed blades. Hence, a 50% reaction design is normally used.

If, in an attempt to reduce the number of stages, the rate of divergence of the passages between the blades is made too great, there is a tendency, particularly when the passages are curved, for the fluid to break away from the blades and flow back in the direction of the pressure gradient. Hence, the aerodynamic shape of the blades is important and the phenomenon of boundary layer separation limits the work which can be absorbed and hence the pressure ratio for each stage. Any attempt to raise the pressure ratio per stage above about 1.2 results in a serious reduction in efficiency.

Unlike the positive displacement compressor, there is only a limited range of flow rates at any given speed within which the compressor can operate. If the flow rate is reduced too much, the flow pattern breaks down completely and the compressor is said to *surge*. Even over a restricted range of flow rates, the efficiency varies considerably and can only be maintained at a high level by varying the speed of rotation or the angle of some or all of the fixed blades during operation. Both of these techniques are expensive to implement and it

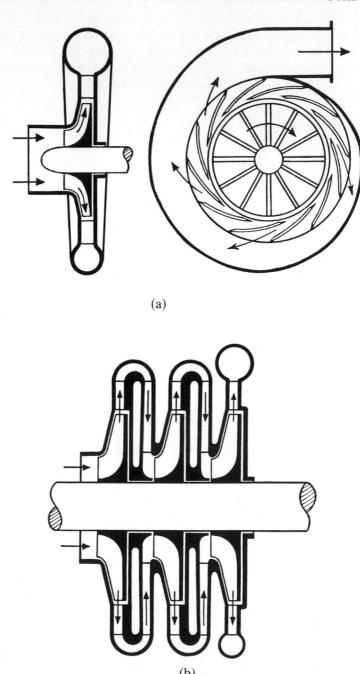

(a)

(b)

Figure 5.24. Centrifugal compressor: (a) single stage; (b) multi-stage

is the lack of flexibility of the axial flow compressor which has led to the development of large centrifugal compressors. It can be seen from Figure 5.16 that axial flow machines are used to compress very large quantities of gas to comparatively low pressures. Under design conditions, the isentropic efficiency is high and interstage coolers are seldom used.

(b) Centrifugal compressor

The centrifugal compressor consists of an *impeller*, i.e. a disc on which one or more rings of radial or curved blades are mounted, which is rotated at high speed. Fluid admitted to the centre or 'eye' of the impeller leaves with a high velocity, and the kinetic energy is converted into a pressure increase in a ring of stationary diffusing blades or a free vortex diffuser which surrounds the impeller, see Figure 5.24a. The pressure ratio of each stage is restricted to about 1.6; so for overall ratios greater than this, several stages are mounted on a common shaft, vanes in the outer casing being used to guide the gas inwards from one stage to the next as in Figure 5.24b. A total pressure ratio of about 20 can be achieved in a single unit, but when the pressure ratio exceeds 5, the fluid must be cooled either by water-jacketing the ducts or by passing the gas through intercoolers between each or every few stages.

Developments in centrifugal compressor design during the past decade, which have been largely empirical, have had a far-reaching effect on the size and design of chemical processes. For example, it was the high pressure centrifugal compressor which made possible the 1000 ton/day ammonia plant. In this instance, a final pressure of 500 bar can be achieved with three or four multi-stage units in series. Except for very high pressure applications, the centrifugal compressor has largely replaced the reciprocating piston compressor. At present it is practicable for flow rates of 3 to $15 \, \text{m}^3 \, \text{s}^{-1}$, but, because of the tortuous path between stages, power consumption is 5% greater and the size three times that of a comparable axial flow machine. As in these, the efficiency decreases as the load decreases, but limited flow regulation can be achieved with inlet guide vanes or variable angle diffuser vanes.

The main advantage of the centrifugal compressor is that it is less expensive, more robust and more stable in operation than the axial flow machine. The chief factor which determines the minimum size of a centrifugal compressor is the amount of gas which can be handled by the final impeller. It is now possible to produce impeller blades which have a width of only a few mm and flow rates of $0.15 \, \text{m}^3 \, \text{s}^{-1}$ are possible, but the efficiency is low. At the other extreme, suction volumes in excess of $7.5 \, \text{m}^3 \, \text{s}^{-1}$ are best handled by an axial flow compressor, a radial compressor being used to boost the pressure should more than about 9 bar be required.

5.13 Efficiency of turbo-machinery

As fluid expands through a turbine, irreversible effects such as friction and leakage lead to an increase in entropy and a reduction in the enthalpy drop.

Furthermore, work delivered by the shaft is less than that calculated from the change of enthalpy because of bearing friction and other external mechanical losses. Unlike the internal losses, however, these do not affect the state of the fluid. Irreversible effects increase the entropy of the fluid flowing through a turbo-compressor also, resulting in an additional enthalpy increase, above that of the corresponding reversible machine. Thus, the efficiency of a turbo-machine may be expressed in at least two ways, depending on whether external losses are included. Here we are concerned only with internal efficiency and we assume that the external losses have been deducted from the shaft work to give the 'actual work'.

For any turbomachine, the work input per unit mass of flowing fluid is

$$w = (h_2 - h_1) - q + \tfrac{1}{2}(\mathscr{V}_2^2 - \mathscr{V}_1^2) \tag{5.98}$$

For simplicity we consider only processes in which the heat, q, and the change in kinetic energy, $\tfrac{1}{2}(\mathscr{V}_2^2 - \mathscr{V}_1^2)$, can be neglected, giving the actual work, w_a, as

$$w_a = h_2 - h_1 = \Delta h_a \tag{5.99}$$

Turbomachines generally contain more than one stage and Figure 5.25 represents the thermodynamic process for a five stage expansion turbine (a) and a five-stage turbocompressor (b). The cross-hatched line, so marked since the process is irreversible, links the states of the fluid between each stage of the machine. Equation (5.99) can therefore be applied either to the individual stages, or to the machine as a whole.

As was indicated in Section 5.5(f), there are many ways of calculating the 'ideal work' in order to evaluate the efficiency of a machine. We examine two ways. Neither is perfect, but both are widely used and we show the usefulness and limitations of each.

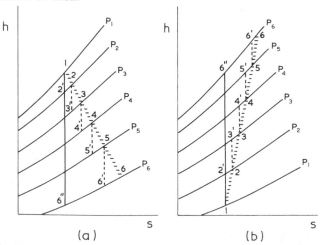

Figure 5.25. Effect of irreversibility in turbo-machinery: (a) five stage turbine; (b) five stage compressor

(a) Adiabatic efficiency (see also Section 5.5(f))

For the purposes of calculating the adiabatic efficiency, ideal work is calculated as the work which would have been involved in a reversible adiabatic, i.e. isentropic, process, starting at the same point as the actual process and ending at the same final pressure. Thus, for the first stages of the turbine and compressor in Figure 5.25, the ideal work, w_s^1, is given by

$$w_s^1 = h_2' - h_1 = \Delta h_s^1$$

for stage 2 by

$$w_s^2 = h_3' - h_2 = \Delta h_s^2$$

and similarly for the other stages. For the whole machine,

$$w_s = h_6'' - h_1 = \Delta h_s$$

Thus, for a turbine, the adiabatic efficiency of the first stage is given by

$$\eta_s^1 = (h_2 - h_1)/(h_2' - h_1) = \Delta h_a^1/\Delta h_s^1 \qquad (5.100)$$

etc., and for the whole machine by

$$\eta_s = (h_6 - h_1)/(h_6'' - h_1) = \Delta h_a/\Delta h_s \qquad (5.101)$$

If the adiabatic efficiency of each stage is the same and equal to η_s^n, then,

$$\eta_s = \eta_s^n \left(\sum \Delta h_s^n \right) \Big/ \Delta h_s \qquad (5.102)$$

Since $(\partial H/\partial S)_P = T$, the isobars diverge from left to right in Figure 5.25 and $\sum (\Delta h_s^n)/\Delta h_s$, known as the *reheat factor*, is greater than 1. Thus, for a turbine consisting of stages of equal adiabatic efficiency, the overall efficiency is greater than that of any one of them. This is a rather illogical conclusion and casts doubt on the wisdom of using adiabatic efficiency as a measure of machine performance, particularly since the 'reheat factor' is merely an artefact of the way in which we define the ideal work. Similar objections occur to the use of adiabatic efficiency for analysing a turbo-compressor but, since the definition of efficiency is the inverse of that for a turbine, the *'reverse reheat factor'* reduces the efficiency of the overall machine to less than that of the individual (equal) stages, a result which is only slightly less illogical than that found for the turbine.

(b) Polytropic efficiency

The difficulties inherent in adiabatic efficiency can be overcome to a large extent by basing the definition of ideal work on a reversible polytropic process between the actual initial and final states. The polytropic efficiency η_P is defined as

$$\eta_P = \frac{w_a}{w_P} \qquad (5.103)$$

where, for a process operating between states 1 and 2, and using a polytropic path as defined by equation (5.49)

$$w_P = h_2 - h_1 - c(T_2 - T_1) \qquad (5.104)$$

Thus, for the first stage of turbine of Figure 5.25(a)

$$\eta_P^1 = (h_2 - h_1)/(h_2 - h_1 - c\{T_2 - T_1\}) \qquad (5.105)$$

and similarly for the other stages and for the whole machine.

For a perfect gas with a constant heat capacity ratio γ, this expression is simplified considerably, since

$$h_2 - h_1 = c_P(T_2 - T_1) \qquad \text{(pg)}$$

This gives

$$\eta_P^1 = \frac{c_P}{c_P - c} \qquad \text{(pg)} \qquad (5.106)$$

If each stage of the turbine of Figure 5.25a has the same polytropic efficiency, it follows that each stage has the same value of c as the overall machine. Thus,

$$\eta_P^0 = (h_6 - h_1)/(h_6 - h_1 - c\{T_6 - T_1\})$$

$$= \frac{c_P}{c_P - c} = \eta_P^n \qquad \text{(pg)} \qquad (5.107)$$

That is, the polytropic efficiency of the whole machine has the same value as each of its (equal) stages.

Exercise

Show that, for the multistage compressor of Figure 5.25b, the same conclusion holds and that

$$\eta_P^0 = \frac{c_P - c}{c_P} \qquad \text{(pg)} \qquad (5.108)$$

For a real gas, these conclusions are only approximations, albeit good ones in practice. Calculations show that, in most cases, the assumption of constant η_P, or alternatively constant c, for each stage results in an overall η_P^0 which differs from the individual η_P by little more than the experimental errors in their determination. We see, therefore, that the concept of polytropic efficiency has considerable advantages over adiabatic efficiency when examining multistage turbo-machinery.

The usefulness of these and other definitions of efficiency lies not so much in permitting us to assess the performance of a given process, as in allowing us to predict the performance of some other process. We illustrate this by describing how measurements on a centrifugal compressor operating under one set of conditions can be used to predict its performance under a second set of conditions in which the gas, inlet pressure, pressure ratio, impeller speed, etc., are different. The method can be applied to a single stage or to a multistage machine, provided there is no intercooling. For simplicity, we assume that heat losses are negligible.

The principle of 'similarity' can be applied to centrifugal compressors and, although the results are not exact, they are usually adequate. Subject to certain restrictions on flow velocity of the gas and rotational speed of the impeller which are satisfied by standard machines operating close to design conditions, a given compressor is operating under 'similar' conditions, 1 and 2, if

$$(v_{in}/v_{out})_1 = (v_{in}/v_{out})_2$$

$$(\dot{m}v_{in}/\Omega)_1 = (\dot{m}v_{in}/\Omega)_2 \qquad (5.109)$$

$$(w_P/\Omega^2)_1 = (w_P/\Omega^2)_2$$

where v_{in} = volume/unit mass of gas under inlet conditions;
   v_{out} = volume/unit mass under outlet conditions;
   $\dot{m}$ = mass flow rate;
   Ω = rotational speed of impeller;
   w_P = polytropic work between inlet and outlet conditions.

When these conditions are satisfied, the compressor has a constant value for the polytropic efficiency η_P, $(\eta_P = w_P/w_a)$. Thus, for example, by making a series of fully instrumented tests on a compressor which include measurement of the work, w_a, supplied by the driver when compressing, say, air, we can calculate the work and the operating conditions when compressing, say, methane, with the same compressor, provided that the tests have been carried out at the values of v_{in}, v_{out}, $\dot{m}$ and Ω required by the similarity conditions (5.109). The calculation of w_P by the methods of Section 5.5 requires the use of thermodynamic charts or tables.

5.14 Refrigeration and gas liquefaction

The uses of sub-ambient temperatures produced by refrigeration include the recovery, liquefaction and storage of gases, the crystallisation of salts from solution, the dewaxing of petroleum products, and the separation of oxygen and nitrogen from air.

Any change which produces work can be used to absorb heat and so generate low temperatures, but to make the cooling continuous, that is, to develop a method of *mechanical refrigeration*, we must devise a flow process in which the working fluid or *refrigerant* absorbs heat at a sub-ambient temperature and rejects it at a higher temperature. Thus, mechanical refrigeration may be thought of as a process for 'pumping' heat.

It was shown in Section 3.5, that any steady-state flow cyclic process which absorbs heat at one temperature and rejects it at a lower temperature serves as a refrigerator when the cycle is reversed. For reasons which are discussed later, the reversed Carnot cycle* cannot be used without modification and in the cycles used in practice, the temperature of the refrigerant is reduced by evaporation, irreversible expansion, or reversible expansion, according to the state of the refrigerant.

Although we are concerned primarily with the principles involved in the design of refrigeration processes, it is important to consider their applications, since, as was shown in Section 3.26, 'loss' of availability, i.e. thermodynamic irreversibility, occurs in the exchanger used to transfer heat from the process stream to the refrigerant. The simplest application is the removal of heat at

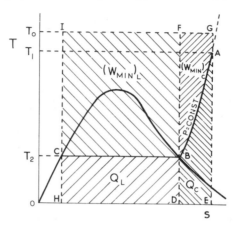

Figure 5.26. Relationship between the refrigeration effect and the required minimum work

constant temperature, as in the condensation of a saturated vapour. Other applications involve reducing the temperature of a material without change of phase. Figure 5.26 represents a combination of both processes, in which gas initially at pressure P and temperature T_1, is cooled isobarically along AB to its condensation temperature T_2, then latent heat is removed isothermally along BC until condensation is complete at C. Thus, it is important to match the temperature profile of the refrigerant along the length of the heat exchanger to that of the process fluid, if large irreversibilities are to be avoided.

5.15   Minimum work of refrigeration

The *refrigeration effect* is the heat which is removed in a cooling process. To maintain consistency with the convention that heat added to a system is positive we formally define the refrigeration effect as the heat taken in by the

---

*Throughout the remainder of this Chapter, we omit the word *reversed* where there is no possibility of ambiguity.

refrigerator from the process stream being cooled. It is therefore a positive quantity. Thus, when as in Figure 5.26, a process stream is cooled isobarically from A to B the refrigeration effect Q_C is (neglecting heat losses)

$$Q_C = \text{heat taken in by refrigerator}$$

$$= \text{heat given up by process stream}$$

$$= -(H_B - H_A) = -\int_{T_1}^{T_2} T \, dS_P \tag{5.110}$$

and is equal to the area ABDE.

The minimum work which must be supplied to the refrigerator to bring about this cooling is equal to the change in availability, B, which from (3.255) is given by

$$(W_{min})_C = B_B - B_A = (H_B - H_A) - T_0(S_B - S_A) \tag{5.111}$$

and is the area ABFG. Note, $(W_{min})_C$ is a positive quantity.

For the liquefaction process, BC, the refrigeration effect Q_L is the area BCHD, and the minimum work $(W_{min})_L$ is the area BCIF, whilst for the combined process the effect and minimum work are the areas ABCHE and ABCIG respectively. The *refrigeration duty* is the effect per unit time and the corresponding minimum work per unit time is the minimum power.

It is logical to define the efficiency of refrigeration as the ratio of the minimum work needed to produce a given refrigeration effect to the actual work required, and we use this definition when we consider gas liquefaction. However, in the case of removal of heat at constant temperature, it is customary to use the coefficient of performance, β, defined in Section 3.5 as the ratio of heat extracted at the lower temperature to the work input to the machine, i.e. the ratio of the refrigeration effect to the work done. Thus

$$\beta = Q/W = \dot{Q}/\dot{W} \tag{5.112}$$

This definition of the coefficient of performance does not imply that work is always needed to operate a refrigerator; it is shown in Section 5.16(c) that the energy input may be in the form of heat.

The minimum work for the isothermal process illustrated in Figure 5.26 enables the maximum value for coefficient of performance to be calculated. Thus,

$$\beta_{max} = \frac{\text{area BCHD}}{\text{area BCIF}} = \frac{T_2}{(T_0 - T_2)} \tag{5.113}$$

which we recognise from (3.48) as the coefficient of performance of a Carnot cycle operating between T_0 and T_2.

This equation shows the rapid rise in the minimum power required for a given refrigeration duty as the temperature T_2 decreases. For example, if heat is absorbed at 240 K and rejected at 303 K, then $\beta_{max} = 240/(303-240) = 3.8$, i.e. the expenditure of 1 kW produces a refrigeration duty of 3.8 kW.

On the other hand, the same power input would produce a potential duty of only 72 W if the heat were absorbed at 20 K.

Another criterion of performance which will become less common as SI units are more widely adopted is the horse-power input per ton of refrigeration. A ton of refrigeration is the rate of heat transfer needed to produce 1 short ton (2000 lb) of ice at 32 °F in 24 hours from water at the same temperature, and is equivalent to 3.52 kW.

Exercise

Show that 1 h.p./(ton of refrigeration) is equivalent to 4.7/(coefficient of performance).

The coefficient of performance of a Carnot cycle is used as a standard against which the efficiency of other refrigeration cycles can be judged, since, for given temperature limits, it cannot be exceeded. We now consider some actual cycles to show how they depart from the Carnot. First we discuss the absorption of heat at constant temperature and later in the Chapter, combined cooling and liquefaction.

5.16   Refrigeration cycles

(a) Vapour compression cycle

It would be difficult to design a steady-state flow cyclic process which operated entirely in the gaseous phase, and which would absorb heat isothermally as in the Carnot cycle described in Section 3.5. Consequently, for constant temperature refrigeration, we use a vapour compression cycle in which the refrigeration effect is produced by the continuous isothermal evaporation of a liquid.

Figures 5.27a and b show the essential components and the ideal thermodynamic path in T-S co-ordinates of the simplest cycle used in practice. Saturated vapour, A, leaving the evaporator is compressed reversibly and adiabatically, then the superheated vapour, B, is cooled at constant pressure until it has condensed. When saturated liquid, C, expands irreversibly and adiabatically through a valve, i.e. with no change in enthalpy, part of the liquid flashes into vapour to produce mixture D. The lines of constant H within the two phase region are such that, for all substances, this results in a decrease in temperature. During DA, the remaining liquid in the mixture evaporates at constant suction pressure absorbing heat until it is converted to saturated vapour A to complete the cycle. Comparison of Figures 5.27b and c shows that this cycle differs from a Carnot cycle operating entirely in the two phase region, in two ways. First, compression takes place in the superheated region because it would be difficult to stop the evaporative process at a state

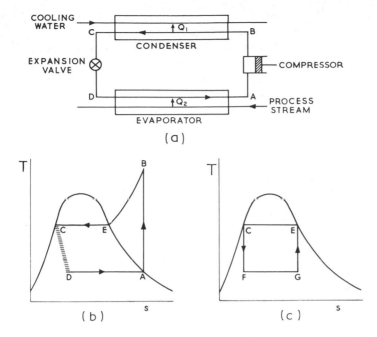

Figure 5.27. Vapour-compression refrigeration cycle: (a) flow diagram; (b) ideal cycle; (c) Carnot cycle

represented by G, see Figure 5.27c; furthermore, as was mentioned in Section 5.12, it is difficult to compress wet vapour efficiently so as to discharge saturated vapour. Secondly, saturated liquid is expanded isenthalpically through a valve instead of isentropically in an engine or turbine. The reason for including an irreversible step in the cycle is that the maximum work which can be recovered by an expander is small compared with the minimum work needed to compress the vapour and, except in the largest installations, the value of the work saved by using an expander is more than offset by the increased cost of the plant. Where, however, an expander is used instead of an expansion valve, its output is coupled to the compressor to reduce the net work input.

The type of compressor depends on the temperature required in the evaporator and on the refrigeration duty. In general, reciprocating compressors are used when the duty at, say, $-20\,^{\circ}\mathrm{C}$ is less than about $500\,\mathrm{kW}$ (150 tons), whereas centrifugal compressors are used for higher duties up to about $20\,\mathrm{MW}$ (6000 tons). The pressure ratio at which the compressor operates is the ratio of the saturation pressures of the refrigerant at the condensation and evaporation temperatures. In the case of a reciprocating compressor this ratio is restricted to about 9 per stage, whereas 5 is more usual for a centrifugal machine. Hence single-stage reciprocating machines are used for small duties at low temperatures, but screw compressors may ultimately replace them because of their lower maintenance costs. When the evaporator pressure is below atmospheric it is desirable to use a hermetically sealed compressor to avoid ingress of air. This is practicable for up to 75 kW reciprocating and 750 kW centrifugal compressors. The condenser may be of the water-cooled shell and tube or evaporative type, but the need for economy in the use of water has led to the wide application of air-cooled condensers on larger installations. In some plants, process streams are used as heat sinks. The stream to be cooled by the refrigerant may be passed directly through a shell and tube evaporator or, alternatively, a secondary refrigerant, such as trichlorethylene or an aqueous solution of NaCl, $CaCl_2$ or propylene glycol, may be used to transfer the heat from the process stream to the primary refrigerant, but this does introduce further irreversibilities.

If, as in Figure 5.27b, the compression is isentropic and the expansion isenthalpic, then, for flow of unit mass of refrigerant round the cycle,

heat transferred in the evaporator $\quad q_2 = h_A - h_D$

heat transferred in the condenser $\quad q_1 = h_C - h_B$

work of compression $\qquad\qquad w = -(q_1 + q_2) = (h_B - h_A)$

Hence, the coefficient of performance

$$\beta = q_2/w = (h_A - h_D)/(h_B - h_A) \qquad (5.114)$$

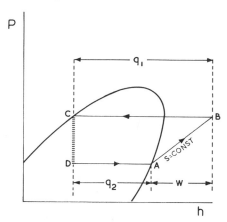

Figure 5.28. Ideal vapour-compression refrigeration cycle in P-h co-ordinates

The enthalpies of refrigerants can be obtained from thermodynamic tables or charts (see Sections 4.17 and 4.18), and it is convenient to use P-H charts for this since, as shown in Figure 5.28, the work and heat can be read from the enthalpy axis once the pressure limits have been fixed from a knowledge of the refrigeration and cooling water temperatures. In practice, the temperature of the condensing refrigerant must be 5 to 10 K above that of the cooling water so that the heat can be transferred in a condenser of economic size. Similarly, the temperature of the refrigerant in the evaporator must be below that of the process stream or secondary refrigerant. These necessary temperature differences place a limit on the efficiency of the overall process. In an actual vapour compression cycle, each process is also, to some degree, irreversible. In Figure 5.29, ABCD represents the ideal and A'B'C'D' an actual cycle. Irreversibility in the compression process, A'B', leads to an increase of entropy and the actual work has to be calculated from the adiabatic or polytropic efficiency, as shown in Section 5.13. Fluid friction in the condenser and evaporator results in pressures at the outlets being lower than those at the inlets. Furthermore, sub-cooling of the condensate and superheating of the vapour occur because the temperature of the cooling water in the condenser has to be lower than that of the condensate, whereas the temperature of the process stream has to be higher than that in the evaporator. Hence A' and C' do not lie on the saturation boundary. Finally, leakage of heat into the expansion valve results in an increase in enthalpy along C'D'. In Section 5.17, we discuss common modifications to vapour

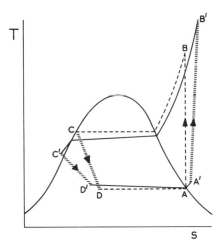

Figure 5.29. Actual vapour-compression refrigeration cycle in T-s co-ordinates

compression plant on the basis of an ideal cycle, since this simplifies the analysis, but it is important to bear in mind the differences between the ideal cycle and that which is realised in practice.

(b) Choice of refrigerant

The variety of processes requiring cooling has led to the use of a large number of halogenated hydrocarbons as refrigerants. To end the confusion caused by different manufacturers supplying the same compound under different trade names, international agreement has been reached on a number designation for refrigerants.[10] Here we describe each refrigerant by its chemical name, and give the number in parenthesis. A recent development is the use of azeotropic mixtures such as (R500) which is 73.8 wt% dichloro-difluoromethane (R12) and 26.2 wt% 1,1-difluoroethane (R152a). It will be seen in Chapter 7 that an azeotrope does not change its composition on condensation or evaporation; hence, it behaves in a vapour compression cycle as if it were a pure substance, but with thermodynamic properties different from those of its components.

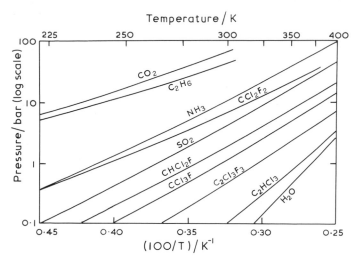

Figure 5.30. Vapour-pressure curves for common refrigerants

The most important property in choosing a refrigerant is its saturated vapour pressure, since this establishes the range of operating pressure for the compressor. Vapour pressure curves for several refrigerants are given in Figure 5.30; more comprehensive data may be found in handbooks.[11]

At one time it was customary to choose a refrigerant so that the pressure in the evaporator was slightly above atmospheric to prevent ingress of air. However, the use of non-flammable refrigerants, the development of efficient purge systems and of hermetically sealed compressors has led to the use of lower evaporator pressures, but with a consequent increase in the required compressor displacement for a given duty.

Since the size, and hence the cost of the plant, is governed by the volume flow rate of refrigerant, the enthalpy of evaporation per unit volume of saturated vapour at the suction pressure should be large. On the other hand, the vapour pressure of the refrigerant at the condensation temperature should be low, so as to reduce the cost of the compressor and the other high pressure parts of the machine. However, as can be seen from Figure 5.30, such choice is limited since the slopes of the vapour pressure curves do not vary widely.

If the ideal vapour compression cycle were a Carnot cycle, the coefficients of performance would be equal for all refrigerants operating between the same two fixed temperatures; hence, when considering the choice of refrigerant, we must bear in mind how the ideal cycle deviates from the Carnot. In Figure 5.31, the coefficient of performance of the Carnot cycle AJDGA based on the ideal vapour compression cycle ABCDEA is given by

$$\beta_{max} = \frac{\text{Area } (2+3)}{\text{Area } 4} = \frac{T_2}{T_0 - T_2} \tag{5.115}$$

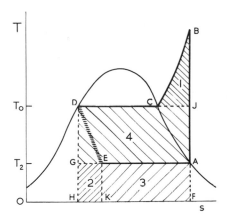

Figure 5.31. Deviations of an ideal vapour compression cycle from an equivalent Carnot cycle

In the ideal vapour compression cycle, the work done, w, is the difference between areas $(1+2+3+4)$ and area 3, the former being numerically equal to the heat transferred from the refrigerant in the condenser, q_0, and the latter to that transferred in the evaporator, q_2. Thus the coefficient of performance is given by

$$\beta = \frac{q_2}{w} = \frac{h_A - h_E}{h_B - h_A} = \frac{\text{Area } 3}{\text{Area } (4+1+2)} = \frac{\text{Area } (2+3) - \text{Area } 2}{\text{Area } 4 + \text{Area } (1+2)} \tag{5.116}$$

Comparison of (5.115) and (5.116) shows that β approaches β_{max} of the equivalent Carnot cycle as area 1, the superheat loss, and area 2, the loss in cooling arising from irreversible expansion, are reduced. A $T\text{-}S$ chart shows that the shape of the saturation boundary is such that, as the condensation temperature approaches the critical, the relative importance of areas 1 and 2 increases in relation to the refrigeration effect, area 3. Thus, the coefficient of performance of a cycle in which $T_0 - T_2$ is fixed falls off rapidly as T_0 approaches T^c. The low critical temperature of carbon dioxide (31 °C) thus accounts for the fact that it is seldom used as a refrigerant. On the other hand, when the condensation temperature is well below the critical, the power required to produce a given refrigeration duty is relatively insensitive to the choice of refrigerant, since the sum of the superheat and expansion losses tends to be fairly constant. However, the ratio of the two is by no means so. Dichlorodifluoromethane (R12) has a high value of $-(\partial T/\partial S)_\sigma$ along the saturated vapour boundary and a low value of $-(\partial T/\partial S)_H$ in the two-phase region; hence, the decrease in performance with this refrigerant occurs mainly as a result of the expansion process. With ammonia the relative magnitudes of the two derivatives are reversed and the superheat loss is the larger. Although the efficiency of a simple vapour compression cycle may not vary much with the choice of refrigerant, it will be seen later that the thermodynamic properties of the refrigerant have an important bearing on the way in which the cycle should be modified to improve its coefficient of performance.

(c) Absorption refrigeration

Absorption refrigerators use two working substances, a refrigerant, and an absorbent for the refrigerant. The principle is essentially that of a vapour compression refrigerator, except that the compressor is replaced by an absorber-stripper, the main energy input to which is in the form of heat rather than work. A detailed description of current absorption refrigeration is outside the scope of this book, and can be found in reviews.[12]

The most common absorption system uses ammonia as the refrigerant, and water, or occasionally aqueous solutions of calcium chloride and strontium chloride, as the absorbent. The essential components of an ammonia absorption refrigerator are shown in Figure 5.32a. Ammonia vapour leaving the evaporator at A is dissolved in cold water in the absorber with the evolution of heat and the concentrated solution is pumped to a higher pressure, at which the dissolved ammonia is stripped with the absorption of heat and enters the condenser at B. The absorber-stripper cycle is completed by returning the weak solution to the absorber via a heat exchanger. This reduces the heat input to the stripper by transferring heat from the weak to the concentrated solution as the latter is pumped to the stripper. The work of compression is much less than that in a conventional vapour-compression cycle since, as we have seen, pumping a liquid requires much less work than compressing a vapour between the same pressures. The heat to the stripper may be supplied in any convenient form, and it is the availability of waste heat which makes this process particularly attractive in chemical plant. However, there is a limit to the coefficient of performance of an absorption cycle. Heat is transferred at three temperature levels. First, atmospheric temperature, T_0, at which heat is rejected in the condenser and absorber. Secondly, refrigeration temperature, T_2, at which heat is absorbed in the evaporator and, thirdly, source temperature, T_1, at which heat is added to the stripper. A small quantity of energy is also added as work in the pump, but this is negligible compared with

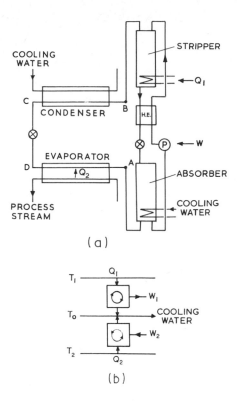

Figure 5.32. Absorption refrigerator: (a) flow diagram; (b) equivalent arrangement of reversible machines

the heat transfers. Figure 5.32b shows two reversible machines which perform an equivalent function.

First a reversible engine receives heat, Q_1, at temperature T_1, and rejects heat at T_0, while producing work W_1, which is negative, with an efficiency

$$-\frac{W_1}{Q_1} = \frac{T_1 - T_0}{T_1} \tag{5.117}$$

Secondly, a reversible refrigerator receives heat Q_2 at T_2, and rejects heat at T_0, while absorbing a quantity of work W_2, the coefficient of performance being given by

$$\frac{Q_2}{W_2} = \frac{T_2}{T_0 - T_2} \tag{5.118}$$

If $-W_1 = W_2$, the combined machines are equivalent to an absorption refrigerator for which the pump work is zero. The coefficient of performance which may be defined as Q_2/Q_1 is given by

$$\beta = \frac{Q_2}{Q_1} = \frac{T_2(T_1 - T_0)}{T_1(T_0 - T_2)} \tag{5.119}$$

The temperature of the cooling water, T_0, and the refrigeration temperature, T_2, are fixed; hence, only that of the heat source, T_1, can be varied. Equation (5.119) shows that in theory the higher T_1, the greater the coefficient of performance, the limiting value $T_2/(T_0 - T_2)$ being that of a Carnot cycle. However, in practice, the thermodynamic properties of the ammonia solution are such that the heat absorbed in the evaporator, Q_2, is not independent of that absorbed in the stripper, Q_1, as is implied by (5.119). The ratio of these, and hence the coefficient of performance, is usually only about 0.9, but this low value is unimportant if waste heat is available. On the other hand, the actual coefficient of performance of the absorption cycle, unlike that of the vapour compression cycle, decreases only slowly as the temperature difference between the condenser and evaporator $(T_0 - T_2)$ is increased. For further information, reference should be made to worked examples of the heat and mass balances necessary to calculate the coefficient of performance of an ammonia absorption refrigerator.[13]

If circulation of the refrigerant is maintained by convection currents caused by density gradients, the pump may be dispensed with, but this type of refrigerator, sometimes referred to as the Electrolux or Servel, is used only in the home.

Water/lithium bromide absorption plants are now used extensively to provide chilled water at temperatures above 5 °C. The principle is similar to that of the ammonia system, and depends upon the ability of a concentrated solution of lithium bromide to absorb the refrigerant water endothermically. At 5 °C, the vapour pressure of water is only 0.009 bar and it was the development of hermetically sealed equipment which has made possible absorption plants of 5.4 MW (1500 tons) duty.

(d) Vacuum refrigeration

Water is a satisfactory refrigerant for many processes requiring cooling to temperatures not below 5 °C. Its chief disadvantage is the large specific volume of saturated vapour at low temperatures which calls for large compressors. Reciprocating compressors cannot handle the volumetric flow rate required for large duties and, although centrifugal compressors have been used, steam-jet ejectors are preferred, in spite of their low efficiency, because they are cheaper and involve less maintenance.

Figure 5.33 shows a vacuum refrigerator for chilling water which uses a steam-jet ejector. The water is sprayed into a thermally insulated flash chamber, A, where part of it evaporates at the low pressure maintained by ejector, B. Thus, the cooling effect is provided by the latent heat of

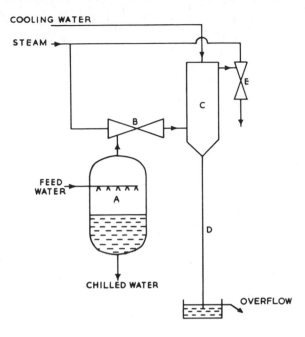

Figure 5.33. Vacuum refrigerator

evaporation. The ejector discharges into a condenser, C, in which the pressure is determined by the temperature of the available cooling water. Since this pressure is below atmospheric, a pump or barometric leg, D, must be used to remove the condensate, and another ejector, E, to remove air, originally entrained in the cooling water. Steam supplied to the ejector, when condensed, serves as make-up water to replace the spray water carried away as vapour. Thus, unlike the previous steady state flow processes, this is not a closed cycle.

Vacuum refrigeration systems using ejectors or centrifugal compressors can handle fluctuating loads much better than conventional vapour compression or absorption processes. Details of equipment and the economic factors of units having duties up to 7.0 MW (2000 tons) have been described.[14]

5.17 Modification to the vapour-compression cycle

We now consider modifications to the simple vapour-compression cycle, either to improve its performance or to lower the temperature at which heat is absorbed. Figure 5.31 shows that the reduced coefficient of performance of the ideal cycle, compared with an equivalent Carnot cycle operating between the same temperatures, arises from superheat and expansion losses. The relative importance of these losses has been shown to depend on the shape of the saturation line, the condensation and evaporation temperature limits and the critical temperature of the refrigerant in relation to the condensation temperature. With halogenated hydrocarbons, most of the loss is caused by irreversible expansion; consequently, to improve the performance we should reduce the entropy increase across the valve. On the other hand, refrigerants such as ammonia have large superheat losses which can be reduced only by incorporating interstage coolers in the compressor, a process which is sometimes called *desuperheating*.

(a) Sub-cooling the condensed refrigerant

The duty of a vapour-compression cycle operating at a given condensation temperature can be increased by sub-cooling the condensate before it reaches the expansion valve. As has been shown, some sub-cooling occurs in all cycles, but the effect may be exploited by using an auxiliary cooling system, or by heat exchange with cold gas leaving the evaporator. In the latter case, the improvement in performance depends strongly on the thermodynamic properties of the refrigerant. Since the heat capacity of the vapour is less than that of the liquid, the temperature change of the vapour is greater than that of the liquid, and sub-cooling the condensate at the expense of increasing the vapour superheat is beneficial only for refrigerants, such as monochlorodifluoromethane (R22) for which $-(\partial T/\partial S)_\sigma$ is large along the saturated vapour boundary.

(b) Multi-stage compression

As the temperature in the evaporator is decreased whilst maintaining the condensation temperature constant, the required pressure ratio of the compressor increases but, since that of a single stage machine seldom exceeds 9, the refrigeration temperature of an ammonia cycle is limited to about $-25\,°C$ for a condensation temperature of $30\,°C$. Lower temperatures require multistage compression with interstage cooling, but the method differs from that used in gas compression at ambient temperatures because the temperature of the compressed vapour cannot be reduced by water cooling. Several methods employ refrigerant as coolant; that shown in Figure 5.34 uses two-stage expansion. Liquid refrigerant, E, from the condenser expands to F in an *open flash intercooler*, sometimes known as an *economiser*, in which the pressure is the same as the compressor interstage pressure. Saturated liquid, G, flows through the second expansion valve into the evaporator, while the vapour, J, from the flash intercooler is mixed with vapour, B, leaving the first stage compressor, so that the combined suction stream to the second stage is at a temperature corresponding to C. The optimum interstage pressure depends on the adiabatic efficiencies of the compressors and can be selected

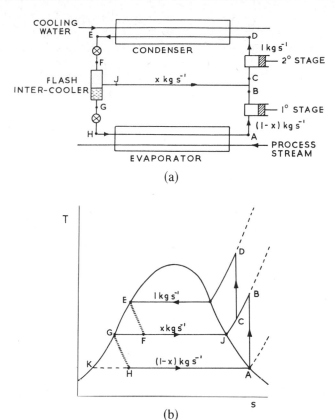

Figure 5.34. Two stage vapour-compression cycle with flash intercooler

by an iterative calculation to maximise the coefficient of performance. Often it is sufficient to assume equal compression ratios for each stage.

Note that the mass flow rates in the different parts of the cycle shown in Figure 5.34b are not equal; the T-S diagram shows only the state of unit mass of the fluid at each point. Due allowance must be made for this when interpreting areas on the diagram as heat transferred.

The improved coefficient of performance of this two-stage cycle, compared with that of a single-stage cycle operating between the same temperatures, arises not only from the reduction in work by interstage cooling, but also from the smaller amount of vapour to be compressed in the first stage. Multistage compression is commonly used with centrifugal machines operating on refrigerants such as ammonia and carbon dioxide which have large superheat losses.

A three-stage vapour-compression process, see Figure 5.35, is used to produce solid carbon dioxide but, unlike the two-stage arrangement, this does

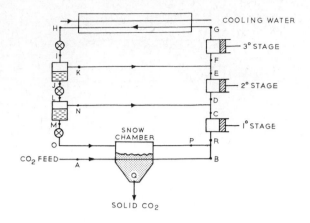

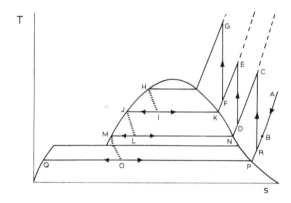

Figure 5.35. Three stage vapour-compression process for the production of solid carbon dioxide

not operate as a cycle. When liquid carbon-dioxide, M, passes through the expansion valve into the snow chamber, it flashes into a solid-vapour mixture, O, if the pressure in the chamber (usually atmospheric) is below the triple point pressure, 5.18 bar. Solid carbon dioxide, Q, is collected and the vapour fed to the first stage compressor together with fresh feed pre-cooled by passing through a coil in the snow chamber.

Example

Calculate the coefficient of performance of an ideal two-stage ammonia vapour compression cycle operating between $-30\,^{\circ}C$ and $26\,^{\circ}C$ assuming that the open flash intercooler is at $-10\,^{\circ}C$.

In Figure 5.34, second compressor delivers $1\,kg\,s^{-1}$. Mayhew and Rogers' tables (see Preface) give $h_E = 303.7\,kJ\,kg^{-1}$ for saturated liquid ammonia entering first throttle at $26\,^{\circ}C$. We read off also h_G and h_J for the intercooler at $-10\,°C$ (values given below). Since $h_F = h_E$ for the throttle, quality at F is

$$x = (h_F - h_G)/(h_J - h_G) = (303.7 - 135.4)/(1433.0 - 135.4) = 0.13$$

For second throttle, $h_G = h_H$, and after reading h_A (saturated vapour at $-30\,°C$) from the tables, we obtain refrigeration duty as

$$\dot{q}_2 = (1 - x)(h_A - h_H) = 0.87 \times (1405.6 - 135.4) = 1105\,\text{kW}$$

From tables, $s_A = 5.785\,\text{kJ K}^{-1}\,\text{kg}^{-1}$, $s_J = 5.475\,\text{kJ K}^{-1}\,\text{kg}^{-1}$, $h_J = 1433.0\,\text{kJ kg}^{-1}$ and for vapour at J superheated by 50 K along isobar JCB, $h = 1551.7\,\text{kJ kg}^{-1}$ and $s = 5.891\,\text{kJ K}^{-1}\,\text{kg}^{-1}$. For first compressor, $s_A = s_B$, thus by interpolation

$$h_B = h_J + (1551.7 - h_J)(s_B - s_J)/(5.891 - 5.475) = 1521.4\,\text{kJ kg}^{-1}$$

power $\qquad \mathcal{P}_1 = (1 - x)(h_B - h_A) = 0.87 \times (1521.4 - 1405.6) = 100.7\,\text{kW}$

We characterise state C as

$$h_C = x h_J + (1 - x)h_B = 0.13 \times 1433.0 + 0.87 \times 1521.6 = 1510.0\,\text{kJ kg}^{-1}$$

$$s_C = s_J + (h_C - h_J)(5.891 - s_J)/(1551.7 - h_J) = 5.745\,\text{kJK}^{-1}\,\text{kg}^{-1}$$

From tables, $s = 5.458\,\text{kJ K}^{-1}\,\text{kg}^{-1}$, $h = 1605.3\,\text{kJ kg}^{-1}$ for saturated vapour at $26\,°C$ superheated by 50 K and $s = 5.790\,\text{kJ K}^{-1}\,\text{kg}^{-1}$, $h = 1729.6\,\text{kJ kg}^{-1}$ for 100 K. For second compressor, $s_D = s_C$, thus

$$h_D = 1605.3 + (s_D - 5.458)(1729.6 - 1605.3)/(5.790 - 5.458)$$

$$= 1712.7\,\text{kJ kg}^{-1}$$

power $\mathcal{P}_2 = h_D - h_C = 1712.7 - 1510.1 = 202.6\,\text{kW}$. Hence coefficient of performance

$$\beta = \dot{q}_2/(\mathcal{P}_1 + \mathcal{P}_2) = 1105/(100.9 + 202.6) = 3.64$$

(c) Compound vapour compression cycle

This cycle, illustrated in Figure 5.36, combines the thermodynamic advantages of condensate sub-cooling with interstage cooling. Liquid refrigerant from condenser, F, is split into two streams; the larger flows at condenser pressure through intercooler 1, while the other is expanded to an intermediate pressure P_i and is then evaporated in the intercooler. The liquid refrigerant is further sub-cooled in intercooler 2 by saturated vapour, A, leaving the evaporator. For optimum efficiency, the pressure ratio for each compression stage should be approximately the same and the temperature at K should approach that at G as closely as possible. Suction intercooler 2 is omitted with refrigerants having large superheat losses, and the compound cycle is then similar to the two-stage process shown in Figure 5.34, except that the closed intercooler 1 replaces the open-flash intercooler. Thermodynamically, the flash intercooler is equivalent to a heat exchanger with zero temperature approach, but this advantage is offset by difficulties of control which account for the wider use of closed intercoolers.

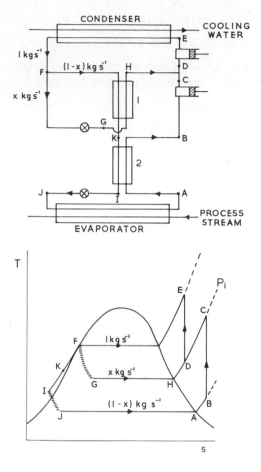

Figure 5.36. Two stage compound vapour-compression cycle

(d) Binary cascade cycles

In theory, the lower temperature limit of a multistage cycle is fixed only by the triple point of the refrigerant. In practice, there are difficulties if the pressure on the suction side of the compressor is substantially less than atmospheric (see page 238); thus for ammonia, the lower limit is about $-35\,°C$. This limit may be lowered by using ethane or ethylene (cf. Figure 5.30), but then the pressure in the condenser is high if it is water cooled. A high condenstation pressure can be avoided by using a binary cascade cycle (sometimes known as *split-stage* compression), in which two simple cycles each using a different refrigerant are connected via a heat exchanger, as shown in Figure 5.37. The refrigerant of higher vapour pressure is condensed by evaporating the other refrigerant which, in turn, is condensed by water cooling.

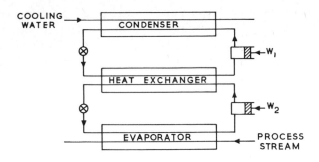

Figure 5.37. Binary cascade refrigerator

Exercise

Show that the overall coefficient of performance of a binary cycle, β_0, is related to the coefficients of performance of the component cycles, β_1, and β_2, by

$$(1 + \beta_0^{-1}) = (1 + \beta_1^{-1})(1 + \beta_2^{-1}) \qquad (5.120)$$

Equation (5.120) requires that β_0 is less than both β_1 and β_2. At temperatures down to about $-30\,°C$, the coefficient of performance of the two-stage expansion process is higher than that of a cascade system, because

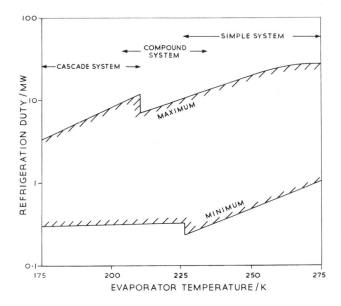

Figure 5.38. Duties of actual vapour-compression cycles

an additional source of irreversibility is introduced into the latter by the non-zero temperature difference between the condensing and evaporating refrigerants in the heat exchanger. As will be seen in Section 5.19, ternary cascade systems are widely used for the liquefaction of natural gas.

(e) Selection of vapour-compression cycles

Figure 5.38 shows the duties of the different vapour compression cycles currently used,[15] based on the assumption that the minimum number of compressors is employed; one compressor for a simple cycle and two for compound and cascade cycles. The maximum and minimum duties relate to centrifugal compressors; if the required duty falls below this minimum, it is best handled by a reciprocating machine. The overlapping ranges arise from the possible use of more than one refrigerant at a given duty and temperature.

5.18 Low temperature gas liquefaction

Gas can be liquefied by either of the paths shown in Figure 5.39a. Path ABC involves cooling at constant pressure down to the condensation temperature followed by liquefaction at this same constant pressure. Path ADEC involves isothermal compression (to D), isobaric cooling (to E) and then conversion to saturated liquid (C) by adiabatic expansion. Table 5.1 gives the refrigeration effect and equivalent minimum work needed to cool various gases at atmospheric pressure down to their condensation temperature, the normal boiling point, and then to condense them completely. These values have been calculated from equation (5.111) by assuming a heat sink temperature, T_0, of 303 K and an initial gas temperature, T_1, of 293 K. It will be noted that the fraction of the total work required for cooling increases as the normal boiling point decreases. If the processes in Figure 5.39a are both reversible, the total

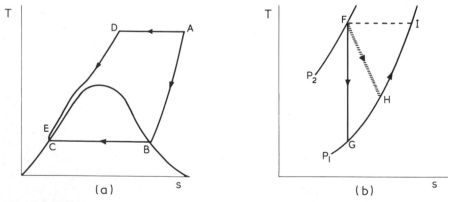

Figure 5.39. (a) Two types of path leading to liquefaction. (b) Cooling effect caused by gas expansion

Table 5.1. Refrigeration effect, Δh, and minimum work, w_{min}, needed to cool and liquefy various gases

| Gas | Normal boiling point/K | $\Delta h/\text{kJ kg}^{-1}$ | | | $w_{min}/\text{kJ kg}^{-1}$ | | |
		Cooling	Lique-faction	Total	Cooling	Lique-faction	Total
Ethylene	169.4	163	485	648	75	396	470
Methane	111.8	397	512	908	277	870	1 147
Oxygen	90.2	197	213	410	133	498	631
Nitrogen	77.8	224	199	423	197	580	777
Neon	27.3	275	86	361	482	859	1 341
Hydrogen	20.4	3 413	434	3 847	6 100	6 090	12 190
Helium	4.2	1 509	21	1 530	6 901	1 488	8 389

work required and the total refrigeration effect are independent of path and the figures given in Table 5.1 apply to path ADEC also.

When the practical implementation of these alternative paths is considered, differences arise. Isothermal compression is impossible, although it may be approximated by a multistage compressor with interstage cooling. This counts against path ADEC, but by far the most important difference arises from the difficulty in providing efficient cooling for the steps DE and ABC. Whichever path is used, we must have a supply of cold refrigerant, usually a gas, with which the process stream to be liquefied can exchange heat in a counter-current heat exchanger. This supply of cold gas can be obtained by reversible adiabatic expansion from pressure P_2 to P_1 along path FG, see Figure 5.39b; or by irreversible expansion through a throttle, provided that F is below the upper inversion temperature at pressure P_2, but the temperature drop will be much smaller (to H in Figure 5.39b). The initial temperature is assumed to be room temperature in each case. Thus, as the cold refrigerant gas flows through the heat exchanger countercurrent to the process stream being liquefied, it follows the isobaric path back to I. Since the isobar is smooth without any discontinuities in slope, the heat exchange will take place with less loss of availability, see page 116, if the process stream follows DE rather than ABC, for in the former case it is possible to realise small temperature differences across the heat exchanger, whereas in the latter the absorption of latent heat during BC makes this impossible. Path DE, therefore, is well 'matched' to the refrigerant stream and in practice less power is needed to operate the compressors (refrigerant stream + process stream) than for path ABC (refrigerant stream only—there are no compressors in the process stream).

Practical liquefaction processes, see Section 5.19, tend to be very much more complex than either of the two paths illustrated in Figure 5.39, but in all cases the design is such as to try to keep the temperature differences between the two countercurrent streams as small as possible compatible with mechanical and economic limitations.

In view of the importance of heat transfer over a range of temperature, we begin by examining the efficiency of gas refrigeration cycles. A gas refrigeration cycle is one in which there is no change in phase at any part of the cycle. Hence the evaporator and condenser of the vapour compression cycle are replaced by heat exchangers which transfer heat over a range of temperature. This discussion should also lead to a better understanding of the more complex steady-state flow liquefaction processes.

Gas refrigeration cycles are not based on the Carnot cycle because, in the absence of a second phase, it is impractical to absorb or reject heat isothermally. An ideal cycle which can be simulated is the reversed Joule, usually known as the reversed Brayton in the U.S.A., the flow and T-S diagrams for which are shown in Figure 5.40. After isentropic compression

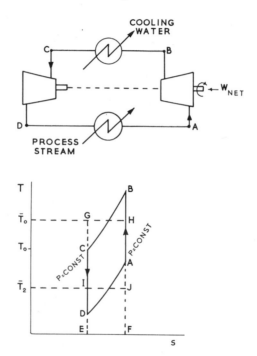

Figure 5.40. Ideal reversed Joule (Brayton) cycle

from A to B, the gaseous refrigerant is cooled by isobaric heat transfer to the surroundings at T_0. During isentropic expansion of the gas to the suction pressure of the compressor, the temperature drops to T_D, after which the refrigerant absorbs heat isobarically in returning to A. If the output from the expander is used to drive the compressor, the net work input for this cycle is the area ABCD, the refrigeration effect the area EDAF, and the coefficient of performance the ratio of the two.

We define the mean temperature $\bar{T}_0$ at which heat is rejected by

$$\bar{T}_0 = \frac{\displaystyle\int_B^C T \, ds_P}{s_C - s_B} \tag{5.121}$$

Similarly, the mean temperature $\bar{T}_2$ at which heat is absorbed is

$$\bar{T}_2 = \frac{\displaystyle\int_D^A T \, ds_P}{s_A - s_D} \tag{5.122}$$

Thus, $\bar{T}_0$ is such that the heat rejected is equal both to area FBCE and to area FHGE. Similarly $\bar{T}_2$ is such that the heat absorbed is equal to both area EDAF and to area EIJF. Hence, the coefficient of performance, β, of a gas refrigeration cycle is given by

$$\beta = \bar{T}_2/(\bar{T}_0 - \bar{T}_2) \tag{5.123}$$

which has the same form as that for a Carnot cycle but is in terms of the mean temperatures at which heat is rejected and absorbed.

Exercise

Show that, for a perfect gas for which the heat capacity is independent of temperature, the coefficient of performance of the reversed Joule cycle is given by

$$\beta^{-1} = (P_2/P_1)^{(\gamma-1)/\gamma} - 1 \qquad \text{(pg)} \tag{5.124}$$

where P_2/P_1 is the pressure ratio of the compressor.

Equation (5.124) shows that decreasing the pressure ratio increases the coefficient of performance, but the refrigeration effect can only be maintained by increasing the flow rate. Thus, the low thermodynamic efficiency and the large size of the plant accounts for the fact that the Joule cycle is seldom used for *constant temperature* heat absorption duties. Clearly, from Figure 5.40, if we wished to absorb heat at a constant temperature T_A, a vapour-compression cycle operating between T_A and T_C would be more efficient than a gaseous cycle operating between T_D and T_B. However, as a non-cyclic process, it is used to cool air, the air acting as its own refrigerant, and the T-S diagram for the process is similar to that shown in Figure 5.40 except that step $D \rightarrow A$ is omitted.

Figure 5.40 shows that the difference between the mean temperatures at which heat is absorbed and rejected is determined by the pressure ratio of the compressor. However, the difference may be varied independently of this ratio if a heat exchanger is incorporated, the resulting cycle (see Figure 5.41) being known as the reversed regenerative Joule or *Bell-Coleman*. We assume that the transfer of heat in the exchanger is reversible, i.e. there is an infinitesimally small temperature difference between the two gas streams at

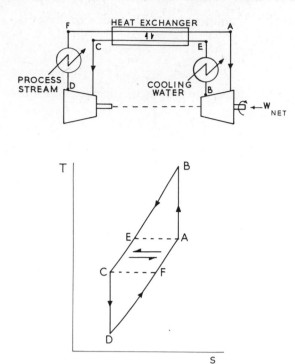

Figure 5.41. Ideal Bell-Coleman refrigeration cycle

all points along the heat exchanger, a situation which, strictly, is possible only for perfect gases of constant heat capacity ratio. Thus, in the limit $T_A = T_E$ and $T_C = T_F$. A cycle in which heat is transferred reversibly from fluid in one part of the cycle to fluid in another part, is known as a *regenerative cycle* and the exchanger with which this is accomplished is sometimes called a *regenerator* or *regenerative heat exchanger*.

Exercise

Show that, for a perfect gas for which the heat capacity is independent of temperature, the coefficient of performance of the ideal reversed regenerative Joule cycle is given by

$$\beta^{-1} = \left(\frac{T_A}{T_C}\right)\left(\frac{P_2}{P_1}\right)^{(\gamma-1)/\gamma} - 1 \qquad \text{(pg)} \tag{5.125}$$

where P_2/P_1 is the pressure ratio of the compressor, T_A is the suction temperature to the compressor, and T_C the inlet temperature to the expander.

If it were possible to compress and expand gas reversibly and isothermally, the regenerative Bell-Coleman cycle would have the form shown in Figure 5.42a, known as the reversed *Ericsson cycle*. Similarly, if the regenerative principle were employed at constant volume, instead of at constant pressure, the resulting cycle known as the reversed *Stirling cycle* would be as shown in Figure 5.42b.

In both of these ideal cycles, heat transfer to and from the surroundings occurs only during the isothermal processes. Heat transfer shown by the arrows within the cycle is assumed to take place reversibly, i.e. across an infinitesimally small temperature difference and to be completely independent of the surroundings. Hence, the coefficient of performance of both cycles approaches that of a Carnot cycle operating between the same temperature limits.

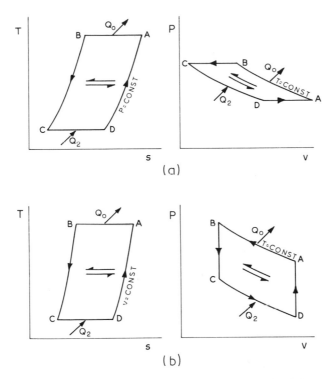

Figure 5.42. (a) Reversed Ericsson cycle. (b) Reversed Stirling cycle

Exercise

Show that the coefficients of performance of the Stirling and Ericsson cycles are equal to that of a Carnot cycle operating between the same temperature limits only if the working fluid is a perfect gas.

We now show how these cycles are used in actual liquefaction processes.

5.19 Liquefaction processes

(a) Single stage throttle

The first continuously operating air liquefier was developed by Linde in Germany in 1895. The process (known as the Hampson in the U.K. and the Linde elsewhere) makes use of the drop in temperature which occurs when compressed air is throttled adiabatically. It may seem surprising that the small Joule-Thomson effect can be used to lower the temperature sufficiently to liquefy air, but it is only by combining the expansion with heat exchange as shown in Figure 5.43 that the cooling may be made cumulative.

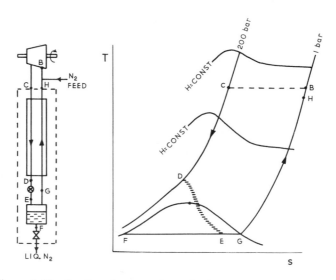

Figure 5.43. Gas liquefaction using a single stage throttle expansion

We shall discuss the steady-state processes developed for liquefying air on the assumption that pure nitrogen is being liquefied. This simplifies the calculations without detracting from the thermodynamic principles. For a discussion of the separation by distillation of a mixture such as liquid air, into its constituents, see Section 7.6.

Nitrogen compressed to a super-critical pressure in a multi-stage compressor, then cooled to ambient temperature, enters the heat exchanger at C. Initially, when the whole system is at ambient temperature, the gas leaves the heat exchanger at D uncooled, and suffers only a small fall in temperature on throttle expansion. However, passage through the heat exchanger countercurrent to the incoming gas cools the latter so that it arrives at D colder than ambient, and becomes still colder after expansion. The temperature at E falls until liquid nitrogen is produced and a steady-state established, when the rate of feed of gaseous nitrogen into the system equals that of liquid removed. Figure 5.43 shows the steady state liquefaction in T-S co-ordinates. For convenience, the compression is represented as isothermal, but although the initial temperature at B is the same as the final at C, the path of the multistage compression process with interstage and after-cooling is similar to that shown in Figure 5.14b; hence the line joining the initial and final states of the compression is shown broken. If fraction ε of the gas entering the heat exchanger is liquefied, an enthalpy balance on the system enclosed by the dotted line in Figure 5.43 gives, if there are no heat losses to the surroundings,

$$h_C = h_F + (1 - \varepsilon) h_H$$

or

$$\varepsilon = (h_H - h_C)/(h_H - h_F) \qquad (5.126)$$

Thus no liquid is produced unless the specific enthalpy of the nitrogen leaving the heat exchanger is higher than that of the warmer gas entering.

In order to compare the performance of various liquefaction processes we define the *thermodynamic efficiency* η as the ratio of the minimum work needed to liquefy unit mass of gas, w_{min} [with the environment at atmospheric temperature, see (5.111)], to the actual work, w_a

$$\eta = w_{min}/w_a \qquad (5.127)$$

Example

In the process shown in Figure 5.43, nitrogen initially at 300 K is compressed to 200 bar with an isothermal efficiency η_T of 0.70. If the minimum approach temperature in the heat exchanger $(T_C - T_H)$ is 5 K, calculate the thermodynamic efficiency of the process, assuming that the temperature of the surroundings is 300 K.

With reference to Figure 5.43 and thermodynamic tables for the properties of nitrogen[16]

$$s_B = 6.831 \text{ kJ K}^{-1} \text{ kg}^{-1}, \quad s_C = 5.152 \text{ kJ K}^{-1} \text{ kg}^{-1}, \quad s_F = 2.843 \text{ kJ K}^{-1} \text{ kg}^{-1}$$
$$h_B = 556.3 \text{ kJ kg}^{-1}, \quad h_C = 524.2 \text{ kJ kg}^{-1}, \quad h_F = 125.7 \text{ kJ kg}^{-1}$$

Work for isothermal compression from B to C is given by

$$w = (h_B - h_C) - T(s_B - s_C) = (556.3 - 524.2) - 300(6.831 - 5.152)$$
$$= 471.6 \text{ kJ kg}^{-1}$$

Actual work per kg nitrogen compressed $= 471.6/0.70 = 674.0 \text{ kJ}$

$$T_H = T_C - 5 = 300 - 5 = 295 \text{ K}$$

Hence from tables, $h_H = 551.3 \text{ kJ kg}^{-1}$. From (5.126)

$$\varepsilon = (h_H - h_C)/(h_H - h_F)$$
$$= (551.3 - 524.2)/(551.3 - 125.7)$$
$$= 27.1/425.5 = 0.0638$$

Actual work per kg nitrogen liquefied, $w_a = 674.0/0.0638 = 10\,570 \text{ kJ}$. From (5.111)

$$w_{min} = (h_B - h_F) - T_0(s_B - s_F)$$
$$= (556.3 - 125.7) - 300(6.831 - 2.843)$$
$$= 765.8 \text{ kJ kg}^{-1}$$

From (5.127)

$$\text{thermodynamic efficiency } \eta = w_{min}/w_a = 765.8/10\,570$$
$$= 0.073$$

(b) Two stage throttle

Figure 5.44 shows that for nitrogen at constant temperature, the enthalpy change between 1 and 20 bar is only a small fraction of that between 20 and 200 bar. Thus, virtually the same cooling effect can be obtained by circulating the gas between 20 and 200 bar with a reduction in the work of compression in the ratio log(200/1) to log(200/20), i.e. 2.3 to 1. This saving is exploited in the Linde double expansion process, a simple version of which is shown in Figure 5.44. An enthalpy balance over that part of the plant enclosed by the

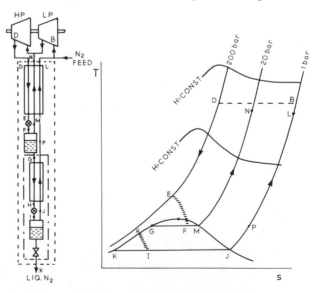

Figure 5.44. Gas liquefaction using a two stage throttle expansion

dotted line shows that

$$h_D = \varepsilon h_K + (1-x)h_N + (x-\varepsilon)h_L \qquad (5.128)$$

where x is the fraction of high pressure feed liquefied after the first throttle expansion and ε is the fraction liquefied as a result of both expansions, note $x > \varepsilon > 0$.

An enthalpy balance over the low pressure part of the plant enclosed by the dashed line shows that

$$xh_G = \varepsilon h_K + (x-\varepsilon)h_P \qquad (5.129)$$

From a knowledge of the pressures and the temperatures of the various streams entering and leaving the heat exchangers the enthalpies may be read off a T-S chart and (5.128) and (5.129) solved for x and ε. If it is assumed that the intermediate pressure is 20 bar, then making the same assumptions as in the previous example, calculations show that[17]

$$x = 0.102, \qquad \varepsilon = 0.0635, \quad \text{and} \quad \eta = 0.148$$

The performance can be improved further by pre-cooling the feed in an auxiliary refrigerator. This reduces the temperatures of all three streams at the warm end of the main heat exchanger, and the increasingly imperfect gas behaviour which results enhances the enthalpy differences at this point. In practice, this procedure increases the efficiency of the liquefaction process by about 7%, after allowance for the extra work required by the precooler.

(c) Liquefaction processes using an expander

Liquefaction by means of an expander, see Figure 5.45, is often called the Claude process after the French engineer who pioneered the development of

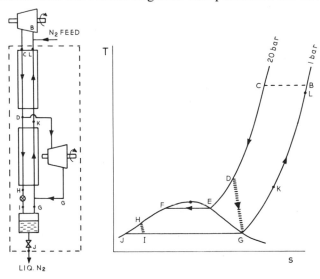

Figure 5.45. Gas liquefaction using an expansion engine

the low-temperature expansion engine. Like the Linde process it uses a heat exchanger to make the cooling cumulative. Today, a turbine would be used instead of the less reliable and less efficient expansion engine and only part of the gas would be expanded, the remainder being throttled to avoid problems caused by liquefaction in the turbine. The pressure of the feed gas would be restricted to about 20 bar, since an expansion ratio of 20:1 is the highest that can be handled in a single unit. For most gases, including nitrogen, this pressure is subcritical, and the removal of the latent heat at constant temperature during step EF is poorly matched to the refrigeration output of the expander. Hence, although we might expect a higher thermodynamic efficiency by the use of an expander rather than a throttle, this advantage is partially offset by the irreversibilities of heat exchange. The thermodynamic efficiency of the process is critically dependent on the efficiency of the turbine and is of the order of 0.31 to 0.35 for a machine having an adiabatic efficiency of 0.80.

The Heylandt process, see Figure 5.46, combines the best features of both

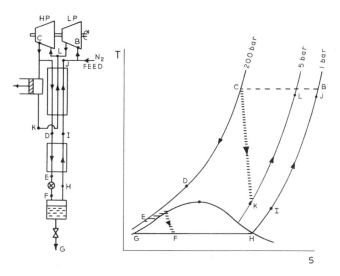

Figure 5.46. Heylandt gas liquefaction process

the Linde and Claude processes. By raising the feed gas pressure above the critical, the expander need not exhaust saturated vapour and the cooling load is distributed almost uniformly along the length of the heat exchanger. Furthermore, the cooling performance and work output of the expander increases as the inlet temperature rises. This arrangement eliminates one heat exchanger, but in view of the high feed pressure the gas must be expanded in an engine rather than a turbine. For the conditions shown in Figure 5.46 assuming the adiabatic efficiency of the engine to be 0.75 the thermodynamic efficiency of the process is about 0.31.

(d) Stirling cycle

In Section 5.18 we showed how it is possible for heat to be transferred reversibly during a non-isothermal process by using a regenerator to absorb heat during part of the cycle and to return the same amount of heat during another part. For the operation to be reversible heat must be transferred between the system and the regenerator across an infinitesimal temperature difference. This is the essential thermodynamic feature of the Philips refrigerating machine, which employs a reversed Stirling cycle, see Figure 5.47.

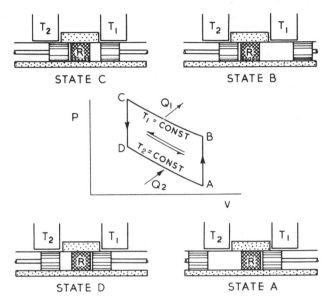

Figure 5.47. Diagramatic representation of the reversed Stirling cycle used in the Philips refrigerator

The machine consists of a cylinder with two pistons and which contains a regenerator, R, formed from a plug of very fine wire gauze, or a mat of fine copper wires lying perpendicular to the flow direction and held between two screens. The regenerator is a poor conductor of heat so that even though there is a temperature gradient along it, there is a negligible flow of heat along the cylinder axis. The cylinder is insulated except for contact with the 'hot' reservoir, T_1, at one end and the cold reservoir, T_2, at the other. The operation of the machine, is as follows:

Process A to B. Both pistons move to the right at the same rate, to keep the volume constant, and no heat transfer takes place with either reservoir. The gas is heated as it passes through the regenerator and reaches temperature T_1 as it leaves the right-hand side. For this heat transfer to be reversible, the temperature of the regenerator at each point must be the same as that of the gas, i.e. there must be a temperature gradient along the axis from T_2 at the left to T_1 at the right. No work is done during this process since it is at constant volume.

Process B to C.   Heat Q_1 is removed from the gas at T_1, or strictly speaking at $T_1 + \delta T_1$, by the reservoir at T_1. During this reversible isothermal process the right hand piston moves inwards, work being done on the system as the pressure increases.

Process C to D.   Both pistons move to the left at the same rate to maintain a constant volume. They are closer together during this process than they were during the process A to B because $V_D = V_C < V_B = V_A$. No heat is exchanged with either reservoir. As the gas passes back through the regenerator it is cooled so that it emerges from the left-hand end at T_2. Again no work is done.

Process D to A.   Heat Q_2 is transferred to the gas at T_2 (or $T_2 - \delta T_2$) from the reservoir at T_2. In order to hold the gas temperature constant, the piston moves outwards, doing work as the pressure falls.

Thus during this reversible cycle the system exchanges heat only with the two reservoirs T_1 and T_2.

Stirling refrigerators usually operate on hydrogen, the maximum pressure during compression being about 45 bar, and the minimum pressure during expansion, 20 bar. A thermodynamic analysis of an actual machine is complicated, even when it is assumed that the working fluid is a perfect gas and that all components are frictionless. The performance is highly dependent on the thermal efficiency of the regenerator; for example when the machine is used for liquefying air, the temperature gradient along the regenerator is more than 40 K cm^{-1} and it is claimed that the mean temperature difference between the gas and the regenerator does not exceed 2 K at any point. When used for refrigeration at a constant temperature of 78 K (the normal boiling point of nitrogen) with rejection of heat taking place at 300 K, a large Stirling machine can achieve a thermodynamic efficiency of 0.42. But this falls to 0.26 when the machine is used as a nitrogen liquefier, mainly because heat for both cooling from ambient temperature and for liquefaction are removed by a refrigerant, hydrogen, which is at a constant temperature of 78 K or below. The temperature profiles in the heat exchanger are therefore badly matched and large irreversibilities result. Clearly, the Stirling refrigerator is much better suited to constant temperature cooling duties.

A later development of the machine incorporating two stages of compression and expansion has permitted temperature down to 12 K to be attained.*

(e) Bell-Coleman cycle

For this cycle to have the same performance as a Carnot cycle, the working fluid would have to be a perfect gas and the compression from A to B', Figure

---

* See G. Walker, *Stirling Cycle Machines*, Oxford University Press, 1973.

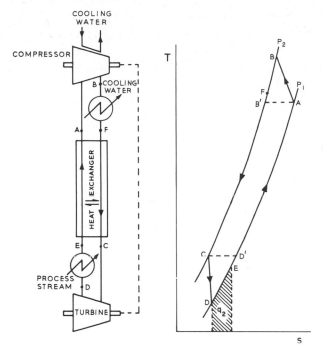

Figure 5.48. Actual Bell-Coleman refrigeration cycle

5.48, and the expansion from C to D' would have to be isothermal. Neither path can be realised in practice, and the actual compression and expansion follow AB and CD respectively. The cooling effect as the refrigerant warms from D to, say, E to allow for a non-zero temperature difference at the cold end of the heat exchanger, limits the refrigeration effect q_2 to the area under the lower isobar from D to E whilst the net work is equivalent to area ABCD. Thus it may be seen that the coefficient of performance of the cycle is critically dependent on the efficiency of the compressor and expander. Losses caused by adiabatic expansion not being isentropic are reduced if the pressure ratio of the cycle is decreased. However under these conditions turbo-machines are relatively inefficient and losses due to the pressure differences across the heat exchanger become significant; on the other hand the losses arising from the approach temperature at the cold end of the heat exchanger are reduced by using a large pressure ratio since under these conditions $(T_{D'} - T_E)$ is small compared with $(T_{D'} - T_D)$. Thus there is an optimum design for each refrigeration duty. For nitrogen liquefaction it is appropriate to compress a gas such as hydrogen or helium, which show small deviations from perfect gas behaviour, through a pressure ratio of 2. Even if the approach temperature is only 2 K, the pressure drop through the exchanger 5% of the inlet pressure, and the adiabatic efficiencies of the turbo-machine 0.9, the thermodynamic efficiency of the cycle is unlikely to exceed 0.25.

(f) Cascade liquefiers

Figure 5.49 shows a simplified cascade for liquefying nitrogen which uses three auxiliary refrigerants, ammonia, ethylene and methane, whose normal boiling points are 239.7 K, 169.5 K and 111.7 K respectively. An analysis of this plant shows that it is possible to liquefy nitrogen with an efficiency of 0.476 and that this could be raised by 5% to 10% of this by using additional heat exchangers to pre-cool all liquids before throttling. Thus, much less power is used in a cascade system to liquefy nitrogen than in the customary Heylandt process. This greater efficiency has not led to the cascade liquefier being used for large scale liquefaction of air, mainly because of the complexity of the plant, but also because methane, the only readily available refrigerant to bridge the interval between 110 and 170 K, is a serious hazard in the presence of liquid oxygen. Cascade refrigeration is widely used, however, to produce liquefied natural gas (LNG), which consists mainly of n-alkanes, of which methane has the lowest boiling point. One commercial plant operating on this principle illustrated uses propane, ethylene and methane as refrigerants. As in the case of nitrogen, it is necessary to pre-cool the natural gas at the temperature of evaporating propane, ethylene and methane before

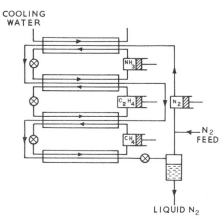

Figure 5.49. Simplified cascade system for liquefying nitrogen

the liquefied gas is finally cooled by throttling expansion to atmospheric pressure. Figure 5.50 shows the temperature profile along the length of a heat exchanger when natural gas is progressively cooled and then liquefied. This curve differs from that for a pure substance since liquefaction of a mixture occurs over a range of temperature (see Section 7.5). If the cooling were to be carried out in a heat exchanger using a heat sink at the normal boiling point of liquid methane, as shown in Figure 5.50a, the heat exchange would be highly irreversible. By passing the natural gas through the three heat exchangers cooled successively by evaporating propane, ethylene and methane, the

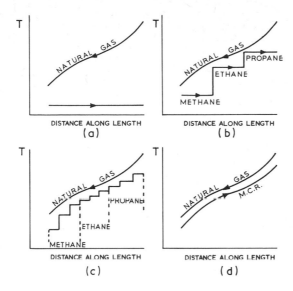

Figure 5.50. The temperature profiles along the length of a counter-current heat exchanger when natural gas is cooled by: (a) the evaporation of a single refrigerant; (b) the evaporation of three refrigerants in cascade; (c) the evaporation of three refrigerants, each at three temperatures; (d) the evaporation of a multi-component refrigerant

irreversibility is decreased, see Figure 5.50b. Large capacity plants requiring high thermodynamic efficiency use multistage compression and interstage expansion of each refrigerant so as to obtain a closer approach to reversibility, as is shown in Figure 5.50c, but the complexity of this makes it difficult to control. Recently *multicomponent refrigerants* (MCR) have been used to extend the cooling range of a single stage vapour compression cycle so as to reduce the number of independent compressors. With MCR condensation and evaporation take place over a range of temperature, and the composition of the refrigerant can be adjusted so that the temperature of the evaporating refrigerant is closely matched to that of the condensing natural gas, see Figure 5.50d. The optimum temperature difference is obtained by an economic balance between the cost of heat exchange area and power.

Figure 5.51 shows a MCR plant, sometimes known as an *auto-refrigerated cascade* plant. Natural gas at a pressure of 42 bar is cooled continuously in a heat exchanger, split into a number of sections until it is condensed and sub-cooled sufficiently to prevent flash evaporation when the pressure is reduced to atmospheric. The MCR, a mixture of hydrocarbons and nitrogen, is compressed in a water cooled centrifugal compressor and passed to a water cooled condenser B in which about 25% of the refrigerant condenses. The condensate and residual gas are separated in C and passed through the first stage of the exchanger HE1 in which the condensate is sub-cooled whilst the

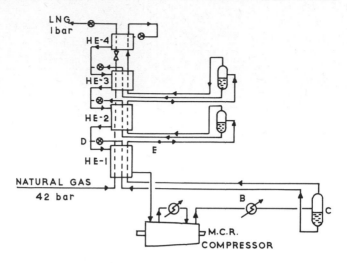

Figure 5.51. Natural gas liquefaction using a multi-component refrigerant

residual gas mixture undergoes further condensation. The sub-cooled condensate is now expanded via throttle D into the shell of the heat-exchanger, where it evaporates with diluent gas from the next stage of the exchanger. The refrigeration available from the combined stream is sufficient not only to condense partially the refrigerant needed in the next stage of the heat exchanger, but also to cool the natural gas feed. The partially condensed residual refrigerant stream E, leaving the first section of the heat exchanger is separated into two phases which pass to the next stage of the main heat exchanger. By successive partial condensation and evaporation, the temperature is progressively lowered; each stage supports the cooling requirements of the next lower one until finally the multicomponent refrigerant is completely condensed, sub-cooled and fed, after throttling, into the cold end of the heat exchanger.

For ease of reference the calculated thermodynamic efficiency of the various processes for the liquefaction of nitrogen have been collected in Table 5.2. Also included are the results of similar calculations for methane although the conditions are not necessarily strictly identical.[18] It must be borne in mind that the efficiency is dependent on the thermodynamic properties of the gas to be liquefied and the irreversibilities of heat exchanger and work transfer. Although these results serve as general guidance they are no substitute for detailed calculations which make allowance for all known sources of irreversibility.

The production and utilisation of temperatures below those used in nitrogen liquefaction plants, say, below 70 K is known as *cryogenics* a subject which has assumed increasing importance in recent years because of the

Table 5.2. Comparison of the performance of various processes for the liquefaction of nitrogen and methane

Process	Thermodynamic efficiency η	
	N_2	CH_4
Single stage throttle	0.073	0.18
Two stage throttle	0.148	0.26
Two stage throttle with pre-cooling	0.218	0.33
Claude	0.314–0.346	—
Heylandt	0.312	0.37
Philips machine	0.26	0.21
Bell-Coleman cycle	0.25	0.23
Cascade	0.47	0.40

demand for liquid hydrogen and liquid helium. The problems of extending conventional techniques to lower temperatures are acute, first because the minimum power requirement increases rapidly as the temperature is lowered and secondly because the additional power needed to compensate for irreversibilities in the process is inordinately high. As yet developments in this field are mainly confined to laboratory equipment and reference should be made to other texts.[19]

5.20 Production of power

The chemical industry uses both mechanical power and heat and it is normal practice at the larger plants to produce these on site rather than take electrical power from the grid. The usual procedure is to generate high pressure steam using as the source of heat either the products of combustion of a conventional fossil fuel or preferably a waste product; or alternatively, to use by-product heat from an exothermic chemical reaction as, for example, would be available from an ammonia synthesis plant. The steam can be used directly for process heating, or, by passing through a turbine, for the production of mechanical power for driving compressors, pumps, electrical generators etc. In this section, we discuss the performance of relatively simple steam plant used for these purposes.

In Chapter 3, we showed that the most efficient heat engine is the Carnot, which absorbs heat, Q_1, at temperature T_1, and rejects some of it at a lower temperature, T_2, providing net work, W. From (3.2) and (3.47), the efficiency of the engine is given by

$$\eta = -W/Q_1 = (T_1 - T_2)/T_1 \qquad (5.130)$$

and it increases as T_1 increases and T_2 decreases.

It is impracticable, however, to use the Carnot cycle as a basis for a power plant in view of the impossibility of transferring heat at a constant temperature since removal of heat from hot combustion gases reduces their temperature. But we can use the Carnot cycle to give us a rough estimate of the maximum efficiency which we can compare with that of the ideal steam power plant cycles we discuss in this section. If we take 2000 K as the temperature of the products of combustion of fossil fuel and 300 K as ambient temperature, then a Carnot engine operating between the mean temperature of 1150 K and ambient would have an efficiency of

$$(1150 - 300)/1150 = 0.74$$

(a) Ideal Rankine cycle

In the simple power plant shown in Figure 5.52, high pressure water enters the boiler of the steam generator at low temperature and leaves the superheater as high-pressure steam at high temperature, heat being transferred from the products of combustion to the fluid at constant pressure. The

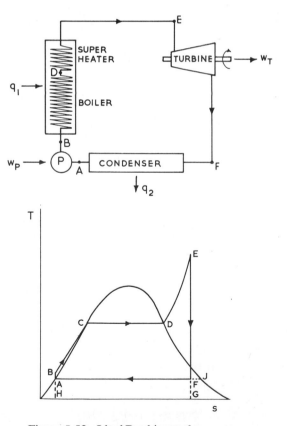

Figure 5.52. Ideal Rankine cycle

steam flowing through the turbine performs useful work as it expands from generator to condenser pressure. After expansion, the low temperature exhaust steam which is usually slightly wet, is condensed at constant pressure by rejecting heat to cooling water and the condensate returned to the boiler by a feed-pump. The ideal cycle, shown in T-S co-ordinates in Figure 5.52, is known as a *Rankine cycle*. The temperature rise in the feed pump has been exaggerated to show clearly the nature of the ideal process; in fact, it is so small that state B is indistinguishable from A. In practice, this cycle can never be realised because of pressure drops through the condenser and boiler caused by fluid friction and because the flow through the turbine and feed-pump is never adiabatic and frictionless. To simplify the discussion, we confine our attention to ideal cycles. The effects of irreversibility in a power cycle, unlike a refrigeration cycle, are usually small and should it be necessary to allow for them, this can be done using the procedures outlined in Section 5.5(f).

The heat absorbed in the generator, $q_1 = h_E - h_B$, is the area HBCDEG; that transferred from the steam in the condenser, $h_A - h_F$, is numerically equal to area GFAH. The net work, w_{net}, which is equal to the output from the turbine, w_T, plus the input to the pump, w_P (note w_P is negative), is

$$w_{net} = w_T + w_P = (h_F - h_E) + (h_B - h_A) \tag{5.131}$$

and is numerically equal to the area enclosed within cycle ABCDEFA.

Thus,

$$\eta = \frac{-w_{net}}{q_1} = \frac{-[(h_F - h_E) + (h_B - h_A)]}{(h_E - h_B)} \tag{5.132}$$

Since the pump work is small in comparison with the output from the turbine, little error is introduced by assuming that water is incompressible. Hence, from (5.33)

$$w_P = h_B - h_A \approx v'_A(P_B - P_A) \tag{5.133}$$

If, as is usually the case, the pump work is sufficiently small to be neglected, then

$$\eta \approx (h_E - h_F)/(h_E - h_B) \tag{5.134}$$

Example

Calculate the efficiency of the ideal Rankine cycle shown in Figure 5.52, assuming that the boiler operates at 30 bar and the condenser at 0.04 bar and that the steam is superheated to 450 °C.

From tables of thermodynamic properties of steam:

$h_A = 121 \text{ kJ kg}^{-1}$ $\qquad h_E = 3343 \text{ kJ kg}^{-1}$, $\qquad h_J = 2554 \text{ kJ kg}^{-1}$

$s_A = 0.422 \text{ kJ K}^{-1} \text{ kg}^{-1}$, $\quad s_E = 7.082 \text{ kJ K}^{-1} \text{ kg}^{-1}$, $\quad s_J = 8.473 \text{ kJ K}^{-1} \text{ kg}^{-1}$

$v'_A = 0.00100 \text{ m}^3 \text{ kg}^{-1}$

The heat added in the steam generator, $q_1 = h_E - h_B$.

If we assume $h_B \approx h_A$.

Then,

$$q_1 = 3343 - 121 = 3222 \text{ kJ kg}^{-1}$$

Now,

$$s_F = s_E = 7.082 \text{ kJ kg}^{-1} \text{ K}^{-1}$$

and from the lever rule

$$x_F = \frac{s_F - s_A}{s_J - s_A} = \frac{7.082 - 0.422}{8.473 - 0.422} = 0.83$$

Hence

$$h_F = x h_J + (1 - x) h_A$$

$$= 0.83 \times 2554 + 0.17 \times 121 = 2141 \text{ kJ kg}^{-1}$$

Turbine work $w_T = (h_F - h_E) = (2141 - 3343) = -1202 \text{ kJ kg}^{-1}$

From (5.133),

Pump work $w_P = v'_A (P_B - P_A) = 0.001 \times 29.96 \times 10^2 = 3 \text{ kJ kg}^{-1}$

Hence, w_P may be neglected in comparison with w_T and the net work taken as -1202 kJ kg^{-1}. From (5.132),

$$\eta = \frac{-w_{net}}{q_1} = \frac{1202}{3222} = 0.373$$

In practice, it is more usual to specify the *heat rate* of power plant which is numerically equal to the ratio of the heat absorbed in the steam generator to the net work output, i.e. the reciprocal of the cycle efficiency.

The efficiency of this ideal Rankine cycle is only half of that for a Carnot cycle operating between 1150 K and 300 K. Clearly, if it is to be improved, some way must be found to increase the mean temperature at which heat is absorbed from the high temperature flue gases or to reduce the temperature at which heat is rejected to the cooling water. A lower limit to the condensation temperature is set by the inlet temperature of the cooling water and the economic size of the condenser. The maximum temperature of the steam is governed by the mechanical strength of the materials available for the highly stressed parts of the plant such as the superheater tubes and the turbine blades. At present, an upper temperature limit of about 600 °C is fixed by economic considerations because, at temperatures above this limit, superheater tubes made of expensive creep-resistant stainless steels have to be used. Increasing the temperature of the steam as it enters the turbine is desirable however, see Figure 5.53a, since it increases not only the mean temperature at which heat is absorbed, and hence the efficiency of the cycle, but also the quality of the steam exhausted to the condenser. In a real plant, this has the effect of increasing the polytropic efficiency of the turbine and

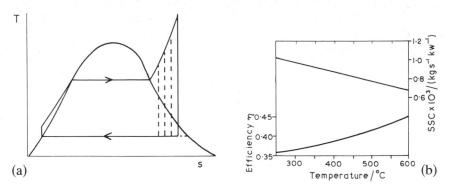

Figure 5.53. Effect of increasing the superheat temperature on the efficiency and specific steam consumption SSC of the ideal Rankine cycle

hence the work output, so there is an additional increase in cycle efficiency above that shown in Figure 5.53b for the ideal cycle.

In addition to the thermodynamic efficiency, a criterion of performance is needed by which the relative sizes of different plants can be compared. In general, the size of the components will depend on the volumetric flow rate, but this varies enormously around the cycle and it is more convenient to consider the mass flow rate of steam per unit power output, a quantity known as the *specific steam consumption* (SSC). This is equal to the reciprocal of the net work output per unit mass flow, thus

$$\text{SSC}/(\text{kg s}^{-1}\,\text{kW}^{-1}) = (w_{\text{net}})^{-1}/(\text{kJ}^{-1}\,\text{kg})$$

It may be seen from Figure 5.53b that increasing the superheat temperature not only raises the efficiency, but decreases the specific steam consumption, hence, the size of the plant for a given power output.

Raising the steam pressure, whilst keeping the temperature of the superheated steam constant, see Figure 5.54a, also increases the mean

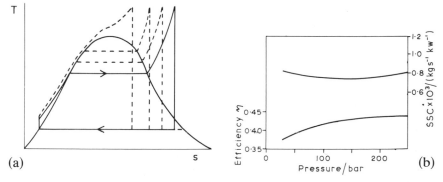

Figure 5.54. Effect of increasing the boiler pressure on the efficiency and specific steam consumption of the ideal Rankine cycle

temperature at which heat is absorbed, and hence cycle efficiency. However, it may be seen from Figure 5.54b that the effect becomes less important as the pressure approaches the critical pressure P^c, because $(\partial T/\partial P)_\sigma$ decreases. In a real cycle the advantage of raising the steam pressure is partly offset by the resulting decrease in the quality of steam leaving the turbine, which has an adverse effect on the polytropic efficiency, and hence on the work output.

It may be seen from Figure 5.54a that, if the pressure is increased too much whilst maintaining the superheat temperature constant, the quality of the steam leaving the turbine will drop below about 0.88 and water droplets will cause rapid erosion of the turbine blades. In order to prevent this it is necessary to use two turbines and reheat the steam leaving the high pressure unit with flue gases before it enters the lower pressure one. Apart from this modification, shown in Figure 5.55, the flow diagram is similar to that of Figure 5.52.

The efficiency of the reheat cycle is

$$\eta = \frac{-\sum w}{\sum q} = \frac{-(w_{HP} + w_{LP} + w_P)}{q_1 + q_{RH}} \tag{5.135}$$

where w_{HP}, w_{LP} and w_P are the work for the high pressure turbine, the low pressure turbine and the pump, while the heat terms q_1 and q_{RH} are the heat

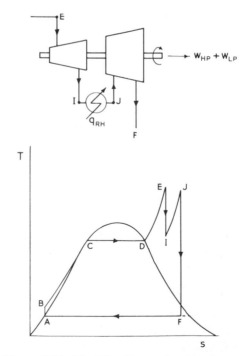

Figure 5.55. Ideal Rankine cycle with reheat

transfer in the generator and re-heater. Thus

$$\eta = \frac{-[(h_I - h_E) + (h_F - h_J) + (h_B - h_A)]}{(h_E - h_B) + (h_J - h_I)} \qquad (5.136)$$

or, if the feed pump work is neglected,

$$\eta = \frac{-[(h_I - h_E) + (h_F - h_J)]}{(h_E - h_B) + (h_J - h_I)} \qquad (5.137)$$

If, as shown in Figure 5.55, the temperature of the steam leaving the reheater is the same as that leaving the superheater, then there is an optimum re-heat pressure between that of the boiler and that of the condenser for which the efficiency of the cycle is a maximum. For an ideal cycle this is about 20% of the boiler pressure. The effect of reheat on the efficiency and specific steam consumption of two cycles, one sub-critical (160 bar) and the other supercritical (350 bar) is shown in Table 5.3. In both cases it is assumed that

Table 5.3. Efficiency and specific steam consumption of Rankine power cycle

Cycle	P/bar	η	SSC × 10³/ kg s⁻¹ kW⁻¹
No-Reheat	160	0.453	0.642
Reheat	160	0.468	0.489
No-Reheat	350	0.468	0.658
Reheat	350	0.485	0.500

the steam leaves the superheater and reheater at 600 °C and that reheating commences when the steam is saturated.

Although re-heat does not have a marked effect on the efficiency, it decreases the specific steam consumption. Clearly, large increases in cycle efficiency cannot be obtained solely as a result of increasing the pressure, and further progress in this direction must await the development of cheap creep-resisting alloys.

(b) Regenerative feed-water heating

We have seen how increasing the temperature and/or pressure of the steam as it enters the turbine raises the mean temperature at which heat is absorbed, and hence the efficiency of the cycle. Figure 5.52 shows that the low mean temperature, defined as in Section 5.18, arises largely from the heat needed to increase the feed-water temperature to that in the boiler. Another way of raising the mean temperature is to pre-heat the feed-water internally within the cycle, using the regenerative principle discussed in Section 5.18, whereby heat is transferred from steam expanding in the turbine to feed-water flowing between pump and boiler.

In the hypothetical plant shown in Figure 5.56, this is achieved by passing the feed-water from the condenser at constant pressure through successive heat exchangers, each of infinite area, located between the stages of a turbine consisting of an infinite number of stages. It is assumed that the pressure and temperature at G are such that the steam becomes saturated, state H, just as it reaches the first heat exchanger. Between H and J, the steam is alternately

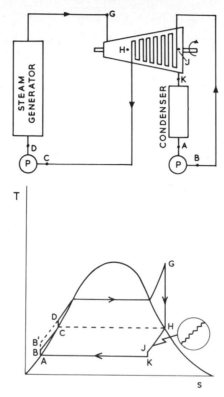

Figure 5.56. Hypothetical plant for regenerative feed-water heating

expanded isentropically in a turbine stage and condensed isobarically in an interstage heat-exchanger. Consequently, the expansion curve between H and J takes the form of a series of steps, shown in the inset, which for an infinite number of stages becomes a smooth line. Since the mass flow rate round the cycle is constant, the cooling line for the steam, HJ, must be parallel to line BC, which represents the isobaric heating of the feed-water, if the heat released by the condensing steam is equal to that absorbed by the feed-water. As a result of this heat exchange within the cycle, which is assumed to take place across an infinitesimally small temperature difference, the feed leaves the exchanger at T_C and, after its pressure has been raised, enters the boiler at T_D, instead of T_B', as in a conventional ideal Rankine cycle. Heat absorption from the external source occurs now only between T_D and T_G; hence, the mean temperature is raised and, since this has been accomplished reversibly, the cycle efficiency is increased. Many ingenious hypothetical systems have been devised in standard texts[1] for the reversible transfer of heat from superheated steam to feed-water, so that the latter enters the boiler at saturation, thus achieving the maximum possible gain. These schemes like the one discussed here are impractical and serve only to illustrate the principle of regenerative feed-water heating.

A practical solution is to extract or 'bleed' steam from the turbine at a number of intermediate pressures in the expansion process and transfer the heat in feed-water heaters. Flow and T-S diagrams of a steam power cycle, using a single *open feed-water heater*, are shown in Figure 5.57. The bleed

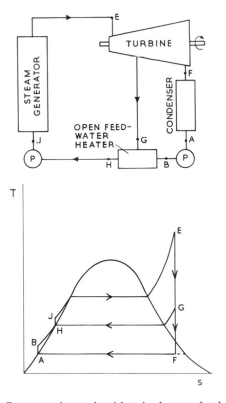

Figure 5.57. Regenerative cycle with a single open feed-water heater

stream, state G, and condensate pumped from the condenser, state B, enter the heater, where under optimum conditions they mix to give saturated water, state H. The heater operates at the bleed-point pressure, so a second pump is needed to force the water into the steam generator. Flow and T-S diagrams for an alternative arrangement, which removes the need for a separate pump, are shown in Figure 5.58 in which condensate is pumped through a *closed feed-water heater,* where it exchanges heat with the bleed stream without mixing. Bleed condensate leaves the counter-current heater as sub-cooled liquid, state K, and is passed through a *steam trap* (a device in which water is throttled to a lower pressure and in which steam is retained). Thus, sub-cooled condensate K is throttled to state M and the resulting wet steam

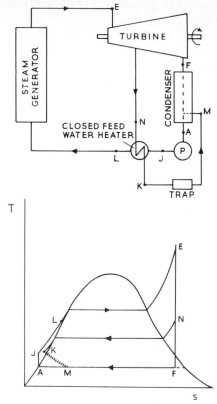

Figure 5.58. Regenerative cycle with a single closed feed-water heater

returned to the condenser, whilst the feed-water leaves the heater at temperature T_L, which ideally is equal to T_N. Clearly neither of these cycles is ideal. In Figure 5.57, the mixing process between steam, N, and water, J, is irreversible. In Figure 5.58, apart from losses caused by the irreversible expansion, K $\rightarrow$ M, there is a non-zero temperature difference across the feed-water heater, so that $T_N > T_L$ and $T_K > T_J$. However, the number of feed-water heaters and streams bled from the turbine at different pressures may be increased so that the losses arising from irreversibilities become progressively smaller and a large (350 MW) power plant may use up to ten such streams. As a rule, closed heaters are used whenever possible to obviate the need for separate pumps.

Exercise

A cycle consisting of n open feed-water heaters is illustrated in Figure 5.59. Show that, if the pump work is neglected, the ratio of the mass flow rate of steam leaving the steam generator, $\dot{m}_S$, to that entering the condenser, $\dot{m}_C$, is given by

$$\dot{m}_S/\dot{m}_C = \prod_{j=1}^{j=n}\left[1+\frac{(\Delta h_F)_j}{(\Delta h_B)_j}\right] \tag{5.138}$$

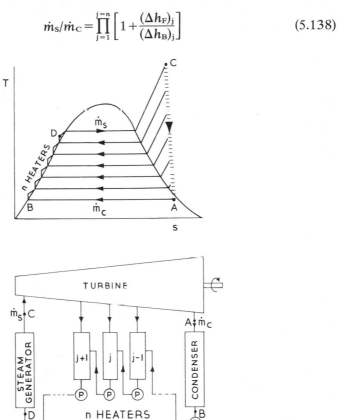

Figure 5.59. Regenerative cycle with n open feed-water heaters

where Δh_F is the enthalpy rise of the feed water and Δh_B is the enthalpy decrease of the bleed stream, in feed-water heater j.

The efficiency of the cycle employing n feed-water heaters is

$$\eta = \frac{-w}{q_1} = 1+\frac{q_2}{q_1}$$

$$= 1+\frac{\dot{m}_C(h_B-h_A)}{\dot{m}_S(h_C-h_D)} \tag{5.139}$$

where $\dot{m}_S/\dot{m}_C$ is given by (5.138).

The optimum number of feed-water heaters and the proper choice of bleed pressures depends on economic as well as thermodynamic considerations, which are outside the scope of this book. In general, a single feed-water heater can produce a gain in efficiency which is about half that which is theoretically possible with an infinite number of heaters, but the incremental gain in efficiency decreases as the number increases. Typically, four or five heaters might be used in a modern sub-critical pressure power plant which would result in an increase in cycle efficiency of about 10%. Regenerative feed-water heating facilitates the design of the turbine, since it reduces the volume of low pressure steam, and so reduces the size of the condenser. However, it would have an adverse effect on the overall efficiency of the plant, as opposed to the cycle efficiency, if steps were not taken to reduce the temperature of the flue gases leaving the boiler by other means, such as pre-heating the air required for combustion.

(c) Process heating

In most chemical plants, heat has to be supplied to the process at relatively low temperatures and in the interests of economy every effort is made to extract this heat from other process streams using heat exchangers. If waste heat is not available, it may be necessary to evaporate a liquid at the required temperature in a boiler fired by fossil fuel, then transfer the heat to the process fluid by condensing the vapour in a heat exchanger and return the condensate to the boiler as in Figure 5.60. From a thermodynamic point of

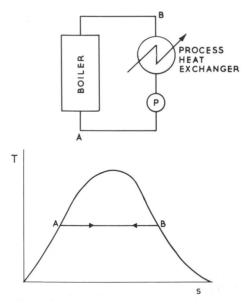

Figure 5.60. Closed cycle for process heat

view, such a scheme is wasteful because the large temperature difference between the products of combustion and the process stream is not used to produce work. This may be unavoidable in an isolated plant which has small demand for work, but in most installations there is a simultaneous need for both heat and work. In these circumstances, it may be more economical to use the plant shown in Figure 5.61, in which high temperature steam is used to

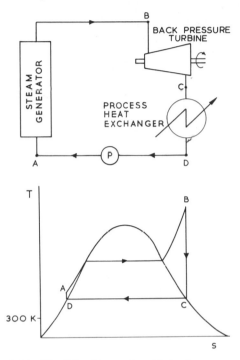

Figure 5.61. Ideal Rankine cycle with back pressure turbine

produce work and process heat is obtained by condensing the steam leaving the turbine at an appropriate pressure. This arrangement is practicable only if the requirements for heat and work are constant and well matched. In the plant shown in Figure 5.62, steam at the appropriate pressure is extracted from the turbine, condensed in the process heat exchanger and returned to the boiler, whilst the remainder is condensed in the usual way. Thus, variation in power and heating duty may be accommodated by controlling the amount of steam which is extracted.

Example

Steam is supplied to a pass-out turbine at 100 bar and 550 °C. In the high pressure stages it expands reversibly and adiabatically to 10 bar at which

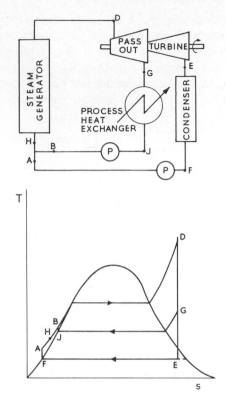

Figure 5.62. Ideal Rankine cycle with pass-out turbine

pressure, 3 kg s^{-1} of dry saturated steam is extracted for process heating and the remainder is reheated to $500\,^\circ\text{C}$ and expanded reversibly and adiabatically to 0.050 bar. If 5 MW of power is required from the plant, estimate the amount of steam required from the generator, neglecting the work required to operate the feed pump.

What percentage of the heat supplied to the steam generator is used in the reheater if the condensate from the process heat exchanger and that from the condenser are returned to the boiler in a saturated state?

With reference to Figure 5.63 and thermodynamic tables for the properties of steam,[20]

$$h_D = 3500 \text{ kJ kg}^{-1}, \qquad s_D = 6.756 \text{ kJ K}^{-1} \text{ kg}^{-1}$$

Since expansion is reversible and adiabatic, $s_G = s_D$.

By linear interpolation, $h_G = 2853 + (23 \times 0.011)/0.048$

$$= 2858 \text{ kJ kg}^{-1}$$

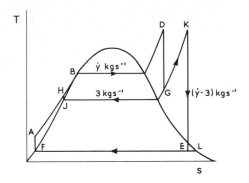

Figure 5.63. Pass-out turbine (see example p. 279)

Work transfer in high pressure section of turbine $= (h_G - h_D) = (2858 - 3500) = -642$ kJ kg^{-1}

From tables,

$s_K = 7.898$ kJ K^{-1} kg^{-1}, $s_L = 8.394$ kJ K^{-1} kg^{-1}, $s_F = 0.476$ kJ K^{-1} kg^{-1}

$h_K = 3587$ kJ kg^{-1}, $h_L = 2561$ kJ kg^{-1}, $h_F = 138$ kJ kg^{-1}

Since expansion is reversible and adiabatic, $s_E = s_K$.

By the lever rule, quality, x, at $E = (7.898 - 0.476)/(8.394 - 0.476)$

$$= 0.94$$

Hence

$$h_E = xh_L + (1 - x)h_F = (0.94 \times 2561) + (0.06 \times 138)$$
$$= 2416 \text{ kJ kg}^{-1}$$

Work transfer in low pressure section of turbine $= (h_E - h_K) = (2416 - 3587) = -1171$ kJ kg^{-1}

Assume $\dot{y}$ kg s^{-1} of steam leaves the boiler. Hence mass flow rate through low pressure section of turbine $= (\dot{y} - 3.0)$ kg s^{-1}

Total work from both sections of turbine $= \dot{y} \times 642 + (\dot{y} - 3.0)1171$, which is given as 5000 kW. Hence

$$\dot{y} = 8513/1813 = 4.68 \text{ kg s}^{-1}$$

Heat to boiler $= \dot{y}(h_D - h_H) + (\dot{y} - 3.0)(h_H - h_A) + (\dot{y} - 3.0)(h_K - h_G)$. If we neglect feed pump work, then

$$h_H = h_J = 763 \text{ kJ kg}^{-1}, \qquad h_A = h_F = 138 \text{ kJ kg}^{-1}$$

Heat to boiler $= 4.68(3500-763)+1.68(763-138)+1.68(3587-2858)$

$= 15\ 083$ kW

Heat to reheater $= 1.68(3587-2858) = 1225$ kW

Hence percentage of heat supplied to reheater $= 8.12$.

Problems

1. Show that for the frictionless flow of an incompressible fluid through a venturi in which the approach velocity $\mathscr{V}_1$ cannot be neglected, the mass flow rate is given by

$$\dot{m} = \mathscr{A}_t\left[\frac{2(P_1-P_t)}{v[1-(\mathscr{A}_t/\mathscr{A}_1)^2]}\right]^{1/2}$$

where subscripts t and 1 relate to conditions at the throat and upstream pressure tappings respectively. Comparison of the above equation with (5.15) shows that the two differ by the factor $[1-(\mathscr{A}_t-\mathscr{A}_1)^2]^{1/2}$ which is often referred to as the 'approach factor'.

2. Nitrogen, which may be assumed to behave as a perfect gas, enters a converging nozzle at 10 bar 480 K and discharges into a receiver where the pressure is 4 bar. Assuming the flow to be isentropic calculate the temperature, pressure and velocity at the exit to the nozzle.

3. What type of nozzle is required to expand 0.2 kg s^{-1} argon at 3.5 bar 300 K to 1.4 bar assuming that argon behaves as a perfect gas? If the velocity of the gas entering the nozzle is low and the coefficient of discharge is 0.97 calculate the minimum cross-sectional area.

4. A safety valve consisting of a simple convergent nozzle with a discharge area of 3 cm^2 when fully open is set to relieve saturated steam at 2.8 bar. If the inlet velocity is negligible and the pressure at the discharge area is 1.7 bar calculate the maximum relieving capacity of the valve assuming that the expansion is isentropic and that phase equilibrium is maintained.

If instead of maintaining phase equilibrium, the steam goes supersaturated during expansion, along a path which may be represented by $Pv^{1.3} = $ const, what will be the discharge pressure and by how much will the capacity be increased?

5. From thermodynamic tables for the properties of steam calculate the work required to compress saturated water at 1 bar to 100 bar.

6. It is found that the power required to compress 1 mol s^{-1} of nitrogen from 1 bar 300 K to 20 bar is 13.0 kW. Presuming nitrogen behaves as a perfect gas

for which $\gamma = 1.4$ is constant calculate the isothermal and adiabatic efficiency of the compression process.

7. The molar heat capacity at 1 bar and the molar volume of gaseous ammonia may be represented by

$$c_P/(\text{J mol}^{-1}\,\text{K}^{-1}) = 31.4 + 0.0174\ T/K$$

$$(RT/P - v)/(\text{m}^3\,\text{mol}^{-1}) = 20.5(K/T)^2$$

Show that the temperature of ammonia discharged continuously from a compressor in which the pressure is raised adiabatically and reversibly from 1 bar, 300 K to 10 bar is 497 K.

8. The van der Waals constants for ammonia are

$$a/(\text{N m}^4\,\text{mol}^{-2}) = 0.4243$$

$$b/(\text{m}^3\,\text{mol}^{-1}) = 3.72 \times 10^{-5}$$

and the heat capacity at 1 bar is given by

$$c_P/(\text{J mol}^{-1}\,\text{K}^{-1}) = 31.4 + 0.0176(T/K)$$

If 1 mol s^{-1} of ammonia is compressed reversibly and adiabatically from 1 bar 300 K to 15 bar, calculate the temperature of the gas after compression and the power required.

Check the results obtained from tables of the thermodynamic properties of ammonia, Ref. 6, page 173.

9. If the polytropic exponent n for the reversible compression of nitrogen from 1 bar 300 K to 5 bar, in a water cooled compressor is 1.2, calculate the heat transfer per mole of gas compressed. It may be assumed that nitrogen behaves as a perfect gas and that $c_P = 29.0\ \text{J K}^{-1}\,\text{mol}^{-1}$ is independent of temperature.

10. A reciprocating compressor having a clearance ratio of 0.05 is used as a vacuum pump. What is the minimum suction pressure which can be developed, assuming the discharge pressure to be 1 bar? Assume that the air being pumped behaves as a perfect gas and that $\gamma = 1.4$ is independent of temperature. If the suction pressure is maintained at 0.05 bar, what is the volumetric efficiency of the pump?

11. A single-stage single-acting water-cooled reciprocating compressor with a swept volume of 0.08 m^3 and a clearance ratio of 0.03 runs at 5 Hz and is to be used to compress oxygen from 1 bar, 300 K to 10 bar. If the reversible polytropic exponent, n, for the compression and expansion processes is 1.30

and if c_P for oxygen, assumed perfect, is $30 \, \text{J mol}^{-1} \, \text{K}^{-1}$, calculate

    (a) the capacity of the compressor;
    (b) the power required;
    (c) the rate of heat transfer to the cooling water;
if the exhaust pressure is allowed to vary, calculate
    (d) the pressure ratio for which the power required is a maximum;
and (e) the capacity of the compressor at the pressure ratio for maximum
       power.

12. A multi-stage compressor with interstage cooling is required to compress helium reversibly and adiabatically from 1 bar to 300 bar with minimum work input. How many stages are required if the gas discharge temperature for each stage is not to exceed 200 °C, the suction temperature to each stage being 25 °C, and what is the pressure ratio of each stage?

13. A vane pump has a capacity of $0.125 \, \text{m}^3 \, \text{s}^{-1}$ when compressing air through an overall pressure ratio of 3. The pressure ratio arising from the internal volume reduction in the pump is 2. Calculate the power input to the pump and compare it with that required by a Roots blower which has the same capacity and overall pressure ratio, assuming that the inlet conditions, $95 \, \text{kN m}^{-2}$, 18 °C, are the same.

14. Steam at 20 bar, 500 °C is admitted to a turbine and discharged at 0.70 bar. The turbine, which is neither reversible nor adiabatic, has an adiabatic efficiency of 0.8. Evaluate the work output per kg of steam. What is the loss in availability during the expansion process if heat loss to the surroundings at 20 °C caused by imperfect insulation is $12 \, \text{kJ kg}^{-1}$?

15. In an ammonia vapour-compression refrigerator designed to absorb 30 kW of heat, the temperature of the saturated ammonia in the condenser is 30 °C and that in the evaporator is −6 °C. Assuming the cycle to be ideal, see Figure 5.27, calculate (a) the coefficient of performance, (b) the mass flow rate of refrigerant, (c) the pressure ratio of the compressor, (d) the power required, and (e) the coefficient of performance if the throttle is replaced by an expander in which the process is assumed to be isentropic.

16. Calculate the minimum power required to liquefy $5 \, \text{mol s}^{-1}$ of air at 1 atm ($= 1.013 \, 25$ bar) assuming that the initial temperature of the air is 300 K (Tables for the thermodynamic properties of air given in Ref. 6, page 173).

17. Air is to be liquefied by the simple Linde plant shown in Figure 5.43 in which it enters the heat exchanger at 300 K and 100 atm ($= 101.33$ bar) and expands to 1 atm (1.0133 bar). If the air flow rate to the plant at 1.0133 bar, 290 K is $0.025 \, \text{m}^3 \, \text{s}^{-1}$ and a temperature approach of 5 K is achieved at the

warm end of the heat exchanger, calculate the rate of production of liquid air. How will the rate of production change if (a) the heat exchanger ceases to be adiabatic and a heat leak of 80 J per mole of air entering the heat exchanger develops, and (b) the pressure of the air entering the exchanger is increased to 200 atm (202.65 bar) assuming that the inlet temperature and heat leak remaining unchanged.

18. Steam at 10 bar, 250 °C is throttled through a pressure reducing valve to 1.5 bar and used to supply 0.5 MW of process heat, the condensate leaving the process heat exchanger at 85 °C. It is proposed to use a turbine in place of the reducing valve in order to obtain mechanical power whilst supplying the same amount of heat. If the turbine, which discharges at 1.5 bar, has an adiabatic efficiency of 0.85 calculate (a) the power output from the turbine and (b) the increase in steam consumption.

Answers

2. $P = 5.3$ bar, $T = 400$ K, $\mathscr{V} = 12.9$ m s^{-1}.

3. Converging-diverging nozzle required. Throat area $= 0.60$ cm^2.

4. If phase equilibrium maintained mass flow rate $= 0.126$ kg s^{-1}. If super-saturated, discharge pressure $= 1.53$ bar, mass flow rate $= 0.130$ kg s^{-1}.

5. Work $= 10.3$ kJ kg^{-1}.

6. Isothermal efficiency $= 0.57$, adiabatic efficiency $= 0.91$.

8. Exit temperature $= 540$ K, power 9.32 kW.

9. Heat $= -1.92$ kJ mol^{-1}.

10. Suction pressure $= 0.014$ bar, volumetric efficiency $= 0.63$.

11. (a) 0.34 m^3 s^{-1}, (b) 104 kW, (c) 17.4 kW, (d) 26.5, (e) 0.26 m^3 s^{-1}.

12. 5 stages required, pressure ratio $= 3.13$ per stage.

13. Power of vane pump $= 16.3$ kW, power of Roots blower $= 22.5$ kW.

14. Work output $= 661$ kJ kg^{-1}, availability loss $= 141$ kJ kg^{-1}.

15. (a) 6.45, (b) 0.0269 kg s^{-1}, (c) 3.42, (d) 4.65 kW, (e) 6.50.

16. Power $= 127$ kW.

17. Mass liquefied $= 0.0304$ kg s^{-1}, (a) decrease in production of 19.0%, (b) increase in production of 120%.

18. Power output $= 67$ kW, increase in flow rate $= 0.027$ kg s^{-1}.

Notes

1. R. W. Haywood, *Analysis of Engineering Cycles*, Pergamon Press, Oxford, 1967. G. F. C. Rogers and Y. R. Mayhew, *Engineering Thermodynamics, Work and Heat Transfer, SI Units*, Longmans, London, 1967.

2. A. H. Shapiro, *The Dynamics and Thermodynamics of Compressible Fluid Flow*, Vols. I and II, Ronald Press, New York, 1953, 1954.
H. W. Liepmann and A. Roshko, *Elements of Gas Dynamics*, Wiley, New York, 1957.

3. R. H. Perry and C. H. Chilton, *Chemical Engineers' Handbook*, 5th edn. McGraw-Hill, New York, 1973.

4. A. B. Greene and G. G. Lucas, *The Testing of Internal Combustion Engines*, English Universities Press, London, 1969, Chapter 5.

5. For a simple example of the use of Lagrange multipliers, see F. van Zeggeren and S. H. Storey, *The Computation of Chemical Equilibrium*, Cambridge University Press, 1970, Appendix 1.

6. V. Chlumsky, *Reciprocating and Rotary Compressors*, E. and F. N. Spon Ltd., London, 1965.

7. 'Industrial Reciprocating and Rotary Compressors', *Proc. Inst. Mech. Eng.* **184**, Part 3R, 1969–70.

8. J. E. Blackford, P. Halford and D. H. Tantam, chapter 8 in *Cryogenic Fundamentals* (ed. G. G. Haselden), Academic Press, London, 1971.

9. E. E. Ludwig, *Applied Process Design for Chemical and Petrochemical Plant*, Vol. 1, Gulf Publishing Co., Houston, 1964.

10. *Brit. Stand.* 4580:1970, 'Number designation of organic refrigerants'.

11. *ASHRAE Thermodynamic Properties of Refrigerants*, Amer. Soc. Heating, Refrig., Air Cond. Engrs, New York, 1969.

12. R. W. Zafft, *Hydrocarbon Processing*, **46**, no. 6 (1967), 131–5.

13. *ASHRAE Handbook of Fundamentals*, Amer Soc. Heating, Refrig., Air Cond. Engrs, New York, 1972.

14. E. Spencer, *Hydrocarbon Processing*, **46**, no. 6 (1967), 137–40.

15. D. F. Ballou, T. A. Lyons and J. R. Tacquard, *Hydrocarbon Processing*, **46**, no. 6, (1967), 119–30.

16. F. Din, (Ed.), *Thermodynamic Properties of Gases*, Vol. 3, Butterworth, London, 1961.

17. *Cryogenic Fundamentals* (ed. G. G. Haselden), Academic Press, London, 1971, 40.

18. N. R. Barber and G. G. Haselden, *Trans. Inst. Chem. Engrs.* **35** (1957), 77.

19. G. G. Haselden (Ed.), *Cryogenic Fundamentals*, Academic Press, London, 1971, pp. 59–90.

20. *N.E.L. Steam Tables*, H.M.S.O., Edinburgh, 1964.

6 Mixtures and Solutions

6.1 Introduction

We have considered so far the properties of a single substance, for example a pure chemical compound, or a mixture, such as air, which may be treated as a single substance if we do not subject it to any changes which alter its composition. We now extend the discussion to mixtures of substances which are mutually inert. Chemically reacting systems are described in Chapter 8.

The word *mixture* is used here to describe a system in which we treat all substances on an equal footing. This is the most convenient view-point for the discussion of gas mixtures or of mixtures of two or more liquids. When one component is present in great excess and is singled out for special treatment, we speak of a *solution*; the component in excess being termed the *solvent* and the remaining component(s) the *solute*(s). This second view-point is convenient for a discussion of, for example, the solution of a gas or a solid in liquid and is obligatory for the discussion of ionic solutions.

The composition of a mixture or solution may be specified in many ways, but the most convenient for a mixture is through the amount (in moles) of each component present. If there are n_i moles of component i and C components in all, then we define the *mole fraction* of each component by

$$x_i = n_i \Big/ \sum_{j=1}^{C} n_j \qquad \sum_{j=1}^{C} x_j = 1 \qquad (6.1)$$

The sums are taken over all C components, including $j = i$. The second part of this equation makes it clear that only $(C-1)$ of the mole fractions are independently variable.

Exercise

By analogy with (6.1) define *mass fractions* in a mixture. Why can we not define volume fractions in the same way? The reason will be clear from the next section.

6.2 Partial quantities

The thermodynamic (and other) properties of a system change with composition, and so we must supplement the fundamental equations (3.174)–(3.177), which were based on the assumption that only two independent variables, such as P and V, were necessary to specify the state of the system, by adding terms to the right-hand sides of these equations which describe such changes. What new functions must we introduce to define these terms? When we mix two liquids we find, in general, that the volume, heat capacity etc. of the mixture is not the sum of those of the unmixed components. How much of the volume etc. is to be ascribed to each component? We shall see that there is no unambiguous answer to this second question, but we introduce functions known as partial molar quantities which provide the most useful answer to both these questions. We call these simply *partial quantities*,[1] since the word molar may be suppressed without risk of confusion.

Let us consider an extensive property of a system which, for the sake of a concrete example, we take to be the volume V. In the case of a homogeneous system at equilibrium under conditions of constant intensive properties, i.e. P, T, composition, all fields etc., an extensive property is one whose magnitude is proportional to the amount of substance present (see Section 1.4).

The *partial volume* etc. in a system of C components is defined by the derivative

$$v_i = (\partial V/\partial n_i)_{P,T,n_j} \qquad (6.2)$$

where the subscript n_j indicates that all $(C-1)$ amounts other than n_i are kept constant. To be quite consistent with (6.1) we should strictly write $j \neq i$ in (6.2), but in practice do not.

We can visualise this function by supposing that we have a beaker containing a liquid mixture with n_1 moles of component 1, n_2 of component 2, etc. We add from a burette a drop of component i and measure the change in volume. The ratio of this change to the amount (in moles) in the drop is v_i. This partial volume clearly depends on the pressure, temperature and composition of the liquid in the beaker, but is independent of the amount already present; that is, a partial quantity is itself formally an intensive property, although it is of a different physical nature from pressure and temperature.

Let us now take the liquid mixture of composition n_1, n_2, etc. and set up above it a battery of C burettes each containing one of the pure components and each arranged so that it can deliver in a fixed time an amount of that component proportional to its mole fraction in the mixture. We now turn on all burettes simultaneously and allow them to run for a certain time stirring the mixture throughout the addition to maintain a constant and uniform composition.

We have now 'created' in the beaker an extra amount of mixture, and since the pressure, temperature and composition have remained constant, so have the partial volumes of each component. Hence the volume of this extra amount is given by

$$V = \sum_i n_i v_i \qquad (6.3)*$$

where n_i is the amount of component i that has been added. By differentiation of this equation at constant P,T, we obtain

$$dV = \sum_i v_i \, dn_i + \sum_i n_i \, dv_i \qquad (6.4)$$

or setting all dn_i equal to zero except for dn_1

$$(dV)_{n_j} = v_1(dn_1)_{n_j} + \sum_i n_i(dv_i)_{n_j} \qquad (6.5)$$

that is,

$$\left(\frac{\partial V}{\partial n_1}\right)_{P,T,n_j} = v_1 + \sum_i n_i \left(\frac{\partial v_i}{\partial n_1}\right)_{P,T,n_j} \qquad (6.6)$$

where, again, the subscript $_{n_j}$ means that all except n_1 are held constant. If we compare this equation with (6.2) we see that the last term must be zero. There is nothing to distinguish component 1 from the others and so the differentiation $(\partial/\partial n_1)_{P,T,n_j}$ can refer equally to any arbitrary addition of a trace of any component, provided it is added at fixed P and T. Hence the sum that is zero in (6.6) can be written

$$\sum_i n_i \, dv_i = 0 \qquad (6.7)$$

where it is understood that the changes dv_i are those caused by any arbitrary change of composition at fixed P,T. This equation is an example of a *Gibbs-Duhem equation*, an important class of equations which show that partial quantities are not mutually independent. The consequences of these are examined below.

At first sight it appears that this relation is without real meaning, for we have integrated (6.2) to obtain (6.3), differentiated the latter to obtain (6.6) and concluded that the sum of the extra terms is zero. The important step is the first integration, for the passage from (6.2) to (6.3) is justified only

---

* For simplicity, a summation over all components from $i = 1$ to $i = C$ is denoted henceforth simply by the symbol i below the summation sign.

because the v_i are intensive properties, and it was to emphasise this point that the experiment with the burettes was introduced.

Exercise (for the mathematically inclined)

Show that the Gibbs-Duhem relation (6.7) is a mathematical consequence of Euler's theorem,[2] and the fact that V is homogeneous of first degree in n_i.

The partial volumes are formally an answer to the question, how much of the volume is to be ascribed to component i, since the sum of $(n_i v_i)$ is the total volume (6.3). However, it is clear from the experiment of adding one drop from the burette that they are more properly a measure of the response of the whole system to the addition of a small quantity of component i, rather than a property of i alone. It is true that in many mixtures v_i will be reasonably close to the molar volume of pure i at the same P, T, but this is not always so. There are even cases known where v_i is negative; thus if we dissolve sodium chloride in supercritical steam we find the partial volume of the salt is about -1000 to $-4000 \text{ cm}^3 \text{ mol}^{-1}$. Each ion pair attracts to itself a shell of water molecules, and this solvation leads to a reduction in volume which is numerically much larger than the space occupied by the added salt.

The volume was chosen for discussion since it is a property which is particularly easy to visualise, but it is clear that similar equations would have been obtained had we chosen any other extensive quantity, e.g. U, H, S, A or G. Thus the partial enthalpy h_i and the partial Gibbs free energy g_i, etc. are defined by

$$h_i = \left(\frac{\partial H}{\partial n_i}\right)_{P,T,n_j} \qquad g_i = \left(\frac{\partial G}{\partial n_i}\right)_{P,T,n_j} \qquad \text{etc.} \qquad (6.8)$$

Partial quantities are mutually related by the same equations as the extensive functions of a single substance. Thus by differentiating with respect to n_i the equations

$$G = H - TS \qquad C_P = T(\partial S/\partial T)_P \qquad (6.9)$$

we obtain

$$g_i = h_i - T s_i \qquad (c_P)_i = T(\partial s_i/\partial T)_{P,n} \qquad (6.10)$$

where the subscript n means that all n_j are held constant, including $j = i$, in the differentiation with respect to temperature.

Partial quantities are difficult to measure experimentally, and it is therefore useful to introduce also the more accessible *mean quantity* defined (for the volume) by

$$v = V \bigg/ \sum_i n_i \qquad (6.11)$$

Clearly, a set of volumes $(n_i v)$ also sums to the total volume V, thus satisfying (6.3) and showing that the partial volumes are not a unique way of ascribing part of the volume to each component. They are, however, unique in their thermodynamic importance, as will be seen below.

Since, in practice, we measure mean properties, and require partial properties, we need to know the relations between them. For simplicity, consider only a binary mixture whose composition is specified by one independent variable, say x_1. Divide (6.3) by n, the total amount of substance, to produce the mean volume v,

$$v = \sum_i x_i v_i = x_1 v_1 + x_2 v_2 \qquad (6.12)$$

and differentiate with respect to x_1 at fixed P,T.

$$\left(\frac{\partial v}{\partial x_1}\right)_{P,T} = v_1 - v_2 + x_1 \left(\frac{\partial v_1}{\partial x_1}\right)_{P,T} + x_2 \left(\frac{\partial v_2}{\partial x_1}\right)_{P,T} \qquad (6.13)$$

where in the second term we have used the identity $dx_2 = -dx_1$, a consequence of (6.1). The last two terms of this equation are just the sum of the changes $x_1 dv_1$ and $x_2 dv_2$, consequent on a change dx_1. These are related by the Gibbs-Duhem equation (6.7), if this is written for the unit amount of substance by dividing by n. Hence the sum of the last two terms of (6.13) is zero and we obtain

$$(\partial v/\partial x_1)_{P,T} = v_1 - v_2 \qquad (6.14)$$

Which, together with (6.12) gives the required relations between the mean and partial quantities,

$$v_1 = v - x_2 (\partial v/\partial x_2)_{P,T}$$
$$v_2 = v - x_1 (\partial v/\partial x_1)_{P,T} \qquad (6.15)$$

These equations enable us to obtain the partial volumes v_1 and v_2 from a knowledge of the mean volume v and its change with composition. They can be generalised to multi-component mixtures, but the results are not so simple.[3]

The equations for a binary mixture (6.15) have a simple geometric interpretation which is illustrated in Figure 6.1. As we change the composition the tangent rolls along the curve of mean volume v as a function of x. Clearly, as one end moves up the other moves down, and it is this restriction which is formally embodied in the Gibbs-Duhem relation (6.7). When we reach one end (e.g. $x_1 = 1$) then the partial volume and the mean volume are both equal to the molar volume of pure component 1, that is $v_1 = v = v_1^o$.

Exercise

Sketch a curve of v against x which leads to a maximum in v_1. How does v_2 behave at this composition? Water + ethanol and water + dioxan show this behaviour. Do the results of V. S. Griffiths (*J. Chem. Soc.* (1954), 860) for the latter system satisfy the Gibbs-Duhem relation?

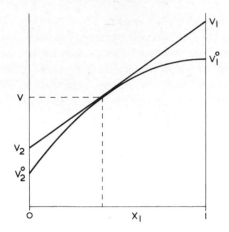

Figure 6.1. The curve is the mean volume, v, as a function of x_1. Its intercepts are the molar volumes of the pure components, v_1^o and v_2^o. At the composition shown by the dashed line, the tangent has a slope of $(\partial v/\partial x)_{P,T}$, and so, by (6.15), its intercepts are the partial volumes, v_1 and v_2

6.3 Chemical potential

We have seen that in systems of one component the molar Gibbs free energy determines the state of equilibrium of a system held at fixed pressure and temperature (Section 3.23). The partial Gibbs free energy plays an equally important role in determining the equilibrium of mixtures, and is therefore given a special name, *chemical potential*, and a special symbol, μ.

$$\mu_i = (\partial G/\partial n_i)_{P,T,n_j} \tag{6.16}$$

If we substitute $(A + PV)$ for G we obtain by the usual rules of partial differentiation (see Appendix, A.13)

$$\mu_i = (\partial A/\partial n_i)_{P,T,n_j} + Pv_i$$
$$= (\partial A/\partial n_i)_{V,T,n_j} + [(\partial A/\partial V)_{T,n} + P]v_i$$
$$= (\partial A/\partial n_i)_{V,T,n_j} \tag{6.17}$$

where the subscript n denotes that all amounts are kept constant, and hence, by (3.184), the derivative $(\partial A/\partial V)_T$ is equal to $-P$.

Exercise

Show by means of similar manipulations that μ_i is given also by

$$\mu_i = (\partial U/\partial n_i)_{S,V,n_j} = (\partial H/\partial n_i)_{S,P,n_j} = -T(\partial S/\partial n_i)_{U,V,n_j} \tag{6.18}$$

Hence we see from (6.16)–(6.18) that μ_i is the derivative of each of the fundamental thermodynamic functions with respect to n_i under conditions where the 'proper' or 'natural' variables for each function are maintained constant. By proper variables is meant here those used earlier in the fundamental equations (Section 3.20). We can, therefore, now answer the first question at the beginning of Section 6.2. The appropriate new functions needed to describe the change of U, H, A and G with composition are, in each case, the chemical potential. The following equations combine (3.174)–(3.177) with (6.16)–(6.18) above

$$dU = T\,dS - P\,dV + \sum_i \mu_i\,dn_i \tag{6.19}$$

$$dH = T\,dS + V\,dP + \sum_i \mu_i\,dn_i \tag{6.20}$$

$$dA = -S\,dT - P\,dV + \sum_i \mu_i\,dn_i \tag{6.21}$$

$$dG = -S\,dT + V\,dP + \sum_i \mu_i\,dn_i \tag{6.22}$$

However, there are conceptual difficulties associated with (6.18) in that it is not obvious at first sight what is meant by a change in amount of substance at constant S or U since the matter added inevitably carries with it its own entropy, energy, etc. We do not wish to enter here into this problem which is bound up with the question of zeros of the functions. In practice we use only (6.21) and (6.22), of which the latter is the more important. From it we can obtain the most widely used form of the Gibbs-Duhem relation (indeed, the form to which the name is sometimes restricted) by subtracting (6.22) from the analogue of (6.4), namely

$$dG = \sum_i \mu_i\,dn_i + \sum_i n_i\,d\mu_i \tag{6.23}$$

We thus obtain

$$S\,dT - V\,dP + \sum_i n_i\,d\mu_i = 0 \tag{6.24}$$

or, the more restricted form with constant pressure and temperature

$$\sum_i n_i\,d\mu_i = 0 \tag{6.25}$$

The fundamental equations (6.21) and (6.22) and the Gibbs-Duhem equation (6.24) enable us now to extend to mixtures the results obtained for substances of fixed composition in the first three chapters. In the rest of this chapter we discuss the properties of systems of one phase and two or more components. We also discuss some aspects of equilibrium between two phases, particularly liquid and gas, but defer the general discussion of phase equilibria in mixtures to the next chapter.

6.4 The perfect gas mixture

The discussion of the properties of a gas in Chapter 3 was greatly simplified by the introduction of the concept of a perfect gas. The same is true for mixtures, and so we consider first the generalisation of the equations of Section 3.13 to mixtures.

The most obvious feature of a perfect gas is its conformation to Boyle's and Charles's laws, and hence we could make the generalisation by requiring that a mixture of perfect gases (or perfect gas mixture) conforms to the same laws. However, we have seen in (3.184) and (3.178) that pressures and volumes are related to free energies by differentiation, namely

$$P = -(\partial A/\partial V)_T \qquad V = (\partial G/\partial P)_T \qquad (6.26)$$

Hence if we start by defining a perfect gas mixture in terms of its equation of state, that is, its pressure and volume, then we shall have to integrate to obtain the free energies. We have then the problem of determining the constants of integration. We evade this by defining a perfect gas mixture in terms of free energies, not the equation of state, and then we can obtain all other thermodynamic functions P, V, S, U and H etc., by the simpler operations of differentiation.

We start with the Gibbs free energy of a pure perfect gas. By integration of the equation for an isothermal change, $dG = V\,dP$ (6.26) with $V = nRT/P$, we obtain for the difference in free energy between an arbitrary pressure P and a fixed or standard pressure $P^{\ominus}$

$$G(P, T) - G(P^{\ominus}, T) = nRT \int_{P^{\ominus}}^{P} \frac{dP}{P} \quad \text{(pg)} \qquad (6.27)$$

$$= nRT \ln(P/P^{\ominus}) \quad \text{(pg)} \qquad (6.28)$$

$G(P^{\ominus}, T)$ is proportional to n, since G is an extensive function, and is otherwise a function only of T, since $P^{\ominus}$ is fixed. Hence we can write it as $n\mu^{\ominus}(T)$ where $\mu^{\ominus}$ is the chemical potential of a pure perfect gas at a pressure $P^{\ominus}$, since the chemical potential (or partial Gibbs free energy) of a pure substance is equal to the molar Gibbs free energy. (Cf. the discussion of volume in Section 6.2.) The standard pressure $P^{\ominus}$ is usually chosen to be 1 atm, but we defer more detailed discussion of standard pressure and standard potential to Section 6.6 and later sections.

We, therefore, write (6.28) as

$$G(P, T) = n[\mu^{\ominus}(T) + RT \ln(P/P^{\ominus})] \qquad \text{(pg)} \qquad (6.29)$$

and the corresponding expression for the Helmholtz free energy is given by

$$A = G - PV = G - nRT$$
$$= n[\mu^{\ominus} + RT \ln(P/P^{\ominus}) - RT]$$
$$= n[\mu^{\ominus} + RT \ln(nRT/P^{\ominus}V) - RT] \qquad \text{(pg)} \qquad (6.30)$$

This is the equation we generalise in order to define a perfect gas mixture; it is a mixture whose Helmholtz free energy is given by

$$A = \sum_i n_i \mu_i^{\ominus} + RT \sum_i n_i \left[\ln\left(\frac{n_i RT}{P^{\ominus}V}\right) - 1 \right] \quad \text{(pg)} \qquad (6.31)$$

By differentiation with respect to volume we see that it conforms to the equation of state of a perfect gas,

$$P = -(\partial A/\partial V)_{T,n} = nRT/V \quad \text{where} \quad n = \sum_i n_i \quad \text{(pg)} \qquad (6.32)$$

It is useful to define a *partial pressure* of component i as (Px_i)

$$Px_i = n_i P/n \qquad (6.33)$$

but it is important to note that this is *not* a partial quantity in the sense of Section 6.2 since pressure is not an extensive property.

The chemical potential of component i follows from (6.31)

$$\mu_i = \left(\frac{\partial A}{\partial n_i}\right)_{T,V,n_j} = \mu_i^{\ominus} + RT \ln\left(\frac{n_i RT}{P^{\ominus}V}\right) \quad \text{(pg)} \qquad (6.34)$$

or, changing to pressure as the independent variable,

$$\mu_i(P, T, x) = \mu_i^{\ominus}(T) + RT \ln(x_i P/P^{\ominus}) \quad \text{(pg)} \qquad (6.35)$$

$\mu_i^{\ominus}(T)$ is the potential of pure i at pressure $P^{\ominus}$ and temperature T. If we are considering changes of composition but not of pressure it is useful to replace this standard potential by that of the pure component at the prevailing pressure, for which we write μ_i°. From (6.35) with $x_i = 1$

$$\mu_i^{\circ}(P, T) = \mu_i^{\ominus}(T) + RT \ln(P/P^{\ominus}) \quad \text{(pg)} \qquad (6.36)$$

and by subtracting this from (6.35)

$$\mu_i(P, T, x) = \mu_i^{\circ}(P, T) + RT \ln x_i \quad \text{(pg)} \qquad (6.37)$$

This equation has been obtained here as a consequence of (6.31), the definition of a perfect gas mixture. It has, however, a value which transcends gas mixtures, for it serves to define an important kind of mixture, the *ideal mixture*, in any phase, solid, liquid or gas. This aspect of the equation is deferred to the next section.

The equations for the pressure and partial pressures of a perfect gas (6.32) and (6.33) lead to two laws, *Dalton's law of partial pressures* and *Amagat's law of additive volumes*.

Dalton's Law: The partial pressure of a component in a mixture is equal to the pressure that the same amount of substance would exert if it alone occupied the same volume at the same temperature. This statement merely puts (6.32) and (6.33) into words.

Amagat's Law: The volume of a mixture is equal to the sum of the volumes of the components when each is held separately at the same total pressure and temperature as the mixture.

Exercise

Show that (6.32) and (6.33) imply this law.

Although real gas mixtures do not conform exactly to Dalton's and Amagat's laws, these laws are often useful approximations; we return to them in Section 6.6, but meanwhile consider further properties of the ideal mixture in the next section.

6.5 The ideal mixture

An *ideal mixture*, like a *perfect gas*, is one of those concepts which simplify the discussion of the thermodynamic properties even of those real systems which do not satisfy their postulates. Here we distinguish between the two words *perfect* and *ideal*; we reserve the former for a pure substance or mixture whose Helmholtz free energy is given by (6.30) or (6.31), and hence whose equation of state is (6.32); we use the latter only in the sense that an *ideal mixture* is, by definition, one whose chemical potentials satisfy (6.37). The former is, therefore, the more restricted class, for a perfect gas mixture is, as shown above, necessarily an ideal mixture, but the latter may be an imperfect gas, a liquid or a solid mixture.

Even as idealised concepts these two classes have a different status, for *any* real gas mixture can be made to approach arbitrarily close to the equation of state (6.32) by lowering the density, whilst a real liquid mixture (say) cannot be brought arbitrarily close to satisfying (6.37) by changing the pressure or temperature. Since the concepts have been established by means of definitions these statements cannot be derived 'from thermodynamics'—they are statements of experimental fact added to the thermodynamic formalism. The concept of an ideal mixture serves in general as a standard of behaviour with which real mixtures can be compared, but which they may never attain.

We now examine the consequences of (6.37). We observe, first, that the equation allows us to calculate μ_i if we know μ_i°, that is the potential of the pure component at the same pressure and temperature as the mixture, and, by implication, in the same phase. This last restriction means that we can readily use this equation for the discussion of the properties of a mixture of gases (e.g. nitrogen + methane) or of two liquids (e.g. benzene + toluene), but cannot use it directly at (say) room temperature for the discussion of a solution of a gas in a liquid (e.g. nitrogen in benzene) or of a liquid in a gas (e.g. benzene vapour in nitrogen) or of a solid in a liquid (e.g. naphthalene in benzene). At room temperature and pressure liquid nitrogen, gaseous benzene and liquid naphthalene do not exist, and so μ_i° is not experimentally accessible. This difficulty can, in some degree, be evaded by extrapolations into unstable regions of pressure and temperature and these evasions are widely used since the concept of an ideal mixture is a valuable one. However, we defer such systems to Sections 6.10 and 6.11, and assume for the moment that μ_i° is accessible.

From the definition of an ideal mixture, (6.37) we obtain the thermodynamic properties, as follows

$$G = \sum_i n_i \mu_i = \sum_i n_i \mu_i^\circ + RT \sum_i n_i \ln x_i \qquad (6.38)$$

$$S = -(\partial G/\partial T)_{P,n}$$

$$= \sum_i n_i s_i^\circ - R \sum_i n_i \ln x_i \qquad (6.39)$$

$$H = G + TS = \sum_i n_i h_i^\circ \qquad (6.40)$$

where $\mu_i^\circ = h_i^\circ - Ts_i^\circ$ since μ is a partial Gibbs free energy, cf. (6.10).

Exercise

Show from (6.38) that the volume and heat capacity of an ideal mixture are given by

$$V = \sum_i n_i v_i^\circ \qquad C_P = \sum_i n_i (c_P)_i^\circ \qquad (6.41)$$

We see from (6.38)–(6.41) that the enthalpy, volume and heat capacity of an ideal mixture are simply the sum of those of the same amounts of the pure components at the same pressure and temperature. However, the Gibbs free energy and entropy are not linear in the amounts of substances. We denote by ΔZ the change in any function Z on forming a mixture from its components at fixed P,T; that is,

$$\Delta Z = Z(P, T, n) - \sum_i n_i z_i^\circ(P, T) \qquad (6.42)$$

Hence, for an ideal mixture,

$$\Delta G = RT \sum_i n_i \ln x_i = -T \Delta S \qquad (6.43)$$

$$\Delta H = 0 \qquad \Delta V = 0 \qquad \Delta C_P = 0 \qquad (6.44)$$

ΔS is positive and ΔG is negative, since mole fractions are necessarily less than unity. Figure 6.2 shows the functions (6.37) and (6.43) for a binary ideal mixture. Since ΔS is positive and ΔG negative we see that the formation of an ideal mixture from its components is a spontaneous process whether carried out in a closed system of fixed energy and volume, or at constant pressure and temperature.

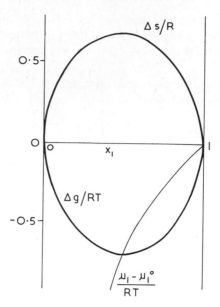

Figure 6.2. The chemical potential of component 1, μ_1, and the molar entropy and Gibbs free energy of mixing, Δs and Δg, for an ideal binary mixture, from (6.37) and (6.43)

6.6 Real gas mixtures: the virial expansion

We have seen in Chapters 3 and 4 that the perfect gas law is an adequate representation of the properties of a real gas only at low densities. This is true also for gas mixtures. Any of the empirical equations of state used for real gases can be extended to mixtures by allowing their characteristic parameters (e.g. a and b of van der Waals' equation) to become explicit functions of composition. Classical thermodynamics cannot tell us how to do this; it is a matter for experiment and for molecular or statistical thermodynamics, and so is deferred to Chapter 9. There is, however, one form of the equation of state for which both theory and experiment tell us unambiguously how the characteristic parameters depend on composition. This is the virial equation (4.20), and since this is particularly useful for representing the equation of state of a vapour in equilibrium with a liquid mixture, we discuss its properties at this point.

As was pointed out in Chapter 4, statistical thermodynamics teaches us that the second virial coefficient, B, arises from the interactions of molecules in pairs, the third, C, from triplets, and so on. It follows that in a mixture B is a quadratic function of composition, C a cubic, etc. Since we wish to use the equations of this section in conjunction with those of the next, on real liquid mixtures, we now adopt the usual convention of using x_i for the mole fractions in the liquid and y_i for those in the gas. With this convention, and with the rule above derived from statistical thermodynamics, we can write for the composition dependence of B, C, etc.

$$B(T, y) = \sum_i \sum_j y_i y_j B_{ij}(T) \qquad (B_{ij} = B_{ji}) \tag{6.45}$$

which in a binary mixture reduces to

$$B(T, y) = y_1^2 B_{11}(T) + 2 y_1 y_2 B_{12}(T) + y_2^2 B_{22}(T) \tag{6.46}$$

For the third coefficient

$$C(T, y) = \sum_i \sum_j \sum_k y_i y_j y_k C_{ijk}(T) \tag{6.47}$$

Here we introduce new coefficients B_{11}, B_{12}, B_{22}, C_{111}, C_{112}, etc. Clearly B_{11}, C_{111}, etc. are the virial coefficients of pure component 1, but the cross terms B_{12}, C_{112}, C_{122}, etc. are properties of the mixture, and cannot be determined from those of the pure substances; their estimation is a matter for experiment or for estimation by the methods of Chapter 9. They are functions only of temperature and, of course, of the nature of the components denoted by the subscripts.

Exercise

Show that the lth virial coefficient of a mixture of C components is formed of $[(l+C-1)!/l!(C-1)!]$ individual coefficients. (Cf. 6.46, where $l = C = 2$, and this number is 3.)

The virial equation of state of a mixture is

$$\frac{PV}{nRT} = 1 + B\left(\frac{n}{V}\right) + C\left(\frac{n}{V}\right)^2 + \cdots \tag{6.48}$$

where B, C, etc. are given by (6.46)–(6.47). We restrict further discussion to the first term of first order in the density in (6.48), that is to the second virial coefficient, B, for several reasons. First, this degree of accuracy suffices for the discussion below of the properties of saturated vapours at near atmospheric pressure; secondly we know little about C for real mixtures; and thirdly, we usually wish to use this equation for calculating $\mu_i(P, T, y)$, and (6.48) loses its simple form if the general expansion is inverted to make P the independent variable.

We proceed from (6.48) to the chemical potential via the Helmholtz free energy, by integrating $(\partial A/\partial V)_{T,n} = -P$; the constant of integration is determined from (6.31) since A approaches that of the perfect gas as the density approaches zero. If we denote A from (6.31) as A_{pg} we find from (6.48)

$$A = A_{\text{pg}} + n^2 RT(B/V) + \cdots \tag{6.49}$$

$$= A_{\text{pg}} + (RT/V) \sum_{j=1} \sum_{k=1} n_j n_k B_{jk} \tag{6.50}$$

where we have started the running suffixes at j so as to leave the letter i free for the component in which we are interested. Hence from (6.17) and (6.34), by differentiation of (6.50) with respect to n_i,

$$\mu_i = \mu_i^{\ominus} + RT \ln\left(\frac{n_i RT}{P^{\ominus}V}\right) + 2RT\left(\frac{n}{V}\right) \sum_j y_j B_{ij} + \ldots \tag{6.51}$$

We can express μ more conveniently in terms of P by substituting for V from (6.48). The result is, to the first order in the pressure,

$$\mu_i = \mu_i^{\ominus} + RT \ln(P y_i / P^{\ominus}) + P(B_{ii} + DB_i) + \ldots \tag{6.52}$$

where

$$DB_i = \sum_{j \neq i} \sum_{k \neq i} y_j y_k (\delta B_{ij} + \delta B_{ik} - \delta B_{jk}) \tag{6.53}$$

$$\delta B_{ij} = B_{ij} - \tfrac{1}{2} B_{ii} - \tfrac{1}{2} B_{jj} \qquad (\delta B_{ii} = \delta B_{jj} = 0) \tag{6.54}$$

Exercise

Derive (6.51) and (6.52) from (6.50). The first step is straightforward; the second requires care in deciding which terms are first order in P, and in manipulating the double sums. Those who find the last task too difficult should carry out the derivation for a binary mixture, for which (6.52) reduces to

$$\mu_1 = \mu_1^{\ominus} + RT \ln(P y_1 / P^{\ominus}) + P(B_{11} + 2y_2^2 \, \delta B_{12}) + \ldots \tag{6.55}$$

with an equivalent expression for μ_2.

The potential $\mu^{\ominus}$ is, as before, a function only of temperature, but it is no longer the potential of the real gas at the standard pressure $P^{\ominus}$. We can say that it is the potential of the equivalent, but hypothetical, perfect gas at this pressure, where by the word equivalent we mean a gas composed of the same substance but with all virial coefficients, B, C, etc. put equal to zero. Those who rightly dislike such hypothetical entities can take $\mu^{\ominus}$ as a standard potential operationally defined by (6.52), or (6.55) for a binary mixture. If the virial equation of state is not sufficiently accurate or convenient for the gas in question, then the more general definition of (6.67) in the next section must be used.

The potential $\mu^{\ominus}$ is related to that of the real gas at an arbitrary pressure $P^{\dagger}$ by writing (6.52) for $y_i = 1$, $P = P^{\dagger}$

$$\mu_i^{\circ}(P^{\dagger}) = \mu_i^{\ominus} + RT \ln(P^{\dagger}/P^{\ominus}) + P^{\dagger} B_{ii} + \cdots \tag{6.56}$$

By subtracting this from (6.52) we obtain a more useful form of this equation which relates $\mu_i(P, T, y)$ to the potential of the real pure gas at an arbitrary pressure $P^{\dagger}$, namely

$$\mu_i(P, T, y) = \mu_i^{\circ}(P^{\dagger}, T) + RT \ln(P y_i / P^{\dagger})$$
$$+ (P - P^{\dagger}) B_{ii}(T) + P[DB_i(T)] + \cdots \tag{6.57}$$

This equation is a complete solution to the problem of defining the properties of a gas mixture in terms of the virial equation to the second term, for all other properties can be obtained from μ_i. Thus, by differentiating with respect to P we obtain the partial volume, exactly as we do for a pure substance, for which $v = (\partial g/\partial P)_T$. We obtain

$$v_i = RT/P + (B_{ii} + DB_i) + O(P) \tag{6.58}$$

We must now notice a difference of language between various classes of scientist. The chemist discusses multicomponent equilibria in terms of the potential μ_i, the physicist uses either μ_i or the entirely equivalent *absolute activity* λ_i, a pure number,

$$\lambda_i = \exp(\mu_i/RT) \tag{6.59}$$

whilst the engineer often prefers the fugacity f_i, which has the dimensions of pressure. An operational definition of f for a pure substance was given in (4.18). For a mixture the corresponding definition is given in (6.66) below, but both may be expressed in terms of the chemical potential

$$f_i = (Py_i)\exp[(\mu_i - (\mu_i)_{pg})/RT] \tag{6.60}$$

where $(\mu_i)_{pg}$ is the potential of the hypothetical perfect gas at the same P, T and y (for a pure substance, $y = 1$ and $\mu = g$).

From (6.60) and (6.35) we obtain

$$\mu_i = \mu_i^{\ominus} + RT \ln(f_i/P^{\ominus}) \tag{6.61}$$

where $\mu^{\ominus}$ is the potential of a perfect gas at the standard pressure, $P^{\ominus}$, and hence also of the real gas at the same standard fugacity $f = P^{\ominus}$. A comparison of this equation with (6.35) shows that fugacity plays the same role in a real gas mixture as partial pressure plays in a perfect gas mixture.

Here we use both chemical potential μ_i and fugacity f_i, but not absolute activity λ_i, with the emphasis on the former since it leads to the most commonly used forms of the equations used to describe ionic solutions and the surface properties of mixtures. We emphasise, however, that the functions μ, f and λ are entirely equivalent. To each equation below written in terms of μ there is a corresponding form in terms of f and one in terms of λ. We give explicitly some of the former. By subtracting (6.35) from (6.52) substituting $[\mu_i - (\mu_i)_{pg}]$ in (6.60) and expanding the exponential we obtain the virial expansion of f_i.

$$f_i/Py_i = 1 + P(B_{ii} + DB_i)/RT + \cdots \tag{6.62}$$

Example

The ratio f/Py is close to unity at pressures close to atmospheric. Thus for a mixture of nitrogen (1) and carbon dioxide (2) at 30 °C, the second virial coefficients[4] are

$$B_{11} = -4 \text{ cm}^3 \text{ mol}^{-1} \qquad B_{12} = -41 \text{ cm}^3 \text{ mol}^{-1} \qquad B_{22} = -119 \text{ cm}^3 \text{ mol}^{-1}$$

Hence

$$\delta B_{12} = +20 \text{ cm}^3 \text{ mol}^{-1}$$
$$DB_1 = +(40y_2^2) \text{ cm}^3 \text{ mol}^{-1}$$
$$DB_2 = +(40y_1^2) \text{ cm}^3 \text{ mol}^{-1}$$

Hence from (6.62)

$$f_1/Py_1 = 1 + (P/\text{bar})[-4 + 40y_2^2]/25204 + \cdots$$
$$f_2/Py_2 = 1 + (P/\text{bar})[-119 + 40y_1^2]/25204 + \cdots$$

If P is less than about 5 bar (and higher terms of the virial equation are needed if it is greater) then f/Py is slightly less than unity for carbon dioxide and for pure nitrogen, but exceeds unity for nitrogen in mixtures rich in carbon dioxide.

Clearly fugacity is equal to partial pressure in a perfect gas mixture, or in a real gas mixture in the limit of zero pressure. In general the ratio (f_i/Py_i) which is sometimes called the *fugacity coefficient* of component i depends not only on the pressure but also on the composition of the mixture. Suppose, however, that the coefficients B_{ij} are the arithmetic means of the self-coefficients B_{ii} and B_{jj}, then from (6.54) and (6.53), δB_{ij} and DB_i are zero and, from (6.58) and (6.62) or from the example above we see that v_i and (f_i/Py_i) are now independent of composition. This important rule is a restricted version of that of Lewis and Randall. They proposed, in general and not merely for a gas for which we can terminate the equation of state at the second virial coefficient, that

$$f_i(P, T, y) = y_i \, f_i^\circ(P, T) \qquad\qquad (6.63)$$

with its corollary

$$v_i(P, T, y) = v_i^\circ(P, T) \qquad\qquad (6.64)$$

Clearly, (6.64) is a statement of Amagat's law of additive volumes; hence if this law holds at all pressures, the rule of Lewis and Randall is valid. In general neither is exact, although both may be useful approximations. For an equation of state terminated at the second virial coefficient both are equivalent to putting all δB_{ij} equal to zero. Methods for estimating virial coefficients are discussed in Chapter 9; here it suffices to say that this quantity is often far from zero as is shown in the example above. The difference δB is relatively smaller if the components have molecules which are physically and chemically similar e.g. two alkanes, but is relatively larger if hydrogen or helium is one of the components. Thus for hydrogen (1) + nitrogen (2) at 0 °C,

$$B_{11} = +14.0 \text{ cm}^3 \text{ mol}^{-1} \qquad B_{12} = +12.5 \text{ cm}^3 \text{ mol}^{-1} \qquad B_{22} = -11.0 \text{ cm}^3 \text{ mol}^{-1}$$

$$\delta B_{12} = +11.0 \text{ cm}^3 \text{ mol}^{-1}$$

Exercise

Show that if the rule of Lewis and Randall holds for each component, the gas mixture is ideal, i.e. it satisfies (6.37) and hence (6.43) and (6.44).

6.7 Real gas mixtures: general relations

If the density is too high for us to use the virial equation of state, or if we prefer to use some closed equation such as that of Redlich and Kwong, then the expressions above are not the appropriate route to the chemical potential and fugacity. Expressions of general validity are obtained by integrating $(\partial \mu_i / \partial P)_{T,y} = v_i$, both for the real gas and for the perfect gas, for which $v_i = RT/P$ (6.58). By subtraction

$$\mu_i - (\mu_i)_{\text{pg}} = \int_0^P \left(v_i - \frac{RT}{P} \right) dP \tag{6.65}*$$

(There is no constant of integration since the difference on the left becomes zero as P approaches zero.) Hence from the definition of fugacity (6.60)

$$RT \ln(f_i/Py_i) = \int_0^P \left(v_i - \frac{RT}{P} \right) dP \tag{6.66}$$

This integral can be evaluated along a line of fixed composition and temperature if the equation of state of the mixture is known in the form of V as a function of P, T and n_i. Unfortunately, most equations of state are in the form of P as a function of V, T and n_i. The necessary inversion is usually made by iterative solution on a computer.

The potential of the perfect gas can be eliminated from (6.65) by substituting (6.35) for $(\mu_i)_{\text{pg}}$

$$\mu_i(P, T, y) = \mu_i^{\ominus}(T) + RT \ln(Py_i/P^{\ominus}) + \int_0^P \left(v_i - \frac{RT}{P} \right) dP \tag{6.67}$$

The potential of the standard state or of hypothetical pure perfect gas, $\mu^{\ominus}$, can be eliminated in favour of that of the real gas at a pressure $P^\dagger$, as was done in going from (6.55) to (6.57) for the virial equation of state. The result is

$$\mu_i(P, T, y) = \mu_i^{\circ}(P^\dagger, T) + RT \ln(Py_i/P^\dagger)$$
$$+ \int_0^P \left(v_i - \frac{RT}{P} \right) dP - \int_0^{P^\dagger} \left(v_i^{\circ} - \frac{RT}{P} \right) dP \tag{6.68}$$

---

* Note the 'shorthand' in writing this integral. The same symbol, P, is often improperly used both for the variable and for its limit. When defining the fugacity of a pure gas (4.18) we avoided this impropriety by denoting the limit P'. When discussing mixtures, however, we revert to the simpler and widely used convention in order to avoid an excess of subscripts and superscripts. Care is needed in handling such integrals. For example if we differentiate the right hand side of (6.65) with respect to pressure we get simply the integrand, $v_i - (RT/P)$, and must not differentiate this further.

Integrals of this kind can be evaluated if we know the equations of state of the pure and mixed gases. All other properties can be found from the potential (6.68), or, what is entirely equivalent, from the fugacity (6.66) by the usual manipulations.

The standard potential $\mu^\ominus$ was introduced originally in (6.29) as the potential of a perfect gas at a standard pressure $P^\ominus$. It reappeared in (6.51) since we obtained the properties of a real gas by integrating $(\partial A/\partial V)_T = -P$, and used the known properties of the perfect gas to determine the constant of integration. By similar reasoning it appears also in (6.61), as a consequence of the definition of fugacity by (6.60). We can, of course, always eliminate $\mu^\ominus$ from the equations in favour of the potential of the pure real gas at some arbitrarily chosen pressure $P^\dagger$, as in (6.57) and (6.68). However, $\mu^\ominus$ is an important quantity in chemical thermodynamics and we must now consider more carefully the standard state of which it is the potential.

In the previous chapters we met the problem that thermodynamic functions do not, in general, have absolute values. If we wish to tabulate U, H, A, G or S we must choose, more or less arbitrarily, a reference state in which the function is assigned the value zero, as for example in the charts in Appendix C. The conventions followed there are typical of the practice of the engineers concerned with the compilation and use of such charts. However, the chemists who have drawn up tables of free energies and enthalpies for use in calculating the equilibria of chemical reactions follow a different convention, which requires the use of the standard state denoted here by the 'plimsoll', or, in London, the 'underground', namely $\ominus$.

It was stated above (6.61) that $\mu^\ominus$ is the potential of the pure gas at a fugacity $f = P^\ominus$, and also the potential of an equivalent (but hypothetical) pure perfect gas at a pressure $P = f = P^\ominus$. Although both gases have the same potential, they are not identical; they have, for example, different enthalpies. We must therefore choose between them in defining our standard state, and, for reasons which will become clear, the choice is the second alternative. By definition:

> *The standard state of a gas at a temperature T is that of the pure equivalent perfect gas at the same temperature and a standard pressure $P^\ominus$. The most common choice of standard pressure is $P^\ominus = 1$ atm.*

If we wish to avoid hypothetical entities such as the 'equivalent perfect gas', then we must abandon the notion that there is a standard state at all. We still need standard potentials, and standard values of other thermodynamic functions, but these need not be ascribed to any particular state of the system, real or hypothetical. They can, if we wish, be defined purely by equations such as (6.67). We retain here the first concept since we think it useful to be able to visualise what is meant by $\mu^\ominus$ etc. Both points of view lead, of course, to the same physical consequences. What we measure cannot be affected by changes of view point.

A standard pressure of 1 atm is not what is loosely called unit pressure unless we are using atm as our unit of measurement. In the SI the fundamental unit is $N\,m^{-2}$ and the practical unit the bar (see Preface). A pressure of 1 atm is thus a *standard* pressure, and although it may be irritating that the standard is not a round number of metric units and yet is so close to the bar, this fact should cause no more real difficulty than the fact that the often used 'standard temperature' of 25 °C is not a round number of kelvin.

The enthalpy and entropy are obtained by differentiating (6.61) with respect to temperature. Thus

$$h_i = \mu_i - T(\partial\mu_i/\partial T)_P$$
$$= [\mu_i^{\ominus} - T(d\mu_i^{\ominus}/dT)] - (RT^2/f_i)(\partial f_i/\partial T)_P$$
$$= h_i^{\ominus} - (RT^2/f_i)(\partial f_i/\partial T)_P \tag{6.69}$$

And so, for a pure substance, we have

$$\mu_i^{\circ}(P, T) = \mu_i^{\ominus}(T) + RT\ln(P/P^{\ominus})$$
$$+ \int_0^P \left(v_i^{\circ} - \frac{RT}{P}\right)dP \tag{6.70}$$

$$h_i^{\circ}(P, T) = h_i^{\ominus}(T) + \int_0^P \left[v_i^{\circ} - T\left(\frac{\partial v_i^{\circ}}{\partial T}\right)_P\right]dP \tag{6.71}$$

$$s_i^{\circ}(P, T) = s_i^{\ominus}(T) + \int_0^P \left[\frac{R}{P} - \left(\frac{\partial v_i^{\circ}}{\partial T}\right)_P\right]dP \tag{6.72}$$

where $\mu^{\ominus}$, $h^{\ominus}$ and $s^{\ominus}$ are the properties in the standard state defined above. It is the occurrence of the derivative of μ at constant pressure (and not at constant fugacity) in the first line of (6.69) which determines how the standard state is most conveniently defined.

Exercise

Obtain from (6.70)–(6.72) the enthalpy and entropy of the real gas in the state $f = P^{\ominus}$ by using the virial equation to the second coefficient. Show that $f = P^{\ominus}$ at a pressure given by

$$\frac{P}{P^{\ominus}} = 1 - \frac{BP^{\ominus}}{RT} \tag{6.73}$$

and that $h^{\ominus}$ is the same as h for the real gas at zero pressure.

Figure 4.9 shows the fugacity/pressure ratio for methane. This ratio is usually a more convenient function to plot than the fugacity itself. From this figure it can be seen that the ratio is close to unity at a pressure of 1 atm and hence that the distinctions drawn above between the different states of the gas are often of little practical importance. It is, however, important to have our conceptions clear in the formal definition of the standard state of a gas. We shall later extend the meaning of the superscript $\ominus$ to cover standard states of liquids and solids, but we defer discussion of this point to Section 8.3, where the need for such definition first arises.

6.8 Liquid mixtures

In a gas mixture at sufficiently low pressures the virial equation of state allows us to express the change of fugacity etc. with composition in terms of the virial coefficients B_{ij}, C_{ijk}, etc. We have no such results for a liquid, and so must be content with more general descriptions. In this section we consider the measurement of the fugacity of each component in a liquid at low pressure, and we see that the ideal mixture of Section 6.5 provides a useful standard of comparison for real liquid mixtures. We defer to the next sections of this chapter the discussion of solutions of gases and solids in liquids, and to the next chapter the wider ranging problems of the phase equilibria between liquids and their vapours at high pressures, and between partially immiscible liquids.

Since we know more about the fugacity of a gas than that of a liquid we measure the latter in terms of the former. If we have a liquid mixture in equilibrium with its vapour, then the following three conditions must be met. First, the temperatures of liquid and vapour must be equal for there to be thermal equilibrium, secondly, the pressures must be equal for there to be mechanical equilibrium, and thirdly, the Gibbs free energy must be at a minimum with respect to a transfer of any component from liquid to gas—or vice versa (the prior conditions of equality of temperature and pressure enforce the choice of G being a minimum as the appropriate condition of thermodynamic equilibrium. See Chapter 3.) This last condition can be expressed formally by equating to zero the small change δG on transferring δn_i of component i from liquid to gas

$$\delta G = [\mu_i(\text{gas}) - \mu_i(\text{liquid})] \, \delta n_i = 0 \tag{6.74}$$

If this is to be true for all components, the chemical potentials, and hence the fugacities, of all components are the same in the liquid as they are in the gas. Hence we measure the fugacities of the components of a liquid by finding the composition of the gas in equilibrium with it and measuring the fugacities of the latter by the methods of the last section.

The condition for liquid-vapour equilibrium in a pure substance (Section 3.23) is the equality of the molar Gibbs free energy. In a mixture it is equality of each chemical potential. The latter result reduces to the former if the number of components is reduced to one, since, in a pure substance $\mu_i^\circ = g$ (Section 6.3). However in a mixture the mean Gibbs free energy g is not the same in both phases, since their compositions are different. In both cases the fundamental criterion of equilibrium is (6.74), namely that the total Gibbs free energy G is a minimum with respect to all transfers of material from one phase to another at constant pressure and temperature.

In order to compare the measured values of chemical potential or fugacity more easily with those of an ideal liquid mixture it is convenient to introduce *activity coefficients* γ_i which are a measure of the difference in the properties of a real and an ideal mixture. These coefficients are defined by the equation

$$\mu_i(P, T, x) = \mu_i^\circ(P, T) + RT \ln(x_i\gamma_i) \tag{6.75}$$

which is seen to be the equation defining an ideal mixture (6.37) but with the extra term $RT \ln \gamma_i$. If μ_i° is still to be the potential of pure i then (6.75) must be supplemented with the requirement that

$$\gamma_i = 1 \quad \text{at} \quad x_i = 1 \tag{6.76}$$

We shall see later that we may abandon the notion that the composition-independent potential in equations defining activity coefficients is necessarily that of pure i (i.e. μ_i°), and require only that it is the potential of some defined state which may be chosen at will. The most common alternative to (6.76) is to choose γ_i to be unity as x_i tends to zero, a choice made below in Section 6.13 when discussing ionic solutions. Activity coefficients, like the potentials they represent, are functions of pressure, temperature and composition.

The introduction of activity coefficients into the vocabulary used for discussing mixtures is a second example of a device that is widely used in thermodynamics. If we have some standard of normality to which we hope our system may conform approximately, then we introduce an arbitrary coefficient into the equations that define the normal systems, and re-phrase our discussion in terms of those coefficients. Thus in discussing a real gas mixture it is natural to take a perfect gas as the standard of normality. We 'make' our real gas conform to this on paper by introducing the fugacity defined in such a way that equations true for a perfect gas in terms of partial pressure now become true by definition for a real gas when written in terms of fugacity. Compare (6.61) and (6.35). In the same way, we here introduce the *activity* $(x_i\gamma_i)$ into our discussion of a real mixture, so that we can write (6.75) in place of the equation defining an ideal mixture, (6.37). Such a substitution is, of course, merely a convenient formalism; until we know how to measure γ_i, and how to express their change with composition, there is no physical content in (6.75).

At a fixed pressure and temperature

$$d\mu_i = RT \, d \ln(f_i/P^\ominus) \quad \text{(cf. 6.61)} \tag{6.77}$$

hence, by integrating (6.77), (6.75) can be re-written in terms of the fugacity as

$$f_i(P, T, x) = (x_i\gamma_i) f_i^\circ(P, T) \tag{6.78}$$

In an ideal mixture $\gamma_i = 1$ and f_i is linear in composition. In a non-ideal mixture (6.75) and (6.78) allow us to express the departure of potential and fugacity from their ideal values in terms of the activity coefficients.

Let us consider now a binary liquid mixture of mole fractions x_1, x_2, (where $x_1 + x_2 = 1$) in equilibrium with its vapour of mole fractions y_1 and y_2 ($y_1 + y_2 = 1$) at a temperature T and a low pressure P, (say, not more than 3 bar). Let us, for convenience, introduce an arbitrary pressure $P^\dagger$, which we suppose to be close to P, and hence, since the pressure is low, close also to the vapour pressure of the pure components, P_1° and P_2°. From (6.75) and (6.57), we have

Liquid

$$\mu_1(\text{liquid}, P, x) = \mu_1^\circ(\text{liquid}, P^\dagger) + RT \ln(x_1\gamma_1) + (P - P^\dagger)v_1^\circ$$

$$\mu_2(\text{liquid}, P, x) = \mu_2^\circ(\text{liquid}, P^\dagger) + RT \ln(x_2\gamma_2) + (P - P^\dagger)v_2^\circ$$

(6.79)

Gas

$$\mu_1(\text{gas}, P, y) = \mu_1^\circ(\text{gas}, P^\dagger) + RT \ln(Py_1/P^\dagger)$$
$$+ (P - P^\dagger)B_{11} + 2Py_2^2 \, \delta B_{12}$$

$$\mu_2(\text{gas}, P, y) = \mu_2^\circ(\text{gas}, P^\dagger) + RT \ln(Py_2/P^\dagger)$$
$$+ (P - P^\dagger)B_{22} + 2Py_1^2 \, \delta B_{12}$$

(6.80)

The pressure $P^\dagger$ is quite arbitrary in each of these equations (although it must be low) and so we can now enforce the conditions of equilibrium by equating $\mu_1(\text{liquid})$ to $\mu_1(\text{gas})$, putting here $P^\dagger = P_1^\circ$; and $\mu_2(\text{liquid})$ to $\mu_2(\text{gas})$, putting here $P^\dagger = P_2^\circ$. We choose these values for $P^\dagger$ because we know that, as well as being in equilibrium in the mixture at pressure P, pure liquid component 1 is also at equilibrium with its pure vapour at a pressure P_1°. Hence

$$\mu_1^\circ(\text{liquid}, P_1^\circ) = \mu_1^\circ(\text{gas}, P_1^\circ)$$
$$f_1^\circ(\text{liquid}, P_1^\circ) = f_1^\circ(\text{gas}, P_1^\circ)$$

(6.81)

and similarly for component 2. By equating the first of (6.79) to the first of (6.80) we obtain

$$RT \ln(x_1\gamma_1 P_1^\circ/y_1 P) = (P - P_1^\circ)(B_{11} - v_1^\circ) + 2Py_2^2 \, \delta B_{12} \qquad (6.82)$$

and conversely for component 2 by exchanging indices.

These equations allow us to measure the activity coefficients γ_1 and γ_2; we require to know the compositions of liquid and vapour, the molar volumes and vapour pressures of the pure liquid components and the equation of state of the gas mixture expressed in terms of B_{11}, B_{12} and B_{22}. In practice, the terms on the right of (6.82) are small compared with RT. If we neglect them we are assuming that the vapour is a perfect gas mixture, and that the liquids have negligible molar volumes. For rough calculations this is a legitimate approximation and reduces (6.82) to

$$\gamma_1 = Py_1/P_1^\circ x_1 \qquad \gamma_2 = Py_2/P_2^\circ x_2 \tag{6.83}$$

The measurement of P, P_1° and x_1 etc. presents no problems but it is much harder to obtain reliable values of y_1 etc. The vapour above a steadily boiling liquid mixture should have the correct composition, but if a sample is taken it is often found to be either too rich in the more volatile component because some fractionation has occurred by partial condensation of the vapour on the sides of the vessel, or too rich in the heavier component because of the entrainment of small drops of the boiling liquid. There is, however, one other way out of this experimental difficulty, and that is to eliminate the vapour composition from the logarithmic terms of (6.82), and the corresponding equation for component 2. This leads to

$$P = x_1\gamma_1 P_1^\circ \exp\left[\frac{(P-P_1^\circ)(v_1^\circ - B_{11}) - 2Py_2^2\,\delta B_{12}}{RT}\right]$$

$$+ x_2\gamma_2 P_2^\circ \exp\left[\frac{(P-P_2^\circ)(v_2^\circ - B_{22}) - 2Py_1^2\,\delta B_{12}}{RT}\right] \tag{6.84}$$

as the exact equation (i.e. correct to the second virial coefficient, and hence adequate to about 3 bar for most substances), and to

$$P = x_1\gamma_1 P_1^\circ + x_2\gamma_2 P_2^\circ \tag{6.85}$$

for the approximate equation obtained by assuming the gas mixture is perfect and the liquids of negligible volume.

This equation takes a particularly simple form if we are dealing with an ideal mixture, that is, one in which all activity coefficients are unity at all compositions. For such a mixture (6.85) shows that pressure is a linear function of composition; that is, for a multicomponent mixture,

$$P = \sum_i x_i P_i^\circ \tag{6.86}$$

This result is known as *Raoult's law*, and is sometimes taken to be synonymous with the definition of an ideal mixture. However, Raoult's law is obtained not only by putting all $\gamma_i = 1$, but by the neglect of the small terms on the right-hand side of (6.82). These terms are, in fact, just the same as those previously neglected in going from Clapeyron's equation to the Clapeyron-Clausius equation (3.224). Figure 6.3 shows the vapour pressure of a binary mixture which comes very close to satisfying Raoult's law.

Exercise

In Figure 6.3 P is a linear function of x. Show that in such a system P as a function of y is part of a hyperbola.

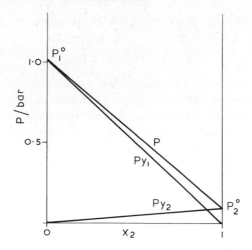

Figure 6.3. Total and partial pressures in the system benzene (1) + bromobenzene (2) at 80 °C. The system is close to obedience to Raoult's law. (M. L. McGlashan and R. J. Wingrove, *Trans. Faraday Soc.* 52 (1956) 470)

We can use (6.84) to measure the activity coefficients γ_1 and γ_2 without knowing accurately the composition of the vapour, since the terms proportional to δB_{12} are so small that even a rough guess at y_i suffices for their calculation.

At first sight we seem to have insufficient information since we have two unknowns, γ_1 and γ_2, but only one equation, (6.84). However, the activity coefficients are not independent since they are measures of the chemical potential and so related by the Gibbs-Duhem equation. From the definition of γ_i (6.75), we have for a change in x_1 at fixed P,T

$$\frac{d\mu_1}{dx_1} = \frac{RT}{x_1} + RT\frac{d\ln\gamma_1}{dx_1}$$
$$\frac{d\mu_2}{dx_1} = -\frac{RT}{x_2} + RT\frac{d\ln\gamma_2}{dx_1} \qquad (6.87)$$

Hence, from (6.25), for one mole of mixture, the sum of these two equations is zero, or

$$x_1\, d\ln\gamma_1 + x_2\, d\ln\gamma_2 = 0 \qquad \text{(fixed } P, T\text{)} \qquad (6.88)$$

This condition, together with the limiting conditions that $\gamma_i = 1$ at $x_i = 1$, enables (6.84) to be solved for γ_1 and γ_2, from a knowledge only of x_1, P_1° and P_2°, and the equation of state of the vapour. Much mathematical ingenuity has been expended on this problem and there is more than one way of handling the results to obtain the required coefficients. One of the best is that of

Barker[5] which takes proper account of the departures of the vapour from the perfect gas laws and which avoids graphical methods.

We have, therefore, two ways of measuring activity coefficients and hence potentials and fugacities. We can either measure total and partial pressures and use (6.82), or we can measure total pressure only and use (6.84) and (6.88). The former leads to experimental difficulties, the latter introduces a differential equation. However, mathematical problems are usually more tractable than experimental and the latter is generally the more reliable route. We shall see below that even the mathematical problem becomes trivial if we are willing to assume some simple analytic equation for the dependence of γ_i on composition.

Figure 6.4 shows schematically a simple form of apparatus, an *equilibrium*

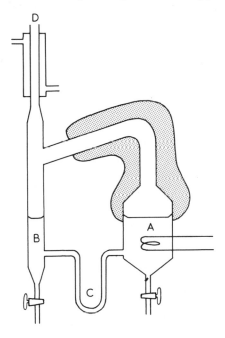

Figure 6.4. An equilibrium still (sketch only)

still,[6] used to measure simultaneously P, x and y. Vapour from a boiling mixture in A is condensed in a small trap B and returns to the boiler through the capillary C. The apparatus is connected, through the condenser, to a manostat at D. The tube leading from the boiler is heated to prevent any partial condensation of the vapour before it reaches B. After the mixture has passed round the still for a few hours, to reach equilibrium, small samples are withdrawn from A and B and analysed, to give x and y respectively. The pressure is measured at D. Measurement of pressure and x only is more simply carried out since the trap B is not needed.

If, however, we can obtain the same information from P alone as we obtain from P and y_i then the partial pressures cannot be mutually independent. There must be some consistency test that they satisfy. This is so, and the test is a useful check on direct measurements of partial pressures. The most obvious form of this test is to calculate the activity coefficients from (6.82) and see that their variation with composition satisfies (6.88), that is, the Gibbs-Duhem equation. However, this equation is, strictly, applicable only to changes at constant pressure and temperature whereas a liquid mixture in equilibrium with its vapour can be studied only at pressures that change from P_1° to P_2° (at fixed T) as x_2 changes from 0 to 1. This complication is generally not serious, but if proper allowance is to be made for it then the consistency test becomes much more complicated. There has been a large amount of work on this problem by chemical engineers, and we refer readers who wish to know more to reviews.[7]

Exercise

A particularly simple form of (6.88) is obtained if we have a perfect gas mixture in equilibrium with liquids of negligible volume, at a low vapour pressure, namely

$$x_1 \, d \ln(Py_1/P_1^\circ) + x_2 \, d \ln(Py_2/P_2^\circ) = 0 \qquad \text{(fixed } T\text{)} \qquad (6.89)$$

where the derivatives are now taken along the saturation line P as a function of y. Derive this equation. This form of (6.88) is commonly called the *Duhem-Margules* equation.

Exercise

The Gibbs-Duhem equation (6.88), and its variant equation (6.89), are restricted to fixed temperatures. In engineering practice we are more usually concerned with fixed pressure and with a temperature that changes with composition from the boiling point of the first to that of the second component. To test for consistency measurements of the boiling point of mixtures we must go back to the most general form of the Gibbs-Duhem equation (6.24). At fixed pressure this becomes, for one mole of mixture,

$$\sum_i x_i \, d\mu_i = -s \, dT \qquad (6.90)$$

where s is the mean molar entropy of the liquid mixture. Show that this equation leads, by arguments similar to that which led to (6.88) to the more general equation for the change of activity coefficients at fixed pressure but variable temperature[8]

$$\sum_i x_i \, d \ln \gamma_i = -\left[h - \sum_i h_i^\circ\right] \frac{dT}{RT^2} \qquad \text{(fixed } P\text{)} \qquad (6.91)$$

Two ratios useful in the discussion of distillation are

(1) the K-value or equilibrium constant for a component, which is simply the ratio of its mole fraction in the vapour to that in the liquid

$$K_i = y_i/x_i \qquad (6.92)$$

(2) the volatility ratio α, where

$$\alpha_{ij} = 1/\alpha_{ji} = K_i/K_j = y_i x_j/y_j x_i \qquad (6.93)$$

The larger the volatility ratio the more readily are two liquids separated by distillation. In a mixture that obeys Raoult's law this ratio is $(P_i^{\circ}/P_j^{\circ})$.

A real mixture generally has values of γ_i that differ from unity at all temperatures and hence at all vapour pressures. Since $\gamma_i \neq 1$, then μ_i, G etc. are not given by the equations for the ideal mixture of Section 6.5. The differences between a real and an ideal mixture are called the *excess functions*, and denoted with a superscript E. Thus we have, by definition

$$G^E = G - G^{ideal} = RT \sum_i n_i \ln \gamma_i$$

$$= RT \sum_i n_i \ln(f_i/x_i f_i^{\circ}) \qquad (6.94)$$

$$TS^E = -T(\partial G^E/\partial T)_{P,x} = H^E - G^E \qquad (6.95)$$

$$V^E = (\partial G^E/\partial P)_{T,x} \qquad (6.96)$$

$$C_P^E = (\partial H^E/\partial T)_{P,x} = -T(\partial^2 G^E/\partial T^2)_{P,x} \qquad (6.97)$$

all of which clearly vanish if γ_i are unity over non-zero ranges of P and T. The measurement of excess functions has thus been reduced to the measurement of γ_i over a range of P, T and x. However, we saw in (6.44) that the heat, volume and heat capacity of mixing are zero in an ideal mixture, and hence the excess function H^E, V^E and C_P^E are equal to the functions of mixing ΔH, ΔV and ΔC_P in a real mixture. In practice it is more accurate to observe ΔH directly by mixing liquids at fixed pressure in a suitable calorimeter than to obtain $H^E = \Delta H$ from the temperature derivative of G^E or γ. The difference in accuracy is even greater than in the formally similar problem of obtaining a heat of evaporation of a single substance in a calorimeter, or from the temperature derivative of the vapour pressure (see Section 3.24).

Similarly, C_P^E is, in practice, better obtained directly from measurements of C_P as a function of composition rather than from (6.97). With the excess volume we have no choice; there is no practicable means of measuring $(\partial G^E/\partial P)$ other than by measuring V^E directly.

Figure 6.5 shows the results of some typical measurement of excess functions and activity coefficients for mixtures of simple, complex and polar molecules. It is seen that for the last the functions are both larger, relative to RT, and have a less simple dependence on composition. In Chapter 9 we take

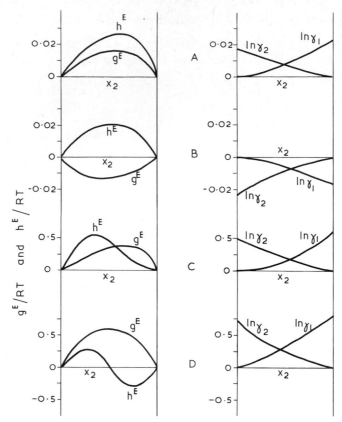

Figure 6.5. Excess Gibbs free energy and enthalpy, and the logarithm of the activity coefficients for four systems

A $\quad$ Ar(1) + O$_2$(2) at 86 K
B $\quad$ n-C$_6$H$_{14}$(1) + n-C$_{12}$H$_{26}$(2) at 25 °C
C $\quad$ C$_6$H$_6$(1) + C$_2$H$_5$OH(2) at 45 °C
D $\quad$ C$_4$H$_8$O$_2$(dioxan)(1) + H$_2$O(2) at 25 °C

Notice the difference of scales between A, B and C, D

up the subject of the prediction of such curves from the properties of the molecules; here we examine only the empirical methods used to represent such behaviour. It can, however, be said shortly that deviations from ideality $(G^E \neq 0, \gamma \neq 1)$ arise from a lack of balance in the intermolecular forces between the different species of molecules. If the molecules are very similar (e.g. benzene + toluene) then the mixture is nearly ideal. If they differ, then the forces are usually stronger between molecules of the same species. Thus in benzene (1) + ethanol (2), Figure 6.5, the mean 1-1 and 2-2 forces are, on average, stronger than the 1-2 forces, and this difference leads to positive values of the excess functions and of ln γ. Each molecule has a lower potential if it is preferentially surrounded by its own kind. If there is a specific complex between molecules of different species, as the hydrogen bonded adduct of $(CH_3)_2CO$—$HCCl_3$, then G^E and $\ln \gamma$ are negative. However, these are crude arguments and cannot be used to explain all the details of curves such as those in Figure 6.5.

Exercise

Calculate the entropy of mixing for the system water + dioxan from the information in Figure 6.5, and estimate the partial quantities h_1 and s_1 for dioxan (1). Comment on the limiting behaviour of these quantities as x_1 tends to zero.

The activity coefficients are well-behaved functions of mole fraction and hence it is natural to express them by polynomials, as was first suggested by Margules. Since $\ln \gamma_1 = 0$ at $x_2 = 0$, we write

$$\ln \gamma_1 = \mu_1^E/RT = \ln(f_1/x_1 f_1^\circ) = a_1 x_2 + b_1 x_2^2 + c_1 x_2^3 + \cdots$$

$$\tag{6.98}$$

$$\ln \gamma_2 = \mu_2^E/RT = \ln(f_2/x_2 f_2^\circ) = a_2 x_1 + b_2 x_1^2 + c_2 x_1^3 + \cdots$$

The coefficients of these series are not independent since the activity coefficients satisfy the Gibbs-Duhem equation. By differentiating the cubic polynomials (6.98) with respect to one of the mole fractions, say x_1, and substituting in (6.88) we see that if the latter equation is to be satisfied at all x_1, then

$$a_2 = a_1 = 0 \qquad b_2 = b_1 + \tfrac{3}{2}c_1 \qquad c_2 = -c_1 \tag{6.99}$$

The first of these relations is the most important, namely that there is no linear term in the polynomials (6.98). Figure 6.5 shows that the graphs of γ_i against x_i have zero slope at $x_i = 1$, which is an experimental verification of this result. We shall see in the next Section that the absence of this linear term leads to some important simplifications in the discussion of dilute solutions.

We can drop the subscripts from b_1 and c_1, and combine the two excess potentials of (6.98) into the excess Gibbs free energy

$$g^E/RT = x_1 x_2 [(b + \tfrac{3}{4}c) + \tfrac{1}{4}c(x_2 - x_1)] \tag{6.100}$$

The particular coefficients obtained in (6.100) are a consequence of stopping the polynomials in (6.98) at the cubic term. Had we taken higher terms in (6.98) we should have had different expressions for b_2, c_2 and, of course, additional equations in (6.99), and so a different result in (6.100). However, the general form of this last equation remains unchanged; a representation of μ_1^E by a polynomial in x_2 results in a representation of $(g^E/x_1 x_2)$ by a polynomial of an order lower by 2 in the difference of mole fractions $(x_2 - x_1)$.

Particularly simple equations are obtained if all coefficients beyond b are put equal to zero in (6.98), namely

$$\mu_1^E/RT = bx_2^2 \qquad \mu_2^E/RT = bx_1^2 \qquad g^E/RT = bx_1 x_2 \tag{6.101}$$

As can be seen from Figure 6.5, g^E is often close to this quadratic form, even for the more complex mixtures.

The polynomial expansion of $\ln \gamma_1$ and $\ln \gamma_2$ (6.98) is the most simple way of representing these functions empirically. It was first proposed by Margules and the equations are usually known by his name. There are, of course, many other functions than a polynomial that could be used. Here we simply mention two, one old, one recent, which have been widely used.

van Laar equation

$$\ln \gamma_1 = A[1 + Ax_1/Bx_2]^{-2} \qquad \ln \gamma_2 = B[1 + Bx_2/Ax_1]^{-2} \qquad (6.102)$$

where A and B are coefficients determined from the experimental results.

Wilson equation

This is most simply given as an equation for g^E

$$g^E/RT = -x_1 \ln(x_1 + \Lambda_{12}x_2) - x_2 \ln(x_2 + \Lambda_{21}x_1) \qquad (6.103)$$

where

$$\Lambda_{21} \neq \Lambda_{12}$$

These empirical parameters are both unity in an ideal mixture.

Exercise

Calculate $\ln \gamma_1$ and $\ln \gamma_2$ that are consistent with (6.103).

These equations and the excess functions are discussed in detail in many books on liquid-vapour equilibria.[9,3]

6.9 The ideal dilute solution

In discussing gas and liquid mixtures we have treated both (or all) the components on an equal footing. A solution is a mixture in which it is convenient to single out one component, usually that present in greatest amount, and call it the *solvent*; the remaining components are the *solutes*. The distinction is one of description, not of physics, but it makes much easier the discussion of liquid systems in which the pure solutes exist as solids or gases at the prevailing pressure and temperature. Here we reserve $i = 1$ for the solvent, and number the solutes $i = 2, 3, 4, \ldots$.

In many solutions the mole fraction of the solvent approaches unity and those of the solutes are 0.05 or less. The activity coefficient of the solvent approaches unity as the concentrations of the solutes fall, and by appeal to (6.98) we can see that this approach is rapid. The linear term is necessarily zero and so the departure of $\ln \gamma_1$ from zero is proportional initially to the square of the mole fraction of the solute, with a constant of proportionality, b, which is of the order of unity, Figure 6.5. Hence if the mole fractions of the solutes are low, we deduce that $\gamma_1 = 1$ with a high degree of accuracy. A solution in which x_i $(i > 1)$ are all sufficiently small for $\gamma_1 = 1$ to be an adequate approximation is called an *ideal dilute solution*. For simplicity we discuss here only the binary solution of solvent and one solute.

The restriction $\gamma_1 = 1$ implies, from the Gibbs-Duhem equation (6.88), that γ_2 is a constant, but does not require this constant to be unity. This less stringent restriction on γ_2 distinguishes the ideal dilute solution from the ideal mixture of Section 6.5. Formally then, a binary ideal dilute solution is one for which

$$\gamma_1 = 1 \qquad \gamma_2 = k$$
$$\mu_1 = \mu_1^\circ + RT \ln x_1 \qquad \mu_2 = \mu_2^\dagger + RT \ln x_2 \qquad (6.104)$$
$$f_1 = x_1 f_1^\circ \qquad f_2 = x_2 f_2^\dagger$$

where k is a constant with respect to changes of composition, but a function of pressure and temperature, and where $\mu_2^\dagger$ is a standard potential (also a function of P and T only) which is related to μ_2° by

$$\mu_2^\dagger = \mu_2^\circ + RT \ln k \qquad (6.105)$$

The difference between the ideal mixture and the ideal dilute solution is shown in Figure 6.6. In both cases the fugacity of both components is a linear function of composition, but in the ideal dilute solution we see that this line passes through the fugacity of the pure liquid component only in the case of the solvent (f_1°). The line for the solute cuts the axis $x_2 = 1$ at a fugacity of $f_2^\dagger$, where the constant k of (6.104) is equal to $(f_2^\dagger/f_2^\circ)$. This definition of an ideal dilute solution is still useful even if the right hand side of Figure 6.6b, that is

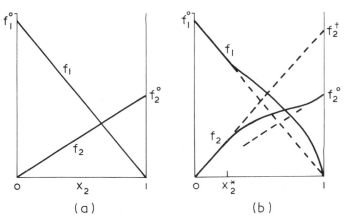

Figure 6.6. Fugacities in (a) an ideal mixture and (b) a non-ideal mixture which is an ideal dilute solution of component 2 in component 1 at mole fractions of x_2 less than x_2^*

$x_2 > x_2^*$, is experimentally inaccessible. For example, if the solvent (1) is water and the solute (2) a solid such as cane-sugar, the curves could be drawn only for values of x_2 less than that of the saturated solution. In such a solution $f_2^\dagger$ and $\mu_2^\dagger$ are still measurable, but f_2° and μ_2° refer to the hypothetical state of supercooled liquid solute, and so are not accessible. It follows from (6.105) that γ_2 of (6.104) is also inaccessible, but we can, if we wish, re-define activity coefficients by basing them on $f_2^\dagger$ rather than f_2° as the state of standard fugacity. That is, by writing for a dilute (but not ideal) solution

$$\mu_1 = \mu_1^\circ + RT \ln x_1\gamma_1 \qquad \mu_2 = \mu_2^\dagger + RT \ln x_2\gamma_2 \qquad (6.106)$$

with the convention that γ_1 and γ_2 are now both unity at $x_1 = 1$. A convention similar to this is adopted below for ionic solutions. We do not do this here since this section treats only the ideal dilute solution, for which all we need to know are f_1 and f_2 as linear functions of composition, as in (6.104).

The equations for the ideal mixture were shown to be equivalent (under certain simplifying approximations) to Raoult's law (6.86), which requires the vapour pressure to be a linear function of all the x_i. The corresponding law for the ideal dilute solution, subject to the same simplifying approximations, is Henry's law, namely the second of the pair of equations,

$$y_1 P = x_1 P_1^\circ \qquad y_2 P = x_2 P_2^\dagger \qquad (6.107)$$

where $P_2^\dagger$ is, under these approximations, equal to the fugacity $f_2^\dagger$ of (6.104). The first of these is the same as in the ideal mixture, and (6.107) may be put into words by saying that if the solvent obeys Raoult's law, the solute obeys Henry's law, i.e. the partial pressure of the solute ($y_2 P$) is proportional to its mole fraction x_2.

The physical cause of the proportionality of f_2 to x_2 in (6.104) is the dilution of the solution. This simple relation is to be expected only when the proportion of solute molecules in a liquid is so low that each is surrounded at all times by solvent molecules alone. Hence each solute molecule is independent of the presence of others of its own kind, and so f_2 is directly proportional to x_2. The solute molecules are, of course, not in the same environments as they are in pure liquid component 2, and so $f_2^\dagger$ is not equal to f_2°.

The simple pairs of equations (6.104) allow us to discuss the two important and related questions of the depression of the freezing-point and the elevation of the boiling-point of a solvent by a solute. Let us consider first a solvent whose freezing-point is T^f (We need not distinguish here between the true triple point and the freezing point at some arbitrary but low pressure). At this temperature pure liquid solvent is in equilibrium with the solid

$$\mu_1^\circ(\text{liquid}, T^f) = \mu_1^\circ(\text{solid}, T^f) \qquad (6.108)$$

If we now add a solute which dissolves in the liquid solvent but not in the solidified solvent (and this is the usual behaviour even for chemically similar substances) then the potential of the solvent is reduced and the equilibrium between liquid and solid is destroyed. If the pressure is fixed, it can be restored only by changing the temperature of the system, and this change is the depression of the freezing-point which we wish to calculate. Let the new equilibrium temperature be T when the mole fraction of solute is x_2.

$$\mu_1^{\circ}(\text{solid}, T) = \mu_1(\text{solution}, T, x) = \mu_1^{\circ}(\text{liquid}, T) + RT \ln x_1 \quad (6.109)$$

where the last potential, $\mu_1^{\circ}(\text{liquid}, T)$ is that of the pure supercooled liquid, since, as we shall show, T is less than T^f. By subtraction of (6.109) from (6.108)

$$RT \ln x_1 = [\mu_1^{\circ}(\text{liquid}, T^f) - \mu_1^{\circ}(\text{liquid}, T)]$$
$$- [\mu_1^{\circ}(\text{solid}, T^f) - \mu_1^{\circ}(\text{solid}, T)] \quad (6.110)$$

Since we have a dilute solution $(T^f - T)$ is small and we can write for both liquid and solid

$$\mu_1^{\circ}(T^f) - \mu_1^{\circ}(T) = -\int_T^{T^f} s_1^{\circ} \, dT \approx -s_1^{\circ}(T^f)[T^f - T] \quad (6.111)$$

Hence

$$RT \ln x_1 = -(T^f - T)[s_1^{\circ}(\text{liquid}) - s_1^{\circ}(\text{solid})]$$
$$= -(T^f - T)[h_1^{\circ}(\text{liquid}) - h_1^{\circ}(\text{solid})]/T^f \quad (6.112)$$

where the heats and entropies are those at T^f. The last step is a consequence of (6.108). We have, therefore, an expression for the depression of the freezing-point $(T^f - T)$ in a dilute solution in which the mole fraction of the solvent x_1 is close to unity;

$$\ln x_1 = -(T^f - T) \, \Delta_f h / RT^2 \quad (6.113)$$

where $\Delta_f h$ is the molar latent heat of fusion of the solvent. Since $x_1 < 1$, then $T < T^f$.

There are several points to be noticed about the argument above. First, it is strictly valid only when T approaches T^f, and so (6.113), which is a useful approximation in practice, has an equivalent and exact differential form

$$\left(\frac{\partial \ln x_1}{\partial T}\right)_{P, T = T^f} = -\frac{\Delta_f h}{R(T^f)^2} \quad (6.114)$$

Secondly, the whole argument rests on the conditions of equilibrium of the solvent which is the only substance present in both phases; no mention is made of the solute. Hence (6.113) and (6.114) are independent of the nature and even of the number of solutes. Since $x_1 \approx 1$, we can expand the logarithm in powers of the sum of the mole fractions of the solutes and obtain

$$\sum_{i=2}^{c} x_i = (T^f - T) \, \Delta_f h / RT^2 \quad (6.115)$$

Exercise

Repeat the arguments above for one or more non-volatile solutes added to a liquid at its boiling-point T^b at pressure P, and show that the equation for the elevation of the boiling-point at this fixed pressure is

$$\sum_{i=2}^{c} x_i = -(T^b - T)\,\Delta_e h/RT^2 \tag{6.116}$$

where $\Delta_e h$ is the molar latent heat of evaporation of the solvent at T^b.

The third point to notice about the argument is that the simplicity of both (6.115) and (6.116) is a consequence not only of the assumption of the laws of the ideal dilute solution, but also of the fact that the solutes are confined to the liquid phase, and are not present in either solid or gas, as the case may be. Results of this kind which depend on the concentration of the solutes in the liquid but not on their nature are often known as the *colligative properties*. Such properties give us an easy way of measuring the relative molar masses (or 'molecular weights') of the solutes, since we can measure the mass fraction, and calculate the mole fraction from the right-hand sides of (6.115) and (6.116).

A third property of this kind is the osmotic pressure of a dilute solution, but this is of less practical importance than the depression of the freezing point or the elevation of the boiling-point and information on it may be sought elsewhere.[10]

6.10 Solubility of a solid in a liquid

The solubility of a solid (2) in a solvent (1) is expressed conveniently by x_2^{sat} as a function of temperature (We neglect any dependence on the pressure, which we again assume to be low and constant).

Let us first suppose that we have an ideal mixture, as distinct from the ideal dilute solution of the last section, but let us retain the names of solvent and solute, respectively, for the component present in the liquid only, and for that present both in the liquid and as a pure solid. In an ideal mixture the equations used in the last section for solvent only (e.g. 6.109) now apply to both components. Thus, taking (6.114), which represents the behaviour of a system containing a solid phase of pure 1 in equilibrium with a homogeneous liquid phase containing both 1 and 2, renaming species 1 as the solute and 2 as the solvent results in a system which is more appropriately described as the determination of the solubility of a solid in a solvent rather than the depression of a freezing point. Hence by this exchange of the subscripts 1 and 2 we have the exact differential result for the *ideal solubility of a solid in a liquid*.

$$\left(\frac{\partial \ln x_2^{\text{sat}}}{\partial T}\right)_{P,T=T^f} = -\frac{\Delta_f h}{R(T^f)^2} \tag{6.117}$$

where T^f and $\Delta_f h$ are now the temperature and molar latent heat of fusion of the solute. Since we have an ideal mixture the liquid solute is miscible with solvent in all proportions, so

$$x_2^{\text{sat}} = 1 \quad \text{at} \quad T = T^f \tag{6.118}$$

and we can use this result in conjunction with the integrated form of (6.117) to give the equation that corresponds to (6.113)

$$\ln x_2^{\text{sat}} \simeq -(T^f - T) \, \Delta_f h / RT^2$$
$$\simeq [(T^f)^{-1} - (T)^{-1}] \Delta_f h / R \tag{6.119}$$

However, in writing the integrated form of (6.117) in this way we have treated $\Delta_f h$ as a constant, independent of temperature, and have ignored any distinction between T and T^f except in the difference $(T^f - T)$. If we try to improve (6.119) by removing these restrictions we come up against a fundamental difficulty. The latent heat of fusion $\Delta_f h$ is defined *only* at $T = T^f$. Above this temperature the solid does not exist; below this temperature the liquid can sometimes have a transient existence in a supercooled state, but such a state may not be sufficiently stable to reversible changes of P and T for it to have measurable thermodynamic properties. Hence a more accurate integration of (6.117) cannot properly be made. There have been attempts at it by calculating the properties of the supercooled liquid by extrapolation from those at and above T^f, but they are scarcely worth while since few real liquid mixtures are sufficiently ideal for the attempted increase in precision to be justified.* However, in so far as the integration can be done more accurately, the second form of (6.119) is strongly preferred to the first.

Exercise

Naphthalene melts at 80.2 °C with a latent heat of fusion of 18.8 kJ mol^{-1}. Calculate its ideal solubility at 20 °C from the second of the two equations (6.119) and compare the result with the solubilities measured by Scatchard,[11] namely

Solvent	x_2^{sat}	Solvent	x_2^{sat}
chlorobenzene	0.256	hexane	0.090
benzene	0.241	acetone	0.183
toluene	0.224	methanol	0.018

* The same point, but applied to changes of P, not T, arises in the discussion of the equilibrium of a liquid mixture with its vapour in Section 6.8. At the pressure P at which we study a binary liquid mixture we have $P_1^\circ < P < P_2^\circ$, where 1 is the less volatile component. Hence pure liquid 2 does not exist at (P, T) and the potential $\mu_2^\circ(P)$ is inaccessible. In equating (6.79) and (6.80) for the second component we put $P^+ = P_2^\circ$, and so tacitly assumed the existence of this potential. The problem is not serious here since the potentials of liquids change little with pressure and the extrapolation into a metastable region can be made with confidence if the pressures P, P_1° and P_2° are low, say less than 3 bar.

It is seen that the solubility approaches the ideal value 0.269 in solvents of similar chemical constitution, but falls a long way below it in those of different type or polarity; these results are typical of the solubility of non-electrolytes. Hildebrand has devoted a life-time's work to the problem of solubility and has shown that if we exclude polar systems or systems with some specific interactions between the molecules, then it is found that the departure of x_2^{sat} from its ideal values in (6.119) is given quite well by the equation

$$\ln[x_2^{sat}/(x_2^{sat})^{ideal}] = -\varphi_1^2(v_2^0)^2(\delta_2 - \delta_1)^2/RT \qquad (6.120)$$

where φ_1 is the so-called volume fraction of component 1, defined by

$$\varphi_1 = x_1 v_1^0/(x_1 v_1^0 + x_2 v_2^0) \qquad (6.121)$$

where v_1^0 and v_2^0 are the molar volumes of the pure liquid components (extrapolated from above T^f in the latter case), and δ_i is Hildebrand's solubility parameter, defined by

$$\delta_i^2 = [(\Delta_e h)_i - RT]/v_i^0 \qquad (6.122)$$

From (6.120) we obtain the estimated solubilities of 0.241 in benzene, 0.228 in toluene, and 0.067 in hexane. The reasons for the choice of this equation are discussed in detail by Hildebrand and his colleagues in two books.[12]

6.11 Solubility of gases in liquids

The discussion in Section 6.8 of a binary liquid mixture in equilibrium with its mixed vapour encompasses the problem of the solubility of a gas (or vapour) in a liquid if we choose to call one of the components the solvent and one the solute, and if the standard states there used for the pure liquid components are both experimentally accessible. If, however, we wish to discuss the solubility of, say, oxygen in water, then the treatment given there is inappropriate since pure liquid oxygen does not exist at any temperature at which we have liquid water. This section deals, therefore, with the case where the asymmetry between the components is more than just a matter of arbitrarily calling the components solvent and solute.

Let us consider the equilibrium between a liquid solvent (1) of low volatility and a gas (2) which may be at a temperature above or below that of its gas-liquid critical point, but which, if below, is at a pressure low compared with its vapour pressure. Under these conditions the gas is sparingly soluble in the liquid, and the solution is usefully described in terms of the laws of the ideal dilute solution. In particular, from (6.104) we have that the mole fraction of gas in the liquid phase is proportional to its fugacity in the gas phase. If the pressure is moderate this fugacity will be close to the partial pressure of the gas, or, if we can neglect the volatility of the solvent, to the total pressure of the system. That is, the solubility of the gas is proportional to the pressure

$$x_2^{sat} = P/P^\dagger \qquad (6.123)$$

where $(1/P^{\dagger})$ is the constant of proportionality, and $P^{\dagger}$ is a pressure large compared with P. This equation is Henry's law, and was obtained previously (6.107) without imposing the restriction of negligible volatility on the solvent.

If this proportionality extended all the way to pure liquid solute then $P^{\dagger}$ would be P_2°; that is, Henry's law would become Raoult's law. In practice this is unrealisable, but we use the result to define the *ideal solubility of a gas in a liquid* by

$$(x_2^{\text{sat}})^{\text{ideal}} = P/P_2^{\circ} \tag{6.124}$$

where P_2° is the vapour pressure of pure liquid 2 at the same temperature. If this temperature is above the critical point then P_2° is the pressure obtained by an extrapolation of the vapour pressure curve ($\ln P$ against $1/T$) to the required temperature.

The concept of an ideal solution thus becomes less precise and, it must be admitted, less useful, as we move from the purely liquid mixtures of Section 6.8 to the solutions of solids and gases in 6.10 and 6.11. Solubilities calculated from (6.124) may be little more than order-of-magnitude estimates, particularly if the temperature is above the critical point. Hence little is to be gained by attempting to improve the estimate by substituting a fugacity f_2° for the pressure P_2°. More is to be gained by attempting to estimate the departure of the real from the ideal solubility, and here again the procedure most commonly used is the calculation of a correction in terms of Hildebrand's equation (6.120). However, the solubility parameter δ_2 is itself not defined by (6.122) if the temperature is above the critical, and is generally taken as an adjustable parameter with which to correlate the solubility of one gas in a range of solvents.

Methane at 25 °C is well above its critical point of 191 K; an extrapolation of the vapour pressure curve using equation (3.225) produces $P_2^{\circ}/\text{atm} = 289$, hence the ideal solubility at 1 atm pressure is the reciprocal of this number, or $x_2^{\text{sat}} = 0.0035$. Observed solubilities run from 0.0083 in the fluoro-carbon C_7F_{16}, to figures close to ideal in hydrocarbons, 0.0033 in cyclohexane and 0.0021 in benzene, down to 0.0007 in methanol and only 0.00002 in water.

Again the fullest discussion of this subject and many of the best measurements are to be found in Hildebrand's books, cited in the previous section. A review by Battino and Clever[13] is useful for its emphasis on experimental methods, definition of the alternatives to x_2^{sat} as a method of representing the solubility (Bunsen coefficient, Ostwald coefficient, etc.) and for its extensive references.

6.12 Polymer solutions

Linear polymers in an amorphous state are often freely soluble in solvents of similar chemical constitution. However, such solutions are not readily described in terms of the concepts so far introduced in this chapter. The difficulty is primarily one of defining mole fraction. A polymer may be a single substance to the chemist but it is composed of molecules of different chain lengths, and hence of different molecular mass. The distribution of lengths may cover several decades and is rarely known with precision. It is always possible to define a mean molecular mass (in fact several, according to the way the averaging is performed) but the concept of mole fraction remains unsatisfactory.

Let us assume, however, that we have a number-average molecular mass and use it to define the number of moles n_2 in a given amount of polymer. If we dissolve this amount in n_1 moles of solvent we find that the entropy of mixing is far from that of an ideal mixture, even if the heat of mixing is negligible. The behaviour is not found in mixtures of molecules of comparable sizes; as can be seen from Figure 6.5, Ts^E is usually of the same magnitude as h^E. The entropy and free energy of mixing of a polymer and solvent are more closely represented by an expression due to Flory and Huggins, and generally known by their names

$$\frac{\Delta G}{RT} = -\frac{\Delta S}{R} = n_1 \ln \varphi_1 + n_2 \ln \varphi_2 \qquad (6.125)$$

where φ_1 and φ_2 are the volume fractions introduced in equation (6.121). Clearly, $\varphi_1 = x_1$ and $\varphi_2 = x_2$ for a solution in which solvent and solute have the same molar volume, $v_1^\circ = v_2^\circ$, and so (6.125) reduces to the usual ideal free energy and entropy of mixing for such a mixture. For a polymer solution the ratio v_2°/v_1°, denoted here by r, is generally between 10^2 and 10^4. The volume fractions defined by (6.121) are expressed in terms of x_i and v_i°, but for work on polymer solutions are more appropriately defined in terms of the actual volume V_i of the samples mixed to form the solution

$$\varphi_1 = \frac{V_1}{V_1 + V_2} = \frac{n_1}{n_1 + r n_2} \qquad (6.126)$$

Exercise

Show that the potential of the solvent consistent with (6.125) is

$$\mu_1 = \mu_1^\circ + RT \ln \varphi_1 + RT\varphi_2(1 - r^{-1}) \qquad (6.127)$$

and hence, if r^{-1} is negligibly small,

$$\ln \gamma_1 = \ln \varphi_1 + \varphi_2 \qquad (6.128)$$

since $x_1 \simeq 1$ in all solutions if r^{-1} is zero.

The thermodynamic properties of a polymer solution are measured by observing γ_1. This can be done, for example, by measuring the vapour pressure as a function of φ_2. The calculation of γ_2 is assisted by the fact that the polymer is quite involatile, hence the total pressure is also the partial pressure of the solvent, but is hindered by the fact that $P_1^\circ - P$ is very small because $x_1 \simeq 1$. This is one of the few situations where the measurement of osmotic pressure is still worthwhile since it is relatively easy to obtain membranes permeable to solvent but not to the polymer solute.

The Flory-Huggins equation (6.125) serves as the standard of normal behaviour for polymer solutions. Real polymer solutions depart significantly from this standard, and have non-zero heats of solution. The best simple representation is the more complete form of the Flory-Huggins equation

$$\frac{\Delta G}{RT} = n_1 \ln \varphi_1 + n_2 \ln \varphi_2 + \varphi_1\varphi_2(n_1 + r\,n_2)\chi \qquad (6.129)$$

where χ, the Flory parameter, accounts for the departure of ΔG from that of (6.125). If χ is proportional to $1/T$, but independent of composition, we see, by differentiation with respect to T, that ΔS is unchanged and remains as given by (6.125) and that, therefore, the last term in (6.129) is simply $\Delta H/RT$. In practice (χT) changes slowly with both variables;[14] the change with temperature implying that the entropy of solution is not given exactly by (6.125).

6.13 Solutions of electrolytes

Electrolytes present several unusual features as solutes; first, the conventional chemical formula does not represent adequately the actual entities present in the solution; secondly, if the electrolyte is a salt then its liquid state is not realisable at the prevailing pressure and temperature, and so a more accessible standard state must be chosen; thirdly, the departures from ideality (however defined) are unusually large; and fourthly, it is conventional to use a concentration scale of *molality*, rather than that of mole fraction which has been used so far in this chapter. We start with the last of these points.

The molality of a solute is proportional to the ratio of the amount of solute to that of solvent and defined by

$$m_i = 1000 \, n_i/\mathcal{M}_1 n_1 \qquad (i > 1) \qquad (6.130)$$

where $\mathcal{M}_1$ is the relative molar mass of the solvent. The molality is therefore a pure number and numerically equal to the amount of solute in moles per kg of solvent. (Some authors define it as $n_i/M_1 n_1$ where M_1 is the mass in kg of one mole of solute. The two definitions lead to the same number, but the latter makes molality a quantity whose units are $\mathrm{mol\,kg^{-1}}$, which is inconvenient in later equations.) Molality is defined independently for each solute; the molality of a solution of a salt in water is not changed if we dissolve a second salt in the same solution. It is this property of independence which makes it more convenient than mole fraction for the discussion of electrolyte solutions.

Since we wish to describe salt solutions in terms of the molalities of their component ions, we must supplement this definition with a condition of electrical neutrality. Let z_+ or z_- denote the charge on an ion, in units of the electronic charge so that for, say, $CaCl_2$ we have

$$Ca^{2+} \quad z_+ = 2 \qquad Cl^- \quad z_- = -1 \tag{6.131}$$

The condition of electrical neutrality requires that

$$\sum z_i m_i = 0 \tag{6.132}$$

where the sum is taken over all ions. The number of ions in a formula unit is called the stoichiometric number of the ion, and denoted by ν_+ or ν_-; thus for $CaCl_2$

$$\nu_+ = 1 \qquad \nu_- = 2 \tag{6.133}$$

These numbers are positive, but the numbers z have the signs appropriate to the charge.

At extremely high dilution a salt behaves as an ideally dilute solute, in the sense of Section 6.8, if we account correctly for the number of ions into which the conventional molecule is divided. It is, however, unusually difficult to reach the necessary degree of dilution. We saw in Section 6.8 that the physical origin of the laws of dilute solution is the independent action of the solute molecules. Ions exert powerful and long-ranged Coulomb forces on each other, and it is, in practice, almost impossible to achieve sufficiently low concentrations for this independence to be reached. Hence we proceed at once to equations which incorporate activity coefficients.

Let G be the Gibbs free energy of a system composed of n_1 moles of solvent, and a fully ionized solute, of stoichiometric numbers ν_+ and ν_-, and of molality of m_+ and m_- in each ion. We can write formally for a change at constant P,T

$$dG = \mu_+ \, dm_+ + \mu_- \, dm_- \tag{6.134}$$

where

$$\mu_+ = (\partial G/\partial m_+)_{P,T,n_1,m_-} \tag{6.135}$$

and similarly for μ_-. However, these chemical potentials are not measurable since we cannot change m_+ at constant m_-; to do so would violate the condition of neutrality, which can be expressed here as

$$m = m_+/\nu_+ = m_-/\nu_- \tag{6.136}$$

where m is the molality of the solute and the only independent variable. Nevertheless, it is convenient at this stage to retain (6.134) and (6.135) as identities since we shall see that linear combinations of these potentials are measurable. We define activity coefficients for each ion from these potentials by writing

$$\mu_+ = \mu_+^{\square} + RT \ln m_+ \gamma_+$$
$$\mu_- = \mu_-^{\square} + RT \ln m_- \gamma_- \tag{6.137}$$

with the convention that γ_+ and γ_- both tend to unity as m and hence m_+ and

m_- tend to zero, but again with the proviso that since μ_+ and μ_- are not accessible to experiment, neither are $\mu_+^\square$, $\mu_-^\square$, γ_+ and γ_-. The potentials $\mu^\square$ are those of a (hypothetical) solution of unit molality in which γ is unity. They have little physical significance.

By substitution of (6.136) into (6.134), we obtain, at constant P and T

$$dG = (\nu_+\mu_+ + \nu_-\mu_-)\,dm \qquad (6.138)$$

and so from (6.137)

$$\mu = \nu_+\mu_+ + \nu_-\mu_-$$
$$= [\nu_+\mu_+^\square + \nu_-\mu_-^\square] + \nu_\pm RT \ln(m_\pm\gamma_\pm) \qquad (6.139)$$

where

$$\nu_\pm = \nu_+ + \nu_- \qquad (6.140)$$

and where the means $m_\pm$ and $\gamma_\pm$ are defined by

$$m_\pm = (m_+^{\nu_+}m_-^{\nu_-})^{1/\nu_\pm} = m(\nu_+^{\nu_+}\nu_-^{\nu_-}) \qquad (6.141)$$
$$\gamma_\pm = (\gamma_+^{\nu_+}\gamma_-^{\nu_-})^{1/\nu_\pm} \qquad (6.142)$$

The molality $m_\pm$ can be calculated from m (it is equal to it for a uni-univalent electrolyte) and hence, since $(\partial G/\partial m)_{P,T} = \mu$ is experimentally accessible, we see that the mean activity coefficient $\gamma_\pm$ and the potential of the standard state $[\nu_+\mu_+^\square + \nu_-\mu_-^\square]$ are also both accessible.

Although the single-ion activity coefficients and potentials cannot be measured, they are not entirely mathematical fictions. If we have a solution of four ions, say Na^+, K^+, Cl^- and Br^-, then we can define four single-ion activity coefficients; but (6.142) allows us to define four mean coefficients of the form $\gamma_{Na^+Cl^-}$ etc., and clearly requires that these satisfy the equation

$$\gamma_{Na^+Cl^-}/\gamma_{K^+Cl^-} = \gamma_{Na^+Br^-}/\gamma_{K^+Br^-} \qquad (6.143)$$

Activity coefficients in electrolyte solutions can be measured in two ways. First, we can measure the activity of the solvent, by measuring its vapour pressure, or by studying the depression of the freezing point (elevation of the boiling point is rarely studied). These methods are, in principle, the same as those described above, and are not further described here. The second method is the measurement of the activity coefficient of the solute and involves chemical equilibria in the solutions (or electro-chemical equilibria if one of the participants in the reaction is an electron). These methods are deferred to Chapter 8. In each case the activity of the component not studied directly is obtained from that measured by solving the Gibbs-Duhem equation. Neither method allows us to study single-ion activity coefficients.

The activity coefficients are defined so that they approach unity at infinite dilution. They reach this limit very slowly, as may be seen from Figure 6.7. It was shown theoretically by Debye and Hückel that the limiting behaviour of $\ln \gamma_\pm$ is proportional to $\sqrt{m}$, a result which is confirmed experimentally. Let us

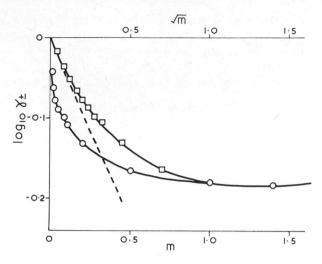

Figure 6.7. The logarithm of the mean activity coefficient of NaCl in water at 25 °C as a function of molality m (circles) and of $\sqrt{m}$ (squares); from Appendices 8.9 and 8.10 of R. A. Robinson and R. H. Stokes, *Electrolyte Solutions*, 2nd. edn; Butterworth, London, 1959. The dashed line is the Dedye-Hückel limiting slope

define the *ionic strength* of a solution, I, by

$$I = \tfrac{1}{2} \sum_i z_i^2 m_i \qquad (6.144)$$

Where m_i is the molality of ion i, and the summation is over all ions present. The factor of $\tfrac{1}{2}$ is inserted so that $I = m_{\pm} = m$ for a uni-univalent electrolyte. Debye and Hückel showed that the limiting behaviour at high dilution can be written

$$\log_{10} \gamma_{\pm} = a(z_+ z_-) I^{1/2} \qquad (6.145)$$

where the product $(z_+ z_-)$, which is negative, is for the ions of the electrolyte under consideration, but the ionic strength is defined, by (6.144), by summation over all ions. The constant a depends solely on the density, dielectric constant and other properties of the solvent; for water at 25 °C it is 0.509.

The results in Figure 6.7 confirm the correctness of (6.145) as a limiting law, but its practical utility is small since it breaks down here at $m \approx 0.05$. In multivalent electrolytes the ionic strength at a given molality is much greater (cf. 6.144), the activity coefficients much lower and the utility of the Debye-Hückel result correspondingly less; thus $\gamma_{\pm} = 0.0175$ for $Al_2(SO_4)_3$ at $m = 1$. It is commonly found that $\gamma_{\pm}$ passes through a minimum with increasing concentration. In NaCl this minimum is at $m = 1.3$, and $\gamma_{\pm}$ has reached unity again at $m = 6$. At higher concentrations it exceeds unity.[15]

6.14 Surfaces of liquids and liquid mixtures

The free energy and hence all the other thermodynamic properties of a two-phase system are found to change not only with such familiar variables as volume, temperature and mole fraction, but, to a small degree also with the area of contact between the two phases. The most familiar manifestation of this effect is the *surface tension* γ, between a liquid and its vapour, or between two immiscible liquids. (This second use of the symbol γ in this chapter may seem to invite confusion with activity coefficients. However, it is the symbol commonly used for surface tension and so it is retained here. Note that it has no subscripts attached to it.) The measurement of this property is described in text books of physics or surface chemistry.[16] Its thermodynamic status is described by saying that the change in G, as defined below, on changing the surface area by $d\mathcal{A}$ at constant pressure and temperature is

$$dG = \gamma \, d\mathcal{A} \qquad (6.146)$$

The dimensions of γ are thus energy/area, or force/length; it is the two-dimensional analogue of pressure. Typical values for a liquid-vapour system run from $9.4 \, \text{dyn cm}^{-1}$ for nitrogen at 75 K, to $28.9 \, \text{dyn cm}^{-1}$ for benzene at 20 °C, to $72.7 \, \text{dyn cm}^{-1}$ for water at 20 °C ($1 \, \text{dyn cm}^{-1} = 10^{-3} \, \text{N m}^{-1}$).

The density of a liquid is many times that of the vapour, except very close to the critical point, but the fall from one density to another is not sharp on a molecular scale. This is shown schematically in Figure 6.8 where the thickness over which there is a detectable departure from the bulk densities on either side is believed to be about 10^{-9} m, or 2–3 molecular diameters. Probably the same is true for the boundary layer between two immiscible liquids.

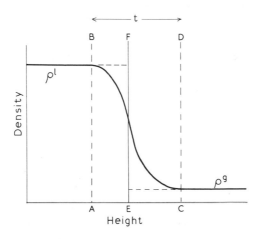

Figure 6.8. The curve shows schematically the change of density with height, in the surface between liquid and gas. The vertical lines AB and CD divide the system into three phases; liquid, surface and gas. The line EF is a Gibbs surface (see text)

Let us restrict our attention to a plane surface between a liquid of C components and its vapour. We may divide the system into three phases, liquid, surface and vapour, Figure 6.8. The position of the dividing planes AB and CD is immaterial as long as they exclude from the liquid and vapour phases any region in which the properties differ from those of the bulk phase. However, for simplicity we place them as close as is possible whilst satisfying this criterion. Let their separation be t, and let the area of the surface be $\mathscr{A}$, so that the volume of the surface phase V^σ is

$$V^\sigma = t\mathscr{A} \tag{6.147}$$

The three phases are in equilibrium and so pressure, temperature and all chemical potentials are the same in each. The work done in reversibly increasing the area of the surface phase by $d\mathscr{A}$ and its volume by dV^σ is

$$-P\,dV^\sigma + \gamma\,d\mathscr{A} \tag{6.148}$$

This takes the place of the familiar expressions $-P\,dV^l$ and $-P\,dV^g$ for the liquid and gas phases. Hence we can write equations for dA etc. that follow the same form as those for the bulk phases. Here we write the equations we need for the liquid phase and for the surface; those for the gas are the same as those for the liquid with the trivial change of superscript.

$$dA^l = -S^l\,dT - P\,dV^l + \sum_i \mu_i\,dn_i^l$$

$$dA^\sigma = -S^\sigma\,dT - P\,dV^\sigma + \gamma\,d\mathscr{A} + \sum_i \mu_i\,dn_i^\sigma \tag{6.149}$$

If we keep the pressure, temperature and all compositions constant, we can integrate these equations since A is first order in the extensive variables V, $\mathscr{A}$ and n_i. The procedure is analogous to the one which we used in deriving (6.3) in Section 6.2. We obtain

$$A^l = \sum_i n_i^l \mu_i - PV^l$$

$$A^\sigma = \sum_i n_i^\sigma \mu_i - PV^\sigma + \gamma\mathscr{A} \tag{6.150}$$

We define the corresponding Gibbs free energies as

$$G^l = A^l + PV^l$$

and

$$G^\sigma = A^\sigma + PV^\sigma \tag{6.151}$$

The one for the bulk phase is the one we are already familiar with, the one for the surface phase is new but intuitively appropriate. This gives us

$$G^l = \sum_i n_i^l \mu_i$$

$$G^\sigma = \sum_i n_i^\sigma \mu_i + \gamma\mathscr{A} \tag{6.152}$$

By differentiation of (6.151) and the use of (6.149)

$$dG^l = -S^l \, dT + V^l \, dP + \sum_i \mu_i \, dn_i^l$$

$$dG^\sigma = -S^\sigma \, dT + V^\sigma \, dP + \gamma \, d\mathscr{A} + \sum_i \mu_i \, dn_i^\sigma \qquad (6.153)$$

The Gibbs-Duhem equations for the bulk and surface phases are obtained by differentiation of (6.152) and subtraction from (6.153), as in Section 6.2,

$$S^l \, dT - V^l \, dP + \sum_i n_i^l \, d\mu_i = 0$$

$$S^\sigma \, dT - V^\sigma \, dP + \mathscr{A} \, d\gamma + \sum_i n_i^\sigma \, d\mu_i = 0 \qquad (6.154)$$

The last result is more usually written, per unit area, by dividing by $\mathscr{A}$

$$(S^\sigma/\mathscr{A}) \, dT - t \, dP + d\gamma + \sum_i \Gamma_i \, d\mu_i = 0 \qquad (6.155)$$

where Γ_i is the ratio $(n_i^\sigma/\mathscr{A})$ or the amount of i per unit area in the surface phase. It is usually called the *adsorption* of component i.

This treatment of a surface as a phase of small but non-zero thickness was due originally to van der Waals and Bakker. Earlier Gibbs had considered the surface to have zero thickness and obtained results which are formally simpler than those above but in which the meanings of n^σ, S^σ, etc. are less obvious. His results can be obtained by supposing that the planes AB and CD of Figure 6.8 are made to coincide at some point within the zone of changing density, say EF. We now define n^σ etc. by the difference between the total amount and that which would be present if liquid and gas continued unchanged to EF; that is

$$V^\sigma = V - V^l - V^g = 0$$

$$n^\sigma = n - n^l - n^g$$

$$A^\sigma = A - A^l - A^g$$

$$S^\sigma = S - S^l - S^g \qquad (6.156)$$

Notice that although V^σ becomes zero when the planes coincide, the quantities n^σ, S^σ, defined by (6.156) are not necessarily zero, and may even be negative. This loss of realism is the price we pay for introducing the formal simplification $V^\sigma = 0$. The equations above now become

$$dA^\sigma = -S^\sigma \, dT + \gamma \, d\mathscr{A} + \sum_i \mu_i \, dn_i^\sigma$$

$$A^\sigma = \sum_i n_i^\sigma \mu_i + \gamma \mathscr{A}$$

$$G^\sigma = A^\sigma = \sum_i n_i^\sigma \mu_i + \gamma \mathscr{A}$$

$$(S^\sigma/\mathscr{A}) \, dT + d\gamma + \sum_i \Gamma_i \, d\mu_i = 0 \qquad (6.157)$$

This last equation is usually called *Gibbs's adsorption equation* and is a particular case of a Gibbs-Duhem equation, see (6.154) and (6.155). It is important to notice that the essentially surface contribution to A and G, namely the term $\gamma\mathscr{A}$, is retained unchanged, and so is independent of the position of EF, which is usually called the Gibbs surface. The values of n^{σ} etc. clearly depend on its position and so may be chosen to satisfy any suitable convention. For a system of one component it is usual to choose n^{σ} to be zero, and so obtain

$$G^{\sigma}/\mathscr{A} = \gamma \qquad A^{\sigma}/\mathscr{A} = \gamma \qquad S^{\sigma}/\mathscr{A} = -(d\gamma/dT)$$

$$\Gamma = 0 \qquad U^{\sigma}/\mathscr{A} = \gamma - T(d\gamma/dT) \tag{6.158}$$

However, these equations have little experimental content; they merely define the surface functions consistent with the two conventions $V^{\sigma} = 0$, $n^{\sigma} = 0$. Surface tension falls with increase in temperature, and necessarily vanishes at the critical point. Hence $U^{\sigma} > A^{\sigma}$. The last equation of (6.158) is formally analogous with the Clapeyron-Clausius equation for the change of vapour pressure with temperature.

In a mixture we cannot choose the position of the Gibbs surface so that all n_i^{σ} are zero, and hence one or more of the quantities must be non-zero. They may be positive or negative and are sometimes called the *surface excess* when we are using the Gibbs convention of $V^{\sigma} = 0$. They are measures of the differences between the amount of component i actually present, and the amount we should expect to be present if both bulk phases continued without change of composition up to the Gibbs surface.

Consider a binary mixture of components 1 and 2, in which we make an arbitrary change of temperature and composition of the liquid phase. From the last equation of (6.157)

$$d\gamma = -(S^{\sigma}/\mathscr{A})\, dT - \Gamma_1\, d\mu_1 - \Gamma_2\, d\mu_2 \tag{6.159}$$

where in the liquid phase

$$d\mu_1 = (\partial\mu_1/\partial T)_{x_2^l}\, dT + (\partial\mu_1/\partial x_2^l)_T\, dx_2^l$$

$$= -s_1^l\, dT + (\partial\mu_1/\partial x_2^l)_T\, dx_2^l$$

and

$$d\mu_2 = -s_2^l\, dT + (\partial\mu_2/\partial x_2^l)_T\, dx_2^l \tag{6.160}$$

where we have omitted the terms $v_1^l\, dP$ and $v_2^l\, dP$ since these are usually negligible. We eliminate $d\mu_1$ and $d\mu_2$ from (6.159) to obtain

$$d\gamma = -[(S^{\sigma}/\mathscr{A}) - s_1^l\Gamma_1 - s_2^l\Gamma_2]\, dT$$

$$-[\Gamma_1(\partial\mu_1/\partial x_2^l)_T + \Gamma_2(\partial\mu_2/\partial x_2^l)_T]\, dx_2^l \tag{6.161}$$

We can eliminate one of the derivatives of the potentials by using the Gibbs-Duhem equation, thus obtaining

$$d\gamma = -[(S^\sigma/\mathscr{A}) - s_1^l\Gamma_1 - s_2^l\Gamma_2]\,dT$$

$$+[x_1^l\Gamma_2 - x_2^l\Gamma_1]\frac{1}{x_1^l}\left(\frac{\partial\mu_2}{\partial x_1^l}\right)_T dx_2^l \qquad (6.162)$$

Hence we see that the terms in square brackets yield expressions for $(\partial\gamma/\partial T)_x$ and $(\partial\gamma/\partial x)_T$ in a binary mixture of negligible liquid volume (i.e. $Pv^l \ll RT$). These quantities are independent of the position of the Gibbs surface, and so we have the result that the quantity

$$\Gamma = x_1\Gamma_2 - x_2\Gamma_1 \qquad (6.163)$$

is the only quantity open to measurement by studying the change of γ with composition. If we wish to ascribe numerical values to Γ_1 and Γ_2 themselves, then we must introduce some non-thermodynamic convention. It is, for example, sometimes convenient to assume $\Gamma_1 = 0$, in which case we can measure Γ_2, and it is now sometimes denoted $\Gamma_2^{(1)}$, where the superscript is a reminder of the convention used. This convention is convenient if we are dealing with a solute which is sparingly soluble in the bulk solvent, but readily concentrates as a so-called *insoluble film* at the liquid-vapour interface. The higher alcohols and fatty acids form such films on water. It is then often legitimate to replace $(\partial\mu_2/\partial x_1^l)_T$ by its value in the ideal dilute solution, *viz.* $(-RT/x_2^l)$.

Alternatively, we can introduce molecular considerations, such as the assumption made by Guggenheim and Adam,[17] that a molecule of each component occupies a fixed area on the surface at all compositions, so that

$$w_1\Gamma_1 + w_2\Gamma_2 = 1 \qquad (6.164)$$

where w_1 and w_2 are constants chosen from our knowledge of the shape and size of the molecules. Γ_1 and Γ_2 become individually accessible if we are prepared to assign values to such constants on non-thermodynamic arguments. However, it is only the sum of (6.163) which can be measured directly. Figure 6.9 shows this quantity for the system water + ethanol at 25 °C. The maximum value of Γ is about 6×10^{-10} mol cm^{-2}.

In a multicomponent mixture, the quantity $(x_i^l\Gamma_j - x_j^l\Gamma_i)$ is experimentally accessible and independent of the choice of the position of Gibbs surface. This function divided by x_i^l is sometimes called the relative adsorption of j with respect to i.

$$\Gamma_{j,i} = \Gamma_j - (x_j^l/x_i^l)\Gamma_i \qquad (6.165)$$

McBain and his colleagues measured relative adsorptions by using a microtome to remove a thin layer of liquid (including all the surface layer) and examined the difference in composition between this layer and the bulk

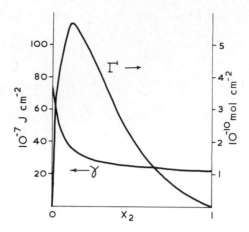

Figure 6.9. The surface tension, γ, and adsorption, Γ, for the system water (1) + ethanol (2) at 25 °C

liquid. The experiment is a difficult one but it provides confirmation of results for $\Gamma_{j,i}$ obtained from change of surface tension with composition.[18]

Problems

1. The results below show the partial volume of benzene, v_B, in a mixture with cyclohexane at 25 °C and 1 atm

x_B	$v_B/\text{cm}^3\,\text{mol}^{-1}$	x_B	$v_B/\text{cm}^3\,\text{mol}^{-1}$
0.042	91.80	0.521	90.01
0.097	91.53	0.618	89.79
0.139	91.33	0.703	89.64
0.202	91.07	0.814	89.50
0.287	90.73	0.926	89.42
0.395	90.36	1.000	89.41

Fit the results to an equation of the form $v_B = a + b x_C^2$. Use the Gibbs-Duhem equation to calculate v_C, the partial volume of cyclohexane. The molar volume of pure cyclohexane is $108.75\ \text{cm}^3\,\text{mol}^{-1}$.

2. The following measurements of the vapour pressure and composition have been reported for the system carbon tetrachloride (1) + chloroform (2) at 55 °C,

x_2	y_2	P/bar
0.0000	0.0000	0.4979
0.0597	0.1035	0.5237
0.1592	0.2505	0.5635
0.3516	0.4786	0.6342
0.4313	0.5557	0.6614
0.5420	0.6584	0.6974
0.6700	0.7578	0.7350
0.7272	0.8017	0.7521
0.9199	0.9418	0.8047
1.0000	1.0000	0.8256

Auxiliary measurements give

$$v_1^\circ = 101 \text{ cm}^3 \text{ mol}^{-1} \qquad v_2^\circ = 84 \text{ cm}^3 \text{ mol}^{-1}$$

$$B_{11} = -1280 \text{ cm}^3 \text{ mol}^{-1} \qquad B_{22} = -970 \text{ cm}^3 \text{ mol}^{-1} \qquad \delta B_{12} = 0$$

Calculate the activity coefficients and excess Gibbs free energy. Check that the former satisfy the Gibbs-Duhem equation, or, alternatively, calculate the excess Gibbs free energy from P and x alone, and compare it with that calculated from P, x and y. (It can be assumed in this last calculation that G^E is a quadratic function of mole fraction.)

3. The following measurements have been reported for the excess Gibbs free energy and excess enthalpy of an equimolar mixture of liquid argon and oxygen.

T/K	83.8	86	89.6	95	100	110
$g^E/\text{J mol}^{-1}$	37.1	—	36	33	32.4	29.5
$h^E/\text{J mol}^{-1}$	60	57	—	—	—	—

Do these results satisfy the Gibbs-Helmholtz equation? Obtain an expression for s^E as a function of temperature.

4. Two liquids A and B are sparingly soluble in each other. At equilibrium the mole fractions of the mutually saturated liquids are $x_A = 0.01$ in one layer, and $x_B = 0.005$ in the other. Estimate the activity coefficients of A and B in both phases.

5. The solubility of natural gas in brine is governed primarily by the fugacity of the components in the gas phase. Estimate the fugacities of nitrogen (1), methane (2) and ethane (3) in a mixture of mole fractions $x_1 = 0.10$, $x_2 = 0.85$, $x_3 = 0.05$, at a pressure of 20 bar and 300 K. At this temperature $B_{11} = -4 \text{ cm}^3 \text{ mol}^{-1}$, $B_{22} = -42 \text{ cm}^3 \text{ mol}^{-1}$, $B_{33} = -183 \text{ cm}^3 \text{ mol}^{-1}$. Estimate cross-coefficients from the rule of Lewis and Randall, or, better, by using the methods described in Chapter 9.

6. A solution of 3.00 g of A in 10.00 g of water boils at 102.30 °C. The latent heat of evaporation of water at its normal boiling point is $\Delta_e h = 40\,655\ J\,mol^{-1}$. Calculate the relative molar mass of A.

7. An aqueous solution of a straight chain carboxylic acid (relative molar mass 150) contains 4.000×10^{-3} kg/kg H_2O at 25 °C. When 2.3×10^{-3} kg of solution is skimmed off 0.031 m^2 of surface by use of a microtome, the concentration of the surface sample is 4.013×10^{-3} kg/kg H_2O. Calculate the surface excess of the acid, and compare your result with the value obtained from the Gibbs adsorption equation using the following surface tension data:

Concentration kg/kg H_2O	Surface tension $N\,m^{-1}$
0.0035	0.056
0.0040	0.054
0.0045	0.052

How can the orientation of the adsorbed molecules be inferred from the surface excess?

8. The following results show the partial pressures (Py_1) and (Py_2) and surface tension γ for a mixture of water (1) and ethanol (2) at 25 °C

x_2	$(Py_1)/N\,m^{-2}$	$(Py_2)/N\,m^{-2}$	$\gamma/N\,m^{-1}$
0.0	3170	0	0.0722
0.1	2890	2370	0.0364
0.2	2720	3570	0.0297
0.4	2450	4560	0.0263
0.6	2110	5350	0.0246
0.8	1330	6440	0.0232
1.0	0	7870	0.0220

Assume that the vapour is a perfect gas mixture and calculate the adsorption Γ. Compare your results with those in Figure 6.9 and calculate the relative adsorption of one of the components.

Answers

The answers to some of the problems are tables or diagrams. The problems with short answers are the following:

3. The results satisfy the Gibbs-Helmholtz equation but are only of sufficient

accuracy to give

$$s^E \simeq 0.28 \, \text{J K}^{-1} \, \text{mol}^{-1}$$

at all temperatures from 84 to 100 K.

4. First phase $\gamma_A = 99.5$ $\gamma_B = 1$

    Second phase $\gamma_A = 1$ $\gamma_B = 198$

5. By the rule of Lewis and Randall

$$f_1 = 1.99 \, \text{bar} \qquad f_2 = 16.43 \, \text{bar} \qquad f_3 = 0.85 \, \text{bar}$$

6. $\mathcal{M}_A = 65$

7. $6.4 \times 10^{-6} \, \text{mol m}^{-2}$

Notes

1. E. A. Guggenheim, *Thermodynamics*, 5th edn, North-Holland, Amsterdam, 1967, p. 20.

2. This derivation is discussed e.g. by H. B. Callen, *Thermodynamics*, Wiley, New York, 1963, p. 47.

3. See e.g. J. S. Rowlinson, *Liquids and Liquid Mixtures*, 2nd edn, Butterworth, London, 1969, p. 108.

4. For a bibliography of measurements of virial coefficients of mixtures, see E. A. Mason and T. H. Spurling, *The Virial Equation of State*, Pergamon Press, Oxford, 1969.

5. J. A. Barker, *Aust. J. Chem.* **6** (1953), 207.

6. See e.g. E. Hala, J. Pick, V. Fried and D. Vilim, *Vapour-Liquid Equilibrium*, 2nd edn, Pergamon Press, Oxford, 1967, Chapter 5.

7. See e.g. M. B. King, *Phase Equilibrium in Mixtures*, Pergamon Press, Oxford 1969, chapter 7; or the papers by E. F. G. Herrington (p. 3:17), S. D. Chang and B. C.-Y. Lu (p. 3:25) and L. C. Tao (p. 3:35) in *Proceedings of International Symposium on Distillation*, Inst. Chem. Eng., London, 1969.

8. See e.g. J. M. Prausnitz, *Molecular Thermodynamics of Fluid-Phase Equilibria*, Prentice-Hall, New York, 1969, Appendix 4.

9. See e.g. M. B. King, *Phase Equilibrium in Mixtures*, Pergamon Press, Oxford 1969; or the papers by E. F. G. Herrington, S. D. Chang and B. C.-Y. Lu and L. C. Tao in *Proceedings of International Symposium on Distillation*; E. Hala, J. Pick, V. Fried and D. Vilim, *Vapor-Liquid Equilibrium*, 2nd edn, Pergamon Press, Oxford, 1967; J. M. Prausnitz, C. A. Eckert, R. V. Orye and J. P. O'Connell, *Computer Calculations for Multicomponent Vapour-Liquid Equilibria*, Prentice-Hall, New Jersey, 1967.

10. See e.g. K. G. Denbigh, *Principles of Chemical Equilibrium*, Cambridge Univ. Press, 3rd edn, 1971, p. 262; E. A. Guggenheim, *Thermodynamics*, 5th edn, North-Holland, Amsterdam, 1967, Chapter 5.

11. G. Scatchard, *Chem. Rev.* **8** (1931), 329.

12. J. H. Hildebrand and R. L. Scott, *The Solubility of Non-electrolytes*, Reinhold, New York, 3rd edn, 1950; J. H. Hildebrand, J. M. Prausnitz and R. L. Scott, *Regular and Related Solutions*, Van Nostrand, New York, 1970.

13. R. Battino and H. L. Clever, *Chem. Rev.* **66** (1966), 395.

14. See P. J. Flory, *Principles of Polymer Chemistry*, Cornell Univ. Press, 1953; H. Morawitz, *Macromolecules in Solution*, Interscience, New York, 1963.

15. For further discussion, see the book by Stokes and Robinson cited below Figure 6.7 (especially Chapter 8, '*The measurement of chemical potentials*') and E. A. Guggenheim, *Thermodynamics*, 5th edn, North-Holland, Amsterdam, Chapter 7.

16. See e.g. A. W. Adamson, *Physical Chemistry of Surfaces*, 2nd edn, Interscience, New York, 1967, Chapter 1.

17. E. A. Guggenheim and N. K. Adam, *Proc. R. Soc.* **A139** (1933), 231.

18. For further information, see Adamson (loc. cit.), or, for a very full thermodynamic treatment, R. Defay, I. Prigogine, A. Bellemans, *Surface Tension and Adsorption* (trans. D. H. Everett), Longmans, London, 1966.

7 Phase Equilibria

7.1 Introduction

Thermodynamic methods find some of their most useful applications in the descriptions they provide of the changes of the properties of coexistent phases with changes of pressure, temperature and composition. We have had examples of such descriptions in earlier chapters. Thus Clapeyron's equation for a system of one component (Section 3.24) relates the change of vapour pressure with temperature to the less easily measured latent heat of evaporation. The equilibrium between a liquid mixture and its vapour (Section 6.8) provides us with the most convenient way of measuring its thermodynamic properties. We have, however, discussed hitherto only such equilibria as were useful for the problems in hand, and have not sought to establish general relations. In this chapter we turn to this wider problem and see what we can determine of the number and nature of phases in a system at equilibrium.

7.2 The phase rule

The conditions for there to be equilibrium between two or more phases are that the pressure P, the temperature T, and the chemical potential of each substance μ_i, shall have the same value in every phase. These conditions impose a restriction on the possible number of phases that can be in mutual equilibrium, a restriction which is known as the *phase rule* of Gibbs. Both the rule and its derivation are simple, but, as is often the case with thermodynamic results, the difficulties lie in understanding properly the symbols in which the rule is expressed. We start, therefore, with explanations of the terms. These are cast more in the form of descriptions than definitions although it is not intended that there should be any imprecision in the meanings imputed to the symbols.

Phase (symbol P). A phase is a macroscopic portion of matter which, when at equilibrium, is homogeneous with respect to all intensive functions, e.g. pressure, temperature, composition, density, partial enthalpies, dielectric constant, etc. The common examples are gas, liquid and solid. The last is usually a pure substance but if it is a mixture, and if it is to be one phase, then the mixing must occur on a truly molecular level, and not be a mere dispersion of one state of aggregation within another. We consider here only bulk phases, and ignore any properties peculiar to the surfaces of solids and liquids.

Degree of Freedom (symbol F). The degrees of freedom are the number of independent variables whose values we are free to choose at will (within certain limits) without changing the number of phases present in a system. In practice, we are concerned here only with the variables pressure, temperature and (C-1) of the mole fractions x_i of the C components present in each phase of the system. Thus $(C+1)$ variables suffice to define the state of a single phase; that is, all other properties such as density, partial enthalpies, etc., are functions only of these $(C+1)$ variables. We are ignoring here such complications as gravitational, electric or other external force fields.

Component (symbol C). It is in counting the number of components in a system that errors are most frequently made. There is no problem if all the substances are chemically inert; the number of components is the number of molecular species present, and it is in this sense that the word has been used so far in this book, although we saw in Section 3.11 that a mixture of fixed composition, such as air, could be regarded as a system of effectively one component provided we subjected it to no process, such as partial liquefaction, which led to changes of composition in part of the system.

If the system is reactive, and if it is always at equilibrium with respect to those reactions, then the number of components is less than the number of molecular species. We define it then as the smallest number of independently variable constituents by means of which the composition of each phase can be expressed, either directly or by means of a chemical equation. This definition is best made clear by examples (but for a general solution to the problem, see note 1).

1. Water. One component, in spite of its dissociation to H_3O^+ and OH^-, or association to $(H_2O)_2$, $(H_2O)_3$ etc. Each of these molecular species can be expressed in terms of H_2O by means of a chemical equation which proceeds rapidly to equilibrium under all practical conditions.

2. $CaCO_3$ (solid) $\rightleftharpoons CaO$ (solid) $+ CO_2$ (gas)

   $CuSO_4.5 H_2O$ (solid) $\rightleftharpoons CuSO_4.3 H_2O$ (solid) $+ 2 H_2O$ (solid, liquid or gas)

   Each of these systems has two components. In the first these can be any of the trio $CaCO_3$, CaO and CO_2, since we can express the compositions of all phases in terms of any two of these (with if necessary a minus sign, as in $CO_2 = CaCO_3 - CaCO$). Similar arguments apply to the second system.

3. NH_4Cl (solid) $\rightleftharpoons NH_3$ (gas) $+ HCl$ (gas)

Here there is only one component if the gas phase is equimolar in NH_3 and HCl, as it would be if it were derived solely from the sublimation of solid NH_4Cl. If we add excess NH_3 or excess HCl to the gas, we have a system of two components.

Exercise

A description of one stage of the Solvay or ammonia-soda process reads 'the slurry leaving the bottom of the second tower consists of sodium bicarbonate crystals, and a solution of ammonium bicarbonate, ammonium chloride, unreacted sodium chloride, soluble sodium bicarbonate and carbon dioxide'. How many components?

With these preliminary definitions we can readily derive the Phase Rule. Let there be P phases, labelled α, β, γ, etc., C components, labelled 1, 2, 3, etc., and, for generality, let us assume that each component is present in each phase. The maximum number of variables needed to specify the state of all phases is $P(C+1)$, of which P are pressures, P are temperatures and $P(C-1)$ are mole fractions. However, the degrees of freedom are less than this number since the system is constrained by the conditions

$$P^\alpha = P^\beta = P^\gamma = \text{etc.}$$

$$T^\alpha = T^\beta = T^\gamma = \text{etc.}$$

$$\mu_1^\alpha = \mu_1^\beta = \mu_1^\gamma = \text{etc.} \tag{7.1}$$

$$\mu_2^\alpha = \mu_2^\beta = \mu_2^\gamma = \text{etc.}$$

$$\text{etc.} \quad \text{etc.} \quad \text{etc.}$$

There are here $(2+C)(P-1)$ independent equations. Hence

$$F = P(C+1) - (2+C)(P-1) = C - P + 2$$

or, as the equation is usually written

$$P + F = C + 2 \tag{7.2}$$

Since F must be positive or zero, we have $P \leqslant C + 2$. More generally, the phase rule allows us to calculate the degrees of freedom of complex mixtures, and the rest of this chapter is a set of variations on this theme (for a full account of the consequences of (7.2), see note 2).

Exercise

At a conference in 1971 it was stated that ammonia and hydrogen chloride were equally insoluble in liquid ammonium chloride. When the speaker was challenged, his evidence for the statement was that the observed vapour pressure of the liquid was independent of the relative volumes of liquid and gas. Outline his reasoning.

7.3 Systems of one component

Here we have $P + F = 3$; that is a system of one phase (solid, or liquid, or gas) has two degrees of freedom, namely pressure and temperature. A system of two coexistent phases (solid and liquid, or solid and gas, or liquid and gas) has one degree of freedom; either the pressure or the temperature, but not both, may be chosen arbitrarily, within limits. This restriction is most familiar for liquid + gas, when we observe that to each temperature there corresponds a fixed vapour pressure, or to each pressure there corresponds a fixed boiling point. Finally, we have no degrees of freedom ($F = 0$) if there are three phases present, solid + liquid + gas. The invariance of this triple-point pressure and temperature is of use in fixing scales of measurement. We have seen, Section 3.8, that the kelvin is defined as the fraction (1/273.16) of the absolute triple-point temperature of water. The triple-point pressure of carbon dioxide (5.179 bar) has been proposed as a convenient pressure for calibrating pressure gauges.

These familiar results are represented in the phase diagram in which one phase is shown as an area, two as a line, and three as the meeting of three lines at a point. (Section 4.4, Figure 4.3). The solid + gas line ends at zero pressure and temperature, the liquid + gas line at the critical point, whilst the solid + liquid line is believed to continue indefinitely, at least until the pressure is so high (megabars) that atoms and molecules lose their identity, as, for example, in the interiors of stars.

Exercise

In Figure 4.3 it is seen that an extrapolation of each of the two phase lines beyond the triple point takes it into the region of the third phase, e.g. the extrapolation of the liquid + gas line lies in the solid area. Discuss this fact in the light of the conditions for equilibrium between the phases.

Most substances have phase diagrams more complicated than that shown in Figure 4.3. The existence of more than one liquid phase is unusual, but not unknown. The most interesting case is ^{4}He (Figure 7.1) whose solid phase is unstable below 25.3 bar at zero temperature, and which has, therefore, no solid + liquid + gas triple point. However at low pressures and temperatures, that is approximately below 25 bar and 2.2 K, the normal liquid changes to a fluid of unusual thermal and mechanical properties. The boundary between the normal and abnormal liquids has no latent heat of transition, but is marked by a strong maximum, or probably an infinity, in C_P. However, a full description of this thermodynamic anomaly is outside the scope of this book.

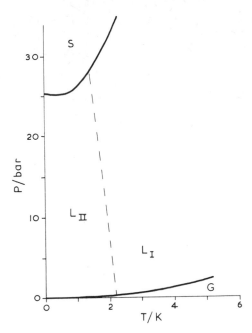

Figure 7.1. The phase diagram of helium. The vapour pressure line ends at the critical point at 5.2 K, 2.3 bar. Above this line there are two liquid phases: the normal liquid (I) and the abnormal (II). The solid exists only at high pressures

Organic substances whose molecules are rigid and shaped either like rods or plates often form *liquid crystals*. This is a state of matter intermediate between the solid and the normal liquid in which the molecules are free to move, but not to rotate. These fixed orientations make the phase highly anisotropic and result in unusual optical properties. A typical example is p-azoxyanisole, which melts to a liquid crystal at 118 °C with a latent heat of 32.3 kJ mol^{-1}, and the liquid crystal changes to a normal liquid at 136 °C with the absorption of a second latent heat of 1.4 kJ mol^{-1}.

The existence of more than one solid phase is much more common than the existence of more than one liquid, and the name *allotropy* is given to this phenomenon. The subject is of great importance to the metallurgist and materials technologist, but, again, only a brief discussion of principles is appropriate to this book.

If each solid phase has a domain of pressure and temperature in which it is stable with respect to all other solid phases, then the phenomenon is termed *enantiotropy*. Thus ice is known to form no less than seven phases, one of which, ice I, is stable in equilibrium with liquid water at pressures below 2.1 kbar and temperatures from −22 °C to 0 °C. The other phases are found only at pressures well above that of the triple point. Another example is that of sulphur (Figure 7.2) which forms rhombic crystals (stable to 96 °C in equilibrium with the gas) and monoclinic crystals (stable from 96 °C to the solid + liquid + gas triple point at 119 °C). One interesting complication is that rhombic sulphur can be heated above its transition point until it melts at a triple point of 110 °C. It is here in equilibrium with both gas and liquid, but all three phases are unstable with respect to the monoclinic crystal.

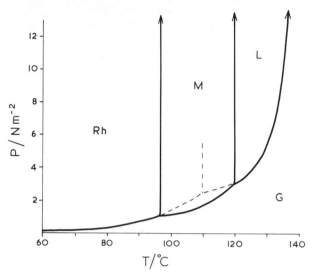

Figure 7.2. The phase diagram of sulphur. There are two solid phases, rhombic and monoclinic. The lines separating the Rh/M and M/L regions meet at a solid-solid-liquid triple point at 151 °C and 1.3×10^8 N m^{-2} (1.3 kbar). The dashed lines show the metastable equilibrium between rhombic solid, liquid and gas

If one solid phase is everywhere stable with respect to all others the phenomenon is called *monotropy*. Thus white phosphorus is a well-known and reproducible state of solid phosphorus; it melts to the liquid at 44 °C, and can, with care, even be boiled at about 300 °C. It is, however, always unstable with respect to the solid red (or violet) phosphorus, which has a sublimation temperature at 1 atm of about 420 °C and which melts at 589 °C. We can draw separate phase diagrams for white phosphorus, liquid and gas, and for red phosphorus, liquid and gas, but cannot properly show white and red on the same diagram. We have seen earlier in discussing liquid-vapour equilibrium (Chapter 4) that there is no impropriety in applying thermodynamic methods to states of a system that are unstable with respect to other states, and hence the melting of rhombic sulphur or white phosphorus is a proper subject for discussion in terms of, say, Clapeyron's equation, as long as the system does not move at a measurable rate towards the more stable state. Indeed, the properties of white phosphorus are experimentally found to be more reproducible than those of red and so the U.S. National Bureau of Standards uses this unstable phase as the standard state! (See Section 8.3).

7.4 Glasses

A glass is a state of matter whose lack of obvious mobility suggests that it is a solid. All other properties suggest that it is more closely allied to liquids. It is isotropic, has no ordered crystalline structure, no cleavage planes, flows slowly under stress, and has no sharp melting point but softens to a true liquid without the absorption of a latent heat. The glassy state is rarely met with in simple substances but is common with polymers, with such organic substances as sugars, and, of course, with the silicates.

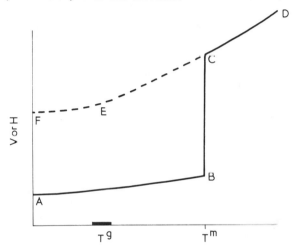

Figure 7.3. The volume or enthalpy of a substance which can form a glass (see text)

The technical importance of many glasses justifies a brief description of their thermodynamic status. This is best made clear from a sketch which shows the volume and enthalpy (for the two behave similarly) of the true crystalline solid state (AB, in Figure 7.3), the sharp increase on melting (BC, at a temperature T^m) and the rise in the liquid state (CD). This latter curve is steeper than that for the solid since the coefficient of expansion and the heat capacity of a liquid are generally greater than those of a solid.

On cooling the liquid it usually fails to crystallise at T^m and passes into the supercooled state (CE). Here it is still mobile, but its viscosity rises as it is cooled. At E it hardens to a glass. The hardening is not sharp but is usually confined to a range of 5–20 K. The transition from supercooled liquid to glass is usually reversible in experiments that last no more than a few hours, but the glass itself is prone to crystallisation (or devitrification) if kept for a long time just below the glass point, T^g. This change is irreversible; the glassy state is unstable with respect to the crystalline, but it is usually sufficiently stable and reproducible for the meaningful discussion of its thermodynamic properties. As can be seen, its volume and enthalpy are larger than those of the crystal, but its coefficient of expansion and heat capacity are similar.

7.5 Two components: liquid and vapour[3]

With two components, the sum $P + F$ is 4. Hence if there is one phase $F = 3$, and its state is specified by pressure, temperature and one mole fraction, say x_2. If there are two phases α and β, then $F = 2$, and the state of the system is specified by any two of the set P, T, x_2^α and x_2^β, where the mole fractions are those of component 2 in each of the two phases. A knowledge only of the overall composition and either P or T is not sufficient to specify the state. We find that if we change the volume of the system at a fixed temperature we vary the proportion of material in phase α, and, by the phase rule, it follows that the pressure and the compositions of both phases vary also. Hence a mixture differs from pure substance in that it does not, in general, have a unique vapour pressure at each temperature, nor a unique boiling point at a fixed pressure (exceptions to these general conclusions are discussed below).

Exercise

An argument based on a cell with partitions was used in Section 3.23 to show that in a one component system the vapour pressure is independent of the ratio of the amounts of substance in liquid and vapour. Why can it not be used in a system with more than one component?

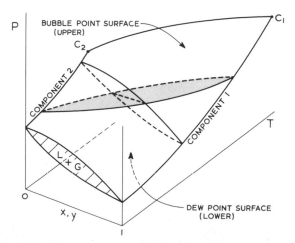

Figure 7.4. The bubble point and dew point surfaces. Each is a sheet in P, x, T space, and they are joined at the edges of the diagram ($x = 0$ and $x = 1$) along the two vapour pressure lines of the pure components

The most important example of two-phase equilibrium is that between a liquid mixture and its vapour since this equilibrium is the basis of many methods of separation, e.g. distillation, absorption, stripping. The equilibrium can be represented graphically as a pair of surfaces (P, T, x) and (P, T, y) drawn in a pressure, temperature, composition space (Figure 7.4). These surfaces are known, respectively as the bubble-point and dew-point surfaces since on expansion of a liquid mixture they mark the point of the first appearance of a bubble of gas and the point of disappearance of the last drop of liquid respectively. For many purposes it is easier to work not with these three-dimensional surfaces, but with their two-dimensional sections (Figure 7.5). One of these, the (P, x) or (P, y) section at constant T (and at low pressures) was discussed in some detail in the previous chapter, since it is the section whose thermodynamic analysis is most straightforward.

For practical purposes the (T, x) or (T, y) sections at constant P are often more useful since separation equipment is usually run under conditions of essentially fixed pressure. The analysis, which we give below, is necessarily less complete than that of the (P, x) and (P, y) sections since for the latter we can take fixed T and, simultaneously, fixed P by working at sufficiently low pressures for the behaviour of the system to be essentially the same as that in the limit $P = 0$. For the (T, x) and (T, y) sections, we have fixed P, but cannot simultaneously have fixed T since there is no limiting process equivalent to letting P approach zero as in the isothermal case. At high pressures (above about 3 bar) we lose this simplification even in the isothermal case, and both sections can then be analysed only with the more formal descriptions of this and the following section.

Table 7.1. Resumé of symbols used in Section 7.5. Two similar sets of symbols are obtained by replacing h by v (volume) or by s (entropy)

Symbol	Meaning or Definition	
h	molar enthalpy	in phase indicated
h_1, h_2	partial enthalpy of species 1, 2	by superscript g, l
Δh	$h^g - h^l$	
Δh_1	$h_1^g - h_1^l$	
Δh_2	$h_2^g - h_2^l$	
y_1, y_2	mole fraction of species 1, 2 in vapour	
x_1, x_2	mole fraction of species 1, 2 in liquid	
Δx_2	$y_2 - x_2$	
g_{2x}	$(\partial^2 g^l / \partial x^2)_{P,T}$	
g_{2y}	$(\partial^2 g^g / \partial y^2)_{P,T}$	
$(dT/dx_2)_P$		
$(dP/dx_2)_T$	Derivatives taken along the equilibrium	
$(dT/dy_2)_P$	(P, T, x) or (P, T, y) surfaces	
$(dP/dy_2)_T$		

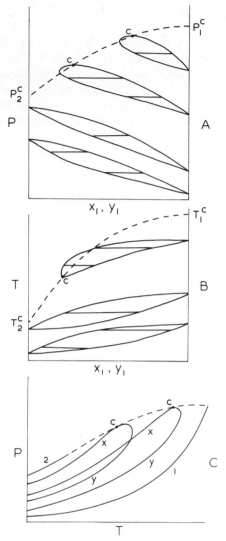

Figure 7.5. Sections of the (P, T, x) and (P, T, y) surfaces. A shows sections of constant temperature, B of constant pressure and C of constant composition. The surfaces cut each other at the pure components $(x = y = 0$ and $x = y = 1)$, and meet to form a continuous surface along the critical locus (see Section 7.7)

The third section, (P, T) at fixed composition, is useful mainly for discussing the behaviour of mixtures near their gas-liquid critical points (see below). If we are working at fixed pressure and are not particularly interested in temperature as a variable, then it is sometimes useful to plot y as a function of x, as a line running from $x_2 = y_2 = 0$ to $x_2 = y_2 = 1$ along which temperature varies parametrically. Such a plot is called a *McCabe-Thiele diagram*; on it we can plot supplementary lines to represent the operating conditions of a distillation column, but such operations are represented more satisfactorily on a chart of h as a function of x and y, and we defer discussion to the next section.

The state of the system in the two-phase region bounded by the dew-point and bubble-point surfaces is found by drawing tie-lines of constant pressure and temperature (Figure 7.5). Each point in this region lies on one tie-line only, and it is readily seen that the lever rule (Section 4.5) is the appropriate geometric construction for calculating the amounts of each phase. If we use a mole fraction scale of composition these amounts are expressed in moles; if we use mass fractions the amounts are the corresponding masses of the

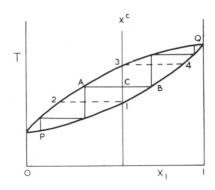

Figure 7.6. The evaporation of a binary mixture at constant pressure

phases. The formal expression of the lever rule is as follows; n^C moles at point C (Figure 7.6) represents n^A at point A and n^B at point B, where, for material balance

$$x_1^A n^A + x_1^B n^B = x_1^C n^C$$
$$x_2^A n^A + x_2^B n^B = x_2^C n^C \qquad (7.3)$$

The sum of these equations gives $n^A + n^B = n^C$, and elimination of n^C gives

$$\frac{n^A}{n^B} = \frac{x_1^B - x_1^C}{x_1^C - x_1^A} \qquad (7.4)$$

which is the lever rule.

If we take a liquid mixture of composition x^C and heat it slowly, then it starts to evaporate at the temperature represented by point 1. This is the bubble-point, and the composition of the first bubble of vapour is that of point 2. As we heat the two-phase system the amount of material in the vapour phase increases in accordance with the lever rule, and its composition moves along the line 2-A-3. The composition of the liquid simultaneously moves along 1-B-4. At the temperature of points 3 and 4 the last trace of liquid, of composition 4, evaporates. This is the dew-point.

The course of a distillation in which the mixture, as it passes up the column, is repeatedly evaporated and condensed to give each time the appropriate equilibrium phase, can be represented formally on a (T, x) section by constructing a lattice of vertical and horizontal lines in the two-phase region. Thus, in Figure 7.6 four successive evaporations are needed for a liquid mixture at P to yield a vapour of composition Q. Each step is a *theoretical plate*; more than four plates are needed in practice since no column is perfect.

At low temperatures, and hence at low vapour pressures, the shapes of the dew and bubble-point curves can be expressed in terms of the thermodynamic functions introduced in the last chapter; that is, the activity coefficients, γ, and the molar excess functions, g^E, etc. This description is useful only at low pressures because of the difficulty over the accessibility of the chemical potentials μ_i° discussed in Section 6.5. At high pressures (say, above about 3 bars) we cannot usefully define excess functions, but we can still use the condition that the chemical potential (or fugacity) of each component shall be the same in both phases to tell us something about the shapes of the dew and bubble-point surfaces. As always, thermodynamic arguments alone cannot give us 'absolute' information, but they can relate the shapes of the surfaces to other properties such as heats of evaporation.

First, we must derive the conditions of thermodynamic stability in a binary system. It was shown in Chapter 4 that a system of one component must be both thermally and mechanically stable. These are necessary but not sufficient conditions of stability in a mixture, which must also be stable with respect to possible local changes of composition. This third condition is called that of material (or, sometimes, diffusional) stability. In an ideal binary mixture Δg, the free energy of mixing at fixed P and T, is a function of mole fraction that is everywhere concave upwards (Figure 6.2). Such a mixture is materially stable. Consider, however, a possible curve of Δg (or of g, since the two functions differ only by a linear function of x) which has a portion which is convex upwards, as in Figure 7.7. A homogeneous mixture of mole fraction x^* could, for example, separate into two phases each containing the same amount of substance and of composition $(x^* + \delta x)$ and $(x^* - \delta x)$. By the lever rule, the free energy of the separated system lies at the centre of the tie-line, and since this point is lower than that of the original homogeneous mixture, it is clear that the latter is materially unstable with respect to the hypothetical change. This argument applies to all parts of the curve where Δg, and hence g, are convex upwards. The formal condition for material stability, which must be added to those of thermal and mechanical stability (4.1) and (4.2) is, therefore,

$$(\partial^2 g/\partial x_1^2)_{P,T} = (\partial^2 g/\partial x_2^2)_{P,T} > 0 \qquad (7.5)$$

It follows from Figure 7.7 that the most stable state of the system at each

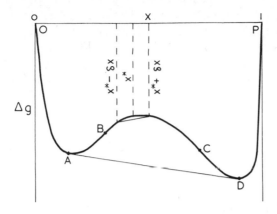

Figure 7.7. The free energy of a system which separates into two phases

composition lies on the piece-wise continuous curve OADP where AD is the tangent to the continuous curve OABCDP. Between B and C the homogeneous state is unstable; on AB and CD the homogeneous state is metastable; that is (7.5) is satisfied, but there is an alternative and accessible form of the system of lower free energy, *viz.* the separation into two phases of compositions represented by A and D, the sum of whose free energies lies on the tie-line joining these points.

It is clear from the geometry of the figure that AD has a lower free energy than any homogeneous state on the line ABCD. We now show more formally that this common tangent satisfies the conditions of equilibrium between coexistent phases, namely

$$\mu_1^A = \mu_1^D \qquad \mu_2^A = \mu_2^D \tag{7.6}$$

Chemical potential is the partial Gibbs free energy and so, from the counterpart of (6.15)

$$\mu_1^A = g^A - x_2^A(\partial g/\partial x_2)_{P,T}^A = \mu_1^D = g^D - x_2^D(\partial g/\partial x_2)_{P,T}^D$$
$$\mu_2^A = g^A + x_1^A(\partial g/\partial x_2)_{P,T}^A = \mu_2^D = g^D + x_1^D(\partial g/\partial x_2)_{P,T}^D \tag{7.7}$$

where we have used the result $dx_1 = -dx_2$. By subtraction of these equations for μ_1 and μ_2, and substitution in the first, we obtain

$$(\partial g/\partial x_2)^A = (\partial g/\partial x_2)^D = (g^A - g^D)/(x_2^A - x_2^D) \tag{7.8}$$

which is the equation of the tangent AD.

We can now use these conditions of stability and equilibrium to determine the shapes of the dew and bubble-point surfaces. Consider a system of two phases in equilibrium at P, T and mole fractions of component 2 in liquid and vapour of x_2 and y_2 respectively. The potentials satisfy (7.6). Consider now a neighbouring state of the system, at $(P+\delta P)$, $(T+\delta T)$, $(x_2+\delta x_2)$ and $(y_2+\delta y_2)$. If, to maintain equilibrium, the potentials are still to be equal then $(\delta\mu_1)$ and $(\delta\mu_2)$ must be the same for each phase. That is

$$\delta\mu_1^l = \left(\frac{\partial\mu_1}{\partial P}\right)_{T,x}^l \delta P + \left(\frac{\partial\mu_1}{\partial T}\right)_{P,x}^l \delta T + \left(\frac{\partial\mu_1}{\partial x_2}\right)_{P,T}^l \delta x_2$$

$$= \delta\mu_1^g = \left(\frac{\partial\mu_1}{\partial P}\right)_{T,y}^g \delta P + \left(\frac{\partial\mu_1}{\partial T}\right)_{P,y}^g \delta T + \left(\frac{\partial\mu_1}{\partial y_2}\right)_{P,T}^g \delta y_2$$

(7.9)

and similarly for component 2. Now $(\partial\mu_1/\partial P)_{T,x}^l$ is v_1^l, the partial volume of 1 in the liquid, and $-(\partial\mu_1/\partial T)_{P,x}^l$ is s_1^l, the partial entropy of 1 in the liquid. Hence, by subtraction of the two sides of (7.9) and of the corresponding equations for component 2, we have

$$\Delta v_1 \, \delta P - \Delta s_1 \, \delta T + x_2 g_{2x} \, \delta x_2 - y_2 g_{2y} \, \delta y_2 = 0$$
$$\Delta v_2 \, \delta P - \Delta s_2 \, \delta T - x_1 g_{2x} \, \delta x_2 + y_1 g_{2y} \, \delta y_2 = 0$$

(7.10)

where $\Delta v_1 = v_1^g - v_1^l$, etc. and where we have used the results, obtained by differentiation of (7.7) with respect to the composition that

$$x_1(\partial\mu_1^l/\partial x_2)_{P,T} = -x_2(\partial\mu_2^l/\partial x_2)_{P,T} = -x_1 x_2(\partial^2 g^l/\partial x^2)_{P,T}$$
$$y_1(\partial\mu_1^g/\partial y_2)_{P,T} = -y_2(\partial\mu_2^g/\partial y_2)_{P,T} = -y_1 y_2(\partial^2 g^g/\partial y^2)_{P,T}$$

(7.11)

for the liquid and gas respectively. We do not indicate whether the second derivatives are to be evaluated by differentiation with respect to component 1 or component 2 since $(\partial^2 g/\partial x_1^2)$ is equal to $(\partial^2 g/\partial x_2^2)$, and similarly for y. The symbols g_{2x} and g_{2y} are abbreviations for $(\partial^2 g^l/\partial x^2)_{P,T}$ and $(\partial^2 g^g/\partial y^2)_{P,T}$. Since, by the condition of equilibrium

$$\Delta\mu_1 = \Delta h_1 - T\,\Delta s_1 = 0$$

(7.12)

we can replace Δs_1 by $(\Delta h_1/T)$, where Δh_1 is the difference in partial enthalpies.

The pair of equations (7.10) connect the four differentials δP, δT, δx_2 and δy_2, and comprise our knowledge of the shapes of the dew and bubble point surfaces. g_{2x} and g_{2y} are abbreviations for $(\partial^2 g^l/\partial x^2)_{P,T}$ and $(\partial^2 g^g/\partial y^2)_{P,T}$. Since, (T, y) lines in Figure 7.5 by solving (7.10) for the ratios $(\delta T/\delta x_2)$ and $(\delta T/\delta y_2)$.

$$\left(\frac{dT}{dx_2}\right)_P = \frac{-Tg_{2x}\,\Delta x_2}{y_1\,\Delta h_1 + y_2\,\Delta h_2}$$

(7.13)

$$\left(\frac{dT}{dy_2}\right)_P = \frac{-Tg_{2y}\,\Delta x_2}{x_1\,\Delta h_1 + x_2\,\Delta h_2}$$

(7.14)

where Δx_2 is $(y_2 - x_2)$, and where $(dT/dx_2)_P$ and $(dT/dy_2)_P$ are used to denote displacements along the equilibrium (P, T, x) and (P, T, y) surfaces. They could, alternatively, be written as partial derivatives $(\partial T/\partial x_2)_{P,\sigma}$ and $(\partial T/\partial y_2)_{P,\sigma}$, where the suffix σ denotes a displacement at saturation. The two notations correspond to writing the slope of the vapour pressure curve of a one-component system either as (dP/dT) or as $(\partial P/\partial T)_\sigma$, both of which are widely used. Here we use the simpler form for the binary systems since we do not wish to make the notation of this section more complicated than is necessary. The denominator of (7.13) is the molar heat of condensation of a drop of gas of composition (y_1, y_2) into the liquid, and that of (7.14) is the molar heat of evaporation of a drop of liquid of composition (x_1, x_2). These may be written in another form by using the counterparts of (6.15).

$$x_1 \Delta h_1 + x_2 \Delta h_2 = \Delta h - \Delta x_2(\partial h^s/\partial y_2)_{P,T}$$
$$y_1 \Delta h_1 + y_2 \Delta h_2 = \Delta h - \Delta x_2(\partial h^l/\partial x_2)_{P,T}$$

(7.15)

We can obtain three more pairs of equations, analogues to (7.13) and (7.14), by imposing conditions of constant temperature, constant x_2 or constant y_2 on the general conditions of equilibrium (7.10). The first is not as useful as (7.13) and (7.14) since we are more often concerned with conditions of constant pressure and with enthalpy changes, than with constant temperature and volume changes. However, it is needed later in this chapter so is recorded here

$$\left(\frac{dP}{dx_2}\right)_T = \frac{g_{2x} \Delta x_2}{y_1 \Delta v_1 + y_2 \Delta v_2}$$

(7.16)

$$\left(\frac{dP}{dy_2}\right)_T = \frac{g_{2y} \Delta x_2}{x_1 \Delta v_1 + x_2 \Delta v_2}$$

(7.17)

Exercise

By considering conditions of constant x_2 or constant y_2, obtain from (7.10) the analogues for a two-component system of Clapeyron's equation for the slope of a vapour pressure curve, namely

$$\left(\frac{dP}{dT}\right)_x = \frac{y_1 \Delta h_1 + y_2 \Delta h_2}{T(y_1 \Delta v_1 + y_2 \Delta v_2)} = \frac{y_1 \Delta s_1 + y_2 \Delta s_2}{y_1 \Delta v_1 + y_2 \Delta v_2}$$

(7.18)

The direct value of equations such as (7.13) and (7.14) is not great since it is generally easier to measure $(dT/dx_2)_P$ etc. than to measure some of the quantities on the right-hand side, the second derivatives of g and the partial enthalpies. If the pressure is low, or if the equation of state of the mixed vapours is known, then g_{2y} and $(\partial h^s/\partial y_2)_{P,T}$ are calculable. In the limit of zero pressure, as for example for a mixture of perfect gases,

$$g_{2y} = RT/y_1 y_2 \qquad (\partial h^s/\partial y_2)_{P,T} = 0$$

(7.19)

and so

$$\left(\frac{dT}{dx_2}\right)_P = \frac{RT^2}{\Delta h}\left(\frac{\Delta x_2}{y_1 y_2}\right)$$

(7.20)

Exercise

Show that in a dilute solution (7.20) leads to the test of consistency used by Wang[4], namely

$$\underset{x_2 \to 0}{\mathrm{Lt}} \left(\frac{\mathrm{d}T}{\mathrm{d}x_2} \right)_P = \frac{RT^2(\alpha_{12} - 1)}{\Delta h_1^\circ} \tag{7.21}$$

where α_{12} is the volatility ratio (6.93), and Δh_1° is the latent heat of evaporation of pure solvent. Although (7.21) follows from (7.20) it is not limited to a liquid mixture in equilibrium with a perfect gas at low pressure, but holds at all pressures. Why?

More general tests for consistency are difficult at high pressures since we rarely have a complete enough knowledge of the thermodynamic properties of both phases[5].

The indirect value of equations such as (7.13) and (7.14) is rather greater, since, as will be shown in the next three sections, they allow us to discuss the latent heats and gas-liquid critical points of binary systems and to investigate the phenomenon of azeotropy.

7.6 Two components: the thermodynamics of distillation*

The separation of the components of a mixture is most commonly achieved by exploiting the change of composition which accompanies evaporation and condensation. To obtain high purity, these operations must be repeated many times, as in the familiar columns for rectification, stripping and absorption. The design of these columns is outside the scope of this book, but we discuss here the compilation and the graphical representation of some of the thermodynamic properties needed before such design can be undertaken. The most important of these is the energy needed for evaporation. This is conveniently represented in tables or charts which show h and s as functions of composition in each phase for a system at a fixed pressure. We consider first, in this section, the definition and measurement of latent heats of evaporation in a mixture; secondly, their representation on (h, x) and (s, x) charts; and thirdly, the use of these charts to analyse the performance of a column. For simplicity, the account is restricted to binary mixtures.

It is clear from Figures 7.4 and 7.5 that there are infinitely many ways of going from the liquid to the gas surfaces, and hence an infinity of latent heats. Here we are concerned with four; the reversible latent heats at constant pressure and at constant temperature, and the throttling latent heats at constant pressure and constant temperature. Each has a differential and an integral form.

The molar latent heat of a pure substance is the heat needed to transfer one

---

* This section is more difficult than the rest of this chapter and may be omitted.

mole from liquid to gas under equilibrium conditions of constant pressure and temperature. The differential latent heat is $T(dS/dn)_{P,T}$ where n is the amount evaporated. (As in the last section, the ordinary differential (d/d) is used to denote a change under the equilibrium conditions implied by the suffixes.) This differential heat is equal to the integral heat $T \Delta s = \Delta h$, since P and T can both be kept constant as the evaporation proceeds. This is not so in a mixture, and we consider first the differential reversible latent heat at constant pressure.

Let n^l and n^g be the amounts of substance in liquid and gas, whose compositions are (x_1, x_2) and (y_1, y_2) respectively. Let a drop dn of composition (z_1, z_2) evaporate at constant pressure where z_1 and z_2 are chosen to maintain equilibrium between liquid and gas. In general z_1 is equal to neither x_1 nor y_1. Let the change of temperature needed to maintain equilibrium be dT. Let dx_1 etc. be the change of x_1 etc. caused by the evaporation. Then, for a material balance

$$dx_1 = -dx_2 = \left(\frac{dx_1}{dT}\right)_P dT = -(z_1 - x_1)\left(\frac{dn}{n^l}\right)$$

$$dy_1 = -dy_2 = \left(\frac{dy_1}{dT}\right)_P dT = (z_1 - y_1)\left(\frac{dn}{n^g}\right)$$

$$(7.22)$$

where $(dx_1/dT)_P$ and $(dy_1/dT)_P$ are the derivatives discussed in the last section. Equations (7.22) can be solved to give dT and the composition of the drop (z_1, z_2) in terms of an arbitrary dn;

$$\left(\frac{dT}{dn}\right)_P \left[n^l\left(\frac{dx_1}{dT}\right)_P + n^g\left(\frac{dy_1}{dT}\right)_P\right] = x_1 - y_1 \tag{7.23}$$

$$z_1\left[n^l\left(\frac{dx_1}{dT}\right)_P + n^g\left(\frac{dy_1}{dT}\right)_P\right] = y_1 n^l\left(\frac{dx_1}{dT}\right)_P + x_1 n^g\left(\frac{dy_1}{dT}\right)_P \tag{7.24}$$

Clearly $z_1 = y_1$ for the first drop to evaporate ($n^g = 0$) and $z_1 = x_1$ for the last drop to evaporate ($n^l = 0$).

The differential latent heat at constant pressure $T(dS/dn)_P$ can be found by considering the change in entropy of the system caused by the evaporation of dn of liquid and the change of temperature dT.

$$(dS)_P = (dS^l)_P + (dS^g)_P$$

$$= \left(\frac{\partial S^l}{\partial n_1}\right)_{P,T,n_2} (-z_1\, dn) + \left(\frac{\partial S^l}{\partial n_2}\right)_{P,T,n_1} (-z_2\, dn) + \left(\frac{\partial S^l}{\partial T}\right)_{P,x} dT$$

$$+ \left(\frac{\partial S^g}{\partial n_1}\right)_{P,T,n_2} (z_1\, dn) + \left(\frac{\partial S^g}{\partial n_2}\right)_{P,T,n_1} (z_2\, dn) + \left(\frac{\partial S^g}{\partial T}\right)_{P,y} dT$$

The notation can be simplified by writing for the partial entropies

$$\left(\frac{\partial S^g}{\partial n_1}\right)_{P,T,n_2} - \left(\frac{\partial S^l}{\partial n_1}\right)_{P,T,n_2} = s_1^g - s_1^l = \Delta s_1 \tag{7.26}$$

and similarly for component 2, and by replacing the entropies S^l and S^g in the derivatives with respect to temperature by the products $(n^l s^l)$ and $(n^g s^g)$

$$(\mathrm{d}S)_P = (z_1\,\Delta s_1 + z_2\,\Delta s_2)\,\mathrm{d}n + \left[n^l\left(\frac{\partial s^l}{\partial T}\right)_{P,x} + n^g\left(\frac{\partial s^g}{\partial T}\right)_{P,y}\right]\mathrm{d}T \quad (7.27)$$

The change of entropy is thus formed of two terms, called the *direct* and *indirect* terms by Strickland-Constable[6]. The first is the change of entropy caused directly by the evaporation of a drop of composition (z_1, z_2), and the second is the change of entropy of each phase caused by the necessary change of temperature $\mathrm{d}T$ which accompanies this isobaric evaporation. The latent heat, $T(\mathrm{d}S/\mathrm{d}n)_P$, is similarly formed from direct and indirect parts.

$$T\left(\frac{\mathrm{d}S}{\mathrm{d}n}\right)_P = T[z_1\,\Delta s_1 + z_2\,\Delta s_2] + T\left(\frac{\mathrm{d}T}{\mathrm{d}n}\right)_P\left[n^l\left(\frac{\partial s^l}{\partial T}\right)_{P,x} + n^g\left(\frac{\partial s^g}{\partial T}\right)_{P,y}\right] \quad (7.28)$$

$$\begin{array}{ccccc}
\text{total} & = & \text{direct} & + & \text{indirect} \\
\text{differential} & & \text{latent heat} & & \text{latent heat}
\end{array}$$

These can be expressed in terms of more accessible quantities by eliminating $\mathrm{d}T$ and the composition of the drop (z_1, z_2) by means of (7.23) and (7.24).

$$\text{direct} = \frac{n^l T\left(\frac{\mathrm{d}x_1}{\mathrm{d}T}\right)_P[y_1\,\Delta s_1 + y_2\,\Delta s_2] + n^g T\left(\frac{\mathrm{d}y_1}{\mathrm{d}T}\right)_P[x_1\,\Delta s_1 + x_2\,\Delta s_2]}{n^l\left(\frac{\mathrm{d}x_1}{\mathrm{d}T}\right)_P + n^g\left(\frac{\mathrm{d}y_1}{\mathrm{d}T}\right)_P} \quad (7.29)$$

$$= \frac{n^l T\left(\frac{\mathrm{d}x_1}{\mathrm{d}T}\right)_P\left(\frac{\mathrm{d}P}{\mathrm{d}T}\right)_x[y_1\,\Delta v_1 + y_2\,\Delta v_2] + n^g T\left(\frac{\mathrm{d}y_1}{\mathrm{d}T}\right)_P\left(\frac{\mathrm{d}P}{\mathrm{d}T}\right)_y[x_1\,\Delta v_1 + x_2\,\Delta v_2]}{n^l\left(\frac{\mathrm{d}x_1}{\mathrm{d}T}\right)_P + n^g\left(\frac{\mathrm{d}y_1}{\mathrm{d}T}\right)_P} \quad (7.30)$$

$$\text{indirect} = \frac{(x_1 - y_1)T\left[n^l\left(\frac{\partial s^l}{\partial T}\right)_{P,x} + n^g\left(\frac{\partial s^g}{\partial T}\right)_{P,y}\right]}{n^l\left(\frac{\mathrm{d}x_1}{\mathrm{d}T}\right)_P + n^g\left(\frac{\mathrm{d}y_1}{\mathrm{d}T}\right)_P} \quad (7.31)$$

$$= \frac{(x_1 - y_1)[n^l(c_P)^l + n^g(c_P)^g]}{n^l\left(\frac{\mathrm{d}x_1}{\mathrm{d}T}\right)_P + n^g\left(\frac{\mathrm{d}y_1}{\mathrm{d}T}\right)_P} \quad (7.32)$$

(7.18) has been used to obtain (7.30) from (7.29); this change enables the direct term to be expressed solely in terms of the 'mechanical' properties P, V, T, x and y, and their equilibrium derivatives along gas and liquid surfaces. The indirect term, however, requires a knowledge of the heat capacities of the two phases.

The total differential latent heat, that is the sum of (7.30) and (7.31), can be reduced to a more simple, but not necessarily more useful form, by replacing the partial derivatives of (7.31) with the equilibrium derivatives (see Appendix A)

$$\left(\frac{\partial s^l}{\partial T}\right)_{P,x} = \left(\frac{ds^l}{dT}\right)_P - \left(\frac{\partial s^l}{\partial x_1}\right)_{P,T}\left(\frac{dx_1}{dT}\right)_P, \tag{7.33}$$

(and similarly for the gas), and by using the following identities which follow from the results of Section 6.2.

$$y_1\,\Delta s_1 + y_2\,\Delta s_2 - (x_1 - y_1)(\partial s^l/\partial x_1)_{P,T}$$
$$= x_1\,\Delta s_1 + x_2\,\Delta s_2 - (x_1 - y_1)(\partial s^g/\partial y_1)_{P,T}$$
$$= y_1 s_1^g + y_2 s_2^g - x_1 s_1^l - x_2 s_2^l = \Delta s \tag{7.34}$$

Here Δs is the entropy difference between a mole of liquid (x_1, x_2) and a mole of gas in equilibrium with it (y_1, y_2). (We consider below the question of the zeros of entropy and enthalpy, whose choice affects the numerical values of such differences between fluids of different composition.).

The result is, for the total reversible differential latent heat at constant pressure

$$\text{total} = T\,\Delta s + \frac{(x_1 - y_1)T\left[n^l\left(\frac{ds^l}{dT}\right)_P + n^g\left(\frac{ds^g}{dT}\right)_P\right]}{n^l\left(\frac{dx_1}{dT}\right)_P + n^g\left(\frac{dy_1}{dT}\right)_P} \tag{7.35}$$

Exercise

Repeat the arguments above to obtain the direct and indirect terms for evaporation at constant temperature. The direct, the analogue of (7.29) is

$$\text{direct} = \frac{-n^l T\left(\frac{dx_1}{dT}\right)_P [y_1\,\Delta v_1 + y_2\,\Delta v_2] - n^g T\left(\frac{dy_1}{dT}\right)_P [x_1\,\Delta v_1 + x_2\,\Delta v_2]}{n^l\left(\frac{dx_1}{dP}\right)_T + n^g\left(\frac{dy_1}{dP}\right)_T} \tag{7.36}$$

and the indirect, the analogue of (7.31) and (7.32) is

$$\text{indirect} = \frac{-(x_1 - y_1)T\left[n^l\left(\frac{\partial v^l}{\partial T}\right)_{P,x} + n^g\left(\frac{\partial v^g}{\partial T}\right)_{P,y}\right]}{n^l\left(\frac{dx_1}{dP}\right)_T + n^g\left(\frac{dy_1}{dP}\right)_T} \tag{7.37}$$

The sum of the two terms can now be expressed in the form of (7.35), but with isobaric temperature derivatives replaced by isothermal pressure derivatives. This is more usefully written in terms of volume by using Maxwell's relations between the partial derivatives $(\partial s^l/\partial P)_{T,x} = (\partial v^l/\partial T)_{P,x}$ etc. The result is, for the total differential latent heat at constant temperature

$$
\text{total} = \frac{-T\,\Delta v\left[n^{l}\left(\dfrac{dx_{1}}{dT}\right)_{P} + n^{g}\left(\dfrac{dy_{1}}{dT}\right)_{P}\right] - (x_{1}-y_{1})T\left[n^{l}\left(\dfrac{dv^{l}}{dT}\right)_{P} + n^{g}\left(\dfrac{dv^{g}}{dT}\right)_{P}\right]}{n^{l}\left(\dfrac{dx_{1}}{dP}\right)_{T} + n^{g}\left(\dfrac{dy_{1}}{dP}\right)_{T}}
\tag{7.38}
$$

It is clear, both from the individual terms (7.36) and (7.37), and from their sum (7.38) in which all derivatives are along the equilibrium surfaces, that the isothermal latent heat can be expressed solely in terms of readily accessible mechanical properties.

The isobaric heat, (7.30)+(7.32), or (7.35) is that to be used for the evaporation of a liquid in a conventional distillation column. The isothermal, (7.36)+(7.37), or (7.38), is that for the pipe-still of the petroleum industry where the fluid is pumped into a hot pipe and evaporates under approximately isothermal conditions[7]. A third important quantity is the differential throttling latent heat at constant temperature. Here the two-phase system expands through a throttle, evaporates in part and is heated back to its original temperature. It is the two-component two-phase version of the isothermal Joule-Thomson coefficient of Section 3.17, and is the latent heat appropriate to the evaporation of a partially liquefied mixture of oxygen and nitrogen, cf. (7.50). The heat absorbed is the change of enthalpy and can be calculated from the reversible heat $T(dS/dn)_{T}$;

$$
\left(\frac{dH}{dn}\right)_{T} = T\left(\frac{dS}{dn}\right)_{T} + V\left(\frac{dP}{dn}\right)_{T}
\tag{7.39}
$$

where the first term on the right is the sum of (7.36) and (7.37). (No terms of the form $\mu_{i}\,dn_{i}$ are needed in (7.39) since, unlike the case considered in (6.20) we have a closed system of fixed amount of each component. The differential dn is an internal change in the amount of substance within one of the phases and not an addition of material to the system.) The second term on the right of (7.39) can be added to (7.37) to give for the whole of the indirect term

$$
\text{indirect} = \frac{(x_{1}-y_{1})\left[n^{l}\left\{v^{l} - T\left(\dfrac{\partial v^{l}}{\partial T}\right)_{P,x}\right\} + n^{g}\left\{v^{g} - T\left(\dfrac{\partial v^{g}}{\partial T}\right)_{P,y}\right\}\right]}{n^{l}\left(\dfrac{dx_{1}}{dP}\right)_{T} + n^{g}\left(\dfrac{dy_{1}}{dP}\right)_{T}}
\tag{7.40}
$$

Since this is again an isothermal latent heat, both direct and indirect terms, (7.36) and (7.40) can be expressed solely in terms of mechanical properties. Their sum, the analogue of (7.38), is the total differential throttling latent heat at constant temperature

$$
\text{total} = \Delta h + \frac{(x_{1}-y_{1})\left[n^{l}\left(\dfrac{dh^{l}}{dP}\right)_{T} + n^{g}\left(\dfrac{dh^{g}}{dP}\right)_{T}\right]}{n^{l}\left(\dfrac{dx_{1}}{dP}\right)_{T} + n^{g}\left(\dfrac{dy_{1}}{dP}\right)_{T}}
\tag{7.41}
$$

A fourth, but less important heat is the throttling heat $(dH/dn)_P$ which, from the fundamental equation for dH (3.74) is equal to the isobaric reversible heat

$$\left(\frac{dH}{dn}\right)_P = T\left(\frac{dS}{dn}\right)_P \tag{7.42}$$

Many discussions of the latent heats of evaporation ignore the indirect terms, and call the direct the differential heats. This is misleading since the differential isobaric and isothermal step implied by the first term of (7.28) is not an equilibrium change, and so cannot be repeated indefinitely until a non-zero amount of material has evaporated. Hence it is not properly a differential heat since it cannot be integrated with respect to dn; as the evaporation proceeds the temperature changes. It is also common for there to be confusion between derivatives along the gas and liquid surfaces, $(d/dT)_P$ etc. in the notation of this chapter, and the partial derivatives $(\partial/\partial T)_{P,x}$ etc. (cf. 7.33).

The indirect heats are small for mixtures of components of similar volatility, but cannot usually be neglected. Figure 7.8 shows the differential reversible heats for the evaporation of an equimolar mixture of carbon dioxide + propene at $0\,°C$, calculated from (7.36) and (7.37).[6]

The isobaric heat of evaporation of an equimolar mixture of oxygen (1) and nitrogen (2) at a pressure of 1 bar can be calculated from Din's measurements[8] of P, T, x and y. At the bubble point $T = 81.5$ K, $x_1 = 0.50$, $y_1 = 0.20$, $(dx_1/dT)_P = 0.0011$ K^{-1}, $(dP/dT)_x = 0.110$ bar K^{-1}; and at the dew point $T = 85.8$ K, $x_1 = 0.80$, $y_1 = 0.50$, $(dy_1/dT)_P = 0.090$ K^{-1}, $(dP/dT)_y = 0.111$ bar K^{-1}. For simplicity, let us assume[9] that $\Delta v_1 = \Delta v_2 = RT/P$, and that $c_P^g = 5R/2 = 21$ J K^{-1} mol^{-1}, $c_P^l = (54x_1 + 58x_2)$ J K^{-1} mol^{-1}. These figures give for the isobaric differential latent heats, (7.30) and (7.32),

direct	bubble point	6000 J mol^{-1}	dew point	6730 J mol^{-1}
indirect		180 J mol^{-1}		110 J mol^{-1}
total		6180 J mol^{-1}		6840 J mol^{-1}

No great accuracy is claimed for these figures, but they show the relative magnitudes of the terms at low pressure. They may be compared with the latent heats of the pure substances which are $\Delta h_1^o = 7120$ J mol^{-1} and $\Delta h_2^o = 5500$ J mol^{-1} at 80 K, and $\Delta h_1^o = 6980$ J mol^{-1} and $\Delta h_2^o = 5350$ J mol^{-1} at 85 K. As in Figure 7.8 the latent heat of the mixture at the dew point, when the last drop of liquid is rich in the less volatile component, is close to the latent heat of that component in its pure state[10].

The total differential latent heats (direct + indirect) can be integrated between bubble and dew points to give the corresponding integral heats. Thus, if we start with n^b moles in the saturated liquid state (where the superscript b denotes the *bubble point*) then the four molar integral heats which

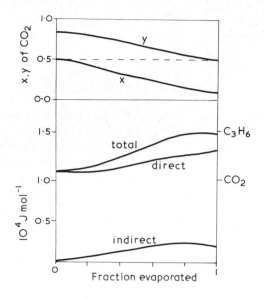

Figure 7.8. The mole fraction of liquid and vapour, and the differential reversible heats of evaporation for an equimolar mixture of carbon dioxide and propene at 0 °C. The markers on the right show the latent heat of evaporation of the pure components

correspond to the differential heats above are:

isobaric

$$\frac{1}{n^b}\int_0^{n^b} T\left(\frac{dS}{dn}\right)_P dn = \frac{1}{n^b}\int_0^{n^b}\left(\frac{dH}{dn}\right)_P dn \qquad (7.43)$$

isothermal

$$\frac{T}{n^b}\int_0^{n^b}\left(\frac{dS}{dn}\right)_T dn; \qquad \frac{1}{n^b}\int_0^{n^b}\left(\frac{dH}{dn}\right)_T dn \qquad (7.44)$$

Thus the first of the isothermal heats, from the area under the *total* curve in Figure 7.8 is $13\,510\,J\,mol^{-1}$. The three integral heats are, respectively

$$x_1^b\,\Delta h_1(x^b, P) + x_2^b\,\Delta h_2(x^b, P)$$
$$x_1^b T\,\Delta s_1(x^b, T) + x_2^b T\,\Delta s_2(x^b, T) \qquad (7.45)$$
$$x_1^b\,\Delta h_1(x^b, T) + x_2^b\,\Delta h_2(x^b, T)$$

where the differences Δh_1 etc. are between vapour and liquid at fixed composition x^b and at fixed pressure P. That is if the liquid mixture of composition x^b is completely evaporated isobarically, $\Delta h_1(x^b, P)$ is the difference between h_1 in the final (gaseous) and initial (liquid) states of the system. These differences are not the same as the equilibrium differences of (7.26)–(7.41). In general, integral heats must be found by graphical or numerical integration of (7.43) and (7.44), since there are scarcely any calorimetric values.

Exercise

In the following simple isothermal case, the integrations can be made analytically. We have amount n^b composition (x_1^b, x_2^b), of an ideal liquid mixture of negligible volume, initially at its bubble point in equilibrium with the vapour, which is a perfect gas mixture. The bubble and dew point pressures are, respectively,

$$P^b = x_1^b P_1^\circ + x_2^b P_2^\circ \qquad P^d = P_1^\circ P_2^\circ (P_1^\circ + P_2^\circ - P^b)^{-1} \qquad (7.46)$$

The amount evaporated, n, is related to the pressure by

$$n = n^b P(P - P^b)(P - P_1^\circ)^{-1}(P - P_2^\circ)^{-1} \qquad (7.47)$$

where $P^b \geqslant P \geqslant P^d$. Let the zero of enthalpy of each substance be the pure saturated vapour, so that $h_1^g = h_2^g = 0$, $h_1^l = -\Delta h_1^\circ$, $h_2^l = -\Delta h_2^\circ$.

The isothermal reversible heat can now be found by writing (7.36) and (7.37) as explicit functions of P, and changing the first integral of (7.44) to $(dS/dn)_T (dn/dP)_T \, dP$. Show that the integral heat so obtained is

$$x_1^b T[\Delta s_1^\circ + R \ln (P_1^\circ/P^d)] + x_2^b T[\Delta s_2^\circ + R \ln (P_2^\circ/P^d)] \qquad (7.48)$$

where the terms in Δs_1° and Δs_2° come from the direct term (7.36) and the logarithms from the indirect term (7.37). Show further that (7.48) is equal to the second line of (7.45).

The isothermal throttling heat is the sum of (7.36) and (7.40). Show that the latter is zero for this idealised case, and hence that the integral throttling heat is here

$$x_1^b T \, \Delta s_1^\circ + x_2^b T \, \Delta s_2^\circ = x_1^b \, \Delta h_1^\circ + x_2^b \, \Delta h_2^\circ \qquad (7.49)$$

Show that the second form of (7.49) is obtained directly by integrating both parts of (7.41), and is equal to the third line of (7.45).

If this idealised case is applied to an equimolar mixture of liquid oxygen + nitrogen at 90 K, then the sources cited above (Din,[8] Rowlinson[9]) give 5150 J mol^{-1} for the integral isothermal throttling heat (and hence here for the integral of the direct term of the isothermal reversible heat), and 5270 J mol^{-1} for the whole of the isothermal reversible heat.

The Joule-Thomson coefficient for the isenthalpic expansion, and hence evaporation, governs the cooling obtained when a mixture of oxygen and nitrogen expands through the throttle of a Linde cycle (see Section 5.19). It can be calculated from four of the functions obtained above

$$\left(\frac{dT}{dP}\right)_H = -\frac{(dH/dP)_T}{(dH/dT)_P} = -\frac{(dH/dn)_T(dT/dn)_P}{(dH/dn)_P(dP/dn)_T} \qquad (7.50)$$

The slope of an isenthalp in the two-phase region of a (T, S) chart can be obtained at once from (7.50) by using the fundamental equation for dH (3.74) for a fluid of fixed overall composition.

$$\left(\frac{\partial T}{\partial S}\right)_H = -\frac{T}{V}\left(\frac{\partial T}{\partial P}\right)_H \tag{7.51}$$

For a pure substance in the two-phase region the derivative $(\partial T/\partial P)_H$ is the reciprocal of the slope of the vapour-pressure line, (dT/dP). For a mixture, the right-hand side can be calculated from (7.23) and its isothermal equivalent, $(dP/dn)_T$, and from (7.39) and (7.42).

The equations above enable the latent heats to be calculated from a knowledge of the gas and liquid surfaces as functions of temperature, pressure and composition, and from auxiliary measurements (or estimates) of densities and heat capacities. This information can be combined with that of the enthalpy and entropy of the homogeneous liquid and gaseous phases to produce charts of h and s as functions of composition at constant pressure. Cross-plotting then gives the isobaric (h, s) chart. These charts play a similar role in the analysis of the thermodynamics of separation to that of (T, s) charts in refrigeration. They are discussed most fully by Bosnjakovic, in a book in which they are applied to almost every aspect of chemical engineering[11]. In this section we restrict our attention to the liquid-vapour equilibrium, an aspect of the use of these charts discussed more fully by Ruhemann[12], and Strickland-Constable[13], whose accounts are followed here.

Figure 7.9 is a sketch of the isobaric (h, x) graph, both as a perspective drawing and in projection on a plane of fixed temperature. Isotherms are shown in each, two of which are for temperatures between the boiling points of the two components. These isotherms connect the dew and bubble points lines by straight lines whose projections on the base of the perspective drawing (plane of constant h) are the familiar tie lines of Figures 7.5 and 7.6.

The integral latent heats fix the spacing of the gas and liquid surfaces on lines of fixed composition. The zero of enthalpy can be chosen independently for each substance and here is conventionally taken to lie in the undercooled liquid for both components. These heats, together with the boiling point diagram Figure 7.6, fix the positions of the dew and bubble point lines and the tie lines connecting them. The enthalpy of the homogeneous gas and liquid phases can be found from calorimetric measurements and from P, V, T measurements, as described in Chapter 4. If the pressure is low the gas isotherms are close to straight lines (i.e. $h^E = 0$ in the gas phase). The independence of the two chosen zeros of enthalpy means that the vertical spacing between two points on a (h, x) chart represents a true difference Δh, that is one which is, in principle, experimentally measurable, only if the two points have the same composition. Nevertheless, enthalpy (and entropy) differences read from such charts and used in expressions of the kind derived above, or in the constructions described below, are all independent of the

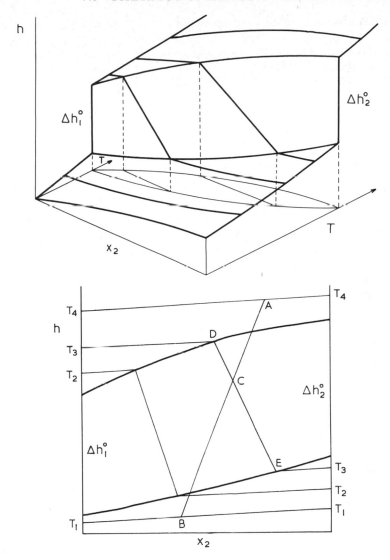

Figure 7.9. The isobaric (h, x) graph. The upper sketch shows the (h, x, T) surface and its projection on the (x, T) plane. The lower is the projection on the (h, x) plane

choices of zero; that is, all differences of experimental significance are unchanged if an (h, x) chart is transferred to a new set of coordinates such that a term of the kind $(k_1x_1 + k_2x_2)$ is added to each $h(x)$, where k_1 and k_2 are independent of temperature, pressure and composition. Thus in (7.41) a change of zeros of enthalpy would change the numerical value of Δh, but it also changes the second term in such a way that the whole quantity is unaltered. Similar arguments apply to the entropy difference in (7.35).

The construction which is of most use on a (h, x) chart is the lever rule (Figure 7.9), which is also invariant to linear changes of coordinates of the kind just described. If we have amount n^A in state A (that is, h^A, x^A, T^A) and n^B in state B (h^B, x^B, T^B), then properties of the two states *jointly* (the word is defined below) are those of state C, where

$$n^A x_1^A + n^B x_1^B = n^C x_1^C$$

$$n^A x_2^A + n^B x_2^B = n^C x_2^C \qquad (7.52)$$

$$n^A h^A + n^B h^B = n^C h^C$$

The first two of these equations can be added to give $n^A + n^B = n^C$. Hence state C is represented on the (h, x) chart by a point on the line AB such that $AC/CB = n^B/n^A$. It remains to define the word *jointly*. It can mean either that the state C is merely a formal representation of the sum of the properties of the separate states, or it can mean that A and B are mixed adiabatically at fixed pressure and that C represents the properties of the new state. Both interpretations are used below. The second rests on the thermodynamic fact that a process which is adiabatic and isobaric is one in which enthalpy is conserved (First Law). Thus, in Figure 7.9, if amount n^A at state A is mixed adiabatically with n^B at state B, the result is a mixture at state C (by the second interpretation). Since C is on a tie-line it represents (by the first interpretation) n^D in state D and n^E in state E, where n^D and n^E can again be found by the lever rule.

We now consider the use of these charts to calculate some of the thermodynamic information needed to design columns for rectification and stripping, which, for simplicity, are assumed to be adiabatic and to operate at constant pressure.

The lever rule can be applied either to a column or process as a whole, or to each individual step. As a simple example of the first consider the calculation of the minimum refrigeration needed to separate a gas mixture into its two liquid components. If the gas at room temperature and pressure is at state A and the liquids at B and C (Figure 7.10), then the heat to be removed is

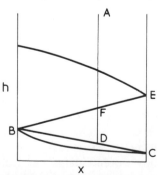

Figure 7.10. The minimum refrigeration effect needed to separate gas at A into liquids B and C, or into liquid B and gas E

represented by AD. If we were content to have the second component as a gas E then the minimum refrigeration would fall to AF.

Figure 7.11 shows a column operating in a steady state with a feed point between plates 0 and 1. The plates are given positive numbers in the rectifying section and negative in the stripping section. Let $(\dot{n}_1^g)_i$ be the rate of flow of component 1 into the gas phase above plate i in the rectifying section,

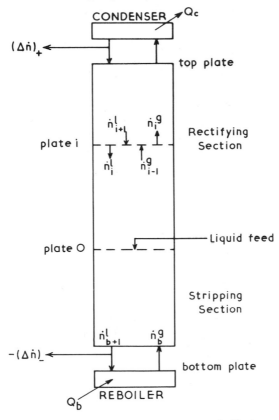

Figure 7.11. The flows of gas and liquid in a distillation column

and let $(\dot{n}_1^l)_{i+1}$ be the rate of return of liquid to this plate from the one above. In a steady state

$$(\dot{n}_1^l)_{i+1} - (\dot{n}_1^g)_i - (\dot{n}_1^l)_i + (\dot{n}_1^g)_{i-1} = 0 \qquad (7.53)$$

or

$$[(\dot{n}_1^g)_i - (\dot{n}_1^l)_{i+1}] = [(\dot{n}_1^g)_{i-1} - (\dot{n}_1^l)_i] = \text{constant} \qquad (7.54)$$

since if this difference is the same for two neighbouring plates it is the same for all plates in the rectifying section. (7.54) can be written

$$(x_1^g \dot{n}^g)_i - (x_1^l \dot{n}^l)_{i+1} = (\Delta \dot{n}_1)_+ = x_1 (\Delta \dot{n})_+ \qquad (7.55)$$

where $(\Delta n_1)_+$ and $(\Delta n_2)_+$ are constants for this (positive) section of the column, known as the *net stream* of each component, and their sum $(\Delta n)_+$ is the net stream of the mixture as a whole of composition (x_1, x_2). Since these equations apply to all plates they apply also to the condenser, so that $(x_1^g \dot{n}^g)_t$ enters it as vapour, $(x_1^l \dot{n}^l)_{t+1}$ is returned as reflux to the *top* plate, and $x_1(\Delta \dot{n})_+$ emerges as product; and similarly for the second component.

By similar reasoning the enthalpy balance on each plate in an adiabatic column gives

$$(h^g \dot{n}^g)_i - (h^l \dot{n}^l)_{i+1} = h(\Delta \dot{n})_+ \qquad \text{(for all } i\text{)} \qquad (7.56)$$

where h is an enthalpy defined by this equation which can be called the molar enthalpy of the net stream. A comparison of (7.55) and (7.56) with (7.52) shows that the equations for the net stream satisfy the lever rule. Hence, in Figure 7.12 the point $h(x_1)$ is common to all plates and is the intersection of the lines connecting $(h^g)_i$ and $(h^l)_{i+1}$.

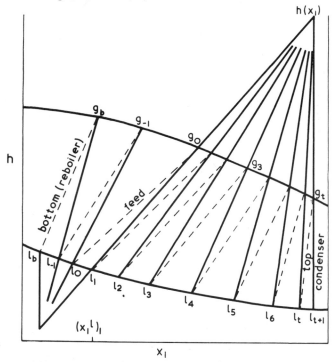

Figure 7.12. The enthalpies of gas and liquid phase in a column

If the second component is also to be obtained pure then the stripping section must be used. The same arguments lead to the calculation of the properties of the net stream withdrawn as liquid product and of the amount of material returned to the column by the reboiler where $(\Delta \dot{n})_-$ of (7.55) is negative for this section. The rate of feed is, of course, the sum of the net streams leaving as gas and liquid products. The line joining the enthalpies of the net streams passes through that of the feed, and relates the ratio of reflux to product at the top of the column to the heat to be removed from the condenser and to be supplied to the reboiler. Thus in Figure 7.12 the reflux ratio $R (R = \dot{n}^l_{t+1}/(\Delta \dot{n})_+)$ is equal to $(h - h^g_t)(h^g_t - h^l_{t+1})^{-1}$ and the heat removed from the condenser Q_c is $(\Delta \dot{n})_+(h - h^l_{t+1})$ or $(R+1)(\Delta \dot{n})_+(h^g_t - h^l_{t+1})$.

If we know the composition of the liquid feed $(x^l_1)_1$, the specified purity of the products, that is, x_1 of the net streams, and either the reflux ratio or the heat supplied to the re-boiler or that withdrawn from the condenser, then we have sufficient information to calculate the number of plates needed and the enthalpy of the net stream. This is shown in Figure 7.12 where the insertion of a lattice of tie lines joining $(h^g)_i$ and $(h^l)_i$, the straight *operating lines* joining $(h^g)_i$, $(h^l)_{i+1}$ and h of the net stream, complete the graphical representation of a rectifying column. Seven rectifying and two stripping plates are needed here to effect the required separation. It is usual for both product streams to be liquid, for the condenser to operate at total reflux, but for the re-boiler to act as a bottom plate and so effect a separation. This difference accounts for the lack of symmetry in the two end sections in Figure 7.12.

Such columns are used for separating substances whose boiling points are above ambient, when heat can be supplied and removed independently and without doing work. In the fractionation of air this is not so. If the column is to produce gaseous nitrogen of high purity at the top, then the temperature there must be that of the boiling point of pure nitrogen. The most convenient coolant is the liquid oxygen, but this boils at a higher temperature than nitrogen, a difficulty which led to the development of the double Linde column, in which one section is at a pressure of about 5 bar. At this pressure the boiling point of nitrogen is about 94 K and so the condenser can be cooled with liquid oxygen at 1 bar, whose boiling point is 90 K.

So far we have considered only balance of material and of enthalpy. If we wish to calculate the work needed to achieve a given separation of, for example, liquefied gases, then we must consider also the entropy changes. From the First Law, the net work (that is, excluding work done by or on the atmosphere) is

$$W = \Delta H - Q \tag{7.57}$$

where ΔH is the difference of enthalpy between the separated substances and the original mixture, and Q is the heat supplied from the surroundings. If S is the entropy of the plant and its contents, and S_0 that of the surroundings; then

$$\Delta S + \Delta S_0 \geq 0 \tag{7.58}$$

If the heat from the surroundings is supplied reversibly $\Delta S_0 = -Q/T_0$ where T_0 is the ambient temperature. Hence, if there are no irreversible steps in the plant $\Delta S_{rev} = Q/T_0$ is the difference of entropy between the separated substances and the original mixture, and so the minimum or reversible work of separation is

$$W_{rev} = \Delta H - T_0 \, \Delta S_{rev} \tag{7.59}$$

This expression is general; it is not restricted to separation by distillation for it is an example of availability (Section 3.25). If the whole process is carried out at ambient temperature (as, for example, is approximately the case for separation by gaseous effusion through a membrane) then the reversible work is just the change in free energy $W_{rev} = \Delta G$.

Thus to separate isothermally an ideal C-component mixture (see Section 6.5) containing amount n_i of species i into C samples (not necessarily pure), each of total amount n_i' and containing amount n_{ij}' of species j, requires a minimum expenditure of work of

$$W_{rev}/RT = \sum_i^C \sum_j^C n_{ij}' \ln\left(\frac{n_{ij}'}{n_i'}\right) - \sum_i^C n_i \ln\left(\frac{n_i}{n}\right) \tag{7.60}$$

where

$$\sum_j^C n_{ij}' = n_i' \qquad \sum_i^C n_i' = \sum_i^C n_i = n \tag{7.61}$$

Complete separation of 2 moles of an equimolar binary mixture at 300 K ($n = 2$ mol; $n_1 = n_2 = n_1' = n_2' = n_{11}' = n_{22}' = 1$ mol; $n_{12}' = n_{21}' = 0$ mol) needs a minimum work of 3458 J. This falls to 2467 J if we are content with 95% purity ($n_{11}' = n_{22}' = 0.95$ mol; $n_{12}' = n_{21}' = 0.05$ mol); that is, we pay heavily for the removal of the last traces of impurity.

We have seen, in Section 3.26, that reversible processes in a system of one component require that there is contact only between streams of equal temperature. If, as here, there is direct contact between the phases rather than the indirect contact through the walls of a heat exchanger, then there must also be equality of pressure. In a mixture we must add the condition of equality of the chemical potential, or fugacity, of each component. This is clearly unattainable in practice. Just as a heat exchanger of economic size has non-zero differences of temperature between the streams, so a distillation column must have non-zero differences of fugacity between gas and liquid if there is to be substantial transfer of material in a column of finite size. Hence, from (7.58) we write

$$\Delta S = Q/T_0 + \Delta S_{irr} \tag{7.62}$$

and

$$W = W_{rev} + T_0 \, \Delta S_{irr} \tag{7.63}$$

The irreversible increase of entropy that accompanies the separation in a column can be calculated by combining the (h, x) chart of Figure 7.12 with an (h, s) chart. The lever rule can be used to calculate the properties of a *joint* state on the latter diagram only if we restrict ourselves to the first of the two interpretations of this word given on page 364. The entropies of two states are, in general, additive only if the two do not interact by exchange of heat or by mixing. If, on an (h, s) chart we join two pairs of coexistent points (say l_2 and g_2 on Figure 7.12) and produce each line to a point which represents h of the net stream, then these points will be separated by a distance ΔS_{irr}, which is the increase in entropy that accompanies this step in the operation of the column.

This section has shown the importance of the latent heats of evaporation in studying the thermodynamics of distillation. The size of the latent heats and the disposition of the tie-lines determine the principal features of the (h, x) and (s, x) charts, and hence, by cross-plotting of the (h, s) charts. From these charts we can calculate the essential heat and work requirements for an insulated column composed of theoretically perfect plates in which the gas and liquid streams come to local equilibrium.

7.7 Two components: gas-liquid critical points

The vapour pressure lines of pure liquids end at critical points and so it is to be expected that the same phenomenon will occur in a liquid mixture. This is so, but these critical points, although physically similar to those of single component systems, are governed by quite different thermodynamic considerations. The critical point in a single component system is a point of limiting mechanical instability (Section 4.12). The critical point in a mixture is one of limiting material instability, that is, from (7.5), a point where $(\partial^2 g/\partial x^2)_{P,T}$ is zero.

Although the instabilities differ, similar methods are used to describe the two kinds of critical point. This is best seen by comparing Figure 4.11b for a as a function of v at fixed T, with Figure 7.7 for g as a function of x at fixed P and T. The classical equations that define the critical point in a system of one component are (4.26), which, when written in terms of the Helmholtz free energy, are

$$(\partial^2 A/\partial V^2)_T = 0 \qquad (\partial^3 A/\partial V^3)_T = 0 \qquad (\partial^4 A/\partial V^4)_T > 0 \qquad (7.64)$$

For a two-component system the corresponding equations can be obtained from Figure 7.7 by exactly the same arguments as those used in Section 4.12. They are

$$(\partial^2 g/\partial x^2)_{P,T} = 0 \qquad (\partial^3 g/\partial x^3)_{P,T} = 0 \qquad (\partial^4 g/\partial x^4)_{P,T} > 0 \qquad (7.65)$$

Again the fourth derivative must be positive if the second is to be positive and non-zero everywhere except at the critical point itself.

The current concern about the exact nature of the zero of $(\partial^2 A/\partial V^2)_T$ for the system of one component, which was discussed in Section 4.14 has given rise to equal concern about the zero of $(\partial^2 g/\partial x^2)_{P,T}$ for a binary mixture. However, less is known about the behaviour of mixtures and so we retain here the classical analysis based on (7.65) but with reservations similar to those made previously.

The numerators and denominators of (7.13) and (7.14) each contain terms of the order of Δx_2, that is terms proportional to a variable which may, with a certain lack of precision, be called the difference in properties between gas and liquid phases. Such terms vanish at the critical point since this is defined as the point at which the phases become identical. However, in addition to these terms, the numerators contain also the factors g_{2x} or g_{2y}, which also become zero at the critical point. Hence it follows that $(dT/dx)_P$ and $(dT/dy)_P$ are themselves zero, as is shown in the second of the diagrams in Figure 7.5. The dew and bubble point curves meet at an extremum (in this case a minimum) of the (T, x) and (T, y) loop. From (7.16) and (7.17) we can show, by the same argument, that the derivatives $(dP/dx)_T$ and $(dP/dy)_T$ are also zero at the critical point, as is shown in the first diagram of Figure 7.5. A third derivative $(dP/dT)_x$ is related to the first and second kinds by the identity

$$\left(\frac{dP}{dT}\right)_x \left(\frac{dT}{dx}\right)_P \left(\frac{dx}{dP}\right)_T = -1 \tag{7.66}$$

and, in general, is finite and non-zero at the critical point, as is shown in the third diagram. The critical locus is there not the locus of the extrema of the loops, but forms their envelope.*

The rounded ends of the (P, x), (T, x) and (P, T) loops of Figure 7.5 are a natural and inevitable consequence of the incipient breakdown of material stability at the critical point, as expressed by the conditions (7.65). They lead, however, to experimental behaviour which is, at first sight, somewhat unexpected.

Consider the (P, T) loop at fixed composition, shown in more detail in Figure 7.13. The heavy line shows the dew and bubble point curves which meet at the critical point. The lighter lines show the relative amount of substance in the gas state, that is the quality (Section 4.5). An isothermal path across this tongue at low temperatures leads to the usual processes of condensation (increasing P) and evaporation (decreasing P), in which the fraction of the system in the liquid state rises, or falls, monotonically, from zero to one, or vice versa. Similarly, an isobaric path results in the usual processes of evaporation (increasing T) and condensation (decreasing T). Consider, however, an isothermal compression, AB, at a temperature between that of the critical point, T^c, and the point T^m, which is the maximum temperature of the dew point line. The compressed gas starts to condense where AB cuts the dew point curve, the amount of liquid increases until about 1/4 of the system has been condensed, and then falls to zero again as the line

---

* The arguments used in this paragraph are correct in their conclusions. They are not, however, entirely rigorous since they include no analysis of the orders of the various zeros. They can be made more precise, at the cost of greater length, and still within the limitations of the classical picture, by consideration not of the Gibbs free energy as a function of P and x, but of the Helmholtz free energy as a function of v and x, see e.g. J. S. Rowlinson, *Liquids and Liquid Mixtures*, 2nd edn, Butterworth, London, 1969, Chapter 6.

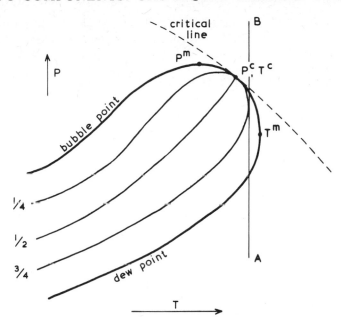

Figure 7.13. The (P, T) loop near the gas-liquid critical point of a binary mixture

leaves the two-phase region at a second dew point. Hence we have here a system in which an increase of pressure leads to evaporation of the liquid, or, conversely, where a decrease produces condensation. A similarly 'unnatural' process occurs on heating or cooling the system at constant pressure if this pressure lies between P^c and P^m. These unusual processes of condensation and evaporation are given the collective name of *retrograde condensation*.

These phenomena are observed in substantial regions of the P, T graph only if the liquid-vapour tongue is wide so that P^m is not close to P^c, nor T^m to T^c. These points of maximum pressure and temperature are generally called the *cricondenbar* and *cricondentherm* respectively. Mixtures of liquids of similar volatility (e.g. normal and isobutane) have a small separation of dew and bubble point curves and so have small regions of retrograde condensation. Mixtures of substances of very different volatility (e.g. methane and butane) have a wide separation, and so much wider retrograde regions. Since methane is an important constituent of natural gas and of many petroleum-bearing strata, the phenomenon is commonly encountered in the handling and compression of natural gas.

Exercise

The critical point does not necessarily lie between P^m and T^m, as is clear from the curves shown in Figure 7.5. Sketch the curves equivalent to those shown in Figure 7.13 for the two cases of (a) the critical point lying at a temperature below that of P^m, and (b) at a pressure below that of T^m.

7.8 Two components: two liquid phases

Many pairs of liquids are only partially miscible, or even so mutually insoluble as to be crudely described as *immiscible*. (There is never complete immiscibility; the logarithmic terms in the chemical potential (6.75) ensure that, however large G^E, the addition of the first trace of any solute reduces the Gibbs free energy of the mixture.). A system of two components and of two liquid and one gaseous phase has one degree of freedom. Hence, it has a well-defined vapour pressure at given temperature, and boils at a fixed temperature at a given pressure. It is represented on a (P, T) graph by a line, since the dew and bubble point pressures are the same although the compositions of all three fluid phases are different. These results are shown in Figure 7.14 for a pair of liquids of very different volatility, e.g. aniline + n-hexane. The (P, x) and T, x sections show that the bubble point surface is interrupted by the region of liquid immiscibility, and it is a consequence of the phase rule that the three-phase line, gas + liquid + liquid, is horizontal in both sections.

The mutual miscibility of two liquids changes with temperature. It may rise or fall with increasing T, but the former is much the more common. If the solubilities of component 1 in component 2, and of 2 in 1, both increase indefinitely with temperature then clearly a point of complete miscibility must be reached. Such a point is a critical point since, as for a gas-liquid critical point, it marks a state of the system in which two phases become identical. It is called either a liquid-liquid critical point or, more usually, a *critical solution point*. If it marks the upper temperature limit of the region of two liquid phases, then its temperature is called the *upper critical solution temperature* (U.C.S.T.). That for aniline + n-hexane is at 69.1 °C at a pressure at which the two liquid phases are in equilibrium with the gas (see Figure 7.14).

Critical solution temperatures of apparently similar systems may be markedly different. Thus, that of aniline + 2,2-dimethylbutane is at 81 °C, and that of aniline + 2,3-dimethylbutane at 71 °C. This sensitivity to the structure of the hydrocarbon is the basis of the so-called *aniline point* for the characterisation of petroleum fractions. This point is the temperature at which a mixture of aniline and an equal volume of petroleum throws down a second liquid phase as the temperature is lowered.

Exercise

The curves shown in Figure 7.14 comprise two (P, x) and two (T, x) *sections* and one (P, T) *projection* of the complete (P, T, x) surface. Make a perspective sketch, similar to that in Figure 7.4, of this three-dimensional surface.

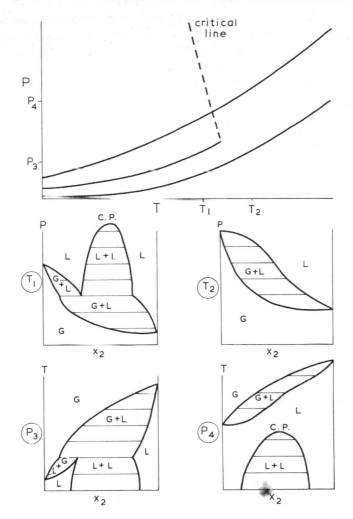

Figure 7.14. The (P, T) projection, two (P, x) and two (T, x) sections of the (P, T, x) surfaces of a binary system which has a U.C.S.T. The variables shown ringed in the four lower sketches are those held constant, and correspond with T_1, T_2, P_3 and P_4 of the top sketch

Liquids are generally immiscible if their molecules belong to widely different chemical types; e.g. paraffin hydrocarbons with lower alcohols or with polar aromatic substances such as aniline or nitrobenzene; water with most organic liquids; mercury with almost everything. The molecular reason for the immiscibility is that the energy, and hence the enthalpy, of a liquid mixture is generally lowest if the molecules are surrounded by their own kind. This tendency to separation is opposed by the tendency to mix implied by the rise in entropy consequent on mixing. This balance between enthalpic effects and entropic effects is swayed in favour of the latter by raising the temperature; the thermodynamic measure of the balance being, as always, at a given P and T, the Gibbs free energy, $G = H - TS$. Hence, miscibility generally rises with increasing T, until the system reaches its U.C.S.T.

There are, however, a few systems in which miscibility increases with decreasing temperature, and which have lower critical solution temperatures (L.C.S.T.).Water is almost always a component of such systems if the phenomenon occurs at low pressures, and the molecular explanation is that in these systems a hydrogen bond can be formed between the water and a polar group in the second component. The formation of this complex lowers the free energy, and so promotes mixing. The complex is unstable at high temperatures, and its dissociation leads to the usual immiscibility of water and an organic liquid.

Critical solution temperatures are little affected by changes of pressure, as is to be expected from the low compressibilities of liquids. Some U.C.S.T. rise with increasing pressure; others, such as aniline $+ n$-hexane, fall, as shown in Figure 7.14. All known L.C.S.T. rise with increasing pressure.

The thermodynamic discussion of gas-liquid equilibria and critical points in the last three sections is based on general criteria of equilibrium and stability, (7.6) and (7.65), and although phrased in terms of gas and liquid, is equally applicable to two liquids. Let x and y be replaced throughout by x^α and x^β, the mole fraction of a component in phase$^\alpha$ and phase$^\beta$; Figure 7.7, equations (7.9) to (7.15), and those of Section 7.7 apply now to liquid-liquid equilibrium and to critical solution points.

Since $(\partial^2 g/\partial x^2)_{P,T}$, or g_{2x} is zero at a U.C.S.T. and, to maintain stability in the homogeneous phase, positive at all higher temperatures, then its temperature derivative, $-s_{2x}$, must also be positive; and conversely at a L.C.S.T. Hence we have the following inequalities

$$
\begin{array}{llll}
\text{U.C.S.T.} & g_{2x} = 0 & s_{2x} < 0 & h_{2x} < 0 \\
\text{L.C.S.T.} & g_{2x} = 0 & s_{2x} > 0 & h_{2x} > 0
\end{array}
\tag{7.67}
$$

These second derivatives are related to those of the excess functions (6.94)–(6.97) by

$$
s_{2x}^E = s_{2x} + R/x_1 x_2 \qquad h_{2x}^E = h_{2x}
\tag{7.68}
$$

The signs of s_{2x}^E and h_{2x}^E are generally the opposite of those of s^E and h^E, (see Figure 6.5) so that we see that we have positive excess enthalpies in mixtures that exhibit U.C.S.T., whilst we have negative h^E and strongly negative s^E at L.C.S.T. These signs are confirmed by experiment and are intuitively consistent with the molecular reasoning above.

The shape of the (T, x) coexistence curve is related, via the condition of equality of chemical potential, to the detailed form of the deviations from ideality discussed in Section 6.8. Thus a knowledge of γ_1 and γ_2 or of G^E, as functions of composition and temperature implies a knowledge of the shape of the coexistence curve, although the necessary equations can only be solved numerically. The converse is not true; a knowledge of the shape of the coexistence curve is not sufficient to calculate G^E as a function of composition and temperature.

Exercise

Assume that the excess chemical potential has the simplest possible form, (6.101) and hence show that b (a function of temperature) is related to x^α and x^β the mole fractions in the two phases (also functions of temperature) by

$$b = \frac{\ln (x_2^\alpha/x_1^\alpha)}{x_2^\alpha - x_1^\alpha} = \frac{\ln (x_2^\beta/x_1^\beta)}{x_2^\beta - x_1^\beta} \qquad (7.69)$$

(The symmetry of (6.10) implies that $x_1^\alpha = x_2^\beta$, $x_1^\beta = x_2^\alpha$.) Show that (7.69) has no solution unless $b > 2$; that is, there is no immiscibility until departures from ideality are sufficiently large and positive. Show further, that for $b > 2$ the *continuous* curve of Δg as a function of x has a portion which is convex upwards, as in Figure 7.7.

Exercise

Show similarly that a polymer solution in which the free energy can be represented by the Flory-Huggins equation (6.129) is stable only if $\chi < \frac{1}{2}$, in the limiting case of polymer of infinite molecular weight. The critical solution point is then at zero volume fraction of polymer.

The formal identity of the thermodynamic description of gas-liquid and liquid-liquid critical points in binary mixtures raises the question as to whether there is always a clear physical distinction between them. In some systems there is, thus in aniline + n-hexane which has been used as an example so far in this section, there is a liquid-liquid critical point at 69.1 °C and a pressure of the order of 1 bar. Increasing the pressure lowers the temperature until the critical line is terminated by the freezing of the aniline at about -10 °C. There is also a gas-liquid critical line which connects the critical points of pure hexane (235 °C) and pure aniline (426 °C), of the kind shown in Figure 7.5. The two critical lines are quite distinct and one can be described unequivocally as liquid-liquid, and the other as gas-liquid.

There are, however, many systems in which this distinction cannot be drawn, and these include such technically important mixtures as those of paraffin hydrocarbons, and also polymer solutions. Consider the binary mixtures formed from methane and the higher alkanes. Methane: + ethane, + propane, + n-butane, + n-pentane are all quite normal; the liquids are completely miscible, and the gas-liquid critical lines resemble that in Figure 7.5. Their (P, T) projections are shown in Figure 7.15. However, with methane + n-hexane, we have a different story, Figure 7.16. The liquids are

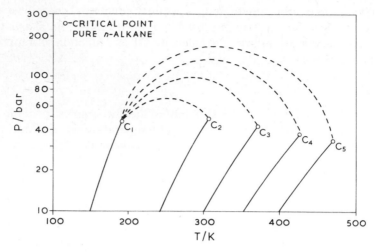

Figure 7.15. The gas liquid critical lines of the binary systems formed from methane and the normal alkanes up to pentane

completely miscible up to 183 K, which is only 7 K below the gas-liquid critical point of pure methane. At this temperature there is a L.C.S.T., that is, the liquid phase separates into two liquid phases, the critical composition being a mass fraction of hexane of 0.3. On further heating we find that there is a second critical point at about 192 K, at which the gas phase of almost pure methane becomes identical with the upper liquid layer, that is the layer poorer in hexane. Clearly, we should say, at first sight, that the first critical point is liquid-liquid and the second gas-liquid, but the situation is not as clear-cut as this, for if we add hexane to the system at the L.C.S.T. of 183 K

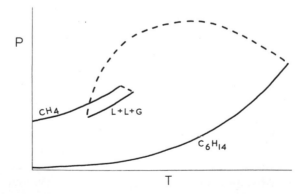

Figure 7.16. Sketch of the critical lines and the three-phase line in the system methane + n-hexane. The vapour pressures of the pure components end at critical points at 191 K and 508 K. The three-phase line is bounded by two critical solution temperatures (see text) at 183 K and 192 K

and simultaneously change the pressure and temperature so that the system stays at a critical point, we find that we move continuously along a path in (P, T, x) space which ends at the *gas-liquid* critical point of pure *n*-hexane at 508 K. A detailed study of this type of system is beyond the scope of this book, but it is one that is very widespread[14]. All *n*-alkanes above *n*-pentane are partially immiscible with methane if their liquid range extends to sufficiently low temperature. Liquid propane, which is used as a de-asphalting agent in the petroleum industry, is likewise only partially miscible with hydrocarbons in the lubricating oil range (C_{35} upwards) if the temperature is above 60 °C.

7.9 Two components: azeotropes

The general equations for liquid-vapour equilibrium are (7.13)–(7.17). In Section 7.7 we considered the limiting case when Δx_2, Δh, Δv, g_{2x} and g_{2y} all became zero at a gas-liquid critical point, and in Section 7.8 extended the argument to liquid-liquid critical points. Here we examine another important special case, that in which Δx_2 alone becomes zero. This condition is that liquid and vapour have the same composition, and hence it describes a mixture that distils unchanged. Such a system is called an *azeotrope* and clearly the existence of such systems is a serious limitation on our ability to separate these liquids by fractional distillation, for $\Delta x_2 = 0$ implies that the *K*-factors and volatility ratios α, (6.92) and (6.93) are all unity.

If follows from (7.13)–(7.17) that the condition $\Delta x_2 = 0$ leads to

$$(dT/dx_2)_P = (dT/dy_2)_P = 0 \qquad (7.70)$$

$$(dP/dx_2)_T = (dP/dy_2)_T = 0 \qquad (7.71)$$

that is, that both isobaric boiling point and isothermal vapour pressure are at extrema at the azeotropic composition. Since Δh_1, Δh_2, Δv_2 and Δv_2 are all positive, it follows that a maximum in P is associated with a minimum in T, and vice versa. This conclusion, and the equations above, are known collectively as the *Gibbs-Konowalow laws*. It is conventional to describe a system with a maximum vapour pressure and minimum boiling-point as a *positive azeotrope*, and the converse as a *negative azeotrope*; the former are much the more common (Figure 7.17).

Exercise

Sketch McCabe-Thiele plots (see Section 7.5) for systems with positive and negative azeotropes.

In many ways an azeotrope behaves as a system of one component; the condition $x_2 = y_2$ imposes a loss of one degree of freedom. The denominators of (7.13) and (7.14) are greatly simplified, since, from (7.15) with $\Delta x_2 = 0$, both are equal to Δh, the molar latent heat of evaporation of the azeotrope;

and similarly for the denominators of (7.16) and (7.17). Hence from (7.13) and (7.16)

$$\left(\frac{dP}{dT}\right)_{x,y} = \frac{dP_{az}}{dT} = \frac{\Delta h}{T \, \Delta v} \tag{7.72}$$

The first equality here follows from (7.70) and (7.71) where the derivative (dP_{az}/dT) is that along the dashed line in Figure 7.17. This equation shows that an azeotrope conforms to the simple form of Clapeyron's equation that is found usually only for systems of one component. Similarly, it follows from $\Delta x_2 = 0$ that the indirect terms in the latent heats (7.31), (7.32), (7.37), (7.40) and the second terms in (7.35), (7.41), all vanish for an azeotrope. Figure 7.18 shows that $\ln(P_{az}/\text{bar})$ is close to being a linear function of $1/T$ for the well-known azeotrope formed from ethanol and water. The second diagram shows the composition of the azeotrope as a function of temperature. It is

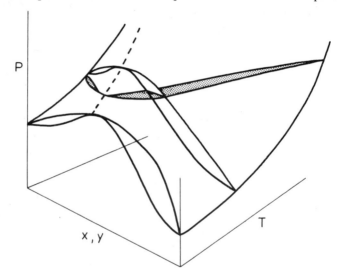

Figure 7.17. The (P, T, x) and (P, T, y) surfaces for a system with a positive azeotrope. Two isothermal sections and one isobaric section (shaded) are shown

seen that there is no azeotrope below 25 °C; that is, the dashed line in Figure 7.17 has reached the PT plane which forms the $x_{H_2O} = 0$ side of the figure. It is, of course, the existence of this prositive azeotrope which is responsible for the well-known failure to obtain pure alcohol by distillation of spirits. The best that can be achieved at atmospheric pressure is a mole fraction of ethanol of 0.9. Figure 7.18 shows that distillation below 25 °C and so at a pressure below 0.1 bar, would overcome this problem, but this leads to large volumes of vapour, and so to expensive equipment. A different method of tackling the problem is described in Section 7.11.

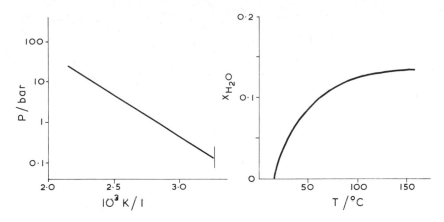

Figure 7.18. The azeotropic pressure and composition as functions of temperature in the system water + ethanol

A system which forms an azeotrope at all temperatures between the freezing of the system and its gas-liquid critical point is said to show *absolute azeotropy*. A system in which the azeotropic temperature range is bounded above or below by the disappearance of the azeotrope at $x = 0$ or $x = 1$ is said to show *limited azeotropy*. The latter is the more common behaviour. Azeotropes are formed only from pairs of liquids of similar volatility, and it is unlikely that the volatility of a pair will run parallel over the whole of this liquid range. Thus water + ethanol and water + acetone are azeotropic at high temperatures but not at low. Ethylene + carbon dioxide is azeotropic at low, but not at high. Ethane + carbon dioxide and benzene + cyclohexane show absolute azeotropy.

All the systems quoted so far are positive azeotropes, which comprise the great majority of the 16 000 binary systems listed by Horsley[15]. Negative azeotropes, that is systems of minimum vapour pressure, and hence maximum boiling point, are relatively rare. They are formed only between substances which can complex together usually through a hydrogen bond, as in chloroform + acetone.

Exercise

Show by straightforward reasoning from the shape of the (P, T, x) surface in Figure 7.17 that (1) the closer the vapour pressures of the components the more likely is azeotropy—it is inevitable if the vapour pressures are the same—(2) a positive excess free energy g^E can lead to positive azeotropy, and if g^E is symmetrical in composition the azeotrope is richer in the component of higher vapour pressure, and (3) for a positive azeotrope an increase in temperature increases the mole fraction of the component whose vapour pressure increases most rapidly with temperature.

If two liquid phases are present the dew- and bubble-point surfaces are cut by the liquid-liquid surface. This is shown in Figure 7.14 for non-azeotropic* systems. The corresponding (T, x) section for a positive azeotropic system is shown in Figure 7.19. The composition of the gas phase now lies between those of the coexistent liquid phases, whereas in Figure 7.14, it lies outside them. Hence, fractional distillation of the type of Figure 7.14 results in complete separation of the components, but fractional distillation of the type shown in Figure 7.19 leads to a mixture of the composition of the gas point on the three-phase line. Such a point represents, therefore, a true azeotropic system since it distils unchanged. However, the Gibbs-Konowalow laws (7.70) and (7.71) are clearly inapplicable and, to distinguish the system from the homogeneous azeotrope of Figure 7.17, it is usually called a *heterogeneous azeotrope*.

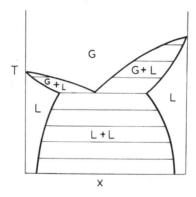

Figure 7.19. The (T, x) section at constant pressure of a binary system with a positive heterogeneous azeotrope (cf. Figure 7.14)

Exercise

Plot the McCabe-Thiele diagram for a system with a positive heterogeneous azeotrope.

Positive heterogeneous azeotropes are very common, for almost all immiscible liquids of even roughly comparable volatility show this behaviour, e.g. water + hydrocarbons, fluorocarbons + hydrocarbons and methanol + cyclohexane. Since the azeotropic composition is not the same as that at the C.S.T. it follows that such systems change to the type shown in Figure 7.14 when very close to the C.S.T.

Exercise

Figure 7.19 is equivalent to one of the five diagrams of Figure 7.14. Sketch the other four.

---

* Those who dislike the double negative may call them *zeotropic* systems, but the word is not widely used.

7.10   Two components: liquid and solid

The nature of the equilibrium between two solids and the liquid formed on melting is determined mainly by the degree of miscibility of the solids. We have here two components, one or two solid phases and (usually) one liquid phase. This is formally analogous with some of the systems already discussed in which we had two components, one or two liquid phases and a gas phase. In fact most of the phase diagrams we need can be obtained from those of earlier Sections by relabelling. This identity of topology is an example of the fact that the restrictions imposed by the Phase Rule are quite general and do not depend on whether the systems under discussion are solid, liquid or gas.

It is rare for two crystalline solids to be miscible in all proportions. This occurs only when their molecular units (atoms, molecules or ions) are so Sections by re-labelling. This identity of topology is an example of the fact appreciable distortion. The energy, and hence the free energy, of an almost rigid crystal is greatly increased by local distortions, and this increase readily leads to instability and hence immiscibility, as described for fluids in Figure 7.7. The rare examples of complete miscibility are mainly alloys, (e.g. gold + silver, bismuth + tin) and the occasional salt pair of closely similar ionic size (e.g. sodium and silver chlorides). In these systems there is a continuous rise of melting point from the first to the second component, and a pair of coexistence curves, the *liquidus* and the *solidus*, exactly analogous with the dew and bubble point curves of Section 7.5. The equations of that section describe the shapes of these curves if x and y are interpreted as mole fractions in solid and liquid, not liquid and gas. The principal physical difference is that melting temperatures, unlike boiling points, are almost independent of pressure, and so it is only the isobaric (T, x, y) section (as in the shaded cut in Figure 7.4) which is of interest. There are also miscible alloys (e.g. gold + nickel) in which the melting temperature has a minimum, and whose (T, x, y) sections have, therefore, the shape of that for a positive azeotrope, as in the shaded cut of Figure 7.17.

However, miscibility is the exception, not the rule; it is much more common for two solids to be essentially completely immiscible. The equilibrium between two immiscible solids, and one liquid, at a fixed pressure (or, which is usually equivalent, in equilibrium with the vapour) can be obtained by re-labelling Figure 7.19 and allowing the area marked L + L to expand to cover the whole of the composition range. The result is shown in the first diagram of Figure 7.20. This diagram is formed from the two curves that represent the solubility of each solid component in the mixed liquid as the temperature is lowered below its melting point. The curves meet at what is called the *eutectic point*, where we have three phases, and hence, if the pressure has been fixed, no further degree of freedom. The eutectic point at a pressure at which the system is in equilibrium with its vapour is a truly invariant state $(F = 0)$, and is called the *quadruple point*, by analogy with the

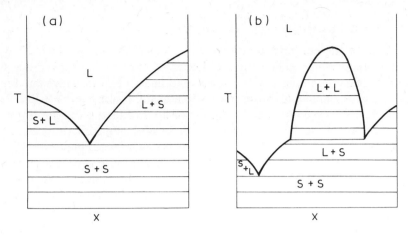

Figure 7.20. Melting diagrams or (T, x) sections for the melting of two immiscible solids to (a) one liquid and (b) to a liquid which forms two partially immiscible phases

correspondingly invariant triple point in a system of one component. A eutectic is generally a finely dispersed mixture of the two pure crystals.

Exercise

Justify the assumption made in parenthesis in the second sentence of the paragraph above.

Exercise

Zone-refining is a method of purifying solids. The impure material is cast into the form of a rod which is enclosed in a tube. By means of an external annular heater a molten zone is made to traverse the rod repeatedly from, say, left to right. After many passes it is found that the impurities have accumulated at the right-hand end. Analyse the performance of this apparatus by reference to Figure 7.20a.

The melting of immiscible solids to partially immiscible liquids leads to a diagram of the second kind shown in Figure 7.20. Notice that the eutectic is still present; it cannot be 'covered' by the region of the two liquids; it generally lies on the side of the component of lower melting point. It is scarcely necessary to quote examples of the types of behaviour shown in Figure 7.20; almost any pair of miscible organic liquids (e.g. benzene + cyclohexane) will give a diagram of the first kind, and any partially immiscible pair with a U.C.S.T. (e.g. phenol + water) a diagram of the second.

The most important variant of these simple systems is the complication of the formation of a solid compound. Consider first a system where the reaction goes essentially to completion at all compositions. Thus acetic anhydride + water react in equimolar proportions to form acetic acid. At all compositions between anhydride and pure water the system contains the acid together with whichever component is present in excess; there is no detectable dissociation of the acid to anhydride + water in the liquid state. The phase diagram for this system is shown in the first diagram of Figure 7.21, which can be regarded as a pair of diagrams, anhydride + acid and acid + water, placed alongside each other. However, most such compounds are less stable in the liquid phase, so that if A and B form compound AB, there is still some free B in the liquid, even when the overall mole fraction of A exceeds $\frac{1}{2}$. This behaviour is common with double salts (e.g. $NH_4Cl + ZnCl_2$ which form a compound with a ratio of $1:2$), with hydrates (e.g. $Mg(NO_3)_2 + H_2O$) and in

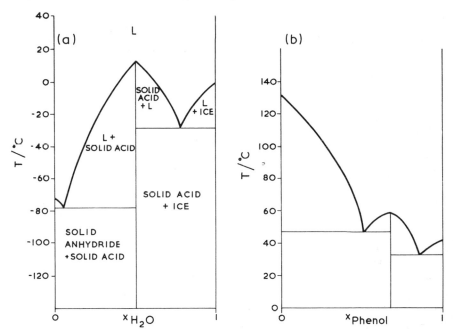

Figure 7.21. Melting diagrams for (a) the system acetic anhydride + water, and (b) for the system urea + phenol

organic compounds (e.g. the urea-phenol adduct $CO(NH_2)_2 + 2C_6H_5OH$). The last of these is shown in the second diagram of Figure 7.21, in which it can be seen that the effect of dissociation is to round the melting curve at and near the composition of the compound.

If the compound is a salt hydrate, it may dissociate before it reaches its true melting point. Such a substance is said to melt *incongruently*, and one of the best known examples, $Na_2SO_4.10\,H_2O$, is shown in Figure 7.22. The system of four phases, solid salt, solid hydrate, liquid solution and water vapour is

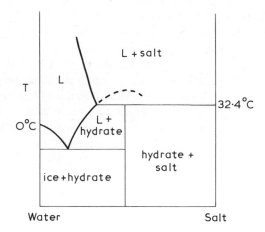

Figure 7.22. Melting diagram of the system water+sodium sulphate showing the incongruent melting of the solid $Na_2SO_4 \cdot 10\,H_2O$

invariant and its temperature, 32.4 °C has been used as a thermometric substandard. This temperature is little changed by pressure, falling only by $10^{-3}\,K\,bar^{-1}$.

Exercise

Figure 7.22 is drawn for a fixed pressure of 1 bar. Continue the sketch to a temperature of 150 °C.

7.11 Three components

For three components we have two independent composition variables, say x_2 and x_3. If we plot these in Cartesian coordinates the composition of a system is represented by a point in the right-angled triangle bounded by the two axes and the line $x_2 + x_3 = 1$. However, this representation is not symmetrical in the three components and it is more usual to use an equilateral triangle as the coordinate system, as shown in Figure 7.23. Here each apex represents a pure component, each side a binary mixture, and the body of the triangle a ternary mixture. The composition at each point is found by dropping perpendiculars to the three sides; the perpendicular joining a point to the binary mixture $i + j$ is proportional to x_k $(i, j, k = 1, 2, 3)$. This construction uses the theorem that the sum of the lengths of the three perpendiculars is a constant for all points in the triangle.

Exercise

Prove this theorem.

A straight line through an apex represents a set of compositions in which the ratio of the amounts of two of the components is fixed. Thus if we take a

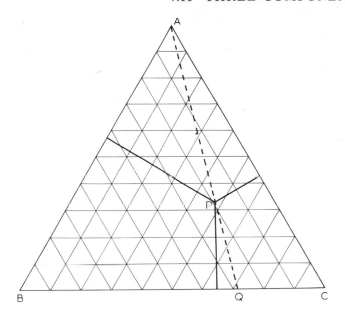

Figure 7.23. The coordinate system used to represent the composition of a ternary mixture. Point P has the composition $x_A = 0.33$, $x_B = 0.19$, $x_C = 0.48$

binary mixture of B and C at point Q ($x_B = 0.28$), and add to a fixed amount of this mixture an increasing amount of pure A, the composition follows the path QPA, and eventually approaches arbitrarily close to the apex A. Tie-lines across two-phase regions connect phases in equilibrium, as in a binary system.

With three components the number of possible phase diagrams becomes too large for systematic discussion; this account is restricted to three types of greatest importance to the chemical engineer.

1. *Equilibrium between liquid and vapour.* We cannot represent geometrically the simultaneous changes of P, T, x_2 and x_3, and even if we hold one variable constant (say fixed P) a representation of T as a function of x_2 and x_3 needs a three-dimensional figure. This is usually drawn as a triangular prism whose base is the composition diagram of Figure 7.23, and whose height is the temperature. In such a space the dew and bubble point surfaces form a pair of sheets which meet at each corner of the prism (the boiling points of the pure components) and which cut the sides of the prism in the dew and bubble point lines of the three binary systems. An azeotrope in one of the binary mixtures produces an extremum in one of the pairs of dew and bubble point lines and the two sheets touch at that point. However, such a binary extremum becomes only a valley or a ridge in the centre of the prism. This is not a true extremum, the sheets do not touch, and mixtures in a valley or on a ridge are not azeotropic, that is, they do not distil unchanged. If there are azeotropes in two or more of the binary mixtures, it is common for the resulting valleys or

ridges to meet in a true extremum, a hole or a peak, at which the dew and bubble point sheets touch, and which is, therefore, a ternary azeotrope.

If two or more of the liquids are immiscible then the surfaces become complicated, and binary and ternary hetero-azeotropes are formed. These are exploited in the technique known as *azeotropic distillation*, of which dewatering processes are the best known examples. Thus water + ethanol form a homogeneous binary positive azeotrope (boiling point 78.15 °C at 1 atm) which contains 4.43% by mass of water, and whose existence prevents pure alcohol (b.p. 78.30 °C) being obtained by fractional distillation. With benzene the system forms a heterogeneous ternary azeotrope (b.p. 64.85 °C) which contains 7.4% of water and 18.5% of alcohol. Hence on adding benzene to 95.6% alcohol, and distilling, the ternary azeotrope comes off first and takes with it all the water. The excess benzene is then removed as a binary homogeneous azeotrope with the alcohol (b.p. 68.25 °C), leaving behind a residue of pure alcohol.

2. *Equilibrium between liquid and liquid.* From three liquids we can form three binary systems, of which zero, one, two or three may be partially immiscible. The first class is of little interest. An example of the second is water + ethyl acetate + propanol, in which only the first pair are partially immiscible. The addition of propanol to the system water + ethyl acetate increases the solubility of the ester in the aqueous layer and of water in the ester layer. The increases continue until the phases become identical at a critical point sometimes called a *plait point*. This is shown in Figure 7.24 as

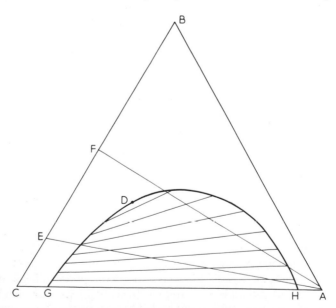

Figure 7.24. Two partially miscible liquids, A and C, are each completely miscible with B

point D, the point at which the tie lines have shrunk to zero length. The locus of the mid-points of these lines passes through D, and the plotting of this locus is the best way of determining the critical composition.

It is seen from Figure 7.24 that the addition of A to a homogeneous mixture of B and C, represented by point E, leads to a locus of compositions which cuts the two-phase 'tongue' at two points. These points lie on opposite sides of the critical point, that is, one in the phase rich in A and one in the phase rich in C. However, if we start with a mixture of B and C of composition F, then the two points of intersection lie on the same side of the critical point.

Exercise

Sketch the amounts and compositions of the two liquid phases as the composition approaches A along the two paths EA and FA, and justify, by comparison with the binary gas-liquid systems discussed in Section 7.7, the name of *retrograde solubility* for the phenomenon exhibited on the second path.

The tie lines that are close to that for the binary system GH have slopes that change linearly with increasing amounts of B, as long as this amount is small. That is, if we add a solute B to a solvent formed of two partially immiscible liquids GH, the solute distributes itself between the two phases in such a way that the ratio of the amounts in each phase is a constant, independent of the total amount of the solute, providing only that this amount is small. This result is called *Nernst's distribution law*, and the constant ratio is called the *partition coefficient*, K. The law is a simple consequence of the laws of the ideal dilute solution established in Section 6.9. The fugacities of the solute in each phase (α, β) are given by (cf. 6.104).

$$f_B^\alpha = x_B^\alpha (f_B^\dagger)^\alpha \qquad f_B^\beta = x_B^\beta (f_B^\dagger)^\beta \qquad (7.73)$$

The partition coefficient is found by equating the fugacities of the solute in each phase

$$K = x_B^\alpha / x_B^\beta = (f_B^\dagger)^\beta / (f_B^\dagger)^\alpha \qquad (7.74)$$

This ratio of standard fugacities is a function of pressure and temperature, but is independent of x_B as long as this is small. It depends also, of course, on the chemical nature of all three substances A, B and C. Nernst's law, and the expression of the partition coefficient in terms of standard fugacities (or Henry's law constants, see Section 6.9) provide the thermodynamic basis for the separation of substances by liquid-liquid extraction. The partition coefficient plays the same role as the K-value of (6.92) plays in distillation.

It must be emphasised that the partition coefficient is independent of concentration only within the range of validity of the laws of the ideal dilute solution. If the solute ionises or associates in one or both layers, then the necessary degree of dilution may be physically unattainable. However, if there is association but not ionisation, then it is often possible to apply Nernst's law to each molecular species, rather than to the solute as a whole. Thus, if we partition benzoic acid between water and a hydrocarbon we find that it is present in the aqueous layer as single molecules C_6H_5COOH (the ionisation of these molecules is negligible), but that in the hydrocarbon layer it is partially associated to dimers $(C_6H_5COOH)_2$. At equilibrium the fugacities of the monomer are the same in both layers, and so it is the ratio of mole fractions of the monomer in the two layers which is independent of concentration. The total concentration of the acid in the hydrocarbon layer can be calculated from a knowledge of the mole fraction of monomer and the chemical equilibrium constant appropriate to that environment (see next chapter). Similar arguments can be applied to weak electrolytes which dissociate partially in the aqueous layer, but not in the hydrocarbon layer.

If two or more of the liquid pairs are immiscible then the phase diagram is more complex. There may be two or three two-phase 'tongues', or two of these can merge to form a two-phase band crossing the triangle from one side to another, as in the first diagram of Figure 7.25. If all three pairs are

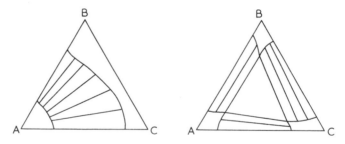

Figure 7.25. Partial immiscibility in two and three of the binary pairs of a ternary system. For example; in the first diagram A might be nitrobenzene and B and C paraffin hydrocarbons; in the second A might be nitrobenzene, B a paraffin, and C, water

immiscible it is usual for the ternary mixture to form three layers, as is shown in the second diagram of Figure 7.25. In the interior triangle of this diagram we have three phases and so, at a fixed P and T there is no further degree of freedom.

Exercise

How may the amounts of each of the three coexisting phases be calculated for a point in the interior triangle of the second diagram in Figure 7.25?

3. *Equilibrium between liquid and solid.* The range of possibilities is now so great that this chapter is brought to an end by an exercise based on one typical example.

Exercise

Complete Figure 7.26 by labelling the areas and drawing tie-lines in the appropriate ones. Use the diagram to decide what concentration of alcohol is needed in an alcohol+water solution that can be used to produce the anhydrous salt by washing the hydrate.

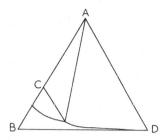

Figure 7.26. Incomplete sketch of the equilibrium between a solid anhydrous salt A, water B, a solid hydrate C, and ethanol D

Problems

1. Phenol and water are completely immiscible in the solid state and partially immiscible in the liquid. Phenol melts at 41 °C and the liquid-liquid system has an upper critical solution point at 66 °C. The normal boiling point of phenol is 182 °C and the aqueous solution forms a positive azeotrope in which the mole fraction of phenol is about 0.03. Sketch the phase diagram of this system in the solid, liquid and gaseous states at a constant pressure of 1 atm. How would the diagram at 0.1 atm differ from that at 1 atm?

2. A homogeneous mixture of 70% (molar) water and 30% of an amine boils at 1 bar at 93 °C. If distillation is allowed to proceed the mixture may be heated further until, at 16% amine, a stable boiling point is reached of 104 °C. When a mixture containing 46% amine is heated from room temperature two liquid layers appear at 62 °C. Analysis of these layers at 75 °C gives compositions with respectively 34% and 58% amine, and at their common boiling point (88 °C) 36% and 56% amine. From this a new distillate containing 71% amine may be obtained which, by fractional distillation, reveals that the pure amine has a boiling point of 77 °C.
   (a) Draw the $(T, x)_P$ diagram for 1 bar.
   (b) How many degrees of freedom has this system:
       (i) in each area of the diagram
       (ii) at $T = 88$ °C
   (c) Describe the properties of the phase transition points with highest and lowest temperatures in this diagram.
   (d) Sketch a free energy-composition diagram at $T = 75$ °C, and $T = 88$ °C, and $P = 1$ bar.

3. Benzene melts at 279 K and chlorobenzene at 228 K. The latent heats of fusion are, respectively, 9.83 and 7.53 kJ mol^{-1}. The substances are completely immiscible in the solid phase, and form an ideal liquid mixture. Construct the phase diagram between 100 K and 300 K.

4. The vapour pressure of a mixture of benzene (1) and perfluorobenzene (2) at 70 °C is given in the table:

x_2	0.0000	0.1847	0.7852	1.0000
P/bar	0.7341	0.7432	0.7129	0.7185

Sketch the (P, x, y) diagram at this temperature, and comment on its form.

5. At 344 K, the vapour pressure of ethanol (1) and ethyl acetate (2) are $P_1^\circ = 0.766$ bar, $P_2^\circ = 0.840$ bar. The system forms an azeotrope at this temperature with $P_{az} = 1.000$ bar and $(x_2)_{az} = 0.54$. Estimate the activity coefficients in the azeotropic mixture, making whatever simplifying assumptions are necessary.

6. A gas mixture of carbon dioxide (1) and methyl chloride (2) with $x_1 = 0.41$ is compressed isothermally at 378 K. Condensation starts at 73 bar, the quality falls to 0.9 at 81 bar, and then rises until evaporation is complete at 84 bar. The critical temperatures of the pure substances are $T_1^c = 304$ K, and $T_2^c = 416$ K. Sketch a phase diagram, including the dew and bubble point curves for $x_1 = 0.41$.

7. Carbon dioxide (1) and ethylene (2) form an azeotrope. The table below shows the vapour pressures of the pure substances and of the azeotrope.

$T/°C$	-10	0	10	20
P_1°/bar	26.5	34.8	45.0	57.3
P_2°/bar	32.4	40.9	—	—
P_{az}/bar	33.9	43.5	54.9	—
$(x_1)_{az}$	0.314	0.359	0.416	—

The critical pressures and temperatures are

$$P_1^c/\text{bar} = 73.8 \qquad T_1^c/°C = 31.0$$
$$P_2^c/\text{bar} = 50.8 \qquad T_2^c/°C = 9.5$$

Draw as accurately as possible the (P, x, y) lines at each temperature, paying particular attention to the behaviour in the critical region. It can be assumed that P^c of the mixture is approximately a linear function of composition.

Answers

The answers to the problems of this chapter are phase diagrams except for:

5. $\gamma_1 = 1.28$ $\gamma_2 = 1.20$

if we assume that the excess functions have the quadratic form of (6.101) and if imperfections of the vapour are neglected.

Notes

1. S. R. Brinkley, *J. Chem. Phys.* **14** (1946), 563, 686.
2. J. Zernike, *Chemical Phase Theory*, Kluwer, Deventer, 1956.
3. For further discussion of subjects covered in the rest of this chapter, see H. R. Null, *Phase Equilibrium in Process Design*, Wiley, New York, 1971, but use the diagrams and recommendations with discrimination.
4. D. I. J. Wang, *Adv. cryogenic Eng.* **3** (1960), 224.
5. For further work see, e.g. J. M. Prausnitz, *Molecular Thermodynamics of Fluid-Phase Equilibria*, Prentice-Hall, New Jersey, 1969, Appendix 9 and references therein.
6. R. F. Strickland-Constable, *Proc. Roy. Soc.* **A209** (1951), 14; G. G. Haselden, F. A. Holland, M. B. King and R. F. Strickland-Constable, ibid. **240** (1957), 1.
7. See e.g. D. C. Freshwater, *Distillation Equipment*, Vol. 5, Chapter 12 of *Chemical Engineering Practice* (ed. H. W. Cremer and T. Davies), Butterworth, London, 1958.
8. F. Din, *Trans. Faraday Soc.* **56** (1960), 668.
9. J. S. Rowlinson, *Liquids and Liquid Mixtures*, 2nd edn, Butterworth, London, 1969, Chapter 2.
10. For further examples of such calculations, see M. B. King, *Phase Equilibrium in Mixtures*, Pergamon Press, Oxford, 1969, Chapters 3 and 9.
11. F. Bosnjakovic, *Technical Thermodynamics*, Holt, Rinehart and Winston, New York, 1965.
12. M. Ruhemann, *Separation of Gases*, 2nd edn, Oxford Univ. Press, 1949.
13. R. F. Strickland-Constable in *Chemical Engineering Practice* (ed. H. W. Cremer and T. Davies), Vol. 4, Butterworth, London, 1957, pp. 1–235.
14. See e.g. ref. 9, Chapter 6.
15. L. H. Horsley, *Azeotropic Data*, Amer. Chem. Soc., Washington, 1973.

8 Chemical Equilibria

8.1 Introduction

The first five chapters covered the properties of pure substances and of mixtures of unchanging composition. The next two covered systems in which the compositions of the phases were variable, but in which there was a fixed set of chemical species. We now extend the discussion to cover systems in which there are also chemical reactions. The essential difference between this chapter and the last two is that instead of conservation of molecules we have now only conservation of atoms. Because of this condition we can express chemical reactions by means of the familiar balancing equations, e.g.

$$C_2H_6(gas) + \tfrac{7}{2} O_2(gas) = 2\ CO_2(gas) + 3\ H_2O(gas)$$
$$CaCO_3(solid) = CaO(solid) + CO_2(gas) \tag{8.1}$$

Such equations have several interpretations. They are used, for example, to express the fact that ethane can be burnt or limestone decomposed to give, in 100% yield, the products shown on the right. We shall be interested in the change of enthalpy etc. accompanying such transformations. The equations are also used to express the fact that there can be a dynamic equilibrium between the components on the two sides, with the rate to the right equal and opposite to the rate to the left. Here we use both interpretations, but start with the latter; that is, we enquire into the conditions of equilibrium when the reaction is free to flow either way in response to changes of composition, pressure and temperature. Systems in which the reactions are not completely free to make this response, whose rates are comparable with those of the changes of pressure, etc. in which we are interested, are outside the scope of classical thermodynamics.

The rate at which a reaction proceeds is of great importance from an industrial standpoint. A reaction which goes very slowly might require such a large reactor to achieve a reasonable rate of production that the process would be uneconomic. It is, however, important to know the composition when equilibrium is finally reached, for this determines the maximum extent to which reactants can be converted into products under given conditions. With some reactions it is difficult to distinguish by experiment between a system in true equilibrium and one in which the rate of change is too small to detect in any reasonable time. Thermodynamics provides us with a means of calculating the extent of reaction at equilibrium so that we can avoid this experimental difficulty. This is of practical importance because, if reaction rate is the limiting factor, we may hope to find some catalyst to speed up the reaction, but if it does not go further because it is already at equilibrium, then we must modify the reactor conditions so as to shift the equilibrium in the desired direction.

Ideally, we should like the reaction to go to equilibrium, thus providing the maximum yield under the prevailing conditions. However, this might require unacceptably long reaction times, and there will be cases in which a given reactor can produce greater amounts of product per unit time if the reacting mixture is removed before equilibrium has been reached, and is then replaced by fresh reactants. A flow reactor is a convenient way of doing this. We do, of course, use more reactants this way, but this is a penalty we have to pay if we are to achieve greater production. If, however, we can separate the unused reactants from the reacted mixture, they can be recycled.

We ask then what information relevant to the study of chemical reactions is provided by thermodynamics. In Chapter 1 we pointed out that thermodynamics deals with changes from one equilibrium state to another, but is unable to say anything about the rate at which the change takes place. This is as true for chemical reactions as it is for physical systems. Thus, as we shall see, we can, by thermodynamic analysis, calculate the composition of a reacting mixture when it reaches equilibrium but we can say nothing about how long it takes to get there. We can determine what factors influence the position of equilibrium, but not what factors influence the rate of reaction. We are, therefore, able to give only a partial solution to the problem of designing a reactor in which the mixture leaves before equilibrium is achieved. Nevertheless, a computation of the equilibrium composition gives a maximum performance against which these reactors may be judged.

The value of thermodynamics in studying reactions is not limited to the determination of equilibrium. The principles developed in the early part of this book apply to chemical as well as to physical systems, although the applications discussed so far have all been to the latter. Thus, for example, the first law applies to any system in which a chemical reaction is occurring. If a reaction is carried out in a closed vessel, the first law gives

$$\Delta U = Q + W \tag{8.2}$$

and if it is carried out in a steady state flow reactor,

$$\Delta H = Q + W \qquad (8.3)$$

provided that changes in kinetic and potential energy can be neglected, otherwise these terms must be included as in (2.14) and (2.15). There is usually no shaft work from a steady state flow reactor (a gas turbine is a case where this is not true) and thus

$$\Delta H = Q \qquad (8.4)$$

On the other hand, closed reactors are usually of one of two types, (i) constant volume and (ii) constant (atmospheric) pressure. We have seen in Chapter 2, (2.48) and (2.49), that, provided no work is involved other than expansion against the constant pressure in (ii), then

$$\Delta U = Q \qquad (\text{const } V)$$
$$\Delta H = Q \qquad (\text{const } P) \qquad (8.5)$$

Thus, the use of the first law to calculate the heat released or absorbed by a reacting system involves the calculation of the internal energy or enthalpy change associated with the making or breaking of chemical bonds. This knowledge is fundamental to the design of all chemical reactors, as for example in many steady state flow reactors, where it is necessary to use the heat generated by an exothermic reaction to preheat the unreacted gases to reaction temperature, before they enter the reactor. Further examples are considered later.

We return now to equations (8.1) but write them so that both products and reactants appear on the right-hand side, the latter with negative signs, e.g.

$$0 = 2\,CO_2 + 3\,H_2O - C_2H_6 - \tfrac{7}{2}O_2 \qquad (8.6)$$

The number of formula units of each substance which enters into a reaction written in this form is its stoichiometric coefficient ν_i. Thus those for carbon dioxide, water, ethane and oxygen, ν_1 to ν_4 in (8.6) are, respectively, $+2$, $+3$, and -1 and $-\tfrac{7}{2}$ (compare this convention with that used for ions in Section 6.13).

If, for example, we start with a stoichiometric mixture of ethane and oxygen, then the composition of the partially reacted mixture for the reaction represented by (8.6) can lie anywhere between $(C_2H_6 + \tfrac{7}{2}O_2)$ and $(2\,CO_2 + 3\,H_2O)$, and we introduce a single variable ξ, *the extent of reaction* (*le degré d'avancement* of De Donder), to describe how far the reaction has gone. It is conventional for ξ to increase as the reaction moves from left to right in (8.1), that is from reactants (negative ν_i) to products (positive ν_i) in (8.6). The system may contain species other than products or reactants; these are the inerts, and since, as we shall see later, they influence a chemical reaction merely by being physically present, we formally incorporate them into this description by ascribing values of zero to their stoichiometric coefficients. Thus if the oxidant in (8.6) is air rather than oxygen, the nitrogen present would be included in a thermodynamic analysis of the reaction but be given the value $\nu_i = 0$.

It is not necessary that we have an initially stoichiometric mixture to apply the idea of extent of reaction. Let us start with a mixture of, for example, carbon dioxide, water, ethane, oxygen and nitrogen of any arbitrary composition represented by n_i^* moles of component i (where i runs through all reactants, products and any inerts which are present) and let the reaction proceed until these amounts are changed to n_i etc. The conservation equation (8.1) requires that the change in each amount is proportional to its stoichiometric coefficient. We therefore define the extent of reaction ξ by

$$n_i - n_i^* = \xi \nu_i \quad \text{(for all } i\text{)} \tag{8.7}$$

The extent of reaction therefore measures the displacement from the original composition n_i^*. Clearly, if $n_i > n_i^*$ for products, then $n_i < n_i^*$ for reactants and $n_i = n_i^*$ for inerts, and so ξ is positive; and vice versa, if $n_i < n_i^*$ for products etc., ξ is negative. Although (8.7) is a general definition, the extent of reaction is particularly easy to formulate if we start with a system which is composed solely of reactants in their stoichiometric ratios, and in which the reaction proceeds until everything is transformed to products, for then ξ increases from zero to $[n_i^*/|\nu_i|]$, where here n_i^* is either the starting amount if i is a reactant, or the final amount if i is a product. The extent of reaction is, therefore, not a pure number, but is an amount of substance, measured in moles.

We saw in Chapter 3 that when a system is at equilibrium at constant pressure and temperature, the Gibbs free energy is a minimum with respect to changes in any independent variable which does not alter P or T. In the case of a chemical reaction, the change in composition, as measured by ξ, is just one such variable (see, for example, Figure 8.1 which gives the variation of G with ξ for the Exercise on p. 400, and thus for any chemically reacting mixture at constant P and T, when the system is at equilibrium,

$$-(\partial G/\partial \xi)_{P,T} = 0 \tag{8.8}$$

This derivative (with the minus sign) is called the *affinity* of the reaction; if the affinity is positive, the reaction tends to proceed from left to right, and vice versa. If it is zero there is no tendency to displacement, i.e. there is equilibrium. The affinity can be expressed in terms of the chemical potentials by using the fundamental equation (6.22), remembering that P and T are constant. It is

$$-\sum_{i=1}^{c} \mu_i \left(\frac{\partial n_i}{\partial \xi} \right)_{P,T} \tag{8.9}$$

which, by using (8.7), becomes

$$-\sum_{i=1}^{c} \mu_i \nu_i \tag{8.10}$$

Hence from (8.8) the condition of equilibrium is

$$\sum_i \nu_i \mu_i = 0 \tag{8.11}$$

Thus the oxidation of ethane reaction is at equilibrium when

$$2\mu_{CO_2} + 3\mu_{H_2O} - \mu_{C_2H_6} - \tfrac{7}{2}\mu_{O_2} = 0$$

Equation (8.11) is the basic equation whose consequences are explored in this chapter. Sums of this pattern are used repeatedly and it is convenient to have a simple notation to represent them. It is usual to adopt the symbol for a change, Δ, for this purpose, and to write Δq as an abbreviation for the sum $\sum_i \nu_i q_i$, where q is any property of interest. Thus (8.11) can be written $\Delta \mu = 0$.

This convention is consistent with that used earlier for Δ since such sums always describe changes, from reactants to products.

Exercise

Show that the affinity is also equal to

$$-(\partial A/\partial \xi)_{V,T}, \quad -(\partial U/\partial \xi)_{V,S}, \quad -(\partial H/\partial \xi)_{P,S} \quad \text{and} \quad T(\partial S/\partial \xi)_{U,V}$$

and hence show that (8.11) is also the condition of equilibrium under all the pairs of constraints implied by the subscripts to these derivatives.

Several points arise in using this basic condition of equilibrium. First, it is applicable to reaction in solids, liquids, gases, or mixtures thereof, since if a reaction is at equilibrium in (say) the gas phase, each molecular species must be at equilibrium with, and therefore at the same chemical potential as (see Chapter 6), the same species present in any solid or liquid phase. Hence the condition of chemical equilibrium in the gas is also that for chemical equilibrium in the other phases. Secondly, although the chemical potential of any inert substance present does not contribute to equation (8.11), since $\nu = 0$, the inert does influence the chemical potential of all of the other substances present (see Section 6.7). Thirdly, there may be more than one reaction occurring; this complication is postponed to Section 8.7. Fourthly, nothing that has been written so far in this book has allowed us to ascribe absolute values to G, A, H or U, and hence there have been only statements about the existence of conventions regarding the zeros from which the potentials in (8.11) are to be measured. Many of the conclusions that are to be drawn from this equation are not affected by this lack of a unique definition, and so discussion of this point is also deferred, to Section 8.4.

8.2   Equilibria in gas mixtures

The chemical potential of a component in a gas mixture (composition y) is related to its fugacity f by (6.61), namely

$$\mu_i(P, T, y) = \mu_i^{\ominus}(T) + RT \ln(f_i/P^{\ominus}) \tag{8.12}$$

The pressure $P^{\ominus}$ is a standard pressure and $\mu_i^{\ominus}$ is the standard potential of pure component i as a (hypothetical) perfect gas at a pressure of $P^{\ominus}$ (see Section 6.7). Throughout this chapter we choose $P^{\ominus}$ to be $1\,\text{atm} = 101\,325\,\text{N}\,\text{m}^{-2}$, since this is the standard pressure always used in chemical thermodynamics. The symbol $P^{\ominus}$ is retained in all equations where it properly belongs so as to avoid any confusion between the standard pressure and the units we use to measure it. (See again Section 6.7.) It will help to understand the first part of this section to remember that for a perfect gas mixture, the fugacity of component i is equal to its partial pressure, a point we return to later, but the derivation we give here does not require this assumption.

Substitution of (8.12) into (8.11), the condition for a system to be in chemical equilibrium, gives

$$\sum_i \nu_i(-\mu_i^{\ominus}/RT) = \sum_i \nu_i \ln(f_i/P^{\ominus}) \tag{8.13}$$

The left-hand side is a function only of temperature, being independent of composition and the pressure of the mixture, and so can be written $\ln K$, where K is also a function only of temperature.

$$\ln K = \sum_i \nu_i(-\mu_i^{\ominus}/RT) \tag{8.14}$$

or

$$K = \prod_i (f_i/P^{\ominus})^{\nu_i} \tag{8.15}$$

where the symbol $\prod$ means that we are to take the product of all factors from $i = 1$ to $i = C$. The number K is called the *equilibrium constant*, since, at a given temperature, it is independent of pressure and composition. Since ν_i are positive for products and negative for reactants we can write (8.15) as a ratio with products in the numerator and reactants in the denominator. Thus, for the first example in (8.1)

$$K = \frac{(f_{CO_2}/P^{\ominus})^2(f_{H_2O}/P^{\ominus})^3}{(f_{C_2H_6}/P^{\ominus})(f_{O_2}/P^{\ominus})^{7/2}} \tag{8.16}$$

This equation or the more general (8.15), together with the conservation equation (8.6) allows us to determine the composition of any mixture when it reaches equilibrium, whatever the initial composition may be, provided we know sufficient about how the fugacities depend on composition and pressure. In general there is a different equilibrium mixture from each initial composition.

The equilibrium constant defined by (8.14) is necessarily a pure number, but its numerical value depends on the choice of $P^{\ominus}$ in (8.15) and hence of $\mu_i^{\ominus}$ in (8.14). An alternative convention is sometimes used in which the factors of $P^{\ominus}$ are omitted from (8.15) and (8.16), so that K becomes a quantity of the dimensions of P^{ν}, where

$$\nu = \sum_i \nu_i \tag{8.17}$$

Thus, on this convention, the equilibrium constant given in (8.16) has the dimensions of $P^{1/2}$. The value of the sum in (8.17) is zero only if the number of formula units entering the equation as reactants equals the number leaving as products, as, for example, in

$$0 = HCl - \tfrac{1}{2} H_2 - \tfrac{1}{2} Cl_2$$

The numerical value of K in (8.16) depends also on how the reaction is written. Thus, if we choose to write, not (8.6), but

$$0 = 4\,CO_2 + 6\,H_2O - 2\,C_2H_6 - 7\,O_2 \tag{8.18}$$

then all ν_i are doubled and K is squared. Subject to these provisos, the larger the value of K the further the equilibrium is displaced towards the products of reaction. In the case of the particular example (8.6) the equilibrium is displaced well to the right and K is very large.

A warning must be given against a 'kinetic' interpretation of (8.15) or (8.16). We might naively assume from (8.1) that the *rate* of combustion of ethane is proportional to the product of its fugacity, and the fugacity of oxygen to the power $\tfrac{7}{2}$; and that the rate of the reverse reaction is proportional to the product of the square of the fugacity of carbon dioxide, and the cube of that of water. If this were so, and since the rates must be equal at equilibrium, then (8.16) would follow at once. However, the supposition is false; the combustion of ethane is a complicated chain reaction whose rate cannot be expressed simply in terms of the fugacities. Nevertheless, (8.16) is true, as we have shown, and its validity is quite independent of the mechanism, or kinetics, by which equilibrium is reached.

Fugacities are complicated, and often imperfectly known functions of pressure and composition. At low pressures, however, they become equal to the partial pressures (see 6.62) and so in this limit we can re-write (8.15) in terms of a constant now called K_P

$$K_P = \prod_i (Py_i/P^{\ominus})^{\nu_i} = \left(\frac{P}{P^{\ominus}}\right)^{\nu} \prod_i (y_i)^{\nu_i} \qquad (pg) \tag{8.19}$$

where Py_i is the partial pressure of component i (P is the total pressure of the mixture, y_i is the mole fraction of component i). There is, of course, nothing to stop our using this constant at higher pressures where the gaseous imperfections become significant, but it will no longer be independent of pressure and composition. Its invariance under changes of pressure and composition is restricted to those circumstances under which the system is (apart from the chemical reaction) a perfect gas mixture.

It is fortunate that for most gas reactions taking place at pressures not exceeding a few bars, the perfect gas approximation is adequate. But for reactions taking place at higher pressures, such as the synthesis of ammonia from hydrogen and nitrogen, which is usually carried out at pressures in the range 200 to 1000 bar, the equilibrium constant in terms of fugacities (8.15)

Table 8.1

Total Pressure P/atm	450 °C		475 °C	
	$K_P \times 10^3$	$K \times 10^3$	$K_P \times 10^3$	$K \times 10^3$
10	6.59	6.5	5.16	5.1
30	6.76	6.6	5.15	5.0
50	6.90	6.5	5.13	4.9
100	7.25	6.5	5.32	4.8
300	8.84	6.5	6.74	5.0
600	12.94	7.4	8.95	5.3
1000	23.28	9.9	14.93	6.8

Values of K_P are taken from the experimental work of A. T. Larson and R. L. Dodge (*J. Amer. Chem. Soc.*, **45**, 2918 (1923), **46**, 367, (1924)). Fugacities are calculated from recent correlations of the *P-V-T* properties of hydrogen, nitrogen and ammonia using the Lewis and Randall rule.

should be used. Although for the very highest pressures the composition dependence of the fugacities must be allowed for, an adequate approximation at intermediate pressures is to use the rule of Lewis and Randall (6.63) which states that the fugacity of component i in the mixture is equal to y_i multiplied by the fugacity of *pure* gaseous i at the same temperature and total pressure as the equilibrium mixture. Table 8.1 gives, for the ammonia synthesis reaction, the equilibrium constants K_P and K, defined as

$$K_P = \frac{(y_{NH_3}P/P^\ominus)}{(y_{N_2}P/P^\ominus)^{1/2}(y_{H_2}P/P^\ominus)^{3/2}}; \qquad K = \frac{(f_{NH_3}/P^\ominus)}{(f_{N_2}/P^\ominus)^{1/2}(f_{H_2}/P^\ominus)^{3/2}}$$

with $P^\ominus = 1$ atm. We see that whereas the perfect gas approximation begins to break down when the total pressure reaches 50 bar, the Lewis and Randall approximation is valid to nearer 600 bar. A test using the true, composition dependent, fugacities is not possible as the required thermodynamic properties have not been measured.

A third form of the equilibrium constant is obtained by using molar concentrations (or densities) as the variables. We define these by

$$c_i = n_i/V \qquad (8.20)$$

and introduce a standard concentration $c^\ominus$ by

$$c^\ominus = P^\ominus/RT \qquad (8.21)$$

In a perfect gas mixture (cf. 6.32 and 6.33)

$$Py_i = n_iRT/V = c_iRT \qquad (pg) \qquad (8.22)$$

and so, by substitution in (8.19) we obtain K_c

$$K_c = \prod_i (c_i/c^\ominus)^{\nu_i} = \left(\frac{nRT}{P^\ominus V}\right)^\nu \prod_i (y_i)^{\nu_i} \qquad (pg) \qquad (8.23)$$

Clearly, K, K_P and K_c are all equal in a reacting mixture of perfect gases. However, the right-hand members of (8.15), (8.19) and (8.23) are not equal in real gas mixtures and only the first is a function of temperature only; that is, it is independent of pressure and composition. It owes this distinction to the simple fact that fugacities were defined, in Section 6.6, to have a direct relation to chemical potential.

Exercise

From $G = \sum_i n_i \mu_i$, and equations (8.7) and (8.12), obtain a general expression for G as a function of the extent of reaction. Apply this equation to the simple case of the isomerisation of two perfect gases, $A = B$, and show that, for n moles of this mixture, G is given by

$$\frac{G(\xi') - G(0)}{nRT} = \xi' \ln \xi' + (1 - \xi')\ln(1 - \xi') - \xi' \ln K_P \qquad \text{(pg)} \qquad (8.24)$$

where $\xi' = \xi/n$ is zero when the system is pure A and unity for pure B, and $G(0)$ is the Gibbs free energy of pure A. Plot $G(\xi')$ for different values of K_P and note that it always has a minimum however large or small K_P may be. In this simple example the equilibrium value of ξ' is related to K_P by $\xi' = (1 - \xi')K_P$. Figure 8.1 shows the function (8.24) for $K_P = 2$.

We now return to the first of the two interpretations of the equations of reaction mentioned at the beginning of this chapter, and ask what is the change in free energy when a reaction proceeds from pure (i.e. unmixed)

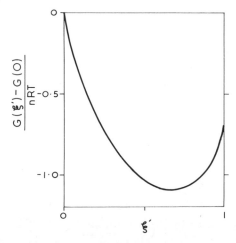

Figure 8.1. The Gibbs free energy as a function of the (dimensionless) extent of reaction, for the isomerisation of two perfect gases with $K_P = 2$

reactants at a temperature T, and in their standard states, to pure products at the same temperature and standard state. We denote this change $\Delta G^{\ominus}$ for an arbitrary amount of reacting material, but it is more convenient to reduce this to a molar quantity by dividing by n where $(|\nu_i| n)$ is the initial amount of one of the reactants. This molar quantity is $\Delta g^{\ominus}$, and by writing the reaction in the form of (8.6), we have at once

$$\Delta g^{\ominus}(T) = \sum_i \nu_i \mu_i^{\ominus}(T) \tag{8.25}$$

and so from (8.14)

$$\Delta g^{\ominus} = -RT \ln K \tag{8.26}$$

This is the change of free energy when stoichiometric amounts of one set of *unmixed* substances react completely to produce a second set of substances, also *unmixed*. It is not the same as the change when the reaction, written as in (8.1) proceeds from mixed reactants on the left to mixed products on the right. Thus the change of free energy between the unmixed perfect gases, one mole of C_2H_6 and $\frac{7}{2}$ moles of O_2, and the mixed reactants, $\frac{9}{2}$ moles of $(C_2H_6 + \frac{7}{2}O_2)$, is given by the expression for the ideal free energy of mixing (6.43),

$$\frac{\Delta G}{nRT} = \frac{2}{9} \ln \frac{2}{9} + \frac{7}{9} \ln \frac{7}{9} = -0.530 \qquad (n = \frac{9}{2} \, \text{mol}) \qquad (\text{pg})$$

That is, the free energy of the unmixed gases is, in this case, higher by $0.530(nRT)$ than the intercept of the curve $G(\xi)$ at $\xi = 0$. We need not, however, generally concern ourselves with calculating such differences as long as we remember to use $\Delta g^{\ominus}$ correctly as a difference between unmixed reactants and unmixed products, all in their standard states.

The standard Gibbs free energy change of (8.26) can be positive or negative, corresponding to values of K less than or greater than 1 respectively. But however large (positive) or small (negative) $\Delta g^{\ominus}$ may be, there is always a state of the system lying between that of wholly products and that of wholly reactants at which G has a minimum, as in the simple example above. This is illustrated in Table 8.2 where we see that reactions showing large

Table 8.2. The significance of the equation $\Delta g^{\ominus} = -RT \ln K$ when the temperature is 298 K

K	$\Delta g^{\ominus}/\text{J mol}^{-1}$	Inference
10^4	$-23\,000$	Reaction 'almost complete'
10	$-5\,700$	Reaction 'favourable'
1	0	Reaction 'central'
0.1	$5\,700$	Reaction 'just feasible'
10^{-4}	$23\,000$	Reaction 'very unfavourable'

negative value of $\Delta g^\ominus$ have a position of equilibrium so close to the right-hand side, that we loosely speak of the reaction as being 'complete'. Increasing $\Delta g^\ominus$ reduces the value of K until one reaches reactions with large positive values of $\Delta g^\ominus$ where the reaction is usually considered 'unfavourable'.

We shall find it useful to define changes of standard thermodynamic functions analogous to $\Delta g^\ominus$ (8.25). Thus, we can define standard changes in enthalpy, entropy and heat capacity as

$$\Delta h^\ominus = \sum_i \nu_i h_i^\ominus \tag{8.27}$$

$$\Delta s^\ominus = \sum_i \nu_i s_i^\ominus \tag{8.28}$$

$$\Delta c_P^\ominus = \sum_i \nu_i (c_P)_i^\ominus \tag{8.29}$$

and like $\Delta g^\ominus$, they are all functions of temperature. Thus $(c_P)_i^\ominus$ in (8.29) are the heat capacities, at standard pressure, of each of the pure unmixed components, both reactants and products, taking part in the reaction. Relationships exist between these standard thermodynamic changes just as they do between the basic functions themselves. Thus for the reaction $A = B + C$,

$$\frac{d\,\Delta h^\ominus}{dT} = -\frac{dh_A^\ominus}{dT} + \frac{dh_B^\ominus}{dT} + \frac{dh_C^\ominus}{dT}$$

$$= -(c_P)_A^\ominus + (c_P)_B^\ominus + (c_P)_C^\ominus$$

$$= \Delta c_P^\ominus \tag{8.30}$$

and

$$\Delta s^\ominus = -\frac{d\,\Delta g^\ominus}{dT} = R\left[\ln K + \frac{d\ln K}{dT}\right] \tag{8.31}$$

$$\Delta h^\ominus = \Delta g^\ominus - T\left(\frac{d\,\Delta g^\ominus}{dT}\right) = RT^2\left(\frac{d\ln K}{dT}\right) \tag{8.32}$$

where the right-hand expressions in terms of K have been obtained from (8.26).

If we neglect the gas imperfection at 1 atm we may also treat $\Delta h^\ominus$ as the change in enthalpy Δh when a premixed set of reactants is transformed at constant temperature and pressure, since, unlike free energy, the enthalpy of mixing perfect gases is zero (6.44). Thus for the combustion of ethane at 100 °C and a *total* pressure of 1 atm to give products at the same temperature and pressure, we write

$$C_2H_6(g) + \tfrac{7}{2}O_2(g) = 2\,CO_2(g) + 3\,H_2O(g) \qquad \Delta h = -1426.3 \text{ kJ mol}^{-1} (100\,°C)$$

and this value of Δh is, to the number of figures quoted, indistinguishable from $\Delta h^\ominus$ of (8.32) at 100 °C. The change Δh is closely related to what is measured in a combustion calorimeter. It is a large negative quantity; that is, heat is evolved if the reaction is carried out isothermally. This positive heat, $-\Delta h = 1426.3$ kJ mol^{-1}, is sometimes called the *heat of combustion,* but care is needed here, for it is easy to overlook the change of sign in this convention. In practice, it is better to avoid such expressions as *heat of combustion* or *heat of reaction,* and always to specify the enthalpy change Δh for the process in question.

The change of $\Delta h^{\ominus}$ with temperature is related to the difference of the heat capacities of products and reactants in their standard states by (8.30). This equation is sometimes called Kirchhoff's Law when it is applied to a reaction carried out at an arbitrary pressure (see also Section 2.9); that is

$$(\partial \Delta h / \partial T)_P - \Delta c_P \tag{8.33}$$

We shall see below that we often use measurements of K at one temperature to calculate the value at another. To do this we need to know Δh as a function of temperature, or Δh at one temperature and Δc_P as a function of temperature. We can then integrate (8.32). This is often written

$$\frac{d \ln K}{d(1/T)} = -\frac{\Delta h^{\ominus}}{R} \tag{8.34}$$

and called van't Hoff's equation. We thus obtain $\ln K$ as a function of temperature. An obvious approximation, but in general valid only over a small temperature range, is to assume that $\Delta h^{\ominus}$ is independent of temperature. Integration of (8.34) then gives

$$\ln K = -\frac{\Delta h^{\ominus}}{RT} + c$$

This equation is sometimes used for extrapolation over wide ranges of temperature, but the equilibrium constants so calculated are liable to be inaccurate and the method should be used only for order-of-magnitude calculations. Both (8.32) and (8.34) show that for an endothermic reaction ($\Delta h^{\ominus}$ positive) the equilibrium constant K increases with temperature.

The conservation of atoms in a chemical equation, and the fact that enthalpy is a function of state (see Chapter 3) implies that the change Δh from a set of reactants, in a defined state, to a set of products, also in a defined state, is independent of the path, that is, of how we write the equation or set of equations that link the two states. This fact allows us to calculate Δh for reactions that are difficult to study directly, or to use tables of Δh for a set of reactions to calculate that for a reaction not listed in the table. Thus, suppose we want Δh for the hydrogenation of ethylene at 100 °C, and know only Δh for the combustion of ethane (see above), ethylene and hydrogen at 100 °C.

$$C_2H_4(g) + 3\,O_2(g) = 2\,CO_2(g) + 2\,H_2O(g) \qquad \Delta h = -1322.2 \text{ kJ mol}^{-1}$$
$$H_2(g) + \tfrac{1}{2}\,O_2(g) = H_2O(g) \qquad \Delta h = -242.6 \text{ kJ mol}^{-1}$$

By addition and subtraction of these equations

$$C_2H_4(g) + H_2(g) = C_2H_6(g)$$

for which $\Delta h = (-1322.2 - 242.6 + 1426.3) = -133.5 \text{ kJ mol}^{-1}$ at $100\,°C$.

This procedure is usually called *Hess's Law*; it is a particular statement of the first law.

Exercise

By considering a similar conservation of standard free energies, formulate a similar law connecting the equilibrium constants of a linked set of reactions.

8.3   Equilibria between gases and solids

The discussion above concerns the equilibrium between gases, and it is convenient, although not strictly necessary, to modify it if some of the components are solids. Consider the combustion of graphite

$$0 = CO_2(g) - C(s) - O_2(g) \tag{8.35}$$

The vapour pressure of graphite is not zero, although it is almost immeasurably small at most accessible temperatures. At equilibrium the chemical potential of the solid is equal to that of this tenuous vapour, which, in turn, is related to those of oxygen and carbon dioxide by (8.11). We could, therefore, use this equation as before to derive an expression for the equilibrium constant (8.15). We do not do this in practice since we can calculate the difference between μ of the solid and $\mu^{\ominus}$ of the perfect gas at $P = P^{\ominus}$ from (8.12) only if we know the fugacity of graphite, and this is hard to measure. However, at low or moderate pressures the chemical potential of a condensed phase is relatively insensitive to the total pressure $[(\partial\mu/\partial P)_T = v$, see (6.24)] and we can replace the fugacity of graphite in the reacting mixture by the fugacity (or in effect the vapour pressure) of graphite in equilibrium with its pure vapour. This latter fugacity is a function only of temperature, a consequence of the phase rule (Section 7.3). The equilibrium constant K is also a function only of temperature, and hence if we omit the term $(f/P^{\ominus})$ for the gaseous carbon from (8.15) we obtain a new constant K', also a function only of temperature. That is, we first re-write (8.13)

$$\sum_i \nu_i(-\mu_i^{\ominus}/RT) - \sum_i'' \nu_i \ln(f_i/P^{\ominus}) = \sum_i' \nu_i \ln(f_i/P^{\ominus}) \tag{8.36}$$

where the primed sum is taken over the purely gaseous components and the double-primed over those present as solids. For the latter

$$\mu_i^{\circ}(s) = \mu_i(g) = \mu_i^{\ominus} + RT \ln(f_i/P^{\ominus}) \tag{8.37}$$

and so, substituting for the fugacities of these in (8.36)

$$\sum_i' \nu_i(-\mu_i^{\ominus}/RT) + \sum_i'' \nu_i(-\mu_i^{\circ}/RT) = \ln K' = \sum_i' \nu_i \ln(f_i/P^{\ominus}) \tag{8.38}$$

The sum of standard potentials on the left is a function only of temperature, and, by definition, is the logarithm of the modified equilibrium constant K'.

Thus, for the reaction (8.35) we have

$$K' = \exp[(-\mu^{\ominus}_{CO_2} + \mu^{\circ}_C + \mu^{\ominus}_{O_2})/RT] = (f_{CO_2}/P^{\ominus})/(f_{O_2}/P^{\ominus}) \qquad (8.39)$$

and for

$$0 = CaO(s) + CO_2(g) - CaCO_3(s) \qquad (8.40)$$

with two solid phases

$$K' = \exp[(-\mu^{\circ}_{CaO} - \mu^{\ominus}_{CO_2} + \mu^{\circ}_{CaCO_3})/RT] = f_{CO_2}/P^{\ominus} \qquad (8.41)$$

In the second example $(K'P^{\ominus})$ is the fugacity, or, in effect, the saturated vapour pressure, of CO_2 above $CaCO_3$.

Henceforth, we follow the usual convention, omit the terms due to the solids from the product of fugacities, and so use the symbol K both for the constant of (8.14)–(8.15) and for that of (8.38). We can, however, make this simplification only if the condensed phases are totally immiscible and so in independent equilibrium with the gases. If, for example, CaO and $CaCO_3$ formed a solid solution, then their potentials would depend on the composition of this solution and so not be functions only of temperature. The simplification above is, therefore, valid for most equilibria involving solids, since these are usually totally immiscible, but not for liquids which are usually at least partially miscible with each other, and which also dissolve the gaseous components. To discuss equilibria between liquid mixtures and gaseous reactions we must return to the basic equation (8.11) and enquire into the factors that determine each potential, by using the methods of Chapter 6.

The equilibrium between reacting gases was shown always to lie somewhere in the partly reacted state, neither pure products nor pure reactants, although in many practical cases some of the equilibrium n_i may be immeasurably small. This is no longer so if there are solid components, for if the equilibrium fugacity of a component in the gas is less than that of the solid at the prevailing temperature, then the solid will react to completion. Thus, if a mixture of air and CO_2 is passed over heated limestone the solid will remain (or become) pure $CaCO_3$, or pure CaO, according to whether the fugacity of CO_2 in the gas stream is below or above $(KP^{\ominus})$ of (8.41).

The symbol $\mu^{\ominus}$ was introduced in Section 6.4, and the conventional definition of the standard state denoted by the superscript symbol $^{\ominus}$ was given in Section 6.7. The meaning of this symbol must now be extended to cover pure liquids and solids. We have seen above that it would be possible, but inconvenient, to discuss equilibria between solids and gases by replacing the former by their saturated vapours and using the equations of the last section. If we did this then $\mu^{\ominus}$ would still be the potential of the hypothetical perfect gaseous state of (say) graphite vapour at 1 atm. However, we do not do this in practice, but modify the treatment as described above. This convention requires that we define the standard state of a substance in the gas, liquid or solid state, thus:

The standard state of a pure substance at a temperature T is defined as follows:

(a) *if the substance is a gas at T and $P = P^{\ominus}$, then the standard state is that of the equivalent perfect gas at this temperature and pressure,*

(b) *if the substance is a liquid or solid at T and $P = P^{\ominus}$, then the standard state is that of the actual solid or liquid at this temperature and pressure.*

The most common choice of standard pressure is $P^{\ominus} = 1$ atm.

If there is more than one allotrope then the stable form of the solid is chosen, e.g. graphite rather than diamond at 25 °C. Phosphorus is an exception; the less stable white form is chosen since this has more reproducible properties than the imperfectly crystalline red form (Section 7.3).

The first part of this definition is a repetition of that given in Section 6.7; the second part is consistent with the definition of the restricted equilibrium constant in (8.38) above, and the relation of that constant to the standard change of free energy by (8.26). That is (8.38) can be re-written in the simpler notation

$$K = \prod_i{}' (f_i/P^{\ominus})^{\nu_i} = \exp\left[-\sum_i \nu_i(\mu_i^{\ominus}/RT)\right] \qquad (8.42)$$

where the primed product is taken over gaseous components only, but the sum on the right is over all products, with $\mu_i^{\ominus}$ defined for both gases and solids by the statements above.

Notwithstanding this definition of the standard state, it is occasionally convenient to speak of the 'standard state of the gas' at, say, 25 °C for a substance which is liquid or even solid at this temperature and a pressure of 1 atm. This usage is to be found in many of the tables discussed in the next section.

Tables of thermodynamic functions list the entropy, enthalpy and free energy of substances in their standard states, most commonly at 25 °C, but occasionally at other temperatures also. The tables list the functions as numbers, and so we must now enquire into the zeros (or reference states) from which these numbers are reckoned. We met this problem in Chapter 4 in choosing the zeros for tables and charts to represent the properties of pure substances, and saw that there were several common choices of zero, the choice between which was solely a matter of convenience. This is no longer so once we wish to discuss chemical reactions between the substances. There is still an element of choice but is it circumscribed by the physical and chemical facts in rather a subtle way which we must now explore.

8.4 The third law of thermodynamics

If we are to tabulate $g^{\ominus}$, $h^{\ominus}$, $s^{\ominus}$ and $c_P^{\ominus}$ for a set of substances which we can react together, then we have to choose two independent zeros; that for $h^{\ominus}$

and that for $s^\ominus$. The heat capacity has an absolute value and needs no artificial zero, and that for $g^\ominus$ is fixed by those for $h^\ominus$ and $s^\ominus$, and the relation $g^\ominus = h^\ominus - Ts^\ominus$.

The first law of thermodynamics guarantees that we can choose zeros for $h^\ominus$ for a set of substances in such a way that addition and subtraction of the set of $h^\ominus$ always yields the correct value of $\Delta h^\ominus$ for any possible reaction. The choice made in practice is to list for each compound the enthalpy of formation in its standard state from its elements, also in their standard states. This *standard enthalpy of formation* is denoted here by the symbols $\Delta_f h^\ominus$. The consistency of this choice is ensured by the fact that any compound can be made only from one set of elements in fixed amounts. Some typical values are—

Substance	$\Delta_f h^\ominus (25\ ^\circ C)/kJ\ mol^{-1}$
$C(s)$	0
$O_2(g)$	0
$H_2(g)$	0
$CO(g)$	-110.52
$CO_2(g)$	-393.51
$H_2O(l)$	-285.83

That is for CO, we have:

$$C(s) + \tfrac{1}{2} O_2(g) = CO(g) \qquad \Delta_f h^\ominus = -110.52\ kJ\ mol^{-1} \text{ at } 25\ ^\circ C$$

From these values we have:

$$C(s) + CO_2(g) = 2\ CO(g) \qquad \Delta h^\ominus = \Delta(\Delta_f h^\ominus) = (2 \times -110.52 + 393.51)$$
$$= 172.47\ kJ\ mol^{-1} \text{ at } 25\ ^\circ C$$

$$CO_2(g) + H_2(g) = CO(g) + H_2O(l) \qquad \Delta h^\ominus = (-110.52 - 285.83 + 393.51)$$
$$= -2.84\ kJ\ mol^{-1} \text{ at } 25\ ^\circ C$$

Hence we do not need tables listing $\Delta h^\ominus$ for every reaction of interest; we need only a table of $\Delta_f h^\ominus$ for every compound of interest, and can find $\Delta h^\ominus$ by appropriate additions and subtractions. Notice the small value for the enthalpy change in the water-gas reaction. This is typical of reactions whose equilibrium position is fairly 'central' under ambient conditions, and it is the smallness of such changes which requires the tabulation of $\Delta_f h^\ominus$ with the high accuracy of the results listed above.

To obtain $\Delta h^\ominus$ at other temperatures from $\Delta_f h^\ominus$ at 25 °C requires a knowledge of c_P as a function of temperature, or what is equivalent, of $[h^\ominus(25\ ^\circ C) - h^\ominus(T)]$ as a function of T. This enthalpy difference is determined experimentally for each separate substance and is independent of the choice of zero implied above. The value most commonly found in tables which list also $\Delta_f h^{\ominus}$ is* $h^{\ominus}(25\,°\mathrm{C}) - h^{\ominus}(0\,\mathrm{K})$, but, in using such tables, it is important to see if $h^{\ominus}(0\,\mathrm{K})$ refers to the true standard state at zero temperature; i.e. the crystalline solid, or to that of the hypothetical perfect gas at zero temperature. The former is always used if the standard state at 25 °C is a liquid or solid, but the latter is often used if the standard state at 25 °C is a gas. From $\Delta_f h^{\ominus}(25\,°\mathrm{C})$ and these differences of enthalpy we obtain $\Delta_f h^{\ominus}(0\,\mathrm{K})$, and hence $\Delta h^{\ominus}(0\,\mathrm{K})$ for all reactions.

$$\Delta_f h^{\ominus}(0\,\mathrm{K}) = \Delta_f h^{\ominus}(25\,°\mathrm{C}) - \Delta[h^{\ominus}(25\,°\mathrm{C}) - h^{\ominus}(0\,\mathrm{K})] \tag{8.43}$$

Thus, for some of the substances listed above:

Substance	$[h^{\ominus}(25\,°\mathrm{C}) - h^{\ominus}(0\,\mathrm{K})]/\mathrm{kJ\ mol}^{-1}$
C(s)	1.050
O_2(g)	8.680
CO(g)	8.668
CO_2(g)	9.363

(For the last three substances the standard state at zero temperature is here the hypothetical perfect gas.) Hence, for the formation of CO and CO_2 from their elements

$$C(s) + \tfrac{1}{2}O_2(g) = CO(g)$$
$$\Delta_f h^{\ominus}(0\,\mathrm{K}) = -110.52 - [8.668 - \tfrac{1}{2} \times 8.680 - 1.050] = 113.80\ \mathrm{kJ\ mol}^{-1}$$
$$C(s) + O_2(g) = CO_2(g)$$
$$\Delta_f h^{\ominus}(0\,\mathrm{K}) = -393.51 - [9.363 - 8.680 - 1.050] = -393.14\ \mathrm{kJ\ mol}^{-1}$$

and for the reaction of CO_2 with C

$$C(s) + CO_2(g) = 2\,CO(g)$$
$$\Delta h^{\ominus}(0\,\mathrm{K}) = 172.47 - [2 \times 8.668 - 9.363 - 1.050] = 165.55\ \mathrm{kJ\ mol}^{-1}$$

or, alternatively,

$$\Delta h^{\ominus}(0\,\mathrm{K}) = -2 \times 113.80 + 393.14 = 165.54\ \mathrm{kJ\ mol}^{-1}$$

Such calculations require only careful book-keeping to obtain the appropriate change of enthalpy. When we come to the entropy, however, a new principle emerges. This is best made clear by some examples of changes of entropy at zero kelvin.

First example

The entropy difference $s^{\ominus}(T) - s^{\ominus}(0)$ can be calculated from measurements in a calorimeter, (Section 3.15). The standard state at zero temperature is,

---

* In general $h^{\ominus}(0)$ is an unambiguous representation of $h^{\ominus}$ at $T = 0\,\mathrm{K}$, but when this quantity is subtracted from $h^{\ominus}(25\,°\mathrm{C})$ etc. it is advisable to write it in full as $h^{\ominus}(0\,\mathrm{K})$.

for the entropy, always taken to be that of the crystalline solid, whatever the state of the substance at 25 °C. Eastman and McGavock[1] measured this difference of entropy separately for the two allotropes of sulphur. They obtained

monoclinic sulphur $s^{\ominus}(368.6 \text{ K}) - s^{\ominus}(0 \text{ K}) = 37.8 \pm 0.2 \text{ J K}^{-1} \text{ mol}^{-1}$

rhombic sulphur $s^{\ominus}(368.6 \text{ K}) - s^{\ominus}(0 \text{ K}) = 36.9 \pm 0.2 \text{ J K}^{-1} \text{ mol}^{-1}$

The temperature 368.6 K is the transition point at which rhombic and monoclinic are in equilibrium at atmospheric pressure (see Section 7.3). They measured the latent heat of transformation, and so obtained

$$s^{\ominus}(\text{monoclinic}, 368.6 \text{ K}) - s^{\ominus}(\text{rhombic}, 368.6 \text{ K}) = 1.08 \pm 0.05 \text{ J K}^{-1} \text{ mol}^{-1}$$

Hence

$$s^{\ominus}(\text{monoclinic}, 0 \text{ K}) - s^{\ominus}(\text{rhombic}, 0 \text{ K}) = 0.2 \pm 0.4 \text{ J K}^{-1} \text{ mol}^{-1}$$

Thus this difference of entropy is zero within experimental error.

Second example

Benton and Drake[2] measured the pressure of oxygen above Ag_2O from 173 °C to 188 °C and so, by means of an equation similar to (8.41), obtained $\ln K$ for the reaction

$$2 Ag(s) + \tfrac{1}{2} O_2(g) = Ag_2O(s)$$

They fitted their results to the equation

$$\Delta g^{\ominus} = a + bT \ln(T/\text{K}) + cT \tag{8.44}$$

with

$$a = -30.30 \text{ kJ mol}^{-1} \qquad b = -4.2 \text{ J K}^{-1} \text{ mol}^{-1}$$
$$c = 91.07 \text{ J K}^{-1} \text{ mol}^{-1}$$

By differentiation of (8.44) with respect to temperature, they obtained

$$\Delta s^{\ominus}(25 \text{ °C}) = -63 \text{ J K}^{-1} \text{ mol}^{-1}$$

Calorimetric measurements yield

	$[s^{\ominus}(25 \text{ °C}) - s^{\ominus}(0 \text{ K})]/\text{J K}^{-1} \text{ mol}^{-1}$
Ag(s)	42.7
$O_2(g)$	205.0
$Ag_2O(s)$	121.7

Hence

$$\Delta s^{\ominus}(0 \text{ K}) = -63 - [121.7 - 2 \times 42.7 - \tfrac{1}{2} \times 205.0] = +3 \text{ J K}^{-1} \text{ mol}^{-1}$$

Again the result is probably zero within the error of measurement and extrapolation of $\Delta s^{\ominus}$ to 25 °C.

Third example

Yost and Russell[3] quote an equation for the standard free energy of the reaction

$$PCl_5(g) = PCl_3(g) + Cl_2(g)$$

in the form of (8.44) above, but with $a = 83.68 \text{ kJ mol}^{-1}$, $b = -14.5 \text{ J K}^{-1} \text{mol}^{-1}$ and $c = 72.26 \text{ J K}^{-1} \text{mol}^{-1}$. The entropy difference $s^{\ominus}(25 \,°\text{C}) - s^{\ominus}(0 \text{ K})$ for these three substances are; PCl_5, 364.5; PCl_3 311.7; Cl_2 223.0 J K^{-1} mol^{-1}. Hence, by the arguments above

$$\Delta s^{\ominus}(0 \text{ K}) = -0.8 \text{ J K}^{-1} \text{mol}^{-1}$$

which is again zero, within experimental error.

Exercise

Why is the form (8.44) used to fit $\Delta g^{\ominus}$ as a function of T? Identify a, b and c in terms of $\Delta h^{\ominus}$ and $\Delta c_P^{\ominus}$.

There is nothing in the first and second laws of thermodynamics which leads us to expect that there is no change of entropy in a physical or chemical reaction between solids at zero temperature. However, the three examples above suggest strongly that this is so, and hence that a new physical principle is involved. This principle is generally called the *Third Law of Thermodynamics*.

This law, like the second, can be stated in many different forms, but in this case the variety of statements is not so much because of the wideness of the implications of the law, but because of the need to avoid a certain narrow class of apparent exceptions. Its earliest formulation was due to Nernst and arose from the consideration of entropy changes similar to those in the three examples above. This form of the third law is called *Nernst's Heat Theorem*, of which a modern version, due to Simon, is, as follows:

Let ΔS be the change of entropy for an isothermal process between internally stable states, or for a process in which the internal metastability is unaffected by that process. Nernst's Heat Theorem states that ΔS tends to zero as the temperature approaches zero.

Clearly the physical content of this theorem depends on the precise meaning of the words 'internally stable', and this is a question which cannot be fully explored here. Suffice it to say that such a state must be crystalline solid, since supercooled liquids and glasses are 'internally metastable' in the sense of this theorem. Helium is an exception, for the liquid state is the stable state at zero temperature and pressures below 23 bar (Section 7.3). However, the peculiar properties of the liquid state formed below 2.2 K ensure that the third law is not violated.

From the first of the examples above we deduce that *both* forms of crystalline sulphur are 'internally stable', notwithstanding our conclusion in

Section 7.3 that monoclinic is unstable with respect to rhombic at all temperatures below 368.6 K. Equally, we see that the crystalline forms of Ag, O_2, Ag_2O, PCl_5, PCl_3 and Cl_2 are all stable.

The commonest substances whose crystals are not 'internally stable' in this sense are H_2, CO, N_2O and H_2O. The first of these has two distinct nuclear spin states, *ortho-* and *para*-hydrogen, and these do not come to equilibrium on cooling. The remainder are crystals in which the molecules have fixed positions, but in which there is a certain degree of random orientation, e.g. in CO and N_2O, which are linear molecules, the crystal is formed with molecules arranged either as CO or OC, or as NNO or ONN, quite at random. This disorder implies lack of internal stability with respect to orientation; they are, in fact, 'orientational glasses'. The remedy for dealing with these special cases is described below.

The Nernst heat theorem implies a wider-ranging result, to which the name of the third law is usually given; namely

It is impossible by any procedure, no matter how idealised, to reduce the temperature of a system to zero in a finite number of finite operations.

Here we simply state this important theorem of the unattainability of zero temperature.[4]

In the next chapter we shall see that by an appeal to statistical thermodynamics we can adduce molecular reasons for the truth of the third law, and find an entirely non-calorimetric method for calculating $s^{\ominus}(T) - s^{\ominus}(0)$. These results not only 'explain' the law, but also lead to experimental evidence in its favour which is stronger than that obtained from the three examples above. However, for the purposes of this chapter, we need only the restricted version of the law embodied in Nernst's heat theorem, as set out above.

This theorem greatly simplifies our choice of zeros for $s^{\ominus}$, for it is now natural to put $s^{\ominus}(0) = 0$ for all substances. This conforms to the theorem and allows us to write what has been called above $[s^{\ominus}(T) - s^{\ominus}(0)]$ simply as $s^{\ominus}(T)$. The zeros for H_2, CO, N_2O and H_2O are taken to be not those of the actual or 'internally metastable' crystal at zero temperature, but those of the hypothetical internally stable crystal. The difference in entropy between the real and the hypothetical state can be calculated by methods explained in the next chapter. Here we need only note that the values of $s^{\ominus}(T)$ listed for these substances in the commonly used tables are based on the second standard or hypothetical state. They exclude contributions from nuclear spin. Such entropies are called *conventional* or *practical entropies*, and can be used, without change, in calculations of chemical equilibria.

An important consequence of the third law is that we can now calculate $\Delta g^{\ominus}$ and $\ln K$ purely from calorimetric measurements, without having to measure directly the composition or fugacities of the system at equilibrium. Thus for

$$C(s) + CO_2(g) = 2 \ CO(g)$$

at 25 °C, we have $\Delta h^{\ominus} = 172.47 \text{ kJ mol}^{-1}$, indirectly from the heats of combustion of CO and of graphite (see above). Measurements of the heat capacities and latents heats of the individual components yield $s^{\ominus}(25\ °C)$; for C, 5.74; for CO_2, 213.64; and for CO, 197.56 J K^{-1} mol^{-1}. Hence

$$\Delta s^{\ominus}(25\ °C) = 2 \times 197.56 - 213.64 - 5.74 = 175.74 \text{ J K}^{-1}\text{ mol}^{-1}$$

$$\Delta g^{\ominus}(25\ °C) = 172.47 - 298.15 \times 0.17574 = 120.07 \text{ kJ mol}^{-1}$$

$$\ln K = -\Delta g^{\ominus}/RT = -48.44$$

So small a value of K implies that the equilibrium fugacity of CO is negligibly small at this temperature. The signs of the $\Delta h^{\ominus}$ and $\Delta s^{\ominus}$ require that K increases with temperature; it is of the order of unity at 1000 K.

Hence the third law not only gives a rational choice of zeros for standard entropies, but also adds to our resources in that it leads to an indirect but often convenient method of obtaining equilibrium constants. Values of $\ln K$ obtained via the third law are often more accurate than those obtained by direct measurement of fugacities, as, for example, in the case of the decomposition of Ag_2O.

8.5 Use of tables

In this section we summarise the contents and conventions of those sets of tables which list values of the enthalpy, entropy and Gibbs free energy in forms suitable for the calculation of chemical equilibria. The most widely used sets fall into four groups.

First, there is a pair of tables from the National Bureau of Standards. The first of these[5] NBS Circular 500, was issued in bound form in 1952, and is now being superseded by successive issues of the series[6] NBS Technical Note 270. These list, among others, the following functions, shown here first in the NBS notation and then in that used in this book. At zero kelvin there is the molar enthalpy of formation in the standard state from elements in their standard states, ΔHf_0°, written here $\Delta_f h^{\ominus}(0)$. They follow the convention, described in the last section, that a standard state at zero kelvin is the solid if the standard state at 25 °C is solid or liquid, and is the perfect gas if the standard state at 25 °C is the gas. At 25 °C they list ΔHf° and ΔGf°, written here $\Delta_f h^{\ominus}$ and $\Delta_f g^{\ominus}$, the enthalpy difference $H_{298}^\circ - H_0^\circ$, written here $h^{\ominus}(25\ °C) - h^{\ominus}(0\ K)$, the conventional or practical entropy S° (see last section) and the heat capacity C_P°, that is $s^{\ominus}$ and $c_P^{\ominus}$.

The second group of tables is built around those known familiarly as API 44. These, like NBS 500, had their origin in the work of Rossini and his colleagues and use similar conventions. The original version[7] has now been superseded by two closely related sets of tables,[8] published by the Thermodynamics Research Center. The earlier list, as before, $H^\circ - H_0^\circ$, ΔHf° and ΔFf° for 25 °C, written here $h^{\ominus} - h^{\ominus}(0)$, $\Delta_f h^{\ominus}$ and $\Delta_f g^{\ominus}$, and also the quantities $(H° - H_0°)/T$ and $(F° - H_0°)/T$, written here $[h^\ominus - h^\ominus(0)]/T$ and $[g^\ominus - h^\ominus(0)]/T$. These last are called the *heat content function* and the *free energy function*. The names are unsatisfactory for the word *function* does not properly describe the operation of subtracting a constant and dividing by T. However, the functions are useful since they generally vary more slowly with T than $h^\ominus$ and $g^\ominus$, and so may be more easily interpolated. The later tables prepared by TRC extend slightly these definitions and change the name of the second. They list, amongst other properties, $(H - H°)/T$ and $(G - G°)/T$, written here as $(h - h^\ominus)/T$ and $(g - g^\ominus)/T$, as functions of pressure and temperature. These are described as the heat content function and Gibbs energy function for the real gas, less that for the gas in its standard state at the same temperature.

A third group of tables stems from the work of Stull and his colleagues at Dow Chemical Co. These comprise a book,[9] and a second edition of the JANAF tables.[10] These tables list $\Delta Hf°$, $\Delta Gf°$, $H° - H_{298}°$, $S°$, $C_P°$, and yet another variant of the Gibbs energy function, namely $(G° - H_{298}°)/T$, written here $[g^\ominus - h^\ominus(25\ °C)]/T$. Here the Gibbs free energy is that of a substance in its standard state, as in Giauque's and Rossini's original definition for the NBS tables, but the constant subtracted is the enthalpy in the standard state at 25 °C, not at 0 K. In the JANAF tables[10] this is written both in the form above and, in that part of the tables compiled before 1966, with F for the Gibbs free energy. The Gibbs energy function is there called the gef and measured in *gibbs* (calorie per degree), but these neologisms are not recommended. Both sets of tables are most useful for temperatures above 25 °C.

The fourth group of tables are those in Landolt-Börnstein.[11] They list $C_P°$, $S°$, $(H° - H_0°)/T$ and the enthalpy and free energy of formation in the forms $\Delta H_B°$ and $\Delta G_B°/T$, that is $\Delta_f h^\ominus$ and $\Delta_f g^\ominus/T$ (the subscript B is for *Bildungs*). These tables are again particularly useful for temperatures above 25 °C. Many of these are in joules, whilst all those of the American groups are in *thermochemical calories* (1 thermochemical calorie = 4.184 J, by definition). However, quotations in this book from these tables have been re-converted to joules to conform with the SI ('re-converted' since all modern calorimetry is carried out in joules and tables in calories are derived from such measurements by dividing by 4.184).

The methods by which these functions are obtained in practice can be deduced from the equations above, but are conveniently summarised here.

$c_P^\ominus$ The heat capacity can be measured directly in a flow calorimeter, or, for a perfect gas, can be calculated by the methods of statistical thermodynamics (see next Chapter).

$$s^\ominus(T) = \int_0^T \frac{c_P^\ominus(T)}{T}\, dT + \sum_{\text{transitions}} \left(\frac{\Delta_t h^\ominus}{T_t}\right) \qquad (8.45)$$

$s^\ominus$ By integration of $c_P^\ominus$ and the addition of entropies of phase transitions.

where $\Delta_t h^{\ominus}$ is the latent heat of the transition at temperature T_t, and the sum is over all solid-solid, solid-liquid and liquid-gas transitions between 0 and T. For the last of these $\Delta_t h^{\ominus}$ is the enthalpy change from the liquid at $P = P^{\ominus}$, $T = T_t$ to the perfect gas at $T = T_t$, not to the saturated vapour, in order to conform to the definition of standard state.

$s^{\ominus}$ can also be calculated by the methods of statistical thermodynamics (see next Chapter).

$h^{\ominus}(T) - h^{\ominus}(0)$　　By integrating c_P and adding the enthalpies of transition

$$h^{\ominus}(T) - h^{\ominus}(0) = \int_0^T c_P^{\ominus}(T)\, dT + \sum_{\text{transitions}} \Delta_t h^{\ominus} \quad (8.46)$$

This enthalpy difference can be obtained by the methods of statistical thermodynamics if $h^{\ominus}(0)$ refers to the enthalpy of the hypothetical perfect gas at zero kelvin, when the sum over transitions disappears from (5.2). If $h^{\ominus}(0)$ is the enthalpy of the crystal then the sum is included, and $h^{\ominus}(T) - h^{\ominus}(0)$ must be obtained calorimetrically.

$[h^{\ominus}(T) - h^{\ominus}(0)]/T$ from $h^{\ominus}(T) - h^{\ominus}(0)$ as a function of T.

$[g^{\ominus}(T) - h^{\ominus}(0)]/T$ from the equation

$$[g^{\ominus}(T) - h^{\ominus}(0)]/T = [h^{\ominus}(T) - h^{\ominus}(0)]/T - s^{\ominus}(T) \quad (8.47)$$

$\Delta_f h^{\ominus}$　　It is occasionally possible to measure $\Delta_f h^{\ominus}$ directly, e.g. for water by burning H_2 in a calorimeter, but more usually enthalpies of formation must be deduced from enthalpies of more accessible reactions by using Hess's Law. Enthalpies of combustion are particularly useful here, see Section 8.2. In principle $\Delta_f h^{\ominus}$ can be derived from the temperature change of the equilibrium constant (8.32) or of $\Delta_f g^{\ominus}$, but such values are rarely sufficiently accurate.

$\Delta_f h^{\ominus}(0)$　　from $\Delta_f h^{\ominus}(T)$, and from $h^{\ominus}(T) - h^{\ominus}(0)$ for the compound and for each of its elements, (8.43).

$\Delta_f g^{\ominus}$　　In principle, from K for the formation of the substance from its elements (8.26), but this is seldom possible. More practicable is the measurement of K for a set of related reactions which can be combined algebraically to give K for formation from the elements. The most accurate route, however, is often via the Third Law, that is to combine $s^{\ominus}$ for each component with $\Delta_f h^{\ominus}$ (Section 8.4).

$$\Delta_f g^{\ominus} = \Delta_f h^{\ominus} - T\, \Delta_f s^{\ominus} \quad (8.48)$$

This quantity can also be obtained from standard electrode potentials (see Section 8.9).

Examples of these functions are shown in Table 8.3 (p. 433) which is taken from the sets of Tables discussed above.

Exercise

Such tables generally contain redundant, if convenient, information. Check Table 8.3 by

1. Calculating $s^{\ominus}$ from columns 3 and 4 and verifying that $s^{\ominus}(500\,\text{K}) - s^{\ominus}(300\,\text{K})$ agrees with the difference of entropy calculated by integrating $c_P^{\ominus}/T$.
2. Calculating $\Delta_f h^{\ominus}(0)$ for each compound. The results should be independent of the temperature at which $\Delta_f h^{\ominus}$ is given. The figures in this Table give

CO(gas)	$\Delta_f h^{\ominus}(0)/\text{kJ mol}^{-1} = -113.8$
CO₂(gas)	$= -393.2$
H₂O(gas)	$= -238.9$
HCHO(gas)	$= -112.0$
CH₃OH(gas)	$= -190.2$

The results for the first three compounds are known accurately, but there is some uncertainty about the last two whose enthalpy of combustion is difficult to measure. These values are from the book by Stull, Westrum and Sinke,[9] but NBS 270-3 gives $-113.4\,\text{kJ mol}^{-1}$ for HCHO, and $-189.8\,\text{kJ mol}^{-1}$ for CH₃OH.
3. Calculating $\Delta_f g^{\ominus}$ from $\Delta_f h^{\ominus}$ and the entropies obtained in (1). The results agree with those in the last column within $0.1\,\text{kJ mol}^{-1}$.

Problems based upon this table are given at the end of this chapter. In solving them, and, more generally, in using thermodynamic tables to calculate yields of chemical reactions, three important limitations must be borne in mind. First, the results are those for a system which is at equilibrium with respect to the reaction or reactions under consideration. They tell us nothing about the rates at which the reactions go to this equilibrium position, and they give no guarantee that there may not be other reactions between the same substances which proceed, perhaps more rapidly, to quite different products (see, for example, Problem 11 below). A second restriction on the usefulness of the calculated yields is that the figures in the tables may not be sufficiently accurate for a reliable estimation of K. We have seen already that there is an uncertainty of at least $0.4\,\text{kJ mol}^{-1}$ in the enthalpy of formation of methanol, and $1.2\,\text{kJ mol}^{-1}$ in that of formaldehyde. Enthalpies of reaction are usually calculated from the differences of enthalpies of formation, and so may be even more uncertain.

Exercise

The enthalpy of a gaseous isomerisation A = B is $\Delta h^{\ominus} = 10.0 \pm 1.0 \text{ kJ mol}^{-1}$, and the entropy of reaction is zero. Calculate the uncertainty in the composition of the gas at different temperatures due to the uncertainty of $\Delta h^{\ominus}$.

A third limitation on the accuracy of calculated yields arises from the implied restriction to the perfect gas. The equilibrium constant K is expressed in terms of fugacities (8.15) and, when so written, is independent of pressure. However, it is common practice to replace these fugacities by partial pressures, and this step is justified only if the mixture is a perfect gas. Little error arises if the components are simple molecules, if the temperature is high, and the total pressure low. If the mixture is not perfect then the substitution of partial pressures is not justified, and the fugacities themselves must be related to composition and total pressure by the methods of Chapter 6.

8.6 Adiabatic reactions

The methods described so far in this chapter permit the calculation of the equilibrium constant at a known temperature. However, in continuous processes a stream of gas may enter a reactor, come to equilibrium without appreciable exchange of heat with the surroundings, and emerge with a different composition and at a different temperature. In this section we discuss the calculation of the equilibrium state in such systems.

The flow of gas requires a small but usually negligible fall of pressure between inlet and outlet. We have, therefore, a system which is both adiabatic and at constant pressure; hence the enthalpy is constant. We use this condition to obtain a relation between the initial and final temperatures and compositions. Let $n_i(T_1)$ moles of species i enter the reactor at temperature T_1, and let $n_i(T_2)$ emerge at T_2. The first law requires that

$$\sum_i n_i(T_1)h_i(T_1) = \sum_i n_i(T_2)h_i(T_2) \tag{8.49}$$

The sums are taken over all components of each stream; reactants, products and inerts. Each partial enthalpy at T_2 is related to that at T_1 by

$$h_i(T_2) - h_i(T_1) = \int_{T_1}^{T_2} (c_P)_i \, dT \tag{8.50}$$

Elimination of $h_i(T_2)$ gives

$$\sum_i n_i(T_2) \int_{T_1}^{T_2} (c_P)_i \, dT = -\sum_i [n_i(T_2) - n_i(T_1)]h_i(T_1) \tag{8.51}$$

The change in the amount of component i is proportional to the extent of reaction at T_2 (8.7).

$$n_i(T_2) - n_i(T_1) = \nu_i \, \xi(T_2) \tag{8.52}$$

Hence

$$\sum_i n_i(T_2) \int_{T_1}^{T_2} (c_P)_i \, dT = -\xi(T_2) \sum_i \nu_i h_i(T_1)$$

$$= -\xi(T_2) \, \Delta h(T_1) \tag{8.53}$$

where the sum on the left is over a mixture of (fixed) outlet composition. An equivalent equation in terms of the inlet composition is found by eliminating $h_i(T_1)$ from (8.49)

$$\sum_i n_i(T_1) \int_{T_1}^{T_2} (c_P)_i \, dT = -\xi(T_2) \, \Delta h(T_2) \tag{8.54}$$

The second is more useful since usually we know $n_i(T_1)$ and wish to calculate $n_i(T_2)$ and hence $\xi(T_2)$. Clearly, we cannot do this from either equation since they involve T_2 (as the upper limit of the integrals) but provide no means of determining it. To do this we must introduce a further condition, namely that the outlet stream is at equilibrium. This requires that $\ln K$ and hence $n_i(T_2)$ and $\xi(T_2)$ are related to the free energy by (8.12) and (8.13). The solution of these coupled equations is not easy since we cannot obtain $\xi(T_2)$ from the thermodynamic table of $\Delta g^{\ominus}$ until we know T_2, and this is itself related to $\xi(T_2)$ by (8.53) or (8.54). Hence, we have to start with a guess either at T_2 or at ξ, and solve the equations by iteration.

This iterative process is illustrated in Figure 8.2, a and b, which show adiabatic reaction paths for typical exothermic and endothermic reactions. With an exothermic reaction $\Delta h < 0$ and the temperature of the reactants increases with the extent of the reaction in accordance with (8.54). However from (8.32)

$$\frac{d \ln K}{dT} = \frac{\Delta h}{RT^2} < 0 \tag{8.55}$$

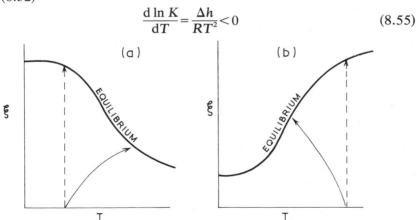

Figure 8.2. Reaction paths for (a) exothermic and (b) endothermic reactions. The isothermal paths are shown by dashed lines and the adiabatic paths by full lines

and hence $\xi(T_2)$ at equilibrium is a decreasing function of temperature as shown in Figure 8.2a. The temperature and extent of the adiabatic reaction at equilibrium is the intersection of the reaction path and equilibrium curve. In the endothermic case, $\Delta h > 0$, the reaction temperature decreases, but the extent of reaction at equilibrium increases with temperature. For both exothermic and endothermic reactions the heat effect is adverse in that a greater extent of reaction would be achieved if the temperature were held constant as shown by the broken lines. From (8.54) the slope of the adiabatic reaction path is given by $(\partial\xi/\partial T)_P$, but this is a complicated expression which changes with T. Hence the reaction paths in Figure 8.2 are generally curved.

One way of making an initial guess at a solution in order to solve iteratively the coupled equations is to assume that the heat capacity of the stream C_P is independent of ξ; that is, that $\Delta C_P = 0$. This is a useful approximation if the stream contains a high proportion of inerts. It implies that Δh is independent of temperature, and so (8.53) and (8.54) reduce to

$$\sum_i n_i(T_1)\int_{T_1}^{T_2}(c_P)_i\,dT = \sum_i n_i(T_2)\int_{T_1}^{T_2}(c_P)_i\,dT = -\xi(T_2)\,\Delta h \qquad (8.56)$$

where the sums are again over mixtures of fixed inlet and outlet composition. This equation is a considerable simplification of (8.53) and (8.54), but if we go further and assume that all c_P are independent of T then the slope of the reaction path is constant and given by

$$\frac{d\xi}{dT} = \frac{\sum_i n_i(c_P)_i}{-\Delta h} = -\frac{C_P}{\Delta h} \qquad (8.57)$$

where C_P is the total heat capacity of the stream.

An increase in the extent of an exothermic reaction can be achieved by cooling the reacting stream at intermediate positions along the reactor. Figure 8.3 shows a fixed bed reactor such as might be used for the production of ammonia from hydrogen and nitrogen, in which the reaction sections (stages 1–3) are filled with catalyst and are arranged alternately between heat exchangers contained within the reactor. In Figure 8.3a it is assumed that each reaction stage is adiabatic and that the reactants leaving each stage are in equilibrium before being cooled to the feed temperature T_1. If, in addition, the heat capacity of the reactants is assumed to be constant, then the slope of each adiabatic reaction path is the same, and is given by (8.57). A simple geometric construction then provides a preliminary estimate of the extent of reaction after any number of stages. The extent approaches that of an isothermal reactor as the number of stages increases.

An alternative and widely used method for achieving a similar effect is shown in Figure 8.3b in which the reactants are cooled by introducing cold feed gas between stages. The cold feed at T_0 is preheated to T_1 before adiabatic reaction in the first stage to an extent corresponding to equilibrium

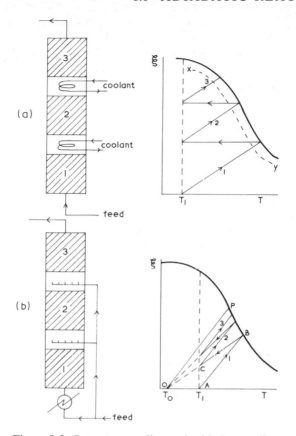

Figure 8.3. Interstage cooling and cold-shot cooling

at B. The state C of the feed to the second stage, resulting from the mixing of the hot reactants leaving the first stage with cold feed, usually known as *cold shot*, lies on line OB, the position being determined by the relative amount of the streams represented by points O and B. It is clear from the construction of the diagram that the adiabatic paths never go beyond the line OP parallel to AB. Hence the conversion in this type of reactor, unlike that in reactors with interstage cooling, is limited to the equilibrium adiabatic conversion that could be obtained from the original feed had the reaction been fast enough at this lower temperature.

In practice, in order to reduce the residence time and hence the size of the reactor, reaction is seldom allowed to proceed to equilibrium in any stage but is stopped at a point near to the locus of maximum reaction *rate*, as calculated from kinetic considerations. Furthermore, for optimum design, careful consideration is given to the feed temperatures of the reactant entering each stage of an interchanger cooled reactor, which are not necessarily the same, and to the pre-heat temperature of a cold shot reactor. However, these design considerations in no way distract from the utility of the simple geometric constructions illustrated in Figure 8.3, in which the line XY might represent the locus of conditions at which the reaction rate is a maximum.

8.7 Calculation of the equilibrium composition

We have assumed so far that the problem of calculating the position of equilibrium is solved once we have found $\Delta g^{\ominus}$ and hence K. In practice this is not so, particularly if there is more than one reaction, for the equations relating the equilibrium constant(s) to the extent(s) of reaction, and so to the n_i, are both non-linear and subject to constraints of mass-balance. This problem is primarily computational not thermodynamic, and so is not discussed here in detail, but it may be useful to indicate the ways in which it can be tackled.

If there is only one reaction then the problem is straightforward, although even here the solution must usually be obtained iteratively. Thus consider the simple reaction

$$2 \, CH_4 + C_2H_4 = 2 \, C_2H_6$$

in which we start with n_1^* mol of CH_4, n_2^* of C_2H_4 and n_3^* of C_2H_6, and calculate K from tables of free energy. Let the extent of reaction at equilibrium be ξ mol, so that the mole fractions are

$$CH_4 \quad \frac{n_1^* - 2\xi}{n_1^* + n_2^* + n_3^* - \xi} \qquad C_2H_4 \quad \frac{n_2^* - \xi}{n_1^* + n_2^* + n_3^* - \xi} \qquad C_2H_6 \quad \frac{n_3^* + 2\xi}{n_1^* + n_2^* + n_3^* - \xi}$$

In a perfect gas mixture these are the ratios of the fugacities to the total pressure, and so K is given by

$$K = \frac{(n_3^* + 2\xi)^2(n_1^* + n_2^* + n_3^* - \xi)}{(n_1^* - 2\xi)^2(n_2^* - \xi)(P/P^{\ominus})} \tag{8.58}$$

Thus, even for so simple a chemical reaction, the calculation of ξ from K requires the solution of a cubic equation.

If there is more than one reaction then there is a set of equations to solve. Consider the possible synthesis of CH_4 from CO and H_2

$$2 \, CO + 2 \, H_2 = CH_4 + CO_2 \qquad (1)$$

$$CO + 3 \, H_2 = CH_4 + H_2O \qquad (2)$$

At 1000 K the equilibrium constants of these reactions are 0.046 and 0.034. If the extents of reaction are ξ_1 and ξ_2, then we have two equations similar to (8.58) but both fourth order in both variables.

Exercise

Show that the equilibrium yield of CH_4 at 1000 K and 25 bar from an initial mixture of 1 mol of CO and 3 mol of H_2 is about 0.721 mol ($\xi_1 = 0.128$ mol, $\xi_2 = 0.593$ mol).

Many problems concerned with combustion involve a large number of possible reactions between many different species. Thus burning CH_4 in excess air could yield N_2, N, O_2, O, NO, H_2O, OH, H, CO, CO_2, etc. as possible products. Clearly it is impossible to solve equations similar to (8.58) by trial-and-error methods. Many systematic ways of tackling the problem have been devised, and these fall into two main classes. Either they first choose a minimum number of independent reactions which yield all the required species and then solve the 'mass-action' equations [that is, of the type of (8.58)] by systematic methods of iteration, or they take the Gibbs free energy as an explicit function of the amount of each species, and minimise G subject to the constraints of mass-balance. The two procedures are, of course, thermodynamically identical, since mass-action equations are derived by minimising G, but computationally they are different. The first requires criteria for choosing the minimum set of reactions from which all species can be formed. This is the same problem as that of finding the number of independent components C in a mixture of M species ($M \geq C$) needed to calculate the degrees of freedom by means of the phase rule. Examples are given in Section 7.2, and the problem is not discussed further here.

The thermodynamics of the second method is as follows. The Gibbs free energy of a mixture of M perfect gases is

$$\frac{G}{RT} = \sum_{i=1}^{M} \left[\frac{n_i \mu_i^{\ominus}}{RT} + n_i \ln\left(\frac{n_i P}{n P^{\ominus}} \right) \right] \tag{8.59}$$

where

$$n = \sum_{i=1}^{M} n_i \tag{8.60}$$

All M species are formed from L elements ($M \geq L$); let $a_{i\alpha}$ be the number of atoms of element α in one molecule of species i. The L conditions of mass-balance are then

$$n^{\alpha} - \sum_{i=1}^{M} a_{i\alpha} n_i = 0 \qquad (\alpha = 1, 2, \ldots, L) \tag{8.61}$$

where n^{α} is the total amount of element α, free and combined. There is, in general, a further set of restrictions on the n_i, namely that

$$n_i \geq 0 \qquad (i = 1, 2, \ldots, M) \tag{8.62}$$

but this set may be ignored if we are dealing only with gases since the dependence of G on n_i is such that the right-hand side of (8.59) when constrained by (8.61) always has a minimum for a positive set of n_i. However, if there may be one or more solid phases present (for example, solid carbon in a fuel-rich flame) then (8.62) is required. This set of inequalities is more troublesome than the set of linear equations (8.61). Hence, this account is restricted to gas mixtures.

The problem to be solved is, therefore, to find the values of n_i which make G a minimum and also satisfy the equations of mass-balance. The usual technique for dealing with problems of constrained extrema is that of Lagrange multipliers. Each equation of (8.61) is multiplied by an (initially) undetermined parameter χ_α, and the set added to (7.2) to give the Lagrangian $\mathscr{L}$

$$\mathscr{L} = \sum_{i=1}^{M} \left\{ \frac{n_i \mu_i^{\ominus}}{RT} + n_i \ln\left(\frac{n_i P}{n P^{\ominus}}\right) + \sum_{\alpha=1}^{L} \chi_\alpha (n^\alpha - a_{i\alpha} n_i) \right\} \qquad (8.63)$$

The condition for $\mathscr{L}$ to be at an extremum can be found by differentiating (8.63) with respect to each n_i, treating now all n_i as if they were independent variables

$$\left(\frac{\partial \mathscr{L}}{\partial n_i}\right)_{n_j} = \frac{\mu_i^{\ominus}}{RT} + \ln\left(\frac{n_i P}{n P^{\ominus}}\right) + \frac{n - n_i}{n} - \sum_{\alpha=1}^{L} \chi_\alpha a_{i\alpha} = 0$$

$$(i = 1, 2, \ldots, M) \quad (8.64)$$

Thus, we have two sets of equations (8.61) and (8.64), the former having L members and the latter M. These can be solved for the $(L+M)$ unknowns, χ_α and n_i, in terms of the known values of n^α, the amount of each element present, and $\mu_i^{\ominus}$, the standard potential of each species. The mathematical techniques for solving these equations are outside the scope of this book; they may be found in a review by Klein and a book by van Zeggeren and Storey.[12]

8.8 Equilibria in solution

Each component in a liquid mixture or solution has, in principle, a non-zero partial pressure in the vapour in equilibrium with that mixture. If the system is at chemical equilibrium in both phases then we have seen that the chemical potentials in the gas satisfy (8.11), namely

$$\sum_i \nu_i \mu_i = 0 \qquad (8.65)$$

Physical equilibrium between liquid and gas requires that μ_i for each component is the same in the two phases. Hence (8.65) is also the condition for chemical equilibrium in the liquid, where μ_i are now the potentials in this phase. To obtain the condition of equilibrium in terms of the composition of the liquid we substitute into (8.65) the appropriate expressions for the change of μ_i with composition. These were discussed fully in Chapter 6 where it was found convenient to use three different conventions for expressing such changes, according to the nature and relative amounts of the substances in the liquid. (Throughout this section we neglect the small dependence of μ_i on pressure in the liquid phase.) The three conventions are as follows.

Liquid mixtures. All components are treated on the same basis and compositions are expressed in mole fractions

$$\mu_i = \mu_i^\circ + RT \ln(x_i\gamma_i) \tag{6.75}$$

with

$$\gamma_i = 1 \quad \text{at} \quad x_i = 1 \quad \text{(all } i\text{)} \tag{6.76}$$

Dilute solutions. Composition is still expressed in mole fractions but there is an unsymmetrical definition of activity coefficients. For component 1, the solvent, (6.75) is retained, but for the solutes $(i > 1)$ we have

$$\mu_i = \mu_i^\dagger + RT \ln(x_i\gamma_i)$$

with

$$\gamma_i = 1 \text{ (all } i\text{) at } x_1 = 1 \tag{6.106}$$

Solutions of electrolytes. The potential of the solvent is again expressed by (6.75) but molality is used for the ionic species. For single positive ions

$$(\mu_+)_i = (\mu_+)_i^\square + RT \ln(m_+\gamma_+)_i \tag{6.137}$$

and similarly for negative ions. These equations are more usefully combined to give

$$\mu_i = \mu_i^\square + (\nu_\pm)_i RT \ln(m_\pm\gamma_\pm)_i \tag{6.139}$$

in terms of the mean molality of each electrolyte, (NaCl), (H_2SO_4) etc.

The three conventions introduce the three standard chemical potentials, each a function of temperature; μ_i°, the potential of pure liquid i; $\mu_i^\dagger$, the potential of i in a hypothetical state defined by extrapolating the properties of the solution to infinite dilution, and $\mu_i^\square$, the potential in a solution of unit activity on the molality scale (i.e. $m_\pm\gamma_\pm = 1$). Which convention we use is a matter of convenience; for example, the second is not necessarily restricted to dilute solutions, although it is generally most useful for them. The third is always used for electrolytes, but it can be, and often is, used also for un-ionised solutes. The choice is governed by the information available in tables such as those discussed in Section 8.5. If we can find there the free energy of formation from the elements in one of these standard states, that is $\Delta_f g^\circ$, $\Delta_f g^\dagger$, or $\Delta_f g^\square$, then it is convenient to use the corresponding convention to describe the change of μ_i with composition, and to define the equilibrium constant for a reaction in which that component is involved. For a liquid solvent for which we can neglect the dependence of g on pressure, g° is equal to $g^\ominus$.

Thus, with the first convention for all compositions we have, as in (8.13)–(8.15)

$$\sum_i \nu_i \ln(x_i\gamma_i) = \sum_i \nu_i(-\mu_i^\circ/RT) = \ln K = -\Delta g^\circ/RT = -\Delta(\Delta_f g^\circ)/RT \tag{8.66}$$

where $g°$ is the molar free energy of a pure component, $\Delta g°$ is the difference on reaction, and $\Delta(\Delta_f g°)$ is the same difference of the free energies of formation of the pure liquids $\Delta_f g°$ (cf. Section 8.4).

Similarly, for other conventions. Thus, for equilibrium between several solutes

$$\sum_{i>1} \nu_i \ln(x_i \gamma_i) = \sum_{i>1} \nu_i(-\mu_i^\dagger/RT) = \ln K = -\Delta g^\dagger/RT = -\Delta(\Delta_f g^\dagger)/RT \quad (8.67)$$

where $\Delta_f g^\dagger$ is the free energy of formation from elements in their standard states (as defined in Section 8.3) to the compounds in solution in standard states defined by (6.106). If the solvent itself is a participant in the reaction then we add terms with $i = 1$ to (8.67); that is, $\nu_1 \ln(x_1 \gamma_1)$ to the first sum, and $\nu_1(-\mu_1°/RT)$ to the second.

In the third convention, we have for reactions between electrolytes

$$\sum_{i>1} \nu_i(\nu_\pm)_i \ln(m_\pm \gamma_\pm)_i = \sum_{i>1} \nu_i(-\mu_i^\square/RT)$$

$$= \ln K = -\Delta g^\square/RT = -\Delta(\Delta_f g^\square)/RT \quad (8.68)$$

and again add terms of $\nu_1 \ln(x_1 \gamma_1)$ and $\nu_1(-\mu_1°/RT)$ if the solvent is a participant. There are here two kinds of stoichiometric coefficient, $\nu_\pm$, which is the number of ions formed from one formula unit of electrolyte, and ν_i, the number of formula units entering into the reaction. The former are positive, the latter positive for products and negative for reactants. Thus for the oxidation of ferrous chloride by permanganate in acid solution we have

$$5\,FeCl_2 + KMnO_4 + 8\,HCl = 5\,FeCl_3 + MnCl_2 + KCl + 4\,H_2O \quad (8.69)$$

Here the solvent is a product so $\nu_1 = 4$, and we add $4 \ln(x_1 \gamma_1)$ to the first sum in (8.4). If we take $FeCl_2$ as the second component we have $(\nu_\pm)_2 = 3$, and $\nu_2 = -5$, so that the second term $(i = 2)$ of the first sum is $-15 \ln(m_\pm \gamma_\pm)_2$, etc. Thus, if we take the solvent as species 1 and number the others in the order in which they occur in the equation, we have

$$+4 \ln(x_1 \gamma_1) - 15 \ln(m_\pm \gamma_\pm)_2 - 2 \ln(m_\pm \gamma_\pm)_3 - 16 \ln(m_\pm \gamma_\pm)_4$$

$$+20 \ln(m_\pm \gamma_\pm)_5 + 3 \ln(m_\pm \gamma_\pm)_6 + 2 \ln(m_\pm \gamma_\pm)_7 = \ln K$$

Exercise

This reaction is essentially the oxidation of Fe^{2+} to Fe^{3+}, and several of the apparent components of (8.69) do not, in fact, take part in the reaction, which can be written more succinctly

$$5\,Fe^{2+} + MnO_4^- + 8\,H^+ = 5\,Fe^{3+} + Mn^{2+} + 4\,H_2O \quad (8.70)$$

Show that equations similar to (8.68) but written in terms of single-ion molalities and activity coefficients, m_+, γ_+, etc., lead to the same equilibrium constant K as is obtained from (8.68) and (8.69) (Use the definitions of m_+ and γ_+ in Section 6.13).

Mixing the conventions leads to 'mixed equilibrium constants' expressed in terms of more than one scale of concentration. Such constants retain, however, their essential property of being functions only of temperature (and strictly of pressure) and of being independent of composition. As an example of the mixing of conventions, and hence of a mixed equilibrium constant, consider the equilibrium of gaseous carbon dioxide and gaseous ammonia with an aqueous solution of urea[13]

$$CO_2(g) + 2\,NH_3(g) - CO(NH_2)_2(aq.) + H_2O$$

The choice of conventions is governed by the fact that we can find values for the free energies of formation at 25 °C of gaseous CO_2 and NH_3 at a fugacity of 1 atm, of liquid water, and of a hypothetical ideal aqueous solution of urea at $m = 1$. For the two gases we therefore express μ in terms of fugacity (as in Section 8.2), for water in terms of mole fraction, with $\gamma_1 = 1$ at $x_1 = 1$, and for urea in terms of molality. The information available at 25 °C is

$CO_2(g)$	$\Delta_f g^{\ominus} = -394.4\ \text{kJ mol}^{-1}$
$NH_3(g)$	$\Delta_f g^{\ominus} = -16.5\ \text{kJ mol}^{-1}$
$H_2O(l)$	$\Delta_f g^{\ominus}$ or $\Delta_f g^{\circ} = -237.2\ \text{kJ mol}^{-1}$
$CO(NH_2)_2(\text{ideal aq.},\ m = 1)$	$\Delta_f g^{\square} = -203.8\ \text{kJ mol}^{-1}$
	$RT = 2.479\ \text{kJ mol}^{-1}$

[Two symbols can be used for water, since pure liquid water is the standard state in the sense of Section 8.3 (superscript$^{\ominus}$) and also for the first convention above (superscript$^{\circ}$).]

From an appropriate mixture of the equations above we have

$$\ln[m(CO(NH_2)_2) \cdot \gamma(CO(NH_2)_2)] + \ln[x(H_2O) \cdot \gamma(H_2O)]$$
$$- \ln[f(CO_2)/P^{\ominus}] - 2\ln[f(NH_3)/P^{\ominus}]$$
$$= [-\mu^{\square}(CO(NH_2)_2) - \mu^{\circ}(H_2O) + \mu^{\ominus}(CO_2) + 2\mu^{\ominus}(NH_3)]/RT$$
$$= \ln K$$
$$= [-(-203.8) - (-237.2) + (-394.4) + 2(-16.5)]/2.479 = 5.68$$

These equations relate the fugacities of the gases to the concentrations and activity coefficients of the liquid components. If we assume that the solution is very dilute, so that $x(H_2O) \simeq 1$ and hence $\gamma(H_2O) = \gamma(CO(NH_2)_2) = 1$, and replace the fugacities by partial pressure we have the simple result

$$\frac{m(CO(NH_2)_2)(P^{\ominus}/P)^3}{y(CO_2)y^2(NH_3)} = K = 293$$

If these simplifying assumptions are not valid then we return to the exact equation, and must make auxiliary measurements to find $\gamma(CO(NH_2)_2)$ and/or $\gamma(H_2O)$ in the liquid ('or', since they are related by the Gibbs-Duhem equation), and to find the fugacity/pressure ratios for CO_2 and NH_3 in the gas mixture.

Exercise

Show that a condition of equilibrium between a solid salt and its ions in solution is that $(m_\pm\gamma_\pm)$ is independent of the composition of the solution, and hence a function only of temperature (and, in principle, of pressure). From the definitions of mean molality and activity coefficient, it follows that the following product is also a function only of temperature

$$(\gamma_\pm)^{\nu_\pm}m_+^{\nu_+}m_-^{\nu_-} = K_s, \qquad \text{the } solubility \text{ } product \qquad (8.71)$$

Only in solutions of very low ionic strength [see (6.145)] can $\gamma_\pm$ be put equal to unity.

The transfer of a proton from one molecular ion in solution to another is an example of *acid-base equilibrium*, the species losing the proton being the acid and that receiving it being the base. Water molecules can both give and receive protons, and hence can be either acid or base. Examples are*

Acid	Base
H_2O	OH^-
H_3O^+	H_2O
$(COOH)_2$	$COOH \cdot COO^-$
$COOH \cdot COO^-$	$(COO)_2^{2-}$
NH_4^+	NH_3

The equilibrium constant for the removal of a proton from a (weak) acid

$$\text{Acid} + H_2O = \text{Base} + H_3O^+$$

in dilute solution ($\gamma_i = 1$) is

$$\frac{m(\text{base})\gamma(\text{base})m(H_3O^+)\gamma(H_3O^+)}{m(\text{acid})\gamma(\text{acid})} = K \qquad (8.72)$$

where K is the *acidity constant* of the acid. Typical values are 1.8×10^{-5} for the moderate acid, acetic acid, and 6.1×10^{-10} for the much weaker acid NH_4^+ (both in water at $25\,°C$). The symbol pK is often used as a convenient abbreviation of $(-\log_{10} K)$. Thus pK for acetic acid is 4.75.

This convention is similar to that by which the acidity of a solution is

---

* It is here more convenient, and no doubt chemically more proper, to write the hydrogen ion in its solvated form H_3O^+, rather than the bare form H^+. The latter is, for convenience, often written in equations such as (8.70). Adding '8 H_2O' to both sides of (8.70) does not affect the form or value of the equilibrium constant.

specified by means of its pH. This was originally defined as the negative of the logarithm of the activity of the hydrogen ion (in suitable units). We have seen, however, that single-ion activities are experimentally inaccessible and so pH now has an operational definition in terms of the e.m.f. of certain cells. Over most of the range of pH this operational definition gives a number which is close to that expressed by

$$pH = -\log_{10}[m_{H^+}\gamma] \tag{8.73}$$

where γ is the activity coefficient of a typical uni-univalent electrolyte in the solution.

If the acid is water we have $2\,H_2O = OH^- + H_3O^+$ and here the constant

$$m(H_3O^+) \cdot \gamma(H_3O^+) \cdot m(OH^-) \cdot \gamma(OH^-)$$

is denoted K_w, the *ionisation product* of water. It is 1.01×10^{-14} at 25 °C.

The temperature dependence of the equilibrium constant for reactions in solution is given in terms of a standard enthalpy of reaction by

$$\frac{d \ln K}{dT} = \frac{\Delta h^*}{RT^2} \tag{8.74}$$

where Δh^* is the appropriate difference of enthalpies of the components in the same standard states as are used to define K; that is $h^\dagger$, h°, $h^\ominus$, or $h^\square$, or a mixture of them, as is appropriate.

8.9 Electrochemical equilibria

An electrochemical reaction is one in which free electrons are participants. Since a solution is electrically neutral, such reactions can take place only at electrodes, which are conductors through which electrons can be added to or withdrawn from the solution. The condition of neutrality requires that we must have two electrodes, anode and cathode, for there to be an electrochemical reaction. Familiar, but chemically complicated, examples are the wet and dry batteries used to supply direct currents. This discussion is, however, restricted to electrodes at which simple reactions take place reversibly. These are amenable to simple thermodynamic description and, in turn, are useful tools for measuring thermodynamic properties. Electrochemistry is a large subject in its own right, in which thermodynamics plays an important role, but of which a full description is beyond the scope of this book.

Reactions at electrodes can be grouped into the following types:

1. *Element to ion.* If metallic copper or zinc is placed in a solution containing the derived cations, the following reactions occur quite readily

$$\tfrac{1}{2}\,Zn = \tfrac{1}{2}\,Zn^{2+} + e \tag{8.75}$$

$$\tfrac{1}{2}\,Cu = \tfrac{1}{2}\,Cu^{2+} + e \tag{8.76}$$

These reactions are the basis of the familiar Daniell cell. It is less easy to bring a gaseous element into equilibrium with its ion, but it can be done by bubbling the gas over a platinum electrode, covered, if necessary, with a deposit of finely divided metal (platinum black). At such an electrode

$$\tfrac{1}{2} H_2 = H^+ + e \qquad\qquad (8.77)$$

$$e + \tfrac{1}{2} Cl_2 = Cl^- \qquad\qquad (8.78)$$

In practice, free chlorine is an objectionable gas and its use can be avoided by using one of the second group of electrodes.

2. *Metal to insoluble salt.*   If a silver wire is covered with a thin deposit of AgCl, or if mercury is made into a paste with calomel then we have electrodes at which the following reactions take place reversibly

$$e + AgCl = Ag + Cl^- \qquad\qquad (8.79)$$

$$e + HgCl = Hg + Cl^- \qquad\qquad (8.80)$$

These reactions are all oxidation-reduction reactions, but that name, in the abbreviated form of *redox* is applied particularly to one of the third group of electrodes.

3. *Ion to ion.*   If a clean platinum wire dips into a solution containing ferrous and ferric ions, then the reaction

$$Fe^{2+} = Fe^{3+} + e \qquad\qquad (8.81)$$

takes place reversibly at the electrode.

These electrode reactions can be combined in pairs to give overall cell reactions from which the free electrons are eliminated. There are often mechanical problems in designing a cell in which the reaction of interest is the only chemical or physical process that occurs, but we assume for the moment that these can be overcome or ignored. Thus (8.77) and (8.80) can be combined by dipping both a hydrogen and a calomel electrode into a solution of HCl of molality m. This is represented schematically by the cell

$$Pt, H_2 \,|HCl(m)|\, HgCl, Hg \qquad\qquad (8.82)$$

where the vertical lines mark the boundary between one phase and the next; that is, in this example, between gaseous H_2 and aqueous HCl, and between aqueous HCl and the semi-solid paste of Hg and HgCl. The cell reaction is the sum of (8.77) and (8.80),

$$\tfrac{1}{2} H_2(g) + HgCl(s) = Hg(l) + H^+(aq) + Cl^-(aq) \qquad\qquad (8.83)$$

The convention followed here is to write the cell diagram (8.82) in the same sense as the reaction (8.83); that is, H_2 is on the left of both and Hg on the right.

A potentiometer connected across the mercury and platinum electrodes would show a potential difference of about $E = 0.3$ V when the molality of the

HCl is unity and no current is passing. Convention again requires that the sign of E is that of the polarity of the right-hand electrode. If we reverse the order of (8.82) and (8.83) then we write $E = -0.3$ V. If the potentiometer produces an opposing potential of just less than the e.m.f. of the cell, then the reaction proceeds slowly from left to right, if it equals it the reaction stops, and if it exceeds it then it drives the reaction backwards. We have here, therefore, a reversible process analogous to that of the compression or expansion of a gas in a cylinder fitted with a piston to which an external force is applied. The maximum electrical work the cell can do in an external circuit is that when the reaction proceeds against a balancing external potential at a rate slow compared with the times taken by the ions to diffuse through the solution, so as to eliminate unwanted gradients of concentration.

Let δn mol of electrons pass through this circuit under these conditions, so that δn mol of H^+ appear at the platinum electrode and δn mol of HgCl yields $Hg + Cl^-$ at the mercury electrode. The quantity of electricity passing through the cell, and hence also through the external circuit is $(F\,\delta n)$ coulombs where F is Faraday's constant (96 487 coulombs per mole of electrons). If the cell reaction involves multivalent ions then we generalise this to $(zF\,\delta n)$ where, as in Section 6.13, z is the signed number of elementary charges carried by any ion of which δn mol passes from left to right as the reaction proceeds. This quantity of electricity falling through a potential difference of E volts can do work of $(zFE\,\delta n)$ joules. This maximum work done by the cell is equal to its decrease of Gibbs free energy, since the whole system is operated at constant pressure and temperature. Hence

$$zFE\,\delta n = -\delta G = -\sum_i (\nu_i\,\delta n)\mu_i \qquad (8.84)$$

where $\nu_i\,\delta n$ is the change in the amount of a product or a reactant in the cell reaction. The fundamental electrochemical equation between the e.m.f. of the cell and the chemical potentials of the products and reactants is, therefore,

$$\sum_i \nu_i\mu_i = -zFE \qquad (8.85)$$

Equations (8.11) or (8.65) can be regarded as a special case of (8.85) for a system in which there is no transfer of electrons and hence for which $E = 0$. Equation (8.85) relates the μ_i, and hence the molalities and activity coefficients of the reactants to the e.m.f. of the cell. On substitution of (6.139) we obtain the electrochemical version of (8.68)

$$\frac{zFE}{RT} + \sum_{i>1} \nu_i(\nu_\pm)_i \ln(m_\pm\gamma_\pm)_i = \sum_{i>1} \nu_i(-\mu_i^\square/RT)$$

$$= zFE^\square/RT = -\Delta g^\square/RT = -\Delta(\Delta_f g^\square)/RT \quad (8.86)$$

where, as before, $\mu_i^\square$ and $\Delta_f g^\square$ refer to solutes in the standard state of $(m_\pm\gamma_\pm)_i = 1$. The standard potential $E^\square$ is, therefore, the e.m.f. of a reversible cell in which all reactants and products have $(m_\pm\gamma_\pm) = 1$. Again we add to (8.86) terms for the solvent ($i = 1$) if this species takes part in the reaction and use other standard states for non-solutes, as appropriate. This relation between E, $E^\square$ and the activities $(m_\pm\gamma_\pm)$ is known as *Nernst's equation.*

Measurements of E can serve two purposes; first to measure the activity coefficients $\gamma_\pm$, and secondly to measure standard free energies of reaction $\Delta g^\square$. As an example, consider the cell reaction (8.83), for which (8.86) becomes

$$E + \frac{2RT}{F}\ln(m_\pm\gamma_\pm)_{\text{HCl}} - \frac{1}{2}\frac{RT}{F}\ln(f_{\text{H}_2}/P^\ominus) = -[\mu_{\overline{\text{HCl}}}^\square + \mu_{\text{Hg}}^\ominus - \mu_{\text{HgCl}}^\ominus - \tfrac{1}{2}\mu_{\text{H}_2}^\ominus]/F$$

$$= E^\square = -[\Delta_f g_{\overline{\text{HCl}}}^\square - \Delta_f g_{\overline{\text{HgCl}}}^\ominus]/F \qquad (8.87)$$

There are no terms for the Hg or HgCl in the first part of this equation since they are already in their standard states (i.e. $\mu = \mu^\ominus$), and there are, of course, no terms for the elements Hg and H_2 in the last part. If the H_2 at the electrode has a fugacity of 1 atm then a knowledge of E as a function of $m_\pm$ allows us to measure $\gamma_\pm$ by writing (8.87) as

$$E + 2(RT/F)\ln(m_\pm)_{\text{HCl}} = E^\square - 2(RT/F)\ln(\gamma_\pm)_{\text{HCl}} \qquad (8.88)$$

At high dilution $\ln\gamma_\pm$ is proportional to $(m_\pm)^{1/2}$, the Debye-Hückel equation of Section 6.13, and so a plot of the left-hand side of (8.88) against $(m_\pm)^{1/2}$ allows us to determine $E^\square$ by extrapolation, and hence find $\gamma_\pm$ at each molality. In Chapter 6 there are described methods of determining γ_1, the activity coefficient of the solvent. From them $\gamma_\pm$ could be found by solving the Gibbs-Duhem equation, but it is usually more convenient to use a cell to make a direct measurement. Moreover, once we have found the standard potential $E^\square$ we can find the standard free energy of reaction $\Delta g^\square$, and so the difference between the free energies of formation of the product compounds and the reactant compounds. This, again, is a valuable alternative to the methods described earlier in this chapter, which required the measurements of heats of reaction and of practical entropies, or the measurement of equilibrium constants.

There are, however, drawbacks to the use of cells, of which the principal one is the difficulty (or strictly, the impossibility) of studying the desired chemical process in isolation from all other physical and chemical effects. Thus, even in so simple a cell as (8.82) we have electrodes made of different materials and hence there will be small (but unknown) contact potentials in the external circuit. Moreover, the platinum electrode dips into a solution saturated with H_2 but containing no HgCl, whilst the mercury electrode is in a solution saturated with HgCl but free of H_2. There is, therefore, a small concentration gradient in the cell which contributes, in principle, to the e.m.f. Were this not present, then the reaction of H_2 with HgCl might occur spontaneously (or irreversibly) and so reduce the e.m.f. In practice these complications are quite negligible for this cell because of the smallness of the contact potentials, the negligible solubilities of H_2 and HgCl and the slowness of the spontaneous reaction. However, in other cells these difficulties can be troublesome, and lead to the introduction of such devices as a porous pot (as in a Daniell cell) or a salt bridge to separate solutions of different composition. Finally if cells are to be used for thermodynamic measurements, they must be operated with no current flowing. If current is taken from them they are not at equilibrium.

Tables of $E^\square$ play the same role in the calculations of electrochemical equilibria as tables of $\Delta g^\square$ in equilibria which do not involve electrons. Clearly, we do not wish to have to list $\Delta g^\square$ or $E^\square$ for every reaction of interest. In Section 8.5 we saw that we avoided this for the free energies by adopting the convention that we list only $\Delta_f g^\square$ for each compound, a convention which is numerically equivalent to assigning a value of zero to $g^\square$ for each element. Similarly we adopt a conventional zero to simplify the tabulation of standard potentials. Here we choose to equate to zero $E^\square$ for the half-cell formed from a standard hydrogen electrode. That is, by convention

$$\text{Pt, } H_2(f = 1 \text{ atm}) \mid H^+(m_+\gamma_+ = 1) \qquad E^\square = 0$$

or, what is equivalent

$$\tfrac{1}{2} H_2(f = 1 \text{ atm}) = H^+(m_+\gamma_+ = 1) + e \qquad \Delta g^\square = 0$$

(The problem of determining the single-ion activity coefficient γ_+ is evaded by extrapolation to solutions sufficiently dilute to enable the Debye-Hückel theory to be used with confidence.) The standard electrode potentials of other half-cells are then the standard e.m.f. of the cell in which they are placed on the right and a hydrogen electrode on the left. Thus, at 25 °C

$$\text{Pt, } H_2 \mid H^+(aq) \mid Fe^{2+}, Fe^{3+}(aq) \mid Pt \qquad E^\square = 0.77 \text{ V}$$

or, for

$$\tfrac{1}{2} H_2(g) + Fe^{3+}(aq) = H^+(aq) + Fe^{2+}(aq)$$
$$\Delta g^\square = -zFE^\square = -74.3 \text{ kJ mol}^{-1}$$

where here $z = 1$ since the reaction advances by 1 mol when 1 faraday of electricity passes. Tables of $E^\square$ commonly list only the half-cell reactants and products separated by a solidus. Typical values are

Half-cell	$E^\square/V$
$\tfrac{1}{2} Cl_2/Cl^-$	1.36
Ag^+/Ag	0.80
Cu^+/Cu	0.52
$AgCl/Ag, Cl^-$	0.22
Cu^{2+}/Cu^+	0.15
$H^+/\tfrac{1}{2} H_2$	0
$\tfrac{1}{2} Fe^{2+}/Fe$	−0.44
$\tfrac{1}{2} Zn^{2+}/Zn$	−0.76
Na^+/Na	−2.71

This series is called the electrochemical series, the half-cells above $H^+/\frac{1}{2}H_2$, that is those with $E^{\ominus}>0$, being the *electronegative* end, and that below the *electropositive* end (the names derive from an older convention of ascribing signs to cells). Thus the metal Na is said to be electropositive with respect to Zn, which, in turn, is electropositive with respect to Cu. The standard potentials, and hence standard changes of free energy, for systems which do not involve the $H^+/\frac{1}{2}H_2$ equilibrium can be found by difference. Thus for

$$Fe \mid FeCl_2(aq) \mid AgCl, Ag$$

for which the cell reaction is

$$\tfrac{1}{2}Fe + AgCl = Ag + \tfrac{1}{2}Fe^{2+} + Cl^-$$

we have

$$E^{\ominus}/V = 0.22 - (-0.44) = 0.66$$

Problems

(Those marked * require information from Table 8.3)

1. Calculate $\Delta g^{\ominus}$ and K for the reaction $2\,NO_2 = N_2O_4$ at 300 K. The mixture has a mole fraction of N_2O_4 of 0.461 at a pressure of 0.3 bar.

2. The standard enthalpy change on combustion of pent-1-ene and 2 methyl but-2-ene are -3155.8 and $-3134.2\ kJ\ mol^{-1}$ at 25 °C. The standard Gibbs free energy of formation at the same temperature are 78.60 and 59.69 kJ mol^{-1} respectively. Which is the stable form in the standard states, and what is the enthalpy of isomerisation?

3. Sulphuric acid is made by the oxidation of sulphur dioxide to trioxide. Calculate the mole fraction of SO_3 in a stream of initial mole fractions SO_2 0.083, O_2 0.125, N_2 0.792, brought to equilibrium at 900 K and 2 atm.

$\Delta_f g^{\ominus}$	SO_2	$-296.3\ kJ\ mol^{-1}$	at 900 K
	SO_3	$-310.3\ kJ\ mol^{-1}$	at 900 K

4. At 300 K we have for the reaction

$$H_2(g) + \tfrac{1}{2}S_2(g) = H_2S(g)$$

$$\Delta g^{\ominus} = -72.99\ kJ\ mol^{-1} \qquad \Delta h^{\ominus} = -84.71\ kJ\ mol^{-1}$$

$$\Delta c_P^{\ominus} = -11\ J\ K^{-1}\ mol^{-1}$$

Estimate K at 700 K.

5. 100 mol s^{-1} of steam at 1300 K and 5 atm pressure enter a reactor in which

Table 8.3. Thermodynamic functions of substances in standard states

T K	$c_P^{\ominus}$	$[h^{\ominus}(T) - h^{\ominus}(0)]/T$	$[g^{\ominus}(T) - h^{\ominus}(0)]/T$	$\Delta_f h^{\ominus}$	$\Delta_f g^{\ominus}$
		J K^{-1} mol^{-1}		kJ mol^{-1}	
	C(s)				
300	8.72	3.56	−2.19	0	0
400	11.93	5.25	−3.46	0	0
500	14.63	6.86	−4.80	0	0
700	18.54	9.69	−7.58	0	0
1000	21.51	12.88	−11.60	0	0
	O$_2$(g)				
300	29.37	29.11	−176.10	0	0
400	30.10	29.26	−184.51	0	0
500	31.08	29.52	−191.07	0	0
700	32.99	30.26	−201.10	0	0
1000	34.87	31.39	−212.10	0	0
	H$_2$(g)				
300	28.85	28.4	−102.4	0	0
400	29.18	28.6	−110.6	0	0
500	29.26	28.7	−116.9	0	0
700	29.43	28.9	−126.6	0	0
1000	30.20	29.1	−137.0	0	0
	CO(g)				
300	29.16	29.2	−169.1	−110.5	−137.4
400	29.33	29.2	−177.4	−110.1	−146.5
500	29.79	29.2	−183.9	−110.0	−155.6
700	31.17	29.6	−193.8	−110.5	−173.8
1000	33.18	30.4	−204.5	−112.0	−200.6
	CO$_2$(g)				
300	37.20	31.5	−182.5	−393.5	−394.4
400	41.30	33.4	−191.8	−393.6	−394.7
500	44.60	35.4	−199.5	−393.7	−394.9
700	49.5	38.8	−211.9	−394.0	−395.4
1000	54.3	42.8	−226.4	−394.6	−395.8
	H$_2$O(g)				
300	33.6	33.3	−155.8	−241.8	−228.5
400	34.3	33.4	−165.3	−242.8	−223.9
500	35.2	33.7	−172.8	−243.8	−219.1
700	37.4	34.5	−184.3	−245.6	−208.9
1000	41.2	35.9	−196.7	−247.9	−192.6
	HCHO(g)				
300	35.4	33.7	−185.4	−115.9	−109.9
400	39.2	34.6	−195.2	−117.6	−107.6
500	43.8	35.9	−203.1	−119.2	−104.9
700	52.3	39.4	−215.7	−122.0	−98.7
	CH$_3$OH(g)				
300	44.0	38.4	−201.6	−201.2	−162.3
400	51.4	40.7	−212.9	−204.8	−148.7
500	59.5	43.7	−222.3	−207.9	−134.3
700	73.7	50.3	−238.1	−212.9	−103.9

equilibrium is reached in the reaction

$$3 \, Fe(s) + 4 \, H_2O(g) = Fe_3O_4(s) + 4 \, H_2(g)$$

Calculate the equilibrium rate of production of hydrogen. At 1300 K

$$\Delta_f g^{\ominus} \qquad H_2O(g) \quad -176 \, kJ \, mol^{-1}$$
$$Fe_3O_4(s) \quad -669 \, kJ \, mol^{-1}$$

6. The standard changes in Gibbs free energy for the reactions

$$2 \, CO_2(g) = 2 \, CO(g) + O_2(g) \tag{1}$$
$$Mn_2O_3(s) + CO_2(g) = 2 \, MnO_2(s) + CO(g) \tag{2}$$

are given by

(1) $\Delta g^{\ominus}/kJ \, mol^{-1} = 565.98 - 0.1736(T/K)$

(2) $\Delta g^{\ominus}/kJ \, mol^{-1} = 200.52 + 0.0061(T/K)$

Calculate the temperature at which the oxygen in equilibrium with Mn_2O_3 and MnO_2 has a pressure of 1 atm.

7. * Carbon dioxide is passed over coke at 1000 K and atmospheric pressure. Calculate the equilibrium composition of the emerging gas.

8. * Calculate K and $\Delta h^{\ominus}$ for the reaction at 500 K

$$CO_2 + H_2 = CO + H_2O$$

and show that the yield of CO is negligible. Estimate K and $\Delta h^{\ominus}$ at 900 K, and hence calculate the extent of reaction of an equimolar mixture of $CO_2 + H_2$ which is brought to equilibrium at this temperature and at atmospheric pressure.

9. * An equimolar mixture of CO, H_2 and H_2O, at a total pressure P is brought to equilibrium with respect to the reaction

$$CO(g) + H_2(g) = C(s) + H_2O(g)$$

Show that no carbon is precipitated unless $(KP/P^{\ominus})$ exceeds 3. Calculate the minimum pressure for precipitation at 1000 K.

10. * Methanol is synthesised from CO and H_2.

$$CO + 2 \, H_2 = CH_3OH$$

Calculate K at 500 K and 700 K and hence show that low temperatures and high pressures favour a good yield. If CO and H_2 are mixed in stoichiometric proportions, what is the equilibrium mole fraction of CH_3OH at 500 K and a total pressure of 100 atm. (Assume perfect gas behaviour.)

11. * It has been suggested that formaldehyde might be made by dehydrogenation of methanol

$$CH_3OH = HCHO + H_2 \tag{1}$$

Show that it appears at first sight that the process is quite promising, but that it is likely that dehydrogenation would not stop at HCHO

$$HCHO = CO + H_2 \tag{2}$$

Show that a more useful route might be by the oxidation of methanol

$$CH_3OH + \tfrac{1}{2}O_2 = HCHO + H_2O \tag{3}$$

Show that $\Delta h^\ominus$ is positive for (1) and negative for (3), so that it might be economical to combine the two reactions.

12. * A mixture of 1 mol of carbon monoxide and 2 mol steam enter an adiabatic reactor at 400 K. If the stream comes to equilibrium with respect to the reaction

$$CO + H_2O = CO_2 + H_2$$

calculate the temperature and composition of the emerging gas. (Use the approximation $\Delta C_P = 0$ for the first estimate.)

Answers

1. $\Delta g^\ominus = 4.14$ kJ mol^{-1}
   $K = 5.35$

2. 2 methyl but-2-ene
   $\Delta h^\ominus = -21.6$ kJ mol^{-1} for Pentene = Me Butene

3. Mole fraction $SO_3 = 0.064$.

4. $K = 1.6 \times 10^4$

5. 31 mol s^{-1}.

6. 888 K.

7. Mole fractions CO_2 0.28, CO 0.72, O_2 negligible.

8. At 500 K $K = 7.8 \times 10^{-3}$
   $\Delta h^\ominus = 39.9$ kJ mol^{-1}

At 900 K $K = 0.23$

$$\Delta h^{\ominus} = 35.0 \text{ kJ mol}^{-1}$$

$$\xi = 0.32 \text{ mol}$$

9. 8.0 bar.

10. At 500 K $K = 6.0 \times 10^{-3}$
700 K $K = 6.2 \times 10^{-6}$

Mole fraction methanol 0.60.

11. See article by E. Jones and G. G. Fowlie, *J. Appl. Chem.* **3** (1953) 206

12. $T = 735$ K. $\xi = 0.90$ mol.

Notes

1. *J. Amer. Chem. Soc.* **59** (1937), 145.
2. *J. Amer. Chem. Soc.* **54** (1932), 2186.
3. *Systematic Inorganic Chemistry*, Oxford Univ. Press, 1946, p. 241.
4. For a derivation from Nernst's heat theorem, see e.g. E. A. Guggenheim, *Thermodynamics*, 5th edn, North Holland, Amsterdam, 1967, p. 157.
5. F. D. Rossini, D. D. Wagman, W. H. Evans, S. Levine and I. Jaffe, *Selected Values of Chemical Thermodynamic Properties*, National Bureau of Standards Circular 500, Washington, 1952.
6. D. D. Wagman, W. H. Evans, V. B. Parker, I. Halow, S. M. Bailey and R. H. Schumm, *Selected Values of Chemical Thermodynamic Properties*, National Bureau of Standards Technical Note 270. This is being issued in parts; Part 270–3 (1968) supersedes 270–1 and 270–2 and covers 34 elements. A further 19 are covered by 270–4 (1969) and more in 270–5 (1971) etc.
7. F. D. Rossini, K. S. Pitzer, R. L. Arnett, R. M. Brown and G. C. Pimentel, *Selected Values of Physical and Thermodynamic Properties of Hydro-Carbons and Related Compounds*, American Petroleum Institute, Research Project 44, Carnegie Press, Pittsburgh, 1953.
8. Thermodynamics Research Center, Texas A and M University, *Selected Values of Properties of Hydrocarbons and Related Compounds*, API Research Project 44, and *Selected Values of Properties of Chemical Compounds* (formerly Manufacturing Chemists Association Research Project); College Station, Texas; 1971, but including earlier tables.
9. D. R. Stull, E. F. Westrum and G. C. Sinke, *The Chemical Thermodynamics of Organic Compounds*, Wiley, New York, 1969.
10. D. R. Stull and H. Prophet, *JANAF Thermochemical Tables*, 2nd edn, NSRDS–NBS 37, 1971. The acronym stands for Joint (U.S.) Army, Navy and Air Force.
11. Landolt-Börnstein, *Tabellen*, Vol. 2, Part 4: 'Kalorische Zustandsgrössen', Springer-Verlag, Berlin, 1961.
12. M. Klein, 'Practical Treatment of Coupled Gas Reactions', Chapter 7 of *Physical Chemistry: An Advanced Treatise*; Vol. 1, Thermodynamics', Academic Press, New York, 1971; F. van Zeggeren and S. H. Storey, *The Computation of Chemical Equilibria*, Cambridge Univ. Press, 1970.
13. This example is due to K. G. Denbigh, who gives a fuller discussion of the subject of this section in Chapter 10 of *Principles of Chemical Equilibrium*, 3rd edn, Cambridge Univ. Press, 1971.

9 Prediction of Thermodynamic Properties

9.1 Introduction

We have emphasised throughout the first eight chapters that classical thermodynamics is primarily a method of inter-relating the experimentally measurable properties of systems in equilibrium states. Thus the change with temperature of the equilibrium composition of a reacting mixture can be related to the heat of reaction at a fixed temperature. We cannot use the methods developed in these eight chapters to tell us anything about the absolute size of a heat of reaction, a heat capacity, a pressure, or any other thermodynamic property, since these depend ultimately on the properties of the molecules of which the system is composed, and classical thermodynamics tells us nothing about molecules. Modern experimental techniques, of which spectroscopy is the most important, have, however, told us a lot about molecular masses, shapes, sizes and internal structures, and it would be valuable if we could exploit this storehouse of information in order to calculate *a priori* the absolute values of thermodynamic functions. The branch of science which enables us to do this is called *statistical thermodynamics* (or *statistical mechanics*, the two names are used almost indifferently). The word *statistical* is appropriate since we have to take averages over the behaviour of many individual molecules in order to calculate the behaviour of the macroscopic systems in which we are interested.

We describe here the use of statistical thermodynamics for the prediction of some of the properties of use to the chemical engineer, but do not discuss in detail its theoretical foundations.[1] Instead we found our discussion on a plausible and familar result—Boltzmann's distribution law—and proceed from this to our working equations as quickly as possible.

First, however, we must discuss the kind of information we can expect from spectroscopy and other sources about the energies of molecules and of assemblies of molecules. A system formed of N molecules in a container of fixed shape and volume adopts one of the very many states allowed by the quantum mechanical (or *quantal*) description of the system. Each state, α, has a particular energy, E_α. It often happens that more than one state has the same energy, in which case we denote the number of these states by ω, and say that ω is the *degeneracy* of the energy level E_α.

A classical* mechanical description replaces the discrete set of states, and hence of energy levels, by a continuous distribution of permitted states and energies. For many kinds of system this is an adequate description, but we start with the quantal description because, not only is it more correct, but it is conceptually simpler.

9.2 The working equation of statistical thermodynamics

In a gas at low density each molecule spends most of its time in isolation, colliding only rarely with the other molecules. In such a system it is meaningful to say that each molecule has an energy, ε_α. In a compressed gas or liquid such a statement is not meaningful since each molecule is always close to many others which exert forces on it. We can now ascribe an energy E_α to the whole system of (say) 10^{23} molecules, but cannot break this energy down into that of individual independent molecules.

We start with the simplest case, that of the dilute gas of independent molecules and *assume* that Boltzmann's distribution law holds; that is, that the probability p_α that a molecule in such a system at equilibrium is in a state of energy ε_α is proportional to $\exp(-\varepsilon_\alpha/kT)$.

$$p_\alpha = \text{const } e^{-\varepsilon_\alpha/kT} \quad \text{(pg)} \tag{9.1}$$

where k is Boltzmann's constant, $k = R/N_A = 1.380\,54 \times 10^{-23}\ \text{JK}^{-1}$, and N_A is Avogadro's constant. An assumption of some kind is needed to link molecular mechanics with classical thermodynamics and although (9.1) is not the simplest assumption, it is one which leads most directly to the establishment of this link. Its validity is, of course, tested by the subsequent agreement of theory and fact.

The constant in (9.1) can be found at once since each molecule must be in some state and so, summing over all states (infinite in number), we have

$$\sum_\alpha p_\alpha = 1 = \text{const } \sum_\alpha e^{-\varepsilon_\alpha/kT} \quad \text{(pg)} \tag{9.2}$$

If we denote the sum of Boltzmann factors by z (9.1) and (9.2) become

$$p_\alpha = z^{-1} e^{-\varepsilon_\alpha/kT} \quad \text{where} \quad z = \sum_\alpha e^{-\varepsilon_\alpha/kT} \quad \text{(pg)} \tag{9.3}$$

---

*The word *classical* is used in this field with two quite different meanings. We distinguish between the *classical*, or macroscopic, thermodynamics of Chapters 1–8 and the *statistical* thermodynamics of Chapter 9. We distinguish also between the *classical*, or Newtonian, mechanics of individual molecules and the more correct *quantal* description of their motions.

The sums in (9.2) and (9.3) are over all allowed *states* of the molecule, not its energy levels, hence if there are levels of degeneracy ω, these appear as ω separate terms in the sum, each with the same energy ε.

We could now use (9.3) to develop the statistical thermodynamics of the dilute, or perfect, gas but instead defer this until we have developed a more powerful equation which is applicable also to systems in which the molecules are not independent.

Let us consider a set of M systems, each of which contains N interacting molecules in a volume V, where both M and N are of the order of 10^{23}. We can meaningfully ascribe an energy E_α to each of the M systems, although we cannot break this down further to molecular energies ε_α. If, however, the M systems are in thermal contact and mutually at equilibrium, then they are exactly analogous with the individual molecules considered above. We may again assume that the probability that a system of N molecules is in a state of energy E_α is given by

$$p_\alpha = \text{const } e^{-E_\alpha/kT} \tag{9.4}$$

or

$$p_\alpha = Z^{-1} e^{-E_\alpha/kT} \tag{9.5}$$

where

$$Z = \sum_\alpha e^{-E_\alpha/kT} \tag{9.6}$$

The sum Z is again a sum over all allowable states, and is called the *phase integral* (for historical reasons we need not enter into), or the *partition function*, since it governs, through (9.5), the partition of systems between states of energy E_α.

The average energy of the M systems is found by multiplying the energy of each state, E_α, by its probability p_α, and summing over all states

$$\bar{E} = \sum_\alpha p_\alpha E_\alpha \tag{9.7}$$

We tentatively identify this average energy with the thermodynamic internal energy U. If the identification is false then our conclusions will not match the facts. Hence

$$U = \sum_\alpha p_\alpha E_\alpha = Z^{-1} \sum_\alpha E_\alpha e^{-E_\alpha/kT} \tag{9.8}$$

$$= kT^2 Z^{-1} \left(\frac{\partial}{\partial T} \sum_\alpha e^{-E_\alpha/kT} \right)_V \tag{9.9}$$

$$= kT^2 Z^{-1} (\partial Z/\partial T)_V \tag{9.10}$$

or

$$-\frac{U}{T^2} = \left(\frac{\partial}{\partial T} (-k \ln Z) \right)_V \tag{9.11}$$

The differentiation in (9.9) and later equations is restricted to constant volume since the energy levels E_α are functions of V.

Equation (9.11) is reminiscent of the Gibbs-Helmholtz equation

$$U = A - T(\partial A/\partial T)_V \qquad (9.12)$$

for this can be rewritten

$$-\frac{U}{T^2} = \left(\frac{\partial(A/T)}{\partial T}\right)_V \qquad (9.13)$$

By comparison of (9.11) and (9.13) we identify the Helmholtz free energy with $(-kT \ln Z)$, that is,

$$A = -kT \ln Z \qquad \text{or} \qquad Z = e^{-A/kT} \qquad (9.14)$$

This equation provides the link we are seeking, for if we know the energy levels $E_\alpha(V)$ open to a system of volume V, then we can, from (9.14) compute $A(V, T)$. All other thermodynamic properties follow by the usual manipulations of classical thermodynamics.

$$U = A - T\left(\frac{\partial A}{\partial T}\right)_V = kT^2\left(\frac{\partial \ln Z}{\partial T}\right)_V \qquad (9.15)$$

$$S = -\left(\frac{\partial A}{\partial T}\right)_V = (U - A)/T \qquad (9.16)$$

$$P = -\left(\frac{\partial A}{\partial V}\right)_T = -kT\left(\frac{\partial \ln Z}{\partial V}\right)_T \qquad (9.17)$$

$$C_V = T\left(\frac{\partial S}{\partial T}\right)_V = 2kT\left(\frac{\partial \ln Z}{\partial T}\right)_V + kT^2\left(\frac{\partial^2 \ln Z}{\partial T^2}\right)_V \qquad (9.18)$$

At first sight it seems dangerous to identify (A/T) with $(-k \ln Z)$ when we know only that they have the same temperature derivative. We merely state here, without proof, that the absence of any constant difference, independent of T, between these two functions is the content of the third law. Moreover, we shall see that if $P = -(\partial A/\partial V)_T$ is to be nRT/V in a gas for which E_α are the energy levels of independent molecules, then (A/T) cannot contain any term which is a function of volume only.

In the rest of this chapter we use (9.14) to predict the thermodynamic properties of fluids from a knowledge of the states and their energies E_α. It is the working equation of statistical thermodynamics.

9.3 The perfect gas: principles

A perfect gas is formed of independent molecules and so could be discussed by means of the simple equations (9.1)–(9.3). However, the more general and powerful equations (9.4)–(9.14) are applicable equally to independent and to interacting molecules. We, therefore, use (9.14) first to obtain the partition function Z by specifying the states, and their energies E_α, for the molecules of a perfect gas.

An independent molecule can move as an entity, it can (if polyatomic) rotate as it goes about one or more axes, its atoms can vibrate in different ways with respect to the centre of mass, and its electrons can occupy either a ground state or one of several excited states. The states open to one molecule comprise all allowed states of each kind of motion, so that when we denote a state by the subscript α, we mean in general one particular translational-cum-rotational-cum-vibrational-electronic state. However, these internal states are, to a good approximation, themselves mutually independent; that is, the rotational states open to a molecule are almost the same whatever vibrational state it is in, etc. In particular the translational states are always strictly independent of the others, and so we start with a gas in which this is the only kind of motion.

(a) *Translational states.* A monatomic molecule such as argon has only translational and electronic states; it cannot rotate or vibrate. It is true that the electrons can acquire a net angular momentum about the nucleus but such a state is of high energy and is classed as electronically excited, not as a rotational state. This and other electronically excited states are energetically so far above the ground state that they are important only in the kilokelvin range of temperature, and are ignored here.

In order to compute Z we need to know the allowable energies of the translational states, and these can be found explicitly by quantum mechanical calculation only for containers of certain simple shapes, such as a rectangular prism or a sphere. However, the thermodynamic properties at temperatures high enough for there to be a gas at all depend only on the distribution of states; that is, on the number in the range ε to $\varepsilon + \delta\varepsilon$, for values of ε of the order of kT. (This point is discussed below, after (9.27)). This distribution is independent of the shape of the container and so we can, without loss of generality, restrict ourselves to a rectangular prism of sides a, b and c. Here a state is specified by three quantum numbers, p, q, r, where $p \geqslant 1$, $q \geqslant 1$, $r \geqslant 1$, and its energy is given by

$$\varepsilon_{p,q,r} = \frac{h^2}{8m}\left(\frac{p^2}{a^2} + \frac{q^2}{b^2} + \frac{r^2}{c^2}\right) \tag{9.19}$$

where h is Planck's constant and m the mass of one molecule. If we add a second molecule of the same species it can occupy one of the same set of states, since the molecules are independent. Hence the energy of one state of the whole set of N molecules is

$$E_\alpha = \sum_{l=1}^{N} \varepsilon_{p(l)q(l)r(l)} \tag{9.20}$$

where $p(l)$, $q(l)$, and $r(l)$ are the quantum numbers of molecule l, and where α is merely a symbol which denotes the whole set of numbers $p(1)$, $q(1)$, $r(1) \ldots p(N)$, $q(N)$, $r(N)$. The partition function Z of (9.6) is

$$Z = \sum_\alpha \exp\left[-\sum_{l=1}^{N} \varepsilon_{p(l)q(l)r(l)}/kT\right] \quad \text{(pg)} \tag{9.21}$$

Since the exponential of a sum is the product of the exponentials

$$Z = \sum_{\alpha} \prod_{l=1}^{N} \exp\left[-\varepsilon_{p(l)q(l)r(l)}/kT\right] \quad \text{(pg)} \tag{9.22}$$

or, exchanging the order of the sum and product, and writing the sum over α explicitly as sums over p, q and r,

$$Z = \prod_{l=1}^{N} \sum_{p=1} \sum_{q=1} \sum_{r=1} \exp\left(-\varepsilon_{p(l)q(l)r(l)}/kT\right) \quad \text{(pg)} \tag{9.23}$$

Since all terms in the product are the same (that is, the molecules are identical), this can be re-written

$$Z = z^{N} \quad \text{where} \quad z = \sum_{p=1} \sum_{q=1} \sum_{r=1} \exp\left(-\varepsilon_{p,q,r}/kT\right) \quad \text{(pg)} \tag{9.24}$$

There is, however, a minor flaw in the argument leading to (9.24). We have assumed that a state in which, say, molecule l has quantum numbers p', q', and r', and molecule m has p'', q'', r'', is different from the state in which l has numbers p'', q'', r'' and m has p', q', r'. Since the molecules are identical this is not so; no experiment could distinguish between the two states. We have therefore, grossly over-estimated the size of Z. We can correct for this very simply if, as is the case in practice, there are very many more accessible states than there are molecules to put in them. It is then extremely unlikely that there will be more than one molecule in any one state, and so the correction is to divide the partition function of (9.24) by $N!$, the number of ways of permuting N molecules. That is, we have

$$Z = \frac{1}{N!} z^{N} \quad \text{(pg)} \tag{9.25}$$

where z is again given by (9.24).

Exercise

Check the formal manipulation of sums, products and permutations by writing out explicitly the partition function for two molecules (l and m) distributed over three states (1, 2 and 3). Equation (9.21) is composed of nine exponential terms, in three of which the molecules are in the same state, e.g. $\exp\left[-(\varepsilon_{l1} + \varepsilon_{m1})/kT\right]$, and in six of which they are in different states, e.g. $\exp\left[-(\varepsilon_{l1} + \varepsilon_{m2})/kT\right]$. These nine terms can be rearranged into (9.23) as the product of two sums of exponentials, each of the form

$$z_l = \left[\exp\left(-\varepsilon_{l1}/kT\right) + \exp\left(-\varepsilon_{l2}/kT\right) + \exp\left(-\varepsilon_{l3}/kT\right)\right].$$

To obtain (9.25), we divide $(z_l z_m)$ by (2!). This division avoids counting $(\varepsilon_{l1} + \varepsilon_{m2})$ as a different state from $(\varepsilon_{l2} + \varepsilon_{m1})$ in (9.21), and so correctly reduces six of its terms to three. However, it wrongly divides the three terms of the form $(\varepsilon_{l1} + \varepsilon_{m1})$ by 2 also. In practice, the set of accessible levels, 1, 2, 3, . . .

greatly exceeds the number of molecules, l, m, $\ldots$, and the number of terms handled incorrectly is negligible compared with those in which each molecule is in a different level.

We can now evaluate z in (9.24). It can be written as the product of three separate sums over p, q and r, since the exponential can be correspondingly factorized when $\varepsilon_{p,q,r}$ is given by (9.19). The first sum can be written

$$\sum_{p=1}^{\infty} \exp\left(-\chi_a p^2\right) = \int_0^{\infty} \exp\left(-\chi_a p^2\right) dp \tag{9.26}$$

where

$$\chi_a = \frac{h^2}{8mkTa^2} \tag{9.27}$$

The replacement of the sum by the integral in (9.26), and the changing of the lower limit to $p = 0$, are legitimate if χ_a is very small. In practice it is about 10^{-9} for typical simple molecules and for accessible temperatures. The definite integral is the error integral,

$$\int_0^{\infty} \exp\left(-\chi_a p^2\right) dp = \frac{1}{2}\left(\frac{\pi}{\chi_a}\right)^{1/2} = \left(\frac{2\pi mkT}{h^2}\right)^{1/2} a \tag{9.28}$$

Hence, by summing similarly over q and r,

$$z = V\left(\frac{2\pi mkT}{h^2}\right)^{3/2} \quad \text{(pg)} \tag{9.29}$$

where $V = abc$ is the volume of the rectangular prism.

The thermodynamic properties follow at once from (9.14)–(9.18). The partition function Z is

$$Z = \frac{z^N}{N!} = \left(\frac{e}{N}\right)^N V^N \left(\frac{2\pi mkT}{h^2}\right)^{3N/2} \quad \text{(pg)} \tag{9.30}$$

where we have used Stirling's approximation for the factorial of a large number,

$$N! \simeq N^N e^{-N} \tag{9.31}$$

From (9.30) and (9.14)–(9.18)

$$A = -NkT \ln\left[\frac{eV}{N}\left(\frac{2\pi mkT}{h^2}\right)^{3/2}\right] \quad \text{(pg)} \tag{9.32}$$

$$P = NkT/V \quad \text{(pg)} \tag{9.33}$$

$$U = \tfrac{3}{2}NkT \quad \text{(pg)} \tag{9.34}$$

$$S = \tfrac{5}{2}Nk + Nk \ln\left[\frac{V}{N}\left(\frac{2\pi mkT}{h^2}\right)^{3/2}\right] \quad \text{(pg)} \tag{9.35}$$

$$C_V = \tfrac{3}{2}Nk \quad \text{(pg)} \tag{9.36}$$

We see, first, that we obtain correctly the equation of state of a perfect gas (9.33), and secondly, that the heat capacity C_V is $\frac{3}{2}Nk$, and hence C_P is $\frac{5}{2}Nk$, so that the molar heat capacities are $\frac{3}{2}R$ and $\frac{5}{2}R$ respectively. These conclusions are amply confirmed for the inert gases at low densities.

The third verifiable result is the expression for the 'absolute' entropy, (9.35), which is called the Sackur-Tetrode equation. This is, in fact, the increase in entropy of a gas in the condition specified by V and T over that in a condition where all molecules are confined to one state (we do not prove this statement here, but merely assert it). If such a condition can be realised experimentally it can only be in the crystal at zero kelvin. For argon, and for many other substances, this is indeed the case. The conventional absolute molar entropy of Section 8.4 for argon in its standard state as a gas at its normal boiling point of 87.29 K is $s^{\ominus} = 129.0\,\text{J K}^{-1}\,\text{mol}^{-1}$. The entropy calculated from (9.35) is $129.20\,\text{J K}^{-1}\,\text{mol}^{-1}$. The agreement is within the error of the calorimetric value. Such a comparison illustrates the value of statistical thermodynamics when, as here, we know sufficient about the molecular mechanics of our system. Equation (9.35) requires only a knowledge of the mass of the argon atom; that is of its 'molecular weight' and of Avogadro's constant. The calorimetric value requires painstaking measurements of heat capacities, latent heats, and the second virial coefficient (to correct to the standard state of the perfect gas). However, in most cases, as we shall see below, the balance of accuracy and convenience is not so heavily weighted on the side of the statistical calculation.

(b) *Rotational states.* Molecules which rotate but which are without significant vibration are the next most simple class to consider. At room temperature and below, such molecules include the tightly bound diatomic molecules, hydrogen, nitrogen, oxygen and carbon monoxide, and radicals such as CH, NH' and OH.

The rotational motion is strictly independent of the translational, and so the partition function of such a molecule can be factorized into the product of the translational partition function, given by (9.24), and an independent rotational partition function. The corresponding contribution to the thermodynamic functions are therefore additive since (9.14)–(9.18) depend solely on ln z. We have, therefore,

$$\varepsilon = \varepsilon_{\text{trans}} + \varepsilon_{\text{rot}}; \qquad z = z_{\text{trans}}z_{\text{rot}}; \qquad \text{and so}$$

$$U = U_{\text{trans}} + U_{\text{rot}}, \qquad \text{etc.} \tag{9.37}$$

We now compute z_{rot} from the allowed rotational states. These depend on the number of orthogonal axes about which the molecule can rotate, which is two for a linear and three for a non-linear molecule (a linear molecule cannot rotate about the axis which contains the nuclei for the same reason that a monatomic molecule cannot rotate at all).

The states open to a heteronuclear diatomic molecule have energies given by

$$\varepsilon_j = \frac{j(j+1)h^2}{8\pi^2 I} \tag{9.38}$$

where I is the moment of inertia about an axis through the centre of mass and perpendicular to the nuclear axis and $j(=0, 1, 2 \ldots)$ is the quantum number. There are $(2j+1)$ states each with energy ε_j; that is, the jth energy level is $(2j+1)$-fold degenerate. Hence

$$z_{rot} = \sum_{j=0} (2j+1) \exp[-j(j+1)h^2/8\pi^2 IkT] \tag{9.39}$$

If the levels are closely spaced with respect to kT we can again replace the sum by an integral

$$z_{rot} = \int_0^\infty (2j+1) \exp[-j(j+1)h^2/8\pi^2 IkT] \, dj \tag{9.40}$$

$$= \int_0^\infty \exp[-\Theta x/T] \, dx \tag{9.41}$$

where $x = j(j+1)$, so that $(2j+1) \, dj = dx$ and where Θ is a characteristic temperature

$$\Theta = h^2/8\pi^2 Ik \tag{9.42}$$

The integral is readily evaluated

$$z_{rot} = T/\Theta \tag{9.43}$$

and so the rotational contributions to U and C_V are, by (9.15), (9.18), (9.25) and (9.37),

$$U_{rot} = NkT \qquad (C_V)_{rot} = Nk \tag{9.44}$$

The states open to a homonuclear diatomic molecule differ in detail from those of (9.38). They are approximately half in number and lead to a partition function half that of (9.42), namely $T/2\Theta$. This factor of $\frac{1}{2}$ is the reciprocal of the *symmetry number*, 2, and corrects for the fact that, whereas the two ends of CO are experimentally distinguishable, the two ends of N_2 are not. Hence the number of distinguishable states of N_2 is only half the number for CO. Nevertheless, as shown below, the contributions to U and C_V (but not A and S) are unchanged. The replacement of the sum (9.40) by the integral (9.41) is legitimate if $T \gg \Theta$, and this is valid for all gases other than hydrogen.[2]

We have, therefore, for the diatomic rotator of symmetry number σ,

$$z_{rot} = \sigma^{-1}(T/\Theta) \tag{9.45}$$

and for the contributions to the thermodynamic functions

$$A_{rot} = G_{rot} = -NkT \ln (T/\sigma\Theta) \tag{9.46}$$

$$U_{rot} = H_{rot} = NkT \tag{9.47}$$

$$S_{rot} = Nk[1 + \ln (T/\sigma\Theta)] \tag{9.48}$$

$$(C_V)_{rot} = (C_P)_{rot} = Nk \tag{9.49}$$

The equations, although obtained specifically for diatomic molecules apply to all linear molecules. Thus the rotational states open to N_2O (whose structure is NNO) are the same as those open to CO, but with a different moment of inertia. Similarly, the symmetric molecule CO_2 (structure OCO), has, like N_2, only half this number of levels open to it; that is, its symmetry number σ is 2.

The three-dimensional rotators (that is, all non-linear molecules) are a more difficult problem. Fortunately, only the classical limits of z_{rot} and of the thermodynamic properties are needed since such molecules do not have very small moments of inertia. This limit is that reached when the spacing of the energy levels is so close that the sums can be replaced by integrals. We have then

$$z_{rot} = \sigma^{-1}(\pi T^3/\Theta^3)^{1/2} \tag{9.50}$$

where the moment of inertia in the definition of Θ by (9.42) is the geometric mean of the three so-called principal moments of inertia.[3] As before, we divide z by the number of orientations which would be distinct if the nuclei were distinguishable, but which are identical in the real molecule. The symmetry numbers of some common molecules are $\sigma = 3$ for NH_3 and CH_3Cl, $\sigma = 12$ for CH_4, $\sigma = 24$ for SF_6. It is 12 for C_6H_6 and 4 for C_2H_4 since either side of these molecules can be placed 'upwards'.

Exercise

What are the symmetry numbers of NH_2Cl, BF_3, C_2H_3Cl and $C_{10}H_8$ (naphthalene)?

Hence the rotational contributions to the energy and heat capacity of a three-dimensional rotator are

$$U_{rot} = \tfrac{3}{2}NkT \qquad (C_V)_{rot} = \tfrac{3}{2}Nk \tag{9.51}$$

the addition of a third axis about which rotation can take place increasing the energy from $\tfrac{2}{2}NkT$ of (9.47) to $\tfrac{3}{2}NkT$ of (9.51).

Exercise

Write down the analogues of (9.46)–(9.49) for the other thermodynamic functions of a non-linear rotator.

(c) *Vibrational states.* The most important type of distortion of the molecule is the molecular vibrations, that is the periodic internal oscillations of the nuclei with respect to the centre of mass of the molecule.

Consider a molecule of n atoms, whose positions in space are described by $3n$ independent coordinates. It is convenient to divide these $3n$ coordinates, as follows; three to describe the position of the centre mass of the molecule, three to describe its orientation (or two if it is a linear molecule), and the remaining $3n - 6$, and $3n - 5$, describe the internal dispositions of the nuclei with respect to the centre of mass. Thus a diatomic molecule, which must be linear, has only one 'internal coordinate', a linear triatomic molecule has four, and a non-linear triatomic molecule has three. The number of independent ways in which a molecule can vibrate is equal to the number of internal coordinates. These independent vibrations are called the *normal modes*. This is not the place for an account of the analysis of the oscillations of molecules into their normal modes (as is given, for example, by Herzberg[4] or by Wilson, Decius and Cross[5]) but we state only that the energy levels open to the oscillating molecule are just those of the $3n-6$, or $3n-5$, normal modes. It is these levels that appear in the infrared and Raman spectra, and the identification of the frequencies of the normal modes is the first task of the molecular spectroscopist.

As a first approximation the molecule can be treated as a group of simple harmonic oscillators each of which has the frequency of one of the normal modes. More than one mode can have the same frequency.

Hence we extend our molecular partition function, cf. (9.37), to cover now both rotational and vibrational motions, and conveniently call these together the internal motions,

$$z = z_{trans}z_{int} \qquad z_{int} = z_{rot}z_{vib} \qquad (9.52)$$

where z_{vib} is a product of $(3n-6)$ or $(3n-5)$ factors, z_v, one for each vibration of frequency v. The factorisation of the partition function in (9.52) follows from the independence of the energy levels (cf. 9.37). The translational levels are always strictly independent of the rotational and vibrational, and it is usually a good approximation to assume that the rotational and vibrational are mutually independent.

The energy levels of a harmonic oscillator of frequency v are

$$\varepsilon_n = (n+\tfrac{1}{2})hv \qquad (n=0,1,2,\ldots) \qquad (9.53)$$

and all are non-degenerate. Hence

$$z_v = \sum_{n=0}^{\infty} \exp\left[-(n+\tfrac{1}{2})hv/kT\right] \qquad (9.54)$$

This is a geometric progression whose sum is

$$z_v = e^{-\beta/2}(1-e^{-\beta})^{-1} = (2\sinh\tfrac{1}{2}\beta)^{-1} \qquad \beta = hv/kT \qquad (9.55)$$

Hence, each of the $(3n-6)$ or $(3n-5)$ vibrations contributes to the energy and heat capacity a term given by

$$U_v = NkT[\tfrac{1}{2}\beta \coth \tfrac{1}{2}\beta] \qquad (9.56)$$

$$(C_V)_v = Nk[\tfrac{1}{2}\beta \operatorname{cosech} \tfrac{1}{2}\beta]^2 \qquad (9.57)$$

$$= Nk\beta^2 e^{\beta}(e^{\beta}-1)^{-2} \qquad (9.58)$$

These functions are often called the Einstein functions since they were first derived for his model of a crystal in which all atoms were supposed to execute harmonic oscillations of uniform frequency. At low temperatures, where β is large,

$$U_\nu = \tfrac{1}{2}Nh\nu + O(e^{-\beta}) \tag{9.59}$$

$$(C_V)_\nu = O(\beta^2 e^{-\beta}) \tag{9.60}$$

At high temperatures, where β is small

$$U_\nu = NkT[1 + \beta^2/12 + \ldots] \tag{9.61}$$

$$(C_v)_\nu = Nk[1 - \beta^2/12 + \ldots] \tag{9.62}$$

The Einstein functions (9.56) and (9.57) are shown in Figure 9.1. The minimum of the energy is $\tfrac{1}{2}Nh\nu$, that is $\tfrac{1}{2}h\nu$ for each molecular vibrator of frequency ν. This zero-temperature energy is thermodynamically unimportant since it corresponds only to a shift of zero; it is, however, conventional to measure vibrational energy from the (hypothetical) stationary or non-vibrating system, although in practice the energy cannot be reduced below $\tfrac{1}{2}h\nu$, as is shown in (9.53) and in (9.59). The area between the asymptote $C_V = Nk$ in Figure 9.1, and the quantal curve for C_V is clearly equal to the zero-temperature energy, $\tfrac{1}{2}Nh\nu$.

Many tables of the thermodynamic properties of the harmonic oscillator have been published. The sixth edition of Landolt-Börnstein[6] (1961) has a table in which the argument is β and in which the functions are in joules. Mayer and Mayer[7] have a table in the form of the argument in β and the functions as dimensionless ratios such as $(C_V)_\nu/Nk$. A more extensive set of tables of this kind is published by the National Bureau of Standards in Washington.[8]

However, (9.56)–(9.58), on which all these tables are based, are exact only if all the vibrations are, in fact, harmonic oscillations, and if the

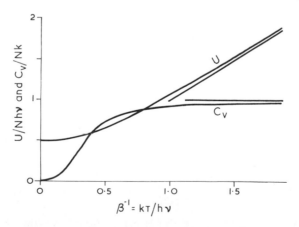

Figure 9.1. The Einstein functions for U and C_V of a simple harmonic oscillator

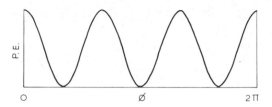

Figure 9.2. Change of potential energy with angle of solution ϕ, for an internal rotator with three equal minima

vibrational motion can be treated independently of the rotational. Neither assumption is strictly correct, and for precise work at high temperatures it is necessary to use a more accurate description of the energy levels open to the molecules. A molecule that is performing anharmonic oscillations does not have the same moment of inertia as a molecule at rest. Conversely, a molecule that is stretched by rapid rotation does not have the same frequency of vibration as one without rotational energy. This coupling of the vibrational and rotational motions can be expressed by writing a combined set of energy levels, ε_{nj}. However, the details of this coupling and the mathematical techniques for summing the partition function over this combined set of levels are not discussed here.

(d) *Internal rotations.* We have assumed so far that a molecule has a rigid structure; that is, that there is only one arrangement of the nuclei which corresponds to a minimum in its potential energy. This is true of all molecules with small numbers of atoms, e.g. N_2, CO_2, H_2O, CH_4, but not necessarily for the larger ones. Thus, in C_2H_6, C_3H_8 or CH_3OH a methyl group can rotate with respect to the rest of the molecule, and as it does so the potential energy passes through a set (usually 3) of maxima and minima (Figure 9.2). Such distortion is called internal rotation and it is intermediate in character between the rotational and vibrational motions discussed above.

Exercise

Why is there no internal rotation in CH_3CN?

If the barrier restricting the rotation of the methyl or other group is low compared with kT, then the motion is a fairly free rotation with only one degree of freedom. It can be handled in the same way as the external rotation and, if the moment of inertia is not too small, leads to a contribution to U and C_V of $\frac{1}{2}NkT$ and $\frac{1}{2}Nk$ respectively. If the barrier is high compared with kT, then the motion is, for all practical purposes, a vibration about one of the minima, with but rare incursions into a different minimum. This switch of structure may be important to the chemist in that it may be fast enough to prevent him isolating isomers of different internal rotational configuration, but it is unimportant thermodynamically. The internal rotation can now be treated as a normal vibration.

In most cases, however, the barrier is neither sufficiently low nor sufficiently high for these two simple limits to be reached; that is, it is comparable with kT. Thus that in CH_3OH is $4.5\,kJ\,mol^{-1}$ which is about twice the value of (N_AkT) at $0\,°C$. The levels open to the internal rotator are then a complex set which change in character from a vibrational type at low energy to a rotational at high. The difficult computation of the thermodynamic properties is facilitated by the extensive tables of Pitzer and his colleagues.[9]

9.4   The perfect gas: applications

The formal results of the last section give us the tools for calculating the thermodynamic properties of a pure perfect gas. We now summarise the use of these methods for gases of technical interest.

The contribution of the translational motion is given always by (9.32)–(9.36), and requires only a knowledge of the mass of the molecule (for S, A and G) and not even that for U, H, C_V and C_P. To this contribution we add those of the rotations of the molecule as a whole, obtained from (9.45)–(9.49) or by substituting the partition function (9.50), raised to the power N, into the general equations (9.15)–(9.18). The shape and size of most gaseous molecules are sufficiently well-known for an accurate estimation of the moment (or moments) of inertia for the calculation of S, A and G. The internal energy U, the enthalpy H, the heat capacities C_V and C_P, are independent of the moments of inertia.

It is only the translational partition function (9.29) which depends on the volume, and which therefore is the only part of z to contribute to the pressure. Similarly, it is only the translational part of Z to which we have to apply the correction of division by $N!$ needed to go from (9.24) to (9.25) (perhaps it would be more accurate to say that this correction for the indistinguishability of the molecules is to be applied once to the term z^N, and is not be be repeated for its internal factors, z_{rot} and z_{vib}).

The contributions from translational and rotational motion are usually straightforward; it is the calculation of those from the vibrations and internal rotations that is more difficult. The first question to be settled is whether or not the latter are present. If not, then it is likely that the spectroscopists have been able to determine the frequencies of all the vibrations. On this point it may be necessary to take expert advice, or to read fairly extensively in the large literature of this field. A review by Frankiss and Green[10] gives useful guidance both on the principles and on the calculations for some typical molecules. In any case it is advisable to check carefully that the correct number of frequencies (with their degeneracies) has been taken into account, by seeing that the total number adds up to $(3n-6)$, or $(3n-5)$ for a linear molecule, where n is the number of atoms in the molecule.

Example

The calculation of $c_P^\ominus$ and $s^\ominus$ for carbon dioxide at 25 °C, from the following information: Relative molar mass (i.e. 'molecular weight') 44.01; Structure, a linear symmetric molecule with C—O bond length of 1.159×10^{-10} m and $\sigma = 2$, and $(3 \times 3 - 5) = 4$ normal modes of vibration of frequencies* 2349 cm^{-1}, 1310 cm^{-1} and 2 of 667 cm^{-1}.

From the Sackur-Tetrode equation (9.35), and from (9.36), we have for the translational contributions

$$(c_P^\ominus)_{\text{trans}} = \tfrac{5}{2}R = 20.786 \text{ J K}^{-1} \text{ mol}^{-1}$$

$$(s^\ominus)_{\text{trans}} = 18.756R = 155.94 \text{ J K}^{-1} \text{ mol}^{-1}$$

For the rotational contributions from (9.48) and (9.49) with $I = 7.13 \times 10^{-46}$ kg m^2, and hence $(T/2\Theta) = 256.25$

$$(c_P^\ominus)_{\text{rot}} = R = 8.314 \text{ J K}^{-1} \text{ mol}^{-1}$$

$$(s^\ominus)_{\text{rot}} = 6.581R = 54.72 \text{ J K}^{-1} \text{ mol}^{-1}$$

For the vibrational contributions from tables of the Einstein functions

'Frequency'/cm^{-1}	$h\nu/kT$	c/R	s/R
2349	11.34	0.002	0.000
1310	6.34	0.072	0.013
667	3.22	2×0.450	2×0.175

giving

$$(c_P^\ominus)_{\text{vib}} = 0.973R = 8.09 \text{ J K}^{-1} \text{ mol}^{-1}$$

$$(s^\ominus)_{\text{vib}} = 0.363R = 3.02 \text{ J K}^{-1} \text{ mol}^{-1}$$

The total functions are, therefore:

$$c_P^\ominus = 37.19 \text{ J K}^{-1} \text{ mol}^{-1}$$

$$s^\ominus = 213.68 \text{ J K}^{-1} \text{ mol}^{-1}$$

Calorimetric values[11] are

$$c_P^\ominus = 37.14 \text{ J K}^{-1} \text{ mol}^{-1}$$

$$s^\ominus = 213.9 \text{ J K}^{-1} \text{ mol}^{-1}$$

The agreement is excellent; the calculated value of $s^\ominus$ is probably more accurate than the calorimetric.

If the molecule is not rigid then it is unlikely that the spectroscopists can give a sufficiently complete specification for a direct calculation of the thermodynamic properties. For some hydrocarbons and other important

---

* Spectroscopists usually quote frequencies of vibration by stating the number of wave-lengths of light of that frequency per centimetre. 1 cm^{-1} is equivalent to 2.9979×10^{10} s^{-1} or 29.979 GHz. A frequency of 1 cm^{-1} is equivalent to a value of $h\nu/k$ of 1.4388 K.

molecules the barriers hindering the internal rotations are known and progress is possible.[12] In making such calculations each internal rotation replaces a vibration in the check that the correct number of $(3n - 6)$ term is included.

With complex molecules, which generally means those with more than about six atoms, it is unusual to know all the frequencies, or to know much about internal rotations or other forms of internal flexibility such as is found in cycloparaffins. Hence, we must resort to methods of approximation which are based on estimates of the unknown frequencies. Such estimates can be made since the normal modes can, in some degree, be ascribed to oscillations of particular parts of the molecule. Thus all organic molecules have frequencies around 3000 cm^{-1} which arise from the stretching of the C—H bond. Unfortunately, the lower frequencies which contribute most heavily to the thermodynamic properties arise from distortions of the carbon skeleton of organic molecules and so cannot be estimated for complicated molecules with the same confidence as the CH stretching frequency. Nevertheless, there is now a sufficient body of knowledge to support semi-empirical schemes for estimating the frequencies from the structural formula by ascribing a bending and a stretching frequency to each bond, in such a way that the total number of vibrations adds up to $(3n - 6)$. The first of these schemes was devised by Bennewitz and Rossner (1938) and modified to include internal rotations by Dobratz (1941). Most of the later schemes are but modifications of these. They are discussed in detail by Reid and Sherwood[13] who recommend the best way of estimating the thermodynamic properties of a wide range of organic molecules in the perfect gas state.

The accuracy of the estimation of thermodynamic properties depends on the detail of the spectroscopic information. If the molecules are simple then heat capacities are usually good to a few parts per thousand, and generally more accurate than calorimetric measurements. If the molecules are flexible, with internal rotations or other easily excited deformations, then the accuracy may fall to 1–2%. If the frequencies are not all known so that it is necessary to use one of the semi-empirical methods, then the accuracy may be no better than 3–5%, or even worse, depending on the complexity of the molecule.

9.5 Mixed gases and chemical reactions

One of the most valuable uses of statistical thermodynamics is the calculation of the position of chemical equilibrium between reacting gases at low pressures; that is, in the calculation of K_P of (8.19). We approach this problem by generalising the working equation (9.14) and the partition function for a perfect gas (9.25) to a mixture of N_i molecules of species i; N_j of species j, etc. We find that (9.14) is unchanged but that, since molecules of species i are distinguishable from those of j, but not from each other, (9.25) becomes

$$Z = \prod_i (z_i^{N_i}/N_i!) \tag{9.63}$$

Stirling's approximation (9.31) can be applied to each factorial to give

$$\prod_i N_i! = \prod_i N_i^{N_i} e^{-N_i} = e^{-N} \prod_i N_i^{N_i} \tag{9.64}$$

where

$$N = \sum_i N_i \tag{9.65}$$

Hence

$$A = -NkT - kT \ln\left[\prod_i (z_i/N_i)^{N_i}\right] \quad \text{(pg)} \tag{9.66}$$

$$= -NkT - \sum_i N_i kT \ln (z_i/N_i) \quad \text{(pg)} \tag{9.67}$$

We can convert this expression from molecular to molar amounts by substituting for N_i,

$$N_i k = N_i(R/N_A) = n_i R \tag{9.68}$$

where N_A is Avogadro's constant. Hence

$$A = -nRT - \sum_i n_i RT \ln (z_i k/n_i R) \quad \text{(pg)} \tag{9.69}$$

This is, therefore, the Helmholtz free energy of a perfect gas mixture in terms of the molecular partition functions, z_i, of each species i. The Gibbs free energy is $(A + nRT)$. The chemical potential follows directly from (9.69)

$$\mu_i = \left(\frac{\partial A}{\partial n_i}\right)_{V,T,n_j} = RT \ln (n_i R/z_i k) \quad \text{(pg)} \tag{9.70}$$

It is now convenient to extract from each z_i its dependence on volume through the translational partition function (9.29). That is, we write

$$z_i = V z_i' \quad \text{where} \quad z_i' = \left(\frac{2\pi m k T}{h^2}\right)^{3/2} (z_i)_{\text{int}} \tag{9.71}$$

where $(z_i)_{\text{int}}$ is the rotational and vibrational partition function for species i, and so z_i' is a function only of temperature. On substituting (9.71) into (9.70) and using the perfect gas equation $V = nRT/P$, we have

$$\mu_i = RT \ln (y_i P/z_i' kT) \quad \text{(pg)} \tag{9.72}$$

where y_i is the mole fraction of species i. This result conforms with that given previously for the dependence of μ_i on pressure and composition (6.35). The standard potential is

$$\mu_i^{\ominus} = RT \ln (P^{\ominus}/z_i' kT) \tag{9.73}$$

We can use (9.72)–(9.73) to obtain the equilibrium constant K_P, by substituting them in the fundamental condition of equilibrium (8.11), namely $\sum_i \nu_i \mu_i = 0$. We obtain,

$$\sum_i \nu_i \ln\left(\frac{y_i P}{z_i' k T}\right) = 0 \quad \text{(pg)} \tag{9.74}$$

or, by comparison with (8.13), (8.14) and (8.19),

$$\sum_i \nu_i \ln\left(\frac{z_i' k T}{P^\ominus}\right) = \sum_i \nu_i \ln\left(\frac{y_i P}{P^\ominus}\right) = \ln K_P \quad \text{(pg)} \tag{9.75}$$

Hence

$$K_P = \prod_i \left(\frac{z_i' k T}{P^\ominus}\right)^{\nu_i} \quad \text{(pg)} \tag{9.76}$$

This equation is correct, but is misleading. It is implicit in this equation that all partition functions are to be measured from the same zero of energy. The equations for z_i' developed in Section 9.3 are all based on a zero of the ground electronic state of each substance, and we can use such zeros as long as the molecules retain their identity. In a chemical reaction, however, there is a large release or absorption of electronic energy, as the chemical bonds are re-arranged. Thus in a decomposition of A_2 to $2A$ the atoms have an electronic energy higher than that of the molecule by an amount equal to the bond energy. This manifests itself as the molar energy of reaction between the (hypothetical) perfect gases at zero kelvin, Δu_0. It is convenient in using (9.70) to be able to retain the convention that each z_i' is calculated from its own ground electronic state, but if we are to do this consistently we must raise all the levels of the products by Δu_0 with respect to those of the reactants. Since energy levels enter z_i' through Boltzmann factors this change requires a factor of $\exp(-\Delta u_0/RT)$ on the right-hand side of (9.76). That is, we write

$$K_P = \exp\left(\frac{-\Delta h_0}{RT}\right) \prod_i \left(\frac{z_i' k T}{P^\ominus}\right)^{\nu_i} \quad \text{(pg)} \tag{9.77}$$

Where each z_i' is now to be reckoned from its own ground electronic state, and where Δh_0 may be written for Δu_0 since at zero kelvin $\Delta h = \Delta u$ for a reaction between perfect gases.

Equation (9.77) shows that an entirely statistical calculation of K_P is not possible for the term Δh_0 must always be obtained experimentally. In some cases it can be measured spectroscopically; for example the heats of dissociation of diatomic molecules.[14] In general it must be found calorimetrically[15] or estimated from a scheme which assigns values to the strength of each chemical bond C—H, C—C, C=C, etc.[16] However, the principal use of (9.77) is that it allows Δh_0 to be calculated from a knowledge of K_P at one temperature, if the partition functions z_i' can be obtained from spectroscopic data as in Sections 9.3 and 9.4. This means that if K_P is known at one temperature, it is known at all, and is equivalent to the use of the third law in Section 8.4. Indeed, a comparison of (8.26) and (9.77) shows that the product of partition functions is directly related to the standard entropy of reaction.

Many examples could be given of calculations based on (9.77). An early one on a reaction of industrial importance was Kassel's calculation of the water-gas equilibrium.[17] A more recent one is its use by Gilmore[18] to obtain the equilibrium concentrations of N_2, O_2, NO, N, O, N^+, O^+, Ar, Ar^+, e, etc. in air at temperatures up to 24 000 K.

9.6   Real gases: the virial equation of state

The results obtained in the last three sections are all based on the factorisation of Z into the N-fold product of molecular partition functions, z ; that is, on (9.25) for pure gases and (9.63) for mixtures. To handle states other than the perfect gas we must go back to the fundamental equation (9.6) in which Z is given by a sum of Boltzmann factors, $\exp(-E_\alpha/kT)$, where E_α is now the energy of state α of the whole system of N molecules. This energy can be broken down into some of the terms we have discussed already, for the molecules are moving, rotating and vibrating. We start, however, by ignoring all internal motions; that is, the discussion is restricted to monatomic species. A dense gas or liquid composed of such molecules has translational energy and another form of energy which we have not discussed so far in this chapter, namely the potential energy of the intermolecular forces. When molecules are packed closely together their mutual forces of attraction can lower the energy by amounts large compared with NkT. The clearest manifestation of this energy is the latent heat of evaporation which is the enthalpy needed to separate the molecules of a liquid and disperse them as a gas of much lower density. This potential energy is a smooth function of the mutual separations of all N-molecules. We call it the configurational energy and denote it $\mathcal{U}(\mathbf{r})$, where the symbol $\mathbf{r}$ represents all the vectors $\mathbf{r}_1 \ldots \mathbf{r}_N$, needed to specify the positions of the N molecules in a volume V. In general $\mathcal{U}$ is a function also of the orientations of the molecules, but it is to avoid this complication that we assume, for the moment, that we have spherical molecules.

We do not need to use the more exact methods of quantum mechanics to handle this configurational energy, for the methods of classical mechanics suffice for all molecules heavier than hydrogen and helium. Moreover, we have seen that classical mechanics suffices also for the translational motion in that we were able to replace the sum over discrete states in (9.26), by an integral over a continuous distribution of states.

We wish, therefore, to obtain the partition function Z of (9.6) for a system in which the total energy of the molecules, each of speed v_l and position $\mathbf{r}_l$, is given by

$$E = \sum_{l=1}^{N} \tfrac{1}{2}mv_l^2 + \mathcal{U}(\mathbf{r}) \tag{9.78}$$

where **r** is a symbol for $\mathbf{r}_1 \ldots \mathbf{r}_l \ldots \mathbf{r}_N$. We see that the difficulty of calculating Z for such a system is our inability to break $\mathcal{U}$ down into N independent terms. To obtain the classical analogue of (9.6) we re-write the translational energy of each molecule in terms of its momentum $\mathbf{p}_l$, so that we have

$$E = \sum_{l=1}^{N} \frac{1}{2m} \mathbf{p}_i^2 + \mathcal{U}(\mathbf{r}) \tag{9.79}$$

where

$$\mathbf{p}_i^2 = \mathbf{p}_l \cdot \mathbf{p}_l = (p_x)_i^2 + (p_y)_i^2 + (p_z)_i^2 \tag{9.80}$$

The partition function is

$$Z = \frac{1}{N!} \frac{1}{h^{3N}} \int \ldots \int e^{-E/kT} \, d\mathbf{p}_1 \ldots d\mathbf{p}_N \, d\mathbf{r}_1 \ldots d\mathbf{r}_N \tag{9.81}$$

where $d\mathbf{r}_l$ denotes a volume element, that is $(dx \, dy \, dz)_l$ in Cartesian coordinates, and where $d\mathbf{p}_l$ is a similar element of momentum 'space'. This integral is the semi-classical version of the quantal sum (9.6), and the presence of the factor h^{-3N} in it requires some comment. Z in (9.81) is called *semi-classical* since it is derived from classical mechanics (and so is an integral, not a sum over discrete states) but it contains also the factor of h^{3N}, which would have no place in a strictly classical expression. The sum (9.6) is a set of exponential functions and so is a pure number. The integral (9.81) is over all values of $\mathbf{p}_l$ and $\mathbf{r}_l$ (within the volume V), since there are no restrictions on these values in classical mechanics. However, the variables of the integral $d\mathbf{p}_l \, d\mathbf{r}_l$ are not pure numbers and so a factor of dimensions of (momentum × distance)^{3N} must be inserted into the denominator of (9.81) if Z is still to be a number. The size of this constant is chosen to be h^{3N}, since this is the size needed to make (9.81) yield the same partition function for the perfect gas as we have obtained already from the energy levels of (9.19). We now demonstrate this.

On substituting (9.79) into (9.81) it is seen, first that the term containing the configurational energy is independent of those containing the momenta and so can be factorised out as a separate integral. That is, we have

$$Z = \frac{Q}{h^{3N}} \int \ldots \int \exp\left[-\sum_{l=1}^{n} (\mathbf{p}_i^2/2mkT) \right] d\mathbf{p}_1 \ldots d\mathbf{p}_N \tag{9.82}$$

where

$$Q = \frac{1}{N!} \int_V \ldots \int \exp\left[-\mathcal{U}(\mathbf{r})/kT \right] d\mathbf{r}_1 \ldots d\mathbf{r}_N \tag{9.83}$$

The factor of $(1/N!)$ is conventionally taken with Q and the factor of $(1/h^{3N})$ with the rest of Z, (9.82). The integration over each of the $3N$ variables of momentum $(dp_x)_1 \cdots (dp_z)_N$ can be made at once, since all are independent, and can take any value between $+\infty$ and $-\infty$. Each integral is an error integral and the result is (9.29) without the volume factor. That is, we can write (9.81) as

$$Z = \left(\frac{2\pi mkT}{h^2}\right)^{3N/2} . Q = Z_{mol} . Q \qquad (9.84)$$

where Q is given by (9.83), and Z_{mol} is defined by this equation for molecules without rotation and vibration.

In a perfect gas $\mathcal{U}(\mathbf{r})$ is zero for all configurations, so that the *configuration integral* Q becomes

$$Q = \frac{1}{N!} \int_V \dots \int d\mathbf{r}_1 \dots d\mathbf{r}_N = V^N/N! \qquad \text{(pg)} \qquad (9.85)$$

since each integration of an element $d\mathbf{r}(= dx\, dy\, dz)$ over the volume V gives rise to a factor of V in Q. The substitution of (9.85) into (9.84) gives again the result for a perfect gas

$$Z = (z_{trans})^N/N! \qquad \text{(pg)} \qquad (9.86)$$

where z_{trans} is the partition function of (9.29).

Equation (9.84) is, therefore, a factorising of Z into two parts, a 'molecular' part and a configurational part Q. It is, however, not a factorising of Z into a product of partition functions since the volume factor of the translational partition function remains with Q whilst the rest goes into the molecular part of Z in (9.84). Thus, although Z is a pure number, neither of the factors into which is has been decomposed is a pure number; one has dimensions of V^{-N} and the other V^N. Since the thermodynamic properties depend on the logarithm of Z this division does not correspond to an easy division of these two properties into two parts, a molecular and a configurational part.[19] Nevertheless, the division is the one usually made, and is followed here. The problem of calculating the properties of real fluids is the problem of evaluating the configurational integral Q. In the previous sections, on the perfect gas, there were no difficulties of statistical thermodynamics, only of molecular mechanics. If the latter could be overcome, we had in Sections 9.3–9.5 exact equations for calculating the thermodynamic properties. For a real gas we have two problems. First the molecular interactions which make up $\mathcal{U}$ may not be known accurately; that is, we may not be able to specify how $\mathcal{U}$ depends on all the configurations $\mathbf{r}$. Secondly, and this is a difficulty we did not have with the perfect gas, even if $\mathcal{U}$ is known, we may not be able to tackle the problem in statistical thermodynamics of evaluating the integral in Q since it is, in general, a $3N$-fold integral that defies factorisation.

We can make some progress by using the fact that, to a reasonable approximation, $\mathcal{U}$ is a sum of the independent interaction of molecules in all possible pairs. That is

$$\mathcal{U}(\mathbf{r}) = \sum_{l<m}^{N-1} \sum^{N} u(r_{lm}) \qquad (9.87)$$

where $u(r_{lm})$, or u_{lm}, is the energy of interaction of a pair of molecules at a separation r_{lm} (we are still neglecting any dependence of u on the orientation of the molecules). Since every molecule interacts with every other there are, in principle, $\frac{1}{2}N(N-1)$ terms in (9.87), but in practice u falls off so rapidly with r that only a number of the order of N are different from zero at any one time. The dependence of the intermolecular potential u on the separation r has been the subject of a vast amount of work, but quantitative results are still few.[20] Figure 9.3a shows the functions for a pair of argon atoms and for a pair of krypton atoms. Other molecules behave qualitatively in a similar way; that is u is large and positive at short separations (leading to a repulsive force between the molecules), it then becomes negative with a depth comparable with kT^c, and finally goes rapidly to zero, being proportional to r^{-6} as it does so.

Substitution of (9.87) into (9.83) gives

$$Q = \frac{1}{N!} \int \underset{v}{\cdots} \int \prod_{l<m}^{N-1 \; N} [\exp(-u_{lm}/kT)] \, d\mathbf{r}_1 \ldots d\mathbf{r}_N \qquad (9.88)$$

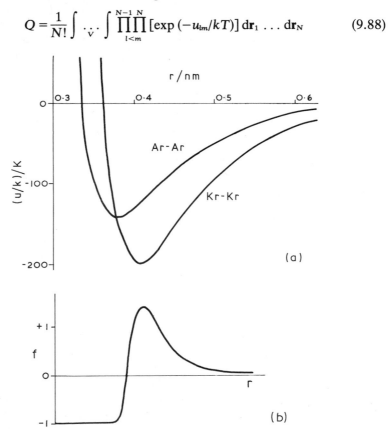

Figure 9.3. (a) The potential energy between a pair of argon atoms, and between a pair of krypton atoms, (b) A sketch of the function f of (9.89) for a potential function similar to those shown in (a)

but this is still an integral which is impossible to evaluate without approximation. We know, however, that in a perfect gas, when each exponential factor is
unity, the integration is trivial, (9.85). Let us therefore introduce (Figure
9.3b) the function of f_{lm} defined by

$$f_{lm} = \exp\left(-u_{lm}/kT\right) - 1 \tag{9.89}$$

so that (9.88) becomes

$$Q = \frac{1}{N!} \int_V \cdots \int \prod_{l<m}^{N-1} \prod^{N} [1 + f_{lm}] \, d\mathbf{r}_1 \ldots \, d\mathbf{r}_N \tag{9.90}$$

We can now attempt to evaluate Q by multiplying out all the products and
collecting terms in order of increasing complexity in products of f_{lm}. If we take
unity from each term and integrate over all $d\mathbf{r}$ then we recover the perfect gas
term, V^N. If we take f_{lm} from one term and unity from all the others then we
can integrate at once over all molecules except $d\mathbf{r}_l \, d\mathbf{r}_m$ and so get a factor of
V^{N-2}. However, since f falls off so rapidly with r, the integrand which is left is
zero except when molecules l and m are close. In these circumstances we can
first change the coordinate system for one of these variables, say $d\mathbf{r}_m$, from
that based on a set of coordinates fixed with respect to the vessel containing the
gas to that based on molecule l as origin. We can let the pair at separation r_{lm}
move as a unit over the whole volume. That is, we have

$$\iint_V f_{lm} \, d\mathbf{r}_l \, d\mathbf{r}_m = \int_V d\mathbf{r}_l \int_V f_{lm} \, d(\mathbf{r}_l - \mathbf{r}_m) \tag{9.91}$$

$$= V \int_V f_{lm} \, d\mathbf{r}_{lm} = V \int_0^\infty f_{lm} 4\pi r_{lm}^2 \, d r_{lm} \tag{9.92}$$

The volume element $d(\mathbf{r}_l - \mathbf{r}_m) \equiv d\mathbf{r}_{lm}$ has been expressed in polar coordinates,
and the upper limit of the integral can be taken to be infinite since f_{lm} falls off
so rapidly with distance.

Thus the N terms obtained by taking one f-function and $(N-1)$ factors of
unity from the product in (9.90) give rise to a term in Q of the form

$$NV^{N-1} \int_0^\infty f 4\pi r^2 \, dr \tag{9.93}$$

There are, however, many other terms from the product which can be
reduced to a similar form. Suppose we have a term $(f_{lm}f_{pq})$ multiplied by
$(N-2)$ factors of unity, then the short-range of each function and the
argument that led from (9.91) to (9.92) allow this term also to be reduced to a
product of two integrals over single f-functions. The same is true of terms
$(f_{lm}f_{mp})$ or of $(f_{lm}f_{mp}f_{pq})$, which can be represented formally by the *graphs*

where each 'bond' represents an f-factor. The simplest product which cannot be factorised to integrals over single f-functions is $f_{lm}f_{mp}f_{pl}$. or

Here the molecules are linked in such a way that there can be no further factorisation. Such a cluster (and its graph) are called *irreducible*—each point is connected to every other by more than one independent route. This graph leads to a term in Q of the form

$$V^{N-2} \int\int f_{lm}f_{mp}f_{pl}\, d\mathbf{r}_{lm}\, d\mathbf{r}_{mp} \tag{9.94}$$

By collecting together all the terms from the product of $(1+f)$ functions, counting the number of each type, and integrating each over all coordinates that are not tied together irreducibly by the f-functions we can express Q as a sum of integrals, and sums of products of integrals, each term of which is composed of an irreducible cluster. The combinatorial problem of counting all these terms is formidable, and here we state only the result.[21] The integral Q starts with the term V^N and then contains terms in V^{N-1}, V^{N-2}, etc. (cf. 9.93 and 9.94). On taking the logarithm of this series to form the Helmholtz free energy (9.14), and differentiating with respect to V to form the pressure, we lose all the products of irreducible graphs and are left with a series in powers of $1/V$ that can be expressed

$$\frac{PV}{NkT} = 1 + B\left(\frac{N}{V}\right) + C\left(\frac{N}{V}\right)^2 + D\left(\frac{N}{V}\right)^3 + \dots \tag{9.95}$$

where

$$B = -\frac{1}{2}\int_0^\infty f_{12}4\pi r_{12}^2\, dr_{12} \tag{9.96}$$

$$C = -\frac{1}{3}\int\int\int f_{12}f_{13}f_{23}8\pi^2 r_{12}r_{13}r_{23}\, dr_{12}\, dr_{13}\, dr_{23} \tag{9.97}$$

where the integration in C is to be taken over all values of r_{12}, r_{13} and r_{23} which form a triangle. This integral is written here in bipolar coordinates. D is a sum of ten integrals each of which has an integrand formed from one of the ten ways of joining four points (i.e. molecules) into an irreducible graph with four, five or six bonds.

The equation of state generated by integrating Q in this way is the virial expansion of Sections 4.11 and 6.6 with the trivial difference that B, C, etc., the second, third, etc. virial coefficients are now expressed in molecular not molar units. This derivation of the virial equation is valuable in several ways. First, we see that since B involves only a pair of molecules, C a triplet, etc., then we can deduce how they will vary with composition in a mixture of gases.

We have already used this result in Section 6.6. Secondly, we have now a link by means of (9.89), (9.96) and (9.97) between the intermolecular potential u, and thermodynamically measurable properties B and C. In practice, this link has been used principally to go from B, and to a lesser extent from C, to u. That is, measurements of B have been one of the most important sets of data used to establish the form of u shown in Figure 9.3. We can, however, now use the link in the reverse direction. For those molecules for which we know u, or can estimate it, we can calculate B and C by means of (9.96) and (9.97) at any temperature of interest. Figure 9.4 shows B calculated for argon from the potential shown in Figure 9.3. Alternative sources of information on u are the viscosity of the gas, the scattering of molecular beams, the ultra-violet spectra of collisional dimers such as Ar_2, and direct quantal calculations. The interpretation of none of these is easy. More useful is often the use of B and other information to estimate u, and then the use of u to re-calculate B at higher or lower temperatures than it has been measured. Such extrapolation is more reliable than the extrapolation of purely empirical equations for B as a function of T. These calculations are not easy nor free from pitfalls, but they are becoming of increasing use for estimating the equation of state of gases.[22] The use of the properties of the perfect gas and of the virial equation of state for estimating the thermodynamic properties of real gases has been discussed in Chapter 4.

This evaluation of Q by series expansion in powers of the density is, perhaps, the only direct evaluation which is of use to the chemical engineer. The virial equation, to which it leads, is however, useful only for moderately

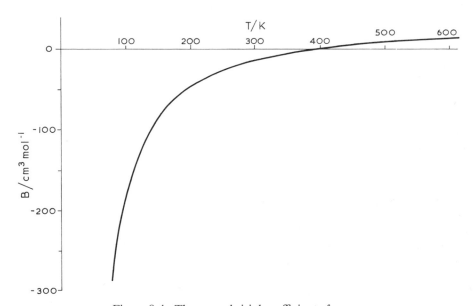

Figure 9.4.   The second virial coefficient of argon

dense gases and not for highly compressed gases or liquids. There are now more sophisticated methods[23] of evaluating Q, which are valid even at liquid densities, but these have not yet yielded results of direct value to the engineer. There are, however, methods of relating Q for one system to Q for another which fall a long way short of a direct evaluation, but which nevertheless yield information of practical value. In the next three sections we examine some of these.

9.7   The principle of corresponding states

The intermolecular potential, shown for argon in Figure 9.3a, is of similar form for other simple molecules. That is, it is a reasonable approximation to characterise each potential by only two parameters, first, a distance σ, which is the *collision diameter*, or the separation at which the potential is zero, $u(\sigma) = 0$, and secondly, an energy ε, which is the depth of the 'bowl', or min $u = -\varepsilon$. If we have a set of substances whose potentials are of the same functional form but which differ only in the values of σ and ε, then we say their potentials are *conformal*. We can write for any member, i, of this set

$$u_{ii}(r) = f_{ii}\, u_{00}(r/h_{ii}^{1/3}) \tag{9.98}$$

On the left of this equation we write u_{ii} since the energy is that between two molecules of species i (in Section 9.9 we generalise the treatment to mixtures, and shall need potentials also for the interaction of molecules of different species, u_{ij}). Equation (9.98) asserts that the potential energy between two molecules of species i at a separation r can be obtained from that for a reference potential u_{00} at a different separation $r/h_{ii}^{1/3}$, by multiplying it by a factor f_{ii}. The two scaling factors f_{ii} and h_{ii} characterise the $i-i$ potential, and are readily seen to be related to ε and σ by

$$f_{ii} = \varepsilon_{ii}/\varepsilon_{00} \qquad h_{ii} = (\sigma_{ii}/\sigma_{00})^3 \tag{9.99}$$

The factor f_{ii} is a pure number and should not be confused with the *function f* of (9.89). The factor h_{ii} is taken to be the cube of the ratio of σ_{ii} to σ_{00} of the reference potential so that, when we come to discuss macroscopic properties, we are able to relate h to volume and f to temperature.

Let us consider now a set of substances, i, whose potentials are all of the common geometric form denoted formally by u_{00}; that is whose potentials can be obtained from u_{00} by scaling the ordinate and abscissa of u as a function of r by the factors f_{ii} and $h_{ii}^{1/3}$. Can we express the configurational thermodynamic properties of substance i in terms of those of the reference substance, 0? Let N molecules of substance i be in a volume $(h_{ii}V)$ at a temperature $(f_{ii}T)$, and let N molecules of the reference substance be in a vessel of the same shape but of volume V, and at a temperature T. For each configuration of the molecules of reference substance there is a corresponding configuration of those of substance i, in the sense that

$$\frac{\mathcal{U}_i[\mathbf{r}_1 h_{ii}^{1/3} \ldots \mathbf{r}_N h_{ii}^{1/3}]}{k(f_{ii}T)} = \frac{\mathcal{U}_0[\mathbf{r}_1 \ldots \mathbf{r}_N]}{kT} \tag{9.100}$$

There is thus a one-to-one correspondence between all values of the integrands of Q_i at $(h_{ii}V)$ and $(f_{ii}T)$ and those of Q_0 at V and T. There is a minor difference that the integrations $d\mathbf{r}_1 \ldots d\mathbf{r}_N$ in Q_i are taken over a volume larger by a factor of h_{ii}. Hence

$$Q_i(h_{ii}V, f_{ii}T) = h_{ii}^N \cdot Q_0(V, T) \tag{9.101}$$

If we replace V and T by Vh_{ii}^{-1} and Tf_{ii}^{-1} we can write this equation in the more useful form

$$Q_i(V, T) = h_{ii}^N \cdot Q_0(Vh_{ii}^{-1}, Tf_{ii}^{-1}) \tag{9.102}$$

We have for the Helmholtz free energy

$$A = A_{mol} + A_{config} \tag{9.103}$$

where A_{mol} arises from the molecular part of Z in (9.84) and A_{config} from Q. All other thermodynamic functions can be divided similarly. From (9.101) we have for A_{config},

$$(A_{config})_i(V, T) = -kT \ln [Q_i(V, T)]$$
$$(A_{config})_0(Vh_{ii}^{-1}, Tf_{ii}^{-1}) = -k(Tf_{ii}^{-1}) \ln [Q_0(Vh_{ii}^{-1}, Tf_{ii}^{-1})] \tag{9.104}$$

and so

$$(A_{config})_i(V, T) = f_{ii} \cdot (A_{config})_0(Vh_{ii}^{-1}, Tf_{ii}^{-1}) - NkT \ln h_{ii} \tag{9.105}$$

Differentiation with respect to volume gives

$$P_i(V, T) = (f_{ii}h_{ii}^{-1}) \cdot P_0(Vh_{ii}^{-1}, Tf_{ii}^{-1}) \tag{9.106}$$

The last two equations are a recipe for calculating the presumed unknown properties of substance i from the presumed known properties of a conformal reference substance, 0. If we require A_{config} or P for substance i at V, T, we find it from the same property for substance 0 at Vh_{ii}^{-1}, Tf_{ii}^{-1} by means of (9.105) and (9.106). Other properties follow from A_{config} by the usual manipulations of classical thermodynamics.

The last equation (9.106) has a particularly simple interpretation, for it implies that if we have the equation of state of the reference substance as a three-dimensional surface in P-V-T space, then we can obtain that for substance i by multiplying the volume scale by h_{ii}, the temperature scale by f_{ii} and the pressure scale by $(f_{ii}h_{ii}^{-1})$. This is the geometric interpretation of the equation. It follows that all singular points on the surface such as the solid, the liquid or the gas at the triple point, or the fluid at the critical point, have values of P, V and T in the ratios of these scale factors. In particular

$$P_i^c = (f_{ii}h_{ii}^{-1})P_0^c; \quad v_i^c = h_{ii}v_0^c; \quad T_i^c = f_{ii}T_0^c \tag{9.107}$$

Hence substance i and substance 0 have the same *reduced equation of state*; that is, P/P^c is the same function of V/V^c and T/T^c for both substances. They are said, therefore, to conform to the *principle of corresponding states*.

This principle has, of course, been used for many years for calculating approximate values of the properties of a substance whose critical constants are known, from those of another for which we have an extensive knowledge of the P-V-T surface and possibly of other properties. This derivation from the principles of statistical thermodynamics is, nevertheless, useful in several ways. First, it emphasises that the thermodynamic properties which can be scaled in this way are only those arising from the configurational part of the partition function, and so of the free energy. This includes all the P-V-T properties, but not the heat capacity at constant volume of the perfect gas. Such 'molecular' parts of the thermodynamic properties must be dealt with separately by the methods of Sections 9.3–9.5 before the configurational properties are obtained by scaling the configurational properties of the reference substance (we discuss this point more fully in the next section.). Secondly, the essentially 'dimensional' arguments which led from a set of conformal potentials (9.98) to a set of conformal P-V-T surfaces (9.106) show us that the principle of corresponding states is followed closely only by groups of molecules which are closely related in the forms of their inter-molecular potentials. In practice, the group Ar, Kr, Xe is the only set which conforms almost within the experimental error of most of their properties.[24] This brings us, however, to the third point; once we know what are the molecular conditions which lead to strict conformation with the principle, then we can ask usefully what are the causes of the small or large departures that more complicated molecules show from the simple behaviour of the inert gas group. This problem is taken up in the next section. Fourthly, and finally, since the technique used in obtaining this principle is essentially one of relating Q for one substance to Q for another, then it may be possible to adapt it to obtain Q for a mixture from Q for one or more of the pure components. We take up this point in Section 9.9.

Meanwhile the principle itself, without further discussion or embellish-ment, remains one of the most useful of all generalisations that yield moderately accurate estimates of thermodynamic properties.[25]

9.8 Deviations from the principle of corresponding states

The derivation of this principle given above rested on the premises that (1) the classical (i.e. non-quantal) expression for the configuration integral Q (9.83) is an exact link between the thermodynamic properties and the intermolecular energy $\mathscr{U}(\mathbf{r})$, (2) that $\mathscr{U}(\mathbf{r})$ could be broken down into a sum of pair potentials $u(r)$ (9.87), and (3) that these $u(r)$ formed a conformal family (9.98). If any of these conditions are violated then the principle may break down. In practice, it is usually the first and the third which give trouble. Thus He, H_2 and, to a lesser extent Ne, are light molecules whose motions cannot be described adequately by classical statistical mechanics, and which therefore depart from the reduced behaviour of the set Ar, Kr and Xe, although their potentials are probably fairly conformal with those of the heavier molecules.

More widespread, and more important are departures from the principle caused by the failure of the potentials to conform. This failure can arise from a different dependence of u on r, or from the dependence of u also on the orientation of the molecule. Examples of the first are such molecules as CCl_4 and SF_6 where much of the 'source' of the intermolecular potentials resides in the peripheral halogen atoms. Such molecules are not far from a spherical shape, but nevertheless show strong departures from the reduced behaviour of the inert gases, which arise in the main from a different functional form of u.

It is, however, the dependence of u on the orientations of molecules as well as on their separations that is the most common cause of departures from the principle, since it is only the inert gases, and a few metallic vapours such as mercury, which have truly spherical molecules. We therefore return to the point which we evaded at the beginning of Section 9.6 of how to deal with the rotational and vibrational motions in a system of interacting non-spherical molecules.

The latter are quickly disposed of, since spectroscopy shows that the frequencies of the normal modes are almost the same in a dense gas or a liquid as they are in a dilute gas. The vibrational energies are, therefore, independent of the translational, rotational and configurational energies. As before, we factorise out the $(3n-6)$ vibrational partition functions z_v of (9.54) and incorporate them, as multiplicative factors, in the molecular part of Z (9.84), and so as additive terms in the molecular parts of the thermodynamic functions (9.102). The rotational motion is more closely linked with the dependence of $\mathcal{U}$ on orientation and needs a fuller discussion.

We saw that for all molecules except H_2 the moment(s) of inertia is(are) large enough for the quantal rotational partition function (9.39) to be replaced by the semi-classical integral (9.40). We can, therefore, treat the rotational motion of interacting molecules in the same way as we treated their translational motion. In (9.79) we divided that into two terms, a sum over momenta and a potential energy. We can write similarly for a diatomic molecule with both translational and rotational energy

$$E = \sum_{i=1}^{N} \left[\frac{1}{2m} \mathbf{p}^2 + \frac{1}{2I} \left(p_\theta^2 + \frac{1}{\sin^2 \theta} p_\varphi^2 \right) \right]_i + \mathcal{U}(\mathbf{r}, \boldsymbol{\omega}) \qquad (9.108)$$

where $\mathbf{p}$ is the translational momentum, as before (9.79), and p_θ and p_φ are rotational momenta about two orthogonal axes with respect to which the orientation of the molecule is defined by the angles θ and φ. The potential energy $\mathcal{U}$ is now a function of all molecular positions, denoted formally by $\mathbf{r}$, and all orientations, denoted by $\boldsymbol{\omega}$.

For non-linear molecules there is a similar, but more complicated expression for the rotational kinetic energy as a function of three angles θ, φ and ψ. However, the result of inserting either (9.108) or its more complicated analogue for non-linear molecules, into the partition function Z is that we can again integrate explicitly (and independently) over all momenta, both translational and rotational.[26] We recover the semi-classical translational and rotational partition functions, (9.29) and either (9.43) or (9.50). Hence we obtain again the division of Z into a molecular and a configurational part (9.84), but where Z_{mol} now contains not only the translational part $(2\pi mkT/h^2)^{3N/2}$ but also the products of $(z_{\text{rot}})^N$ and $(z_{\text{vib}})^N$, and where the configuration integral Q differs from (9.83) in that its integrand is now a function of molecular orientations

$$Q = \frac{1}{N!} \int \ldots \int \exp\left[-\mathcal{U}(\mathbf{r}, \boldsymbol{\omega})/kT\right] d\mathbf{r}_1 \ldots d\mathbf{r}_N \, d\boldsymbol{\omega}_1 \ldots d\boldsymbol{\omega}_N \quad (9.109)$$

The integrals over $d\mathbf{r}$ are to be taken over the volume V, and those over $d\boldsymbol{\omega}$ over all orientations.

In general we cannot evaluate (9.109), as we could not the more simple integral (9.83). However, in liquids and gases the thermodynamic effects of the dependence of $\mathcal{U}$ on orientations are often quite small, and it is therefore natural to seek a method for calculating the ratio of integrals (9.109) and (9.83) even if we cannot evaluate either. Let us suppose that $\mathcal{U}$ is again a sum of the interactions of molecules in pairs, as in (9.87), and that the pair-potential $u(r, \boldsymbol{\omega})$ can be separated into a spherical and an orientational part

$$\mathcal{U}(\mathbf{r}, \boldsymbol{\omega}) = \sum_{l<m}^{N-1} \sum^{N} u(r_{lm}, \boldsymbol{\omega}_{lm}) \quad (9.110)$$

$$u(r, \boldsymbol{\omega}) = u_0(r) + u_1(r, \boldsymbol{\omega}) \quad (9.111)$$

The division in (9.111) is arbitrary, but we can make it in a unique way if we require that the average of $u_1(r, \boldsymbol{\omega})$ over all angles is to vanish at each separation r. We have then that u_0 is defined by

$$\int u(r, \boldsymbol{\omega}) \, d\boldsymbol{\omega} = u_0(r) \quad (9.112)$$

whilst

$$\int u_1(r, \boldsymbol{\omega}) \, d\boldsymbol{\omega} = 0 \quad (9.113)$$

The variable in these integrals is a formal representation of the two or three angles (hence the vector notation) needed to specify the mutual orientation of a pair of molecules, and the integrals have been normalised by dividing by 4π or $8\pi^2$, as is appropriate, so that

$$\int d\boldsymbol{\omega} = 1 \tag{9.114}$$

For fairly simple and not too polar molecules (e.g. N_2, C_2H_4, CO_2, HCl, SO_2) the orientational part of u is small with respect to the spherical part for most configurations. For grossly non-spherical or highly polar molecules (e.g. n-C_6H_{14}, CH_3COOH, H_2O, NH_3) this is not so and u_1 of (9.111) is at least as large as u_0. For the former class we can take u_1 to be small and so expand each Boltzmann factor which appears in Q (9.88).

$$\exp\left[-u(r, \boldsymbol{\omega})/kT\right] = \exp\left[-u_0(r)/kT\right]\left\{1 - \frac{u_1(r, \boldsymbol{\omega})}{kT} + \frac{[u_1(r, \boldsymbol{\omega})]^2}{2(kT)^2} - \cdots\right\} \tag{9.115}$$

Both sides of this equation can now be averaged (that is, integrated) over all orientations $\boldsymbol{\omega}$, an operation we denote by means of a bar above the expression. On using (9.113) we find that the term on the right which is linear in $u_1(r, \boldsymbol{\omega})$ vanishes, and so

$$\overline{\exp\left[-u(r, \boldsymbol{\omega})/kT\right]} = \exp\left[-u_0(r)/kT\right]\left\{1 + \frac{\overline{[u_1(r, \boldsymbol{\omega})]^2}}{2(kT)^2} + \cdots\right\} \tag{9.116}$$

$$\simeq \exp\left[-u^*(r)/kT\right] \tag{9.117}$$

where

$$u^*(r) = u_0(r) - \frac{1}{2}\frac{\overline{[u_1(r, \boldsymbol{\omega})]^2}}{kT} \tag{9.118}$$

The average of the square of $u_1(r, \boldsymbol{\omega})$ is necessarily a positive quantity and, since it is an average over all angles, it is a function only of the separation r.

If, therefore, we can break $\mathcal{U}(\mathbf{r}, \boldsymbol{\omega})$ into a sum of two-body terms (9.110), and if it is legitimate to integrate over all angles by taking a separate average over each two-body Boltzmann factor, then we see that Q becomes that of a system of (hypothetical) spherical molecules with an effective energy $u^*(r)$ which is a function of temperature. In practice, this separate integration for each molecular pair is sometimes legitimate and sometimes not[27]; it depends on the form of $u_1(r, \boldsymbol{\omega})$. If this arises solely from an electrostatic interaction between dipoles or higher multipoles of otherwise spherical molecules, then the separation is legitimate. If it arises from other terms, e.g. from the change with orientation of the repulsive parts of the potential as, e.g. with N_2 or C_2H_4, then the separation is not legitimate. However, even in these cases, the thermodynamic consequences are close to those implied by (9.118) and we do not enter here into these complications.

It does not follow from (9.118) that, even if the potentials $[u_0(r)]_i$ form a conformal set, that the set $[u^*(r)]_i$ is also conformal. It may be conformal as, for example, when $u_1(r, \omega)$ arises solely from the interaction of point dipoles, but even if it is not, the dependence of $u^*(r)$ on r is usually close to that of u_0. Its dependence on temperature is that which distinguishes u^* most obviously from u_0. We can expect, therefore, that non-spherical molecules will depart from the reduced behaviour of the inert gases in such a way that it will appear that their potentials are deeper at low temperatures than at high, and that the departures will increase with the strength of the orientational forces. Hence a small molecule like N_2 will be closer to Ar than an elongated molecule like C_2H_4. We can expect, therefore, that departures from the corresponding states of the inert gases will increase regularly as the non-sphericity of the molecules becomes more pronounced and that, for all substances, these departures will depend in a similar way on temperature.

These expectations are borne out and the development of this section is the theoretical justification for the well-known methods by which chemical engineers handle such departures, of which the most widely used is Pitzer's *acentric factor*,[28] ω (the symbol ω is here a parameter which characterises each molecular interaction and not the general symbol for angles used above. It is difficult to avoid the coincidence without violating customary usage). Pitzer proposed that the increasing departure from the reduced behaviour of the inert gases shown by increasingly non-spherical molecules could be measured most conveniently by its effect in lowering the reduced vapour pressure P_σ at a temperature near the normal boiling (the departure is always a *reduction* of vapour pressure because u^* has a deeper bowl (Figure 9.3) than u_0, since from (9.118) $u^* < u_0$ for all r). For Ar, Kr and Xe, (P_σ/P^c) is almost exactly 0.1 at a reduced temperature of $T/T^c = 0.7$. Hence Pitzer defined ω by the equation

$$\omega = -1.000 - \log_{10}(P_\sigma/P^c) \tag{9.119}$$

This parameter[29] is 0.021 for O_2, 0.040 for N_2, 0.013 for CH_4, 0.105 for C_2H_6, 0.152 for C_3H_8, 0.215 for C_6H_6 and 0.348 for H_2O.

If ω is small (say, less than 0.2) then the departures from corresponding states are approximately linear in ω, as $u^*(r)$ is linear in $[u_1(r, \omega)]^2$ the value of which may be taken as a measure of the size of ω. Hence, for compression factor Z (not to be confused with the partition function) we can write

$$Z(P_r, T_r) = Z_0(P_r, T_r) + \omega Z_1(P_r, T_r) \tag{9.120}$$

where $Z_0(P_r, T_r)$ is the compression factor of the inert gases at a reduced pressure and temperature of

$$P_r = P/P^c \qquad T_r = T/T^c, \tag{9.121}$$

where $Z_1(P_r, T_r)$ is an auxiliary function which must be found empirically, and $Z(P_r, T_r)$ is the compression factor of the system of non-spherical molecules. These functions Z_0 and Z_1 are shown in Figures 9.5 and 9.6. The value of this

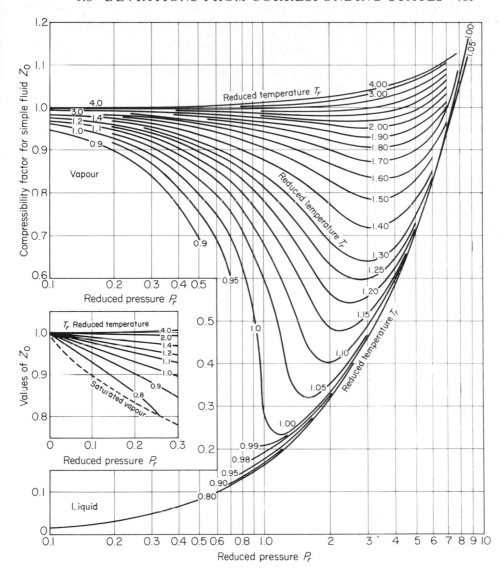

Figure 9.5. Compression factor, Z_0 (based on W. C. Edmister[28])

relation is clear. Since we know Z_0 and can determine Z_1 from the observed behaviour of several well-studied fluids for which ω is not zero, then all we need, to calculate Z for any substance of interest, are its critical constants P^c and T^c and a knowledge of its vapour pressure at $T_r = 0.7$. This last piece of information is usually available since it is close to the normal boiling-point of most substances. The resulting value of Z is substantially more accurate than

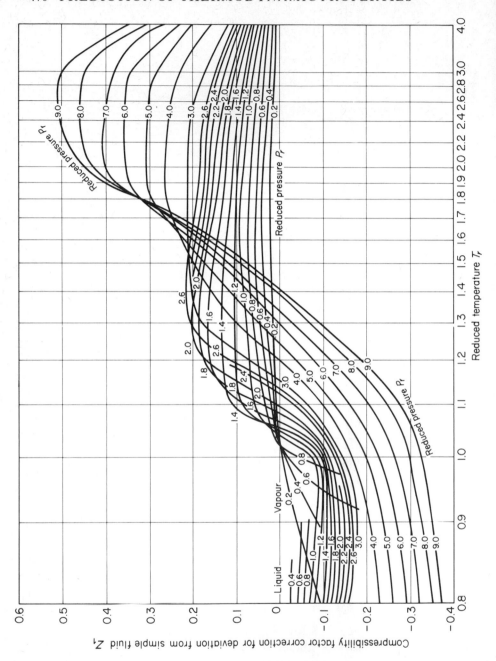

Figure 9.6. Correction to the compression factor, Z_1 (based on W. C. Edmister[28])

that obtained by using the principle without this correction for the 'shape' of the molecules.

If the theoretical treatment above were an exact description of the way real molecules interact, then Z_1 would be a calculable function. This is, in fact, quite close to being the case,[30] but for the highest accuracy it is preferable to treat it as a function which is found from the observed behaviour of real substances composed of non-spherical molecules.

Once the compression factor is known, then the departures of all other configurational properties from the principle of corresponding states can be found by the usual methods of classical thermodynamics.[31] Auxiliary tables have been prepared to help in these calculations.[32] The departures from the principle of different features of the P-V-T behaviour, e.g. the virial coefficients B and C, can also be represented by means of a reference part and a non-spherical part which is proportional to the acentric factor ω.

A scheme closely related to the use of Pitzer's acentric factor is that devised by Hougen and Watson[33]. If all substances obeyed the same reduced equation of state, then the compression factor at the critical point would have a universal value. In practice, it is found to fall as the orientational forces become more powerful and is found to be related to ω by the empirical and approximate equation

$$Z^c = 0.293/(1+0.375\omega) \tag{9.122}$$

so that Z^c for Ar, Kr and Xe is 0.293. Hougen and Watson use the departure of Z^c from this value as the third parameter with which to correlate departures from the principle of corresponding states, in the same way that Pitzer used ω. They tabulate reduced properties such as V/V^c and h/RT^c, separately for each value of Z^c as functions of P_r and T_r. Their scheme, although it is by (9.122) entirely equivalent to Pitzer's, is less useful in practice since it is much harder to measure Z^c accurately than it is to measure the saturated vapour pressure at $T_r = 0.7$.

Example

According to Din's tables (see Section 4.19) propane has a molar volume of $v = 303.0 \text{ cm}^3 \text{ mol}^{-1}$ at 500 K and 100 atm pressure. Hence the compression factor Z is 0.738. We can use the schemes of Pitzer and of Hougen and Watson to calculate Z at these values of T and P. For the former we need to know that $T^c = 370.0$ K and $P^c = 42.10$ atm (Din), and the vapour pressure near the normal boiling point, which leads to an acentric factor of $\omega = 0.152$ (Reid and Sherwood). For the latter we need T^c and P^c, as before, and $v^c = 195.7 \text{ cm}^3 \text{ mol}^{-1}$ (Din).

Pitzer: From the figures above $T_r = 1.351$, $P_r = 2.375$. Interpolation in the Figures 9.5 and 9.6 gives

$$Z_0 = 0.700 \qquad Z_1 = 0.210$$

and so, from (9.120)

$$Z = 0.700 + (0.152 \times 0.210) = 0.700 + 0.032 = 0.732$$

Hougen and Watson: Interpolation at $T_r = 1.351$ and $P_r = 2.375$ in their table of Z which is appropriate for $Z^c = 0.27$, gives

$$Z = 0.731$$

Thus the two predictive schemes agree together, but are about 1% low. Had we attempted to calculate Z from the reduced equation of state for argon without correction for the deviation from the principle of corresponding states, we should have obtained $Z = 0.700$ (that is, Z_0 of Pitzer's scheme), which is 5% low.

There are other ways of representing the P-V-T behaviour of systems of non-spherical molecules. We can, for example, fit the data for any substance, spherical or non-spherical, to an empirical equation, as described in Section 4.13, and provided the fitting equation is flexible enough it will almost always represent P-V-T values and quantities derived therefrom with greater accuracy than the method of corresponding states can predict the properties of one substance from those of another. Such representation is, however, not a prediction unless we have a means of estimating, independently of the P-V-T data themselves, the parameters of this equation. Such representation is merely the fitting of a convenient interpolating function. It is the virtue of the treatment of deviations from corresponding states discussed above that it does have this predictive value; we can obtain the compression factor from a few facts, the values of critical constants and vapour pressures, which are independent of the P-V-T behaviour we wish to know, and independent also of derived thermodynamic properties, such as enthalpies, which we wish to derive from this P-V-T behaviour. In the next section we shall see, however, that empirical equations such as the BWR equation can have genuine predictive value for estimating the properties of mixtures.

9.9 The properties of mixtures

It may be a reasonable objective, although one not achieved, to measure experimentally all the properties of every pure substance of interest to the chemical engineer and so to be able to restrict the methods of estimation described in the previous sections of this chapter to ranges of temperature that are difficult to reach. It is inconceivable however, that we shall ever have experimental values for all the properties of every multi-component system of interest. Hence the prediction of the properties of mixtures is, and will be, one of the most important fields in the application of thermodynamics to chemical engineering. We cannot hope to describe here more than a small proportion of the work in this field, and lay most emphasis on those methods which have a strong theoretical foundation in statistical thermodynamics.

The principle of corresponding states is a simple relation between the configuration integrals of two substances, one of whose properties we know, and one whose we wish to calculate. Such an approach seems ideally suited to the calculation of the properties of a mixture if we could obtain a similar relation between Q of the mixture and the Q of one or more of the components from which it is made. We can assume, for this purpose, that we know by experiment or by calculations of the kind described above, what are the properties of each of the components.

We can at once generalise (9.83) to give the configuration integral of a mixture of spherical molecules.

$$Q = \frac{1}{\prod_{i=1}^{C} N_i!} \int \cdots \int_V \exp\left[-\mathcal{U}(\mathbf{r})/kT\right] d\mathbf{r}_1 \ldots d\mathbf{r}_N \qquad (9.123)$$

where

$$\sum_{i=1}^{C} N_i = N \qquad (9.124)$$

The configuration energy $\mathcal{U}$ now depends not only on the positions of the N molecules, but also on what may be called their assignment by species to these positions. That is, the value of $\mathcal{U}$ is changed if the chemical species of a pair of molecules at two positions $\mathbf{r}_l$ and $\mathbf{r}_m$ is changed from say, species 1 at l and 2 at m, to say, 3 at l and 4 at m, etc. In a pure liquid $\mathcal{U}$ is a function only of the positions and not of the assignment of the indistinguishable molecules to these positions.

In a mixture of C components we have $\frac{1}{2}C(C+1)$ different pair potentials of the kind $u_{ij}(r)$. Thus in a pure component, 1, we have the single potential $u_{11}(r)$; in a binary mixture we have the three potentials $u_{11}(r)$, $u_{12}(r)$ and $u_{22}(r)$, etc. Clearly, we can learn nothing about the cross-terms, $u_{12}(r)$, etc. from a study of pure 1 and pure 2 alone. We return later to the problem of how we can estimate these terms, but deal first with the more fundamental problem of how we can calculate Q even if we assume that all potentials are known.

The dependence of $\mathcal{U}$ on assignment-by-species precludes the use of the simple dimensional arguments which led from (9.98) to (9.102). If $\mathcal{U}$ is independent of this assignment then we can still proceed, but this is the case only when the pair potentials $u(r)$ are the same for every species, as for example in an isotopic mixture. In this case, we have for the difference between the Helmholtz free energy of the mixture $A_{mixt}(V, T)$ and that of any one of the same number of molecules of one of the pure components, $A_0(V, T)$

$$A_{mixt}(V, T) - A_0(V, T) = -kT \ln (Q/Q_0) = kT \ln\left(\prod_i N_i! \middle/ N!\right) \quad (9.125)$$

Applying Stirling's approximation (9.31) to each of the factorials (9.125) leads to the result that a mixture in which all potentials are the same is an ideal mixture. That is,

$$A_{\text{mixt}}(V, T) - A_0(V, T) = NkT \sum_i x_i \ln x_i \qquad (9.126)$$

where $x_i = N_i/N$. This result has been obtained only under very restrictive conditions, and these cannot be relaxed if we are to derive the laws of the ideal mixture. Any difference in intermolecular potentials, whether arising from differences in molecular size, shape, polarity or strength of attractive forces, leads, in principle, to deviations from ideality. In practice, as we have seen in Chapter 6, these deviations are small if the potentials are closely similar as, for example, in a mixture of benzene and toluene.

If we are to make progress in the case of more general potentials then we must introduce some approximations. Since (9.125) was obtained by assuming that $\mathcal{U}$ was independent of the assignment of molecules by species to the positions of every configuration, then it is tempting to approximate $\mathcal{U}$ by taking, for each configuration $\mathbf{r}$, an average of $\mathcal{U}$ over all assignments by species to each position of $\mathbf{r}$. We then have a system in which $\mathcal{U}$ is again a function only of $\mathbf{r}$, since its dependence on assignment has been removed by the averaging. That is, we have approximated Q, and so the Helmholtz free energy of the mixture, by that of a hypothetical one-component system, which we denote by a subscript x, whose potential is the average of all the potentials in the mixture. That is, $u_x(r)$ is given by

$$u_x(r) = \sum_{i=1}^{C} \sum_{j=1}^{C} x_i x_j u_{ij}(r) \qquad (9.127)$$

since the average probability of finding molecule i at one position of a configuration r is x_i, and the average probability of finding species j at a second position of r is x_j. The sum is taken over C^2 terms, that is over the $\frac{1}{2}C(C+1)$ different interactions between like and unlike molecules. In a binary mixture we have $(x_1^2 u_{11} + 2x_1 x_2 u_{12} + x_2^2 u_{22})$; four terms of which three are different.

This device of averaging over assignments is, at first sight, an attractive solution to the problem. We say that each mixture of composition x behaves like an ideal mixture of hypothetical identical substances, subscript x, between each of which there acts the average potential $u_x(r)$ or (9.127). That is

$$(A_{\text{config}})_{\text{mixt}} = (A_{\text{config}})_x + NkT \sum_i x_i \ln x_i \qquad (9.128)$$

where

$$(A_{\text{config}})_x = -kT \ln Q_x \qquad (9.129)$$

$$= \frac{1}{N!} \int_v \cdots \int \exp\left[-\mathcal{U}_x(\mathbf{r})/kT\right] d\mathbf{r}_1 \ldots d\mathbf{r}_N \qquad (9.130)$$

and

$$\mathcal{U}_x(\mathbf{r}) = \sum_{l<m}^{N-1} \sum^{N} u_x(r_{lm}) \qquad (9.131)$$

and u_x is the average potential of (9.127). The ideal free energy of mixing is still present in (9.128) since although we have in Q approximated the mixture by a set of identical potentials, and so, in a sense, replaced it by a hypothetical pure substance, the terms in $(x_i \ln x_i)$, which arise from the factorials outside the integral, are still present.

This approximation is quite good if we have a mixture of molecules of the same size which differ only in the strengths of their attractive forces, that is, in the depths of the bowl in Figure 9.3a. If, however, we have a dense liquid mixture of molecules of different sizes, that is, of different σ in Figure 9.3a, then the approximation is bad. Equation (9.127) implies that we are as likely to find a molecule i as a molecule j at each position in an equimolar mixture. This is clearly unrealistic if some molecules are larger than others; we cannot expect a large molecule to fit as easily as a small one into every position of a densely packed configuration. Nevertheless, the concept behind (8.128)–(9.131) is a valuable one which can be divorced from the particular expression for u_x given in (9.127).

A set of equations of the form of (9.128)–(9.131) is called a *one-fluid approximation*, since it replaces the calculation of $(A_{\text{config}})_{\text{mixt}}$ by that of the calculation $(A_{\text{config}})_x$, the configurational Helmholtz free energy of a hypothetical single component. If the potential u_x, which is so far undetermined, now that we have abandoned (9.127), is conformal with those of the pure components from which mixture is made, u_{11}, u_{22}, etc., then we can calculate $(A_{\text{config}})_x(V, T)$ by the principle of corresponding states. This leads to what chemical engineers usually call a *pseudocritical approximation*, and can be expressed by saying that we calculate $(A_{\text{config}})_x$ from the configurational Helmholtz free energy of some reference substance, usually one of the components of the mixture, by means of the corresponding states equation (9.105) which we re-write

$$(A_{\text{config}})_x(V, T) = f_x (A_{\text{config}})_0 (Vh_x^{-1}, Tf_x^{-1}) - NkT \ln h_x \qquad (9.132)$$

where

$$f_x = T_x^c/T_0^c \qquad h_x = v_x^c/v_0^c \qquad (9.133)$$

and

$$u_x(r) = f_x \cdot u_0(rh_x^{-1/3}) \qquad (9.134)$$

To use such a one-fluid or pseudocritical approximation we need a recipe for the calculation of f_x and h_x, or T_x^c and V_x^c, from the parameters of the pair potentials f_{ij} and h_{ij}. We have seen that the recipe (9.127) is not accurate for mixtures of molecules of different sizes.

The first rule of this kind to be widely used in chemical engineering calculations was that of Kay[34] who put

$$T_x^c = \sum_i x_i T_i^c \qquad P_x^c = \sum_i x_i P_i^c \qquad (9.135)$$

which, because of the relation of T^c and P^c to the parameters of the potential implied by the principle of corresponding states (9.107), is equivalent to

$$f_x = \sum_i x_i f_{ii} \qquad h_x = \frac{\sum_i x_i f_{ii}}{\sum_i x_i f_{ii} h_{ii}^{-1}} \tag{9.136}$$

(9.135) is a simple linear rule for the calculation of T_x^c and P_x^c, but it does not imply that T_{mixt}^c and P_{mixt}^c are linear functions of x. The hypothetical substance of subscript x represents the mixture for the purposes of calculating Q, but the Helmholtz free energy of the mixture contains also the ideal mixing terms (9.128). In fact, (9.135) usually leads to a value of P_{mixt}^c which, correctly, exceeds the linearly interpolated value of P_x^c (see Section 7.7). Nevertheless, (9.135) and (9.136) are still not accurate approximations and, in particular, ignore the dependence of the properties of the mixture on the forces between unlike molecules—only terms of the form f_{ii} and h_{ii} are used in (9.136), there are no cross-terms f_{ij}, h_{ij}, $(i \neq j)$.

There have been many attempts to improve on Kay's recipe for the calculation of f_x and h_x, and it is probable that the best results are to be obtained by writing

$$f_x = \left(\sum_i \sum_j x_i x_j f_{ij} h_{ij} \right) \left(\sum_i \sum_j x_i x_j h_{ij} \right)^{-1}$$
$$h_x = \sum_i \sum_j x_i x_j h_{ij} \tag{9.137}$$

where the double sums are taken over all C^2 terms as in (9.127); that is, over both like and unlike interactions. The theoretical and empirical reasons[35] for preferring these equations are too difficult to be explained here, but it seems unlikely that there is a superior one-fluid approximation. Equation (9.137) is usually called van der Waals' approximation because if it is applied to a fluid mixture which conforms to his equation of state, then it implies the following rule for computing his parameters a and b.

$$a_x = \sum_i \sum_j x_i x_j a_{ij} \qquad b_x = \sum_i \sum_j x_i x_j b_{ij} \tag{9.138}$$

These are the rules which he himself used. However, (9.137) and the equations with which it is to be used, (9.128)–(9.131) and (9.134), are a method of calculating $(A_{config})_{mixt}$ which uses the principle of corresponding states but not van der Waals' *equation*.

We cannot make further progress until we can determine the parameters f_{ij} and h_{ij} to be used with (9.137). Those for the like interactions f_{ii}, h_{ii}, present no problem in a mixture of conformal substances; they are related to the critical constants by (9.107). The unlike terms f_{ij}, h_{ij} $(i \neq j)$ are in many cases likely to be close to some kind of average of the like terms. We write

$$f_{ij} = \xi_{ij} (f_{ii} f_{jj})^{1/2} \tag{9.139}$$
$$h_{ij} = \eta_{ij} (\tfrac{1}{2} h_{ii}^{1/3} + \tfrac{1}{2} h_{jj}^{1/3})^3 \tag{9.140}$$

thus transferring the problem to that of estimating the parameters ξ_{ij} and η_{ij}.

The form of these equations is partly an historical accident, but is justified since we find in practice that both ξ and η are close to unity. If we are to make calculations on an unstudied binary mixture of chemically similar substances, then we will usually take

$$\xi_{ij} = \eta_{ij} = 1 \qquad (9.141)$$

It is, however, better to determine these parameters empirically from such observed properties of the binary mixture as are available, and to use the results so obtained either for a calculation of these same or other properties of the binary mixtures at different values of V and T, or to use them to calculate the properties of a multicomponent mixture in which i and j are two of the components. One of the virtues of this treatment of mixtures is that it makes full use of the fact that, to a reasonable approximation, the forces between molecules arise from their interactions in pairs (9.87). Hence a study of the properties of each pure component and each of their binary mixtures tells us, in practice, all we need to know about the like and unlike parameters, f_{ii}, h_{ii} and f_{ij}, h_{ij}. There are no specifically multicomponent parameters f_{ijk} etc. which we need to calculate. Nevertheless, the experimental study of even all the binary mixtures in which we might be interested is a formidable programme, and we still must often guess the parameters ξ_{ij} and η_{ij} for $i \neq j$.

In the absence of direct information it is often best to put all $\eta_{ij} = 1$ but to take ξ_{ij} as slightly less than unity. The more dissimilar the molecules the further from unity is ξ_{ij}. Some typical values are[36] $Ar + O_2$, 0.99; $N_2 + CO$, 0.99; $N_2 + CH_4$, 0.97; $CO + CH_4$, 0.99; $CH_4 + C_2H_6$, 0.99; $CH_4 + C_3H_8$, 0.97; $C_2H_6 + C_3H_8$, 1.00; $C_3H_8 + n\text{-}C_4H_{10}$, 0.99; $CO_2 + CH_4$, 0.94; $CO_2 + C_2H_6$, 0.91; $CH_4 + CF_4$, 0.92; $C_6H_6 + \text{cyclo-}C_6H_{12}$ 0.97. These figures are subject to an uncertainty of at least 0.01, since the theory is not exact and since the use of different properties (e.g. second virial coefficient B_{ij}, T^c_{mixt}, or G^E) leads to slightly differing values of ξ_{ij}. Nevertheless, the list above shows some typical values and should allow more accurate choices than $\xi_{ij} = 1$ to be made for systems which have not been studied.

One point has been passed over in listing these values. Many of the molecules are far from spherical and so deviate from the reduced behaviour of Ar, Kr, and Xe. We saw in the last section how Pitzer's acentric factor could be used to correlate the reduced properties of non-conformal substances. That treatment can be combined with the discussion of corresponding states in mixtures given above, to produce a method for predicting the properties of mixtures of non-conformal substances. However, the details of this combination are too long to discuss here.[37]

Example

From the evaporation of a liquefied natural gas we obtain a mixture of CH_4 ($x_1 = 0.719$) and N_2 ($x_2 = 0.281$). What is the compression factor Z at

$T = 192.65$ K and $v = 252.62$ cm³ mol⁻¹? Here the two substances are close to mutual conformality, and we can use the equations above without correction with Pitzer's acentric factor.

We take methane as the reference substance since we have a recent and accurate table of PVT data.[38] Hence, from (9.107), we have for the pure components

$$f_{11} = h_{11} = 1$$
$$f_{22} = T_{N_2}^c / T_{CH_4}^c = 0.6605$$
$$h_{22} = v_{N_2}^c / v_{CH_4}^c = 0.9027$$

The cross parameters are obtained from (9.139) and (9.140) with $\xi_{12} = 0.97$ (see above) and $\eta_{12} = 1$. Hence

$$f_{12} = 0.7883 \qquad h_{12} = 0.9505$$

We now use the van der Waals one-fluid recipe (9.137) to obtain f_x and h_x

$$f_x = 0.8915 \qquad h_x = 0.9724$$

The pressure of the mixture could now be calculated from that of methane by using the principle of corresponding states, that is, (9.106) with f_x and h_x as the parameters of the hypothetical one-fluid which has the properties of the mixture substituted for f_{ii} and h_{ii}. Since we wish to calculate Z we re-arrange this equation into the more convenient form

$$Z_x(V, T) = Z_0(Vh_x^{-1}, Tf_x^{-1}) \qquad (9.142)$$

That is, we have

$$Z_x(252.6 \text{ cm}^3 \text{ mol}^{-1}, 192.65 \text{ K}) = Z_0(259.4 \text{ cm}^3 \text{ mol}^{-1}, 216.10 \text{ K})$$

We look up Z_0 in the table of the properties of methane at these values of v and T and obtain

$$Z = 0.708$$

The experimental value[39] is 0.706. The excellent agreement is due here to the facts that methane and nitrogen are simple and similar molecules and that the density is quite low ($P = 44.85$ bar).

The treatment of mixtures given above has been set out at some length because it is the treatment which, whilst usable by chemical engineers, is most directly grounded in the theory of statistical thermodynamics. The resulting equations are not simple and the calculation of, say, a K-value for a component in a multi-component mixture of non-conformal molecules needs a computer programme of some length and complexity, as may be seen from the references cited.

Much of this complexity arises from the difficulties of the numerical analyses, not of the thermodynamics. Thus, to compute a K-value for a liquid-vapour mixture we have to find a pressure and temperature, and a composition of each phase, at which each component has the same fugacity in the liquid as it has in the vapour. We illustrate the procedure by examining the case of a binary system which forms an equilibrium liquid mixture of composition (x_1, x_2) at temperature T.

First, we must choose a reference substance. For the most accurate results we would choose the molecular species present in greater amount in the mixture. However, it may be that the required information about this species is not available, and we must turn to a minor component, or even to a substance which is not present in the mixture, but if we do this there is always some loss of accuracy. The properties of this reference substance can be given in tables or charts or represented by an equation of state. We assume the latter and, furthermore, require that the equation be applicable to the whole fluid region (that is both liquid and gas) and that it is of the form

$$P_0 = P_0(V, T) \tag{9.143}$$

(subscript zero indicates that the equation is for the reference substance). The BWR equation, see Appendix B, satisfies these requirements.

For equilibrium between a liquid (composition x, molar volume v^l) and a vapour (composition y, molar volume v^g) of a binary mixture of species 1 and 2

$$P(v^l, T, x) = P(v^g, T, y) \tag{9.144}$$

$$\text{fugacity}_1 (v^l, T, x) = \text{fugacity}_1 (v^g, T, y) \tag{9.145}$$

$$\text{fugacity}_2 (v^l, T, x) = \text{fugacity}_2 (v^g, T, y) \tag{9.146}$$

That is, we have three equations in the three unknowns, v^g, v^l and y, and in view of the complexity of the equations, a solution, if it exists, will be found only by iterative techniques. This procedure requires trial values of the three unknowns, and we presume that these are available.

Using our trial values of v^g, v^l and y, we require the six quantities (2 pressures and 4 fugacities) in (9.144) to (9.146) in terms of the 'corresponding' properties of the reference substance. To do this we first calculate f_x and h_x, using (9.137), as in the example above, for the hypothetical one-component fluid which is to represent the liquid phase and similarly f_y and h_y for the vapour phase. These parameters enable us to compute the configurational properties of the two hypothetical substances in terms of properties of the reference substance:

$$P_x(v, T) = (f_x h_x^{-1}) P_0(v h_x^{-1}, T f_x^{-1}) \tag{9.147}$$

$$\text{fugacity}_x (v, T) = (f_x h_x^{-1}) \cdot \text{fugacity}_0 (v h_x^{-1}, T f_x^{-1}) \tag{9.148}$$

$$(u_{\text{config}})_x (v, T) = (f_x) \cdot (u_{\text{config}})_0 (v h_x^{-1}, T f_x^{-1}) \tag{9.149}$$

$$Z_x(v, T) = Z_0(v h_x^{-1}, T f_x^{-1}) \tag{9.150}$$

$$(s_{\text{config}})_x (v, T) = (s_{\text{config}})_0 (v h_x^{-1}, T f_x^{-1}) + R \ln h_x \tag{9.151}$$

$$(h_{\text{config}})_x (v, T) = (f_x)(h_{\text{config}})_0 (v h_x^{-1}, T f_x^{-1}) \tag{9.152}$$

and similarly for y. Equation (9.147), is (9.106) in terms of x, (9.150) is a repetition of (9.142) and (9.148) to (9.152) are derived from equations given by Rowlinson and Watson.[40] Subscript zero again refers to reference substance. Algebraic expressions for these configurational properties are given for the BWR equation in Appendix B. If we assume the mixture is conformal, the fugacity of component i in the mixture is[40]

$$\text{fugacity}_i\,(v,\,T,\,x) = x_i\,.\,\text{fugacity}_x\,(v,\,T)$$

$$\times \exp\left\{\frac{(u_{\text{config}})_x(v,\,T)\psi_{1i}}{RT} + [Z_x(v,\,T) - 1]\psi_{2i}\right\} \quad (9.153)$$

where

$$\psi_{1i} = 2\left(\frac{\sum\limits_j x_j f_{ij} h_{ij}}{\sum\limits_j \sum\limits_k x_j x_k f_{jk} h_{jk}} - 1\right) - \psi_{2i}$$

$$\psi_{2i} = 2\left(\frac{\sum\limits_j x_j h_{ij}}{\sum\limits_j \sum\limits_k x_j x_k h_{jk}} - 1\right) \quad (9.154)$$

If the mixture is not conformal, similar but more complex equations[40] must be used. We now apply (9.153) to components 1 and 2 in each phase of our binary mixture to give the four fugacities needed for equations (9.145) and (9.146). Equation (9.147) gives the two pressures for (9.144). Thus, by iteration, our trial values of v^g, v^l and y can be modified until (9.144) to (9.146) are satisfied.

The solution of the liquid-vapour equilibrium is now, in principle, complete, except in as far as we may also require the enthalpy and entropy of the two phases at equilibrium. These may be calculated from the configurational properties of the hypothetical one-component fluids, as given by (9.151) and (9.152), by the addition of the contributions from the molecular part of the partition function and, in the case of entropy, from the ideal entropy change on mixing. The last term arises from the difference between $(A_{\text{config}})_{\text{mixt}}$ and $(A_{\text{config}})_x$. The results are, however, more conveniently expressed in terms of the so-called 'residual' properties, which we define, for a given property, as the difference between the values in the real state and in the perfect gas state at the same v and T (An alternative definition, which we do not use here, compares the values at the same P and T). For further details on the relation between residual and configurational properties see Appendix B. We obtain, for the enthalpy and entropy of a mixture of composition x,

$$h(v,\,T,\,x) = f_x \cdot (h_{\text{res}})_0(vh_x^{-1}, Tf_x^{-1}) + \sum_i x_i h_i^\dagger(T) \quad (9.155)$$

$$s(v,\,T,\,x) = (s_{\text{res}})_0(vh_x^{-1},\,Tf_x^{-1}) + R \ln\,(P^\dagger v/RT)$$

$$+ \sum_i x_i s_i^\dagger(T) - R \sum_i x_i \ln x_i \quad (9.156)$$

where $h_i^\dagger(T)$ and $s_i^\dagger(T)$ are the molar enthalpy and entropy of pure species i in the perfect gas state at temperature T and standard pressure $P^\dagger$. For a substance which is a gas at $(P^\dagger, T)$, this is the standard state designated in Chapter 8 by $\ominus$.

The results obtained are generally quite accurate by comparison with other methods of predictions. However, in view of their complexity, it is natural to ask, before starting on such calculations, if there are not easier ways of getting results of comparable accuracy. We give a brief account of some of the methods.

There are, first, empirical methods. We have seen in Section 4.13 that multi-parameter equations such as BWR or Bender's equation, can represent accurately the $P\text{-}V\text{-}T$ properties of pure substances in both gas and liquid phases. It is natural to attempt to extend these equations to mixtures. This can be done in a number of ways, all of which require that we have a rule or rules for obtaining the parameters of the mixture in terms of the parameters of the pure components. In the case of the BWR equation (4.44), which we choose as our example in view of its wide usage, it is customary to represent each parameter for the mixture, X_{mixt}, by a sum over the parameters for the pure components X_i in the following way

$$X_{\text{mixt}} = \left(\sum_i x_i X_i^{1/n} \right)^n \qquad (9.157)$$

The original authors of this equation proposed that the index n should be 1 for B_0 in (4.44), 2 for A_0 and γ and 3 for a, b, c and α, but the choice is empirical.

The simplest way in which to use the BWR equation for prediction of the properties of a mixture is to take the parameters determined from experimental data on the pure components, as mentioned in Section 4.13, and to form the mixture parameters from these by use of (9.157). All configurational thermodynamic properties can then be computed from the resulting equation. Since this method uses pure component data only, it resembles that of Kay (9.136) and suffers from the same defect in that it neglects the dependence of the properties of the mixture on the forces between unlike molecules. Nevertheless, its use can be justified on the grounds of convenience and the fact that for many multicomponent systems it works surprisingly well. This is particularly so if an extended form of the equation is used (that is, one which includes additional temperature-dependent terms, see Section 4.13) and which can reproduce more accurately the properties of the pure components.[41]

The crude nature of the way in which the BWR equation is used for mixtures can be reduced by incorporating experimental data for mixtures either into the formulation of the equation or into the mixing rules, or both. Thus, if we wished to use the method for binary mixtures of oxygen and nitrogen we could assume the mixing rules (9.157) to hold, and carry out a regression analysis to obtain the BWR constants for oxygen and nitrogen simultaneously, using as experimental information, not only that for the pure components, but also whatever binary information is available as well. In this particular system, we might expect to have available liquid-vapour equilibrium data. The resulting formulation will, in general, give a better representation of the binary mixture data but a slightly worse one for the pure components. We see, of course, that we have now removed the predictive aspect of the use of the BWR equation and replaced it by an interpolatory role, or at most an extrapolatory one.

There are other ways in which binary experimental information can be incorporated, and one very attractive way allows us to leave the pure component parameters untouched. The adjustments to obtain a 'best fit' to the mixture data are made by making the form of one or more of the mixing rules (9.157) composition dependent. This has been done successfully by Bender[42] who used an extended BWR equation to represent the properties of mixtures containing argon, oxygen and nitrogen, but made the mathematical form of the parameter c_{mixt} in (9.157) dependent on the molecular species involved. This was done by taking experimental information on each of the three binaries formed from argon, oxygen and nitrogen in turn, and by a regression procedure determining the form of c_{mixt} for each unlike pair, i.e. $Ar + O_2$, $Ar + N_2$, $O_2 + N_2$. Not surprisingly, this more flexible approach improves the 'goodness of fit' substantially as far as the binary mixtures are concerned, but the procedure remains an essentially interpolatory one. It does, however, assume a predictive aspect if for a ternary argon, oxygen, nitrogen mixture the value of c_{mixt} is formed by a combination of the c_{mixt}'s for the three binary systems, and in this way Bender was able to make very accurate predictions of the properties, including phase equilibria, of the ternary system.

These methods, based on the BWR equation, can obviously be extended to other substances and to systems containing more components, but it is clear that every new component brought into consideration necessitates a large amount of time spent on collecting and collating experimental data and on doing the necessary regression analysis. The resulting equations, due to their flexibility, are capable of very accurate representation of the experimental data, but it is just this flexibility which has destroyed what little predictive character was there in the first place, and has reduced their role to much more of an interpolatory or extrapolatory one. The approach is of use to the designer who is concerned with mixtures containing the same few components (such as the designer of liquid air plants where mixtures of argon, nitrogen and oxygen only are encountered) for whom it is worthwhile spending the time needed to determine the necessary BWR parameters. It is of less use to the designer who is concerned with a 'one-off' job.

We see, therefore, that both the corresponding states one-fluid approximation and the more empirical BWR approaches have their advantages and disadvantages. The one-fluid approximation is complicated and expensive in computing time, but is closely tied to theory and is easily extended to new properties and to new substances, if we know their critical constants and acentric factors. The BWR, and similar equations are more simple and less expensive in computer time, and there is now a considerable amount of experience in their use. They are difficult to extend to new substances for which the whole set of empirical parameters must be determined afresh.

One approach is closely tied to theory, one is frankly empirical. Is there a middle way? Prausnitz has developed methods which are neither as empirical as the BWR equation nor as closely tied to theory as the one-fluid approximation. He calls his methods *molecular thermodynamics*, which he defines as 'an engineering science, based on classical thermodynamics, but relying on molecular physics and statistical thermodynamics to supply insight into the behaviour of matter'. His methods are described in his books, and particularly in the one from which this quotation is taken.[43] There he discusses more fully many of the subjects touched upon in the last four sections of this chapter, and it is recommended as a view of the problem of prediction which is, perhaps, complementary to that given here. The whole field of prediction is an active area of research, and it is too soon to say yet which will become the preferred methods of the future. It is certain, however, that statistical thermodynamics will play an important role in these methods, and the aim of this chapter has been to give a short account of how it is used today.

9.10   Prediction and storage of thermodynamic data by computer

It will be evident that the accurate prediction of those thermodynamic properties of greatest interest to the chemical engineer is no easy task. Furthermore, the methods employed should be suited to the iterative procedures used to 'optimise' plant design; hence they must be carried out by digital computer and be accessed repeatedly by the main design programme.

The computer can be used in two ways: firstly, as a means of storing information as in a library, and secondly, for performing predictive calculations as outlined in the first nine sections of this Chapter. The first needs a computer of large storage capacity but relatively slow operation, the second has no need for large storage capacity but the ability to perform very high speed mathematical operations is crucial. With the equipment currently available, these requirements are to some extent incompatible, but it is unlikely that they will remain so.

Currently, the digital computer is used extensively in chemical engineering design in both the ways described but, as yet, neither can be said to be fully developed. The difficulties are obvious; the computer library is very much smaller than a library of books and selection is necessary, usually by restricting the scope of material included, whereas, in the case of prediction, no satisfactory method exists for highly polar substances, such as water, nor for mixtures containing them. Thus, the two uses of the computer are complementary.

The computer library, or 'data bank' as it is sometimes called, is generally built up from experimental data stored either in 'raw' or 'partially digested' form. As far as thermodynamic properties are concerned, this usually means in the form of largely empirical correlations (this term is used to describe polynomial or similar representations of an experimental quantity, such as C_P, as a function of one or more independent variables, such as P and T) and usually only for pure substances or mixtures of fixed composition, such as air. These constraints are necessary to keep the size of the data bank within reasonable bounds. This does not mean that it cannot be used to provide values for an arbitrary mixture, but only that such quantities must be computed from the values for the pure components. Thus, if the data bank contains a table of values of the BWR coefficients for several pure substances, the coefficients for a mixture can be calculated by the empirical combining rule given in (9.157). However, as we have described in this chapter, this particular procedure can now be replaced by a predictive one soundly based on statistical thermodynamics and, in general, there is much less need for empiricism. The modern computer is just fast enough to cope with the extensive calculations needed to predict the properties of many pure components and their mixtures, but the problems of interfacing design programmes with predictive procedures remain formidable.

Notes

1. There are many introductory texts on statistical thermodynamics. The following are particularly recommended: G. S. Rushbrooke, *Introduction to Statistical Mechanics*, Clarendon Press, Oxford, 1949; T. L. Hill, *Introduction to Statistical Thermodynamics*, Addison-Wesley, Reading, Mass., 1960; F. C. Andrews, *Equilibrium Statistical Mechanics*, 2nd edn., Wiley, New York, 1975.

A book which deals both with the fundamentals and with many of the applications of interest to chemical engineers at greater length than is possible in this chapter is, T. M. Reed and K. E. Gubbins, *Applied Statistical Mechanics*, McGraw-Hill, New York, 1973.

2. For a discussion of the energy levels and thermodynamic functions for H_2, HD and D_2, see e.g. J. S. Rowlinson, *The Perfect Gas*, Pergamon Press, Oxford, 1963, Chapter 3.

3. J. E. Mayer and M. G. Mayer, *Statistical Mechanics*, Wiley, New York, 1940, pp. 192–4.

4. G. Herzberg, *Infra-Red and Raman Spectra of Polyatomic Molecules*, Van Nostrand, New York, 1945, Chapter 2.

5. E. B. Wilson, J. C. Decius and P. C. Cross, *Molecular Vibrations*, McGraw-Hill, New York, 1955.

6. Landolt-Börnstein, *Tabellen*, 6th edn, Vol. 2, Part 4, Springer, Berlin, 1961, p. 731.

7. J. E. Mayer and M. G. Mayer, *Statistical Mechanics*, Wiley, New York, 1940, p. 445.

8. J. Hilsenrath and G. G. Ziegler, *Tables of Einstein Functions*, National Bureau of Standards Monograph No. 49, 1962. A much shortened version of these tables is in M. Abramowitz and I. A. Stegun, *Handbook of Mathematical Functions*, National Bureau of Standards Appl. Math. Series, No. 55, 1964, p. 999.

9. K. S. Pitzer, *J. Chem. Phys.* **5** (1937), 469; K. S. Pitzer and W. F. Gwinn, *J. Chem. Phys.* **9** (1941), 485; J. C. M. Li and K. S. Pitzer, *J. phys Chem.* **60** (1956), 466.

10. S. G. Frankiss and J. H. S. Green, 'Statistical Methods of Calculating Thermodynamic Functions', Chapter 8 of *Chemical Thermodynamics*, Vol. 1 (ed. M. L. McGlashan), Chemical Society, London, Specialist Report Series, 1973.

11. J. F. Masi and B. Petkof, *J. Res. Nat. Bur. Stand.* **48,** (1952) 179; W. F. Giauque and C. J. Egan, *J. Chem. Phys.* **5** (1937), 45.

12. Frankiss and Green, loc. cit. (note 10).

13. R. C. Reid and T. K. Sherwood, *The Properties of Gases and Liquids: their estimation and correlation* 2nd edn, McGraw-Hill, New York, 1966 Chapter 5.

14. A. G. Gaydon, *Dissociation Energies and Spectra of Diatomic Molecules* 2nd edn, Chapman and Hall, London, 1953.

15. T. L. Cottrell, *Strength of Chemical Bonds*, Butterworth, 2nd edn, 1959.

16. Reid and Sherwood, loc. cit. (note 13).

17. L. S. Kassel, *J. Amer. chem. Soc.* **56,** (1934) 1838. This and other examples are discussed by T. L. Hill, *Introduction to Statistical Thermodynamics*, Addison-Wesley, Reading, Mass, 1960, pp. 182–7.

18. F. R. Gilmore, *Rand Corp. Rep.* RM-1543, (1955).

19. For further discussion see e.g. J. S. Rowlinson and I. D. Watson, *Chem. Eng. Sci.* **24** (1969) 1565. For a different, but rarely used, method of dividing Z into two dimensionless factors see R. L. Scott, p. 40 in D. Henderson (ed.) *Physical Chemistry*, Vol. 8A, 'The Liquid State', Academic Press, New York, 1971.

20. H. Margenau and N. R. Kestner, *Theory of Intermolecular Forces*, 2nd edn, Pergamon Press, Oxford, 1971.

21. For a full discussion see e.g. J. E. Mayer and M. G. Mayer, *Statistical Mechanics*, Wiley, New York, 1940, Chapter 13. For a shorter, and probably more easily followed derivation, see N. G. van Kampen, *Physica*, **27** (1961), 783.

22. For an account of how to make such calculations, and estimates of their accuracy, see R. C. Reid and T. K. Sherwood, *The Properties of Gases and Liquids*, 2nd edn, McGraw-Hill, New York, 1966, Chapter 3.

23. J. S. Rowlinson, *Liquids and Liquid Mixtures*, 2nd edn, Butterworth London, 1969, Chapter 8; J. A. Barker and D. Henderson, in D. Henderson (ed.), *Physical Chemistry*, Vol. 8A, 'Liquid State', Academic Press, New York, 1971, Chapter 6.

24. See e.g. Rowlinson, *Liquids and Liquid Mixtures*, pp. 267–270.

25. Reid and Sherwood, loc. cit. (note 13), Chapter 3.

26. See e.g. G. S. Rushbrooke, *Introduction to Statistical Mechanics*, Clarendon Press, Oxford, 1949, pp. 85–88 (linear), 130–133 (non-linear).

27. See e.g. Rowlinson, *Liquids and Liquid Mixtures*, pp. 270–8.

28. Reid and Sherwood, loc. cit. (note 13) p. 29 ff, 55ff, 140–143, 272–283, 571–584; K. S. Pitzer and R. F. Curl, *Thermodynamic and Transport Properties of Fluids*, Inst. Mech. Eng., London, 1958, p. 1; W. C. Edmister, *Petrol Refiner* **37**(4) (1958), 173.

29. A list is given in Reid and Sherwood, loc. cit., Appendix A.

30. Rowlinson, *Liquids and Liquid Mixtures*, pp. 277–283.

31. J. S. Rowlinson and I. D. Watson, *Chem. Eng. Sci.*, **24** (1969), 156.

32. Reid and Sherwood, loc. cit. (note 13).

33. O. A. Hougen, K. M. Watson, and R. A. Ragatz, *Chemical Process Principles*, Part 2, 'Thermodynamics', 2nd edn, Wiley, New York, 1959, p. 569 ff. Reid and Sherwood, loc. cit., Appendix B.

34. W. B. Kay, *Ind. Eng. Chem.* **28** (1936), 1014.

35. R. C. Reid and T. W. Leland, *A. I. Chem. E. J.* **11** (1965), 228; T. W. Leland, J. S. Rowlinson and G. A. Sather, *Trans. Faraday Soc.* **64** (1968), 1447; Rowlinson, *Liquids and Liquid Mixtures*, pp. 326–332.

36. Taken mainly from Rowlinson, *Liquids and Liquid Mixtures*, pp. 332–344; A. J. Gunning and J. S. Rowlinson, *Chem. Eng. Sci.* **28** (1973), 521; and A. S. Teja and J. S. Rowlinson, *Chem. Eng. Sci,* **28** (1973), 529; for further values see M. J. Hiza and A. G. Duncan, *A. I. Chem. E. J.* **16** (1970), 733.

37. See e.g. J. W. Leach, P. S. Chappelear and T. W. Leland, *A. I. Chem. E. J.* **14** (1968), 568; J. S. Rowlinson and I. D. Watson, *Chem. Eng. Sci.* **24** (1969), 1565, 1575; A. J. Gunning and J. S. Rowlinson, *Chem. Eng. Sci.* **28** (1973), 521.

38. *Survey of Current Information on LNG and Methane*, National Bureau of Standards, Boulder, Colorado, (1973), NBSIR 73–300.

39. D. R. Roe and G. Saville, unpublished results.

40. J. S. Rowlinson and I. D. Watson, *Chem. Eng. Sci.* **24** (1969), 1565, 1575.

41. See e.g. S. K. Sood and G. G. Haselden, *Am. I. Chem. E. J.* **16** (1970), 891 and the references cited in this paper.

42. E. Bender, *The calculation of phase equilibria from a thermal equation of state, applied to the pure fluids argon, nitrogen, oxygen and their mixtures*, Müller, Karlsruhe, 1973.

43. J. M. Prausnitz, *Molecular Thermodynamics of Fluid-Phase Equilibria*, Prentice-Hall, Englewood Cliffs, N.J., 1969.

Appendix A

Partial differentiation

The use of thermodynamic equations requires frequent manipulation of expressions for one property as a function of several others. Thus we may have pressure as a function of volume and temperature, a relation we can write formally as $P = f(V, T)$. In Section 4.12 we meet, similarly, Helmholtz free energy as a function of volume and temperature. Such a function can be represented as a surface in a three-dimensional graph. Here we summarise some of the properties of such surfaces.

The operation of ordinary differentiation is most easily visualised as taking the slope of a curve in a two-dimensional graph. If $z = f(x)$ then the slope is (dz/dx). Surfaces have different slopes in different directions and *partial differentiation* is a generalisation of ordinary differentiation to include three (and more) dimensions. Let $z = f(x, y)$ be a thermodynamic surface, e.g. x, y, z were V, T, P or V, T, A in the examples above, Figure A1 shows

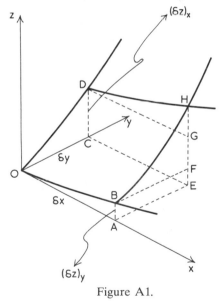

Figure A1.

part of the surface on which, for convenience, we have placed the origin of coordinates at the point at which we wish to calculate the derivatives. Let δx be a small increment along the x-axis. The curve OB is the section of the surface in the z, x plane, and in this plane we can apply the rules of ordinary differentiation. Hence the increment δz, which corresponds to δx is the height AB, or $(dz/dx)\,\delta x$. Since this plane is a section on which y is constant (in fact, $y = 0$ in this example), then we show this constancy by means of a subscript, and a differently shaped letter d in the derivative, and so write for the height AB

$$(\delta z)_y = \left(\frac{\partial z}{\partial x}\right)_y \delta x \tag{A.1}$$

Similarly, in the z, y plane, CD is

$$(\delta z)_x = \left(\frac{\partial z}{\partial y}\right)_x \delta y \tag{A.2}$$

The total increase in z caused by an arbitrary small increment δx, and another arbitrary small increment δy is EH and so is the sum of $(\delta z)_y$ and $(\delta z)_x$, since $AB = EF = GH$ and $CD = EG = FH$. These equalities follow at once from the geometry of the figure if the increments are sufficiently small for all lines to be assumed to be straight. Hence

$$\delta z = \left(\frac{\partial z}{\partial x}\right)_y \delta x + \left(\frac{\partial z}{\partial y}\right)_x \delta y \tag{A.3}$$

The evaluation of the partial derivatives $(\partial z/\partial x)_y$ and $(\partial z/\partial y)_x$ is straightforward since, in differentiation with respect to x we treat y as a constant, and vice versa. Thus if, for example,

$$z = x e^{xy}$$

then

$$\left(\frac{\partial z}{\partial x}\right)_y = (1 + xy)e^{xy} \qquad \left(\frac{\partial z}{\partial y}\right)_x = x^2 e^{xy}$$

The relations we need for the calculation of thermodynamic derivatives all follow from equation (A.3). Thus, if we go to the limit so that δz, δx and δy all become differentials, we have the expression for a *total derivative*

$$dz = \left(\frac{\partial z}{\partial x}\right)_y dx + \left(\frac{\partial z}{\partial y}\right)_x dy \tag{A.4}$$

If the total increment of z is zero then (A.3) becomes

$$0 = \left(\frac{\partial z}{\partial x}\right)_y (\delta x)_z + \left(\frac{\partial z}{\partial y}\right)_x (\delta y)_z \tag{A.5}$$

or

$$\left(\frac{\partial z}{\partial y}\right)_x (\delta y)_z = -\left(\frac{\partial z}{\partial x}\right)_y (\delta x)_z \tag{A.6}$$

where the subscripts z remind us of the additional restriction to constant z. If we divide by $(\delta x)_z$, and let the increments become differentials

$$\left(\frac{\partial z}{\partial y}\right)_x \left(\frac{\partial y}{\partial x}\right)_z = -\left(\frac{\partial z}{\partial x}\right)_y \tag{A.7}$$

which can be written more symmetrically as

$$\left(\frac{\partial z}{\partial y}\right)_x \left(\frac{\partial y}{\partial x}\right)_z \left(\frac{\partial x}{\partial z}\right)_y = -1 \tag{A.8}$$

since, as for ordinary differentials, $(\partial x/\partial z)_y$ is the reciprocal of $(\partial z/\partial x)_y$, but only if both have the same subscript, in this case, y.

If all derivatives are to be taken at a constant value of some fourth variable, say w, then by the same rules as apply to ordinary differentiation

$$\left(\frac{\partial z}{\partial y}\right)_w \left(\frac{\partial y}{\partial x}\right)_w \left(\frac{\partial x}{\partial z}\right)_w = +1 \tag{A.9}$$

This is to be contrasted with (A.8).

Example

If α_P is the coefficient of isobaric expansion, which is defined as $V^{-1}(\partial V/\partial T)_P$; if β_T is the coefficient of isothermal compressibility, defined as $-V^{-1}(\partial V/\partial P)_T$, and if γ_V is the thermal pressure coefficient, defined as $(\partial P/\partial T)_V$, then (A.8) requires

$$\alpha_P = \beta_T \gamma_V \tag{A.10}$$

For a typical liquid α_P is about $10^{-3}\,\mathrm{K}^{-1}$ and β_T about $10^{-4}\,\mathrm{bar}^{-1}$, so that on heating at constant volume the pressure rises by about $10\,\mathrm{bar}\,\mathrm{K}^{-1}$.

Equation (A.8) can also be written

$$\left(\frac{\partial x}{\partial y}\right)_z = -\frac{(\partial z/\partial y)_x}{(\partial z/\partial x)_y} \tag{A.11}$$

This is convenient if it is easier to express z as a function of x and y, rather than x as a function of y and z, or y as a function of x and z.

Example

The adiabatic Joule-Thomson coefficient (Section 3.16) is $(\partial T/\partial P)_H$, but it is inconvenient to have $T = f(P, H)$ or $P = f(T, H)$, and hence we use (A.11) to obtain

$$\left(\frac{\partial T}{\partial P}\right)_H = -\frac{(\partial H/\partial P)_T}{(\partial H/\partial T)_P} \tag{A.12}$$

Both derivatives on the right-hand side are easily calculated.

It often happens that we wish to take the slope of a surface along a line specified by requiring that some property maintains a constant value. Thus we may know $P = f(V, T)$, but wish to calculate the adiabatic coefficient $(\partial P/\partial T)_S$, that is, the reciprocal of the rise of temperature on adiabatic compression at constant entropy. Let the property to be held constant in

(A.3) be denoted w, then, dividing (A.3) by δx, and when the increments δz, δx, and δy are along a line of constant w, we have

$$\left(\frac{\partial z}{\partial x}\right)_w = \left(\frac{\partial z}{\partial x}\right)_y + \left(\frac{\partial z}{\partial y}\right)_x \left(\frac{\partial y}{\partial x}\right)_w \tag{A.13}$$

This is the general equation for 'changing directions' or changing constraints, since it enables us to calculate $(\partial z/\partial x)_w$ from $(\partial z/\partial x)_y$. It can be put into several other forms. Thus from (A.11) with w for z

$$\left(\frac{\partial z}{\partial x}\right)_w = \left(\frac{\partial z}{\partial x}\right)_y - \left(\frac{\partial z}{\partial y}\right)_x \frac{(\partial w/\partial x)_y}{(\partial w/\partial y)_x} \tag{A.14}$$

$$= \left(\frac{\partial z}{\partial x}\right)_y - \left(\frac{\partial z}{\partial w}\right)_x \left(\frac{\partial w}{\partial x}\right)_y \tag{A.15}$$

Thus the adiabatic coefficient $(\partial P/\partial T)_S$ can be written

$$\left(\frac{\partial P}{\partial T}\right)_S = \left(\frac{\partial P}{\partial T}\right)_V - \left(\frac{\partial P}{\partial S}\right)_T \left(\frac{\partial S}{\partial T}\right)_V \tag{A.16}$$

This equation does not quite achieve our aim of expressing the right-hand side in terms of derivatives readily obtained from $P = f(V, T)$. If we use Maxwell's relation and the relation of entropy to heat capacity (Section 3.11), we have

$$(\partial S/\partial P)_T = -(\partial V/\partial T)_P$$

$$(\partial S/\partial T)_V = C_V/T$$

and so, by means of (A.11)

$$\left(\frac{\partial P}{\partial T}\right)_S = \left(\frac{\partial P}{\partial T}\right)_V - \frac{C_V(\partial P/\partial V)_T}{T(\partial P/\partial T)_V} \tag{A.17}$$

which is the desired result. This can be written more simply by using (3.96) for the difference of C_P and C_V, to give

$$\left(\frac{\partial P}{\partial T}\right)_S = \frac{C_P}{(\partial V/\partial T)_P} \tag{A.18}$$

This last equation is the basis of Lummer and Pringsheim's method of measuring the heat capacity of a gas by the 'mechanical' method of observing the fall in temperature on a sudden isentropic expansion.

A useful application of (A.13) is to calculate derivatives along a line of saturated gas or liquid. Thus the heat capacity at saturation of a liquid, C_σ, is the derivative $T(\partial S/\partial T)_\sigma$, where the subscript indicates that the pressure is to be adjusted as the temperature rises so as to maintain the liquid in the saturated state. From (A.13)

$$\left(\frac{\partial S}{\partial T}\right)_\sigma = \left(\frac{\partial S}{\partial T}\right)_P + \left(\frac{\partial S}{\partial P}\right)_T \left(\frac{\partial P}{\partial T}\right)_\sigma \tag{A.19}$$

or, multiplying by T, and using Maxwell's relation for $(\partial S/\partial P)_T$,

$$C_\sigma = C_P - T\left(\frac{\partial V}{\partial T}\right)_T\left(\frac{\partial P}{\partial T}\right)_\sigma \qquad (A.20)$$

The last derivative, $(\partial P/\partial T)_\sigma$, is the slope of the vapour pressure curve, and is commonly written in ordinary differentials without the suffix, (dP/dT). This dropping of an implied constraint (in this case σ), and changing back to ordinary differentials, is used in Chapter 7 to simplify some of the notation. Since σ is not a property (A.19) cannot be transformed to equations analogous to (A.14) and (A.15).

Exercise

Use the definitions above of α_P, β_T, and γ_V to show that the coefficient of thermal expansion at saturation α_σ, is given by

$$\alpha_\sigma = \alpha_P - \beta_T\gamma_\sigma \qquad (A.21)$$

where γ_σ is again the slope of the vapour-pressure curve. This equation can be derived either from the rules for partial differentiation as above, or from the geometry of Figure A2 in which OA represents the change of saturated volume with P and T. OB and AC represent isothermal compression of the liquid, and OC represents heating at constant volume.

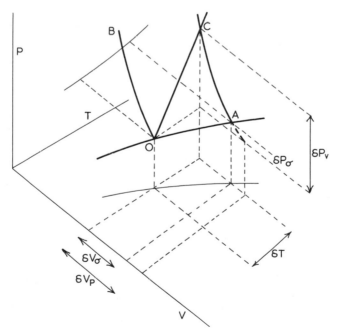

Figure A2

Examples could be multiplied indefinitely, but it will be found in practice that (A.4), (A.8) or its alternative (A.11), and (A.13), will serve for almost all manipulations.

Second partial derivatives can be formed by differentiating the first derivatives. Thus we have $(\partial^2 z/\partial x^2)_y$ and $(\partial^2 z/\partial y^2)_x$. The cross-derivative is

$$\frac{\partial}{\partial x_y}\left(\frac{\partial z}{\partial y}\right)_x = \frac{\partial}{\partial y_x}\left(\frac{\partial z}{\partial x}\right)_y \qquad (A.22)$$

and is usually written without a subscript as

$$\frac{\partial^2 z}{\partial x\, \partial y}$$

Exercise

Verify (A.22) when $z = xe^{xy}$, as above.

If we have a mixture then we may need more than two independent variables. Thus in Chapter 7 it is convenient to discuss the molar Gibbs free energy as a function of P, T and mole fraction x_2, i.e. $g = f(P, T, x_2)$. The equation for the total derivative (A.4) is readily extended by adding further terms, but we neither derive nor need the extensions of the later equations.

Appendix B

Benedict-Webb-Rubin equation for a pure substance

The BWR equation, like most other practical equations of state, is of the form $P = P(v, T)$, which, for convenience, we use in the alternative form $P = P(\rho, T)$ where $\rho = 1/v$. As shown in Chapter 4, changes in enthalpy, entropy, etc. along an isotherm can be calculated from this equation and, by including also the enthalpy, entropy, etc. of the perfect gas in its standard state (for definition of this see Chapter 8), the total value at any ρ and T, such as $h(\rho, T)$ and $s(\rho, T)$, can be written down explicitly.

For use in Chapter 9, we define two other sets of quantities—residual properties and configurational properties. We define a residual property, such as h_{res}, the residual enthalpy, as the difference between the enthalpy of the real substance at a given v and T and the enthalpy of that same substance in its perfect gas state at the same v and T. (We could alternatively require the two states to be at the same P and T, but this gives a different set of values for the residual properties and it is not a definition which we use.) Configurational properties are used extensively in Chapter 9, and are defined in Section 9.6 to which the reader is referred. As is indicated there, calculation of a configurational property often involves taking the logarithm of a dimensioned quantity. They must, therefore, be used with care.

Equation of state

$$P(\rho, T) = RT\rho + (B_0 RT - A_0 - C_0/T^2)\rho^2 + (bRT - a)\rho^3$$
$$+ a\alpha\rho^6 + c\rho^3[\{1 + \gamma\rho^2\} \exp(-\gamma\rho^2)]/T^2 \tag{B.1}$$

Fugacity

$$RT \ln[f(\rho, T)/\rho RT] = \int_0^\rho (1/\rho)\, d(P - RT\rho)$$
$$= 2(B_0 RT - A_0 - C_0/T^2)\rho + 3(bRT - a)\rho^2/2 + 6a\alpha\rho^5/5$$
$$+ c[1/\gamma + \{\rho^2/2 - 1/\gamma + \gamma\rho^4\} \exp(-\gamma\rho^2)]/T^2 \tag{B.2}$$

Internal energy

$$u_{res}(\rho, T) = \int_0^\rho \left\{ P - T\left(\frac{\partial P}{\partial T}\right)_\rho \right\} \bigg/ \rho^2\, d\rho$$
$$= -(A_0 + 3C_0/T^2)\rho - a\rho^2/2 + a\alpha\rho^5/5$$
$$+ 3c\rho^2/T^2[\{1 - \exp(-\gamma\rho^2)\}/\gamma\rho^2 - \{\exp(-\gamma\rho^2)\}/2] \tag{B.3}$$

$$u_{\text{config}}(\rho, T) = u_{\text{res}}(\rho, T) \tag{B.4}$$

$$u(\rho, T) = u_{\text{res}}(\rho, T) + u^\dagger(T) \tag{B.5}$$

Enthalpy

$$h_{\text{res}}(\rho, T) = u_{\text{res}}(\rho, T) + P/\rho - RT$$
$$= (B_0 RT - 2A_0 - 4C_0/T^2)\rho + (2bRT - 3a)\rho^2/2$$
$$+ 6a\alpha\rho^5/5 + c\rho^2/T^2[3\{1 - \exp(-\gamma\rho^2)\}/\gamma\rho^2$$
$$- \{\exp(-\gamma\rho^2)\}/2 + \gamma\rho^2 \exp(-\gamma\rho^2)] \tag{B.6}$$

$$h_{\text{config}}(\rho, T) = h_{\text{res}}(\rho, T) + RT \tag{B.7}$$

$$h(\rho, T) = h_{\text{res}}(\rho, T) + h^\dagger(T) \tag{B.8}$$

Entropy

$$s_{\text{res}}(\rho, T) = \int_0^\rho \left\{ R\rho - \left(\frac{\partial P}{\partial T}\right)_\rho \right\} / \rho^2 \, d\rho$$
$$= -(B_0 R + 2C_0/T^3)\rho - bR\rho^2/2$$
$$+ 2c\rho^2/T^3[\{1 - \exp(-\gamma\rho^2)\}/\gamma\rho^2 - \{\exp(-\gamma\rho^2)\}/2] \tag{B.9}$$

$$s_{\text{config}}(\rho, T) = s_{\text{res}}(\rho, T) + R - R \ln(N\rho) \tag{B.10}$$

$$s(\rho, T) = s_{\text{res}}(\rho, T) + R \ln(P^\dagger/\rho RT) + s^\dagger(T) \tag{B.11}$$

where $u^\dagger(T)$, $h^\dagger(T)$, $s^\dagger(T)$ are the values of the functions for the substance in its perfect gas state at temperature T and standard pressure $P^\dagger$. For a substance which is a gas at $(P^\dagger, T)$ they are $u^\ominus(T)$, $h^\ominus(T)$ and $s^\ominus(T)$ of Chapter 8.

Appendix C

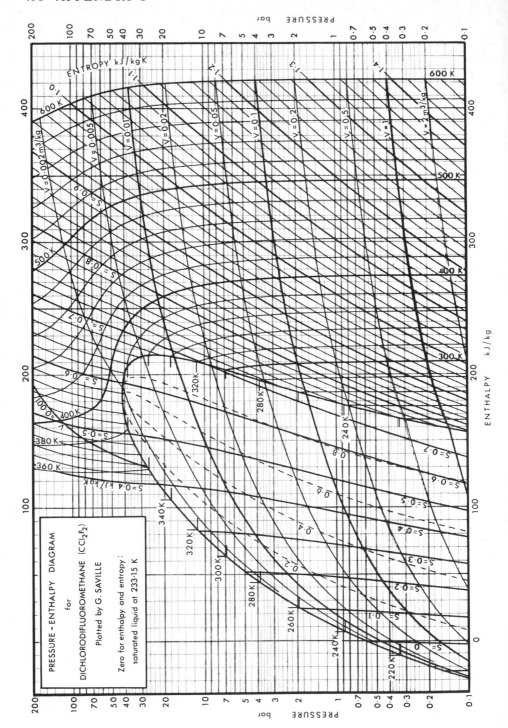

PRESSURE - ENTHALPY DIAGRAM
for
DICHLORODIFLUOROMETHANE (CCl$_2$F$_2$)
Plotted by G. SAVILLE
Zero for enthalpy and entropy:
saturated liquid at 233·15 K

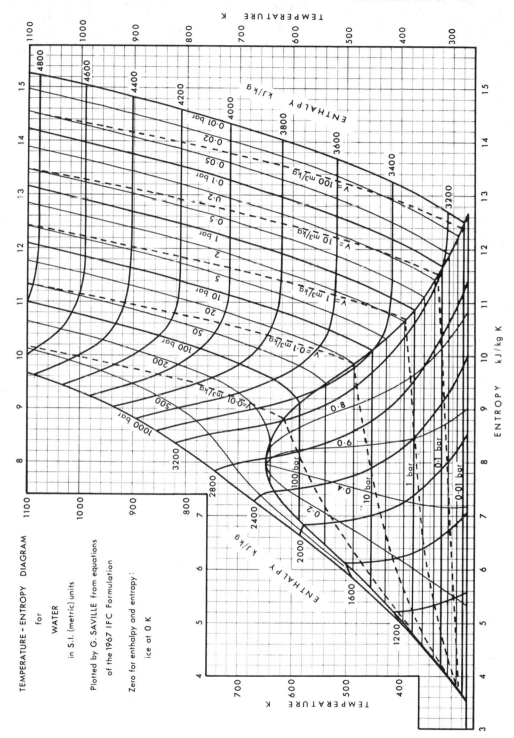

TEMPERATURE - ENTROPY DIAGRAM

for

WATER

in S.I. (metric) units

Plotted by G. SAVILLE from equations
of the 1967 IFC Formulation

Zero for enthalpy and entropy:
ice at 0 K

Index